More Praise for *The Education of a Speculator*

"I highly recommend *The Education of a Speculator*. It provides an excellent combination of glimpses into exciting new areas as well as a rigorous analysis of the latest scientific insights from academe. This is a valuable book into the world of stock and futures trading and investing."

> David N. Dreman
> Chairman, Dreman Value Advisors, Inc.

"Victor Niederhoffer's *The Education of a Speculator* is an educational delight for all readers. The insight and interdisciplinary relationships he provides not only suggest lessons about financial markets, but how the world works. The book is a joy to read, a treat to muse over and an endless source of provocative discernment."

> Herbert London
> John M. Olin Professor of Humanities, New York University

"Highly educational. A treasure trove of insights on all aspects of investments and speculations. Tremendously enjoyable. A book almost too good to be true."

> Edwin Marks
> President, Carl Marks & Company, Inc.

"This book might have been titled, 'Against All Odds,' as Niederhoffer's life has been nothing less than a record of transforming the impossible into the routine. But who could have expected that the travelogue of this journey would be so absorbingly told that the reader feels himself swept into the professional and intellectual life of a remarkable man?"

> Robert D. Kephart
> Founder, Kephart Communications

"After 40 years as a pit trader, I've known hundreds of good traders. I believe that the common denominator among successful traders is an athletic background. Knowing how to lose and come back is the most important factor in trading and Victor Niederhoffer epitomizes this."

> Henry S. Shatkin
> Shatkin, Arbor, Karlov & Co.

The
Education
of a
SPECULATOR

To Michael:

with Appreciation:

Victor Niederhoffer

The
Education
of a
SPECULATOR

Victor Niederhoffer

JOHN WILEY & SONS, INC.

New York • Chichester • Weinheim • Toronto • Singapore • Brisbane

Copyright © 1997 by Victor Niederhoffer.
Published by John Wiley & Sons, Inc.

Library of Congress Cataloging-in-Publication Data:

Niederhoffer, Victor, 1943–
     The education of a speculator / Victor Niederhoffer.
          p.   cm.
     Includes bibliographical references and index.
     ISBN 0-471-13747-2 (cloth : alk. paper)
     1. Commodity futures—United States. 2. Brokers—United States—
Biography. 3. Speculation. 4. Commodity exchanges—United States.
I. Title.
HG6049.N54   1997
332.64'5—dc20   96-30765

In memory of my father
Arthur Niederhoffer

Artist: Susan Slyman

Preface

I'm tired of hearing teachers say to me, "You should know better. Your father is a policeman. You should set an example."

Arthur Niederhoffer,
writing about his son

"Get out! Like the market, they're too big for you; you're in over your head!" The Hungarian voice was directed at my daughter Katie and me as we tested the waters of the Atlantic Ocean in Southampton, Long Island. Hurricane Andrew's waves had been merciless that entire August 1992 weekend. We turned around, and there stood our host, the legendary 60-something sultan of speculation, the man who broke the Bank of England, the invincible George Soros, the palindrome, in his bikini trunks. Like many Europeans of wealth and maturity, George likes to affect a certain riskiness in his recreational apparel.

My former boss, the bilious billionaire, bellowing at me, even as I was vacationing at his summer home—this was too much.

"Oh no," I quickly rejoined, "the recommended procedure, as the great Francis Galton wrote, is to sit down facing the water, with your hands dug into the sand, and just let the waves roll over you after they break." Although I had not enjoyed the luxury of a childhood in Southampton, the air had been as rich, the sun as shiny, and the waves as big for the poor working stiffs like me who grew up next to the ocean in Brighton Beach, Brooklyn. "I'm very familiar with how to handle big waves. That's my niche—going against."

Always aware of the virtue of having an escape route in mind, I hastened to add, "Anyway, good people on shore can rescue a weak swimmer in trouble by firmly holding hands together in a line, with the foremost—that's you, George—ready to clutch me while the wave recedes."

Despite my bravado, a shudder ran through me. I am a speculator, and my daily bread depends on reversing big moves. In economic terms, my function is to balance supply and demand. I sell when prices are high and buy when prices are low. When prices are too high and *consumers* want to exchange cash for goods, I take their cash and let them have their goods. I prevent shortages by pushing prices down so consumers don't have to pay up. Conversely, when prices are down and *producers* want cash badly for their goods, I give them the cash and take their goods. In these bad times, I keep producers from going broke, and prevent waste and spoilage by bringing prices up. I'm like a dynamic refrigerator, or a captain rationing food on an unexpectedly long voyage.

But these waves we were battling, caused by the biggest hurricane in 20 years, had been pounding the shore relentlessly. Although I wouldn't admit it to George, it was very clear to me that something unusual was going on.

Even in today's information economy, extremes in weather tend to coincide with violent moves in markets. Volcanoes, blizzards, and earthquakes all have an impact on stock markets and financial systems around the world.

Sure enough, on the two days following Hurricane Andrew, the markets moved in a horrible trend that almost buried me, exactly as George had predicted. The bond and stock markets plummeted, supposedly because insurance companies would be forced to sell bonds to pay all the storm damage claims. Everything is connected. When bonds fell 2 percent, the dollar fell a like amount. American assets often look less attractive to foreigners during violent stock and bond market declines.

When I tried to reverse the chain of tidal movements set off by the hurricane, I almost went under. Like the poor farmer, I had brought the reversing pot of water to the well once too often. At about this time, George Soros started calling me "the loser." "Nothing personal, Victor, but have you seriously thought of closing up shop and calling it a day?" he'd say.

Weather-related moves have not been the only disaster to befall me. "They" almost always catch me on the wrong side of big moves. During the first quarter of 1995, they caught me long the dollar while it receded 20 percent against the yen. I was also facing the wrong way when the dollar exactly retraced its decline during the last half of that year, going up 20 percent. (I call the study of such moves *LoBagola analysis*, in honor of an African Jew who noted similar paths in the annual movements of elephants.)

A friend, after reading an early draft of this book, wrote me this agitated message:

> [I] respond[ed] to it with grave concern. It's obvious that it's only a question of time until you go under. Why in the world would I ever risk money in the futures market and, if I ever gave in to such folly, why should it be with Niederhoffer!? I know that must come across harshly, but I thought it better to put it that way rather than sugarcoat it.

Like most successful people, secure in their trade and stature, I tend to emphasize my losses. The main reason is that it keeps me humble, an essential for success in a field where one false move can lead to irreversible disaster. I'm aware that it was "unthinkable" to hold a lifeboat drill for the "unsinkable" *Titanic*. (As a reminder, I have a picture of the *Titanic* in the entrances to all my offices.) The other reason is that recalling my losses tends to reduce the envy of others, a trait all too prevalent in our culture and all too directed toward speculators.

I first learned to accent my weaknesses during my career in squash, where I became North American Champion. My humility led to my opponents becoming so fat they didn't notice that I hardly lost a game during ten years of my reign as U.S. Champion. Nothing recedes like success. But as of mid-1996, most of the rating services in my field ranked me number one for most periods up to three years. My first client in managed accounts, Tim Horne, is still with me after 14 years. After all fees, his initial $100,000 investment is now worth about $6 million, a compounded return of about 30 percent per year.

Another early client, Paul Cifrino, wrote to me in June 1995: "Might there not be considered an arrangement for you to receive an additional share of profits based on your results that are extraordinary?" He insisted on "tithing the profits for charity" and requested that I designate a recipient for those profits. In one of the ironies that pervade speculative activities, I dropped 20 percent for Cifrino the day after he wrote his letter.

I am not a great believer in efficient markets, random walks, or rational expectations. My own trading especially refutes these. I trade strictly based on statistical "anomalies," the analysis of multivariate time series, and the quantifications of persistent psychological biases. The only newspaper I read is *The National Enquirer*. I don't own a television, don't follow the news, don't talk to anyone during the trading day, and don't like to read books less than 100 years old. For the past 15 years, I have traded futures with a face value of more than a billion dollars each month (sometimes in one day) for my own account and for my clients. I have had some ups and many downs, with the latter frequently involving losses of seven- and eight-figure amounts, sometimes coming to more than 25 percent of my liquid worth and my clients' net assets in a single day.

In statistical terms, I figure I have traded about 2 million contracts in my life thus far, with an average profit of $70 per contract (after slippage of perhaps $20). This average profit is approximately 700 standard deviations away from randomness, a departure that would occur by chance alone about as frequently as the spare parts in an automotive salvage lot might spontaneously assemble themselves into a McDonald's restaurant.

I don't intend to unload any of my secret money-making systems here, for readers' good as well as mine. If I did hold an "open sesame" to the markets, I wouldn't share it. There is ample opportunity to use wealth in this world, and neither I nor my friends, nor anyone else I have ever met, has so much of it that they are interested in putting themselves at a disadvantage by sharing their secrets. This would only cast their "edge" into oblivion and return them to being mere mortals who struggle for their daily bread. Man cannot live by bread alone, but it helps if others don't bake it using your recipe.

Even if I had decided to give away secrets and systems that I thought would have recurring value, my partners, family, and employees would doubtless have prevailed on me not to spill the beans. After laying a guilt trip on me, they would have ultimately confronted me with outside counsel. "Victor, you and your legatees should be aware of an interesting line of cases concerning conversion of work product generated by employees."

No, it is inconceivable that anyone will divulge a truly effective get-rich scheme for the price of a book. Besides, there is something drastically wrong with most of the systems unloaded on would-be speculators today. Most of the knowledge for sale doesn't have science behind it. Statistical data, other than anecdotal evidence, are almost never available to support the recommended techniques. The techniques are Monday-morning quarterbacking. On the rare occasion when a true guru shares secrets of a recurring, well-defined, systematic nature, the cycles are about to change. Better to go against. What looks good today is encapsulated by the market tomorrow and will change the expected profits, the probabilities, and the path of least resistance in subsequent periods. A good bet is that all systems will stop working when you use them.

I can't show you how to make money by parroting systematic trades. But I can show you something much more valuable: a way of thinking that will lead you to greater success. I am a good student, and my teachers have been the best. They have included average Joes, billionaires, genius cops, a hobo, chairmen of exchanges, bookies, Nobel scientists, eminent statisticians, a "Mistress of the Market," and several world champion game players. But as my chess teacher, International Grandmaster Art Bisguier, puts it, "You have to know the lesson is there in order to use it." I will alert you to the lessons this pantheon of greats taught me.

Successful speculations arise naturally from the ordinary, simple, and humdrum events of life. Games, music, nature, hoodoo, horses, and sex are great teachers. The successful speculator expedites a current price to its inevitable level. The techniques of expediting—and its cousin, hustling—are useful in all fields.

The grand theme of this book will be the lessons I learned from my father, Arthur Niederhoffer. His gentleness, kindness, intelligence, and creative spark caused all who knew him to love him. I will transmit the lessons he taught me so I could survive and succeed in all my speculations. The sources of Arthur's teachings were the countless games he played with me, the ten thousand lessons he chauffeured me to and observed, the daily dose of books and stories he read to and with me, and the several books he wrote about cops and their families.

At the other end of the spectrum of wealth, trading expertise, and hands-on parenthood from my dad, my counter theme will be the lessons I learned from my friend, George Soros, starting in 1981, the year Artie died. George is by popular consensus the greatest speculator in history.

During most of the 1980s, I provided execution and advice for him on most of his commodities and fixed-income trades, served as his partner in numerous ventures, and acted as broker for many of his funds. In addition, we have developed a personal relationship based on our common love of tennis and kids (totaling 11 between us).

What a contrast. Artie would routinely drive from New York to Boston and back overnight so he could type a term paper for me while I rested from a hard squash game. George has never had the pleasure of changing a diaper in his life. Artie was so poor he could never afford to buy a share of stock. George routinely moves markets by tens of billions of dollars when it is rumored that he is granting an interview or giving a speech. Artie drove a 15-year-old car to the airport to pick up and drop off every relative and their relatives. George doesn't attend funerals of his best friends (but surreptitiously supports the widowed and countless others with billions in philanthropy). Artie was the most human man I've had the pleasure of knowing, and George, the greatest humanist.

Join me in seeing how humdrum everyday experiences, combined with the wisdom of the immortals, can help you appreciate and maybe even learn the nitty-gritty of buying low and selling high.

VICTOR NIEDERHOFFER

Weston, Connecticut
November 1996

Acknowledgments

This effort spans so many disciplines, so many calculations, so much history, and so much ground that I couldn't have accomplished it by myself in several lifetimes. So many good people helped in putting this work together that I am embarrassed that the end product doesn't stand on a higher plane. Much of the book is dedicated to telling the good stories that my parents accumulated over forty years of a beautiful marriage. Another large segment recounts the wisdom I have been able to extract from the humble workaday activities of my good friends Caroline Baum, Art Bisguier, Dan Grossman, Rudolf Hauser, Herb London, Jim Lorie, Irving Redel, Marty Reisman, Robert Schrade, George Soros, Steve Stigler, and Joan Kennedy Taylor.

I have tried to quantify much of that wisdom. To do so, I have relied heavily on and benefited greatly from the insights and scientific contributions of my partners, Paul Buethe and Steve Wisdom, and I owe thanks to my colleagues, Richard Allen, Carlos Garcia, Dan Murphy, John Smarra, Michael Cook, Peter Jones, and Robert Wincapaw, for their calculations. Steve Stigler, Ron Volpe, Tim Horne, and Paul Cifrino gave me the initial impetus to become an author. "The Old Trader and the Yen" grew out of efforts with Messrs. Conolley and McKeage.

Some of my friends have been kind enough to collaborate with me on parts of the book. Tom Wiswell contributed to the material on board games, which represents the fruit of 15 years of the World Checkers Champion's thoughts about the meaning of games and life. John Conolley lived at my house for four months, fine tuning, researching, and editing every chapter in this book. His guidance on poker techniques, Dante, and Hemingway was invaluable. Jay McKeage, my assistant during 1994 and 1995, performed yeoman's work at an early stage of the manuscript. His knowledge of the classics provided a timeless anchor, especially on the Delphic Oracle and LoBagola. The material on ecology grew out of successive collaborations with Richard Zeckhauser and Steve Wisdom.

I benefited greatly from chapter-by-chapter critiques and improvements of my efforts by Larry Abrams, Bill Hurd, Herb London, Elaine Niederhoffer, Roy Niederhoffer, Frank Satterthwaite, and Joan Kennedy Taylor.

The following persons made substantial contributions to particular chapters: Bill Bradford, Murray Franck, Pat Graney, Rudy Hauser, Mitchell Jones, Bill Kenworthy, Richard Kostelanetz, Daniel Murphy,

Diane Niederhoffer, Katie Niederhoffer, John Normile, Harry Pincus, Michael Robert, Adam Robinson, Hank Shatkin, and Jim Wynne. Steve Stigler, Steve Wisdom, and Steve (Dr. Bo) Keeley provided lines of attack and historical examples for every chapter.

A number of talented artists contributed their visual interpretations of the tales told and some of their work is reproduced herein.

Last and most important, my editor, Pamela van Giessen, from the inception, when she completely recast a collection of my good stories into this comprehensive opus, to the end, when she came to Connecticut and personally retyped and edited every page (eliminating a few hundred pages in the process), was indefatigable, inspirational, and essential. My deepest appreciation, Pamela. Without you, the book would have ended in Book Hill.

My wife Susan has been my partner during many of the battles narrated here. My romantic inspiration for the past 20 years, she shepherded our four kids (Artemis, Kira, Rand, and Victoria) while I worked night and day for three years putting my touches on these pages.

Some of the names have been changed and a few stories have been telescoped to preserve the privacy of the individuals involved. Only Pamela van Giessen and Steve Wisdom had the opportunity to read the whole manuscript. Despite my diligent efforts to check the accuracy of each of its thousands of facts and citations, I am resigned to the presence of some unnoticed errors. None of the above-named persons is guilty.

V.N.

Contents

Chapter 11: Sex   242

Never the Twain. My Grandfather's Bent. Artie's
Allusions. My Sex Education. An Attractive Reporter.
Keep Your Distance. The Mistress of the Market. History
of Sex and Speculation. Transgressions Close to Home.
The Science of Sex. Sex in the Speculator's Family.

Chapter 12: Returns and Randomness: Academic Style   262

Five Glorious Years. The Lorie Years. A Quantum
Variation. An Historic Chance Phone Call. An
Unfortunate Short. An Ear Full of Cider. The Random
Walk Theory. Competing Hypotheses. Transactions and
Regularities. Blue Monday. Reversal of Fortune. An Ounce
of Testing. The January Effect. Yearly Seasonals. The
Fortunate Illness. Jew or Squash Player? The Western
Frontier. The Goodman Technique. The Chief Rabbi.
Time Series Charts. The Subjective Nature of Academic
Research. Final Days in the West.

Chapter 13: Connections to Monitor   293

Market Chains. Reasons for Interrelations. Bogus
Intermarket Relations. Leiningen and the Markets.
Humility in Interrelations. The October 1987 Crash.
Correlations between Markets. International Connections.
Japanese Case Study. A Japanese Field Trip. A Japanese–
American Web. International Correlations. Profitability
of Intermarket Trading. Connections to Monitor.

Chapter 14: Music and Counting   322

Music in the Market. Funeral Music. Pure Music.
Predictive Music and Markets. Emotional Moves.
Contrast and Repetition. Dissonance and Resolution.
Rules for Success. Rules for Mastering an Elemental
Activity. Music and Counting. Difficulty of Counting.
How to Count. Counting Education. Computer-Assisted
Moves. Musician and Counter Employees. Danger of End.

Chapter 15: The Ecology of Markets   350

The Field at the Board. Ecological Principles. Market
Ecosystem. Public Producers. Managed Futures Public.
Other Publics. Governmental Contributors. The Primary
Consumers. Fixed-Income Herbivores. Carnivores—Hedge
Funds. Decomposers. Rules and Regulations. Maintaining

The Old Trader and the Yen

I wish I was the fish, he thought, with everything he has against only my will and my intelligence.

Ernest Hemingway
The Old Man and the Sea

I am an old trader, and I trade the yen in the cash market. I once had the best record among all the traders. I was rated number one in my field, and my picture was in all the newspapers. Customers crowded my doors. The attractive currency brokers talked sexy to me, told me where their customers' stops were, and where the central banks were buying and selling. The great Soros more than once called to have me trade for his own account.

But I got in over my head. I bought the dollar when the dollar:yen was 93. It went to 88 in just a few hours. I was eaten alive. The banks will not give me credit anymore, and many of my customers have left. I still have some customers—people who are not happy with feeding all their money to the stock market. They are afraid that it will crash as it did in 1929 and 1987. They look to me to land a big return, but without risk or drawdown. I can do it; but they don't want me to gamble, and I cannot do it without gambling. The risk creates opportunity. Still, I am humble because I have lost many times.

Lopez, an 18-year-old student from Mexico, worked at my side for free, just so he could learn from me. He ran computer programs for me, got me tea, and woke me when I was tired. Lopez has now left to trade at a more successful firm in the daytime, but he comes to visit me after hours. "Victor," he says to me, "I could help you tonight. We've made some money together."

"No," I say, "You're with a better firm; stay with them."

"But I remember how the dollar went down for 10 days in a row and you kept buying it. And then it went back up, and we made back all we lost and more."

"Yes, but now the dollar is going up and we're selling it."

"The Bank of Japan and the U.S. Treasury want it up; everyone in the world wants it up and I am fighting it. I am already short $300 million and the forces are against me."

"Can I get you some tea? The dollar's been up many days in a row. Let me run some programs."

"Yes, of course. Between traders," I say.

"Victor, the patterns are bearish. Can I sell alongside?"

"No, you are too young to risk everything. You have to learn to sit it out when the tide is too strong."

At 7 P.M. in New York, it is morning in Asia. The sun is shining there. Men in white shirts are preparing for battle. The banks will wait for their customers to sell the dollar to hedge their export earnings, and then they will buy it. They have a great advantage over me, for I have been sitting in front of my monitor, staring at the screen, eyes burning, for two nights and a day, and now part of another night. They drink *sake* each night with their friends from school and the ministries, and they learn what is going to be announced and where they will be buying and selling. When the poor folks, the outsiders, demand an investigation because a number was leaked, the Central Bank says no investigation is necessary because leaks are impossible.

When I visited Japan, I saw the hotels where the white-shirted men sleep in little coffins on nights when they are too drunk to get home safely. When they do get home, their wives massage them and dress them and put them onto the bullet train for their two-hour commute to work.

My wife has gone to Maine with the kids. She is worried. "Why not get out and call it a day? You can't seem to get it right this year."

"No, It's bearish," I say.

The waters are very deep. Maybe too deep. The Japanese trade balance is scheduled to be announced. If the surplus is lower, there will be no need for the United States to bash the dollar down to save American jobs in the Rust Belt. The dollar will rise, and I will be buried because I am short an amount ten times greater than my worth. Already there are rumors that the surplus is lower. The Bank of Japan is said to leak news of this to cushion the blow of the announcement. Japan has been running a $50 billion annual trade surplus with the United States.

The current Assistant Secretary of State has said that this surplus is unacceptable. I knew him when we were boys at Harvard. He was known as an economist then. Now he doesn't say a word unless it will help his boss. I have to eat, so it is well to know what's good for the Democrats. The great Soros is a Democrat, and he is rich beyond the dreams of such as I. Maybe I'm not as rich as he because I went to Chicago after college.

I dialogue with myself. "I wish that I had never met Milton Friedman or George Stigler, or his son Steve, or Jim Lorie, with their liberalism of the classics."

"Fool! Is this the way for a friend to talk? You love these men!"

"Yes, I revere them, but they make me poor."

"Poverty does not matter!"

I don't talk during the trading day. Noise distracts me from the job at hand. When I played squash, I would wear a sock on my hand before the match so that no one would shake my hand and distract me. But now I talk to calm myself. I should not talk out loud even when there is no one around to think I'm crazy.

I used to listen to music when I traded at night. Now the CD player is broken, and I don't wish to spend the money to get a new one while I am having losses. Besides, in the time it would take to turn on the music, something big might happen to the yen. That would be just my luck, to have the dollar spike down in the two seconds I was away. I need some luck today. But it is better to use my knowledge and tricks than to count on luck.

I think about music. About all the funeral music my traders play when I am down. The Mozart *Requiem*, Beethoven's "Moonlight" sonata. Why couldn't I be long the dollar rather than short? I want to cry. The Beethoven *Marcia Funebre* has a complete cycle in it, from high C sharp to low G sharp and back, in four measures. The dollar:yen has gone down from a high of 105 to 80 and now it is back to 93. What if it goes back to 105?

Now is not the time to think about cycles or music. Now is the time to think of only one thing: the yen.

My only hope is the Bank Negara, the terrible central bank of Malaysia. Bank Negara is like a pirate. It trades violently and takes no prisoners. It is happy to wreck me and my fellow traders. So far, it has lost $10 billion, almost bankrupting the country, by always going against the dollar and bonds. The Malaysians like to stampede the market at 7 P.M. New York time. If they call up all 50 banks in their network at the same time, in Australia, New Zealand, and Singapore, and sell the dollar, I may be able to take my line back with dignity.

A man should never give up hope. But it is better to have science. I know what happens to the yen when the soybeans are up and gold is down. If good luck comes, I will be ready for it.

Soros is long the dollar. He is always with the force when governments and businesspeople want something to happen. His father taught him to survive when the Gestapo was interning the Jews in the concentration camps. My father is dead because he listened to the big shots at the Memorial Hospital, who then shot him up with chemicals that destroyed his heart and lungs.

I played tennis with Soros last night. I hope he is playing tennis now, so he will not be able to buy any more dollars for a while. I wonder whether my father could beat him in a tennis match. We hardly ever lost when I played doubles with my father. When I play with Soros as my partner, I almost always lose. But that is because Soros pays the pros to play against us. The exchanges, the Treasury, the trend followers, the banks, the politicians and policy makers are all against me now. Now is not the time to think of my father or Soros, or fellow traders. Now is the time to do only one thing: watch the screen.

Bank of Tokyo flashes a price of 93. An Australian bank, the Westpac of Sydney, flits over the waters offering dollars at 92.75. But the fish are too big for it. It's gone in a second and now DKB Bank of Tokyo is bidding 93. That's bad. They always seem to know what's going on first.

Just then, I see the dollar:mark drop sharply. Union Bank of Switzerland is offering it down. "Be honest like your country," I say. The mark and yen often swim together. Bank Negara must be hitting the dollar while Europe is asleep. What a huge trade. 1.50, 1.49, 1.48. Please now, move to the yen. Mark:yen must follow. The yen is cheap. Come on, the yen is lovely.

I wish I were rich and powerful. The most important banks would request my advice. I could influence prices directly. I would put up my bids on the Telerate like the other big fish. I could afford direct lines to the banks. Best of all would be a Reuters dealing machine. I would contact four banks at the same time and hit them before they change the yen. Rothschild himself would tremble. I would discuss good books with the learned. Now I must deal with brokers. I pay them points to trade, so I always start behind. The banks know I trade through brokers. When the brokers call on my behalf, the banks change their course and trade ahead of me before I can catch them. It would not spoil the master plan if I were a rich man.

Now, I'll put in some orders with the broker to sell dollars at 93.50. I'll let them have those dollars where they want it. They won't know it's me. Please take it. Come on now, it's beautiful! They can't leave it this cheap. But they don't take it.

Now I see the Deutschebank circling. They offer to sell the dollar at 1.4850. This is good. Where there is dollar:mark selling, dollar:yen selling will soon follow. My phone rings. They are beginning to buy dollars from me at 93.50. "Sell very carefully," I tell the broker. "Take a few yards only. I don't want to frighten them away."

The buying stops. Go down, dollar. Please fall back. I can't hurt you. I am just one old man. I wait with my orders back in full size. Don't be afraid. Please come back to 93.50. Buy my dollars, yen. Smell my millions, hard and cold. Eat them, yen; eat them.

Yes! Three phones ring at the same time. They have swallowed the bait. I have let out a line $100 million long. What a buyer. That must be Bacon. Or Jones. He took my bait as if it were a sardine. I will give him more line at 94. Take it. Price does not matter to you. Give *me* the edge, not the Bank of Japan. Then you will be so far behind that, in the morning, when the stock markets in Europe sink, I will kill you.

I love you, yen. You are so orderly, so loyal, like your country. I don't hold it against you that you would not take my dollars when I tried to buy food in Tokyo for my family of eleven. Now take my dollars. You feel the *gaijin* are dirty. They will not take their shoes off in your crowded restaurants. But I do take my shoes off. I'll build a rock garden and sit and pray to Shinto gods if you'll just take my dollars at 93.50 and then go down to 91.

I know that you want to go down, dollar:yen. The earthquake created tremendous demand for dollars to buy foreign goods from the industries destroyed in Osaka. I realize that your economy is in recession because the West cannot afford to buy your goods at these high prices. But please go up a little first. Fool some buyers into thinking you want to go up. Then, when they sell, you'll go down even harder.

Nothing happens. The dollar is going up steadily. I feel it drawing my balance lower and lower. What will I do if it keeps pulling me down? My brokers will give me a margin call if the dollar goes any higher. 94.00, 94.25, 94.50. I just lost another $4 million. Turn down, dollar. Please go lower. I'd better sell some more dollars to feign strength. They should not know how weak I am. All right. Sell ten yards of the dollar at the market. That will kill the dollar.

The dollar takes my selling like I am a minnow. The dollar is pulling my house along with it.

I am afraid. I have gone too far. The Japanese trend followers will all jump in if the dollar goes above 95.00. The bubble will drown me. The Japanese are very brilliant. Their nine-year-old schoolchildren solve problems that Harvard and Williams students could not solve. But they run in herds. The nail that sticks out gets hammered. If the dollar sticks up any higher, the entire Japanese trading community will jump in to buy it. A higher dollar will become an ever rising bubble.

I wish Lopez were here. I need tea. I need to see what happens when the dollar is at a new high at 8 P.M. on a Tuesday. But he has seen me lose too many times, and he is with another shop. I wish I were young again. Then, if I lost, I could recover. Now it is too hard. When I go out with my wife, I get asked if I am her father. I must survive now so that my children and Susan will live.

Please, I beg of you. I pray: Slow down, then go down. Shame on me. How can one who has no superstition pray? Francis Galton did not pray. He thought of his shared heredity with all other creatures and this made him reverential. But the priests do not die older than others. All my praying will not make the dollar go down. I am a man, and I must do my work.

If the dollar goes up any higher, my customers will kill me. My partners will look at me and say, "We told you not to sell the premium." Then they will say nothing. They will go home to their families and say, "We lost. We're in trouble. Victor did it again."

The dollar is now open in Tokyo. The dollar cannot go up as long as I sell it, and it will not go down until I buy it back. We are in a dead heat.

No one should be alone in his old age. I should be with my six daughters in Maine. But I cannot even urinate for fear that the move down will occur.

Here is the Japanese Ministry of Finance head saying that there is no danger of the discount rate in Japan being decreased again. It is already just 1 percent. That is good for me. The dollar will go down if the rates are high. But the Japanese traditionally deny that they will decrease it three times before lowering. This is their third denial. All the traders know this and the dollar goes up. It touches 94.50.

The Japanese surplus will soon be announced. If it is lower, I will go under. How can I stay in when all hinges on a number that all the traders in Japan already know about! The direct line rings.

"Victor, do you have any stops?" my broker asks. If I tell him, then immediately the price will go to that level and I will be dead. "I don't believe in stops," I say strongly. "Yen, I will stay with you until I am dead," I say softly. The yen will stay with me, too. But I am as patient as the yen. I played squash every day for ten years in a row before winning the big one. I have been watching the screen for 52 hours without sleep. And I am not going to give up.

The yen is my friend, and there is a full moon out. The trends often change when the moon is full. The moon affects the markets just as it affects women, crops, crime, and the tides. I am afraid I have as much chance of killing the dollar as of killing the moon. Still, I will not fail for lack of effort or preparation.

I'm hungry. I have not eaten since lunch and the gnats are starting to come in through the window screen and are biting me all over. Perhaps I should stare at the computer screen harder. Will that make it turn in my favor? It's all I have left.

Just then, the dollar jumps down. Hail to the Chief. The Chairman of the Eminent Persons Council, generally thought to be a mouthpiece for the Administration, is speaking in Japan. He calls for an equilibrium dollar of 80. The dollar drops to 94, 93, 92. Yes! Dollar holders are desperate to get out. This is what I was born to do. To take their dollars when they are afraid to hold them. To give them the dollars back when they want to sell me their goods. I end up with all their dollars and all their goods.

I must buy $400 million without anyone's knowing, or else I will turn the market. But I am all alone. And brokers will rush ahead to buy as soon as they know what I'm doing.

I pick up two phones and press the speaker on another. "What's your dollar bid and offer for 12.5 yards of yen?" I say. I wait a second and then say, "I buy dollars." And with three words, I just bought $375 million against the yen. I am whole again.

I call Susan. My mouth is dry and my ulcers are violently painful. "I'll be coming to Maine tomorrow," I say. "Are you alive?" she asks. "We both killed each other," I say.

I go hit some balls on my racquetball court before finishing my job and writing up all the tickets. But my job is not over yet. I still have 2.5 yards.

By the time I get back, the sharks have hit me. The trade surplus is announced. The dollar moves to 93. I lost a quarter million on just those 2.5 yards, but I just made $3 million. Not to worry. I throw on 4 more yards just for the fun of it.

But then the sharks begin to attack with horrible fury, as if they were maddened by my escape. The Bank of Japan buys dollars. The rumors were true, after all. The price rushes to 94, with resolution and malignancy. It was too good to last. Why did I do something for fun? I never have fun trading. It is too serious. I just dropped a million.

My nerve is going now. I close out all my positions. "I shouldn't have sold so many dollars," I say, "both for your sake and mine."

Like the fisherman in *The Old Man and the Sea*, I think, "Fish that you were, I am sorry that I went too far out. I ruined us both. But we have killed many sharks, you and I, and ruined many others. How many did you ever kill, old fish?"

I fought the dollar in a battle to the death. Shortly after I covered, the Bank of England, the Bundesbank, and the Federal Reserve (acting for the Treasury) all intervened to buy the dollar. By the next morning, the dollar rose to 98. Had I not bought it back, I would have lost $40 million, about 100 percent of my capital.

I am sore from my wounds. I feel like the sole survivor from a plane crash. I am tired. Before I leave, I check my faxes. A memo from my lawyer informs me that a certain agency wishes to review my filings for the past 10 years. Two boxcars of documents.

The sharks are always circling, always tearing at my flesh. Hades, go away; you can't have it. It's mine. I've paid my dues. I cannot keep the sharks from hitting me. They are very powerful and do what they please. But I will continue to fight them while I have strength. I have my resolution, and there are many things I can do.

As I leave my office, my partners are coming in to pick up the pieces of the trades and even out the weights. "What a trade it was," I hear them saying as I drive away.

CHAPTER 1

Brighton Beach Training

This drama unfolds on the handball courts of Coney Island, where people drink lime rickeys on the boardwalk, a knish toss from the center of the one-wall handball universe.

Michael Disend
The Brooklyn Reader

The Losers

Where the city ended, I began. In 1943, I was born at the southern edge of the underdog capital of the world, Brighton Beach, Brooklyn. The mere mention of the name is traditionally good for a raised eyebrow, a snicker, or a joke. A town of second fiddlers, where "da Bums," the Dodgers of baseball, were revered.

In a typical Brooklyn touch, the Dodgers didn't win a modern World Series from the annual event's inception in 1903 until 1955. They lost seven times along the way. Then, two years after finally beating the Yankees in 1955, the team moved to Los Angeles. Ebbets Field, their former home and originally the site of a garbage dump, was torn down and replaced with a housing development. In a typical Niederhoffer touch, I bet on the Dodgers to win the pennant in 1951, when they were ahead by 13 games. Bobby Thompson's homer in the playoff game relieved me of my funds.

The Brooklyn Dodgers took their name from the locals' need to dodge around the world's largest trolley system or perish. The no-fare kids riding on the back edge of the trolleys learned to jump off before the route got too close to the police station, where they risked receiving a clubbing. Brooklyn during that era was a town of cemeteries, breweries, congestion, change, rebels, losers. No war movie of the era was complete without a clip of a heart-of-gold kid from Bensonhurst, chewing gum, bumming a cigarette, and speaking in Brooklynese. Nor would a play about a move from Manhattan be complete without the lament, "Now I'll have to go back to Brooklyn." No wonder that a Society for the Prevention of Disparaging

9

Remarks Against Brooklyn claimed 40,000 members and counted 3,000 slanders in 1946.

The edges of civilization attract a fringe element. Brighton had more than its share of the downtrodden, beach bums, gamblers, hustlers, invalids, lost souls, low lifes, peddlers, and street musicians. But mainly Brighton welcomed families—working stiffs whom the elevated subways deposited on the frazzled edges of civilization for a day of baking sun, cheap and cacophonous revelry, and then a nickel's ticket back to endless drudgery.

THE LITTLE PEOPLE

Brooklyn's legendary street games taught me how to survive. On a typical Sunday in 1951, I'm watching "the Milkman" play a big-money game against my 12-year-old Uncle Howie. The stake is $50, held under a hat by "Louie the Lion." The Milkman calls a time out. He looks overhead. Thunder clouds loom, the humidity's high. He needs to break to take a shower. There are no rules on duration or frequency of time-outs, so a fight breaks out with the referee.

The referee is diminutive Sam Silver, half the size of the players. Sam affects a style borrowed partly from Tomashevsky, the great Yiddish actor and the Charlie Chaplin of Yiddish theater, and partly from Bill Klem, a legendary baseball umpire who believed that the guy in the 25-cent bleacher seat is as much entitled to know a call as the guy in the boxes. Like the wrestling referees of today, Sam frequently ended the games black-and-blue. But these beatings were real, and Sam often had to run for his life when the players chased him off the court.

After three hours of delay, the storm the Milkman is waiting for finally comes and all bets are returned. Howie and I lose our bets.

Some 41 years later, it happens again. It's April 13, 1992. I'm holding a short bond position that I plan to get out of at the close. But a water-main break in Chicago floods the Chicago Board of Trade. Trading is canceled for the first time ever, and by the time the Exchange opens for a full session three days later, I'm down 100 percent on my equity. Whenever I hear the expression "Sometimes you win and sometimes you lose," I always add, "And sometimes you get rained out."

I've learned that around volatile announcements, such as the employment figures and the Consumer Price Index (CPI) number, another outcome is possible—a dead heat. Market orders to buy will be filled at the high of the day, and orders to sell will be filled at the low, leaving me dead on my margin regardless of my direction.

On the street, we stop to admire an Oldsmobile. The owner jumps out. "I'll sell it to you for $100. But it costs you nothing. I got a sure thing at Belmont which I'm going to bet the whole stack on and you're in for a 5 percent carry if you get me the cash before the daily double." We come up with the money, the horse wins, but we don't recoup because the car breaks down on the way to the track.

Often, in my speculations, dealers call me with a bargain. They just happen to have some off-the-run securities left over from an unrelated swap of short-term into long-term paper.

If I buy it now, it costs me nothing because the dealer provides 0 percent financing for two weeks. By that time, I'll doubtless be out with a profit. A moment after I buy it, a massive offering of that off-the-run security hits the street, and I'm down 50 percent on my equity before I can hang up the phone.

The nicknames of the tanned and wizened people I grew up with tell their story: "Bitter Irving," "Bookie," "the Animal," "the Martian," "Rugged," "the Indian," "Nervous Phil," "the Ganef," "the Barber," "the Butcher," "the Milkman," and, of course, "the Refugee." Brooklyn consistently led the nation in number of immigrants arriving and homes built.

In short, I grew up with the little people of Kasrilevka immortalized by Sholom Aleichem in *Fiddler on the Roof*:

> Stuck away in a corner of the world, isolated from the surrounding country, the town stands, orphaned, dreaming, bewitched, immersed in itself and remote from the noise and bustle, the confusion and tumult and greed, which men have created about them and have dignified with high-sounding names like Culture, Progress, Civilization. But transformed by the many mirrors of poverty to [Brighton Beach].[1]

These little people were cooled by the healthful breezes and salt air of the Atlantic Ocean, which were then wafted 10 miles northwestward to be re-breathed by the high financiers in the towers of Wall Street. They, in their rarefied aeries, thought they breathed the sea air first; but it had already been staled and soured by the whole, wide miasma of Brooklyn. "In much the same way," wrote Herman Melville, "do the commonality lead their leaders in many other things, at the same time that the leaders little suspect it."[2] This was true of Brighton. The bird or squirrel or chickweed knows, from the drop in pressure, that a storm is coming. We have to wait until the raindrops splash against our windows. The denizens of Brighton, living on the edge of life as well as on the edge of land, knew, from the sudden drop in income, that the crunch was on. The financiers had to wait until the stale news appeared in *The Wall Street Journal*.

Manhattan and Wall Street seemed miles away when I was growing up. Brighton was the Harvard of my education as a speculator. The games, bargains, music, sex, and fauna taught me to appreciate the earthy and nitty-gritty. That's the proper foundation for buying low and selling high, the trade of a speculator.

A Brighton Pedigree

After the First World War, my paternal grandparents, Martin and Birdie Niederhoffer, were experiencing financial reverses in their residential real estate business. Forced to cut back on their lifestyle, they discovered that the Brighton Beach area, with its inexpensive housing in apartment buildings and its proximity to the Atlantic Ocean, would reduce the family's living and vacation expenses. Their son Arthur was born there in 1917.

My maternal grandparents, Sam and Gertrude Eisenberg, were following doctor's orders by settling in Brighton Beach. After a critical thyroid gland operation, my grandmother was urged by her surgeon to seek out a healthful, iodine-laden sea environment in which to reside. Their daughter Elaine was born in 1924.

My parents met in 1939, when Elaine was made editor of her high school newspaper, *The Lincoln Log.* One of her co-editors was Jane Niederhoffer, who liked to bounce homework assignments off her erudite brother, a football star at Brooklyn College. My mom soon became a regular at these study sessions; romance was born, and eventually so was I, exactly nine months after Elaine and Artie were married in 1943.

Artie was the kind of guy we all meet once or twice in a lifetime, one whom everyone loves and respects. The character in mythology that most resembles him is Balder, the Norse god of light and beauty. He was brave, wise, just, sincere, simple, and generous, the kindest and gentlest of gods.

Artie received his L.L.B. from Brooklyn Law School in 1939 and was admitted to the New York State Bar in 1940, but he was unable to find employment as a lawyer in the still depressed economy. After eight years of the New Deal, the unemployment rate stood at 18 percent. Needing work, my dad decided to join the New York City Police Department in 1940.

A great salary of above $1,000 a year, and a fine pension, plus the job security, made police, fire, and sanitation department jobs seem like real plums. When New York decided to hire 300 new policemen, more than 30,000 would-be applicants lined up to take the test. Artie scored in the top 100 and joined the police force as a patrolman stationed in the Coney Island area. He supplemented his salary with jobs as a night watchman and by loading *The New York Times* onto delivery trucks. Eventually, he resumed his studies at Brooklyn College and NYU, and gained a Ph.D. summa cum laude in sociology. After 20 years' service, he retired from the police force with the rank of lieutenant, and became a founding professor of John Jay College, the criminal justice unit of the city university system. His books, *The Gang* (which Artie characteristically allowed his Ph.D. adviser to claim senior authorship for), *Behind the Shield, The Ambivalent Force,* and *The Police Family* are still considered classics in their field.

Artie and Elaine settled in Brighton Beach in a small, art-deco apartment one block from the four major landmarks of Brighton: the private beach, the boardwalk, the elevated train, and the massive 75,000-square-foot, brick Public School 225.

The jewel of the beach was a "private" club, Brighton Beach Baths. Dating back to the days when mogul Joseph P. Day was developing the area as a roost for gamblers and dandies, this one patch of "PRIVATE" beach was my personal oyster.

For the next 25 years, Artie and Elaine spent most of their nonworking hours on the beach. The sandy beach of Brighton extended 100 yards from the ocean and ran for one mile before being met by the rich people's Manhattan Beach on the east and the carnival-and-fantasy beach of Coney Island on the west. Brighton, in its benevolence, permitted the poor to enjoy the same air, luxurious views, fine cuisine, and opportunity for sport as the rich. The three miles of adjacent beaches, with their fresh salt air, gentle surf, light reflecting off the smooth sand and churning waters, open spaces, sightings of luxurious ocean liners sailing away to exotic lands, and views of the sun setting over the sea provided a panorama that the richest potentate could not have found wanting. As for food, no king's palate ever delighted in delicacies tastier than Mrs. Stahl's knishes, Lundy's oysters, or Nathan's frankfurters, all served in restaurants near the beach, or the Humorettes, celrays, lime rickeys, malteds, egg creams, hot pretzels, kishke, and waffles on sale in the ubiquitous candy stores surrounding the beach. If a communication was urgent, the telephone at the candy store served as well as the private postal services of the nobles or the carrier pigeons of Reuters or Rothschild. As for sport, paddle tennis and handball on concrete were Brighton's version of lawn tennis and squash. Little people play their racquet sports against concrete walls and on cement floors, not on slate and grass. They hole their putts around obstructions of papier-maché windmills rather than on the well-manicured greens of Augusta or Pebble Beach.

The Boardwalk

The boardwalk still runs like a stream from the shtetl that was Brighton, curving gently past the handball courts, alongside the Aquarium, and on to wondrous Coney Island. The old parachute jump from the '39 World's Fair dominates this spot like some ancient symbol of the universe. The sun slowly sinks beyond the endless ribbon of the boardwalk, culminating in a great burst of gold. Soon, only the shimmering necklace of light that is Coney remains, rising out of the welter of bodies, the waves, and the reflections of things past.

Underdogs have a tendency to look surreptitiously and guiltily at those above them. Repeatedly, short stories and remembrances about Brooklyn record voyeurism underneath the crisscrossing planks of the boardwalk, or beneath the crests of one of the roller coasters, so it seems to have been a vivid part of the primal Brooklyn experience.

I chased the filtered light [running below the boardwalk], played games with it: cutting it up, throwing sand on it. . . . Tired of that, I zigzagged between the pillars, my heart pounding, looking up through the thin spacings between the boards in search of ladies who left their underwear home, an Indian, stalking his prey.[3]

Worse than the voyeurism were the activities alluded to in this characteristic passage:

Underneath the secluded, dapper netherworld below the boards were taking place other activities, more intimate ones, which required the special shaded privacy that the boardwalk afforded. Some called it the hotel underworld.[4]

In a legendary incident in family history, Artie caught a young relative (not me) taking part in an indiscreet intimate activity with an adult. He beat up the adult within an inch of his life.

I am not as strong as Artie. But when brokers take the orders of my customers and "bag" the trades in the shaded privacy of their booths rather than in the ring, I sometimes find it difficult to refrain from giving the offenders a tongue-lashing.

I didn't go in for voyeurism. I found it degrading, even as a kid. Today, when half of the dealers and traders in the world are trying to figure out what George Soros and the Dream Team just might be buying, I look upon their unholy interest as a variant of market voyeurism. Instead of overhearing conversations, rummaging through garbage, anticipating actions from telephone rings, positioning sentries at the elevators, attending seminars with a guru, or visiting Delphic oracles to find out how to succeed, they should get out in the sun and do something invigorating.

On the sides of the boardwalk, there were families and workers, and those who will never work. They washed up on the rocks, recumbent, wet, and warmed. They luxuriated in the sands, intimate, almost naked. Three million beachgoers in two square miles on a sunny July 4 can get crowded, but there was always room for two more.

The sky might darken suddenly against the silvery waters. A deluge of rain or wind led to a panicked exodus from the beach. In the most primordial vaults beneath the boardwalk, shivering and sandy, most of the mob waited out the crisis. Some streamed out through the streets of Brighton and went back to little apartments within large buildings of impressive Moorish design, with lobbies decorated with proud sailing ships. I would use the opportunity to rush into a cafeteria and hustle a few nickels in a game of five-card stud.

In winter, the crowd huddled on beach chairs, wrapped up against the coursing winds. The "polar bears" plunged into the Atlantic. My parents retreated to play paddle tennis, sheltered by the high concrete sides of a drained triple-Olympic-size pool.

THE BRIGHTON CYCLES

Brighton's fortunes, like those of most other beach communities, suffered through frequent and ever-changing cycles. At the turn of the century, the area was a retreat for the wealthy. Brighton, among its other distinctions, was the horse racing capital of the world. It boasted three racetracks: Sheepshead Bay, Gravesend, and Brighton Beach. Exclusive hotels such as the Brighton Beach, the Manhattan Beach, and the Oriental catered to the rich and naughty. Coney Island's Feltman's Ocean Pavilion Hotel, where the frankfurter was invented, had nine separate dining facilities, each with its own private band. Well-known speculators, such as Diamond Jim Brady, the Vanderbilts, the Belmonts, and Leonard Jerome, "put on the Ritz" on the boardwalk before driving their trotters to elaborate champagne and quail dinners. Entertainers such as Jimmy Durante and Eddie Cantor performed at music halls crammed with revelers and the overflow from the track.

But that era ended when gambling was declared illegal in 1910. The racetracks were converted to speedways and then to housing developments, fueling the many years when Brooklyn set a record for new-home construction.

The automobile helped to democratize Brighton. The rich could travel to more secluded areas. The establishment of direct public subways to Brighton in 1920 enabled the borough's masses to reach their own beach. Rides, franks, watermelon, and malteds were all priced at five cents each. Brighton became "the nickel empire" rather than "the rich man's paradise." Millions took the subway to the beach each sunny weekend. What they needed first were bathhouses. By the end of the Roaring '20s, there were 30 bathhouses, all linked by the boardwalk.

Running at right angles to the beach was a massive series of wooden and metal beams, up to 30 feet high, that held the decaying wooden track of the Brighton Beach and Coney Island subway lines. Bungalows and apartments in the neighborhood rumbled and shook every ten minutes as the trains made their way out to Coney Island or back to Manhattan.

Underneath the elevated trains was a strip of open-air fruit stands, bakeries, delicatessens, restaurants, and discount apparel stores. Every three years, these stores went through a cycle ranging from 100 percent occupancy to 90 percent vacancy. Brighton ("Little Odessa") is now mainly populated by Russian immigrants, but the stores still invite customers.

The worst market crash of all, in 1929, brought the Great Depression, which lasted until 1946 and scaled back Brighton once again. My paternal grandfather, Martin, was wiped out during the Depression. He routinely speculated in real estate and stocks during the Roaring '20s with an equity of 5 percent of the market value of his holdings. Like many others, he was able to withstand that first 200-point crack, when the Dow went below 200 in November 1929. Then, after tottering ominously for a year, the Dow fell another 75 percent to 50, in May 1932, and Martin was buried alive many times over. He became a kind of Don Quixote thereafter, eternally searching for the stake that would support his rise again, while remaining vigilantly ahead of the rent collector. Fittingly, he read *Don Quixote* in Spanish and committed it to memory to drown his sorrows. He and his ilk were known as "dead ducks" on the street.

His saga was the classic Brighton experience. After some hairbreadth escapes, he and his wife Birdie settled on Brighton First Street, the last street on the Brighton side of the Coney Island border, in a $25-a-month, 400-square-foot apartment. With this exposure to changing fortunes ingrained in me by my heredity and environment, I guess it's natural for me to tend to play a defensive game in my speculations.

BROKERAGE HOUSE BELLWETHERS

I try to protect myself from sucker plays in the market by waiting to buy until things look really grim. Blood in the streets isn't enough. Nathan Rothschild said he liked to buy when the cannons are firing, and sell when the trumpets are blowing. That's good enough for him but not for a weak hand like me.

I heard those cannons on the streets of Taiwan in March 1996, when the Chinese lobbed some missiles in the direction of the April 1996 Taiwan presidential elections. The analysts attributed it to an attempt to drive the Taiwan stock market down. It was good for a 7.8 percent one-day decline in Hong Kong stocks and a 5 percent drop in Taiwan. I immediately sought shelter in some Chinese mutual funds. Within a week, Taiwan began to *rise* whenever the missiles were launched. During the month after the missiles, Taiwan was the best performing stock market of all.

When the *Titanic* sank, a "spine-chilling chorus drifted across the water—a mixture of cries, screams, and shouts. It was the most nightmarish sound imaginable."[5] When I hear the "thunderous roar and hiss of escaping steam" from the market, followed by the "long continuous wailing chants" as magazine articles proclaim the end, I know it's time to jump in. As the Japanese market reeled from the aftermath of the Osaka earthquake and the Barings failure in mid-1995, flirting with 15,000 on the Nikkei, a certain magazine ran one of its notorious cover stories forecasting fair value at 8,000. Brokers were in disarray. I knew then that it was every man for himself, and I rushed into the fray.

The wholesale failure of brokerage firms during a panic is often associated with market bottoms. The bottom of the 1995 slide in the Nikkei came in conjunction with the collapse of Barings and Company. At the bottom of the 1987 crash, the market had teetered precariously on its edge with every vicissitude in the profit and loss that U.S. investment bankers faced on the British Petroleum underwriting. Noted investor and *Barron's* roundtable participant Jim Rogers likes the comfort of complete collapse, as memorialized by the closing of a stock market, when he buys. In early 1996, he indicated he was building up a line of Pakistani stocks because the Pakistan stock exchange had just been shut down. As of mid-1996, Pakistan's up about 35 percent.

Gerald Loeb recounts a story illustrating the other side of the equation. His brokerage house was swimming in luxury at the height of the 1929 crash. When Loeb traveled, his stock dealings were by no means curtailed.

> During these times, Mike Meehan, the famous speculator and floor specialist in the high-flying RCA stock of 1929, opened the first office on a steamer—the North German Lloyd luxury express liner *Bremen*. I sailed on her for Europe in early October 1929. I think it was the maiden voyage of the seagoing board room. At least, so far no firm has opened an office on a plane.
>
> I was not immune to the optimism of this period. I laid the groundwork for a stock market country club. . . . Fine brokerage offices were other straws in the wind. We built a showplace in Palm Beach. The interior wood was all weatherbeaten and genuine, collected along the Atlantic Coast. We had a patio, a fountain, palm trees, of course, a real fireplace, and two or three cars to lend just in case a client needed some transportation . . .[6]

Shortly thereafter, Loeb formed and quickly sold out an offering for a brokerage house in a golf country club. The crash of 1929 came before he could collect the subscriptions. Loeb recommends selling stocks when brokerage profits are at highs and buying them when brokerage houses are in the red.

There was an interesting daily double of broker–stock interactions in conjunction with the stock market panic of July 1996. In the first place, Hambrecht & Quist, one of the leading underwriters of technology and healthcare issues, announced that it would be filing an initial public offering. Some income statement numbers tell the exciting story:

	Yearly Results*					Six-Month Results*	
	1991	1992	1993	1994	1995	1995	1996
Revenues	$81.8	$125.5	$110.5	$119.3	$220.0	$86.8	$204.5
Net income	(9.9)	9.7	15.3	15.9	49.4	18.5	47.6

*Amounts in millions of dollars.

No sooner had the announcement of the filing been made than the NAS-DAQ Index plummeted over 15 percent. In late July, the market rallied and the issue was refiled.

In the second race, a broker jumped out the window and killed himself as the Thailand SET Index registered a decline of 30 percent over the previous two months. My partner in Thailand, the very knowledgeable Mustafa Zaidi, immediately called me, "Victor, I thought you'd want to know." Based on his information, I lucked out. I doubled my Emerging Tiger holdings. In the next three trading days, the SET Index gained 5 percent.

Although Loeb's sensible words of advice have a ring of truth, the problem is that too many things sound reasonable and can also be supported by anecdote. As the Dow ricocheted up and down 100 points a day at the beginning of 1996, several newspaper articles made the case that the market was in strong hands because brokerage house profits were high and "as is well known, these have to fall before the market drops." What good is such advice and how can anyone tell the good from the bad without data or recurring principles?

Lessons from Livermore

From an early age, I have been very cautious about accepting seemingly sensible advice. Martin, my grandfather, had the luck to be taken under the wing of Jesse Livermore, "the Boy Wonder" of Wall Street in the early 1900s. The two of them often traded together at bucket shops on New Street. Afterward, they frequently repaired to the music district where Martin doubtlessly introduced Jesse to pretty young things (a fatal proclivity of the Boy Wonder) at Waterson & Berlin, Irving Berlin's original firm, where Martin was Chief Financial Officer.

Martin idolized Livermore, as though the Boy Wonder were a blindfolded chess player or a composer without a keyboard. Livermore often traded stocks by the sound of the ticker tape, without seeing the prints. Yet Jesse was humble ("The only thing a man should do when he is wrong is cease to be wrong"), flexible ("There is a time for all things"), and selective ("You can beat the market in grains but not the grain market").[7]

When the Boy Wonder had one of his superior insights, he had no hesitancy about going for the jugular. During the 1907 crash, a delegation from the Big Board had to beg the Boy Wonder to hold off his shorting because the stock market itself might cease to exist under his relentlessly accurate selling. Sensing, like Soros at a much later date, that it was in his own self-interest to allow the market to survive ("I'm a player in the market also"), he generously covered his shorts at the bottom.

So prudent was Jesse that he took account not only of his own potential weaknesses, but those of an all-too-devoted wife:

> After I paid off all my debts in full . . . I put a pretty fair amount into annuities. I made up my mind I wasn't going to be strapped and uncomfortable and minus a stake ever again. Of course, after I married I put some

money in trust for my wife. And after the boy came I put some in trust for him.

The reason I did this was not alone the fear that the stock market might take it away from me, but because I knew that a man will spend anything he can lay his hands on. By doing what I did my wife and child are safe from me.

More than one man I know has done the same thing, but has coaxed his wife to sign off when he needed the money, and he has lost it. But I have fixed it up so that no matter what I want or what my wife wants, that trust holds. It is absolutely safe from all attacks by either of us: safe from my market needs: safe even from a devoted wife's love. I'm taking no chances![8]

Livermore's insights are so timeless in their wisdom that I have collected some of them in Table 1–1. They read like a compilation of nuggets from one of the market magician books that are so popular today. Funds supervised by the best of these magicians are currently sold to the public today. Unfortunately, new tricks are always required to stay on top.

The only problem with Martin's reminiscences of the Boy Wonder's genius was the omission of a crucial fact. Jesse had gone bankrupt at least three times before the 1929 crash. He put his last chips in during the early 1930s and was wiped out. He flitted around Wall Street for another ten years, trying to scare up another stake. Finally, near the wolf point, he tried to recoup by selling a book of his insights. When that failed too, he gave up, penned an eight-page suicide letter at the Sherry-Netherland Hotel, and blew his brains out in the hatcheck room in 1940.

I have always found it wise to take Wall Street adages, maxims, and advice with a grain of salt. The best way to taste plausible theories, like those of Loeb and Rogers regarding brokerage houses, is to quantify, test, and analyze them rigorously.

The first thing I did to test the brokerage profits theory was to collect monthly prices for Merrill Lynch, the largest U.S. brokerage house, from the time it was listed on the New York Stock Exchange (NYSE) in 1972 through year-end 1995. Next, I computed the firm's monthly and yearly returns and compared them with the S&P 500. For example, in 1995, Merrill Lynch rose from 35.75 to 51, a return of 43 percent. The S&P 500 in 1995 rose from 459 to 615, a gain of 34 percent. Merrill Lynch thus showed an excess return of 9 percent. If Loeb's theory is true, then the excess returns should be an inverse predictor of future S&P moves.

The correlation between Merrill Lynch's excess return in a month and the S&P return in subsequent months is a positive 0.05 for each of the next seven months.[9] When Merrill Lynch does well, the S&P subsequently tends to perform better, and when Merrill Lynch does badly, the S&P worse. After the ten largest excess monthly returns for Merrill Lynch, the S&P gained an average of 3 percent in the next six months. After the ten largest excess monthly declines for Merrill Lynch, the S&P

Table 1-1.   Insights of Jesse Livermore

On the importance of selective speculation:

There is a time for all things, but I didn't know it. And that is precisely what beats so many men in Wall Street who are very far from being in the main sucker class. There is the plain fool, who does all the wrong things everywhere, but there is the Wall Street fool, who thinks that he must trade all the time. No man can always have adequate reasons for buying or selling stocks daily—or sufficient knowledge to make his play an intelligent play. (p. 21)

On markets and their participants:

But the one thing a Stock Exchange firm will not do is to split commissions. The governors would rather a member committed murder, arson, and bigamy than do business with outsiders for less than a kosher eighth. The very life of the Stock Exchange depends upon their not violating that one rule. (p. 47)

My relations with my brokers were friendly enough. Their accounts and records did not always agree with mine, and the differences uniformly happened to be against me. Curious coincidence—not! But I fought for my own and usually had my way in the end. They always had the hope of getting away from me what I had taken from them. They regarded my winnings as temporary loans, I think. (p. 53)

On mistakes and wisdom:

If a man didn't make mistakes he'd own the world in a month. But if he didn't profit by his mistakes he wouldn't own a blessed thing. (p. 97)

Of course, if a man is both wise and lucky, he will not make the same mistake twice. But he will make any one of the ten thousand brothers or cousins of the original. The mistake family is so large that there is always one of them around when you want to see what you can do in the fool-play line. (p. 119)

A man can excuse his mistakes only by capitalizing on them to subsequent profit. (p. 147)

On the speculator and his emotions:

I sometimes think that speculation must be an unnatural sort of business, because I find that the average speculator has arrayed against him his own nature. The weaknesses that all men are prone to are fatal to success in speculation—usually those very weaknesses that make him likable to his fellows or that he himself particularly guards against in those other ventures of his where they are not nearly so dangerous as when he is trading in stocks or commodities.

The speculators' chief enemies are always boring from within. It is inseparable from human nature to hope and to fear. In speculation when the market goes against you, you hope that every day will be the last day. It is absolutely wrong to gamble in stocks the way the average man does. (pp. 130–131)

From Edwin Lefèvre, *Reminiscences of a Stock Operator* (New York: John Wiley & Sons, 1994). Reprinted with permission of Expert Trading, Ltd.

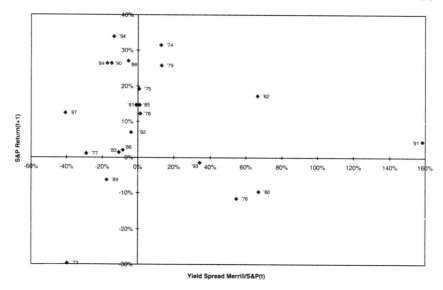

Figure 1–1.   Excess Return of Merrill vs. S&P Return
(Following Year), 1972–1995

declined 4 percent in the next six months. Unfortunately, at least as far as
Merrill Lynch is representative of brokerage stocks, there is no support for
the inverse hypothesis as it relates to monthly returns.

But one interesting finding did emerge. The excess return of Merrill
Lynch in one year and the S&P change the next year were correlated at
−0.3. There were five years when Merrill Lynch's excess return was 30
percentage points or more. In the year immediately following three of
these years, the S&P declined. The odds in favor of a decline in those
years were 3 to 2, compared to 2 to 15 in the other years. The odds ratio of
11 to 1 suggests that, for yearly returns, brokerage house fortunes are a
negative harbinger. Figure 1–1 shows the relation graphically.

RACQUET TRAINING

I seem to have been born with a racquet in my hand. The earliest photographs of me show that my favorite crib and carriage toy was a ping-pong
paddle. I attended my parents' paddle-tennis matches as soon as I was old
enough to crawl, and this formed my introduction to sports.

The paddle tennis courts at Brighton Beach were taken down during
the winter months, but hardy players, including my parents, continued
their matches at such times by stringing up a net in the empty but sheltered cavern of the adjacent triple-Olympic-size swimming pool. Arthur
and Elaine were among the stalwarts who, shielded from the cold blasts off

the Atlantic, would pound the ball back and forth only 100 yards from the shoreline.

With their net set up in the shallow end of the pool, they would place me in the deep end, and the five minutes it took me to crawl up the cement slope to where they were playing would give them time to play a few points. Each time I reached them, they would return me to the deep end—an early Sisyphean experience that was no doubt a harbinger of my future efforts as a speculator. When their match was over, Mom would toss the ball to me while Dad helped me hold the wooden paddle. With the ball in play, he said, "Hit!" and guided me through the motions of a perfect forehand.

I often think of those abortive attempts when I enter the box for yet another day of speculation. During my trading career, involving many hundreds of billions of dollars and at least 5,000 separate days of entering the fray, I have not had one satisfactory day. When I make money, I always want to kick myself for not being more aggressive. On those all-too-frequent occasions when I lose, every dollar hurts. Why didn't I have the sense to stay away? Better yet, I wish my father were alive to show me the markets, sizes, and directions of the perfect trades.

The "toss and hit" drills, begun at the bottom of the swimming pool, eventually moved to a real tennis court. I have continued this tradition with my six daughters, only now with more up-to-date equipment—one-quarter-size racquetball graphite miniracquets. But, my kids and I are opportunistic. In August 1995, after almost being buried by some insider trading by various governmental officials, I beat a hasty retreat to the icy climate of Vinalhaven, Maine, to join a family reunion. I knew it would be too cold to play tennis, so I didn't bring my racquet. But my three-year-old, Kira, insisted on playing tennis anyway. "Daddy, I can use a frying pan to hit," she said. The incident would have evoked a "Vickie, you have another champ coming along" from Artie, but in his absence—in his honor, perhaps—it will invoke a smile from my readers.

By the age of six, I was too skillful for my peers. To win nickels in betting games, I had to play with my left backhand or spot my opponents 15 points a game to even out the odds. At an early age, I learned how to bounce back from initial adversity. Even more important than bouncing back was not getting in the hole at the start.

I took my lessons here from Whitlow Wyatt, a Brooklyn Dodger ace hurler during my youth. His three rules for staying ahead are as good for speculators as for baseball, racquetball, and handball players:

Never let down for a moment. You can't, to be a consistent winner. Pitch to every batter as though [you] were facing him the first time. That helps make you careful.

The second rule is to pitch to every hitter as though you were trying to keep him from getting a long hit. That makes you cut corners or watch weakness more carefully.

Racquets run in the family: The racquet education of Kira (top, with frying pan) and Galt (bottom).

The third idea I keep in mind is that no matter how low a batter's average may be, you cannot afford to show him too much of even your Sunday pitch or he'll hit it.[10]

During the speculating day, I am frequently distracted with divertissements that tend to make me let down. To minimize them, I don't take phone calls, break for lunch, or allow visitors. No signing checks and, especially, no shuffling of those infernal tax and regulatory forms that fill up so much of the average businessperson's workday. These distractions would no doubt cause me to throw in the towel. When Wyatt's rules aren't enough to shield me, I think of another great baseball player of my youth, Ted Williams. When he found that the fuss about his August birthday was distracting him unduly from his batting .400 plus, he simply changed the date of his birthday to October. I do not have the natural flair or wisdom of some traders, or the research skills of others, but I excel in concentration and focus.

I continued the tennis practice sessions on all sorts of courts with my parents throughout my youth. One of the keys was playing every day in the winter at the Coney Island courts on Neptune Avenue. We would bring a shovel to clear the snow, and wear gloves when the temperature dropped below freezing. Unfortunately, I never became a good tennis player. My greatest achievement in the game came when I won the New York City 18-and-under Junior Tennis Championship at the age of 11. My game is on a par with the number-two player on an average college team. I feel and understand all the great shots but simply don't have the skill. It's always humiliating when a friend arranges for me to be trounced handily by a club pro. I feel the same way when a friend introduces me to the promoter of a panacea. I'm in over my head.

The early racquet training was more helpful in squash, where I was fortunate enough to come under the tutelage of Jack Barnaby, the greatest coach in the history of racquet sports. He caught me before I learned the game the wrong way.

My chief idiosyncrasy as I pursued my athletic career was that I practiced against myself four out of seven days. Each day, during these sessions, I would practice one stroke over and over. Almost all other players played matches. First, I'd hit every finesse shot off the forehand side; next, the same shots with the backhand. Then a repetition of the same shots, but starting off the back wall. Ultimately, a game against myself. Mr. Forehand against Mr. Backhand, or Mr. Offense against Mr. Defense. Finally, a burst of wind sprints up and back and around the court until I couldn't take one more step. I kept a diary of these workouts, part of which was published in the book, *Smart Squash: Using Your Head to Win* by Austin Francis. In looking back over the diaries, I calculated I practiced or played at least one match on 3,500 consecutive days, no exceptions.

The training has been helpful in my speculations. I was honored when I heard my partner, Paul Buethe, tell a prospective customer that I concentrated harder and worked more consistently at my job than anyone he knew.

My model in racquet sports has always been "The Crocodile," René Lacoste. In his brilliant autobiography, written shortly after he won Wimbledon in 1928, and undoubtedly one of the best tennis books ever, he describes how he found himself serving once at Wimbledon's center court while his opponent was bowing and everyone in the stadium was standing. Unbeknownst to him, Queen Mary had just entered the stadium, and the spectators were rising to honor her, as is the custom. The 18,000 spectators at Wimbledon knew the Queen had arrived. Lacoste thought only of his serve.[11]

During the French championships, the Crocodile had a great advantage. Rain was the norm during the tournament, and knowledgeable fans always brought umbrellas to the game. When the inevitable downpour came, the stadium was rife with noise and motion as umbrellas unfurled. This was always good for a few points for Lacoste. His opponents were distracted by the noise, but René, concentrating on the match, had not noticed.

Playing competitive games is especially helpful for would-be speculators. The whole purpose of childhood may be viewed as a window for play. One beautiful thing about play is that if you have an inquiring mind and keep records, you can learn which techniques carry the day.

Hank Shatkin, a veteran owner of a clearing firm on the Chicago Board of Trade and an employer of more than 100 floor brokers in his day, believes that a background in competitive athletics is the best training for future speculators. The floors of the exchanges are studded with former professional athletes. At least eight members in the grain pits of the Chicago Board of Trade are former professional ballplayers for the Chicago Cubs or Bears.

Sometimes, the relations between markets and professional athletes can become chaotic. On Thursday, September 25, 1995, a member of the Chicago Board of Trade, who usually played his games on the bond floor, played hookey from an afternoon session to attend a key Chicago Cubs baseball game. He got so angry when the pitcher, Randy Myers, served up a home-run ball that he jumped on the field and rushed the mound to beat up Myers. Showing a ruggedness that could qualify him for a position as a futures trader in Chicago, Myers calmly wrestled the trader to the ground, pinned him to make sure he held no gun, turned him over to uniformed personnel, and then proceeded to pitch his team to a 12–11 win.

THE FINEST GENTLEMAN

The athletes of Brighton were proud of their working-class backgrounds. They used their hands on the job and were proud to use them in their play. Handball and handtennis were the games of choice.

The Milkman was invariably tired during morning matches, after crating bottles from a horse and cart for all the neighborhood. Vic Hershkowitz, the best singles player, had an advantage over the other players. He could practice on the job: the firehouse provided a four-wall court for its operatives. Moey Orenstein, the best doubles player, also had a training advantage: it was rumored that he served as a runner and collector for major bookies. Artie played doubles with "Rugged," named for his construction-worker hands, and "the Plumber."

The players let off steam during the money games. It was a rare game that didn't have at least two fistfights and three changes of referees. The players always emerged black-and-blue because the rules of the game gave a point to a player who hit a shot and blocked the opponent out without moving. The only defense was to knock the obstructing player senseless with one's body or the ball. Those hard black balls can sting the back pretty smartly when hit at 100 miles an hour from two feet away. Invariably, the games stretched on for hours as the players argued with the crowd and the referees.

Professional squash in the old days was every bit as physical as one-wall handball, basketball, or football. Then a genius came up with the "English Let"—awarding the point to the player who hit the other one with the ball. Immediately, everyone started clearing. Today, squash is a gentleman's game.

I took the English Let rule seriously. Once I was winning 11–3 in the finals of the 1971 Nationals. My opponent was in my way, so I belted him with the ball.

"At 11–3?" he cried out.

"At 14–zip," I responded, and I gave him the kind of look that good collectors use to expedite payment.

I still get that same rush when dealers back out of a trade after quoting me a firm market. There are always at least three direct lines in my office taped up so that brokers who recently transgressed can no longer ply their trade with me. The impact on my wealth is as small as it was in my squash game. But I uphold the rules of the game and relive my previous greatness.

In sharp contrast to all the other combatants stood a man who called every ball out against himself; a man who never argued, never bet, and always complimented his opponents on their "beauties." Artie was universally acknowledged to be a paragon of sportsmanship.

When my dad and I lost a hard-fought paddles doubles match during which he called our good shots "Out!" over and over again, while our opponents were cheating like crazy, I could not prevent myself from screaming at him.

"Dad, I have to tell you, I had a nickel riding on us in that match and you lost it for me with all your———bad calls against us. You're supposed to be my partner, not the other guy's."

"So what of it. It's only a game. If you need one or two points that badly that it makes the difference, you don't deserve to win. Give the other side the benefit of the doubt, and you'll get the best out of them. You'll feel better also."

I liked to talk to Soros about how great a guy Artie was. One day I spun the "Doubles" story to him. The red-colored hot-line phone between his desk and mine kept us in close touch. George listened and then mumbled something in Hungarian that I took to mean that he felt this was true about me also.

Three weeks later, he launched an audit of all the trades I had ever done for him. "Victor, I trust you completely . . . but because we're so close I thought I should have this done for mutual protection. Now what was the name of that firm you called to change the ticket of that losing trade from your account to mine? Gary, finish this audit within a week and report directly to Curacao." He later translated the Hungarian he had mumbled into the phone as: "The more he talks about his honesty the faster I count my silver."

I guess this skepticism, which he also applies to himself, is one of the reasons that George is legendary. But, the mere fact that I told him this self-serving story about my honesty was enough to trigger his antennae. I must admit that I am the same way. When someone starts a sentence with "Quite honestly . . ." or "In all frankness . . . ," I put my hand firmly on my wallet.

It took me a while to understand what my father said and longer to apply it. But I knew that the idea had taken root 17 years later, in 1966, when I was playing in the Harry Cowles Squash Tournament in the rarefied atmosphere of the sixth floor of the Harvard Club of New York. The English have a tradition of augmenting all of their commonplace activities with a wager. In homage to the English (who could be counted on for at least eight rounds of toasts—"God save the Queen!"—at the pretournament banquets), the tournament was highlighted by a "Calcutta auction" the evening before the semifinals, following the banquet. In this auction, each semifinalist was "sold," with the proceeds to be divided between the two finalists. My Uncle Howie and I pooled our resources to buy a share of me.

The next day, my opponent was Bobby Hetherington, an Episcopalian minister from Buffalo, and one of the finest sportsmen I have ever met. He was seeded second in the tournament and after a hard-fought first game, I won it, 15–9. In the gallery sat Uncle Howie, watching his first competitive squash match. After laying off some of his expected winnings, he rushed down to see me between games.

"Vic, what are you doing? Of the nine points he won, you called eight down on yourself before the referee even had a chance to call it. If you keep that up, we're a sure thing to lose the Calcutta pool."

"Howie," I said, "That's the way you're supposed to do things in squash. Isn't that how Artie would call it?"

I still remember the mixed emotions on Howie's face as he rushed to the gallery to make sure that I got a fair shake and that he had the proper odds in games two and three.

I try to play fair in my dealings. I don't participate in promotions, regardless of how much I can make out of them. While I hasten to add that I am no more honest or dishonest than the next guy, I have made it a practice to give all the calls to the other side—for exactly the reason that Artie stated. The funny thing is, although I've met many businesspeople since then, I've yet to meet one who didn't consider him- or herself honest also—including the worst crooks imaginable. Doubtless, there's someone out there who feels the same way about me. You are not going to make much progress in business if you let the other party know you think he is a crook. You have to get on the court before you go to court.

CONTROL OF TEMPER

Aside from gambling, my main vice as a kid was my temper. When the ref gave me a bad call, I had no hesitation about giving him a piece of my mind. And I hated playing doubles with my dad because we had to win two points to get one up on the scorecard. He would call all my good killers "Chinese"—point for the other side.

After I lost the first game of a money game, I cursed at my adult opponent for blocking me out, threw my racquet at his head, and grabbed the quarter bet out of the hat and ran away with it.

Artie was right behind me. He caught me in the proverbial Brooklyn spot, under the boardwalk. "If I ever see you act in that disgraceful fashion again, I'll take away your ticket to the beach. Go back and apologize right now or you'll get an even worse tongue-lashing than this. In addition to being a disgrace, you just helped your opponent along by losing your temper because he'll play harder now." With that, he gave me a left cross to my shoulder. He was on Brooklyn College's wrestling and football teams. That punch stings 45 years later.

Since then, I have won countless matches where my opponent stormed at the referee, thereby dissipating his own energies.

As a speculator, the easiest fall guys for my mistakes are the floor traders who execute my orders. It is tempting to take out my wrath on them when I lose money, especially if the loss has been exacerbated by a poor execution. Time and again, they come up with some lame excuse for a bad fill that I know conceals terrible moral turpitude on their part. But "my shoulder still hurts" when I open my mouth, and the maximum invective that I ever disseminate to some pitiful clerk is something like:

> Hi, Doc Niederhoffer here. Just wanted you to know that there are no words in the English language strong enough to describe the incredible improprieties of what you just did to my client. He's incensed and undoubtedly will be canceling his account and bringing an action against me and my agents forthwith. Humbly alert the broker and the head of your clearing firm, as well as all employees in between, not to be surprised if a process server appears at their homes imminently.

Because I often lose money in a trade—purely, of course, as a result of bad broker execution—my brother, Roy, has programmed the computer to deliver the above message via voice synthesizer, along with appropriately demoralizing inflection and rhythm. On one occasion, our currencies broker on the IMM responded to the computer synthesizer, "At least it's good to hear from you personally, even if it's only to hear of our mistakes."

"Well, that's the kind of guy I am," Roy typed into the computer.

In this regard, I have never found the antics of John McEnroe at all unusual. Such tantrums were *de rigueur* for all of the handball players at Brighton. I recall the time when Jack Kramer threw his tennis racquet at the referee in a California 13-and-under tournament. He was delighted to see his dad walking over to the referee. "Finally," he thought, "my dad's sticking up for me by going over to the ref to give him a piece."

The next thing he heard was the referee announcing, "Game and match, Smith. He wins, 4–6, 4–3, default." Jack's father then walked over to him, grabbed the racquet, and broke it over his knee. He informed Jack that he would not be playing for the rest of the summer, and, furthermore, if he ever disgraced himself in that way again, he would never play another tournament. Jack once remarked to me that this was the last time in his great competitive career that he ever argued with a referee. I believe the training Jack and I received was better suited to a successful career in speculation, or any other field, than the training that apparently leads so many pro athletes to dis their opponents with utter impunity.

ECONOMY OF MOTION

Every night, at the end of Artie's 4 P.M.-to-midnight shift, we went through a little ritual. He brought home some coffee danish from the Sea Breeze Bakery, along with a pint of Breyer's banana ice cream from the local candy store.

After the feast, Dad would sit by my bed and we would discuss the things that young sons and fathers talk about most—namely, sports. To be the best at something consistently, Dad said, you had to be economical, using the least amount of input to accomplish the greatest output. Take Marty Reisman, he said, whom we had recently seen playing Dick Miles in a high-stakes money game at the legendary Lawrence ping-pong club on Broadway at 54th Street.

Marty had a consummate stroke. He scraped directly through the ball on his backhand, like a blackjack dealer flipping a card on the table, and on his forehand he spun the ball upward in a salute. Because both sides were equally good and perfectly balanced, he was always ready to return an angle or drop shot. He once went through 50 matches without once being caught by a drop shot. And he frequently defended from ten feet behind the back edge, especially against his nemesis, ten-time U.S. Champion

Dick Miles. Marty's accuracy and the controlled force of his drives were his trademarks. He once finished a quarter-final match in the 1949 World Table Tennis Championship in Stockholm before the game being played at the next table, which had started at the same time as his match, had finished its first point. To be fair, that first point on the adjoining table lasted 20 minutes.

In tennis, Ken Rosewall had that same economy of motion and directness that all champions seem to have—Fred Astaire in dance, Michael Jordan in basketball, Sam Snead in golf, Gayle Sayers in football, and Sugar Ray Leonard in boxing. The written descriptions of the performances of these widely varying great champions frequently contain similar terms: completely effortlessly, never breaking a sweat, smooth as silk, floating like a butterfly.

A typical panegyric to poetry in motion is a description of Josh Gibson, perhaps the greatest home-run hitter in baseball history (whether Babe Ruth was the white Josh Gibson or Josh was the black Babe Ruth is moot), by his first manager, Judy Johnson:

> It was just a treat to watch him hit the ball. There was no effort at all. You see these guys now get up there in the box and they dig and scratch around before they're ready. Gibson would just walk up there . . . .[12]

After the talk about economy in motion in sports, my dad turned to Emily Dickinson's poems. "But Dad, she's a poet," I protested.

"Yes, but every athlete would do well to study the economy of her expression, the sharp impact she gets from words, that builds inexorably to a whole," he replied. There were indeed several athletes who frequented Brighton Beach and were spoken of in terms of "poetry in motion." Vic Hershkowitz never had to dive for a shot. He was always in position, and his natural left *and* right, blazing at 100 mph, enabled him to take the direct path to each shot, rather than having to favor a weak side, the way athletes with a dominant side inevitably and inartistically must play.

"Vic, your main problem in racquet sports is your frilly stroke. Your backswing has a wide arc. You pivot with a military about-face on your cross-court drives. And you end your follow-through with an accelerating flourish, climaxing in a complete stop, with your racquet face saluting the flag. You jump to reach maximum altitude on your serves, and you seem to love to retrieve lobs passing over your head while playing the net, or while running toward the baseline, through the legs. Take it easy. Stay close to the ground. Get on the balls of your feet. Be compact. Get rid of all the folderol and concentrate on the basics. Keep your eye on the ball. Move your racquet to the same place as where you want the ball to go."

I am reminded of my weaknesses and the proper solution when I'm playing squash. The front and back walls serve as an echo chamber. Whenever anyone says anything in the gallery, I can hear it, regardless of how softly it is spoken. When someone new to squash is invited by an aficionado to come and watch me play, within a few seconds of the start of the match comes the inevitable: "That's Niederhoffer!?? He moves like an elephant!"

I try to compensate for my awkwardness by giving myself a good margin of error on all my shots. I always aim at least six inches above the tin, unlike my adversaries, who love to shoot an inch above the tin in a do-or-die effort to win the point outright or lose if it catches the tin. I do the same in my speculations. I never buy a market up on the day or sell one down on the day.

On one occasion, I heard something more flattering from an oldtimer. "When I see big Niederhoffer play at first I think he's awkward, flat, built like a tackle. But he reminds me of Honus Wagner, the best that ever played baseball. Could play any position, stole 700 bases, led the league in batting eight times. The kid's a natural. I just hope he doesn't ruin it with that temper. He should learn from Wagner, who had the sweetest disposition in the world."

I did learn to control that temper, through losing lots of matches in college when I argued with the referee and hit my hand against the wall in disgust. In each of the fields I have played in, I have needed every unit of energy I possess available for output. All waste gives my competitor an edge. Except for naturals I have run into, such as the Marty Hogan in racquetball, or Babe Ruth in baseball, or George Soros in speculating, I have never seen a success in any field who didn't have some internal mechanism for economizing on energy at work at all times.

SOME LESSONS FROM WILLIE SUTTON

On October 3, 1951, I was observing Yom Kippur. While atoning, when the rabbi turned his back, I was secretly listening to the final playoff game for the National League pennant, between the New York Giants and the Brooklyn Dodgers. I had 100 percent of my net worth staked on the Dodgers with Bookie, who was atoning close enough to my radio that he could cover any late-breaking bets.

The pennant race in 1951 came down to the last game of a three-game playoff between the Giants and the Dodgers. Howie was a Yankee fan, but he felt the Dodgers were a shoo-in to win. Dodger ace Don Newcombe (20–9 on the season) would be taking the mound at the Polo Grounds. And Brooklyn had administered a 10–0 licking to the Giants just the day before. Uncle Howie didn't believe in grinding. "Bookie's the only one that can do that," he'd say. "He has the edge." So my Uncle Howie bet his entire net worth, $800, including $2 of mine, on the Dodgers. The Dodgers were ahead, 4 to 1, in the bottom of the ninth. Howie and I were counting our winnings.

We snuck out of Yom Kippur services to catch the play-by-play on our hidden portable radios. And then the tide changed. Alvin Dark singled for the Giants, and Don Mueller followed with a single of his own, which moved Dark to third. But then New York's leading RBI man, Monte Irvin, fouled out. Minutes later, Whitey Lockman hit a stand-up double, moving Mueller to third and scoring Dark. Ralph Branca came in to face Bobby Thompson with two men on and the score 4 to 2. Holding our breath, we pressed the radio to the ear, covering it with a yarmulke. Thompson hit the second pitch into the stands for a home run: 5 to 4 Giants. Next thing, Russ Hodges was screaming into his microphone: "The Giants win the pennant! The Giants win the pennant!"

Howie and I went from riches to rags in five minutes. At the same moment Howie and I were in such dejection, a wealthy handball and chess player was drowning his sorrows in a Borough Hall bar. That sorrowful man, likewise a rabid Dodger fan, left as little to chance as any of the great heroes. He planned, studied, and analyzed every aspect of his equipment and trade before taking a risk. I am referring to the greatest entry and exit man in history, Willie Sutton, the famous bank robber.

Willie had recently escaped from a Pennsylvania prison and was hiding out in an apartment in a mainly Puerto Rican neighborhood near Flatbush and 4th Avenues in Brooklyn. As always, Willie planned his strategy in advance. He taught himself Spanish while in prison. He knew that his neighbors would read only the Spanish-language papers and hence would be unlikely to see his "wanted" photos in the major New York dailies.

The day the Giants upset the Dodgers, Willie was watching the play on television (he avoided the stadium, knowing how many off-duty cops would be there). Later, he wrote about that game:

> I saw Bobby Thompson hit his home run off Branca in the final 1951 play-off game in a tavern a block from Brooklyn police headquarters . . . . As I watched Thompson circle those bases I felt like going into headquarters and giving myself up. I don't think I've ever felt more depressed in my life. Being a Dodger fan shortens your life by years. Even when they win, as they did in 1952, they worry you half to death.[13]

Now if that ball game had such an effect on Willie, causing one of the greatest bank robbers and prison-escape artists of all time to contemplate turning himself in, imagine the impact on ordinary mortals like Uncle Howie and me. In modern times, it has been posited that the performance of the leading Japanese baseball team, the Giants, has a similar effect on the Nikkei stock index. When the Giants are on a roll, a bullish trend in the Nikkei is likely. Probably no baseball team in the United States today is revered the way the Brooklyn Dodgers were in the 1950s or as the Giants are now in Japan. It would be interesting to study the impact of the Chicago Bulls' wins and losses in relation to U.S. Treasury Bonds traded on the Chicago Board of Trade.

Willie Sutton exemplified the rule that "Success in any endeavor requires single-minded attention to detail and total concentration." Willie would spend weeks and months casing a bank before robbing it; he would dress in a cop's uniform. His disguise was so perfect he would find himself answering complaints from passersby and directing traffic.

Subsequently, my dad showed me a few pages in Willie Sutton's *Where The Money Was*. Willie memorialized his training methods:

> I enjoyed playing the different roles. I was always so wrapped up in any job I was planning that as soon as I put on a policeman's uniform I felt like a policeman. The car would usually be parked a block or two away, and while I was strolling to the bank I'd automatically check the doors of the shops with my eyes. From time to time someone would stop me to ask directions. On two separate occasions, motorists asked me if it would be all right to leave their car in a no-parking zone for a couple of minutes—they were just going to run in and pick something up. I lectured them severely. How could they ask a policeman for permission to violate a city ordinance? "Now if you happened to ride around the block," I told them, "I might not be here when you got back."
>
> . . . While I was crossing a busy intersection in Philadelphia in my uniform . . . I was hailed down by a police cruiser. A captain got out and bawled the hell out of me for having a button loose on my collar. I felt just awful about it—yes, sir, you're right, sir; an absolute disgrace, sir—not because a police officer had stopped me right across from the bank I was about to rob but because I was being censured by a superior. I was a very conscientious cop right up to the time I stopped being a cop and started being a thief.[14]

Willie's favorite saying was, "We had a plan." For planning and execution of a bank robbery, most cops think that Sutton's equal never lived. He calculated the risks and always tried to find the weak point in the protection systems set up by a bank. His first robbery, knocking off a department store at the age of ten, was carefully planned. When they put him in prison, he spent every waking minute studying how to get out, either by escaping—by studying architectural blueprints of the prison facilities—or through the legal process—by studying legal precedent. He never went to school, but in the prison libraries he studied psychology, literature, philosophy, medicine, and law. His legal studies finally paid off when he won a pardon after searching for ten years for the legal precedents that saved him long after his lawyers had given up. If you want to be good at speculation or any other job, be as dedicated as Willie.

A THREE-PERSON PARTNERSHIP

In my youth, two friends and I devised a plan to earn some spending money. The Brighton Beach Baths was adjacent to the public beach. On a national holiday, like Memorial Day or July 4, more than two million people visited the beach. Good Humor boys carried 50-pound boxes of ice cream and ice on their shoulders. Candy stores provided bottles of soda for the thirsty. We formed a three-way partnership, collecting the bottles the sunbathers left on the beach. With the two-cent bottle deposit, on a good day, a hard-working team like Stevie, René, and me could earn $15 or $20 (approximately $300 in today's money).

But there were hazards. If we happened to bother two lovers smooching, we were likely to get a kick in the butt. And after we collected the bottles, we had to store and clean them before they could be redeemed for the deposit. But perhaps my biggest risk in this venture was my choice of partners.

We carried our loot in a cardboard box. One day, tired and hot, my partners and I stepped onto the boardwalk to refresh ourselves with a cold drink and a custard. I held the box while my partners ordered. Daydreaming, I barely noticed that my load seemed to be getting heavier. Next thing I knew, the owner of the custard stand grabbed me by the arm and started yelling "Police!" An officer rushed over.

There, in my box, surrounded by empty bottles, were full bottles of Mission Cream Soda, Hoffman Orange Soda, Vernon's Ginger Ale, and Dr. Brown's Celery Tonic.

"Kid, you're only 8 or 9 years old and already a thief. I hate to think of what's going to happen to you when you grow up. Give me your name so I can fill out a J.D. card and contact your parents."

"But I didn't do it," I explained. "My friends planted this stuff on me."

"Then you better get rid of your friends."

When I told my dad what happened, he told me a little story about a steer that worked in a beef slaughtering operation where he had once had a job. "That steer would climb up the ramp to the killing floor just as if it was the best place in the world. All the other cows and steers would follow him. But somehow he always managed to get lost in the shuffle and slide back to the bottom of the ramp by the time the other cattle had met their doom under the knife.

"You are going to meet many 'friends' like that steer in your day. If you want to live a long and successful life, stay away from types like that. And whenever in doubt, check to see if the friend is along with you at the end of the ramp, the same as he was at the beginning."

The markets also like to play the "Judas" steer. They love to move a few wild ticks in one direction just to induce investors to take a wrong position in stocks. Similarly, the screen quotes in many markets are maneuvered to make the live markets look good. When this happens, the boys in the office all start mooing, "This ramp is beautiful."

Since my early partnership in Brighton I have encountered many "friends" who have tried to lead me to slaughter, typically in some tax-oriented investment. My friend will tell me he's planning to invest his life savings with some operator who is the best in the business. Based on this reassurance and my desire to minimize taxes, I'll rush up the investment ramp. But then, after my funds have been committed, I'll find that my friend has decided not to invest in the deal after all. Not that it wasn't a great deal, of course; it's just that some other opportunity came along and claimed all his funds. The predictable result, nine times out of ten, is total loss of my investment as well as the unkindest cut of all: disallowance of the tax deduction that added the extra return that made the deal attractive in the first place. I have seen more investors lose big after being sucked in by a tax break than almost any other sucker play.

After my partners sold me down the river, they generously offered me a chance to get even in a money game.

The game would be my left and Stevie's right (he was a lefty) against René's two hands—two serves each side. But we would spot him 15 points in a 21-point game. The game was arranged, the money placed in a hat, and a referee chosen. But one problem quickly became apparent—my partner was dumping on me, that is, falling down on me. Whenever he served, he hit two shorts—an out. When the ball was hit to him, he buried it in the floor—Chinese, or point to other side. I chased my partner off the court. It turned out that I was playing against both my opponent and my partner, handicapped by 17 points, since it took me 2 points to figure out what was happening.

I eventually evened the score at 18-all and the match was called. No way were my two adversaries, both much bigger than I, going to let me collect on that bet. But never have I accomplished anything as heroic as that comeback, one against two. I learned things from the experience.

First, "dumping" the game occurs much more often than would appear. There is always some way of setting it up that has a ring of probity. "Now look, young man, do you want to win this game by 50 points and embarrass your opponents and flunk out of college next year, a poor man? Or would you be better off giving the other side a little dignity, slacking off a little, and winning by 40 points and ending up rich?" The "under" bet is looking mighty good at this point.

Second, no matter how certain a particular speculation looks, there is always a good likelihood that it will go astray. Frequently, things are not what they seem. A deal that seems too good to be true is likely not to be true, or, as it was so aptly put by Damon Runyon:

> Son, no matter how far you travel, or how smart you get, always remember this: Someday, somewhere, a guy is going to come to you and show you a nice brand-new deck of cards on which the seal is never broken, and this guy is going to offer to bet you that the jack of spades will jump out of this deck and squirt cider in your ear. But, son, do not bet him, for as sure as you do you are going to get an ear full of cider.[15]

CHAPTER 2

———•◦•———

Panics and Hoodoos

Wall Street is as much the natural field for panics as the prairie is for tornadoes.
The Art of Investing

Scott Joplin had his ear finely tuned to Wall Street when he started *The Wall Street Rag*, written in 1908, with the notation "Panic in Wall Street, Brokers feeling Melancholy."[1]

The cascading syncopated minor and diminished chords from a C major base, spanning 3½ octaves, capture the wild dissonance of Wall Street during the 1907 Panic, which undoubtedly inspired Joplin.

At the Panic's height in October 1907, call loan rates reached 150 percent per year, and there were bank runs and failures throughout the country. Cash and certified checks were redeemable at a 5 percent premium. Wall Street was jammed curb to curb with a mob of depositors clamoring for their banks to pay up. Stock markets and exchanges across America closed down. The original illustration on the cover of Joplin's music score shows the universal excitement of the panicked as they descend on the NYSE and the subtreasury from their sanctuary in Trinity Church.

Jesse Livermore gave a good description of the height the Panic reached on October 24, 1907, when no money could be borrowed on the New York Stock Exchange. He likened it to:

> . . . the classroom experiment [of] the mouse in a glass-bell when they begin to pump the air out of the bell. You can see the poor mouse breathe faster and faster, its sides heaving like overworked bellows, trying to get enough oxygen out of the decreasing supply in the bell. You watch it suffocate till its eyes almost pop out of their sockets, gasping, dying. Well, that is what I think of when I see the crowd at the Money Post! No money anywhere, and you can't liquidate stocks because there is nobody to buy them. The whole Street is broke at this very moment, if you ask me.[2]

The Dow Industrials declined from a high of 96.37 on January 7 to a low of 53 on November 16. Declines of 45 percent in the averages can hurt, especially if the average speculator is operating with a margin of just 10 percent, as was the norm in those days.

The business environment of 1907 is a reminder that not much has changed in the forces that move markets. The San Francisco earthquake and fire in 1906 and the Russian–Japanese War that began in 1904 withdrew billions from productive capital. The Barings failure of 1890 was another reminder of the Damoclean sword awaiting. Record business conditions and unprecedented grain crops caused interest rates to rise. New issues of stocks sold like hot cakes, and stocks reached record highs. On March 14, 1907, the high flyers broke from 10 percent to 25 percent, and the Dow dropped from 83 to 76.

The politics–stock connection surrounding the 1907 Panic bears an eerie resemblance to the backdrop today. As prices dropped throughout the world, in what *The Economist* described as the "biggest financial disaster that had overtaken the city since 1857," the President stepped up to the plate.[3] Against the backdrop of the decade of greed that had preceded, and the unconscionable profits of the rich, Theodore Roosevelt's words might have been penned by a populist today: "Certain malefactors of great wealth [have conspired] to bring about as much financial stress as possible." In words strikingly similar to those of the Secretary of the Treasury, who stated, at the height of the Mexican bailout in 1995, "I don't care one bit for the rich who might be hurt by the fall," President Roosevelt told a leading financier trying to extract a favor for the Morgan interests, "I am not interested in your wealthy friends." The President's impact on the market became so negative that when he simply proclaimed that "Honesty is the best policy," there were runs on financial institutions throughout the land.

Panics on Wall Street in the 19th century had the certainty of the sea closing over a shipwreck. In a typical description, Henry Clews remarks that, in 1837, "Prices dropped to zero." He mentions casually a few pages later that the Panic of 1857 was much more severe.[4] A New York broker writes of panics, "No drive of cattle upon the western prairie is more subject to sudden scrapes and erratic rushes."[5] A catalog of some of the more infamous 19th-century panics appears in Table 2–1.

These anecdotal reports must suffice for the days before meaningful stock averages existed. But to understand any event, especially one as broad as a panic, it's necessary to define and quantify. Many definitions would be acceptable. I decided to quantify by identifying a panic as any time when a daily Dow Jones Industrials closing price fell by at least 10 percent from the highest prevailing close during the preceding 30 calendar days (with no overlapping allowed). The following tabulation confirms that panics peaked at 38 in the 1930s and were last heard from in the 1980s, when four were identified for the decade. Panics have all but vanished in the 1990s.

Frequency of Panics, 1890–1996

Decade Beginning	Number of Panics
1890	11
1900	9
1910	7
1920	9
1930	38
1940	4
1950	2
1960	3
1970	9
1980	4
1990–1996	1

BUY AFTER THE PANIC

Nobody has ever figured out what causes a panic. But some form of what biologists call positive feedback—"Why Peacock's Tails Are Big"—or

Table 2–1. Major 19th-Century Financial Panics

Year	Precipitating Cause	Highlights
1812	War with England	Trade paralyzed; 90 bank failures. Interest rates rose.
1837	President Jackson's failure to maintain United States Bank	Rail stocks dropped to zero.
1857	Failure of Ohio Life	Three-fourths of railroads went into receivership.
1861	Outbreak of Civil War	Speculating was suspended.
1869	Black Friday gold panic	Gold dropped 30 percent in one day.
1873	Failure of Jay Cooke & Co.	NYSE closed, stocks declined at least 50 percent. "Much more severe than Panic of 1907."
1884	Excessive speculating	"Stocks went down to perdition," about one-third. "The inferno." In one half-hour, values fell by 10 percent.
1890	Barings & Co. Argentine bonds	Interest rates reached 183 percent. Villard stock declined from 34 to 7.
1893	Agitation for change in gold/silver ratio	Failure of 800 banks attributed to Panic. Dow drops 50% from high to low.
1901	Northern Pacific Corner	"Stocks declined one-third in one hour. Nearest to hell I ever saw on Wall Street."

what Soros calls reflexive behavior is involved. Here's a typical scenario reported in one of my 100-year-old books:

> One of the worst panics that I ever saw in the Street occurred under my own eye. I was seated at the Board one day, and I never saw the room more quiet. Everything was easy and buoyant. Stocks were steady, the 'roads where earning money, and everything was cheerful. A member present belonged to a house that was carrying a very large line of stock. He offered two hundred shares for sale. A man sat opposite to witness the transaction. He said to himself, I have some of that stock; if this man who is so heavily interested in it, is about selling out, something must be the matter. I will sell mine out while I can. He threw his on the markets. Others followed. A scene of indescribable excitement prevailed. Other stocks were affected. The panic became universal, and inevitable ruin followed. It turned out that nothing was the matter, that the broker who had caused the panic had an order to sell.[6]

There's more agreement on what comes after panics—stability and recovery. The weak hands are washed out, and bargain hunters pick up the pieces. Scott Joplin, wise in the ways of Wall Street, saw this clearly. As to whether Joplin's wisdom originated from his royalties negotiations with his publisher or from the guidance my grandfather Martin (the publisher's chief financial officer) gave him from his own experiences, I do not know. But a mere 16 measures from the beginning of *The Wall Street Rag*, the program note "Good times have come" appears. The melody modulates to a major key and returns home to the middle register. Joplin would doubtless have participated in a time-tested method of making money from panics if his attentions had not been concentrated on music.

Old Wall Street hands know to take out their canes and hobble to the Street after panics:

> But few gain sufficient experience in Wall Street to command success until they reach that period of life in which they have one foot in the grave. When this time comes, these old veterans of the Street usually spend long intervals of repose at their comfortable homes, and in times of panic, which recur sometimes oftener than once a year, these old fellows will be seen in Wall Street, hobbling down on their canes to their brokers' offices.
>
> Then they always buy good stocks to the extent of their bank balances, which have been permitted to accumulate for just such an emergency. The panic usually rages until enough of these cash purchases of stock is made to afford a big "rake in." When the panic has spent its force, these old fellows, who have been resting judiciously on their oars in expectation of the inevitable event, which usually returns with the regularity of the seasons, quickly realize, deposit their profits with their bankers, or the overplus thereof, after purchasing more real estate that is on the up grade, for permanent investment, and retire for another season to the quietude of their splendid homes and the bosoms of their happy families.[7]

Once the horrible 1931–1932 period was over, it paid to hobble to Wall Street after panics. Starting with 1940, for example, the Dow was up an average of 1 percent one month after the panics, and 3 percent three months later.

Since the 1987 crash, a big daily decline in the S&P has been a great time to take out the canes. After a decline of 7.50 points in the S&P, the average move one day later has been 1.39 S&P points. Compare this with the .12 points after a randomly selected day and the .88 points after a daily rise of 7.50 points or more. (A 7.50-point move during this period was about 1.5 percent.)

Because of the high variability, however, and the rise of 300 S&P points during the period since 1987, the results are quite compatible with randomness. An interesting sidelight that emerges from examination of the big moves in mid-1996 is that 7.50-point moves are occurring with three times their normal frequency. Batten the hatches.

	Move in S&P Next Day		
	Average Points	Percent Up	Occasions
After decline of 7.50 points	1.39	.55	31
After rise of 7.50 points	.88	.60	30
After any day	.12	.52	2164

Panics also occur in fixed-income markets. The largest decline in bond prices since the 1987 crash came on March 8, 1996, when bond prices plummeted more than three full points. Bond market participants were in a state of complete shock.

On that day, I left the comfortable repose of my home, eluded my loving family, which always urges me to be prudent at times like these, and plunged.

I deposited profits from my bond purchases, which went up 100 percent, on my required margin the next day. Had I the courage to buy stock to the extent of my bank balances the next day, I could have retired on the overplus. Stocks registered the largest one-day Dow rally ever, rising 173 points after opening down some 50 points.

Frequently, such forays don't lead to quietude in my splendid home. In August 1988, I bought after a panic following a Federal Reserve increase in the discount rate. It serves me right. I find, after a complete enumeration, that buying after panics in bonds is not a profitable activity. It almost brought me under. During March 1995, I bought when the dollar versus the yen plummeted 5 percent during one day. During the October 19, 1987, stock market crash, I traded into my maximum long position. Perhaps if I were to hobble myself with a cane or practice my clarinet during these periods, I'd have more chips to deposit with my bankers.

When I started out in business, I liked to buy when panics hit good stocks. But the vigorish was so great that I stopped once I learned about the wonderful world of futures. It would be interesting to enumerate all the 10 percent panics in individual NYSE issues, with a view to "quickly realizing an overplus."

Unfortunately, as noted in Table 2–2, panics have all but stopped in the 1990s.

THE MIGHTY FALLEN

Panics occur in all walks of life, not just in stock and interest-rate markets. Dumas remarks offhandedly in the opening of *The Three Musketeers* that panics were so common in France in the 17th century that the citizens always had their muskets and cutlasses close at hand. Most 19th-century books on stocks enumerate some ditties that make the 1929 and 1987 U.S. crashes seem almost tame by comparison. The panics were so prevalent and violent in the 19th century that fistfights occurred daily in the gentlemanly splendor of the New York Stock Exchange trading floor. An 1893 review of NYSE practices by Edward G. Riggs puts the matter in perspective. "Up to ten years ago, the brokers frequently settled their differences by resorting to fisticuffs. Notably in one week in 1884, during the panic of that year [note the routineness of the mention], there was a downright rough-and-tumble fighting match every day. Since then, the temper of the brokers seems to have improved [doubtless due to the decline in frequency of panics]."[8]

My 10 percent, one-month rule is specific, but perhaps the archetypal description of the eye of the 1864 panic—which brought the great bull leader of his time, Anthony Morse, to his knees—may be more helpful in capturing the qualitative flavor of such an event:

> An appalling stillness, like that which precedes a tornado, followed. Then the storm burst. The board room seemed suddenly transformed into a Cyclopean workshop, where a hundred great trip-hammers were being plied. Pillar after pillar toppled over, till the dome fell. The palace of enchantment, built by a strong and cunning magician of so many golden hopes, passed away like a cloud-pageant.
>
> All day long the panic raged, without pause or hindrance. The Evening Exchange was a pandemonium. A crowd of ruined operators reeled and surged up to the rostrum, half crazed by their losses, and stupefied or maddened by drink, while the whole room rang with yells and curses. The space outside the railing was jammed with weary faces, on which was written only the word—run! Close to the door stood a figure in widow's weeds, wild eyed and shrinking. She had risked her last dollar on Fort Wayne, which was selling for 90. She stood there only for a moment, and then passed out into the damp, chilly night forever.
>
> Above all the chorus of execrations was heard the word "Morse." Human nature now showed its basest side. No epithet too vile with which to couple the name of the prostrate financier. He had fallen like Lucifer in one day,

Table 2–2. Chronology of 10 Percent Crashes in Dow Jones
Industrials, 1890–1990

Observation	Date of Crash	Price	Price Three Months Later
1	Nov. 10, 1890	62	66
2	May 9, 1893	59	48
3	July 17, 1893	52	51
4	July 26, 1893	43	56
5	Dec. 21, 1895	49	54
6	July 14, 1896	49	49
7	Aug. 6, 1896	44	55
8	Nov. 5, 1897	46	50
9	Feb. 24, 1898	45	52
10	Nov. 13, 1899	64	63
11	Nov. 18, 1899	58	63
12	Jan. 2, 1900	68	66
13	May 15, 1900	57	59
14	July 21, 1903	51	45
15	Sep. 24, 1903	47	48
16	Dec. 12, 1904	66	78
17	Mar. 13, 1907	83	79
18	Aug. 12, 1907	71	57
19	Oct. 11, 1907	64	64
20	Oct. 29, 1907	57	62
21	Jan. 3, 1910	88	85
22	July 22, 1910	70	86
23	Dec. 18, 1916	98	96
24	Sep. 4, 1917	81	71
25	Oct. 31, 1917	75	80
26	Aug. 20, 1919	98	108
27	Nov. 28, 1919	104	91
28	Feb. 4, 1920	97	94
29	Aug. 7, 1920	84	85
30	Nov. 17, 1920	75	76
31	Dec. 22, 1920	67	77
32	June 6, 1921	71	69
33	Mar. 20, 1926	145	153
34	Oct. 3, 1929	330	247
35	Oct. 28, 1929	261	258
36	Oct. 29, 1929	230	262
37	Nov. 13, 1929	199	272
38	May 5, 1930	260	220
39	June 14, 1930	244	240
40	June 18, 1930	219	234
41	Sep. 27, 1930	213	160
42	Oct. 17, 1930	187	163
43	Dec. 16, 1930	158	184
44	Apr. 16, 1931	163	142
45	Apr. 29, 1931	144	136
46	May 29, 1931	128	142
47	July 27, 1931	140	101
48	Sep. 12, 1931	124	79

Table 2–2.   *(Continued)*

Observation	Date of Crash	Price	Price Three Months Later
49	Sep. 21, 1931	111	78
50	Sep. 30, 1931	97	77
51	Nov. 21, 1931	97	83
52	Dec. 4, 1931	87	86
53	Dec. 14. 1931	77	81
54	Feb. 9, 1932	72	57
55	Mar. 31, 1932	73	43
56	Apr. 8, 1932	63	41
57	Apr. 29, 1932	56	53
58	May 25, 1932	49	73
59	July 4, 1932	43	71
60	Oct. 5, 1932	66	62
61	Oct. 9, 1932	58	62
62	Dec. 13, 1932	60	54
63	Feb. 14, 1933	57	81
64	Aug. 4, 1933	93	93
65	Sep. 27, 1933	93	97
66	Oct. 21, 1933	84	106
67	May 10, 1934	94	90
68	July 26, 1934	86	93
69	Sep. 7, 1937	164	128
70	Sep. 25, 1937	147	127
71	Oct. 18, 1937	126	132
72	Nov. 20, 1937	120	128
73	Mar. 23, 1938	114	127
74	Mar. 29, 1938	102	136
75	Mar. 29, 1939	132	130
76	May 14, 1940	128	123
77	May 21, 1940	114	125
78	Feb. 14, 1941	118	117
79	Sep. 3, 1946	179	168
80	July 12, 1950	199	229
81	Oct. 22, 1957	420	446
82	Sep. 28, 1960	569	616
83	May 24, 1962	623	616
84	June 21, 1962	550	592
85	May 5, 1970	710	725
86	May 26, 1970	631	760
87	Nov. 14, 1973	870	810
88	July 10, 1974	762	648
89	Aug. 22, 1974	705	615
90	Sep. 13, 1974	627	593
91	Dec. 5, 1974	587	753
92	Nov. 13, 1978	792	830
93	Nov. 6, 1979	806	882
94	Mar. 12, 1980	810	873
95	Feb. 8, 1984	1156	1176
96	Oct. 16, 1987	2247	1956
97	Oct. 19, 1987	1739	1936
98	Aug. 16, 1990	2681	2550

from the zenith of his fame. The men who, but yesterday, extolled him to the skies, now vied with each other in cursing him.[9]

There was an interesting follow-up to the fall of the former king. A few years later, totally down and out, reduced to begging outside Trinity Church, Morse was spotted by a member of the New York Stock Exchange. He relayed the news to his fellow members. The stocks that Morse liked to bull up in his heyday—Fort Wayne, Reading, and Old Southern—immediately rose 5 percent. Perhaps a visit by Bunker Hunt to the New York COMEX, the home of the silver market, would have a similar impact on silver and gold, which have listlessly lagged at less than half their former levels since Hunt's fall.

Former members who are floating around Wall Street bereft of funds are referred to as ghosts or dead ducks. The graveyard watchman at Trinity Church looks out for them, but they are gone in the twinkling of an one-eighth down tick. If you ask how a ghost lives without money on Wall Street, the invariable reply is, "He doesn't. He merely exists." In describing some prominent 19th-century shorts sellers, Riggs issues a prophetic warning that has not lost its punch after 100 years:

> They have studied every influence, every feature that had any bearing on the market, and worked them out in detail; and yet with all their determination to succeed they are now numbered among the hapless ghosts of the Street. They have passed the sixty year limit, and must eventually end their days in an East Side lodging house.[10]

I have sold my membership on the commodity exchanges, but I am not yet a ghost there and I can still afford to eat at Delmonico's and The Four Seasons. But I am a ghost in squash. The game I played, hardball squash, is gone forever, replaced by a soft ball more in keeping with easy living. Occasionally, as a favor to a friend, I make an appearance in a squash doubles tournament. Invariably, my team is seeded first and we are handicapped with 10 points. My efficacy is less than that of the "ghosts" of Wall Street in such appearances.

Artie frequently was called on to remove the bodies and inventory the possessions of dead ghosts in the East Side boarding houses, a euphemism for the Bowery's Skid Row. This entailed delicate negotiations because the landlords often refused to release the bodies before being paid for past-due rent. When the legendary Anthony W. Morse died, a few of his old friends, for whom he made millions, did come forward to pay off the rent, and his funeral rites were held.

"Vickie, what will you do if you get caught in a panic in the market?" Artie often asked me. "They're completely unpredictable—a war, a change in Fed policy, an earthquake, a brokerage house failure, an assassination. They couldn't be subsumed in those computer outputs of yours."

"Dad, I'll just come in with the hard serve."

Artie wasn't convinced at all. He had had much experience with the dangers of time-tested methods of buying during panics. When he was 13, a spell of 16 non-overlapping 10 percent panic declines occurred in a horrible year, from April 16, 1931, when the Dow stood at 163, to July 4, 1932, when the Dow hit 43. Instead of retiring to the shelter and quietude of a splendid home after his dad bought during such tornadoes, Artie's family retired to the public beach. "Take it easy," he said.

I always hear the sounds of the Atlantic Ocean's waves closing over my wretched trades as I get set to take the plunge when a panic is in full force.

WERE YOU SHORT?

The aftermath of the 1931 panics left my grandparents strapped financially for the rest of their lives. I well remember their struggle to scratch up the $25 annual cost of their membership in the Brighton Beach Baths. But during the '50s, when I visited them each week after my music lessons, I could always count on some stock market war stories. The routine started with my music lessons at the home of my teacher, Arnold Fish. Arnold taught theory at the Juilliard School of Music. After finishing the lessons, we'd discuss the music-sports-stock market connection at his outdoor ping-pong table. The 1950s had been as wild and profitable to public speculators as the 1990s. The Dow appropriately ended the 1940s at 200 and ended the 1950s at 679.4. A 240 percent price appreciation carries many stocks with it.

My grandfather Martin lived through a thousand financial deaths during the stock market rise as he shorted the hades out of each rally, waiting for the 1930 crashes to reemerge. I have seen all too many friends victimized by a similar syndrome: they have shorted during the 1990s, waiting for the 1987 crash to reappear. Psychologists tend to study such mindsets in university laboratories. My research institute was the Brighton First Street apartment of my grandparents, where I had the comparative advantage of a view of the Atlantic Ocean and Coney Island. After receiving my weekly allowance of $1.00, I could count on learning some dos and don'ts of speculating (more the latter than the former).

"Martin, how was the market today?" Birdie asked.

"It was up a lot," Martin replied.

"Were you, how do you say it, short?"

"What's short?" I queried.

"Well, in business, a contractor or wholesaler has to agree to sell his goods at a particular price before he buys them. He sells first and then buys what he needs on the open market. The same is true in the stock market. You can borrow shares from someone, sell the shares, and then buy them back at a later time—hopefully, at a lower price."

"It sounds very complicated," I said.

"That's right, that gives the big boys a big edge. They have the connections to borrow the shares. The public, like Birdie, doesn't even know what a short is."

I have often recalled that remark, which contained so much wisdom. The public is trained to buy before it sells. Rather than sell first, it buys initially. Someone has to be on the other side of these trades. They are the pros. In most market conditions, the pros can be anticipated to charge the public for accommodating its instinct to buy first.

"Why is it that when prices went down a lot yesterday you were a bull, and today, when they're way up, you're a bear?"

"Well, yesterday General Motors went on strike and everyone thought they were going to settle it."

"But I've often heard you say that whatever everyone's doing is wrong."

"Birdie, if you'll just attend to the cooking and piano playing, I'll attend to providing a living around here like I'm supposed to."

"But Martin, I could have told you that General Motors wouldn't be able to settle."

"How?"

"We've had eight years of boom since the end of the war. The workers are flush and tired and their union bosses have to show the workers they're working hard for them. Why should they have settled?"

Remembering the 1931 bloodbaths, Martin liked to sell short the first day after a big panic. That's one of the only mistakes I haven't made more than two or three times. I don't like to sell stocks short. The brokers have all sorts of contrived reasons for refusing to pay interest on the credit balances. I lose an interest rate, a dividend, and a risk premium when I short. Soros told me once that he lost more money selling short than on any other speculative activity. My experience is similar. The advice that comes down the pike from authors of stock market doom books—that individual investors should sell short—is a ticket to the poorhouse.

MIDDLEMEN

I have learned that, in medieval times, Niederhoffers were middlemen who facilitated dealings in the court of essential transactions that noblemen found beneath their dignity. Nothing has changed. That's what I do right now for operators like central banks, governments, processors, and big speculators like the great George Soros himself, who still deigns to let me handle some of his trades as long as I maintain proper humility and save him a few bucks in the process.

As the first son of an immigrant family, great things were expected of Martin. He sailed through elementary school and high school and went on to City College, majoring in accounting. He developed an interest in linguistics, and eventually mastered several languages. To help pay his way through school, he worked as a bookkeeper in a publishing enterprise. While there, he developed a reputation as a rake. His new secretary, Birdie, a real looker and former silent movie pianist, was easily eight inches taller than Martin's 5'2". Rumors that he was a degenerate had already circulated in the office. He called her in to take dictation on her first day as his stenographer. "Miss Bertha, I'm going to ask you something now and I'll never ask it again. Will you marry me?"

"I'll have to ask my mother."

"No, I have to know right now."

"Yes." (She figured she'd ask her mother anyway.)

Martin soon branched out into speculations in real estate and the stock market. At one time, he amassed nearly $1 million of wealth, including substantial corner property on Flatbush Avenue and Avenue K, and several six-figure margin accounts in the stock market, at the prestigious firm of DuPont & Company. Unfortunately, the crash of 1929 and the ensuing Depression wiped Martin out. The family was forced into a hand-to-mouth existence. Three children were born, in 1918, 1921, and 1924; money for more children was not available after 1929.

Like many others who lost everything in the Depression, Martin frequented the bankruptcy courts, hoping that he could pick up a foreclosure for a prayer and a song. While he pounded the court steps, the boys in the family worked as door-to-door salesmen to pay the bills. On one of his forays into court, Martin found himself a sinecure. The judge had called out to the courtroom to ask whether anyone could act as interpreter between two litigants, neither of whom could speak English. He needed someone who could handle Yiddish and Spanish. Martin said later that, although he was not fluent in either language, he knew enough to finesse his way through the situation.

Gimme a Hundred HAT

Martin's forays into the stock markets were legendary within the family. He spoke trippingly of classic companies that no longer exist, like TIN, HAT, Foreign Power, Wurlitzer, Allegheny, Nash, Asphalt, Manville, Neon, Horn & Hardart, Cook, Vendo, and Chalmers. These companies had all been standards during the 1920s, and, like many speculators since then, Martin had not adjusted to the fact that the blue chips of yesterday frequently become the laggards of today. The average stock performance was down about 80 percent in the next 30 years. In retrospect, I find about three out of four of his favorites have since entered bankruptcy. This illustrates a general tendency among the former standing. Business is ever-changing and so are consumers' preferences. Of the 12 companies constituting the Dow Jones Industrial Average at the end of the 19th century, only one, General Electric, has withstood the test of time and is still with us. The others have passed into oblivion or have been merged out of existence. Martin was also careful to steer me away from such promotions as Disney, Walmart, Tam Brands, Capital Cities, Merck, and Noxell, which appreciated 4,000 percent to 10,000 percent over the next 30 years. These are the kinds of stocks that Peter Lynch calls forty-baggers that contributed to the stellar performance of the Magellan Fund.

I spent considerable time during the 1960s and 1970s visiting with major listed companies on the NYSE. The merger business I founded purveyed closely held companies to them. In addition, I ran an active investment advisory and stock trading operation. During that time, like most stock pickers, I knew the names, business, and price/earnings ratio of almost every listed company. When I turn to the stock listings 30 years later, I can hardly recognize 10 percent of them. Almost all the former greats have hit the dust, changed their name, been acquired, or been replaced by companies with more glamorous current prospects. The manufacturers that were once the high flyers have now all been replaced by service, communication, and concept plays. Such changing fortunes in returns on capital make me very wary of paying too high a premium over book value or earnings for any current Street favorite, no matter how compelling the niche.

Martin began his day by getting a rundown on the rail stocks. In the 19th century, the rails provided market leadership and sold for prices well above those of the upstart industrials. Martin's favorites included Philadelphia & Reading, New York & New Haven, New York Central, and Baltimore & Ohio. These great rocks of stability, all the rage at the turn of the century, when most of them had three-digit handles, have declined fairly steadily throughout the last 70 years. He who dines with the devil should sup with a long spoon. Yes, they received monopoly status and guaranteed mail freight from Washington. But that made them too fat, too ready to accept ruinous wage settlements and work-rule agreements with unions. Competition from the airlines and other forms of surface transportation eventually did most of them in. Those who were able to play with massive tax losses or land holdings survived.

ONCE BURNED . . .

I realized now that men of Martin's generation, who lost everything in the Depression, were traumatized by the vivid memories of their losses. In addition to their focus on the wrong companies, these men suffered from psychological maladies that had even worse consequences for their bank balances. They assumed that because there had once been a day in 1929 when stocks crashed by 25 to 50 percent, and because an aftermath in 1931 brought a further 78 percent decline, such times could be expected to dawn again. Except for the October 19, 1987, crash, such times have not dawned in 65 years. Forewarned is foredoomed. Whenever Martin held a stock that rose 10 to 15 percent above his initial purchase price, he would sell out for a small profit in order to avoid losing all his chips in another crash. "You can never go broke by taking a profit," Martin loved to say. This rule *was* good for a profit two out of three times, but then Martin's profits would be swallowed up by his losses from hanging on to the old standbys that were slowly deteriorating into nothingness as their franchises with the public evaporated.

But there was still enough money to buy me a round lot of 100 shares of stock for my bar mitzvah. I supposedly had potential. It has been rumored that I once provided the funds for a family meal of Moo Goo Gai Pan at the local Chinese restaurant with my winnings from paddleball speculation.

My First Stock

Martin could afford only a round lot of a stock selling below $1. He chose for me the cheapest stock on the NYSE, Benguet Mining, selling at 50 cents a share. What I didn't realize until later was that, by the time I had paid the minimum fixed commission of 6 cents a share plus the bid/asked spread of $\frac{1}{16}$, I was down 25 percent on my investment before I even started. That's about standard for most tailor-made deals the public likes to speculate in.

1954 was a typical postwar year. The Dow rose 44 percent, from 281 to 404, and almost half of all listed issues were up 50 percent or more. While all the other stocks around Benguet—The Beneficial Finances, Bendixes, Bests, and Bethlehems of the world—were steadily ticking up, Benguet hardly moved at all. It stayed riveted to $\frac{1}{2}$ for four years. Finally, a miracle happened. The stock rose to $1. On my grandfather's advice, I rushed to take my profit of $50. The stock hovered at $1 for a few more weeks after I sold, and then advanced steadily to $30 in three years.

Small Profits

I have repeated the mistake of grabbing at small profits and selling at a targeted round number over and over in my speculative career. I believe many others make this same error. The reason: Many players set their sights at certain reasonable targets. Fast-moving operators, aware of these targets, come in just ahead, ready to take the other side, knowing that there will be considerable pressure to offset at prices not much worse than current. This pressure usually drives the price away from the target. But if the price can overcome these operators and reach the target, something big is about to happen.

I have quantified a number of nonrandom phenomena that occur around target prices. My first efforts examined the moves of commodities and stocks that broke through round numbers. I found that after a breakup and subsequent pullback, markets tend to be quite bullish.

Because I am a reversalist by trade, it is sometimes hard for me to practice what I preach. I am often tempted to sell right after a commodity or stock attempts to break through a round number from below. But then I think back to Benguet and, sometimes, I am able to control my impulse to take a fast profit. It usually doesn't help. A typical mistake: I took a 5 percent profit on my Nikkei position when it hit 18,000 in 1994, after a six-month holding period. In the next three days after I sold, it added another 1,000 points. After two weeks, it went up 2,000 points. I've made this mistake in the Nikkei four times in the past five years. When will I learn?

A GOOD CHEW

After the sale of my first stock, I had $100 in my pocket and was ready for my second investment.

As a special treat, Martin took me to see a ticker tape room in a brokerage. Such rooms are now extinct in the United States, but can still be seen in parts of Asia. In a dimly lit room, there were about 25 chairs filled with ill-clad men and women, all obviously down and out. Most of them were scratching Xs and Os on paper while gazing at a ticker tape meandering by on a screen hardly visible from the back. Someone shouted, "Steel! They're ready to take it up." Martin explained to me that U.S. Steel, then selling at $100, was one of the blue-chip investments you could always feel safe buying. With a book value of $150, the stock was vastly undervalued. Even on the conservative assumption that it sold all of its assets at depreciated cost, the liquidation value of the company was still at least 50 percent higher than current market. Why, its coal reserves alone were worth $200 a share. From that day on, however, Steel never attained a price higher than $100. It gradually withered to about $10 in 1988, then stabilized, and has since crept back up to about $40.

"Martin, what's a great stock for the future?" I asked. "One I can just salt away for after college?"

"For technology, brand name, franchise, and just plain good management, I chose Western Union. Their network of messenger boys, telegraph wires and sets, their brand name—it gives them a franchise akin to printing money. No one could even think of competing with them." Western Union stood at $60 at the time and has steadily declined to $2 now.

"For a consumer product, you might choose Tucker Taffee. Americans love two things, a good sweet and a good chew." Martin pointed out that Tucker had a multimillion-dollar annual advertising budget and a market value of over $100 million, substantially higher than that of Hershey at the time. But, same story. Many years later, I saw the tag-end of the Tucker business, after it had declared bankruptcy. Two girls were hand-wrapping pieces of rock candy, made in old mayonnaise jars from heated sugar water, in a dilapidated storefront in Hampton Beach, New Hampshire.

HARD TIMES ARE HERE

The financial waters at the Arthur Niederhoffers' house were also fairly troubled in those days. When I reached my teens, my parents decided to enlighten me concerning our financial situation. They frequently sat me down and told me that they hoped to be solvent by the time my dad was 60. At that time, our total debt of $25,000 was five times his annual income, and we had no significant assets. The situation was not helped by the expense for music lessons for my sister and me, and the prospect of a $3,000-a-year college tuition expense looming in the near future. My mom, to help out, became a New York City public school teacher.

At my grandparents' home, things were not much better. Martin's shorts all got creamed. By the 1960s, he was ready to go long, just in time for a devastating 23 percent decline in the first six months of 1962. He held on to a few losers until they reached prices in line with those that prevailed 33 years earlier. His future stock market speculations were confined vicariously to my own forays into the market and reminiscences of the greats he had known back in the days before the '29 crash.

LOOKING FOR LOST LUCK

"So long, boys, we're off for a walk." One day, after a long morning of watching the tape. Martin took me on a grand tour of the Wall Street environs so I could take in the full array of Street denizens as they poured out of their buildings for a quick lunch and a stroll around the block.

We passed the bronze doors of the New York Stock Exchange at 11 Wall Street, and many a gloriously named brokerage firm. Most are now forgotten. Either they went bankrupt or they consolidated into new associations. Martin showed me the hallowed cathedral of J. P. Morgan's bank at 23 Wall Street, so imposing that it deigned to advertise no name on its facade. Only the gold-leafed number, 23, showed on its glass doors.

As we turned down New Street, where Martin received his start in a bucket shop, he nodded toward an old-timer painfully making his way along the curb with the help of a silver-handled ebony cane. (The cane was not held out as the emblem of a time-tested method of making money; the experience in the 1930s had warned Martin away.)

"Don't let the fancy cane fool you. Old Fitzie there lost everything in the '30s, and now he haunts Morgan Bank, where he was caught in the bomb blast in 1920. Somebody planted a bomb outside the bank in a pushcart and it nearly killed him; you can still see the pockmarks in the stones of the building over there.

"Fitzie's luck was never any good after that, and he always seems to be looking for the luck he lost that day, along with a piece of his leg. Now he's what we call a dead duck. But there was a time . . . Old Fitz was the toast of the Street. He owned a jet-black Pierce Arrow cabriolet, a princely mansion fronting Union Square, elaborately appointed in gold leaf and marble, and a stud farm out in New Jersey horse country. He plied Long Island Sound in a yacht he kept in Newport. But he got in over his head—the fate of everyone, I guess, who trades with too much debt. Back then the margin requirement in stocks was around 10 percent, and he traded with the full tenfold leverage on his positions. Fitzie took a flyer on a stock that he heard was being cornered. But the clique pulled the plug before Fitzie could get out and he went down with the ship. He finally had to sell his Exchange seat to pay his debts. He should have known he was at the mercy of unscrupulous operators. They always sniff out the players who have gotten in over their heads and crush them like ants underfoot. Make sure they don't do that to you."

"But who are 'They'?" I wondered.

"'They'—I'll tell you, 'They' are what Jung refers to as 'the collective unconscious' of the market. And, Vickie, it's not only stocks they manipulate. They lock up the supplies of corn, wheat, and cattle the same way. Beware of corners whenever you trade." I recalled that remark when I was short a boatload of silver in late 1979 at $5.50 an ounce. It climbed inexorably past $10, limit up every day, before I could get out by the skin of my teeth, saved only by the long position in gold I had "hedged" it with.

MAGNUMS AND JEROBOAMS

As we passed the corner of the NYSE, Martin pointed to a penthouse apartment in an adjacent building. "That's where the infamous Richard Whitney lived. Richard was President of the Stock Exchange and a pillar of the Street in the late 1920s and early '30s. His older brother George was a partner of J. P. Morgan's, and Richard was the 'Morgan broker.' He was famous for defending the Street's interests during Roosevelt's first term, when the SEC was formed, and old Joe Kennedy was appointed the first Commissioner of the SEC. Not many men could stand up to old bootlegger Joe, one of the most ruthless stock manipulators that ever lived, but Richard could. He lived the gilded life, and was a prominent member of the best clubs, like the Porcellian at Harvard, and the Knickerbocker and Links clubs in the City.

"Richard had, besides his New York townhouse, a 495-acre estate in Far Hills, New Jersey, where he was a member of the township committee and master of the foxhounds at the Essex Hunt. They said his farm payroll alone was $1,500 a month, to pay for a superintendent, herdsmen, grooms, a jockey, a gardener, and teamsters; he had horses, prize Ayrshire chickens, and thoroughbred Berkshire pigs. Nobody could doubt that he was a model of probity, standing for all that was noble about American financial affairs.

"But it turned out that Richard had no business sense at all. He borrowed millions from his brother, from the Morgan Bank, and from anyone foolish enough to lend to him, and sank it all in worthless stock like American Colloid Corporation and Distilled Liquors Corporation, makers of Jersey Lightning. He bet his whole fortune and career on the idea that once Prohibition was over, the country would consume huge quantities of New Jersey applejack. The Street turned a blind eye to all of this, figuring that George Whitney, the Morgan partner, would always be there to bail out his brother in a pinch. By 1936, Richard was practically the only buyer of Distilled Liquors stock, and as the price kept sinking, Richard borrowed and finally embezzled more and more money to meet margin calls and to buy more stock in the wild hope he could underpin the market himself.

"Eventually, the whole house of cards came crashing down. Richard embezzled funds from the Stock Exchange's Gratuity Fund, to which he had been appointed trustee. The Gratuity Fund was set up to take care of members' widows and orphans. When the Exchange membership found out about this transgression, their indulgence stopped. Suddenly, all his friends shook their heads, sadly saying there was nothing they could do for poor old Dick. He had even misappropriated assets of the New York Yacht Club, where he was Treasurer.

"When the police came, he was forced to teach them the proper nomenclature for champagne-bottle sizes. 'Gentlemen,' he pointed out with pained noblesse oblige, 'they're not two-quart and six-quart bottles. They're magnums and jeroboams.' Besides the champagne, the police inventoried 47 suits, 12 walking sticks, and four pink riding coats for foxhunting. The judge sent Dick Whitney to Sing Sing for five years, and when he got out his brother George personally saw to it that Richard was packed off to Massachusetts where he managed a dairy farm and then worked in an explosives factory."

HOODOO

"Victor, you know Wall Street has a graveyard at one end and a river at the other," he said to me as we neared the intersection of Broadway and Wall, where the neo-Gothic splendor of Trinity Church loomed over us and the adjacent centuries-old cemetery, where the bones of Alexander Hamilton lie. When Trinity was built in 1846, its spire was the tallest structure in Manhattan. Its parish was chartered in 1697 as part of the Church of England, and the parish still owns a sizable chunk of prime Wall Street real estate granted to the colony by Queen Anne in 1705. As my lesson continued, there issued forth from Trinity's darkened stones the celebrants of the mystery, in sumptuous robes, and the members of their flock who had

just attended the noon service—a throng of freshly forgiven Street operators who spilled out of the massive bronze doors into the sunlight, wafted
along on the brooding strains of the church organ that grandly hummed
their glory.

At that moment, as in so many other histories, an unforgettable character made his appearance—to my lifelong salvation.

As the splendidly tailored crowd swept by us, there suddenly appeared,
near the black wrought-iron gate of the graveyard, a certain ghost, an ap-
palling figure, bedraggled of mien, threadbare of coat, and bloodshot of
eye. I felt Martin stiffen beside me as he said, "Get away now, Paulie, I've
got nothing for you today." Martin grabbed me by the elbow and steered
me around this apparition as Paulie leaned after us, whispering about a tip
on an impending merger. Giving up on us, Paulie tried his line on various
members of the departing congregation, but with no better luck. Before I
could ask, Martin turned to me, "That was Paulie, and he's a hoodoo.
Don't ever take a tip from a hoodoo, Vic; their luck is cursed. Paulie used
to be a top bondbroker for one of the best houses, but then his luck went
against him. Making money was easy until the Fed raised the discount
rate, and suddenly all of Paulie's bond accounts were underwater.

"Then he tried his hand at stocks, and piled heavily into the new computer companies. He was one of the biggest spending Stock Exchange
members during the '50s; the parties he threw at his Park Avenue apartment were legendary. But then his luck turned sour again. I heard he got
his customers into Burroughs at around 90 and held on while it collapsed,
finally selling out around 8. He bought Texas Instruments at over 200, and
his last customer walked out when the stock fell below 25. Paulie moved
from firm to firm and each one fired him. Now he's out of a job and spends
all day on the steps of Federal Hall trying to cadge a living out of old ac-
quaintances by giving them takeover stock tips. Take my word for it, Vic,
when you see a hoodoo, don't ask questions and don't hang around to listen. A hoodoo's bad luck is contagious."

Garet Garrett gives the classic definition of a hoodoo in one of my favorite books on Wall Street:

> There is about him an air of departed prosperity which is unmistakable.
> Nearly everybody knows him. He was once a member of the New York
> Stock Exchange, or the son of one, or what's-his-name that was Gould's
> broker twenty years ago. He is most knowing of speed and would easily fool
> you if you were not warned. All the past he understands, and the why of
> everything, but for the present and future he is a source of fatal ideas and a
> borrower of money.[11]

The legendary Rothschilds would never do business with a hoodoo, no
matter how blue his blood or impeccable his references. They knew it

looked like rank superstition, but they nonetheless had no scruples about basing a credit decision on such a judgment. The Rothschilds knew full well that bad luck could arise from chance alone. But, more likely, excess of greed, rashness, cowardice, bad temper, or plain moral turpitude were the root causes of the hex. Like most successful operators, they made their own luck.

I have found that there are indeed certain persons whose trails are littered with disaster and carnage. They always have an explanation ready, but the record shows that all who associated with them lost money and position. One of my greatest business talents is my ability to identify these hoodoos early and to keep away from them in all my business and personal affairs. My partners have acquired the knack also. Whenever we are sitting through a business presentation for an opportunity that is available because of an incredible series of unlucky breaks, one of them will pass me a note: H-O-O.

Since I absorbed the lesson of the hoodoo in my own life, I have told it to many friends. I usually throw in some quote like "Hoodooism is not confined to steam locomotives. I have known a hoodoo diesel rail car, and a hoodoo bear" in the market or "I started the trade with a heavy hoodoo. The large man was long, also."

Invariably, my friend will reflect for a moment and say something like, "You know, I know a hoodoo in my department too." Or, "I know a stock picker like that. I won't even tell him what I'm buying, for fear . . . ." As they leave, scratching their heads, I say, "The prospect of having your cake and eluding a hoodoo is sublime." I've met numerous hoodoos in all walks of life in my day, inside and outside the rails and boards, and in the racquet courts and law courts.

A Harvard Club Hoodoo

In 1986, my mentor and the father of my speculative business, Jim Lorie, arranged for me to meet Ivan Boesky. Jim apparently believed that Boesky's activities in stock trading might mesh well with the futures trading strategies I was developing. Boesky at this time was in his glory. He liked to convene power breakfasts at the Harvard Club of New York, where the proscription against placing papers on the tables enables profound matters to come under discussion without the risk of any precise numbers or other type of analysis interfering with the grand schemes being contemplated. The sober tone of the high-vaulted, oak-paneled dining hall lends gravity and probity to the personalities there assembled, and the accent of virility is added by the many portraits of Harvard-bred statesmen that line the walls, punctuated by the staring heads of antlered beasts that presumably were dealt a thundering, high-caliber death by Bully old TR, who hated Wall Streeters with a passion. This room provided the perfect backdrop to Boesky's ruddy glow, the result of frequent Palm Beach vacations and a daily workout on the squash court.

Boesky's Club membership was apparently traceable to his having attended a class at Harvard's Extension School. This connection was more than sufficient for the Harvard Club to welcome him with open arms. The Club, always in a delicate financial position, was in such dire straits in those days that it even accepted for membership a Jewish squash player (yours truly), although a friend—the great diplomat Charlie Ufford, who once scored the finest point against me in my multifarious squash career, a lob over my head at a crucial point in the fifth game of the semifinals of the 1965 squash championships—had to intervene to tilt the balance in my favor.

Boesky did not grant me an audience at the Harvard Club. I was not important enough to warrant such treatment. I was invited to the arbitrageur's office for a "breakfast" meeting. I was served a bagel on a silver tray. Splashed everywhere on the walls of his office were photographs of Ivan—speaking at university commencement exercises, shaking the hands of political grandees, being borne aloft in a chair by the muscle-power of 20 worshipful members of a temple he supported, holding up a copy of *Merger Mania*, or seated behind the wheel of one of his pink Rolls Royce phaetons. A soberly groomed secretary in a floor-length skirt freshened my coffee. Ivan himself breakfasted on a glass of grapefruit juice and a Danish, and discoursed on the merits of dietary moderation, in honor, he said, of my attainments on the squash court.

The phone rang, and when I heard words like "We'll tender at 75" wafting about, I got up to give him privacy. Ivan beckoned elaborately for me to stay to listen in on one of his "arbitrage situations." Suddenly, I had a powerful memory of the ghost who once had scratched my back in the chill shadow of Trinity Church. I quietly made my exit as he spoke in a tense whisper to his counterpart.

THE ANTI-HOODOO

The character trait I'm most proud of is my ability to have on my associates an effect opposite that of a hoodoo. My business partners become millionaires. Five of my former assistants have gone on to become centimillionaires.

Except for a few customers who dropped me in the middle of a losing trade, I've never had a client lose money with me. Even though I was a terrible doubles player, I won the national tournament with three separate partners.

In the old days, an anti-hoodoo was watched closely. People followed him around and copied every move. "If he were to tie his necktie under his ear, they would do the same." I don't wear ties or shoes when I trade.

Financial Trader dubbed me "The Shoeless Trader." I'll know my anti-hoodooism has been properly recognized when there is a run on socks around the Chicago Board of Trade.

UNLUCKY DAYS

Martin concluded his disquisitions on the stock market. "Vic, there are a few basic rules in stock speculation. Stay with the tried and true old standards. Don't be deceptive. You never go broke taking a profit. Stay away from the hoodoos. And stay away from Fridays. Old-timers still remember the countless formerly wealthy men who jumped from their windows on Black Friday, September 2, 1869, during the gold panic. Above all, never buy a stock or bond on a Friday the 13th." The part about hoodoos is good advice.

I followed this last injunction carefully for many years. Superstition, even my grandfather's, must be tested. I analyzed Martin's "Friday the 13th Rule" for the 17 years ending Friday, September 13, 1996 (Table 2–3).

The results are eye-opening. On average, bonds have gone up one-third of a point on Friday the 13th. Taking account of the variability of bond prices on all days, results this far away from unchanged would occur less than 1 in 1,000 times by chance variation alone. The results for stocks are too variable for a reliable estimate. On Friday, October 13, 1989, stocks went down 190 Dow points, the third largest one-day decline ever. But the average for the other 21 Friday the 13ths was +5 Dow points. There is sufficient evidence to show that Friday the 13th is indeed a day to beware of—for bond bears.

Friday the 13ths have a way of coming up and passing by without the blowing of horns; one more is scheduled for December 1996, one for June 1997, and three will occur in 1998 (February, March, November).

EVERYONE RETIRES TO THE SOUTH

One day, about 30 years after meeting the hoodoo beneath the Trinity spire, I was visiting my 92-year-old grandmother, Birdie, at the Collins Avenue old-age home in Miami. Her greatest desire was to get a corned beef sandwich at Wolfie's, the famous Jewish delicatessen on 9th Street and Collins Avenue. I wheeled her the four blocks and we made our way into an establishment where three-fourths of the patrons were likewise seated in wheelchairs.

We reminisced about some of Martin's stock market coups: Air Reduction, Allis Chalmers, American Can. These stalwarts of the early 20th century had been bequeathed to her and, like most elderly people in this situation, she had sold the ones that were above cost, only to see them quadruple in the next few years, and had retained the ones that were below

Table 2–3. The Friday-the-13th Effect

Price Changes from Close on Thursday the 12th to Close on Friday	Point Change in Bond Futures, in Decimals	Point Change in Dow Jones Industrial Average	Point Change in S&P Futures Contract
June 13, 1980	1.19	5.80	net yet traded
Feb. 13, 1981	0.00	(7.60)	not yet traded
Nov. 13, 1981	(0.19)	(4.66)	not yet traded
Aug. 13, 1982	0.78	6.47	2.50
May 13, 1983	(0.16)	4.35	0.70
July 13, 1984	0.44	5.30	0.70
Sep. 13, 1985	0.81	(4.71)	(1.00)
Dec. 13, 1985	0.56	23.97	3.25
June 13, 1986	2.00	36.06	5.10
Feb. 13, 1987	0.16	17.58	5.30
Mar. 13, 1987	0.28	(8.68)	(1.40)
Nov. 13, 1987	(0.35)	(25.53)	(2.00)
May 13, 1988	0.47	21.39	3.80
Jan. 13, 1989	0.82	(1.61)	1.00
Oct. 13, 1989	0.34	(189.96)	(30.00)
July 13, 1990	0.34	10.04	1.40
Sep. 13, 1991	(0.09)	(23.56)	(4.20)
Dec. 13, 1991	(0.50)	20.35	3.20
Mar. 13, 1992	(0.22)	27.28	1.40
Nov. 13, 1992	0.00	(6.22)	0.20
Aug. 13, 1993	0.28	0.56	0.40
May 13, 1994	0.79	6.84	1.10
Oct. 13, 1994	0.35	4.92	1.19
Jan. 13, 1995	1.00	49.46	4.80
Oct. 13, 1995	.46	29.63	4.85
Sep. 13, 1996	1.47	66.58	10.75
Averages:	0.42	2.59	0.57

cost, such as Famous Artists, Four Seasons Nursing, and Levin-Townsend, which eventually sank into bankruptcy. I asked Birdie if Wolfie's should stock up on pastrami or ham. The pastrami moves briskly. Taking that perspective, it's easy to see which stocks to unload and which to hold or buy more of.

Quantifying the relative performance of stocks that recently have acted badly versus those that have acted well has led to much pseudoscientific analysis. Academics in the 1990s, who usually belong to the Behavioral Finance cult and are often funded by the National Science Foundation, now point to such studies to show that stocks overreact to bad news. In the

1960s, the studies, à la mode, showed that buying relative strength led to superior returns. The rage today is to find pairs of "matching" stocks—sell the overvalued one and buy the undervalued one. This is often combined with buying stock market futures. I can make one forecast with considerable confidence: Whenever one or the other of those two competing approaches seems to show superior returns, the other approach is a good bet. Fading the published technical analysis of academic systems is always a good horse to ride. Even a professor is shrewd enough to keep the good stuff, if any, private.

I told Birdie that, each year, come Hades or high water, I buy my kids a good stock they can follow in the stock tables for themselves. In 1992, I bought them IBM, noting with pride that I had picked it up at 110, after it had recently traded as high as 140. "Just tuck that away," I said, "you can't go wrong with that one." A few months later, IBM fell to 52, and my kids called to ask if IBM had split 3 for 1 after I had bought it for them (a potential suit?). In a throwback to Martin's advice to his family in the 1950s, all I could muster was, "The stream of dividends, including the final liquidation dividend, is the main determinant of value. IBM has maintained its dividend for decades, so don't worry." Two weeks later, the IBM Board voted to cut the dividend by 40 percent, and the stock fell to 46.

As Birdie recalled Martin's stock market speculations, she admitted that it used to cause her a fair amount of trepidation. And although Birdie had a much better mind for the market than Martin usually gave her credit for, she had been totally unprepared to manage the small portfolio of stocks she inherited from him. For his part, Martin shared the conventional opinion of the 1920s, that Wall Street was "no place for women, since they lack the mental equipment. They have no ballast apart from men, and are liable to perish when adversity arises."

As we left Wolfie's and made our way back to the nursing home, we returned to our remembrances of Martin, and she turned to me saying, "Vickie, I'm worried about you now. The market took a bad knock the other day, and it seems very volatile. I know you're big in futures. Are you short stocks now?"

Before I could reply, her face suddenly paled and her eyes widened. "No, Paulie, I don't have a penny, and leave us alone! Vic, hurry up, I need to get back to my room to make a phone call." As we sped off, she continued, "Don't look back at him. Maybe he'll go away . . . . He usually hangs out at the mutual fund offices on the corner, under the electric stock ticker. I used to give to him, because I remember him from Brighton and Martin's Wall Street days. But then, I figured, look at him—he's doing better than I am on Social Security and with my worthless stocks. So I stopped giving." I turned back and saw him rattling some coins in a paper cup, trying to smooth the wrinkles out of a sports coat. Twentieth-century hoodoos and ghosts like the warmth of Miami over the chill of the Bowery.

CHAPTER 3

Delphic Oracles and Science

Although there are growing signs that cyclical disinflationary pressures may have ended, it is premature to conclude that a U.S. inflation cycle upturn is imminent.

Dr. Geoffrey H. Moore
Former Chairman, Center for
International Business Cycle Research

Ah, the glory that was ancient Greece: the golden age of Pericles, Praxiteles, Aeschylus, Sappho, Sophocles . . . the mysteries of Eleusis, and the riddles of Herakleitos . . . olive trees blowing in the thyme-scented air below Olympus . . . the notes of the oaken flute, the plaint of goats; sweet honey and pungent yogurt; the cries of fishermen drawing in their nets in the bay of Piraeus. The legacy of ancient Greece is with us in every aspect of our lives. Our theater, literature, architecture, philosophy, and natural sciences are so immersed in Greek tradition that it is impossible to imagine our culture without it. And bearing no less debt to Greek tradition is the eminent art of forecasting in our era.

The hallowed summit of Parnassus towers above the ancient Sacred Road leading out of Athens into the austere beauty of Phocis. At the point where the old valley road turns west to climb an incline, one finds the fabled Parting of the Ways, where young Oedipus, disturbed by what he had heard from the Oracle and determined not to return to his supposed parents at Corinth, took the left fork to Thebes and to his dire fate. Over the hill, along the right fork, the road descends to Delphi on the steep cliffside, below the ochre Phaidriades, the twin "Bright Cliffs." There, at Delphia, the shrine of the Sun-God clings to the mist-shrouded hills, dizzily overlooking the mile-deep gorge leading down to the sun-bedazzled Gulf of Corinth, where it gives onto the wine-dark Mediterranean. Behold the terrible and numinous Temple of Apollo at Delphia, the *omphalos*, the very navel of the universe.

Millions of eons ago, golden Apollo found this place and there he slew a dragon, a python (hence "Pytho," Delphi's older name). He slaked his thirst from the spring that bursts forth from the hillside, Telphousa, and courted the lissome but reluctant naiad who made that spring her watery home. Looking about for priests to tend his temple and the Oracle he had installed there—the Pythia, the serpent woman—he leaped into the sea, where, in the shape of a dolphin (hence the supposed derivation of "Delphi"), he carried off an entire ship of Minoans from the island of Knossos to be his votaries.

One day, a goat herder noticed that his animals were friskier than usual when grazing there. He found they had become intoxicated by the vapors issuing from a cleft in the rock. Pythia, who spoke in riddles at the temple, was routinely inspired by these same fumes as she answered the desperate supplications of her visitors with her maddening, enigmatic forecasts, chewing the entrancing toxin from laurel leaves, gyrating to unearthly rhythms. The fame of the place spread, as much for the accuracy of the predictions as for the awesome spectacle of the Pythia and the priests' hexameter translations of her frenzied ululations, which she delivered amid the swirling steam issuing from the bowels of the sacred hill.

The Delphic Oracle emerged from these humble beginnings to sway the Greeks on all matters of import for over 2,000 years. It lives on today, in the gambits of forecasters, ranging from the most humble horoscope to the market-wrenching testimony of Alan Greenspan. Joseph Fontenrose has aptly summarized its influence:

> The Delphic Oracle has captured the imagination of ancients and moderns alike. From the sixteenth century B.C., it was the most popular of Greek Oracles, attracting clients from all Hellas and beyond. Such was its prestige that most Hellenes after 500 B.C. placed its foundation in the earliest days of the world. . . . Whatever the origin of the Oracle, it soon began to acquire fame and prestige and to attract powerful and wealthy clients from distant parts of Greece. Cities as well as individuals began to consult it. It had acquired some pan-Hellenic reputation by 700 . . . and we know that responses were spoken at Delphi at least down to the third quarter of the third century A.D.[1]

The Delphic Oracle was not just an oracle. It was a "happening." The site itself, though separate from any state that might control it, was the most convenient geographic center for the Greek communities. It was easily accessible by two foot paths and the Gulf of Corinth. All who see Delphi remark on its wild and rugged beauty, startling gorges, sparkling streams, and the resonant echoes off the side of the snow-laden Parnassus. Amid such splendor, who would dare quibble with the accuracy of prophecy?

Delphia was also a cultural center. Many fine works of art were gathered there, including the Column of the Dancing Women, the Delphian Twins, the Naxian Sphinx, and the striking bronze Charioteer. The two treasuries on the site doubtless contained surpassing riches. Every four years, all Greece came to the Pythian games. Great bowls of silver were filled with choice wine, and libations to the gods were offered.

The Delphian added to the happening with modern networking techniques. The Oracle was open for divination just one day a month, only nine months a year. All important State matters had to be bounced off it. The crowded conditions enabled the customers or "consultants" ample time to catch up on news, arrange deals, and hunt for jobs, as in modern meetings.

The marketing techniques of the Delphic medium would not play second fiddle to Coca-Cola, Nike, or Procter & Gamble today. As a Harvard graduate, I am frequently exposed to what is acknowledged to be the most outstanding fund-raising organization in the world. The fine wines served to prospects, the abundance of degrees conferred on politicians involved with funding, the honoring of influential cult figures—where am I? In Cambridge, Massachusetts, 2000 A.D., or Delphia, Greece, 800 B.C.?

DELPHIC AMBIGUITY

The first Oracles, the "Pythonesses," were virgins. But when one of the consultants seduced such a one, older women were chosen in their stead. The Oracle prepared herself by chewing the sacred laurel leaves, drinking from the pure water springs, and burning barley meal in the never-dying fire on the altar of the gods. She then sat upon a tripod placed over a cleft in the floor. She breathed in gasses from the fissure, and then broke into wild babblings and cries, which were put into poetic form by an attending priest and then delivered to the consultant.

Forecasting techniques were eclectic. On occasion, the flight of birds acted as the signal; on other occasions, clues were found in the entrails of cows, or divining pebbles, or dreams. But all commentators agree that the usual technique, called the intuitive method, was the prophetic frenzy emanating directly from the gods.

The message itself was frequently delivered in verse marked by Greenspanish ambiguity. Some legendary questions and answers illustrate:

Q. How far can a democracy go on constitutional reforms?
A. Sit in the middle of the ship steering straight; you have many helpers in Athens.
Q. What is the best means of prosecuting Viday's War?
A. You will not take the city until Amhitrites' wave washes my temenos on the sacred shore.
Q. Where lies salvation after defeat in battle?
A. When a goat drinks near Neda, Apollo will no longer preserve Massone for destruction will be near.
Q. How does a nation pursue wealth?
A. Love of money will destroy Sparta.

One accurate prediction plus a regrouping after a miss live on for posterity. Croesus, the rich king of Lydia, wanted to make war on Cyrus. Before consulting an oracle for sanction, he decided to test six of the best known oracles. At a synchronized departure time, he sent envoys to each of the oracles to ask what Croesus was doing at a site 100 days' travel away. He had carefully kept the secret to himself and had chosen an action that was beyond all possible conjecture. The Pythoness answered immediately and accurately. "Engaged in boiling the hard-shelled tortoise and the flesh of a lamb with brass above and brass beneath." After the test, Croesus asked: "Dare I go to war, to challenge the growing might of Cyrus the Persian?" Came the answer in flawless hexameter: "Croesus crossing the Halys will destroy a great empire." True enough; the trouble was, Croesus' empire turned out to be the one that was destroyed.

When Croesus sent an envoy to Delphi to demand an explanation, the Pythoness took the offensive. "Nor," said the oracle, "has Croesus any right to complain . . . . [H]e ought, if he had been wise, to have sent again and inquired which empire was meant, that of Cyrus or his own; but if he neither understood what was said, nor took the trouble to seek enlightenment, he has only himself to blame for the result."[2]

In describing the contemporary Greeks' disillusionment when the Delphic oracle about Croesus was falsified, Frederick Poulsen remarks that it can only be compared to the impression the destruction of Lisbon made on Voltaire and his contemporaries. "Certainly the catastrophe was worse for the reputation of the oracle than the discovery that in certain cases bribery had been tried with success."[3] To find a modern analogy, one would have to turn to the catastrophic disillusionment that long-term bears felt about the outcome of predictions of certain former gurus who have been calling for Dow 1000 since it hit 4000 or so. Yet, in its day, the oracle was known for truth, not obfuscation. Plato, surely nobody's fool, upheld this belief. How, then, did Delphi get its reputation?

Scholars have been trying for thousands of years to uncover the secret of the Delphic Oracle's success. In one masterful analysis, representing the culmination of 60 years of scholarship by one of the most revered students of Greek life, Joseph Faltenras classified the verified historic answers of the Oracle into categories (with percentages indicated):[4]

	Percentage of Occasions
Commands	30%
Statements	40
Prohibitions	25
Nonpredictive future statements	03
Clear predictions	02

Table 3–1.   Delphic Responses and Modern Market Equivalents

Typical Delphic Responses	Modern Market Equivalents
Command: Where the old men have long taken baths, and where unwed maidens dance in chorus to flute accompaniment, in the halls of the womanish man, worship Hera.	Reduce your investment in bonds by 5 percent of your portfolio and increase by 5 percent of your capital your present investment in precious metals stocks.
Statement: The gods forgive all uncontrollable acts [said to a priest who got drunk and had intercourse with a woman].	Volume is very bullish. The stock market rises on rising volume.
Prohibition: Restrain yourself, Roman, and let justice endure, lest Pallas bring a mightier war upon you and empty your marketplaces and you return home with loss of much wealth.	It is so far from its 50-day moving average (29) and its 200-day (18) that it's just too risky for my taste.
Nonpredictive future statement: If he [Kallistratos of Athens, who was fleeing a death sentence] goes to Athens, he will obtain the laws. [He went and was executed.]	We bought Fleming (FLM) at 24. (Current price is 14.25, a 38.40 percent loss.) Fleming fell on meaningless news that the company may have to pay $100–$200 million in compensatory damages for breach of contract. The FLM CEO called the ruling "absurd" and has filed an appeal.
Clear prediction: Honorius will have a glorious reign.	Given ideal upside targets and these support levels, the Dow should fall at least 91.5 percent, but no more than 98.3 percent, from its high (of 3000).

Note that clear predictions represent only 2 percent of the oracles. Therein lies the secret of the Oracle's success. Rather than resting on ambiguity, the rarity of the Oracle's predictions and the difficulty in falsifying any statements that were made ensured their success. Table 3–1 supplies market-world equivalents for some Delphic responses.

LESS GAS, MORE FOG

What, then, is the lesson of Delphi? Oracles, forecasts, and prophecies are a business. They should be evaluated with the same skepticism and savvy that would be applied to a used-car dealership or an Oriental rug auction. Legendary and self-administered reports of forecast accuracy should be taken with eight grains of salt. At Delphi, the sacred rituals, the architecture, and the very vista inspired a belief in accuracy. The art, athletic games, feasts, religious sanctuary, and networking helped attract visitors. The dignity, ambiguity, and caution of the predictions were cover propaganda designed to defuse evaluation.

Based on my study, I have developed some guidance for the oracle business in the new millennium:

- An impressive site that invokes awe, far removed from the clients' neighborhoods, should be selected (Jackson Hole, Santa Fe, New Haven, or Cambridge would be ideal).
- A guru, preferably pushing age 100, should be installed as the head.
- Networking should be preferred over forecasting.
- Forecasting should be rare. Briefings should stick to statements, commands, and warnings.
- If a forecast is mandatory, it should be made conditional on events unlikely to occur in the future. When cornered, the spokesperson should frame the unconditional forecast in an ambiguous fashion that allows a claim of success regardless of the outcome.
- A certain mystical ambiance should be adopted, to preclude down-to-earth comparisons.
- The accuracy of forecasts should be evaluated by the forecaster before anyone else can administer a fatal report card.
- When retrospection shows that one of the forecasts has hit the mark, the methodology should be reviewed in detail at a multimedia press conference.
- When an audience is particularly credulous, a startling forecast should be delivered, provided the answer is known in advance. If advance confirmation is not possible, the forecaster should arrange to obscure the timing of the forecast so that it seems to have occurred before the event.
- A new forecasting technique should be developed at each public meeting so that clients will spend their time evaluating the methodology rather than the oracle's past accuracy.
- Wine, sex, athletics, and song should be *de rigueur*. The frequency with which written reports command and describe rather than predict should be recorded.

The modern market pundits not only follow the Delphic model, but also extend, innovate, and improve on all fronts. They do, in the main, limit themselves tightly to commands and descriptions. Many of the best live in houses far from Wall Street, near pellucid streams or majestic mountains. At the forefront is the self-administered evaluation. Rarely is a market communication not littered with such classics as "As forecasted," "As I've suggested," "Last week's call was right on the mark," "We took profits at," and "While we have been among the foremost in the bullish camp." A more subtle approach invokes "There is a certain element of inevitability in," "It was indeed tested, and so far has resisted as expected," and "Few pundits pushed the notion of X, but yours truly had a sense for it and predicted it back on [date]." In 1996, the U.S. Bureau of Labor Statistics expanded its mandate to forecasting inflation as well as recording it. In patting itself on the back for one such producer price index forecast, the Bureau came up with a classic: "The increase in energy prices dissipated as one could have foretold."

THE AMBIGUOUS PREDICTION

At the forefront of the survival techniques of the Delphian descendants is a forecast that has a high prior probability of success. One elementary variant is seen in the newspapers daily: a guru makes sentient observations on what happened and then gives a three-legged forecast, "There is not a consensus on whether the market will go up, down, or be unchanged tomorrow." A subtler approach, followed by 90 percent of modern practitioners, is the formulation of a forecast in terms of a range. "We anticipate that the dollar will turn in a range-bound day tomorrow, fluctuating within a two-pfennig range from today's close. From these levels, one would target 1.48, then 1.80 and 1.95."

The forecast has the virtue of having a 95 percent prior chance of being true. When the predicted activity transpires, the appropriate follow-up is: "As forecasted, the dollar was range-bound yesterday." Another noteworthy technique in this area is the forecast-for-all-seasons: "The bonds should go up tomorrow unless the employment report is far above expectation." The Delphic counterpart was, "You will be preserved when a goat comes."

No discussion of Delphic utterances would be complete without an analysis of the Federal Reserve, the institution that most clearly rivals Delphi in its prestige and influence. The Fed's role in prophesying the future course of the economy, the plethora of new indicators brought to the table to maintain the illusion of science, the secrecy of their deliberations, the ambiguous quality of their utterances, the ascetic nature of the chairmen, the elaborate protocol, is possibly idempotent with Delphi. Where else could be found an institution of such importance that persistently refuses to release its deliberations? Only after a mole disclosed that the Fed kept transcripts of all of its meetings was there a reluctant agreement to release the transcripts after a five-year hiatus. In what other venue could a trillion-dollar institution, announcing its intentions, hide behind such gobbledygook as "Increase slightly the degree of pressure on reserves"?

Even a cursory study of the Fed's ambiance uncovers such details as the imposing marble-clad temples of the Federal Reserve Banks, the fine food served at the dining halls, the art that lines the inner vestibules, the evasiveness of its utterances, the ascetic attitude, the infinite power, the incessant political intrigues, and the desperate attempt to maintain its independence and perks. Commentators are almost unanimous in referring to the chairmen of the Fed as delphic, monastic, unemotional, inscrutable, evasive, stolid, and disciplined.

William Greider provides a nice mix of the secular and the sacred in his 800-page treatise on this mystique:

> The Federal Reserve was not a sacred temple. The seven governors were not high priests performing mystical rites. Yet the Fed inherited all the resonant feelings that surrounded money, the religious mood and the full freight of irrational meanings. The Federal Reserve's decision making was the essence of secular rationalism, devoted to scientific theory. Yet is was still the modern equivalent of mysterious sanctification, for its officers performed the ancient priestly function: the creation of money. The central bank, notwithstanding its claims to rational method, enfolded itself in the same protective trappings that adorned the temple—secrecy, mystique, an awesome authority that was neither visible nor legible to mere mortals. Like the temple, the Fed did not answer to the people, it spoke for them. Its decrees were cast in a mysterious language people could not understand, but its voice, they knew, was powerful and important.[5]

The only problem in analyzing the Fed is that to analyze the correspondences, the divergences, and the underlying principles adequately would require a Ph.D. dissertation, or at least an all-but-dissertation, the modal degree of the Fed staff—a status "Dr." Alan Greenspan mysteriously graduated from when he assumed the chairmanship at the age of 62. As far as I know, no one has ever seen or read Greenspan's dissertation. Somehow, this uncrossed threshold seems appropriate for the Fed's perennial status at the borders of politics, economics, banking, academics, altruism, growth, deflation, and exchange rate stabilization. The difficulty of formulating an honest mission statement for the Fed boggles the mind. It is somehow reassuring to know that most Fed staffers have only one career path open after leaving the Fed: exchanging insights as to what their former colleagues might be doing.

Almost everything emanating from the Fed has a linguistic quality entirely appropriate for Delphi. As of June 1996, the Fed, as usual, had to appear to be saying something momentous when it had no clues as to which way the economy was going or what it should do when the move became clear. A recent Open Market Committee proclamation was an utterance worthy of the most illustrious Pythonesses: "[T]he economy seemed to have adequate forward momentum, did not appear to require any further stimulus . . . but the economics could change considerably in either direction." The economy will fluctuate when the sacred cows feed on the Elysian Fields.

A TAXONOMY

Delphi is the root from which all market forecasters have sprung. But many branches have developed, and most market advisers and investment newsletter writers are as fresh as a spring day. Here, then, are some of the species I spotted recently, with characteristic quotes that verify their identity:

- The Mystic: "The Fibonacci retracement of 61 percent came within one point of the high. The bonds topped out in October 1993, bottomed 13 months later, and here we are again in November 1995, 13 months later, back at new highs." (I cannot refrain from noting here that there are so many key Fibonacci retracement levels—23.6, 38.0, 50, 61.8, 100, 161.8—that the chances are 50–50 that some high or some low will retrospectively occur within one point.)

- The Unappreciated (lonely, bitter, angry): "This is an angry book and rightfully so. All along we stated that while the Dow continues to set record highs, our paid-up subscribers were reporting that classified advertising in Evansville continued at a five-year low. The container-board market continues its relentless slide reflecting the correction. Futures don't exist. There's nothing but spot."

- The Other World Person (doesn't read newspapers or watch TV for economic insight and hasn't read a book in two years): "The parking lots at the malls in New Jersey were empty over the weekend."

- The Mathematician (applies high mathematics, calculus, chaos theory, evolutionary programming): "We have found that the Machey-Glass equations can robustly estimate the length of a periodic cycle in oil."

- The Traditionalist (relies on the wisdom of Gann, Livermore, or some great historical figure): "I spoke with Colonel Roberts, the greatest living expert on Gann-Elliott analysis, and he agrees."

- The Washingtonian (previously worked for the government, or at least attended a conference in Washington): "Sources I met at the Washington conference inform me that it is three-in-five that [the President] will resign before the end of his term."

- The Correlation Expert (creates new regularities at all times to support the market views): "Soybeans have traditionally fallen into the gutter before a big rally in bonds."

- The Stand-Alone Artist (goes against the crowd; a maverick; can't be bought): "I have booked myself on an around-the-world cruise. If the Dow is above 1000 when I get back, then my forecast was irrelevant; I'll come back and build my kids a treehouse. Otherwise, I'll have my day."
- The Insider (believes the market went up because Soros is buying): "The Dream Team has a bullet bid in."

I have compiled a list of the personal habits and characteristic utterances of gurus in the 1980s. I find it timeless, even though many gurus are deceased or have fallen out of favor or into incarceration. Examples of their wisdom and a collection of their photographs and autographs hang prominently in our trading room. These exhibits provide a certain deflationary ambiance that I find essential to success in my field. And I am the first to admit that the shoe also fits this Other World Person.

HUMBLE PIE WITH WHIPPED CREAM

Harry Browne, best known for his bestseller of the 1970s, *How You Can Profit From the Coming Devaluation* also wrote *Why the Best Laid Investment Plans Usually Go Wrong . . .* , which contains a magnificent modern summary of how far the self-administered performance review has advanced since the days of King Croesus in 500 B.C. Browne's analysis is worth savoring because it seems applicable to almost all self-evaluations:

> One of the best performers turns out 40 or 50 predictions each year in the January issue of his newsletter. As a preface, he reviews the success of last year's forecasts and totals up the score. Amazingly, he almost always seems to have been around 87 percent right. Can you imagine how much money you could make if you had access to forecasts that were correct 87 percent of the time?
>
> His January review doesn't actually reproduce last year's forecasts— probably because of space limitations. Instead, the writer provides a scorecard: so many right, so many wrong, so many that were inconclusive. He refers specifically to only a few of the predictions.
>
> He usually cites one or two forecasts that seem now to have been especially shrewd. But, of course, you expect him to do that.
>
> It's when he cites some that turned out to be wrong that you're won over. You can see that he's being more than open and honest. By treating a near-miss as "wrong," he demonstrates that his talent and even his standards tower far above yours and mine.
>
> For example, reporting in January 1985 on his 1984 forecasts, he said:

> Among the losers: I was a bit too optimistic about the high in gold (said 450 and was only 406). Ditto silver: I said 11.50 high, but was only 10.85.

Any man who's wrong only 13 percent of the time, and who's *that close* when he's wrong, must be a genius. At the time of the review, gold was at $300; so to have missed a top $106 away by only 10 percent seems—well, awesome.

[But] I've never found him to be even 40 percent right—let alone 87 percent. And he almost never repeats last year's forecasts accurately. For example, that no-so-bad gold forecast that he humbly scored as a near-miss was not, in the original, quite as he described it a year later ("said 450 and was only 406"). The original actually said, "Gold forecast: probable high: $450–$500." When he made the forecast, gold was *already* at its $406 high for the year. So he missed the high by 10 percent to 19 percent—and failed to foresee that gold would spend the rest of the year heading downward.[6]

THE LONG NIGHT

It's not just chance that the practices of Delphic and modern speculative forecasts overlap. In speculation, as in politics and science, uncertainty, risk, and partial knowledge are the rule. The scientific method, a framework for verifying predictions, was developed to reduce uncertainty and ambiguity. After a fitful start in the golden days of Aristotle, perhaps held in check by Delphi itself, the scientific method remained moribund until the Scientific Revolution of 1600.

Logic, rather than observation and measurement, settled disputes. All matter was thought to be composed of earth, air, water, and fire. In fact, standard European textbooks of the 18th century still taught this dogma. Alchemists attempted to change base metals into gold. Astrologers tried to predict human behavior from the movements of the planets. Many believed, 100 years after the findings of Copernicus, that Earth was the center of the universe.

Biologists thought that life arose spontaneously. Worms came out of dirt and mice grew out of dirty linen. All the diagrams of the human body were based on the works of Galen, the third-century Greek physician who had dissected dogs for his pictures. Blood was thought to flow from the liver and to pass between the ventricles of the heart. When a patient sought to be cured of an ailment, the diagnostic team consisted of astrologers and alchemists who would treat the ailment as a symptom of planetary misalignment or divine disapproval. Each organ in the body was thought to be under the control of a sign. In Montaigne's celebrated essay of 1576, "Apology for Raymond Sebond," he mentions the new medical science of Paracelsus, and a complaint that up until then medicine "has been good for nothing but killing men."

Here and there, a valid scientific principle was developed (Archimedes is the father of physics), but the discoveries were useless because the true findings were hopelessly mixed with the false. The situation was not helped by the great fire at Alexandria, where the only library of Greek works was burned, nor by the periodic destruction of all books by barbarian invaders.

THE LIGHT DAWNS

All this changed with a series of demonstrations launched by Galileo in the 1590s. The most famous was his experiment at the top of the Leaning Tower of Pisa, where he dropped two spherical iron balls, one weighing 10 pounds and the other 1 pound, in front of an audience of professors and students. Aristotelian physics had previously stated that a 10-pound ball would fall 10 times faster than a 1-pound ball. "The downward movement of a mass of lead or any other body endowed with weight is quicker in proportion as to size."[7] When Galileo's two balls landed with a thud simultaneously, Aristotelian physics died instantaneously.

There is some dispute as to whether Galileo actually performed this experiment (his biographer, Vincenzo Viviani, in 1654, says he did, but his contemporaries don't recall Galileo referring to it). However, there is agreement that the experiment was typical of the vivid employment of the scientific method that he pioneered.

To verify that much of the progress in science has emerged from darkness, one need look no further back than the Middle Ages. Out of this murkiness, in a span of 100 years, came marvelous illumination: Galileo's formulation of the principles of mechanics, Harvey's discovery of the circulation of blood, Gilbert's discovery of magnetism, Newton's discovery of gravitation, Kepler's observation and proof of the elliptical nature of the planetary orbits about the sun, new instruments such as Janssen's invention of the microscope, Napier's discovery of logarithms, Descartes' formulation of analytical geometry, and much more. Along with the discoveries, inventions, tools, and techniques came new methods of communication. Publishers such as Éstienne were started. Great libraries, such as the Bodleian at Oxford, the Bibliothèque Nationale in Paris, and the Biblioteca Ambrosiano in Milan, were founded. Weekly newspapers were formed in the great cities of Europe.

In summarizing the Scientific Revolution, Ariel and Will Durant state:

Science now began to liberate itself from the placenta of its mother, philosophy. It . . . developed its own distinctive methods, and looked to improve the life of man on the earth. This movement belonged to the heart of the Age of Reason, but it did not put its faith in "pure reason"—reason independent of experience and experiment. Too often such reasoning had woven mythical webs. Reason, as well as tradition and authority, was now to be checked by the study and record of lowly facts; and whatever "logic" might say, science would aspire to accept only what could be quantitatively measured, mathematically expressed, and experimentally proved.[8]

The scientific liberation makes for fascinating history. But, as Einstein put it, "If you want to know the essence of scientific method, don't listen to what a scientist may tell you, watch what he does."[9]

MEN AS OTHER MEN

Scientists have been thought of as disinterested superpeople who are above and beyond the fray, ready to bear privation without complaint while seeking truth regardless of the consequences. The prevailing view was that science arose out of serene and halcyon vistas—a cloister, perhaps, or at least a university; a place far from the madding crowd.

Henri Poincaré, the great mathematician, succinctly describes this sublime view of the role of scientists. "Their business is not with the possible, but the actual—not with a world that might be, but with a world that is. They have but one desire—to know the truth. They have but one fear—to believe a lie."[10]

Today, a more realistic view of the scientific process has emerged. Like the confreres Shylock describes in *The Merchant of Venice*, the scientist is "fed with the same food, hurt with the same weapons, subject to the same diseases, healed by the same means, warmed and cooled by the same winter and summer" as the rest of us. When pricked with a needle, a scientist bleeds. I know many scientists, and I've found that they like to get a discount at the supermarket, admire an attractive member of the opposite sex, and root for the home team just like you and I do. When they go into water that's over their head, they don't walk—they swim. And when they lose big by purchasing stocks without book value, they flail. Jim Watson's book, *The Double Helix*, which was made into a popular movie, frankly admitted that scientists are human, have little common sense, and are sincerely interested in fame, money, and recognition. They are insanely competitive about getting to the top rung first when climbing the ladder to a scientific discovery. Jim is humble enough to admit that the paintbrush fits his own hands.

Jim and his wife of 25 years, Liz, a former 'Cliffie who told me she was the only female student of Jim's who beat him to the punch by making the first move, have become my friends through the good office of our common friend, Hobo Keeley. Liz sent me a review of *The Search for DNA* after underlining a passage where the reviewer had noted that Watson, in his spare time, was less likely to be considering the entries in the periodic table than to be contemplating how to make it with Professor Smith's delicious *au pair* girl.

Richard Feynman, one of the greatest American-born theoretical physicists of the 20th century, married an *au pair* 16 years his junior. He met her while admiring her blue bikini on the shores of Lake Geneva, doubtless while preparing a lecture. His most important discoveries involved the fields of weak interactions, superfluidity of liquid helium, and quantum electrodynamics (for which he won the Nobel prize). He went so far as to learn Portuguese well enough so that he could prey upon women in their native tongue when he was lecturing in Brazil.

Feynman was an original outside physics also. He liked to prepare his Caltech lectures at a topless bar close to campus. He loved to disarm safes, decode Mayan hieroglyphics, paint nudes, play bongo drums, act in plays, and play games of all sorts. His lucid demonstration for Congress of the partial cause of the *Challenger* disaster, using an O-ring and a cup of ice water, is reminiscent of Galileo at Pisa. He was the impossible combination of "theoretical physicist and circus barber" according to *The New York Times*. At Caltech seminars, he would ask the students and faculty to bring up any problem discussed in *The Physical Review*, and then would extemporaneously give his own treatment and solution. "It's a game and it's not serious," Feynman said one month before he died in 1988. A good gamester, good musician, good scientist, and good speculator often turn out to be one and the same.

THE METHOD

The scientific method is defined by the *Oxford English Dictionary* as "a method of procedure that has characterized natural science since the 17th century, consisting in systematic observation, measurement and experimentation and the formulation, testing, and modification of hypotheses." Its flavor was described by Davy as analogy confirmed by experiment; by Stanley Jevons as discovering identity among diversity; by Walter Pater as the analysis of rough and general observations into groups of facts that are more precise and minute; and by Herbert Spencer as finding sequences among phenomena and grouping them into generalizations.

Some of the features common to most scientific work are: classification, observation, questioning, testing, measuring, collecting information, experimenting, modeling, and revising theories.

The scientist, as a professional, has been compared variously to a detective who attempts to classify the information and evidence found at the scene of a crime in order to find the perpetrator; or to the supermarket shopper who tests an apple by biting it, feeling it, observing its color, shape, and hardness, and then deciding whether to buy that kind of apple; or to a rat trying to make its way through a maze.

William S. Beck's wise words about the scientific method should be absorbed by anyone wishing to get ahead in the field of scientific speculation or any other scientific pursuit.

A scientist is rather like [Peter], a rat in a maze. Both proceed by observation, insight, hypothesis, and trial, and for both, the hypothesis may arise
from mere hunch. The invention of hypothesis is the truly creative part of
science. It is perhaps this phenomenon that most emphatically distinguishes Peter from Newton.[11]

Like a child, the scientist must be eternally curious. "If you spend any
time spinning hypotheses, checking to see whether they make sense,
whether they conform to what else we know, thinking of tests you can
pose to substantiate or deflate your hypotheses, you will find yourself
doing science," writes astronomer Carl Sagan.[12] Once scientists find the
answer to one thing, they must, like children, ask a host of other questions.

The scientific process consists of reducing the margin of uncertainty
about phenomena. Or, as Karl Popper, the great logician, philosopher,
and mentor to Soros put it, the process proceeds by overturning incorrect ideas. One method of eliminating incorrect ideas involves feedback.
Simple hypotheses are preferred to complex ones because they are easier
to refute. A hypothesis is scientific only if it can be falsified. Another
way of expressing the same idea is: If a hypothesis explains everything
and forbids nothing, it is not scientific because it is consistent with all
states of nature.

APPLIED SCIENCE

Some scientists collect and classify like accountants or inventory counters.
Others formulate deep questions in the fashion of philosophers or poets.
Still others are bold and courageous, like explorers. To many, like Feynman, science is a game. I decided at an early age that I would make my living by applying the scientific method. It seemed a noble pursuit, about as
important and useful as the invention of agriculture, tools, or the printing
press. And, the field seemed vast enough for me to find a niche. My training in collecting data on sporting events, formulating proper odds, betting
on the game, and then revising my theories based on outcomes seemed to
be the right stuff to build on.

I was fortunate to find one area for application of this method—an area
that had not advanced beyond the scientific techniques of the dark ages, an
area where preconceived ideas and logic rather than counting and questioning formed the basis for accumulating knowledge. I found the field of
technical analysis of markets.

But there had to be a spark to activate my interest. In 1980, a friend in
the publishing business told me that, to assist his 100 employees in picking stocks and markets, he had hired a spiritualist who was equally adept
at spoon-bending, diagnosis and healing of disease by touch, and market
prediction. "After you meet her, I'd like you to attend one of her spoon-

bending sessions, where you can get acquainted. Perhaps that will get you out of your slump in the market."

I informed my friend Harry that he was in good company in his reliance on spiritualism for stock picks. Commodore Vanderbilt, the Bill Gates of the 19th century and the founder of the New York Central Railroad, had developed intimate relations with spiritualists on whom he relied heavily for stock picks. In his later days, the Commodore was a great believer in spiritualism and often considered it expedient, before deciding anything of import, to consult mediums in the manner of the ancient Greeks going to Delphi.

"But she [the spiritualist] and Uri Geller have been tested at one of the major academic research institutions. And they assert there is no known physical law that could explain their powers," Harry responded.

"Harry, I've been exposed to academic scientists in a number of different contexts. And I assure you they're just as naïve, and have just as little common sense as the rest of us. The same scientist who will marvel with disbelief and laugh uproariously at the illusion of a magician who has made an elephant disappear in front of him one evening will stake his scientific reputation and honor on the possibility of a psychic being able to bend a one-inch key held in his hand the next day."

Martin Gardner discusses the naïveté of certain academic institutions affiliated with Stanford University concerning the psychokinetic power of Uri Geller, who was best friends with some confidants of the publisher. "And if one psychic can bend a spoon, perhaps a group of psychics could trigger a nuclear explosion in a warhead. Julius Caesar had his oracles. Hitler had his astrologers. Our military complex has SRI."[13] My favorite newspaper, *The National Enquirer*, reported in November 1995, "You really can find water with a stick. The stunning cases are detailed by Dieter Betz, a physicist at the University of Munich, in a study recently published by Stanford University's prestigious *Journal of Scientific Exploration.*"

My friend and I agreed that I would suspend disbelief to the point of sending a member of my firm to the next spoon-bending dinner held by his faith healer. I sent my friend, the hobo-veterinarian, Dr. "Bo" Keeley, to the session. The hobo walks backward and writes in mirror-writing, so I had his report retyped:

Dr. Bo Reports

I attended a dinner at a fancy East Side apartment along with 15 others. The leader, wearing a slinky silk dress exposing considerable cleavage, invoked various spiritual powers to help our success at the task. Occasionally, she brushed against me under the table. The allure was very tempting but I had a job to do. Every now and then, a noise or distraction would occur somewhere in the room. Immediately thereafter, someone in another spot would yell with amazement, 'It bent by itself,' and produce a spoon bent in grotesque fashion.

I warmed up my own spoon during the process while the others were distracted, by rubbing it while no one looked. Then I bent it myself with two fingers, and was able to form the most fantastic shapes imaginable. Everybody rushed around me and I was the subject of general adulation.

I estimate that of the 15 people in the room, 14 were paid confederates or otherwise involved with the leader. One of the confederates asked me what line of business I was in and rather than say "I'm a 'bo," I gave my standard answer. "I'm not wealthy myself, but I represent someone who is." This only increased my presumed importance. If her forecasts of the stock market have the same rationale and integrity behind them as her seances, you'll be bust before long.

To maintain my wealth, I decided that I would base my business decisions on the scientific method rather than the pseudo-scientific method.

Fads and Especially Fallacies

Previously, I had studied pseudoscience in the writings of Martin Gardner, games editor of *Scientific American* for many years. All freshmen at Harvard were required to read his book, *Fads and Fallacies in the Name of Science*. The book is too fresh and comprehensive to summarize in a few sentences. But anyone who reads Gardner should be persuaded that such things as ESP, psychoenergetics, precognition, faith healing, flying saucers, seers, orgone boxes, and Atlantis, are flimflam. Gardner's exposé of the techniques of key-bending is representative:

> Most car keys bend easily, especially if they are long and have a low-cut notch. [The entertainer] Geller prides himself on his strength (he works out with bar bells, Puharich tells us). If you have strong fingers you can bend most car keys simply by resting the key crosswise on the fingers and pressing firmly with the thumb. Stronger keys require pressing the tip against the side of a table, the table leg, the side of a chair, or whatever firm surface is handiest. In any case, the bending can be done in a split second. Of course it must be done at a moment when no one is looking.
>
> To obtain the necessary misdirection [the entertainer] Geller creates a maximum amount of chaos by moving around the room and going quickly from one experiment to another.[14]

Across the Atlantic, the definitive *Oxford Companion to the Mind* devotes some 7,000 words to paranormal phenomena and parapsychology versus 6,750 to "memory," 3,800 to "consciousness," 1,050 to "creativity," and 68 to "correlation."[15] The English have always excelled in keeping their finger on the pulse of the retail customer. *Oxford* examined classic supernatural phenomena such as ghosts, levitation, thought reading, seances, water dowsing, communication with the dead, and precognition. The editors concluded that, after 50 years of research, not a single phenomenon originally classified as a supernatural or, later, as a paranormal phenomenon has achieved general acceptance among the scientific community:

> Not one demonstrable or repeatable, paranormal effect has been discovered, not one characteristic or law has been found which turns up in all these experiments that claim a positive result.[16]

In seeking an explanation for the high degree of belief and continuing extensive research in this discredited field, Christopher Scott sagely notes, "We have only to assume a small but continuing flow of researchers, ready to deceive themselves, or perhaps to deceive others, victims of wishful thinking or conscious fraud."[17]

What struck me, from immersion in the supernatural, was that the techniques of the bogus scientists chronicled by Gardner and *Oxford* are virtually identical to those deployed by the average market guru. In discussing psychic phenomena, physicist J. A. Wheeler noted the difficulty of pinning the opponent to the ground:

> For every phenomenon that is proven to be the result of self-delusion or fraud or misunderstanding of perfectly natural everyday physics and biology, three new phenomena of "pathological science" spring up in its place. The confidence man is able to trick person after person because so often the victim is too ashamed of his gullibility or too mouse-like in his "stop, thief" to warn others.[18]

Wheeler reports the following five symptoms of pseudoscience, developed by Irving Langmuir of General Electric:[19]

1. The maximum effect that is observed is produced by a causative agent of barely detectable intensity, and the magnitude of the effect is substantially independent of the intensity of the cause.
2. The effect of a magnitude that remains close to the limit of detectability; or, many measurements are necessary because of the very low statistical significance of the results.
3. [There are] claims of great accuracy.
4. Fantastic theories contrary to experience.
5. Criticisms are met by *ad hoc* excuses thought up on the spur of the moment.

How It's Done Downtown

After steeping myself in market literature, I have come up with a similar list for written contributions in the field of market analysis. The distinguishing characteristics here are:

1. Appeal to authority.

2. An absence of counting.

3. A framing of predictions in a form that cannot be tested.

4. A tautological prediction guaranteed to be true under almost all conceivable circumstances.

5. No allowance for chance variations; any randomly formed groups exposed to varying conditions will show differences in means and variability. But the differences can be due to sampling variation rather than the true effects of the conditions. That's what statistical analysis is about.

6. A paranoid mien.

7. Disregard of alternative explanations.

8. Self-evaluation of accuracy.

9. Retrofitted systems.

Some examples from recent sources that have crossed my desk, and their key hallmarks among the nine items on my list, appear in Table 3–2.

A PLETHORA OF AUGURIES

For those who don't have a statistical mind or who have not been exposed to card games or gambling, the possibility of a random explanation for many phenomena is hard to grasp. Simply put, what we observe in real life is a sample from a population. Even if the sample is random, the mean of the values observed from the sample is likely to differ from the population mean. The differences observed for many market phenomena are merely due to sampling variations resulting from the large number of samples taken and the high variability within the population.

Consider, for example, the world-famous Superbowl indicator. Germany watches it like a hawk. If the winner of America's Superbowl is a team that hailed originally from the NFL, the signal is bullish. If a team originally from the AFL wins, the signal is bearish. The moves in stocks in the 12 months following NFL and AFL wins are enumerated and summarized in Table 3–3.

The results are striking. The total change in the DJIA during the 12 months following victories by teams originally in the NFL has been 4412.08. The average change is 259 Dow points. During years when AFL teams were victorious, the total DJIA change has been −7.3. Reviewing the average ranks of changes in the Dow with respect to the two origins of winners, it turns out that differences as large as these could be explained by chance only once in 300 occurrences. But how many different sporting events could have served as a benchmark predictor with equal

Table 3–2.   Modern Market Science

Quotations	Scientific Defects
Once again we are back into the range-bound scenario. Interestingly, the Nikkei has become better bid over the last week and this suggests there may be further upside scope into December. A break over the key resistance may precipitate further dollar buying and this would provide confirmation. (Bank technical newsletter)	A little intermarket analysis here. But is strength in Nikkei bullish or bearish for dollars, and if the Nikkei is up, is there more likely futures upside or downside scope in Nikkei or yen? If resistance is broken, there is confirmation of dollar buying. (2, 3, 4, 5, 7, 9)
It is now apparent that this rally is wave E of the larger triangle patterns from the April low, explaining why the dollar is still holding up. The attempt to push the dollar through support at 1.3730 against the deutschmark failed, leaving a double bottom. This important support is serving as the origin for a very sharp impulsive bullwave. (A bank newsletter)	An appeal to the unproved and untested Elliott theory. Triangles can be defined in many different ways, especially after they're no longer triangles. Are double bottoms bullish or bearish? The bullwave is defined as impulsive tautologically after a rally. (1, 2, 3, 4, 5, 7)
What are your fellow shorts thinking? That they should protect their position by putting buy stops in above the market. This is the conventional wisdom. Where will they place them? Right in the unfilled gap area. What should your strategy be? To give it to them right above the gap. There will be an emotional spike up on "stop running." (A day-trading system newsletter)	You and I are one step too smart. Other shorts will respond to the visual chart phenomena of the author's orientation. Enough practitioners of losing methodologies exist to ensure profits to those aware of their tactics. Supposed market phenomena of emotional buying at chart points will continue indefinitely without mutation of form. "Fellow shorts" implies uniformity of motive. Conventional wisdom attempts to lure through an apparently shared condescending attitude. Fading the spike technique raises the question of quantifying and identifying the spike in the first place. (1, 2, 3, 4, 6, 7, 9)
It tests methods such as divergence, volume accumulations, statistics, candlestick formations and . . . systematically discovers the best way to trade each stock. (Advertisement featuring a financial columnist feeling like a kid with a new toy)	Does gross retrospection determine the results? Taking account of all the retrofitting, are the results in accord with chance variations alone? Will conditions in the future be harmonious with those that the backtests emerged from? (2, 3, 4, 8, 9)

(Continued)

Table 3–2. *(Continued)*

Quotations	Scientific Defects
The quick rally to 1.4250 has changed the short-term outlook on the USD from very negative to ranging but still we shoot for a week low around 1.3945. In other words, the Buck has simply hit the wall at 1.4250 and while below 1.4275 is not expected to make significant gains. Our call for 1.36 within a couple of weeks is still well alive with a major pivot level to watch at 1.4075/95. (A Chartist newsletter)	A rise in the dollar is apparently bullish but bearish, but at resistance unless it goes up. To its credit, there is a refutable prediction here, unless an upside pivot reverses the finesse. (2, 5, 7, 9)
The 1.42's should prove to be very tough to break but if they do then we are set to reach 1.46's. Until the bullish breakout occurs we remain resolutely bearish on the U.S. unit with the following targets: . . . . (A bank recap)	A classic. It's bearish unless it's bullish. Nice allusion to being alone. Normal variability makes such range-based forecasts true most of the time by chance. (2, 3, 4, 5, 6, 7, 8)
We adhere to our long-held strategy of selling out-of-the-money puts. This is best done once the herd is stampeded south. Or according to our friend, Vic Niederhoffer, the elephants having once charged in one direction will often return along the same trampled path. (A fax letter)	Are puts generally over- or under-valued after declines or rises? Reliance on work of Niederhoffer, a suspect speculator, a legend from squash but a mortal in trading, fails to mention that Niederhoffer presented no evidence that LoBagola analysis had empirical validity. Random price series have long runs also. (1, 2, 3, 4, 6, 7, 8, 9)
The Japanese move to push down market rates has maintained an attractive 5-percentage-point interest rate differential in favor of the dollar. The turn of the yen is at hand. (A bank commentary)	Is the lower interest rate differential greater or less than inflationary expectations and expected moves in the cost of living? What evidence is there that interest rate differentials favor a strong currency. (1, 2, 3, 7)
Market capitalization of the Nikkei's first section is 3.2 trillion, about 10 percent above where it should be. Japan is worse off than it looks. With shares still fetching an average price/earnings ratio of 50 times estimated earnings, the Nikkei will have to shed 14 percent before it is fairly valued, figures an equity strategist. Even with the index around 12,000 we couldn't say stocks are unequivocally cheap. (Business magazine cover story)	Does a high price/earnings ratio forecast superior or inferior price performance? How have P/E ratios changed recently? Is the quality of earnings different among different countries? Would price/book value ratio comparisons be more relevant? (This forecast of a decline came just before a 25 percent increase.) (1, 2, 7, 9)

Table 3–3. The Superbowl as an Indicator of Change
in the Dow Jones Industrial Average (DJIA)

Year of Superbowl	Winner of Superbowl	DJIA Change during Next 12 Months
1967	NFL	119.42
1968	NFL	−174.13
1969	AFL	69.02
1970	AFL	38.56
1971	AFL	51.28
1972	NFL	129.82
1973	AFL	−169.16
1974	AFL	−234.88
1975	AFL	236.17
1976	AFL	152.24
1977	AFL	−173.48
1978	NFL	−26.16
1979	AFL	33.73
1980	AFL	125.25
1981	AFL	−88.99
1982	NFL	171.54
1983	NFL	212.10
1984	AFL	−47.07
1985	NFL	335.10
1986	NFL	349.28
1987	NFL	42.88
1988	NFL	229.74
1989	NFL	584.63
1990	NFL	−119.60
1991	NFL	535.20
1992	NFL	132.20
1993	NFL	452.90
1994	NFL	80.35
1995	NFL	1356.81
1996 (9/1/96)	NFL	341.27

plausibility—the World Series, the NBA Championship, the NHL Stanley Cup, the New Year's Day bowl games, or the won–lost record of the Chicago Bulls or the New York Yankees over a single season? Each of the winners might provide an independent prediction of the Dow. Reformulating the question: Since 1967, what are the chances that, in five major annual sporting events, a win by one of the ten competitors will be associated with the DJIA's rising at least 250 points in that year? The answer, determined by simulation, turns out to be about one-half. And, if not predictive of the Dow, how do bonds match up with the winners?

The Superbowl analysis shows why the random walk or efficient markets model is often consistent with many of the effects found by technical analysts or the more dressed-up retrospective anomalies of the academics.

When people ask me whether markets are random, I feel as I did when people asked me who, in my opinion, was the best squash player of all time. "Jack Barnaby, my coach," I always replied.

To get a flavor for the randomness of markets, consider a run of moves that occurred on sixteen consecutive Fridays in the yen from close to close during the third quarter of 1995. The chances of finding 16 consecutive declines for a 50–50 series is 1 in 65,536, a seeming anomaly. Table 3–4 contains the data on the changes.

Looking over the past ten years, I find this is indeed the longest run of daily moves that occurred in any major market. But over the past ten years, there were 2,500 different opportunities for one day to show such a run. And with five major markets and two directions of change, there are at least ten other sets of 2,500 separate possibilities to consider. So, the chances should be multiplied (conservatively) by a factor of about 25,000 to put it into perspective. Bearing in mind that looking at corresponding days a week apart is just one of a thousand different ways to classify the data, the original infinitesimal probability becomes much more likely.

Table 3–4. Consecutive Moves in Yen
(Friday Trading), June–October, 1995

Thursday Date	Thursday Close	Friday Close	Change
June 29	12093	12058	−35
July 6	11988	11789	−199
July 13	11674	11627	−47
July 20	11587	11531	−56
July 27	11579	11568	−11
Aug. 3	11249	11142	−107
Aug. 10	10990	10854	−136
Aug. 17	10504	10435	−69
Aug. 24	10528	10505	−23
Aug. 31	10431	10422	−09
Sep. 7	10254	10182	−72
Sep. 14	9897	9748	−149
Sep. 21	10293	10162	−131
Sep. 28	10283	10126	−57
Oct. 5	10161	10045	−116
Oct. 12	10185	10001	−84
Oct. 19	10039	10057	+18

However, this likelihood must be placed in the perspective of the performance of the yen in 1996. From Friday, March 1, to Friday, July 19, 1996, the yen declined (from NY close to NY close) in 19 out of 20 weeks. Table 3–4 tracks a 17-week period in 1995, which had a similar pattern.

Over the nine-year period ending September 30, 1995, the longest run of consecutive days, up or down, for some major markets was as shown in Table 3–5.

Because 2,250 trading days were considered for each market, the results are in line with chance.

All who speculate will inevitably observe countless long runs of consecutive rises, declines, or alternations in markets. On many occasions, one market will consistently lead or lag another, or lags will be a month or a year apart where similar moves occur. Novices who make such discoveries often believe they have found the Rosetta Stone and are willing to stake large amounts on the continuity of the relation they have observed. Academics call such discoveries anomalies, and they rush to consolidate their gains with such naïve procedures as buying stocks in December to take advantage of the January effect.

But there is a simpler explanation. We are all exposed to many occasions when a chance phenomenon might occur. The odds are quite high that we will observe these relations due to chance alone.

Statisticians attempt to adjust multiple exposures through a procedure called the Bonferroni Adjustment. In brief, if you look at 1,000 comparisons, you need to augment the probability of obtaining each observed difference by multiplying by 1,000 to adjust for your retrospection. For people who sit on park benches, waiting to see whether there are clusters of redheaded girls or of short men, the number of comparisons they implicitly consider is in the millions. Thus, they are likely to find unusual coincidences.

Table 3–5. Longest Runs of Consecutive One-Day Changes in Major Financial Markets, 1987–1995

	Up Run		Down Run	
	Number of Days	Date Run Began	Number of Days	Date Run Began
Crude oil	10	Feb. 28, 1988	9	Nov. 9, 1987
Bonds	9	Sep. 8, 1992	13	Apr. 24, 1990
Swiss	9	June 21, 1994	9	Oct. 25, 1993
S&P	10	Jan. 15, 1987	8	Sep. 11, 1991
Yen	12	Feb. 22, 1993	11	Feb. 25, 1992
Deutschemark	11	May 3, 1994	7	June 22, 1993
Gold	8	May 23, 1988	9	Feb. 3, 1988
Soybeans	7	Nov. 9, 1994	7	Aug. 7, 1992

A related phenomenon is the tendency to underestimate the degree of clustering that random shufflings will create. To see this effect, take some candies of different colors and mix them up thoroughly in a big glass jar. Most who see it wonder at the marvelous mosaic that results, attributing it perhaps to gravitation or electrical attraction.

I tried the experiment at home with five one-pound bags of jelly beans of different colors. My kids all shouted, "Birds of a feather stick together. All the reds and blacks and whites are together." But the experiment was tarnished when they noticed that all the jelly beans had different weights. I repeated the mixing experiment with colored M&Ms.

The tendency to attribute order to mainly random constellations also surfaces when we look at the pluses and minuses in the price change column of stocks listed alphabetically in the newspapers. Statisticians call this tendency the bunching effect.

To make some money from this effect, bet a friend even money that there will be at least two people with the same birthday in a room of more than 23. Of course, donate your winnings to a worthy cause as speculators should never engage in casual gambling.

Yet, weighty academic research, usually emanating from warm climates or Parnassian vistas, on such topics as synchronicity, meaningful coincidences, confluential events, hidden memories, dissociation, and related psychic phenomena will continue to be popular. In a similar vein, those you telephone might just have been dialing your number or thinking about you, and you are sure to see the mirror image of your favorite historical character in a crowded theater. Someone in your family is sure to know when something bad happened to a family member miles away, and Soros is likely to have a backache before a major move against his positions.

CHAPTER 4

Losses, Comebacks, Trends, and the Weather

It will be found sometimes that the player who has consistently lost sometimes wins, first one match and then another because by dint of losing he has created within himself a greater desire to conquer.

René Lacoste

HOW TO LOSE

There are so many ways to lose, but so few ways to win. Perhaps the best way to achieve victory is to master all the rules for disaster and then concentrate on avoiding them.

With the increasing specialization in modern times, born losers are commonplace. Think of the Washington Generals, who have not beaten the Harlem Globetrotters since 1971; or the Chicago Cubs, who have not won a World Series since 1908; or Anthony Young, who lost 20 straight games for the New York Mets in 1995. Bob Uecker, formerly of the St. Louis Cardinals, had a lifetime batting average of .200—an overstatement of his talent. He's in demand for television commercials because he makes people feel good about themselves.

I can count my lucky stars that I grew up five yards away from the greatest loser of all time, my uncle, Howie Eisenberg. In a classic article, "Second Place Is Some Place," Howie supports his claim as the man most likely to fail in the final round. Some highlights from his lament capture the flavor:

It was the advent of the USHA national one wall tournaments that really afforded me the opportunity to come into my own as a loser. In the space of 24 hours in 1960, I achieved the Falstaffian accomplishment of finishing second in singles and doubles.

Faced with the spectre of victory within my grasp, I admirably kept my cool, knowing that divine intervention would allow me to remain winless. This came in the form of a horrendous call by the referee after which Oscar

85

was humane enough to hit a fly kill ending the game and leaving the record unblemished.

. . . with the score tied at 18 in the third game, once again the Lord interjected in the guise of human frailty, causing his messengers (referee and linesmen) to make no fewer than three atrocious calls in succession.

. . . we took a 20–12 lead in the second game of the finals, having won the first. Alas, my perfect record of failure was apparently shattered as I hit a flat kill shot. The jig was up—or at least it would have been if a lesser man than the chief referee had been in control.

Lack of conditioning had always been my ace in the hole in insuring a second place finish. Much to my chagrin, in the 1970 tournament my ace was played prematurely and I blew a 20–12 second game lead after I had won the first over Mike Dikman in the wrong crowd, the semi-finals. When I again lost a semi-final three-game match in the 1971 USHA one wall singles, I thought my greatest feats had come to pass.

Not satisfied with having brought the winningest doubles player ever down to my level, I sought out the player whom many regard as the best doubles player who has ever played the game.

A wiser man would have rested on his laurels, content with a record of abject failure that could only be aspired to but never attained by mere mortal losers.[1]

Two examples will suffice. The first came on the occasion of the 1966 National Jewish One Wall Doubles Championship, held in the Brownsville Boys Club in Brooklyn. Howie was serving, his team up 1 game to 0 and 20–8 in a 21-point second game of a two-out-of-three-games match. The tournament was so important that Handball Commissioner Mickey Blechman was in attendance. Before the game even started, Howie had publicly excoriated Mickey about the quality of refereeing on the court. Howie motorcycled to the court, riding double-eagle with his cute girlfriend and arriving just 5 minutes before the match started. He had promised her an ace as the final point. It was their special secret.

Gasping for breath, Howie took a long preparation time for his 125-mile-an-hour serve. He bounced the ball three times, catching it higher each time as he accelerated toward the service line, much like a discus thrower preparing for a toss. The markets like to take a similar series of energizing jabs upward before preparing for a killer upward move.

Suddenly, Commissioner Blechman flew down from the stands, screaming triumphantly, "He's out!" Howie forgot that Blechman, in a bid for lasting fame, had recently revised Rule Number 1,013 of the Handball Regulations to allow no more than three bounces of the ball before serving. "I could still call a time out." Howie screamed. But it was to no avail. A 15-minute rhubarb ensued with Howie dissipating all his remaining energy chasing Blechman around in vociferous Talmudic debate.

Howie was so distracted and enervated that he went on to lose 21–20 in the second game and 21–3 in the third game, a devastating loss.

I asked Howie why so many referees seemed to rule against him when it was a close call. Howie's response was characteristically direct. "Referees are typically ignominious nonentities who could never win their own handball games. That's why they like to suppress the promising young players and decide against them whenever the call is close."

Marty Reisman, the frequent U.S. and English table tennis champion and winner of dozens of championships, had so much natural ability he could get away with fighting with the referee. "You prejudiced son-of-a-gun," he'd tell the referee at the beginning of a match. "Watch out that you don't steal any points from me." Towering over the referee, Marty liked to mime a few karate chops to add emphasis to the warning. When I told him about Howie's bad luck with referees, he responded, "That could be a page from my book. Table tennis also attracted narrow-minded bureaucrats who were intent on siphoning off all the money and glory for themselves. I let them know how I felt. The only time I think it hurt me was when I inadvertently asked the president of the amateur association to hold my bets in an overseas championship match. In the heat of the moment, I thought he was my bookie. The nonentity waited until I was on the boat home to set his revenge. He sent me a telegram announcing that I was suspended from amateur play. But the next year, the English wouldn't pay the official's transportation expenses unless they reinstated me." When I questioned Marty 30 years later as to whether his arguments with the refs hurt him, he admitted wistfully, "Well, it would have been nice not to have been suspended for three years when I was in my prime."

Howie and Marty believed in "in-your-face" confrontation. They let the refs know exactly what they thought of them. I can well imagine that any bitterness rankling in the heart of a failed-player-turned-ref easily switched to outright hatred when he had to listen to a public tirade about his character deficiencies. It's not fun to have a guy twice your size spit insults at you in front of thousands of spectators.

Uncle Howie's approach was diametrically opposed to Artie's. On one occasion, Artie stopped Sam Silver, a diminutive referee of many a match at Brighton Beach, saying, "Sam, your reffing is very good and I fear goes uncelebrated. I'm just on the way to take the family out for a fish dinner; won't you join us?" Later, I asked him why he had done that, especially when Silver had made so many bad calls against Howie and me. Artie replied, "Always make friends with the ref; it can't do you any harm, and it may help in that he may not go out of his way to hurt you." I have followed this advice in my dealings with the commodities exchanges. I make it a point to visit the floor a couple of times a year to talk to the floor traders and clerks. They may not kill themselves to give me a great fill next time I place an order, but at least they won't go out of their way to give me a bad one.

I violated this commonsense advice at the beginning of my career, when I could afford to express my views freely. When my self-regulatory agency applied for an exclusive right to regulate the industry, I protested. I wrote to Washington indicating that there was no need for exclusivity; innovation and diversity would be stifled, the price to the public would be raised, and costs would increase. "I detect some rent-seeking behavior here," I admonished. Adding a few philosophical points about the evils of licensing, I noted that futures people needed licensing about as much as barbers did—and it served exactly the same anticompetitive purpose.

In support of the request for certification, the association proudly remarked that there had been hundreds of letters in support and only one against. Shortly after the certification was approved by a unanimous vote, I found myself in a face-to-face meeting with the association chairman, who was then copping a salary above $500,000 per year. The association was investigating me for technical infractions of its advertising code. We looked at each other quizzically. Neither of us could suppress a smile.

I learned my lesson. To get the benefit of the doubt any time there was a problem, I immediately applied for and became a member of all the major exchanges I traded in. To its credit, the NYSE, a private club with 200 years of experience in keeping potential renegades out, was the only stock exchange to fail to admit me. I am not constituted to be a member of such an exclusive club. Many of the club's rules are necessarily designed to prevent competition and maximize revenues for members. I like the revenue part but not the competition restriction. I felt that I had a great product to proffer to the masses, and the rules cramped my style. To minimize competition, the exchanges enforce strict capital guidelines for all activities. I tried to compensate for the lack of capital with extensive advertising. Catch-22. All advertising was so closely monitored and regimented that cracking the nut became all but impossible.

To enforce their mission, the exchanges conduct frequent audits. Once a year, four auditors from the exchange descended on our office for two months. To be fair, many of the audit procedures and standards do protect the public from abuse. There are so many charlatans associated with the futures industry that, without standards, the advertising would quickly resemble the kind that surrounds horse racing. Furthermore, without capital standards, the public wouldn't have the confidence to trade without fear for the safety of their funds. The audits verify that customer funds are segregated and that reports of returns are accurate. The net result to the public is that no customer has ever lost funds because of the insolvency of a member of a major futures exchange.

The auditing of my activities usually led to a stern letter and a $1,000 fine. To keep up with the compliance requirements, I needed two extra full-time employees. Worse yet was the pall that the prospective audits put on my efforts to generate new business. What if promotional wording offended potential competitors and their agents?

Eventually, a soft commodity exchange socked me with a five-figure fine, even though I hadn't executed a trade on the exchange in three years. I hate being pushed around by a referee who serves as prosecutor, judge, jury, and collector. This was the last straw. I sold all my memberships and became an upstairs trader.

Feigning Injury

The second archetypal Eisenberg loss came during the finals of a singles tournament. Knowing that he had a tendency to tire, Howie decided that, if push came to shove, he would feign an injury and get the benefit of the 15-minute injury time-out to recuperate.

Howie won the first game as usual. The second game was a battle royal; the score was nip and tuck for the whole game up to 14-all. Time for an injury. Howie hit the floor and grabbed his ankle in agony.

"I think it's a fracture. Is there a doctor in the house?" Immediately, "the Farmer," a cop, rushed out and started giving Howie a vigorous series of messages, lifts, and compressions. He wound a huge elastic support bandage around Howie's ankle at least 100 times. The whole thing seemed to be working perfectly. Fifteen minutes elapsed, and Howie, well rested, went to serve. He then proceeded to lose the next 18 points, and registered a 21–4 loss in the third game.

"What happened?" I asked him after the game.

"Well, I wasn't hurt too bad when I stopped to rest. But by the time the Farmer got through fixing me up, I couldn't move at all."

Howie Eisenberg after a hard losing game.

ADVICE FROM AN EXPERT

After reviewing Howie's losses, I came up with a number of rules for losing that should stand speculators in good stead, provided they stand on their head.

- Know that you are the greatest, that winning is a foregone conclusion. Let your opponent know, by your words and deeds, that your winning is assured. Tell your broker how much you like a particular trade and how well you've been trading lately.

- Excoriate the referee and insult his motives. He'll be so intimidated that he will never again call the close ones against you. Write a letter to a newspaper decrying the excessive level of regulation imposed by the SEC, CFTC, and NFA—or, best of all, by the IRS. These agencies are filled with disinterested public servants. As long as the debate is engaged, they are happy.

- Cut your gains when you're ahead. Relax, you're the greatest. Never think about what could go wrong and it won't. Grab at small profits and refuse to take losses.

- When behind, put everything you have into catching up. After you've caught up, coast for a while and give yourself some well-deserved praise. Dwell on your past victories, recalling them to yourself in precise detail. Never look back on defeats, trying to figure out what you did wrong; that activity is for suckers. There's no need to learn from traders who have poor results: losses are just bad luck. The chances of lightening's striking twice are remote.

- Enrage your opponents by downplaying their chances and mocking their ability. Let your opponents know, à la Babe Ruth, exactly how you plan to trounce them: point to where you're going to hit. Let the market know your intentions. It's best to leave limits and stops with a broker at the round numbers; just ask the Hunt brothers.

- Don't dignify the finals with any undue training that you wouldn't put forth in any other game. Nonchalance carries the day in the pinch. Don't worry about announcements or Fed activities. How difficult can it be to make a few dollars trading?

- Call a time-out when you have momentum, to cause your opponent to worry about what you're going to do next. When a market goes your way, get out immediately and think about what to do next. Limit your stock gains to two baggers.

- Invite the opposite sex to the game and let it be known that you're the greatest and that you're saving the winning shot as your special shared secret. When trading, bring your favorite significant other by to see you in action. Hey, if you're good, flaunt it!

- Be sure to indulge in intercourse before you play. It will relax you and make you that much steadier in the pinch. If this diversion is not available, a few drinks or a nice big meal will do almost as well. Take a break with a paramour in the middle of the trading day.

- Adapt new and experimental techniques for your crucial matches. You'll catch your opponent off guard. When in doubt, apply systems without paper trading.

- Arrange to officiate when you have spare time during a tournament, or, better yet, accept a position on the committee. Don't be afraid to attend to other business while involved in a trade. Take your hand-held quote machine to meetings, and trade around your positions during breaks.

- Adopt expensive habits like playing polo or racing yachts. Be sure to make enough money trading each day to cover one special purchase.

- If the score goes against you, stick to your guns. You know best. If the results go against you, don't worry. Gains are bound to come back, especially when the market is wrong.

- Celebrate the victory the evening before, when you won't be too tired to enjoy it. Don't be afraid to tally your profits in a trade. Make sure you don't get less than your due. Don't even show up for trading the next day. Leave an order with your broker to exit at the close.

- Forget about the frictions, the small wastes of energy that grind you down. Great strokes fell great oaks. Let your opponent worry about grabbing all the edges. Don't worry about your fills. What's a tick or two going to matter, anyway?

Even if you don't apply these particular rules of losing, a million and one others are available. Whether the pursuit is poker, sports, gambling, or speculation, losing is the easiest thing in the world.

Practical Losses

I am not immune from succumbing to loss myself. Some of my instructive losses follow:

On October 19, 1987, I had a nice long bond position. But then my partner, Susan, walked through the trading room. She noted that the Dow was down 300 already that Monday, after having dropped 108 points the previous Friday. "I hope you're not playing the stock market today; it's too wild." This was all I needed. I figured that she expressed the fear out there. And, I like to sexulate when she is around. I immediately placed an order with my broker to buy 100 S&Ps. Before I heard the word "Filled," I was down $3 million on the trade. The chairman of the Securities and Exchange Commission chose to say the stock exchange might be closed down just a second after I bought.

Next, I received a call from Tim Horne, my first customer, who runs the most successful valve manufacturing business of all time, Watts Industries. Watts, now a $750 million market value company, had a market cap of $10 million when Tim took over as chairman in 1978. "Victor, the boys at the Metal Manufacturers Trade Show and I have been talking. We're scared to go near the market. It looks terrible. I hope you don't have any stock positions in our accounts."

"Tim, you do the valve manufacturing and I'll do the speculating. That's the division of labor. I'll call you after the close."

If businesspeople were so nervous that they were worrying about the market rather than their own products . . . ; I bought another 50 S&P futures. The S&P futures ended down 80.75 points on the day, a loss of $40.4 thousand per contract. I had taken what would have been my best day ever and turned it into a nightmare.

The next day, the exchange increased the margin requirements to hold futures. This, plus the losses from the existing position, plus the fear of future losses, made it all but impossible to hold for the likely rally. Fortunately, the S&P opened up 22 points the next day. I sold out at the opening. The lesson—perhaps the most important rule for speculators: Don't get in over your head.

On Wednesday, January 9, 1991, I was in fat city: I was long bonds and the S&Ps, and short crude oil. Each position was up 50 percent on my margin. Secretary of State James Baker had scheduled a meeting with the Iraqi foreign minister, Tariq Aziz. The meeting had already lasted 8 hours. Better close your positions out, my partners suggested. This is one of our best profits ever, and anything can happen. "Oh, no, they must be dotting the i's and crossing the t's on the final settlement," I said. After all, considerable progress had already been made regarding the terms of Iraq's withdrawal from Kuwait. Surely neither party would wish a showdown. But then, at exactly 2:30 P.M., Secretary Baker called a press conference. "Regrettably," he began, but reporters were already stampeding for the telephones. No settlement had been reached. Within 2 minutes, the Dow plummeted 80 points, bonds were down 1½ points, and oil was up $3 a barrel. One word from Baker brought a $5 million swing in my equity. The lesson: Political events are often unpredictable, especially when an election is forthcoming or the stock market is on a tear.

On Thursday, February 10, 1983, I had a nice short position in gold, which had been in a bearish trend for several years. And, like magic, it had been going down an average of $3 an ounce from close on Friday to open on Monday for the previous three years. I was sitting pretty. Nothing could go wrong. I shorted heavily at noon that day and smugly began to count my profits.

Then, out of the clear blue, from 2 P.M. to 3 P.M., gold jumped $7. No reason for the rise, just technical buying by the funds, we were told. But that weekend, around 4 A.M. on Sunday, U.S. Navy fighter planes shot down a Libyan jet flying over the Mediterranean. This caused tremendous tension, always good in those days for at least a good run in gold. After all, nuclear war in the Mideast was now possible.

This was just bad luck. No one could have known on Friday that the United States was going to down a Libyan jet 36 hours later. This was some consolation—until I discovered later that the United States had been buzzing over that area of the Mediterranean for several weeks. Apparently, the Pentagon had put out the word that an incident should be precipitated in order to show the Mideast powers who was boss. Somehow, the U.S. gold market, in its wisdom, had anticipated the move. The lesson: Information that seems to be completely fresh is often as smelly as a dead fish.

The occasion for another disaster was the government's monthly announcement of the employment numbers. Often, the volatility of the moves in fixed-income prices on this one day (usually the first Friday of each month) is greater than the sum of the volatilities on all the other trading days. Perhaps I could be pardoned for violating one of my essential rules: Never use stop losses. Other traders always know. Invariably, the price moves to the level of the stop. The order is executed at a loss, and then the market turns around and moves wildly in your original direction. The only consolation is that you played a part in the cosmic market order by reducing your broker's risk.

The price of bonds on this occasion was 108-14. I placed my stop at 107-30. The employment number was released at 8:30 A.M. Joy and jubilation. The Department of Labor was in a bullish mode. They must have subtracted 200,000 from the actuals to help along the favorite sons. I'm golden.

Except, horror of horrors, price is moving against me! I'm stopped out.

What happened? A big hedge fund placed an order to sell 1000 at even. The hedger meant it to be sold at 109 even. But the broker took it to be 108 even. Those 1000 contracts were awfully tempting. Prices moved to 108, 107.31, 107.27. I was stopped out. Immediately thereafter the price moved straight up to 110. My stop turned a 150 percent profit into a 25 percent loss. Three lessons were highlighted:

- Ambiguity in the message sent on an order will work against you; be redundant in communicating it.
- Never be flip, especially when the forces are with you.

- Avoid stops, except when you can't meet a current or prospective margin call.

THE REVENGE FACTOR

There's something important to know about losing, above and beyond the lessons it teaches about winning. *After a loss, victory becomes more likely.* All good athletes know this maxim.

"Watch the revenge factor" and "Don't let up" are drummed into all players, in the Pee-Wee leagues and on up. The best expression of the maxim and its cause was set down by René Lacoste. In addition to winning Wimbledon twice, "the Crocodile" is a pioneer in the sports apparel licensing field. He knows plenty about how to win.

> I have often remarked that an unexpected defeat is generally followed by a series of successes; the best means of willing to win is to be beaten from time to time. That allows for better measurement of the meaning which separates the two expressions "to lose" and "to win," and that renews the desire to win. One is so made that one accustoms oneself much more easily to success than to defeat; a series of victories seems always rapidly naturally to blunt the will. On the contrary, a defeat causes the well-known reaction: the desire to regain what one has just lost.
>
> It will be found sometimes that the player who has consistently lost sometimes wins, first one match then another, because by dint of being beaten has created with himself a greater desire to conquer.[2]

Champions in all fields invariably voice similar sentiments concerning the value of losing. J. R. Capablanca, World Chess Champion from 1921 to 1927, and one of the greatest ever to hold the title, put it this way:

> There have been times in my life when I came near to thinking that I could not lose a single game. Then I would be beaten and the lost game would bring me back from dream land to earth. Nothing is so healthy as a thrashing at the proper time, and from few won games have I learned so much as I have from most of my defeats.[3]

In his *Chess Fundamentals*, "Capa" gives the scores of 14 of his games and appends an instructive commentary. The first six chosen for comment were games he lost.

CHAMPIONS VS. LOSERS

Almost all the great champions are extremely humble relative to their own abilities, and they are endlessly appreciative of the efforts of amateurs. Good players usually understand the difficulty of a game and the many different ways of achieving proficiency. Thus, they are delighted to see someone traveling on the road to mastery, even a beginner.

Boasts about great successes are a giveaway on someone's insecurity. When I was good in squash, I didn't go around telling the whole world about it. "My racquet will do the talking," I'd say. The same is true for speculators. Reading most forecasters' assessments of their own records can bring one back to Delphi and astrology: "As we predicted . . ."; "Yesterday's call was right on target . . ."; "While we have been one of the foremost in the bullish camp throughout the rise . . . ." The strange thing about all this self-praise is that the forecasters actually come to believe their own hype. Psychologists call this tendency the "I knew it all along" phenomenon. After elections, 99 percent of the voters "knew" that the winning candidate was going to win.[4]

During the 10 years I traded for George Soros, I never heard him speak once about a winning trade. To hear him talk, you'd think he had had nothing but losers. Conversely, listening to the biggest losers, you'd think they had had nothing but winners.

The tendency to do better after a defeat—often observed in athletics—is a phenomenon that manifests itself in market action as well. After a loss, markets generally become more bullish. For example, during the ten years ending with 1996, crude oil went up a total of $10 open to close after a decline on the previous day but went down $9 after a rise on the previous day.

When I can't hide my trepidation from my wife, on those nights when I'm experiencing a big loss, she usually urges me to take out the garbage just as I'm in the throes of agony. "But dear, I can't. The currencies are drubbing me in Tokyo." Then she'll say, "That's good. After a fall, it's bullish. Whenever it's way against you overnight, it tends to come back great the next day. The dishwasher needs filling also. You'll find it as relaxing as knitting."

Once I tried a different tack. "George Soros has never changed a diaper. The opportunity cost of his doing so would be prohibitive, maybe $10,000 a diaper." Susan was not moved.

In sports and markets, the most dangerous time is when you are ahead. That is when you are most likely to let up, drop your guard, and make a bad decision out of overconfidence.

Soros gave me this advice on an occasion when I had scored a big win for him: "Climb off your horse. You're only as good as tomorrow's trade. Why are you always fighting the trend? Why do you make it so hard for yourself? Are you a masochist? Haven't you read my books? The markets are reflexive. Positive feedback. That's why we need a supranational altruistic authority to stabilize things."

Far be it from me to question the wisdom of the sages. Capablanca, Lacoste, Soros—the very idea of putting the wisdom of these world champions to a test seems irreverent. Still, even Homer nodded. And some principles that are highly effective in chess, tennis, or diplomacy just might not carry over on a one-to-one basis to speculation.

To put some beef on the plate, I computed the year-to-year changes of 18 major markets from 1985 to 1995 (Table 4–1). The markets may be roughly divided into financials (stock and bonds), currencies, grains, tropicals (sugar, coffee, and cocoa), metals (gold, silver, and copper), and meats (cattle and hogs). To start, I computed the worst performing market among all 18 each year, and looked at the change the next year. The worst markets, with their percentage changes the next year, are as follows: 1986 Corn (22.5), 1987 Hogs (4.8), 1988 Swiss Franc (−3.8), 1989 Coffee (14.3), 1990 Wheat (50.7), 1991 Copper (4.4), 1992 Pound (−2.0), 1993 Copper (66.3), 1994 Hogs (24.6). The average change for the worst performer in the next year is 20.2 percent, a nice return on the usual margin of 5 percent. In statistical terms, the 95 percent confidence interval for the worst performer ranges between 4.5 percent and 36 percent.

In a larger view, there were 42 years in which a market went down by 10 percent or more—about once every 7 years for each market. The average change in the subsequent year was 11.5 percent. Again, this is highly significant, economically and statistically.

Finally, to assess the overall higgledy-piggledy of the moves, I looked at the consistency of the ranks. Do the changes in ranks from year to year exhibit nonrandom properties? The answer is yes. The average rank correlation between consecutive years is −0.28, a highly nonrandom result. The poor speculator has dared to offer some bits of data to the giants. The bits provided nourishment.

THE PIVOTAL QUESTION

The pivotal speculation question is: do prices move in trends?

I do not know the answer. Some indirect evidence, however, is found in the performance of trend followers versus contrarian (or discretionary) traders. According to MAR, the leading rating service for managed accounts, the contrarians outperformed the trend followers in six of the nine years, 1987 to 1996. On average, the contrarians made 26 percent versus 15 percent for the trend followers (Table 4–2). But all of this superiority came during the early years, when the universe was much smaller.

Retrospectively reported results tend to be significantly higher than those from prospective reporting. (Those who performed badly never get to the stage where they have the volition or resources to report.) But all those with superior performance somehow take the trouble to make sure their results are included. Perhaps this explains those average returns of 64 percent and 86 percent for 1987. The results reported by Barclay, which

Table 4-1. Yearly Commodity Returns, 1986–1995 (Percent Change)

Year Ended	Bonds	S&P	DMark	Swiss	Yen	Pound	Gold	Silver	Copper
1986	15.2	14.0	26.5	27.3	27.0	2.3	20.4	-7.9	-6.2
1987	-10.4	1.9	23.2	27.3	30.9	27.9	21.9	24.8	136.9
1988	1.3	13.6	-11.2	-15.4	-3.0	-4.4	-15.1	-10.1	4.6
1989	10.7	27.1	3.6	-3.8	-13.6	-11.7	-2.9	-13.5	-30.4
1990	-3.0	-7.2	13.2	21.6	6.0	20.2	-1.6	-19.8	10.0
1991	9.4	26.5	-2.7	-7.3	8.2	-3.4	-10.1	-7.9	-16.5
1992	-0.1	4.7	-6.2	-7.1	0.2	-18.8	-5.6	-4.7	4.4
1993	9.4	7.3	-6.4	-1.2	11.9	-2.0	17.0	42.2	-18.5
1994	-13.4	-1.8	13.3	14.5	12.8	6.7	-1.9	-6.7	66.3
1995	22.5	34.3	7.9	13.8	-3.3	-0.1	1.2	4.9	-10.2

Year Ended	Cotton	Cocoa	Coffee	Sugar	Soy	Corn	Wheat	Steers	Hogs
1986	-7.7	-16.5	-31.6	14.3	-9.2	-40.6	-29.2	-7.4	-0.5
1987	14.4	-4.8	-9.2	69.6	19.4	22.5	4.4	10.9	-13.6
1988	-13.8	12.9	31.3	18.7	39.1	53.4	40.8	13.7	4.8
1989	15.7	-51.6	-54.8	20.3	-29.5	-14.6	-3.2	7.0	12.1
1990	14.5	20.2	14.3	-28.4	0.2	-1.7	-33.0	1.25	4.1
1991	-25.5	4.8	-1.2	-4.0	-0.9	8.0	50.7	-12.6	-27.3
1992	-0.3	-18.3	-16.4	-9.0	0.7	-16.1	-10.0	10.6	11.7
1993	22.6	31.7	-6.8	27.6	24.8	43.3	41.5	-7.3	0
1994	31.3	4.1	160.6	43.0	-21.3	-24.7	-20.7	-2.1	-15.8
1995	-8.1	-10.3	-38.5	-16.9	32.9	62.5	35.8	-8.4	24.6

Table 4–2. Returns for Trend Followers vs. Discretionary Traders

	S&P	MAR Trend Followers	MAR Discretionary	Barclay Trend	Barclay Overall
1983	48.1%	5.3%			
1984	7.0	24.4			
1985	21.2	27.6			
1986	14.9	−0.3			
1987	1.0	64.3	86.3		
1988	45.5	16.3	27.3		
1989	20.2	−4.6	36.3		
1990	0	28.9	21.4		
1991	26.0	19.0	14.3	4.4%	3.6%
1992	5.0	−0.3	18.5	−0.4	−1.0
1993	10.7	19.6	32.2	9.6	10.1
1994	1.0	−5.7	−1.0	2.1	−0.7
1995	35.0	20.3	12.1	3.6	13.4
1996*	11.9	−4.3	7.7	−3.0	−0.2
Average	19.2%	15.1%	25.5%	2.7%	4.2%

*As of 9/1/96

tend to be more contemporaneous, appear to average 11 percent less than the MAR results.

More direct evidence on whether reversing gets better results than trend following may come from examination of the correlation between consecutive changes for different time periods in some major markets (Table 4–3). A strong tendency for reversal in silver is evident for all periods, and there is a small tendency toward continuations for the one-month changes in all other markets. Other periods show close to zero correlation.

However, even if the correlations had shown a consistent pattern, their usefulness would have been limited. In some seasons, trend following is good; in others, reversing is good. The problem is how to differentiate the two seasons in advance.

Table 4–3. Serial Correlations of Changes for Commodities, 1987–1996

Period	Silver	Oil	Bonds	S&P	Swiss	Yen
1 day	−0.01	0.01	0.00	−0.03	0.02	−0.01
2 days	−0.02	−0.11	0.00	−0.06	−0.02	0.01
10 days	−0.22	0.13	−0.04	−0.06	0.01	0.18
Monthly	−0.15	0.27	0.13	−0.02	0.15	0.18
Yearly	−0.36	−0.04	−0.89	−0.71	0.05	−0.05

PENUMBRA OF FLUCTUATION

Frank Taussig, a Harvard economist, had some good insights on this subject 75 years ago. He found a tendency for markets to reverse between certain bands, and to give way to continuation or trend-following behavior when the bands were broken.

The bands are now referred to by technicians as support and resistance levels. Taussig referred to these zones as a "penumbra within which prices fluctuate . . . . Within this there will be ups and downs, many and perhaps wide fluctuations." In situations tending to disequilibrium, Taussig wrote:

> There is a wider range for unexpected developments in the situation, for the calculations and guesses among dealers and speculators, optimism and pessimism, waves of sentiment and belief. There is a zone of uncertainty, a penumbra of considerable extent.[5]

Forty years later, scholars like Paul H. Cootner and Sidney S. Alexander attempted to reconcile Taussig's ideas with the random walk hypothesis. Alexander studied price fluctuations through "filters" of percentage moves in prices, ignoring the time element. To test the nonrandomness, he paper traded the various filters. A small filter, on the order of 5 percent, was found to yield significantly profitable results (although Alexander left out commission costs). He concluded:

> There *are* trends in stock market prices, once the "move" is taken as the unit under study rather than the week or the month. That is, the nonrandom nature of stock price movement . . . proceeds . . . from transforming the measure over which changes are considered. The many statistical studies which have found speculative prices to resemble a random walk have dealt with changes over uniform periods of time. The filter operation, however, deals with changes of a certain magnitude irrespective of the length of time involved. . . . In fact, medium filters uniformly yield profits, and the smallest filters yield the highest profits, and very high they are.[6]

Cootner specifically tried to merge the penumbra with the random walk:

> . . . [P]rices will behave as a random walk with reflecting barriers. In something like the manner once suggested by Taussig, prices within those upper and lower limits will tend to move like a random walk . . . there probably would also be random changes in the trends around which the random walk takes place.[7]

I threw myself into this controversy and, in a sense, I have never stopped working with it. Since reading these studies 30 years ago, I have devoted a substantial part of my waking hours to quantifying the phenomena of price reversals and breakouts. The studies emanated from Massachusetts

Institute of Technology (MIT) in the late 1960s. They spawned such firms as Commodity Corporation, which manages about $1 billion with techniques that have evolved since those formative days. The MIT Nobelist, Paul Samuelson, has been on the board of the Commodity Corporation since 1975. Our paths crossed in 1996 when I began to manage some money for one of their entities according to the principles of music, nature, deception, gambling, games, et al. Speculation, like most activities, is an art-science. Attempts to answer the pivotal question of speculation invariably raise twice as many questions as they solve. Perhaps all I can say definitively is that prices sometimes move like a wild beast, sometimes like a gentle lamb, and sometimes like a playful trout.

THE WIND IS YOUR FRIEND

When the time came to write my undergraduate thesis, it was natural for me to pursue the question of trends versus reversals. To study it, I immersed myself in my favorite part of Harvard, its library system, which is among the finest in the world.

Harvard maintains over 100 libraries in the Boston area and throughout the world. They contain over 11 million volumes, and most of these books are in the Cambridge campus libraries. Widener Library is said to contain over five miles of books. I made myself at home in Harvard's libraries. A person can commune there with the greatest minds of history, learning any subject in which humans have attained knowledge. One can be transported from there to adventures anywhere in the solar system.

The interaction among the sun, the atmosphere, moisture, and the wind—the four elements that affect our weather—held me in its sway one evening in 1963. I had just finished one of the never-ending league matches against the Union Boat House in Boston. After a hasty meal at Durgin Park, paid for by the friends of Harvard Tennis and Squash, I had rushed back to the library before its 10 o'clock closing hour.

As usual in Boston, it was a rainy 7 on the Beaufort scale. The cold winter air sweeping down from Canada was colliding with the warmer air over the Atlantic Ocean. While I walk, I always perform a Beaufort calculation of the strength of the wind. If the leaves rustle and there's just a slight breeze, that's a 2; if branches are moving and small trees sway in a fresh breeze, that's a 5; if whole trees are moving and walking is difficult, that's a 7, a high wind. In that case, I'm golden. Just a little bit of dust in the air gives me a lock hand in buying grains.

The wind is the speculator's friend. Along with ocean currents, the other key part of the earth's circulatory system, the wind, links us all together. "You're never away," as environmentalists like to say. Wind prevents the air near the equator or the poles from becoming unbearably hot or cold. It exchanges the warm air from the equator, rising toward the poles, with the cold air from the poles, falling toward the equator.

The wind also transfers nutrients all over the world, giving the Brazilian rain forest the benefit of phosphates blown across from the Sahara and nourishing algae in Hawaii with the growth enhancement of iron blown in from the Gobi Desert in China.

As a speculator, the wind has been my friend on several occasions. On May 18, 1980, a titanic cloud of ash hurtled into the sky over Mt. St. Helens in Washington State. The cloud quickly boiled upward and spread downwind, darkening the sky and creating fear among the multitudes who watched it. The wind in its majesty quickly carried the ash as far east as the Great Plains. A starstruck worshipper of the "Sultan of Speculation" remarked that when he played tennis with him that day, he was stunned to find Soros wondering about the impact the volcano would have on the markets.

This time, my statistical bent and love of incunabula gave me the edge. I knew that the darkening ash would combine with the propelling winds to prevent the sun's beneficent rays from shining on the grain crops. I rushed to buy the grains.

In particularly violent eruptions, like Indonesia's Tamboura volcano in 1815, which injected 50 times as much ash into the atmosphere as the Mt. St. Helens eruption in 1980, it's the devil take the hindmost. Europe had a summerless 1816.

Grains showed an enormous rise in 1816: the per-bushel price of wheat in England rose from 9 shillings 0 pence to 16 shillings 6 pence. More portentously, the price of malt more than doubled. In discussing the 100 percent price rise of wheat from year-end 1815 to year-end 1816, Thomas Tooke stated, "The bad harvest of 1816 intervened and gave a respite from the state of distress."[8]

I am not about to palm off some second-hand anecdotes as "research," as do many of the trash sources that I decry. A study is in order. Unfortunately, historical statistics on the amount of ash deposited by volcanoes is not readily available. Volcanologists generally test the acid in ice cores or tree rings to calculate an objective estimate. The written record and the objective estimates have been combined by Facts on File in the *Encyclopedia of Earthquakes and Volcanoes*.

For the top 14 volcanoes, I computed the percentage move in wheat prices for the 12 months following the eruption. PAY DIRT (Figure 4–1). The average change in wheat 8 months after a volcano's eruption is 11 percent, a highly nonrandom and economically important event.

FORECASTING THE WEATHER AND PRICES

Growing up in Brighton, where rain, sun, and wind affected the outcome of every game, I became sensitive to the pervasive impact of weather. Consequently, when I visited libraries, I made it a practice to browse through the meteorology section. To Harvard's everlasting credit, they maintained

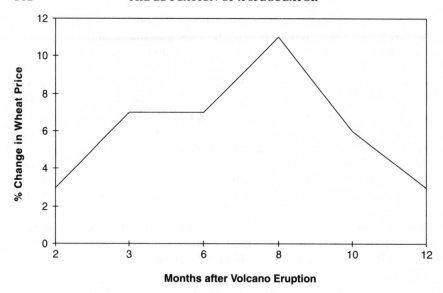

Figure 4–1. The Volcano Eruption/Wheat Price Relationship

bound volumes of all scientific journals in open stacks. I have found that smaller colleges still maintain this practice.

Browsing through the turn-of-the-century meteorological journals, I became fascinated by their discussions of the then nascent science. The early writers in meteorology were attempting, essentially, to create a new field of scientific inquiry complete with a predictive methodology, using for their raw materials a fascinating combination of "folk wisdom" and the first essays at rigorous statistical analysis of strictly quantitative data.

In the area of popular beliefs about the weather, there were allusions to traditional oral history. I came across such items as the following gem, taken from a discussion with an anonymous German-American quoted in the *Cincinnati Enquirer* in September 1884. This elderly man kept tree frogs in a jar with an inch of water on the bottom and a little wooden ladder extending from the bottom of the jar to the top. The frogs were his barometer: when they ascended the ladder, it meant fair weather; when they climbed down into the water, rain was expected. He offered more predictive signs:

> Take the ants. Have you ever noticed the activity they display before a storm, hurry-scurry, rushing hither and yon, as if they were letter-carriers making six trips a day, or expressmen behind time? Dogs grow sleepy and dull, and like to lie before a fire when rain approaches; fowls roll in the dust.

Beetles flying late in the evening foretell a fine day on the morrow; cranes flying high. Hogs when they run squawking about, and won't bite, and jerk up their heads, and see a wind coming, hence the proverb, "Pigs can see the wind."

When you see a swan flying against the wind, toads coming out of their holes in unusual numbers on an evening, worms, slugs and snails appearing, robin redbreasts pecking at our windows, you can put them all down for rain signs.[9]

In their all-encompassing spirit of inquiry, early meteorologists would extrapolate the folklore and then proceed to more scientific analysis without missing a beat. The April 1885 issue of the same journal contains a review of one of the early studies of weather maps and how to use them "to best advantage" in the study of the "fluctuation of weather types."[10]

Weather maps were invented by the ingenious English scientist Francis Galton, whom I consider the greatest mind to have graced the Western world in the past few hundred years. When I make my escape from this all-too-hard current world, should I ascend the stairs to Heaven before being thrust below, I would wish first for a hug and conversation with my dad, and then to sit at Galton's feet for a few hours to observe his great mind at work.

It dawned on me, when reading these journals, that the science of meteorological prediction might have a bearing on stock markets, especially in the area of forecasting price movements. Consider the following editorial from the same journal:

The question as to what may be considered as the verification of a prediction is a particularly important one in meteorology [vis-à-vis the natural sciences]. While in [meteorology] prediction is especially important, and the verification can be tested by anyone, there enters into it the question not only of *what*, but also of *how much*. . . . If a storm is predicted, will a slight increase in wind verify?

In meteorology the energies involved are vastly complex and subject to vast and ever-varied perturbations; the conditions of one day are probably never exactly reproduced, and the "signs" of the time will never be followed by exactly the same weather at another time.[11]

Confirmation of a potential link between predictive approaches to meteorology and markets came when I discovered the work of Herbert E. Jones. Jones' articles appeared in the 1930s, in the then recently founded journal *Econometrica*, and they built on statistical predictive models that had been developed in the field of meteorology. Jones had collaborated with the wealthy investor Alfred Cowles, who, while studying at Yale, decided to apply mathematical methods to predicting stock prices. The latter subsequently formed "The Cowles Commission for Research in Economics" to study phenomena related to stock price prediction.

As Cowles and Jones developed their methodology, they found it expedient to construct a new index of the stock market, one weighted by market value rather than by price, as the Dow Jones index until then had been compiled. They calculated this new index from 1897 to 1926. Their data subsequently formed the foundation of the Standard & Poor's Index, on which the famous S&P 500 futures contract traded on the IMM is based.

Their next step was to compute runs of all different lengths in averages and individual stocks, to see whether there was any momentum or tendency to reversal. The results of these efforts appeared in a series of papers published over the next 15 years. The conclusion from one of them provides a good summary of the pair's findings:

> This type of forecasting could not be employed by speculators with any assurance of consistent or large profits. On the other hand, the significant excess of sequences over reversals . . . represents conclusive evidence of structure in stock prices.[12]

The weight of scholarly study in this field, now called rational expectations and efficient markets theory, has oscillated like a pendulum between the structural school, advanced by Cowles, and the random walk theory, advanced by Cootner, Fama, Malkiel, and others who believe that markets are completely unpredictable. But with the temerity and self-confidence that I picked up during my days as a paddle hustler, I decided I would concentrate on the systematic departures from randomness: the so-called anomalies, rather than the haphazard random observations. This aspect seemed much more alluring.

Many of the price anomalies I focus on relate to runs or sequences and reversals. Measurements are often so imprecise that the only thing one can know with reasonable assurance is whether the series is up or down, large or small, greater or less than something else. For situations like these, runs are natural, and when comparing two elements such as price and volume, a natural extension of runs is to look at co-movements and contra-movements—that is, the concurrent moves of two separate variables in similar and in opposite directions.

BUILDING BLOCKS

I tested co-movements for price and volume in my undergraduate thesis. After a tortuous line of reasoning, which now seems hopelessly naïve, I figured that something big was up in the area of demand when two consecutive increases in volume occur in conjunction with two consecutive increases in price. I called this a positive breakthrough. I defined a negative breakthrough as two negative changes in price occurring in conjunction with two consecutive decreases in volume.

The prediction was that stocks are more likely to rise significantly after positive breakthroughs than after negative breakthroughs. In fact, the prediction was confirmed in my thesis, using monthly post-Second World War data from 1948 to 1961. The chances of a rise in the next month after a positive breakthrough during this period was 73 percent. Negative breakthroughs were followed by advances in the next month only 39 percent of the time.

MIDNIGHT OIL

In my youthful enthusiasm, no extensions of the theory seemed too great to undertake. In addition to working around the clock when I was home, I carried hundreds of newspapers to all my squash and tennis tournaments. In the dormitories, I performed calculations, testing my theory on hundreds of individual stocks and on the stock market averages, until 4:00 or 5:00 in the morning. I looked at expectations, systems, truncated distributions, foreign stocks, and ticker tape data. Baker Library at Harvard University Business School conveniently carried the hard copies of every ticker tape transaction that had taken place on the NYSE from 1890 forward. These were in bound volumes containing the details of up to 25,000 separate market transactions or about 32 pages of transactions daily in those early days.

I grandly concluded Chapter 6 of my thesis: The results indicate that the logarithmic random walk is contradicted by the monthly S&P industrials price and volume behavior from 1928–1961. By selecting stocks that showed recent evidence of structure, I argued, buying these issues after positive breakthroughs and selling after negative breakthroughs, a speculator could have made profits of 260 percent.[13]

I closed the thesis with, "In summary, this study provides support for a model that forecasts systematic and predictable price behavior. It is submitted that the burden of proof has shifted to those who contend that prices move in a patternless fashion, known technically as the random walk in stock prices."

They say that there is nothing as scary as a fact confronting a theory. I remembered the gist of my thesis, but I didn't have a copy of it to refer to.

Fortuitously, I became good friends with Professor Ron Volpe of Youngstown State University. Ron has been my client for the better part of the last ten years. I discovered that Professor Volpe had collected all of my published work, including a copy of my undergraduate thesis.

Now I had no excuse for refraining from further testing of my theory, using the 30 years or 360 months of data subsequent to December 1962, which was the cutoff point for my undergraduate research.

BACK TO THE DRAWING BOARD

The results in a nutshell: My theory does not hold up. For stock market averages, there is no predictive relation between stock prices and volume during the post-WWII period, 1946–1991. The regression of future price changes as a function of previous price and volume changes explains less than 1 percent of the variability of the future price changes. No "t" statistics either, of a univariate or multivariate nature, above 1. Table 4–4 shows some expectations after breakthrough that underline their lack of predictability.

How deflating.

On the other hand, I guess you could say I have spent the intervening 30 years of my professional life refining my theory that price moves show predictive patterns in the laboratory of our trading room.

CONGESTION OF PRICES

I pursued my random property studies by starting at the beginning. I haunted the floors of the exchanges and studied the ticker tape.

My first discovery was that certain exchange members, called specialists, had the exclusive license to make markets in stocks. The specialist system developed in the late 19th century, according to legend, when one of the members broke his leg in an accident and was immobilized. Because he couldn't move around and trade freely with the other members, he requested that members come to him whenever they wanted action in, say, Western Union.

The system had great survival value and lasts to this day, despite the efforts of the major brokerage houses, electronic trading systems, third markets, and rival regional and overseas exchanges. The least reason for survival is that the specialists have traditionally been among the most profitable denizens of Wall Street. Their yearly returns often average more than 50 percent of invested capital.

Whenever a customer has an order that is to be filled at a particular price (a "limit order"), the order is given to the specialist. This tends to

Table 4–4. Moves Following S&P Breakthroughs

Price Move	After Positive Breakthrough	After Negative Breakthrough
Next month	0.90	0.80
3 months later	0.53	1.60
4 months later	(0.46)	1.70
5 months later	1.40	1.90
6 months later	2.00	2.00

create concentrations of orders at certain prices, especially multiples of 5 and 2½ in the larger capitalization stocks, and multiples of ¼ in the lower cap stocks (those with stock prices of less than $10 per share). Stock prices tend to fluctuate, up and down, between the "magic" numbers where the limit orders are concentrated, until the concentration is broken.

When buy market orders come in, they are executed at the price where sell limit orders are concentrated. Conversely, sell market orders are executed at the price where buy limit orders are clustered. For example, if there are buy limits at 99½ and sell limits at 100, the price will fluctuate between 99½ and 100, depending on whether the last order was a buy (at 100) or a sell (at 99½). This creates opportunities for fast-moving professionals. As M.F.M. Osborne and I noted, in a 1966 study:

> In the short run, the limit orders on the [specialist's] book will act as a barrier to continued price movement in either direction. Until all limit orders at the highest bid . . . and the lowest offer . . . are executed, transaction prices will fluctuate up and down between the bid and the offer in accordance with the random arrival of the market orders.
>
> Mr. Alfred Cowles added the following observation in a letter [to us] . . . : "If professionals actually habitually profit from a knowledge of these patterns, that might explain a phenomenon which for many years has intrigued me. As a result of repeated analyses of large numbers of purchase and sales . . . I have noted repeatedly that the average price at which series of 100 or more orders have been executed consistently averaged at prices slightly less favorable to the investors than the average of high and low for the day for each stock purchased or sold." This is a manifestation of the compensation the specialist receives for the stabilizing services he performs for investors.[14]

The net result is that periods of reversals will characterize individual stock movements for a time. But where reversals have ended and continuations are predominating, there is likely to be strong underlying demand or supply. How else could the market orders have overwhelmed the shrewd professional traders, the slow-moving users of limit orders, and the market makers, all of whom are reversal creators?

The speculator strives to comprehend the interaction among the underlying forces of supply and demand, the emotions of the winners and losers, and the weather.

COTTON IN EARS

No one has been more fortunate than I in being exposed to losses from an early age. I say to Uncle Howie, Grandpa Martin, Marty Reisman, and the Brooklyn Dodgers: Please don't consider me ungrateful for not learning better from your lessons on losses. Alas, it hasn't saved me from the cruel fate of losing, at least as a speculator. Soros gave me the nickname "loser" because it happened so often. I can't blame him. "Victor, you lost me $500 million this year," he'd say. As I slunk away, he'd continue, "But who knows how much I would have lost without you."

The one thing I can say in my defense is that at least I am aware of my predilection and have taken steps to overcome it. When I first started speculating in organized markets, I quickly ran a $40,000 initial stake into $22 million. My technique was simple: I bought gold at $290. Each time it went up $10, I pyramided and added to my holdings with my profits.

The one thing that saved me was that my previous experiences in sports and poker playing indicated that momentum had a way of changing. I had learned that much from Howie. Gamblers usually decide to limit how much they will lose, but they rarely limit how much they will win or what percentage of their winnings they will give back in bets if they are lucky enough to get ahead. This seemed a costly omission. I decided to set my loss limit at 50 percent of my winnings. I couldn't lose. My strategy was good for unlimited profits and, at worst, I'd end up with $11 million.

The goddess of losses is a terrible temptress. She does everything possible to prevent her worshippers from allowing friends to protect them from her clutches. The model story on this point is Odysseus. On his voyage home from the Trojan War, he was informed by Circe that his ship would pass by the bewitching Sirens. He desperately wanted to hear their beautiful songs without being lured to destruction. Knowing that he was prone to weakness, Odysseus ordered his crew to put beeswax in their ears and tie him up. He knew that the Sirens' beauty was so great that he would refuse to listen to anyone who tried to stop him from joining the temptresses. To protect against his own weakness, he directed his men, "If I beg you to release me, you must tighten and add to my bonds."

With $22 million in profits in gold, the Siren song of profits lured me to bigger and bigger risks, but I knew I was vulnerable. As the markets heated up, I put on my maximum bullish position and removed myself from the fray. I locked myself inside a racquetball court instead of tying myself to a ship's mast. I issued instructions to my assistant and future wife, Susan: "Do not listen to my entreaties if I wish to double further. If the losses reach 50 percent of the winnings, reduce my positions by one-half. If I beg to be released, sell everything out."

I took a trip to Staten Island, secure that nothing could go wrong. I started my game against my opponent on top of the world. It was calm on the racquetball court, and my opponent and I lost ourselves in the game. After the first two games, I broke for a call to my broker. Some rumors about liquidation by the Hunts had hit the fan. My wealth had dropped severely—perhaps by 50 percent or so! I immediately placed a call to Susan, "Untie me. Disregard everything I said before. Don't sell anything, it will come back." She tightened the bonds, selling out not only 50 percent of my positions, but an additional 50 percent. My faithful companion followed my original directions. Had she not done so (and had I not been astute enough to ask her to tighten the bonds if I relented), my wealth would have dwindled to zero.

To give the goddess of losses her due, however, she managed to take back an additional 45 percent of my winnings, leaving me with just 5 percent of my previous high to continue on my discovery.

Like all too many gamblers, however, I was rueful. For months after, I couldn't refrain from giving Susan that famous Eisenberg-Reisman intimidation technique. "You ignominious nonentity, don't suppress me ever again."

CHAPTER 5

Winning and Self-Reliance

No one before or since has used the front wall from deep in the court with such dev-
astating effect as Harry Cowles. His dew-drop tactic was derided until he defeated
the national champion 3–0 and 15–0 in the third game.

Jack Barnaby
Winning Squash Racquets

THAT AUSTERE TRADITION

Late at night, when Japanese traders close down for lunch for two hours,
hoping for a reversal, I close my eyes and dream. As I slumber, I can taste
the Beef Wellington at Delmonico's, where Jesse Livermore and my grandfather Martin celebrated after a good trade. I can hear my music teacher,
Robert Schrade's father, playing along in a quartet with Brahms; I see the
practice sessions of the great squash players, Cowles and Barnaby; I smell
the flop houses where Artie inventoried the belongings of ghosts and
hoodoos; and I feel the excitement at Scott Joplin's bordello where Martin
ogled the girls.

Yes, that is the kind of education that will prepare a speculator for success. But there's institutional learning also, like the Harvard Colleges and
Lincoln High Schools of Life—the kind that prepares most of us to become good soldiers, true believers, and conformists.

Fortunately, I played racquet sports and music well enough, and my parents were strongly enough behind me to give me the self-confidence to
survive. My resistance to conformity has been the bedrock of my speculative persona.

The squash team at Harvard is the most successful team in the history of
intercollegiate athletics. In 1996, the men's team had a winning streak of 70
matches, and the women had won 40 in a row. Between them, they have won
11 of the last 12 National Intercollegiate team championships. This is typical of the past 70 years. Presumably, some of their winning tradition might
have applicability in some other fields and on boards and exchanges.

I'm not going to apologize profusely for drawing on my squash education, even though the sport I played is gone with the dodo. I realize that except for the handful who still play or remember hardball squash, my experience breaking into the game is of little consequence. But the lessons learned from this intense, closed game are multifarious. The very proximity of the players wielding lethal weapons, unseparated by a net, demands good sportsmanship for survival. The unwritten rules taught the players to restrain their swing when they could kill their opponent, to acquiesce in the opponent's and referee's bad calls, to clear out of the way, and never to use the big, big "D."

Squash is the gentlemen's game replete with worship of the English lords who formerly were the only ones with enough money and leisure to play. The tradition involves the stiff upper lip, the uplifted chin, the fighting spirit, the muddling through thick or thin, the acceptance of victory with grace or defeat with modesty, the understatement of travail.

The tradition at Harvard springs from Harry Cowles, the coach from 1928 to 1936. Cowles is considered by the cognoscenti to have been the best ever to play the game. If one of his champion students was not gracious in victory, Harry was wont to play him a little exhibition game, winning 15–0 in the third and final game.

Harry, who taught at the exclusive Harvard Club of Boston before arriving at the Yard, never could adjust to the less patrician players from the United States who abandoned long white ducks for shorts. In his book, *The Art of Squash Racquets*, Cowles laments:

> As good squash has been and is at present played in long trousers as in shorts. The hindrance, if any, is negligible. On the other hand, there is no doubt that long white trousers lend a niceness to the game that is lost through the adoption of shorts. . . . Now and then a player appears in the court with nothing on at all except an athletic supporter. If such a person could but watch himself a single time from the gallery he would hasten to change his habits.[1]

The new ways, the increasing democratization of the game, doubtless contributed to Cowles's insanity. He spent the last ten years of his life—from 1936 to 1946—in an asylum.

When Jack Barnaby took over in 1936, the English tradition was Americanized. Shorts were permitted. Athletes were encouraged to try out for the team even if they had not previously been polished at Harvard's now notorious finishing clubs. No longer did boys new to the game have to pay for lessons if they wished to learn. Jack regularly took those who had never played before and turned them into nationally ranked players in three years.

Jack's ancestors hailed from Hartford, Connecticut, where the cold weather and no-nonsense mien of the insurance industry precluded year-round tennis. When he entered Harvard in 1930, one of the tennis players suggested he take up squash during the winter. Jack responded, "Why, I thought that was a small, odoriferous pumpkin that climbs over limbs of trees." When Jack showed up and asked Harry Cowles for a chance to try out for the team, Cowles said all positions were filled with current or future national champions.

The only way for Jack to get a chance to play was to pay Cowles for private lessons. Jack studiously attended these for a year, and, as he has often related to his many students, "My game improved to a level equal to the great National Champions on the team at the time, such as Glidden, Pool, and Strachen." On my back as I write these words is a shirt honoring Jack for his 80th birthday. It says, "The older we get, the better we were," a tribute to Jack's stories about his own play during the 1930s. I have looked at the records, and the stories are true. Jack was a finalist and won numerous Massachusetts tournaments and registered wins over such champions as Glidden and Pool in exhibition games.

When I showed up in 1961 to try out for the team, I lacked blue blood but had a surplus of fight. I regularly dove headlong to return a tennis ball, and I could play two five-set matches without tiring. This was the one area I fit in; fighting until death has always been a key part of the Harvard sports tradition.

I'm afraid, however, that I was a little deficient in polishing the front door handles with sufficient care. My persona clashed with the understated, austere, waspy English tradition that permeated the game. Before I had even touched a racquet, I walked up to Jack and said, "I'm going to be the best ever in that other game besides tennis you coach." I could almost hear the agonizing groans coming from the full-size portraits (all in long pants) of past champions that hung in Jack's office. To Jack's credit, he merely responded, "I'd be happy to show you what a squash court looks like in a few days." In describing the incident years later, Barnaby generously said:

> Since he was a beginner who had never seen the court before, his boast seemed to savor of premature arrogance. To Niederhoffer it was simply a statement of fact, comparable to what any of us might say, such as "I'm now going to the Post Office." He was National Junior Champion fourteen months later.[2]

Jack confided in me 35 years later that he had had to bite his tongue to refrain from saying, "You seem like the biggest horse's ass I ever had the displeasure to meet in 40 years at Harvard." This was not the only time I'd cause Jack to bite his tongue.

On one memorable occasion, lord high Ned Bigelow was officiating a game of mine. After I lost, I gave him a cursory, "Thanks!"

"I didn't do much," he responded.

"You can say that again," I retorted.

Jack told me that my flippancy almost led to the cancellation of the annual National Tournament due to a lack of financial support. Yet Jack bided his time, and said to me a few hours later, "That was perhaps an overly caustic comeback you made."

"But Jack, I would have won the whole tournament if he weren't on the Yale guy's payroll," I said.

SELF-RELIANCE

Call it self-confidence or "insufferable arrogance"—I had that quality in all my competitive endeavors. Social scientists now call it fancy names such as "locus of control," "congruence," "self-reliance," "self-efficacy," "self-concept," "internal control," "feeling like an origin rather than a pawn," "lack of self-derogation," and "personal responsibility." The gist of all their findings is that lack of self-confidence causes withdrawal, which leads to displacement into self-destructive and antisocial behavior. Risk taking, one blade of the speculative scissors close to our heart, is positively correlated with how well we feel about ourselves.

Psychologists like to study self-confidence with contrived experiments involving students, professors, and confederates. A typical experiment starts with a student's being told he or she failed an intelligence test. Next, a handsome confederate engages the student in conversation. One thing leads to another and "a date is requested." The student's acceptance or rejection of the date is the dependent variable. There are so many artifices and biases in such a set-up that it makes one want to shout "Professor!"

In contrast, baseball, the all-American sport, provides a setting where the outcome is objective, subjects are mature, and there is strong motivation to succeed. Here are some findings on self-confidence from baseball players:

On favorable self-image:

Nothing is more likely to give a pitcher a positive, confident attitude than eight big ones on the scoreboard. (Jim Brosnan)

When you win, you eat better, sleep better, and your beer tastes better and your wife looks like Gina Lollobrigida. (Johnny Pesky)

On a slump:

You decide you'll wait for your pitch. Then as the ball starts toward the plate, you think about your stance. And then you think about your swing. And then you realize that the ball went past you. (Bobby Murcer)

So if you are not hitting, the fault is yours. Having admitted that, what do you do? You ask everybody on the ball club:

"What am I doing up there that I shouldn't do?"

You'd be surprised at the answers. One fellow tells you this . . . another tells you that . . . somebody else tells you something else. You've changed your stance. Your feet are too close together . . . or too far apart. You're swinging too soon . . . or too late. You take all the advice you hear . . . and what happens? You're lucky you don't get hit in the head. Then one day, you start to hit, and you know that all the time, it was your fault. (Lou Gehrig)[3]

As the baseball quotes make clear, it's much easier to figure out when you lack self-confidence than to remedy it.

HEY, ALL-AMERICAN

Many astute commentators on the market have concluded that the one characteristic most important for success in speculation is self-esteem. A treatise from the 1880s qualifies on my 100-year test-of-time rule, even though it was reprinted as late as 1923 by the *Magazine of Wall Street*:

> A [speculator] must think for himself; must follow his own connections; self-trust is the foundation of successful effort. [Don't] follow the mentally lazy habit of allowing a newspaper or broker or a wise friend to do our security market thinking.[4]

The old books on great stock market operators have numerous descriptions of the sangfroid of this or that legend in the heat of battle. But the feats of Jay Gould, John W. Gates, H. H. Rogers, and Cornelius Vanderbilt are not as well known as those of the legends of today. My own tennis game played with Soros in the midst of the October 19, 1987, stock market crash is perhaps more compelling.

We played while the carnage was at its greatest. The previous day, Soros had dropped at least a billion. Yet he didn't have a care in the world (or so it seemed). He played his best game ever, beating me heads up (I was not as carefree as he). He was confident that the market would open the next day and opportunities for profit would manifest themselves with the same regularity and predictability (to him) as in the past.

I tend to display more self-confidence before I play than after I lose. I expected to win each of the thousands of tournaments I played in, and I was convinced I'd be a successful speculator even before I made my first trade on an organized market. I trace the roots back to the football fields of Brooklyn College in the 1930s.

Artie played fullback in the popular single wing formation. Brooklyn College played a big-time football schedule in those days, with games against Army, Cal, Michigan, and Notre Dame. The great powerhouses enticed Brooklyn with irresistible Depression-era stipends to travel to their stadiums. How much of those teams' frustration was relieved when they won 100–0 against the Jews may only be guessed.

Typically, my dad referred to his team as "the world's worst" and his contributions to it as "least of all." He may have been correct. I subsequently checked the scores of the football games in which he played during his four-year college career. The record tallied one win, one tie, and 33 losses. The cumulative score chalked up against Brooklyn was 705 to 8. During one eight-game stretch, the other team actually gained on Brooklyn's offensive downs because points for safeties were often scored against Brooklyn.

On one occasion that became legendary in our family, the coach yanked Artie out of a game when the score was 50 to 3 against Brooklyn. Grandad Martin could not take it any longer. He fired off a letter to the coach. The gist was this: "With a great All-American like Niederhoffer on the team, how could you waste such talent by calling on other players, mere novices, to run, throw, or kick the ball?"

I still have the second page of the letter, which captures the flavor of the typical Niederhoffer defense of their children. You can imagine the anger coach Lou felt when he received it. But he was able to extract vengeance. The next day, he read the letter out loud to all the players in the locker room. To Artie, that was the most embarrassing moment of his life.

Page 2

You yanked Arthur out in the third quarter and on the *next* play Rockwell ran 20 yards for a touchdown, and the game was lost.

There were about 20 forward passes tried in the game by Brooklyn, only one was completed and that was the only one thrown by my boy. Your comment on this throw which was supposed to be a short flip, was that if a good thrower had thrown it, it would have been a touchdown.

Defensively, the team clicked in the C.C.N.Y. game; offensively, it was worse than in the Alumni game. That same dated uncertainty.

In spite of your criticism, three out of every four tackles made by Brooklyn secondaries in the C.C.N.Y. game were made by Arthur, even after he was injured.

In the Montclair game, the team offensively and defensively outplayed Montclair in three out of the four quarters. The signal calling was daring and flawless, even the play, a buck on the strong side which might have clicked on the weak side, but that is judging results.

Now that you have put Arthur on the second team, for the love of pete, give him the ball to carry on some plays, let him throw and receive, and not block exclusively for a bunch of novices.

Good luck to you Lou and no hard feelings either way.

Yours very sincerely,

Artie's teammates kidded him mercilessly about the letter and called him "All-American Niederhoffer" the rest of his playing days at Brooklyn. Years later, our family met one of his former teammates by chance at Lundy's, the 2,800-seat seafood restaurant in Sheepshead Bay, Brooklyn. He greeted Artie: "Hey, All-American, how's your dad?"

When Artie told his dad about his embarrassment, Martin answered, "If not me to stick up for you, then who?" That's par for the Niederhoffers in all parent–child relations. I once wrote a similar letter to the Chapin School, when Galt was yanked out of a talent show. I referred to her teachers as maggots and destroyers, and told her not to worry. Her talent could not be suppressed and the school's own self-loathing prevented her from appearing. For the next four years, the teachers called me "Mr. Noriegafer." The letter was printed by *Boardroom Reports*. It struck a responsive chord all over the country with parents who had seen their kids suppressed by their teachers. I still get requests for it from parents wishing to keep the flame of individualism alive among their children. When my kids have any little problem at school, I like to raise their hackles by suggesting, "Maybe I should dash off a little note to your teacher." Shortly after, I hear Susan saying, "He's only kidding," over the cries and tears.

My reputation has carried over to the trading floor. When we get a bad fill, my partners say to the counterparty, "Dr. Niederhoffer would like to chat with you after the close on that." After I hear the explanation, I like to say, "Perhaps I should drop you and your boss a little note clarifying our thinking on this." Invariably, the broker responds, "Please don't. You're filled at your price."

Time Not Wasted

One other area of my upbringing gave me a good head start. I was surrounded by books. Just being around them and reading their titles is enough to open a wide world of knowledge to a kid. Artie was fortunately stationed in the 9th Precinct, which included the Manhattan publishing district. In the days before chain stores and remainder sales, publishers were forced to throw out their overstocks. Artie and a few other intellectual cops kindly offered to save the publishers the salvage and crating costs by taking these overstocks off their hands at no charge.

Our 700-square-foot house in Brighton contained more than 10,000 books. We supplemented this with twice-weekly visits to the local library. Books were read to me each night. At Artie's funeral, five librarians showed up to pay their respects to their best customer. The ratio of books to wealth and of librarians to other mourners at his funeral may have been of Guinness Book caliber.

We were too poor, or too self-contained perhaps, to buy a television. I didn't have the luxury of sitting passively in front of the tube, watching sports and all the other great stuff I have always loved to watch. I cajoled, "I'm the only kid in the world without TV. Why can't we have one? I want to watch the Knicks and Sid Caesar."

No luck! My parents were adamant. "Read a book instead. What's good for everyone else isn't necessarily good for us. We don't have TV for a reason. Books can communicate everything that people wish to share; books can make you laugh or cry and transport you all around the world. Books are the most permanent thing in the world because they record the wisdom of the ages that produced them. They can help you live a thousand different lives, unlike television, which is here today, gone tomorrow. Just go to our shelves and pick out a book."

"Yes, but television is more exciting."

"For crying out loud—you're like a zombie in front of that TV set [at my grandparents' house]. Look at you. You're in a trance. TV may stimulate you, but it makes you passive. You're poor. You're not going to have the luxury of having others do things for you. Remember that. If you want something to happen, you're going to have to do it yourself."

"But I need it for my homework," I'd say. No dice.

After such a lecture, I would wait for a propitious time and sneak over to my grandparents' house and glue myself in front of their tube. Unfortunately, I could never relax completely. There was always the possibility that my father would discover my refuge and drag me away from the set. Or that my mom would extort extra piano and clarinet practice in exchange for granting me TV viewing time. At the time, being deprived of TV was the ultimate tragedy of my young life. In retrospect, however, in those leisure hours, precluded from TV viewing, I was able to find time to cultivate a love of and an interest in sports, music, and books that prepared me for a lifetime of entertainment, pleasure, and relaxation.

Like most traders and brokers, I spend most of my working hours glued to a screen watching the high-resolution flashing of prices and the scrolling of news stories. The screen has the same hypnotic effect on me that my parents feared television would have. Watching the exact image that a million or more other people are watching, I become a mass-man. I tend to involve myself in the insular world within the display rather than thinking fresh thoughts that originate from the wide world outside. Brahms and Beethoven liked to start their day with a walk in the woods. I like to interrupt my day with a similar communing with nature. Best of all was to unwind myself at the Botanical Gardens with my Susan. The only problem is that the muse of markets knows when I'm gone. It always makes fantastic moves in the brief time I'm vitalizing myself away from the screen.

Today, I vitalize myself with a library of thousands of old books that I go back to for fresh ideas. In the old days, the authors wrote for a much higher common denominator. I find the old books bracing and invigorating. After reading some old books, distillations of timeless wisdom, I feel I have my hand on a reliable tiller that can help me steer through the ephemera of the modern seas. The old books are like the trunks of trees from which the branches of modern knowledge grow. The only hope for a speculator is to get in touch with the roots because the leaves are as impermanent as a fiddler on the roof. The goods that are changing hands in today's markets may change, but the players show the same reactions—happiness, surprise, anger, disgust, fear, sadness, and contempt—as traders did a thousand years ago.

Drop a Perpendicular

Harvard would have come into my ken merely as a team to bet against in basketball, had it not been for the emphasis it places on scholar-athletes. My first exposure came at high school tennis practice, when a racquet held by one of the kids trying out for the team flew out of his hands and hit my mother in the stomach. Instantaneously, a stampede of awkward youths, all wearing thick tortoise-shell-framed eyeglasses, scrambled toward her. Two of them tripped over each other, and the whole gang fell in a heap about her. All of us were vying for spots on the team. The flying racquet, however, was typical of the skill and coordination of the aspirants. I was the only one who could hit.

These "klutzes," however, turned out to be mathematical whizzes—five of them were Lincoln's math team stars—and all were seniors. They figured out that the major ingredient for admission to an Ivy League college was a letter in tennis. In those days, Harvard chose a few candidates from all of Brooklyn. All-round students fared best.

I was about as good in math as the boys were in tennis. So, I was very hesitant when they suggested that I try out for the math team. "Don't worry," they said. "Whenever you're in doubt, the answer is likely to be 1, *pi* or *e*. Try to figure out which is more likely and then guess." When I told my dad, who skipped grades six times in elementary school because of his math ability, he added, "If that doesn't work, try dropping a perpendicular to the base."

A beautiful symbiosis: I worked on their tennis, and the team worked on my math. Ultimately, the seniors graduated, with several bound for Harvard, and the best tennis player of the lot off to Johns Hopkins. After they left, I finally competed in city meets.

Eventually, I faced my first solo math test. The first question of the exam was: "Find the sum of $(2 + \sqrt{5})^{1/3} + (2 - \sqrt{5})^{1/3}$."

In the three minutes allocated for this problem, there was no way I could simplify the equation. But I remembered the math mavens' admonition. The answer didn't seem to be *pi* or *e*. A light flashed. This was the first question of the year. Also, the first expression was bigger than the second, so the answer couldn't be zero. I guessed 1 and that turned out to be correct.

The second question was: "Calculate the formula for the angle trisector of the unequal angle of an isosceles triangle in terms of its equal and unequal sides."

Again I was stumped. But I remembered my dad's advice and dropped a perpendicular to the base. Then, the problem became quite elementary through application of the Pythagorean theorem and the formula for the area of a triangle. At least that's how I remember it. But "the older we get . . ." The least I can do for my readers is to take the medicine I recommend for everyone else to support my "memories" and "brilliances." In this vein, I ran the problem past my partner, Steve Wisdom, a math major at Harvard. Next I knew, we had three Ph.D.s burning the midnight oil in an attempt to solve it. The moral—kids can be quite as good at logical and geometric thinking as adults.

I did not become much of a math wizard, but I gained enduring values from my experiences on the team, and I never forgot the simple offshoot of "1, *pi*, or *e*."

SIMPLE GUESSES

It's amazing how often simple guesses tend to be accurate. If someone asks about the likely price of a stock at year-end, the best answer is "Unchanged." When a commodity has a big move in the beginning of a week, the best guess for the second half is exactly the opposite. The percentage of the total NYSE issues traded each day that ends unchanged, about 2 percent, is much higher than would be predicted by chance. Also excessive is the number of times the Dow or any commodity closes at exactly the same price as on the previous day. One good way to take advantage of this phenomenon is to sell at the money option straddles—the sale of a call and a put at the current price. Much more often than you would expect, you'll make money on both sides because the expiration will close at exactly the same price you sold it.

I was delighted to find that the stock market shares my love of unchanged issues. In a typical trading day, 3,100 issues are traded on the NYSE and about 725, or 25 percent, show no change for the day. About 10 days a year, the percentage of unchanged issues falls to a low of 15 percent or less. From 1928 to the present, these have been highly bearish events, with the expected change in the S&P over the next 12 months coming to about 10 percentage points below the norm. On the other hand, on the 10 or so days a year when the percentage of unchanged stocks is 30 percent or more, the market is bullish over the next 12 months, going up about 10 percentage points a year above the norm. Differences between means at least as large as these would occur by chance variation alone on fewer than 1 in 5,000 occasions.[5] Apparently, a real phenomenon is at work.

I attribute this result to the tendency for "Mr. Market," the muse of profits, to love days when there are many unchanged issues. On these days, market makers are almost guaranteed a profit because when the public buys above yesterday's close, the market makers sell; and when the public sells below yesterday's close, the market makers buy. If the percentage of stocks closing unchanged is low, the professional traders who copper the public are not happy with the market and they tend to move it lower. The hoary Wall Street rule, "Never sell a quiet market," appears to be upheld for stocks at least. I tried to generalize by applying it to other markets. My empirical conclusion is that it applies to fixed-income markets. In foreign currency trading, many similar returns to previous prices occur. The range in New York is often the exact range of Tokyo and Europe. When futures start ticking wildly in New York, cash quotes invariably shrug it off. Sometimes, the gravitational pull of unchanged is so strong that a whole day of trading passes in which it's impossible to buy the dollar at its low and sell the dollar at its high while copping a profit. It's fat city for the dealers on these days.

I am often stunned when I read books on markets or investments to find that the authors forego even rudimentary attempts to quantify their common sense observations. Examples from two of the most popular investment books illustrate my point. In one, a group of Midwestern ladies recommend buying stocks that make sweets because they all enjoy them. In the other, a retired fund manager quit when he realized he hadn't read any books in the last two years. Worse yet to him, he had not even attended a football game. He recommends purchasing retailing stocks of companies that his daughters patronize at the malls. What grade would a high school chemistry student get for such observation? It would seem that we put more care and research into purchasing a computer or VCR than a stock.

I was very fortunate, while at Harvard, to make the acquaintance of M. F. M. Osborne, a high-energy physicist at the U.S. Naval Research Laboratory. He had more creativity and insight in his left pinkie than all the quants, Ph.D.s in finance, and professors of finance I've met in 35 years (with the notable exception of one or two of my friends). Someday, he will be recognized as the Pasteur of the field of efficient markets and rational expectations. His paper, "Brownian Motion in the Stock Market" (*Operations Research*, vol. 7, no. 2 [March-April, 1959] Cambridge, MA: MIT Press), is still the seminal and most useful paper ever written in this field. He developed it one day while looking into a river and thinking about the migratory behavior of salmon. He noticed the similarity of their behavior to stock prices. He then stepped back and approached the subject of the randomness of stock prices from the standpoint of an observer from

Mars. He saw the moves in stock prices as "a close analogy with the ensemble of coordinates of a large number of molecules."

I contacted him, and we formed a collaboration that lasted for 15 years. Along the way, we took on the most revered economists and game-theorists. "Someone's going to eat crow raw, squawking and fully feathered," Osborne liked to say, "and something tells me it ain't going to be me." He was always right. By the time Osborne got through with Oskar Morgenstern—who knew about as much about stock prices as I knew about nonlinear hat matrixes—Morgenstern was begging for mercy.

Out of respect for Osborne, my readers, and myself, I hereby report the following test of whether small changes in the stock market are bullish, as previously indicated, or random:

Moves in S&P Following Small and Large Daily Changes*

Greater Than	Less Than	Description of Move	Number of Observations	Average Change Next Day	Average Change Next Five Days
0	1.00	Small rise	354	.16	.37
−1.00	0	Small decline	347	−.10	.83
1.00	2.00	Medium rise	260	.09	.13
−2.00	−1.00	Medium decline	227	.12	.70
2.00	3.00	Large rise	185	−.14	.18
−3.00	−2.00	Large decline	140	.27	.67
3.00	4.00	Substantial rise	118	.09	.42
−4.00	−3.00	Substantial decline	102	−.13	.17
4.00	5.00	Steep rise	80	−.04	.63
−5.00	−4.00	Steep decline	60	.68	2.75
5.00	∞	Tremendous rise	106	.76	1.05
−∞	−5.00	Tremendous decline	92	.37	2.91

*Average close-to-close changes in S&P Futures Contract from 1988–1996, following daily changes of indicated magnitude. A change of 1.00 point in the S&P corresponds to eight points in the DJIA.

The results kill two birds with one stone. After a small positive change of less than 1.00 point, the average move the next day is close to zero. The same is true for small negative changes. Furthermore, there are many more large positive changes than large negative changes. This refutes the idea that declines are more violent than rises. There is one interesting byproduct. After the 92 occasions when the S&P registered a daily decline of more than 5.00 points, the average change five days later was 2.91 points. The total move in the five days following such events was a staggering 267.72 points. However, given the high volatility following large daily moves and the substantial upward drift of stocks during the period, results as extreme as this would occur about one in ten occasions from chance variation alone.

ACCEPTED AT HARVARD

I followed in the footsteps of the other athlete-mathematicians in my class and applied to Harvard. The college counselor did everything she could to discourage me from applying, and my principal wrote a letter telling the school "Not." But it worked against them. Some of the interviewers had also been blackballed as they rose through the ranks. Add to this the information that my hobby was stock picking, which meant that someday I might be a big contributor.

I was one of only a handful of students accepted at Harvard from Brooklyn's public schools. Considering that, at my school, a student with a 1,300-point Board score would graduate 250th in the class and that there were many other schools with equal academic excellence in Brooklyn, I'd have to call my acceptance a miracle.

Harvard had been educating for 320 years when I entered in 1961, so it was nothing if not resilient. We both bent a little and, I believe, ended up stronger for the association.

Unlike the students today, members of the class of 1964 were expected to fend for themselves. Neither "Mother Harvard" nor the "Old Boy Network" was available to pay the bills. I needed to work; a policeman's salary of $10,000 a year didn't go very far in those days, even when tuition and board were only $3,000 a year.

THE POSTMAN DOESN'T RING

My first job at Harvard was in the Student Post Office. My duties were to sort the mail and run the route, delivering and picking up mail at departments on the north side of the campus. The pay was the munificent sum of $1.80 an hour.

After a few days on the job, I graduated to full-time mail carrier. My boss, an elderly Irishman, was from the old school. His shoes were polished to a gleaming luster and his tie choked his neck in a perfect knot. As I left for a delivery one day in typical Boston fall weather—freezing rain with winds in the 50-mph range—he gave me some sharp advice. "Keep your head on your shoulders and whatever you do, don't miss picking up the mail at the Watson Laboratory in Biology. Since that professor won that Nobel Prize he thinks he owns the world and when the mail isn't picked up twice a day, he calls to complain. Last time we missed him I found myself apologizing to a vice president of the corporation."

I have never been good at following directions. In retrospect, I see I was not well-suited to a career in mail carrying. My ideal career would probably be as the women's squash coach at a large university or director of research at a flavoring laboratory. But I badly needed the money from that mail job. Perhaps I was distracted by the rain, the secretary, or my studies, but I forgot the pickup at Jim Watson's lab. My boss's dismissal of me was abrupt.

"You're fired. How they let incompetents like you into Harvard, I'll never know. You don't even have enough sense to get out of the rain and go inside to pick up at the one place I told you over and over again not to forget. Get out of here and never come back."

Some 30 years later, through the kind offices of our mutual friends— the Sultan of Speculation and my good friend, Dr. Bo—Jim Watson and I have become reacquainted. I asked him if he had made the call to get me fired. "Not at all. I was too busy doing my research, running two laboratories, and hunting for a wife among my students and assistants."

SKATING THROUGH HARVARD

Anyone who enters Harvard is almost guaranteed to graduate. Of the entering class, 99 percent grab degrees at Harvard versus 95 percent among the rest of the Ivy League schools. Considering that a good part of the student body hardly attends more than half of their classes, and most of the others are so totally committed to their extracurricular activities that they have no time for reading the assigned course work, let alone any outside readings, the graduation rate is amazingly high.

Without these odds in my favor, I certainly wouldn't have made it to the finish line. I have always had a reluctance to attend large lectures. Most of the popular undergrad courses were taught by eminent professors in halls where 500 to 1,000 were in attendance, if not wakeful. The smells in a lecture hall turn me off. I can't breathe well with all that carbon dioxide circulating back into the air. On a more mundane level, I find it difficult to stay awake after strenuous exercise. Besides, I like the idea of feedback. To me, the ideal educational forum has always been a walk with some erudite professor while we talked about areas of common concern. In this day of copiers and desktop publishing, there is no reason for lectures to be delivered without feedback. Notes could be prepared in advance and distributed to students. This would force the instructor to be concise and accurate because the printed word demands more presentational logic and rigor than does the spoken lecture. I have found that only at prestigious universities and cabals do the lecturers balk at providing written notes.

Many of the professors seemed to have been sweet-talked into teaching an undergraduate course, or coerced at a departmental meeting as a punishment for some transgression. Others were over-the-hill pioneers, former stars desperately clinging to contributions they had made in the prewar days. Finally, there were the political types, former ambassadors and officeholders who obviously were out of touch with the recent technical developments in the field. Not yet having mastered the art of blindfold checkers play, the only way I could stay awake in class was to buy an advance copy of the Suffolk Downs Racing Form and handicap the races.

Cultivate Our Gardens

In the concluding paragraph of *Candide*, Pangloss reviews the events of Candide's life, both tragic and triumphant:

> All events are linked up in this best of all possible worlds; for, if you had not been expelled from the noble castle, by hard kicks in your backside for love of Miss Cunegonde, if you had not been clapped into the Inquisition, if you had not wandered about America on foot, if you had not stuck your sword in the Baron, if you had not lost all your sheep from the land of Eldorado, you would not be eating candied citrons and pistachios here.
> "'Tis well said," replied Candide, "but we must cultivate our gardens."[6]

My solution to the problem of passing my courses at Harvard set in motion a chain of events that enabled me to make a living, thereby laying the base for my life as a speculator.

At Harvard's introductory courses, the weekly routine involved one lecture from an eminent professor and two discussions taught by foreign graduate students. The "section men," as they were called, were obviously leading a hand-to-mouth existence with salaries that barely covered their living expenses. Their reward was the certification that a teaching position and a degree from Harvard would provide when they entered the job market. Even then, Eastern Illinois University favored assistant professors who had put in stints as adjunct assistant professors at Harvard.

Harvard in those days spun a masterly web to maintain low salaries among its teaching assistants ("Think of the prestige"). The university also prohibited the hiring of any of its own graduate students until they had taught at some other school for at least five years. This policy was already famous for having lost Paul Samuelson, the famed Nobel mathematical economist who popularized Keynesian economics in his bestselling textbooks of the 1960s. Samuelson is the quintessential Harvard economist. No matter the amount or role of greater government spending and higher taxes, he's likely to be there with an academic justification. Samuelson's work for his doctorate at Harvard in 1948, exploring the mathematics of the interacting effects of consumption and investment on output, is still considered one of the most important expositions in economics. It still wasn't sufficient to break the Harvard taboo against hiring its own.

But there was a quid pro quo for the graduate students. In exchange for low wages and smooth passage, the grad students were graded on a very high curve. The average grade, A−, was considered quite good in the days before grade inflation, egalitarian marking, and numerous pass/fail courses—all of which have made most grade-point averages as meaningful as the lines on a stock chart.

I quickly realized that if I confined myself to graduate courses as an undergraduate, and even consistently copped the worst grade in the class, I could likely pull a B+. And this would more than compensate for my bad study habits.

I was so successful at this approach that, when the time came for a final class ranking of all the economics majors at Harvard, I came in second out of 150. My technique did not pass unnoticed. Anytime an undergraduate of apparently limited intellectual ability took on a curriculum of mainly graduate courses, he or she was said to be "Niederhoffering the curriculum."

Years later, I ran into Professor Wassily Leontief, founder of input-output economics, at a Soros party. He had been my professor in graduate-level Microeconomics 201, where I had received a B+, the worst grade in the class. The professor's basic idea, that there are fixed technological relations between the output of an economy and the inputs of labor and capital necessary to produce them, makes about as much sense as the Russian notion that some genius master-planners in Washington are responsible for all the wonderful variety of goods on American supermarket shelves. I am told that Leontief has renounced the theory, as well as he should. Nevertheless, Leontief had one of the sharpest minds I have ever encountered. He remembered me after 25 years and said, "Here you are Niederhoffering the commodity markets by picking up the detritus of Soros's trades, just as you did in my classes." On occasions I reach the sweet spot in trading by buying at the low, selling at the high, exiting just in time. "You Niederhoffered them," my partners call out.

NIEDERHOFFERING THE GUTS

As with all virtuous acts, one good one led to another. In the process of "Niederhoffering the guts," I came upon the solution to the problem of financial survival. During my first week at Harvard, I noticed a throng of raucous, broad-waisted, thick-shouldered scholars, easily twice my weight, walking closely behind a thin, bespectacled, blond-haired gentleman. The loud group, most of whom I recognized as members of the football team, followed the delicate-looking fellow into a classroom. I asked one of the football players what was going on.

"You know, on the football team we spend about four hours a day practicing and, unlike you Anglophile squash players, we take bodily abuse while we're practicing. By the end of the session, we're really tired. The last thing we have time for is to work our butts off in some pre-med course. Well, the guy we're following is Tommy Terman, a master at finding gut courses. His father taught at Harvard and developed one of the standard intelligence tests. He left money to all his kids based on their grade averages. Terman's on the bridge team and has to travel a lot, so he applies all his intelligence and experience at the beginning of each term, finding the easiest classes. We football players follow him so we can enroll in them as well."

Apparently, this is a tradition that smart undergraduates have followed spontaneously since. Steve Wisdom graduated from Harvard some 20 years after me. He reports: "Will, the pro hockey player, was famous in my day for leading us to the guts. Just as the june bug means that water is near, when Will was in a class we knew that good grades would flow freely. He became so famous for his efforts in this regard that the school newspaper gave him the moniker 'Melonhead.'"

On one occasion, Steve was rather concerned because he had not attended any classes or read the assigned books in an important economics class. However, his fear turned to reassurance when he saw Will entering the halls of Sanders to take the final exam with him. Steve evidently had numerous such experiences because he received no more than one or two grades lower than an "A" in his tenure at Harvard.

HOW TO "NIEDERHOFFER" A CLASS

Nowadays, the art of "Niederhoffering" course work has become virtually institutionalized. Adam Robinson is undoubtedly the master at using contrary thinking to get good grades. Adam is a cofounder of the *Princeton Review*, and his books on how to improve test scores by determining the agenda of the test designers sell more than half a million copies a year.

Adam and my brother Roy, who is also a grand master in this area, have put together a summary checklist on how to get by in course work. Since all speculators—or their kids—have to take courses and tests at some time, I offer the list:

1. Always take a major course in its off-time. Your competitors will be those who either flunked it previously or aren't serious about it.

2. Whenever you are unprepared in class, speak out early so you will be less likely to be called on regarding the assigned material. If you aren't prepared for a particular question on an exam, write your own and answer it.

3. Never take a course with a male instructor when attractive females are sitting in the front row (and vice versa). A related principle is that teachers grade students of the opposite sex more leniently than those of the same sex. Because professors of both sexes grade males

more strictly than females, males should try to conceal their gender on papers and tests as much as possible, and females should make their gender obvious.

4. Try to enroll in courses that are experiencing declining enrollment. The professor will be grading high to keep the course alive.

5. Avoid courses taught by graduate student assistants who seem to be trying to engage you or others romantically.

6. Visit during the professor's office hours as frequently as possible. It will be harder for a professor who knows you well to grade you harshly, especially if item 3 or item 5 pertains.

7. Start slowly in courses that are known to be graded according to improvement during the term; incorporate systematic errors in your initial papers and exams so that you will be seen to improve during the course of the semester.

8. Always recapitulate the professor's favorite catch phrases and clichés on your papers and exams.

9. Study the past exams. Previous questions and themes are often repeated.

I am fortunate to have among my friends a wide array of wise birds and shrewd articles who apply timeless speculative principles in the trenches of their own day-to-day jobs. No one fits this bill better than Adam Robinson, who has become the chief tutor to my family—no small job, with six of my kids constantly taking standardized tests, from the APGAR at birth to the Graduate Record Exam.

When I asked the tutor-in-chief for some late-breaking tips on standardized testing, he came up with the following:

- The questions on most multiple-choice standardized tests are arranged roughly according to the number of students who answer them correctly—allowing a casebook example of contrarian thinking. The answers to earlier (easy) questions will be obvious to the crowd (most students); the answers to those later in a section will always be unexpected. In other words, the answers to earlier questions will always be attractive, and those later in each section will always be unattractive. Put yet another way, the answers to early questions will "seem right," and the answers to later questions will "seem wrong."

- On standardized tests, the old truism "When in doubt, go with your first hunch" is a prescription for failure. The later questions in each section are those that most students get wrong; that is, these are precisely the questions where the crowd's first hunch must be incorrect.

- Standardized tests, like eye charts and high-jump contests, are designed to find one's level of incompetence. Unless a perfect score is your goal, attempting all questions is asking for trouble. Be willing to punt on a few time-consuming questions to save time for the rest. Spend the most time per question on neither the easiest questions nor the hardest, but on the "medium" ones instead.

These rules also apply to trading organized markets. Go with the market at the beginning of a period, but against the market near the close. When in doubt, stay out. Spend your time trading liquid markets about which you have superior insight. Forget about the ones that 200 analysts follow.

During my years at Harvard, the members of the football team were clearly the early pioneers in Niederhoffering. In all fairness to their native intelligence, I found that of 20 individuals listed on the football team in my 25th reunion book, there were five who turned out to be doctors, several professors, six attorneys, and six CEOs. Those who wish to suceed in business might be well-advised to buy shares in their Ivy League football friends at an early age.

PAYING MY WAY

I found it advisable to make Terman's acquaintance at once. We struck a friendship and the next thing I knew I had traded squash lessons for his money-making techniques.

Terman had taken an off-campus apartment. Out of that domicile he ran a weekly poker game to which many of his friends from the football team were invited. Terman suggested I join the game.

I took his advice. Even then, I was patient. I waited the whole length of the marathon 24-hour games we played, until I was dealt the one perfect low hand. By then, my more impatient opponents were so desperate that they were likely to call any big bet just so they could stand a chance of getting even. The urge to get even is one of the most costly habits a speculator can have. Unfortunately, it is also one of the most common. It's especially prevalent after a disastrous move. That's why, when prices make a huge move against and then manage to come back, they're ready to go much further. At least, that's what I always say when I lose 10 percent or 20 percent of my chips in a few days, wait until I'm close to even, and then exit my position in relief—only to see a continued move that would have garnered me a huge profit unfold in the seconds after I'm out. Some speculator could make a fortune by quantifying this tendency.

BLOWING IN THE WIND

Ever since my racquetball hustling days, I have been a master at using obstructions to advantage, such as when the hustling involved playing while sitting in a chair, or using a garbage can cover as my racquet. The consistent 30-mile-an-hour winds that blew off the Charles River into the tennis court at Soldiers Field adjacent to Harvard were quite normal to me. That wind originates from the south, from the more stable air of the Atlantic.

On the Harvard tennis court, my strategy was supreme. I became number one on the freshman tennis team by playing challenge matches on windy days only. The number-two man, Frank Ripley, who subsequently became the U.S. 40-and-over doubles champion, was by far my superior in ability. But I still managed to emerge victorious in all our test matches.

Tennis courts are generally laid out north–south so players don't have to look directly into the sun on a lob or a serve. When I played on the north side of the court, I belted the ball with all my might to my opponent's backhand, knowing the wind would blow it in. When I played on the south side, I applied a spin serve to get the ball in, and the wind would add another 30 miles an hour in velocity to make the shot an ace.

I frequently take account of asymmetry in my trading. Rises tend to occur in the shape of a U. After a day or two of normal rises, there is frequently ample time to join the major move. But declines generally have the shape of an inverted V. They occur spontaneously and quickly, and they usually offer no opportunity to climb on board. Thus, selling into strength becomes *de rigueur*. But I'm ever vigilant of my obligation not to unload so-called plausible common sense without appropriate quantification. I have tested this phenomenon a million ways and I find no support for it whatsoever. Another speculative canard bites the dust.

The wind and rain were so prevalent at Harvard that the fall tennis season lasted only a few days. The tennis players then turned their attention to squash. In typical Niederhoffer fashion, I tried to get a leg up on the game by reading some books on squash. The books pictured great champions such as F. D. Amr Bey taking full backswings with the racquet extended behind and two feet over the head. I copied such strokes and follow-throughs.

Barnaby caught me practicing those swings. He took one look at my books and told me I was a fish out of water. I was studying books about the softball game rather than American hardball, the game I was playing. Jack recommended a short backswing with the racquet cocked close to the shoulder, thereby allowing for accuracy, surprise, and deception.

The same principle holds true for most fast-paced activities like speculation. The best opportunities often emerge out of the clear blue and are gone again in an instant. If you need to go through lengthy preparation just to get your order in, you might as well not bother competing with the faster moving competitors.

After confiscating my books, Jack took me into his office and gave me a little lecture. "Remember, you're not playing golf on an immovable course. You're playing against an opponent. In isolation, a shot that hugs the left-side wall and then takes its bounce one inch from the back wall might be great. But not if your opponent's plastered against the exact spot on the left back corner."

"Use your head and your . . . fanny." (When Jack said "fanny," he scanned the room to make sure no ladies' sensibilities would be offended by such a dreadful word.)

Jack explained the strategy best in *Winning Squash Racquets:*

> Well I once beat an opponent in the finals of the Boston Open by using my fanny. I had been winning with shots. He had then bottled me up in the backhand corner, playing with relentless depth. But I had answered with three-wall nicks. The score was in my favor 2–1, 13–11. How could I get two more points? I decided to hit six shots down the wall with him, then at the first good opportunity fake (but not make) a three-wall nick. We hit the six in an even exchange of good depth, and his ball came off the back wall at about the eighth exchange. I prepared in the usual manner, but just before I played I twisted my fanny around about two or three inches extra as though I had a secret plan to hit the sidewall. He took off forward for the suspected three-waller and my straight drive, the ninth in a row, a foot over the tin, was a clean ace. I needed one more. We exchanged again; again after five or six, I made my tiny fanny move, and hit a hard wide crosscourt. It was an ordinary depth shot but it was an ace for the match. Brainwashing can really pay off even against the best in top play.[7]

I often think of Jack's fanny when I watch the moves of a commodity trying to set the players up on the wrong side. Six days in a row, the market opens down and closes down on the day. The seventh day, it twists its fanny and goes up. Players jump in to buy, thinking it's going to keep rising. Instead, it ends the day down. The next time, it twists its fanny and opens up again, but this time it has a very wide day and closes limit up.

I must have learned the right time to zig and zag in racquet sports. In his inscription to my copy of his book *Winning Squash,* undoubtedly the best book on the game, Jack wrote: "Of all those I taught . . . you never leaned on me to do *your* part as well as mine. Every concept I gave you was seized, made your own, adapted to yourself, and often expanded beyond what I gave you—as in the case of 'self-practice' which you made into a whole genre by itself, with great benefits."

My "self-practice" was consistent and persistent and has extended into my speculative career, where I often sit and stare at the screen for 72 hours straight, waiting for that perfect wave.

LESE MAJESTE

All who seek to raise money should learn from Harvard. Within a week of moving to a new address, the alumnus is certain to receive his first piece of mail from the Harvard fund or one of its affiliates. Twice a year, one of your roommates from undergraduate days will call with a personal appeal for funds. "How's your daughter, Galt, now aged . . . 20 and your significant other [glances at screen] . . . Susan." At Harvard, Bill Gates, Warren Buffett, or George Soros, or the sheik of the Emirates, or another 7 of the top 10 wealthiest, will doubtless soon be, or presently are, or will have recently finished delivering a prestigious invited lecture series. Once a year comes an invitation to dine with the President at the local Harvard Club or the school itself, concerning that urgent new project of "wiring the University."

No wonder the endowment of $7 billion far exceeds that of any other institution in the world.

Such a cornucopia does, on occasion, leave the apparatus a bit fat. In the early 1990s, Harvard needed a new squash facility. They approached me to donate the full $6 million required for 20 composite courts. (Only at Harvard could the cost be $300,000 a court.) I figured that this would be a nice project to attach Artie's name to. I gave them an opening bid of $1 million. The assistant fund-raiser looked at me with the same disdain that the *maître d'* at a fancy restaurant gives me when I bring my friend the hobo. He walked out of my office a minute or two later without even making a counteroffer.

HARVARD INVESTMENTS

The air of invincible arrogance that permeates Harvard extends to the management of its investment portfolio.

In an astonishing piece with reverberations in every chapter of this book, *Forbes* reports that the Harvard endowment fund is one of the world's largest users of derivative securities.[8] As of June 30, 1995, the face value of its outstanding positions totaled $35.3 billion. On a net equity of $7.7 billion, the leverage is far greater than George Soros'. One of the strategies Harvard favors is to buy undervalued securities and sell short comparable overvalued securities within the same industry. For example, on June 30, 1995, it was long Sears Roebuck and short J. C. Penney. Bets on this pairs strategy accounted for about $1 billion of Harvard's short position in stocks. Counters on the street take account of Harvard's shorting. They buy the securities Harvard needs to borrow, and then "pressure Harvard to deliver them," presumably by jacking up the borrowing rate.

In discussing how such strategies reduce risk, Harvard Management Director Jay Light, a professor at the Business School, states that, if the market falls, "We will get hammered less than, no more than, and almost surely less than we would have been hammered had we just had [our portfolio] in domestic equities." "None of the above," I want to answer across the 31-year gulf that separates me from my Harvard days. "What does it mean?" Susan asked me when I read it to her before rolling on the floor in a belly laugh.

Harvard should be reminded of the Duke of Queensbery, who bet his colleagues in the early 1700s that he could deliver a message 50 miles within an hour without the aid of horses, carrier pigeons, etc. His noble colleagues lept at the bet. After some big bets, the Duke enclosed the message in a cricket ball which 24 expert cricketeers passed the full length in under one hour. I only hope that the friction in getting in and out of pairs as well as those pesky takeovers (which have a way of emerging subsequent to a short's seeming overvaluation) don't prevent the Harvard cricketeers from reaching their milestone.

CHAPTER 6

---•◦•---

The Nature of Games

As a kid, I played Monopoly with the twist I invented of buying and selling shares in the bank. Well, today, I do the same.

George Soros,
explaining his success to a friend

VICKIE SAWYER

"Vickie!"

No answer.

"Vickie!"

No answer.

"Where is that darned boy, anyway? Yoo-hoo, Vickie!"

A slight noise. She whips about in time to grab me by the shirt. If I hadn't stopped to hook a piece of watermelon, I would have made it outdoors.

"Where do you think you're going, young man? You have to practice the piano. You promised me you would do it last night."

"But, Mom, it's summer. I promise to practice after I play some games outside."

"I've heard that before. Now you just march—."

"Mom! Look behind you!"

She whirls around. The split second is all I need to dash out the door and down the block.

I know, of course, that I'm going to have lots of explaining to do when my dad gets home, but this day, as on countless days of my youth, I found a Saturday spent playing street games worth bargaining for.

With my baseball cards in my jacket, a pink ball in my pants pocket, a piece of watermelon in one fist and a bag of marbles in the other, I set out to make the most of a summer day. And so began my education on the sidewalks of Brighton on the shore of the Atlantic.

"Schlomo," I yell as I skip the 20 steps from the alley where I live to Brighton 10th Court. "I'll flip you to see who goes first in stoop ball.

Heads I win." Thirty years before I officially become a speculator, I implore luck to be a lady. Tacitus reports that the ancient Germans often staked their liberty on the fall of the dice. "He who lost submitted to servitude and patiently permitted himself to be bound and sold in the market. . . . The Saxons, Danes and Normans were similarly addicted." But if I lose this time, my only punishment will be to stand with my ass facing Schlomo while he hurls a few fast ones at it.

STOOP BALL

Stoop ball is played on the outside stairs of apartment buildings. The object is to catch the ball before it bounces twice. You score 5 for a catch on 1 bounce, 10 for a catch on a fly, and 100 for a fly caught off the edge. First to reach 1,000 points wins. All things considered, there's about the same balance of skill and chance in this game as in many other pursuits. The most important strategy for all such games involves finding the proper balance between aggression and caution.

The Sharpe ratio has been developed in the speculation game to measure the reward per unit of risk. It is closely monitored by all the rating services and their customers in deciding who the best players are. The stoop ball players monitored the average score-per-edge ratio with similar intensity.

In the Brighton variant of stoop ball, timidity rules. And perhaps that's how I became the master of the errorless games I play in squash and aspire to in speculation, where I frequently rack up 12 consecutive winning months before reaping the whirlwind of a disastrous decline. There's always an uncertainty as to those unusual moves that I sometimes forget. In stoop ball, the uncertainty was chaotic. A billionth of an inch led to two vastly different outcomes. If I hit the back edge of the stoop, the ball is liable to hit the door and the owner might come out and throw hot water at us. If the ball sails after hitting the middle edge, it might land across the street in the Cohens' fenced yard, where a Doberman is waiting to tear our pants. To let the punishment fit the crime, the rule is that whoever last touched the ball before it landed in the Doberman's yard has to retrieve it.

Most kids choose to go for it. If we hedge too much by throwing for the low stoop, our opponent is likely to reach 1,000 first. If it was an old one, that ball could sting the posterior. And I don't have a dime for a new pink ball. More important, I certainly don't want the girl I like from the big apartment house on the corner, to see my humiliation.

This time, I'm grinding, going for the low edge so I'm safe from the dog. But the owner of the apartment building is trying to get some rest. He works evenings as a garbage man. Chaos strikes. A Tsunami, as bears like to call sudden rises, occurs. The ball hits the owner's door and he calls the police. They threaten to lock us up if we don't stop playing. As the police arrive, I feel like I do whenever the authorities show up for a surprise audit. "Hi, Officer, thanks for coming. I didn't mean to do it." The ass-kissingness of it all. But that episode with the police will be great training for my future gaming and speculating. The officer's look of smug content-edness at his power over us is the same as that of a government agent who hold our lives in their palm. He grins as we sweat and abjectly apologize.

DISASTER LIES IN THE MIDDLE

"Blondie, grab a stick," I'm being addressed. "We're choosing sides for monkey in the middle." In monkey in the middle, two kids on two bases play catch while the "monkey" in the middle tries to intercept the ball.

The great bulk of money invested in risky transactions is funneled through middlemen. In my industry, the middlemen are called asset allo-cators and trading managers. The fees they charge, 2 percent to 4 percent of assets per year, relieve the customer of making the ultimate decision. The experience and investigatory expertise of the middlemen certify that the ultimate managers meet the standard. They will choose the advisor with the best performance. But after the extraordinary fees these advisors will charge, plus the middleman's fee, what's left?

Humans like the comfort of a herd in choosing risky investments. If presented with the opportunity to trade in the major stock holdings of ag-gressive mutual funds, nine out of ten would choose to short the stock rather than buy it. Who needs a company with no earnings valued by the market at ten million times the number of PhDs on the payroll? But the diversity of the fund's holding, and the certification of the fund's size, rating, and past performance removes the perceived risk of the "invest-ment." A corresponding desire to stay in the middle afflicts most specula-tors, myself included, in their order placement. I am too frightened to buy something at the market when it goes straight down, and too frightened to sell it when it goes straight up. But after it has retraced a good part of the move, I'm all too ready. I often compromise by leaving a limit order in below the market when some market is crashing. That's probably worst of all. Half the time I get filled, I can count on an immediate drubbing as trend followers and other dynamic hedgers jump in. On those occasions when I don't get filled, a fantastic rise is in the cards.

Galton learned about the herdlike or slavish tendencies of humans from his travels with oxen in Africa. The oxen all rushed into enclosures during the evening. The main problem in using them to carry packs was the diffi-culty of finding one to lead. If one ox was separated from the herd, it ex-hibited agony until it found the herd and plunged back into the middle. This, if nothing else, provided comfort for the herdsmen: they knew that the entire herd was safe if but one ox was sighted.

Galton concludes that "an incapability of relying on oneself and faith in others are precisely the conditions that compel brutes to live in herds." He applies this to people: "The vast majority of persons have a natural tendency to shrink from the responsibility of standing and acting alone. They exalt the *vox populi* even when they know it to be the utterance of a mob of nobodies."

A bovine nature explains much of human herding activities. It's every bit as bad in speculating as in choosing lottery numbers, where concentration on picking popular numbers is likely to lead to a shared purse if the miracle occurs.

Trading from the middle is the surest ticket to disaster. You're with the public in the middle, bound to play the losing role. When you choose the middle, you have the comfort of the pack, the security of company, and a feeling of value. You're also more than likely to pick the short stick.

The captain holds the toothpicks in his hand so they all look the same size, but one has been broken. I pick the one in the middle. Sure enough, it is the short stick. And I'm "it."

The game reminds me now of the games I see played around refundings, when the big operators throw billions in bonds between themselves, with small fries like me in the middle. One of the big government dealers made a practice of inventing fictitious bids to corner the market during the refundings. On a few occasions, bids were submitted in my firm's name without my knowledge. The unkindest cut was that I lost heavily on a short position that got squeezed, in part, because bids in my own name had been used to corner the market against me. The relevant regulatory agencies showed up at our door with smug contentedness. I abjectly proved to them that we weren't involved. They departed with a repeated refrain: "You see how fair we are." Artie always waved his hand at me in disgust when I choked up in tennis tournaments, slicing the ball into the middle of the court. "Hit out, go for it," he'd say.

I took my own advice on May 10, 1996, when the expectation was for a 0.5 percent increase in the PPI. I bought heavily on the opening and made a bundle when bonds and stocks both rocketed up 1 percent. I'm always telling my colleagues they're gutless—they don't go for the edge. Faint heart never won fortune or the fair lady.

The penalty for failure to catch the ball during monkey in the middle is "going through the mill." The big kids never liked me and must have used brass knuckles when I was crawling through. My ass was always black-and-blue by the time I got to the end of the gantlet.

When the central banks are intervening against me, I try to wait until someone with inside information about the moves takes profits. Then I strike out to escape my pursuers. Usually, during evenings, there are only three major gantlets to evade: the Bank of Japan, the Bank of England, and the Bundesbank.

I was ambushed by central banks on August 15, 1995 when I was short the dollar against the yen. "You can't outgun them, but you can make them fear you," is how the modest former Harvard boss at the U.S. Treasury described the switching they gave me.

As I sat on my position, realizing that this could be the end, I turned to a picture of the *Titanic*. "Tell Susan I played the game out straight to the end," I told my assistant, Lopez, echoing the dying words of Ben Guggenheim to his buddies on the *Titanic* as the foresection of the ship settled in the water. Unlike Guggenheim, who changed from sports clothes into a tuxedo saying, "I wish to perish like a gentleman," I like to wear loose-fitting clothes in such situations, to reduce the tightness and sweating. Had I been on the *Titanic*, I doubtless would have used the final moments (after supervising Susan and my six kids' departure in a lifeboat) to perfect my squash game. The "indestructible" ship had been built with a squash court above the keel. One of the survivors met the squash pro as the ship was going down and, in an English touch, said, "I guess we better cancel the lessons for tomorrow." Other millionaires on the ship, playing an end game, continued holding their cards in the smoking room as the ship sank. The band provided rhythmic accompaniment, playing uplifting songs until the final hymn, "Autumn."

SEIZE THE MOMENT

Next, a little Ringolevio, a form of team hide-and-seek. The seekers wait until the count of 10 while the others hide. When a hider is firmly captured by the other side, "a mere tag is not enough"; he's placed in the den. The captive can be freed if tagged by one of his team. The side that has made the most captures at the end of a half-hour wins.

Monkey, monkey, bottle of beer.
How many monkeys are there here?

At first I'm not chosen. So the picker adds, "One, two, three, out goes he." He's learned to count syllables and adds the last six so I'll be on the opposite side of Evaso, the block bully who delivers killing tackles. It's good to count when you do science or speculation, or when you bear a grudge. But I'm opportunistic. When I see that I'm being set up for some hard tackling, I pretend to limp. The captain's afraid to put my life in jeopardy for fear my Dad will lock them all up if they "total" me again, like they did the first time they broke my nose. I'm following in the footsteps of Artie, who had his nose broken five times playing tackle football games without helmets on the sands of Brighton Beach.

A speculator must always be ready to adapt to the ever-changing environment. I made one of my biggest coups after I learned, during a 1995 dinner with an Indian squash player and derivatives expert, that the office rental price per square foot in Bombay was 10 times the comparable cost in New York. Yet its stock market was valued, relative to earnings, at only half the U.S. levels. Something had to give. I bought the Indian stock market with abandon.

How speculators should look at Ringolevio could fill a book.

> The simplest secret is patience in picking the time to run for the base.
> Never be so clever and smart as to let the other team see your face.
> When you discover that the other side is distracted a lot,
> Free your teammates while the iron is hot.

My strategy isn't working this time. Evaso and three other big boys have me in their sights. I'm only 10 yards ahead. I was slow as molasses then and have lost speed steadily since. But I've always been great at anticipating and evading. There's only one escape route. I duck into an alley, jump over a fence, and slide into the Doberman's doghouse.

I thus replay the escape route of Colter, one of the intrepid frontiersmen who accompanied Lewis and Clark on their expedition. He was caught by Blackfoot Indians in 1808, stripped naked, and given a chance to run for his life from 500 Indians intent on torturing him to death if they caught him. He was able to save his life by running five miles in 25 minutes, killing one of his pursuers, diving into a stream, and then hiding in a beaver lodge. As is well known, these houses are closed on the outside, the only entrance being under water. He didn't have to wait to undress. He emerged beaverlike in the evening and swam to safety.[1]

Colter's pursuers tramped on top of the beaver lodge but did not find him. It was unthinkable for a man to live underwater in a beaver lodge. My pursuers found it equally unthinkable to enter the Doberman's doghouse. Fortunately, for me, that Doberman liked watermelon.

Thirty years later, I was short silver to the tune of a face value of 20 times my equity when the Hunts started bulling the metal up. It closed limit up two days in a row on its way from $10 to $45 an ounce. I found an escape route as small as the beaver lodge by first buying the spot month up $1 on the day and then "switching" out of my shorts by selling the spot and buying the forward. Within a second of my great maneuver, silver had moved from limit up on the day to limit down on the day. A rumor that the Hunts were selling had been planted. I have never been as furious with myself. Yet, if I hadn't covered my short at $11 an ounce, I'm sure that my remains would be in Boot Hill.

CHAINS

Schlomo produces a deck of cards. "Let's play blob-tag. Low card is it!" He shuffles and deals each kid a card. Evaso, with the three of clubs, is it. Each time he tags someone, they link arms and the blob becomes bigger. Like DNA and RNA molecules, the chain stops at four when we're playing with girls. By the time 20 kids are caught, the chain, moving against the shifting, mixing background of uncaught players, looks to me exactly like the diagrams of proteins in most modern biology books. Like all chain games, the strategy is part speed and strength and part working well with your neighbor. But I slow the chain when I'm caught until we can catch Bea, and can get to run with her.

A good speculator builds his position from a single base linked to a long, flexible chain of trades. Here's a hoary old favorite that emerges once or twice a year and is good for a trillion or so of outright trading on each round. The dollar's going to be weak because the government's going to keep interest rates down so jobs will be good when the election comes. The mark will be the chief beneficiary, so let's buy it. Strong markets will create demand for German bonds and stocks. Let's buy some of those also. Pressure will be put on the pound and the lira to keep pace. Sell them and their stock and bond markets. The whole support system might entangle, which will be bad for Mexico. Sell the peso and, while you're at it, sell the Indian global depository receipts short and calls on Telemex on the CBOE.

DNA and RNA, the basic chain molecules of life, are built from four simple units. The Morse code is built on two units. If you add too many separate units to your position, it becomes unwieldy. If the Bundesbank believes the dollar is substantially undervalued and acts to catch you, this move might lead to the chain's breaking at its base. Exploding links in your position can have lethal consequences.

There's an eerie echo of the resultant overextension in Mahlon Hoagland and Burt Dodson's description of the cancer mechanism in their masterful exposition of biology. "Sometimes a cell turns bad. It becomes a sociopath, dividing at will, jostling its neighbors, and taking off for distant parts. This cell-run-amok is a cancer cell."[2] If I had a dollar for each time a nice dollar decline was attributed to a Bundesbank announcement in exactly the same words ("They've gone amok in their press conference"), I'd be a much wealthier man.

Unfortunately, the patterns are always reshuffling and realigning. "Mix it up!" we used to holler at our teammates, meaning they should vary the pattern of play to keep our opponents confused. Mix it up is what the market does. Only the utmost attention to the principle of ever-changing cycles enables you to stay on the mixer.

LADY, I DID IT

Let's play "Lady, I Did It," the leader shouts.

"Picker up," another yells. Faster than Walter Johnson, who could pitch a lamb chop past a wolf, two others shout, "Stone thrower" and "Wiper off." They're safe. But I'm too late. I'm the one who has to ring a lady's doorbell on the second floor of an apartment building. The object of the game is to ring the doorbell, wait for the lady to open the door, yell out, "Lady, I did it," and then run away before she can shut the door to figure out what tragedy lurks. I get up the nerve to do it. A pretty young woman answers. Before I can utter a word, she chants, "Lady, I did it." How deflating. My hopes were so high.

The game's over. I feel the same way when I call a dealer for a quote. Right after "Hello" but before I request "Kindly bid $10 million," the futures tick 20 points against me. At least I get the "hello" in. When your call does get through, the dealers like to put you "in line" to make sure you don't play a trick on them by ringing two bells at the same time.

Jesse Livermore had a similar front-runner to cope with when he secretly gave instructions to a telegraph operator in Florida to sell a line of steel. Some retired commodity speculators from Chicago were able to intercept the message and translate the sound of the Morse code the operator typed.

During the big bull moves, in gold and silver during 1979–1980, many brokers employed a network of spies to alert them when Bunker Hunt's broker got on the elevator to the eighth floor of the World Trade Center, the COMEX headquarters. By the time he arrived on the floor, the ante had invariably been raised by another half a buck, before the Texan could bull it up himself.

HADES OF A NOTE

The team games are over and it's getting late. Already some of the mothers are whistling and hand-signaling for the kids to come back for supper.

One mother yells for Freddie. When he continues his play, she raises her voice and mimes a karate chop.

Twenty-five years later, I stand on the floor of the CBOT. There's madness in the air as always. As I look down at the concentric circles of the pits, I can't help thinking of the nested circles of Dante's Hell:

> Here sighs and wails and shrieks of every sort
> Reverberated in the starless air,
> So that at first it made me weep to hear.
> In divers tongues, in accents horrible,
> With groans of agony and screams of rage,
> In voices weak and shrill, with sounds of blows,
> A ceaseless tumult's everlasting roar
> Seethed round about that timeless blackened air,
> As sand is tossed before the whirlwind's blast.[3]

To convey information and generate commissions amid the lamentations, the clerks use hand signals. Now, all the clerks' hands are scratching their heads in a frantic parody of confusion, much like souls arrived unexpectedly on the banks of Acheron. Jim Balducci, not bald yet, just sold two thousand.

Now they're touching the backs of their necks feverishly. I think of the Souls of the Violent, slapping away the rain of fire. The large sale is from a "Paine in the neck" broker.

Now there's another order for a large hedge fund that is my main competitor. The clerk's hands are moving in the sign of a cross. This one always gives "saintly" fills.

I see a crowd of a thousand brokers suffused with excitement and waving at one man. He might be a demon standing athwart the Lake of Boiling Blood. They circle around him, and he is engulfed like a new sinner in a horde of capering devils. All the clerks move their right arms in right angles above their left arms in long, hard, rhythmic swings. I tremulously draw closer to my guide. "What hideous wickedness are they signaling now?" It turns out to be my broker, "the Butcher's" hand signal, arising from his knack for butchering orders. He has just filled a limit order from my firm and is being mobbed by other brokers entreating him to give them a piece of the action. My other major broker is "Pockets," whose hand signal is the miming of a wallet being displaced from a pocket.

> I turn my face away with bitter tears
> And groan to God with lamentation sore;
> My eyes beseem a fiery slogan there:
> "Abandon hope, whose trades are entered here."

When my mom calls me, she sometimes moves her hands as if playing a sonata on the piano. "Vickie, it's time to practice." Thirty years later, the virtuoso floor broker is Tom Baldwin. When he plays a 1000 lot, the clerks on the floor use the same hand signals to communicate it to the amateurs upstairs. In 1995, I managed money for one of Baldwin's five affiliated firms, but they dropped me after I played a bad piece on the yen during the first movement.

HEY, THAT'S NOT FAIR!

I challenge a new kid on the block to match tossing faces and backs of baseball cards. One player calls out the number of cards and tosses his cards on the sidewalk. The second player has to match the first player's numbers of faces and backs. The other boy, a stranger in the neighborhood, turns out to be a rogue thrower from Kings Highway. He wears a hat and a button shirt. He starts out by winning each of the first seven throws. I discover his secret when I dive down to count his tosses. His last card thrown appears strange. It has been mutated. It has a head on the front and a head on the back. He has separated the layers of laminated cardboard that made up the faces and backs of each card and artfully reglued them together so he has a supply of two-faced and two-backed cards. Near the end of a session, he can toss the appropriate card to create perfect matches every time. When we discover his deceit, we appropriate his cards and beat him up to within an inch of his life. Rogues have become common on and off the trading floor.

In 1992, at the CBOT, a rogue trader disguised with a wig and shades entered the floor. His trick was to complete trades on some large orders, giving up the name of the correct clearing firm if the trades turned out to be winners and giving up an incorrect clearing firm if the trade was a loser. As he sold the bonds short, prices plummeted precipitously. I covered my longs at a huge loss. A second later, the opportunistic boys on the floor discovered he was a rogue. They bought with abandon knowing his clearing firm would have to cover the shorts. When the rogue was sent to jail, the CBOT instituted a high-tech coded photographic identification system for entering the floor.

In recent times, every speculator who has lost big for his firm has been branded a "rogue" by the media. I offer the following gallery of rogue traders:

Rogue Traders

Name	Amount	Instrument	Institution
Nicholas Leeson	$1.4 billion	Nikkei	Barings
Toshihide Iguchi	1.1 billion	T-bonds	Daiwa
Robert Citron	2 billion	Bonds	Orange County
David Askin	500 million	Mortgages	Granite Fund
Metallgesellschaft	1 billion	Crude oil calendar spreads	Metallgesellschaft
Joe Jett	1 billion	Mortgage-backed securities	Kidder Peabody
Juan Pablo Davila	1 billion	Copper	Chilean Government
Victor Gomez	70 million	Mexican peso	Chemical Bank
Jay Goldinger	100 billion	Bonds	Capital Insight
Yasuo Hamanaka	2.6 billion	Copper	Sumitomo

Whenever one of my traders loses big, my partners and I brand him "The Rogue." Unlike the counterparts in my industry, I don't write memos to my clients attributing my recent losses to an unauthorized rogue. I'm afraid they might ask me whether some of my previous winnings were unauthorized also. "No, those *were* authorized, sir."

GOING FOR BROKE

Hungry for legitimate action, I rush to get my Uncle Howie to challenge Harvey, the second best tosser of cards on the block, to a game of Closest to the Wall.

In my childhood, a kid's net worth was measured by the size of his card collection. The kids in my neighborhood and I would sail the Atlantic Ocean for a Jackie Robinson card. In the Brooklyn variant of this universal game, two players sit in the gutter and toss a card toward the wall of an apartment building six feet away. The one whose card lands closest to the wall keeps both cards. I put up my collection of 200 cards, more than 80 percent of my total net worth, to back my uncle. My uncle flips by compressing the card at the back edges between the thumb and forefinger, thereby springing it toward the wall. At first, he is winning. But as the cards get worn, they lose their spring, and the simple backhand toss that Harvey uses is better. The cycles change as they do in markets and games. After about an hour, my uncle has lost all of his cards plus 199 of mine. At that point he wins a throw, giving us two. The winner gets to choose the size of the next throw and he calls out "two." Seeing certain bankruptcy, I start crying. Howie goes on to win back all but 10 of my cards.

We end up close to where we started. The blood circulates to and from the heart, a bird migrates to the south and back, and we end near death similar to our state at birth. "Every biological circuit, whether a sequence of proteins in the act of consuming a sugar molecule or a complex ecosystem exchanging material and energy, exhibits self-correcting tendencies like those of the steam engine."[4]

Afterward, I scold Howie for risking everything in one toss. He tells me, "If you are going to gamble, the only way to do it is *to gamble*. The only person who can grind out a profit is Bookie, because he takes 5 percent off the top, regardless."

I have never forgotten this advice. Often, when I am down and out after some terrible speculation, I'll come right back with another large trade. "You're going right back?" Susan asks. Desperate times call for desperate measures. "I'm going for broke," I always respond (even when I'm scared out of my wits). If it was right for Howie then, it's true today, some 43 years later.

I'm luxuriating in getting my cards back. There's no victory as satisfying as coming back from the grave, and no loss as horrible as giving back what you've won. Psychologists who have studied the tendency call it the endowment effect. Once you own a product, you require much more than the purchase price to induce you to give it back. But when you bought it, you were just on the fence.[5] My clients were really angry with me, in August 1995, after I had made them 150% in the previous 15 months and gave back 20% in one day. But I was their golden-haired boy in March

1996, after I lost 30 percent in one day and ended the month down 5 percent or so.

AN ANIMAL INSTINCT

I liked to play games when I was young, and I find them equally delightful as an adult.

Animals also like to play. Otters will slide down mud banks over and over. Brown bears will roll and somersault down a hill, then climb back up and do it again. Sea otters toss their babies into the air and catch them. Lion cubs play with their mother's tail, learning how to stalk and pounce. Gorillas play tenderly with their cubs. Sea lions toss rocks into the air and fetch them. Half the reason we keep cats is to watch them play: with a string, with a ball, or, unpleasantly (to us), with a mouse.

Like humans, animals seem to have rules. As Johan Huizinga points out in *Homo Ludens*, perhaps the masterwork on the subject of play, "[Young dogs] invite one another to play by a certain ceremoniousness of attitude and gesture. They keep up the rule that you shall not bite, or not bite hard, your brother's ear."[6]

GAME OF LIFE

Like the animals, we learn from play. Why is it that those lessons are the linchpins of success in all subsequent pursuits?

Perhaps I should be stopped from pursuing an answer by Mark Twain's notice at the beginning of *The Adventures of Huckleberry Finn:* "Persons attempting to find a motive in this narrative will be prosecuted; persons attempting to find a moral in it will be banished; persons attempting to find a plot in it will be shot."[7] Yet I fear that those who don't learn the deep lessons of games will die from bankruptcies, so I persist.

Players, and even most academics, recognize that life is a game. In *Games of Life*, Karl Sigmund's takeoff point is that life, just like a game, is often a matter of gambling payoffs and tradeoffs. Games and play help us explore the world and come to grips with it. If you're game, take your cue. In *Simplicity and Complexity, Games of the Intellect*, Slobodkin makes the point that the simplistic nature of games captures an essential element of culture. The gamer's goal is to reach a standard of excellence, which is exactly what's required in life.

As an academic field, the sociology of sports is a goldmine. There is much weighty talk about how, in team games, we relate to others as allies or opponents, just as we do in life. George Simmel, the founder of interpretive sociology, and Norbert Elias, the founder of figurative sociology, write extensively about how games prepare us to take account of the unintended interdependencies that spring from the intentional interactions.

I doubt there's a sport—golf, tennis, karate, fishing—that doesn't have a book or article linking it with the game (or web) of life. John Updike notes: "Golf is life and life is lessons."[8] Peter Bjarkman concludes, with respect to baseball, "There are the life mirroring seasonals and daily cycles of baseball play; the fluctuating pace and repetitive cycles of the long ongoing summer season are the very essence and mirror of our daily human existence."[9]

In baseball, the metaphor is so common it's considered clichéd. *The Encyclopedia of Baseball Quotations*, one of the most enjoyable and instructive books I've ever read, eliminates as "stale" all quotes about the game as "a metaphor for life, earth, all that is sublime, the order of the cosmos." Yes, but what Willie Mays says about the game is too good to omit: "Baseball is a game. Yet it is also business, but what it most truly is is disguised combat. For all its gentility, its almost leisurely pace, baseball is violence under wraps."[10]

Bart Giamatti, President of Yale in the 1980s and baseball commissioner in 1988, may have best captured the haunting nature of games and life. Referring to how he became commissioner, he said, "Dante would have been delighted . . . there are a lot of people who know me who can't understand for the life of them why I would go to work on something as unserious as baseball . . . if they only knew."[11]

Games affect life. Activities as disparate as suicide and retail transactions dip before such major sporting events as the Superbowl and the World Series.

Game-play is great for relieving tension also, they say, unless you get as involved in it as do the opposing forces in many soccer matches in Europe and South America, where players' deaths are common. More frequently, it's the other way around. *The National Enquirer* reports that the Florida customers of a futures broker were arrested for torturing and killing him as punishment for losses he inflicted on them. Like panics, these tragic events are unpredictable, but it appears they are becoming more prevalent. Seven died and hundreds were severely injured in a cricket game in India in 1995, much to my cost as I was long Indian equities.

A chronology of the panic-up and panic-down moves in major futures markets from 1986 to 1996 appears in Table 6-1. Like their lethal counterparts in sports, big moves in currencies are becoming more prevalent. Five of the eight biggest five-day changes in currencies of the past five years occurred in 1995.

SPECULARE

The game of speculation is one of the most popular and pervasive of all games known to humans. It took its name from the *speculare*, who stood at the back of a Roman ship during sea voyages. His job was to find good

Table 6-1. Largest One- and Five-Day Changes in Major Futures Markets, Adjusted for Limit Moves (1986–1996)

	Commodity	Day of Week	Date	Change	Rise	Day of Week	Date	Change	Decline
1 Day	Bonds	Tuesday	Oct. 20, 1987	694	6.9375	Friday	Mar. 8, 1996	−343	−3.4375
	Copper	Wednesday	Nov. 23, 1988	1180	$.1180	Friday	June 14, 1996	−1125	−$.1125
	Crude	Monday	Aug. 6, 1990	356	$3.56	Thursday	Jan. 17, 1991	−1056	−$10.56
	DMark	Thursday	May 25, 1995	216	$.0216	Thursday	May 11, 1995	−229	−$.0229
	Gold	Friday	Sept. 19, 1986	184	$18.4	Thursday	Jan. 17, 1991	−301	−$30.1
	Heating oil	Monday	Jan. 14, 1991	1162	$.1162	Thursday	Jan. 17, 1991	−2964	−$.2964
	Pound	Friday	Oct. 5, 1990	548	$.0548	Wednesday	Sept. 16, 1992	−800	−$.0800
	Silver	Thursday	Sept. 10, 1987	94	$.94	Monday	Apr. 27, 1987	−186	−$1.86
	Soybeans	Thursday	July 14, 1988	645	$.645	Monday	July 18, 1988	−1095	−$1.095
	S&P	Wednesday	Oct. 21, 1987	4200	42.00	Monday	Oct. 19, 1987	−8075	−80.75
	Sugar	Wednesday	Jan. 3, 1990	120	$.0120	Tuesday	July 26, 1988	−241	−$.0241
	Swiss	Thursday	May 25, 1995	334	$.0334	Thursday	May 11, 1995	−341	−$.0341
	Yen	Monday	Feb. 14, 1994	454	$.000454	Thursday	Aug. 19, 1993	−404	−$.000404
5 Day	Bonds	Monday	Oct. 26, 1987	1041	10.04625	Thursday	Apr. 24, 1986	−619	−6.1875
	Copper	Wednesday	Nov. 23, 1988	2660	$.2660	Wednesday	Nov. 16, 1987	−1760	−$.1760
	Crude	Monday	Aug. 6, 1990	784	$7.84	Monday	Jan. 21, 1991	−1020	−$10.20
	DMark	Tuesday	Mar. 7, 1995	470	$.0470	Wednesday	Jan. 15, 1992	−473	−$.0473
	Gold	Friday	Sept. 5, 1986	381	$38.1	Monday	Mar. 26, 1990	−357	−$35.7
	Heating oil	Thursday	Aug. 23, 1990	2078	$.2078	Monday	Oct. 22, 1990	−2740	−$.2740
	Pound	Monday	Oct. 8, 1990	1022	$.1022	Wednesday	Sept. 16, 1992	−1876	−$.1876
	Silver	Friday	Apr. 24, 1987	242	$2.42	Wednesday	May 27, 1987	−204	−$2.04
	Soybeans	Thursday	Aug. 4, 1988	1195	$1.195	Friday	July 22, 1988	−1410	−$1.410
	S&P	Monday	Nov. 2, 1987	3750	37.50	Monday	Oct. 19, 1987	−11010	−110.10
	Sugar	Friday	July 1, 1988	254	$.0254	Tuesday	July 26, 1988	−324	−$.0324
	Swiss	Tuesday	Mar. 7, 1995	711	$.0711	Monday	May 15, 1995	−568	−$.0568
	Yen	Tuesday	Mar. 7, 1995	808	$.000808	Wednesday	Aug. 16, 1995	−702	−$.000702

fishing areas. The game as we play it is as old as history. Joseph, in the Old Testament, noticed a seven-year cycle of good and bad harvests in ancient Egypt. He convinced the Pharaoh to buy or tax away the excess in good years and warehouse it for lean years. He became immensely wealthy and influential because of his shrewd speculations.

Speculation combines chance and skill and includes elements of hunting, deception, cooperation, competition, creativity, rhythm, and physical strength—in short, all the elements of games we played as children. Here is a brief outline of the game:

Object of Game. To make a profit by buying something at a low price and selling it at a high price.

The Board. An organized stock or commodity exchange such as the New York Stock Exchange (NYSE) or the Chicago Board of Trade (CBOT).

Equipment. A phone and money. For advanced players, a rented quote screen or ticker.

The Play. Arrange with a member of the Board to buy and sell while the Board is open. You can do this on credit. Unless you are a member, you lose when you owe a member more than you have available to pay during the required time frame.

Strategy. Be careful to balance potential reward with risk. Most players lose, so if you find yourself part of the herd, chances are you should change your plan. Combine cooperation with colleagues and competition with opponents to gain the limited chips.

Purpose of Play. A popular 19th-century proverb says: "A child doesn't play because he's young. He's young so he can play." Infants are born helpless, but they learn for themselves how to survive in a world of competition and cooperative play. Nature gives us the rudiments for success but relies on play to focus, sharpen, and strengthen them for the vicissitudes we will meet within the game of life.

Indeed, play is so fundamental that the very language we use to describe it has its own syntax. As Huizinga points out:

Does not this mean that the act of playing is of such a peculiar and independent nature as to lie outside the ordinary categories of action? Playing is not doing in the ordinary sense; you do not "do" a game as you "do" or "go" fishing, or hunting, or Morris-dancing, or woodwork—you "play" it.[12]

Play is so basic, so fundamental to human nature, that the roots of culture grow in it: language, myth, ritual. "Now in myth and ritual," Huizinga says, "the great instinctive forces of civilized life have their origin: law and

Table 6–2. The Sixteen Patterns of Life

Biological Pattern	Speculative Pattern
1. Life builds from the bottom up.	Learn about the market-making process.
2. Life assembles itself into chains.	Stocks-currencies-bonds-grains.
3. Life needs an inside and an outside.	The dealers versus the public.
4. Life uses a few themes to generate many variations.	Every day starts with one of the four patterns: up yesterday, up open; up yesterday, down open; down yesterday, up open; down yesterday, down open.
5. Life organizes with information.	Prices provide the information.
6. Life encourages variety by reshuffling information.	Everyday Mr. Market reshuffles his various themes to extract the maximum amount of energy from his opponents.
7. Life creates with mistakes.	Those figures reported today will be revised downward next month.
8. Life occurs in water.	Don't buy stocks when it's snowing.
9. Life runs on sugar.	The public provides the juice.
10. Life works in cycles.	The full moon is inordinately associated with extremes in markets.
11. Life recycles everything it uses.	After they weaken you, the vultures will send your chips back to the dealers and large hedge funds.
12. Life maintains itself by turnover.	The public must have hope, so they return and tell their friends to join.
13. Life tends to optimize rather than maximize.	Speculation is an intricate dance between risk and reward.
14. Life is opportunistic.	Flexibility and alertness will enable you to discover the penicillin or rubber in speculation.
15. Life competes within a cooperative framework.	The dealers need the speculators who need the floor traders. When you lose, be happy you did your job. Just like the 999,999 sperm that don't get to fertilize the egg.
16. Life is interconnected and interdependent.	Only connect the bonds, stocks, currencies, grains, and metals, and you have it made.

order, commerce and profit, craft and art, poetry, wisdom and science. All are rooted in the primeval soil of play."[13]

The game is never easy. The people you play with and against have their own agendas. Sometimes, the only way you can achieve your agenda is by beating theirs. Their goal is to beat you. At other times, cooperation is the key to joint success.

Play is fundamental. It connects us to our humanity, to our culture and history, to the cycles of nature, where everything has its season, and every season returns in due course.

The elements of games—swimming, hunting, fishing, hitting, throwing, running, climbing, hiding, calculating, deceiving, creating, and singing—are fine raw materials for many recipes. Nature has been kind to provide a fine tableau for tasting them: water that's great for swimming; trees and mountains for climbing; stars, sky, sea, and land for creating; and birds and frogs for singing. Life itself is a great dinner made from the same ingredients. The games it seems to prefer combine competition and cooperation, skill and chance, fixed strategies and opportunism, loops and trends. The "pursuit" of making a living requires the same skills in an endlessly varying and constantly shifting proportion. The lawyer is skilled at hunting and fighting, the construction worker at climbing, the actress at emoting, the professor at calculating, the scientist and designer at creating, and the speculator at all of the above.

Hoagland and Dodson list 16 patterns that all life has in common (Table 6-2). I find that the games I played taught me about all of them.

CHAPTER 7

---◆●◆---

Essential Board Games

Before every game say the following: I can defend myself from my opponent, but who will defend me from myself?

Tom Wiswell

CHECKERS IN MY LIFE

Psychological biologists now agree that the earliest memories tend to be the most pleasant and important. My earliest memory is of watching my father play checkers and chess against a kind opponent at a park in Coney Island. Life without board games for me would be like life without love or art. Speculation, without the lessons of board games, would be just as bereft.

The NYSE building at 30 Broad Street in lower Manhattan was fittingly designed with a large room for playing checkers and chess when the markets were quiet. Artie played these games out of love and necessity. During the Depression, board games were the cheapest form of play. In 1944, in Hungary, George Soros whiled away the time spent hiding from the Gestapo by playing chess with his father, Tivadar, for cookies. After Tivadar had won, and eaten all the cookies, they turned their attention to Monopoly™. The vicarious pleasure of building and renting, combining and selling for millions was as close as anyone could get to the real thing those days.

George continued his chess playing in the United States. He likes nothing better than forgetting his positions and philanthropy over a game (or two, if he happens to lose the first). At my first meeting with him, he challenged me to a game. We played and I lost. I took lessons. The lessons didn't help. I just can't improve my game regardless of the amount of study I put into it. But it has helped George. I arranged for Art Bisguier, International Grandmaster, to give George a series of lessons. Sure enough, George has beaten Art twice. I can't beat Art with a rook spot.

150

I think I know why I can't improve in chess. I'm accustomed to seeing the board as a checker board, where the moves are to adjacent black squares. I just can't visualize all the long diagonal and backward moves of the pieces. So often, a speculator accustomed to one frame of reference fails to drop that frame when entering a new arena. For example, buying and holding is great for stocks but a sure ticket to disaster in futures. I had a chance to make this point in a poignant fashion when I was on a panel with the august director of research of a prestigious investment banking firm that has well-oiled Washington connections. "Our research shows that buying the front months in commodities would have led to a 12 percent compounded return right in line with stocks," the director said. "Buying the front month in oil, in fact, would have led to a 100 percent return in just the last 12 months." As the words flew out of his mouth, something about the disdainful look he cast in my direction reminded me of the look that my exalted Wasp squash competitors from Yale used to give me. "As soon as I leave this forum, I'm going to go out and short some oil," I responded. "Apparently you guys have no shame. The last time I heard talk of these front-month strategies, a gargantuan European firm dropped $2 billion or so by encapsulating such advice. I trust you have those realizations—plus the results of Julian Simon's well-publicized bet with Ehrlich that commodities would decline substantially in the '80s—in your calculations."

George and I often play chess together. Each of us could play against much better players, but chess enables us to relive the endless process of struggle and pleasure that is part of our respective family traditions. As we move back and forth, usually with me falling deeper and deeper into trouble, I remember how Artie would make one move after another in checkers, just beyond my ability to defend. True to our respective traditions, I lose almost every game we play, thereby maintaining the paternal nature of the relationship—and my memories of my dad. George and I do not talk when we play, but I could sense the palpable strength he garnered when he drubbed me three straight games on the weekend following the October 19, 1987, crash.

Artie carried his bibles, the *British Guide to Draughts*, and Lasker's *How to Play Chess*, to work. During lunch breaks and dead time in the squad car, he studied strategy and tactics. After work, he'd play checkers at Seaside Park in Coney Island. He eventually concluded that playing board games displaced other fields where he could be more productive. He agreed with Siegbert Tarrasch that, like life without music, life without chess is not worth living, but he felt there should be a limit. He called that period the fallow years. Board games can become all-consuming. And yet, for me, they turned out to provide the ideal base for my life.

Board games differ from life in one significant aspect, however: Board games are zero sum. There is one winner, one loser. Life, however, is frequently win-win. As you deal with your opponent, you hope to come to a conclusion where you both go away better off.

Perhaps the most famous quote connecting board games and life is from T. H. Huxley:

> The chess board is the world, the pieces are the phenomena of the universe, the rules of the game are what we call the laws of Nature. The player on the other side is hidden from us. We know that his play is always fair, just, and patient. But also we know, to our cost, that he never overlooks a mistake or makes the smallest allowance for ignorance.[1]

One of world's most famous speculators, Warren Buffett, personifies Mr. Market as the omniscient player-opponent in an almost identical fashion. Sometimes, Mr. Market will buy your goods at Walmart prices. On other occasions, he will buy from you at Tiffany retail. The question is: Can you take advantage of his dispositions?

I go a little further in classifying my opponents and the type of game we're playing. On each board I play, I view the position of the pieces, particularly the pawns, as closed or open. The closed position is where my pieces are touching against my opponent's and little space exists between our collective pieces. Strategy reigns supreme. Preparing the pawns for a good end-game is essential. The open position is where the pieces are separated and the center is not covered with offensive or defensive pieces. Time is of the essence. Aggressive tactical play carries the day. In the vernacular of world-class chess, Staunton played for closed positions, and Paul Morphy opted for open positions. I've met many players who are very good at playing in closed positions and others who are great open players. The real champion, the one in a billion, can adapt to either kind of position as the board of life changes.

Bobby Fischer's greatness in chess was that he was equally adept at closed and open positions. When the position on the board of life opened up shortly after he won the world championship, he elected to fall back into retirement and the closed positions of a religious sect.

The market in Eurodollars, now the largest in the world, may be viewed as a closed market. To take delivery requires a million dollar minimum. Eurodollars often spend a week moving in just a five point range. Strategic long-term trading is in order. The market in S&P futures or coffee is the closest thing to an open market. Price often moves $3,000 or more per day per contract.

I believe one of the things that makes Soros great is that he can move from one to the other, deftly changing his strategy to extract the maximum number of billions for the balancing, signaling, and expediting that he gracefully but reluctantly performs. During the open positions, à la the British pound devaluation, there he is fully leveraged, ready to hasten the inevitable adjustment that must be made to set the events on the right course and line Quantum's pockets with a few billion. But during the closed positions, where prices move back and forth between bands of intervention, with slight dipsy doodles in one market or the other enforcing homeostatic adjustments, then George manages to grind out a profit each month, patiently playing the closed game of the moment.

Suiting the correct tactics and strategies to each situation may be considered the mystery of life. The major speculations—education, career, romance, marriage, family, residence—can be thought of as different positions with varying mixes of openness and closedness. How well we play them may be thought of as determining our success. Learning from a master board game player or two would seem to be a helpful building block. He doesn't mind a draw in such a position. "Victor, if I can stay close to even when the door is closed, and come in for checkmate when the door is open, I'm delighted."

A CHECKERS MECCA

My first board games were played on the public boards at Seaside Park in Coney Island in 1950. Coney Island was a thriving amusement area in those days. Seaside Park drew hundreds of checkers players daily. They played on outdoor tables with checker boards painted on top, courtesy of the New York City Department of Parks and Recreation. It didn't get much cheaper than that. All you needed to while away the day there was an initial dime to buy a set of 24 pieces.

The park was full of old-timers who had emigrated before World War I. About half of the players hailed from Scotland, Ireland, or Wales, where cold weather and frugal living apparently combined to create the ideal conditions for incubating checker buffs. To this day, whenever I go there, I can't get a game unless I bring my own checkers. The Scotsmen there are too economical to use their own pieces. A checkers set was cheaper than chess. Brooklyn has always been a mecca for checkers. The 25-year Freestyle World Champion, Tom Wiswell, his predecessor, Millard Hopper, and a host of other champions started out at Seaside Park. The tables are still there and are frequented by clientele whose average age is now in the nineties.

My dad would work the 4:00 P.M.-to-midnight police shift, sleep until morning, then play some tennis and walk over to Seaside Park. I came with him one day.

"Hi, Sully. Are you recovered yet?"

"Yes, but from now on, I'm wearing leather pants. They don't burn."

"What happened, Dad? Where was the fire?" I asked.

"Well, Sully is famous for his concentration at the game. Sometimes he takes 30 minutes for one move. One of the guys, as a practical joke, lit a match and placed it by Sully's rear end while he was concentrating on a move. The match burned right through to the skin and singed him before he noticed it. He didn't put it out, either, until he had moved and punched the clock. That's the way you should concentrate, too, if you want to win."

At another table, a stray chess game was going on. "Hey, McCarthy, what are you doing to that coffee?"

"What do you mean?"

"You're stirring your coffee with a bishop, not a stirrer." He was so focused he hadn't noticed.

Bookie liked to play at an adjacent table with a 65-year-old oddsmaker nicknamed "Schoolboy," who had been making book continuously since the eighth grade (the nickname stuck).

One of the players offered to play me a game. Dad encouraged me, and, before I knew it, I was face-to-face with a man with more hair on his face than I had on my head. My dad told me I played him even for the first five moves. A kibitzer leaned over my shoulder and warned, "Kid, you're in a published loss!"

I hear these words often in my speculations today, and it gives me the same cold shudder. The usual board is a trade I make in some market I'm not overly familiar with. Like Soros, I believe in jumping in before I'm fully conversant with the pitfalls. "Invest now, investigate later" is Soros' ukase. Invariably, right after I've delivered a check, a wrinkle occurs that puts me down 10 percent or more in a heartbeat. I just hadn't taken into account this large seller or that temporary discrepancy in the valuation model before I leapt in. When I'm down 20 percent in a week, I break into cold sweats as I realize I'm in a published loss. That's it, I'm gone.

"You see big Scottie over there," Dad said, pointing to a kindly looking but bedraggled man in his forties. "His wife kicked him out of the house and now he sleeps in the park. I don't want that to happen to you."

"What did he do?"

"His wife didn't know he was a confirmed checkers player. Shortly after he got married, he started staying late at Wiswell's Checker Club on 96th Street. His wife would call and he'd say, 'I'll be home right away.' She'd call again and he would tell the secretary to answer, 'Scottie's not here. He left for home.'

"Finally, she couldn't take it any longer. She showed up at the 96th Street club, dodged through the ping-pong players, and reached over to Scottie at the checkers table, knocked all the pieces off the board onto the floor, and proceeded to drag him home in front of all the guys. So, he then began to invite his checkers buddies home to discuss the games.

"They were always muttering moves like 4–8; 23–18; 11–15, et cetera, and writing them down in books, frequently interrupted by calls to experts like Wiswell or Sam Gonotsky for updates from recent play. Well, his wife thought she had married a bookie by mistake and the marriage was over.

"Whatever you do, marry a woman who understands your profession, and don't invite your friends over every evening, either."

As I trust has become abundantly clear by now, I have followed all my father's advice as closely as the Greeks followed the Delphic oracle. While I was courting the future Mrs. Niederhoffer, who not only understood my profession but helped to create it as my assistant, I figured I should expose her to the board games as a litmus test. I took her to the game tables at Washington Square Park, where I had played many games with my father as a boy. I prevailed on Susan to wait while I tried to get a game. Traditionally, veteran checkers players at the park won't play with a stranger because they don't want to waste time on a "patzer." I asked a number of players for a game, but they all refused. Finally, someone said, "Junior will play you."

Junior turned out to be a ragged, stinking, 70-year-old alcoholic who had obviously lived in the park for years. Taking shallow breaths, but feeling very confident, I sat down across from him. As it became apparent that I could actually play, a crowd gathered around to watch. Soon, I saw a chance to take two men for one. I made my move, only to hear a voice from the crowd say, "Ha, ha, ha. He's got you in 'Jacob's Ladder.'" As I watched in consternation, Junior jumped right up a ladder of my men to the king row.

It was good to play checkers again. It was exhilarating to set my mind against another and find myself matched. Still, defeat was painful, so I resolved to better my game. Like my father, who was a formist, I always try to do things in a proper framework.

The "boys" who surrounded us were quick to suggest that if I were serious about improving my checkers, I should take lessons from Tom Wiswell ("The Kid" at 71). He was a 25-year, undefeated World Board Champion when he retired. I sought him out and arranged for weekly lessons. The lessons commenced in 1981 and continued every Tuesday until 1995, in my firm's New York offices.

BOARD MEETING IN PROGRESS

During 15 years of weekly lessons, Wiswell didn't miss a session. Considering that he was 71 when the lessons began, this is quite a testament to his fortitude, as well as to the life-enhancing attribute of a game that has many champions who are in their 80s. Asa Long, a former foreman at a Jones and Laughlin Plant in Cleveland, won the U.S. checkers championship in 1988 at the age of 88. He had first won the title 65 years earlier in 1923, when he was 23.

The routine of Tom's visits was always the same. He arrived about 2:00 P.M. In an endearing Benny Hill-like fashion, Tom took advantage of the privilege that 70-year-old men used to have of making a sexual allusion to a woman without fear of a harassment action. He would greet a female employee with: "If only I had known a girl like you when I was younger . . . but then perhaps I wouldn't have been World Champion for 25 years and written 17 books"; or, "I'd love to play a game with you . . . and we could play checkers also." "Asa, give me a kiss for good luck," he liked to say to my highly competent office manager, a former model in Sweden.

After Tom arranged a private game or two with the more susceptible members of our firm, the serious play would begin. At 3:00 P.M. (EST), the Board of Trade closed and the board games were opened.

No interruptions were tolerated. We had a sign printed, "BOARD MEET-ING IN PROGRESS," and placed it on the door promptly at 3:00 P.M. If the computer bellowed "New low in crude" or "You're tapped out," Wiswell liked to remind us that King John was playing chess when his assistants came to announce that his city, Rouen, was under siege by Philip Augustus. King John dismissed his assistants until he finished his game. "In deference to King John, the least you can do is play the game without interruption until you reach the king row." If a frazzled voice shouted out that the markets were moving strongly against us, Wiswell reminded us of the many kings who received word of their death sentence while playing chess, but who refused to interrupt their game. Percy reports that when the Elector of Saxony received his death sentence while he was playing a game in prison, he commented on the injustice of it all, finished the game with his accustomed brilliance, and expressed all the satisfaction that is commonly felt on gaining such victories.[2]

Checkers master Jules Leopold often joined these sessions. Invariably, a visitor would mutter, "I thought checkers was a kids' game. You mean there are books on it? Are there people who actually make a living at this?" To this, Leopold had a stock reply: "There are five pieces on the board. Black to move and draw. You've got yourself $120 if you can solve this problem in one week." Next, he offers the opponent $100 for a donut if he wins or loses (a loophole can force a draw). So far, no one has claimed either prize.

TOM WISWELL

Tom arrived at each session with a collection of 15 proverbs that related the game of life to the board game. The first part of the lesson consisted of a discussion of how these proverbs applied to current problems in life and markets. Over 15 years, he drafted over 10,000 proverbs. The game would begin with the introductory statement. "Promise me one thing. If I beat you, we're still friends."

The lessons certainly relaxed me and my colleagues after a day on the roller coaster. The nature of the speculation business for people like me is that the markets never close, even after the final bell. Worse yet, the weight of business, which must of necessity be deferred during the day, all piles up.

Occasionally, Wiswell, who finally wrote 20 books, including the best-seller, *Let's Play Checkers*, said of the proverbs, "Study these carefully. I've worked my whole life on them, and many of these apply." On another such occasion, he slipped in, "This will be the last book I ever write, but it will be the best."

Like most people, I'm guilty of undervaluing goods that are abundant. I'm ashamed to say that in the heat of the trading moment and the abundance of more than 10,000 proverbs, I took Tom's efforts for granted. Then, one day, for the first time in 15 years, Tom did not show up for our Tuesday lesson. He called the next day to tell me that he'd been lost on the elevator and couldn't remember which floor we were on. This from a man who the week before could remember the moves from 10,000 separate games. He kept riding back and forth. "Victor, I need your help. You're all I've got left," he kept calling to say over the course of the next few days. I had just suffered my worst trading loss ever, dropping 40 percent in one hour at the lowest point (the yen again). I didn't take care of Tom the way I would have or should have under other circumstances.

Shortly thereafter, he was transferred from his home of 50 years in Brooklyn to the VA old-age home in Queens. Gradually, in his absence, the awareness sank in that I'd been sitting on a goldmine.

Wiswell's pithy thoughts represented the final effort of a great mind—an undefeated World Champion for 25 years in a game played by millions. And, as I trust I've made clear by now, admittedly with a heavy hand, life and speculation are both games also. Once the realization set in, the only question I had to deal with was how to organize and present Wiswell's gems. The prospect of classifying Wiswell's proverbs has been a daunting one for me. Because games are as big as life, the subjects he covers are infinite. My solution to classification has been to divide the proverbs into the usual stages of the game.

First, there are the rules of the game—the technical aspects of the board, the moves, and the rules. Second are the techniques of preparation before the game, and third, the innumerable techniques for winning during the game. I have taken one subset of the winning techniques and created a fourth category—the techniques of deception, which is a subject close to the hearts and wallets of most speculators. Apparently, game players know a lot more about it and take it into account more frequently than speculators do. A fifth set of proverbs illumines what to do after the game. Wiswell no doubt intended his examination of the end game of checkers to extend to his life, or his approaching death, as well. I find some of these proverbs difficult to read because, in retrospect, I realize the finality of what he had in mind. Lastly, many of the proverbs touch not so much on winning techniques, but on the character of a winner. These are the timeless traits that are endemic to any winning pursuit.

I'm confident that anyone who studies these proverbs will soon be walking with the gods, uplifted and improved in all games he or she plays.

Adding commentary to Wiswell's aphorisms is, to me, the equivalent of paraphrasing Shakespeare. I realize that I am no Charles Lamb. I'm not unmindful of the danger when a mere mortal such as myself attempts to transform or summarize the work of an immortal. Those who edited Beethoven and Dickinson have become the goats of history. Perhaps a better endeavor would have been to forgo work on my own book and devote the rest of my life to disseminating Tom's work to the masses in proper form. But I am not without practical experience in connecting games and life and speculation, which was the animus or intent of Tom's proverbs. Brief comments on some personal favorites and on the particular resonances that the proverbs express do not, therefore, seem a misdirected tribute to their author.

RULES OF THE GAME

The pieces talk, teach, and cure. The proverbs start with Wiswell's favorite "moves that disturb your position the least disturb your opponent the most." Pursuits in life involve struggle and competition, opening up your position, getting in over your head, failure to maintain proper defense. Most pursuits cannot be won with isolated assets. Each move forward creates a weakness. To develop or not is the key.

A theme that runs through many of the proverbs is the importance of the lowly and little things: waiting moves, quiet moves, leaving things alone, the correct decision between two choices. How many times have you neglected the little things and ended up in hot water?

Wiswell says that if you want to be certain of your position, you must begin by doubting it. In trading, one must be ever vigilant because everything can happen. When you become too comfortable in a position, that is usually the time to exit. A string of good trades can sometimes lead to inattention to detail and subsequent losses. The markets usually find a way to take down traders at the height of their hubris.

Moves that disturb your position the least disturb your opponent the most.

The pieces do not come alive until two humans sit down and move them around; then the fun begins.

The easiest thing in the world is to learn the checkers moves; the hardest thing is to learn to play them correctly.

In many games, you have just two possible choices: you must make this move or you must make that move. Deciding is what it's all about.

A draw is a win for both players since each succeeded in avoiding defeat.

The clock is your natural enemy, but there is no reason why it cannot become your friend: that only takes discipline, mental agility, developed visualization, and nerves of steel!

To lose is human, to win is divine, to draw is an art.

A tempo is used in a neutral sense: time. A player who takes two moves where the same objective could be gained in one has "lost" a tempo. If a player forces his opponent to incur such a loss of time, he is said to have "gained a tempo."

There are millions of lines of play, but the one that interests you is the position on the board today; and tomorrow it will be a different one—and the next day still another . . . ad infinitum.

Playing the simple game of checkers is a complicated task; playing the complicated game of chess is a simple task.

Some players have no problem with the game's precepts, but they get in trouble when they have to think.

Remember, you are not allowed to have two moves, but you are permitted second thoughts. If you don't take advantage of that right, you're wrong.

The winner of a match is not always determined by who is right . . . but in the end . . . who is left.

In chess a lowly pawn may checkmate the king, and in checkers a common man may defeat a powerful monarch.

Moves that were once thought to draw are now known to lose; and moves that were once thought to win are now known to draw. Play is always in a state of flux.

Don't try to look too far ahead in the opening. Save that for the endgame, when it is much easier to see far ahead.

The losing genie, once let out of the bottle, can't be put back in that easily, if at all.

We all have losing days, drawing days, and winning days; but not every day is a losing day, and not every day is a drawing day, and although we may not like it, not every day is a winning day.

Most of the masters and experts have their own "grapevine" and "spies"; this is how they keep track of the latest play, and "who is who" among the latest crop of promising Bobby Fischers of tomorrow. If the real Bobby Fischer decides to make a comeback, they would be the first to know . . . although that would not be a secret for long.

There are two basic tenets that usually hold true in checkers and chess: 1. Possession, or control, of the center squares is desirable. 2. Side moves are weak for chess; "A Knight on the rim means you'll be trimmed."

A bridge is often the road to victory, or it may save you from defeat. I live near a great bridge, and I always try to have one in my games.

Behind every master there are analysts and players who supplied much fine play, plus coaches and writers who aided them with cooks and acted as sparring partners. Few players, if any, reach the top alone.

Every exchange makes a fundamental difference in the character of your game; therefore every trade should be made with great care regarding a new formation: Be wary about jumping to conclusions!

A move, once made, can never be unmade!

The player who winds up with the most pieces is the winner; but now and then the player who winds up with the least number of men is the winner.

To develop or not to develop, that is the question. In chess, for attacking purposes, a fast pace is desirable. In checkers, however, it is best to avoid the fast lane.

BEFORE THE GAME

The importance of knowing what to do at the beginning is a common theme. Homework, systematic study of old masters, practice, hard work, and good coaching determine the result. Simplicity, humility, temperance, imagination, visualization, and investigation are the key building blocks of a win. And of course, our old theme: losing is great preparation for winning. I won often in squash in the past. Today I occasionally gain an upper hand in speculation. The game is over before it starts because I did my homework.

The opening is the "planning" stage. You should already have a pretty good idea of this part of the game *before* you even sit down to work, especially if you are playing with a clock. When you have studied the opening you are playing as if you have a safety net under you.

I call the old standard openings "clichés" because they were good in the beginning, and have stood the test of time.

The student should concentrate on the weak openings; the strong ones will take care of themselves.

Not all games are lost in the mid- and endgames; many players go astray in the first ten moves.

It isn't only what you know that counts, it's also what you don't know; and don't know that you don't know.

How do you start a manuscript? You can begin by writing down all your games, win, lose, or draw, but especially when you lose. Check your games with the masters' games, and if you win and cannot find the variation in published play, you may have a "cook," and that goes in your special "Cook Book!" Take care of your manuscript and your manuscript will take care of you. If you don't write, you are wrong. Start your special manuscript today, not tomorrow.

The student playing much, suffering much, and studying much: these are the three pillars of learning.

If you wish to play with the masters: become acquainted with their games, their strengths, and their weaknesses, if any. Watch them when they play, and listen when they talk, and read their books before you play them.

Don't play on a heavy meal; a hungry player is a good player.

Some of my best lines of play I have found when I was not especially looking for anything: so always be on the lookout, you never know what golden nuggets you'll come across.

A good coach is worth a hundred kibitzers.

Chart your course well before you play—if you wish to avoid the shoals.

The young Willie Ryan lost regularly to the great Sam Gonotsky and these many defeats were only stepping stones to future greatness.

Some masters seem to lead charmed lives—escaping certain defeat or winning hopeless games; but behind their charmed lives are years of work and study.

You may not have as much knowledge as your opponent, but you do have as much imagination—use it!

The oldest play is brand new if your opponent has not seen it. I've won many more games and matches with old plays than with new.

The search for the right move—while you are playing—is helped by the research you have done before playing.

When you discover good moves on your own, you are apt to remember them longer than the ones you learn by rote. Look in old books. They helped me win several title matches.

The good moves are all there—waiting to be made: all you have to do is sort them out and put your hand on the right pieces and move them to the right squares. Yet some of the greatest masters have made serious mistakes in carrying out this "simple" transaction.

When you invest in a line of play, investigate for information, and for misinformation.

When it comes to playing top games, the champions are workaholics, but it is work they enjoy.

It's fun trying to master a game, as long as you don't expect to succeed.

The good player doesn't memorize by heart, he memorizes by his brain. That way the plays stay with him or her.

In order to play a game today, you should have studied yesterday.

When you need a win, moderation should not be your guide. This is the time when you must do or die!

Before you ever push a piece, 90 percent of the work has already been done. The winner is the player who has done his homework.

In order to win, you've got to set the stage.

Do not try to remember more plays than you can digest. It is better to know less and understand more.

DURING THE GAME

If it was easy to win, there would be more champions. The techniques are simple. The eternal question is how to balance patience and prudence versus going for the home run. Traders often take positions that have no staying power because future events can force them out. One move makes a difference. Perhaps it is ultimately better to do it wrong than not at all.

Time is always marching on. Wiswell has shown many different ways to make it our friend. Speculators' lot would be much happier if they could follow the common board game practice of sitting on their hands and writing a trade down before sending it to the broker. The game of speculation is played against a clock quite similar to the chess clock. The markets are usually open for six hours a day. The goal is to steer between the Scylla and Charybdis of indecision and haste. I believe that Wiswell's advice to hurry the moves but not the thinking probably provides the clearest perspective on the proper route. But beware: you're in the gravest danger when you may appear safest. Beware of brokers bearing gifts or promising 100 percent returns. During the years I played Wiswell, I never once saw him give up a piece by falling into a trap. As he said: "Prepare to resign when you're getting something for free." Buyer beware: Don't let up.

In trading, pulling the trigger on when to trade is just as important as all the preparation and attention to detail that went before. If a trade does not do well at the start, the trader must be disciplined and have what-if scenarios in place for alternate courses of action. As long as the circumstances for making the trade are still in effect, the trader can stay with the position.

Exercise judgment, exercise caution, exercise patience; and, finally, exercise.

Indecision is fatal. It is better to make a wrong decision than build up a habit of indecision.

The slower you move, the faster you'll "arrive."

It takes a good player to know exactly when a win becomes a draw and a draw become a loss.

Force is not the answer.

The difference between victory and defeat is nearly always a single move.

In few games is attention to minutiae so important as it is in chess and checkers.

Never let the fear of striking out get in your way.

No victor depends on chance; instead, skill, science, and study are the winning words.

The wise player can see the handwriting on the wall *before* there is any handwriting on the wall. *That's* looking ahead!

Use your *eyes* when playing a master; use your *ears* when a champion is talking; and finally, be careful which piece you *touch* when playing anyone, good or bad.

Many a draw is lost for the simple reason that you did not ask for it at the right time.

The true art of playing is not only to make the right move at the right time, but to leave unmade the wrong move at the moment of truth.

I seldom use the word "impossible"; you will see just about everything happen on the board if you play long enough.

When a player errs, he faces a hanging judge.

Pieces on the side of the board are the handwriting on the wall.

Against a player who makes only star moves, it is very difficult to score any wins.

In the openings, you must beware of clever transpositions by your wily opponents, or you may lose the same game that you entered by another door.

Good players seldom hover over the board. After you decide on your move, take a firm hold of the piece and move it to the right square. Hovering shows that you are nervous, undecided, and in doubt about your game. That gives your opponent a decided advantage and you may be headed for a fall.

Success in the opening can lead to a weak middle game, and, finally, defeat in the ending.

Don't give up what looks like a hopeless game; instead, give up a piece. It may draw—or win. You should not overlook the chance to go a piece down and get a game up.

DECEPTION

Who can doubt after reviewing the rules that deception is always below the surface. Good players refuse to fall for tainted material traps, ambushes, masquerades, and bluffs. I want to kick myself after going through them for all the times I made an inviting move only to find myself in a horrible trap in my opponent's parlor. Deception is, unfortunately, timeless, ubiquitous, and complete. Don't make a speculative move without taking it into account.

In trading, one's opponent isn't this person or that person, it's the whole market. When the market setup seems perfect, be doubly careful. Some moves that look very weak turn out to be very strong. In trading, sometimes one's best trades are those that exit losses.

Learning how to refuse proffered material that may be tainted is an art; cultivate it.

A gambit may win, lose, or draw, but one thing is certain: it usually adds spice to the game.

No matter how bad your position is, never let your opponent see you sweat.

Every good player practices a little honest larceny; otherwise they could never win a game.

The best trap is the trap your opponent does not see.

Sometimes you have your opponent exactly where he wants you . . . and then it's too late.

When you sacrifice a piece, try to leave ajar the door to draw.

When your opponent allows you to make a very inviting move, remember the story of the spider and the fly.

You are in the greatest danger when your game appears the safest.

Sometimes a game seems to play itself, and all the moves fit right into place—for a brilliant loss.

You may know a trap but fail to recognize it in a new runup: that is known as defeat by masquerade.

I can stand falling into someone else's trap, but to lose by my own play is unbearable.

Having a champion in a loss—and winning it—are two different things. Champions are master escape artists and know many ways to avoid defeat. So beware!

When your opponent offers you a free piece, it might be wise to "just say no"; the price may be too high.

Bluffing may work in poker, but not in checkers, at least not against top players.

Beware of the player who talks a weak game, but plays a strong game. Play the board, not the player.

If a move is inviting, natural, and looks strong, it's a good move or a good trap—and sometimes it takes a good player to tell the difference.

It is always wise to remember that your opponent may be as Machiavellian and scheming as you are.

The trouble with a loss is that it usually looks like a win or a draw.

Smart gamblers never gamble, and when a master sacrifices a piece, you can usually prepare to resign.

When you spy that far-off trap, make certain you will be the victor, not the victim.

The "obvious" move may be the right move to win . . . to draw . . . or to lose.

When you are offered a tainted pawn or piece, remember the old maxim: Let the buyer beware.

Just because a move does not appeal to your aesthetic sense does not mean it is a bad move. That awful looking move may be a draw . . . or a win.

Be careful, the opportunity that is knocking may, in fact, be defeat, cloaked in the guise of victory.

AFTER THE GAME

The sober reflections of Wiswell, all written in his waning years, from age 71 to 85, herald his own end game. Many of the proverbs were written by Wiswell with speculation in mind. It's hilarious at first to see a group of board players analyzing a game after it's over. The postmortum often takes up ten times as much time as the game. If only speculators would spend one-tenth the time analyzing a completed trade that they spend implementing it, they would have a lot fewer losses.

You may make a move without knowing why, but after you've lost the game, the reason will be apparent.

We can play today's draws and anticipate tomorrow's wins, but we shouldn't forget yesterday's losses.

Who has been my toughest opponent? That's easy; it is old man "Father Time." Eventually, he checkmates everyone, and that should come as no surprise. But a great champion like Asa Long, who is nearly ninety, still puts up a great battle.

I've lived my life, I've done my work, now I'll take my hat and go.

As a writer of checker books—I am often alone—but I am never lonely; to write, and compose problems, one must have *solitude*.

When I was a young patzer, I was told by one old-timer: "You are a genius, you have a genius for making ham moves." He was right, but I soon made him a victim.

Defeat is no respector of players; all are vulnerable.

After suffering a disastrous defeat, listen to some good music.

The losing player who says: "I'll look it up tomorrow," very seldom does look it up. Don't put it off; look it up that day and you'll be sure to remember it.

It is never too late to be the champion you always wanted to be; but the days turn into weeks, and the weeks turn into months, and the months turn into years, and before you know it . . . your dreams are gone with the wind.

Wins are where you find them: Don't discard your defeats, recycle them and score wins against your future opponents. Experience is a good teacher. Capablanca went eight years—from 1916 to 1924—without losing a game, and that record was never seriously challenged.

When you lose a game in a hard match, it is difficult—but even a two-game lead can be overcome or tied as I know from experience; you have got to shut the door and fight back.

When you sit down to play a game, you do not *have* to win; or even draw; if you lose with grandeur and style, it can have a positive effect on your future play. In my Webster's dictionary, "lose" is *not* a four-letter word.

You will play some games that are unique; look for them and file each one away in your memory bank. They will be your wins and draws of tomorrow.

If you are playing or watching a good game, and a very fine move is made, write it down immediately; otherwise it will disappear into the thin air.

After a losing session, begin to prepare for your next game, your next match, your next tournament. Every master loses . . . and then comes back to win it all.

After a victory we are all a bit younger; after a loss we are a little bit older; and, after a draw we remain as we were.

When is a loss not a loss? When you have learned something new and important.

After you lose a tough game there is only one thing to do; set them up and start all over again.

After a winning streak, you'll probably lose several games. What goes up must come down.

A good scare may eventually help you to make a good score.

I know players who would rather lose than think; many often do.

You can't always be on top of your game; when some players lose, they are laughing on the outside and crying on the inside. It happens to all of us sooner or later.

I suggest you study your great victories a long time, and then study your great defeats twice as long. You may well learn a great deal more from the latter.

Whenever we win or draw a game, we feel there is no need to study; and after we lose a game we feel it is too late . . . and it is.

Study yesterday's master games today, and they will be your key to the master games of tomorrow. That is what the old masters did.

You may not realize it—but your time could be running out; watch the clock.

A beautiful game is in the eye of the beholder; and that is usually the winner; but a brilliancy is a game that can be admired by the loser, as well as the winner.

There are not too many hard facts concerning analyzed play, only judgments and opinions, subject to change; Doubting Thomases are always tilting at windmills, and winning victories here and there.

Right after you've made a drawing move—you suddenly realize that would have forced a brilliant winning combination! And everyone in the room saw it but you.

Sometimes, when I win a beautiful game, I think I am either a genius or I'm lucky, and I know I'm not a genius.

Remember, after every defeat, no matter how disastrous, you can start a brand new game. After the night, there is a "new beginning."

Optimists are usually good losers because they expect to win the next game; pessimists are usually sore winners because they *know* they are going to lose the next game.

CHARACTER OF A WINNER

I often think of Beethoven, Shakespeare, and Jefferson after reading these pithy aphorisms.

Only those with passion can become masters.

Only the strongest players can swim in the shark-infested waters of the Masters' Seas.

Success does not come all at once; even for masters it comes in stages, separated by years.

You are the architect of your own victories and defeats.

Some players not only go down to defeat, they run halfway to meet it.

Every player needs confidence—with a dash of self-criticism and skepticism.

The good player is the one who knows he will always have a lot to learn.

Those players who do not learn from experience, will not learn at any other school.

In order to win, you should analyze the play, you need to analyze the player, and you must, above all, analyze yourself.

Masters are like generals, it takes an emergency to reveal their genius.

Champions make the best moves in the best order, thereby creating disorder for their opponents.

You cannot claim all the credit for your success in the game; you owe a good deal of it to your many opponents down through the years. They helped to show you how to win, lose, and draw.

You can't expect to be an expert in a short time. You have to play, and learn, as you go along.

The patzer is a player who cannot defeat anyone but himself. We all start out as patzers.

The lucky winner is often the player who sees a brilliant idea two minutes before the loser. You must have quick reflexes on the board.

Now and then a patient player will win, mainly on strength of a single virtue. Don't underrate patience.

Luck and chance have no hiding place on a board. Caprice may be there, but knowledge and finesse are in charge.

Cocksureness is the sign of conceit and the badge of ignorance.

The player who knows how will usually draw, the player who knows why will usually win.

Your intuition may, at times, lead you to the right move, but it won't really help until you find out *why* it works.

Good players give their best in every match, every game, every move.

The player who does not develop a strong memory will not develop into a strong player.

Chess styles are classified according to two general categories: attacking and positional. The attacking player is the romanticist, he goes all out in order to denude the opposing King in the middle game. Pieces and pawns mean nothing. The positional player is the mechanical materialist of Chess.

Use your mind, use your eyes, use your imagination; and you can go as far as they will take you.

It is often the richly talented but lazy player who fails to reach his full potential, while the less gifted, but plodding player, like the tortoise, slowly makes his way up the ladder of success.

It is good to be a strong player; but it is also important to be a fair player.

Many games are won by players who are smart; many games are lost by players who are too smart.

When all is said, superior knowledge is the mightiest weapon of the masters. One does blunder, perhaps must blunder, now and then; but prepared analysis, classical or contemporary, is nonetheless one's chief asset in the larger struggle for the world titles.

There is such a thing as "dumb luck"—pure chance—and what I call "intelligent luck"—hard work. I don't begrudge any player the former, but I'd rely on the latter if I were you.

Great improvements in play are usually found by a player in solitude, and only rarely discovered in crossboard, tournament, or match play.

The master knows exactly the right moment to do nothing.

On the long road to victory, the player who can go that extra mile will probably come up with that extra move that wins the game.

If you have foresight, you will probably win; if you have insight, you will probably draw; if you have hindsight, you will probably lose. And we all win, draw, and lose.

The popular player loses without an alibi, wins with grace, and draws with a smile.

There are players who keep an "open mind" and are ready, when necessary, to change course and improvise, in order to win or draw; then there are others who have a rigid mindset, and plow ahead, regardless of the consequences. The latter philosophy, or lack of philosophy, often leads to defeat.

CHAPTER 8

---·◦·◦·---

Gambling the Vig

When I was young people called me a gambler. As the scale of my operations increased, I became known as a speculator. Now I am called a banker. But I have been doing the same thing all the time.

Ernest Cassel
Banker to Kings

The fate of a stock operator, at the best, is to be avoided and to avoid it is easy.
Wm. Worthington Fowler
Ten Years on Wall Street

I SPECULATE, YOU GAMBLE

Like most parents, Artie would have preferred that his son become a professor rather than a speculator. But when some altercockers got together to shep a little naches from their kids, Artie couldn't resist some kvelling. At one such gathering of retired policemen, an officer remarked that his daughter was a doctor, another that his daughter was a concert pianist, and another that his son was a professor of astrophysics. Artie chimed in that his two sons were speculators. "Oh, you mean, gamblers," came the loud chorus. There's more truth than beauty in that response. When asked the difference, I reply, "I invest, you speculate, they gamble."

The emotions, motivations, economics, sociology, what have you, are part and parcel. Every nonephemeral purchase is made with the hope of a gain against a backdrop of uncertainty and risk. Where are the lines that distinguish gambling, investing, and speculating to be drawn? The activity of a professional card counter in a casino is much closer to investing than is the buy-and-flip strategy of the millions who play hot new stock and bond issues.

The old stock-picker's tale of buying a stock on speculation and then holding it as an investment when the price falls illustrates the infinitesimal difference between the two in practice. No question about it. Despite the excruciating distinctions in all available treatises, the three are first cousins.

171

The main difference between gambling and speculation is that the risk of gambling is created by the "casino" for entertainment, whereas the risk of speculating is inherent, whether the goal is to raise capital, process a commodity, or buy land. The speculator's activities provide for a transference of risk as well as a discovery of the price that balances what's desired against what's available in quantity, quality, and time. The gambler receives entertainment and a prayer of gain in return for his hard-earned dollars.

Regardless of the differences in function or motivation, I know one thing for sure. Gambling suited me for speculation.

CHRONOLOGY

My first lesson in gambling came when I was 11. Gambling was ubiquitous in Brighton. I have not figured out whether the cause was the transient nature of the citizens attracted by the cool breezes, the destabilizing influences of the adjacent amusement area at Coney Island, or the tendency of those who play sports with their hands to self-destruct. All I know is that most good handball players wouldn't play a point unless a dollar was riding on it.

The routine at Brighton Beach began each day with some high-stakes gin rummy games. A crowd of 50 people would stand behind each player as the hands were played. Next, the crowd gravitated to a handball court where big-money games were held. The best money player was Moey Orenstein. A natural rightie, he was so good that to even out the money games, he had to play with his lefty backhand. Depending on the odds, he played while belted down to a chair, or with his legs tied together, or taking his strokes with his feet only, à la soccer, or allowing his opponent the use of three adjacent courts—and spotting his opponents 15 to 20 points out of 21. The stakes varied from $1 a man to the occasional grudge match involving hundreds of dollars.

One day, during a lull in the activity, I was called to play paddles in a big-money match against the current handball champion, George Baskin. Some large bets were placed, and I emerged the victor, 21–14. My backers gave me a pair of sneakers as my reward. When my dad finished the 8:00 A.M. to 4:00 P.M. shift that day, I ran to tell him. "Dad, I just won a big-money game from George Baskin. And look what I got. A new pair of Keds."

"I'm glad I wasn't there," he responded.

"What do you mean? Wouldn't you have enjoyed seeing it?"

He said, "No. It would have been terrible. I would have stopped the game and given you a beating. I don't ever want to see you gamble. The worst thing in the world for me would be if you became a gambler when you grow up. I know a guy, used to be one of my best friends. He has a great mind and a great job. But he got fired for playing card games during lunch. When his boss told him he was canned, he begged him to hold off until after that

The dangerous lure of gambling: "I don't want you to be a gambler. All gamblers die broke" (Artist: Harry Pincus).

day's game. Once I saw him playing two poker games at the same time. He even got into a card game on the train going to his wedding. He got so involved in it he was late for his wedding and his fiancée called it off. Now, of course, he's a bum; that's the inevitable fate of confirmed gamblers. All gamblers die broke and most of them turn into degenerates along the way. I don't want that to happen to you." I've shown this passage to many friends who had gamblers in their families. Invariably, the reaction has been a few minutes' silence, then the comment, "Yes, my father was a gambler also and unfortunately he died broke." Trying to lighten the atmosphere, I add something like, "Well, at least he didn't die a degenerate." After a few seconds comes the doleful response, "I'm afraid he did."

My next lesson was trivial but haunting. Until I went to college, my maternal grandparents (and their son, the great gambler, Uncle Howie) lived in a dwelling adjacent to ours. They rented their basement out to transients who were down and out in their luck. I challenged one of the tenants to a little five-card stud. I busted him. The next evening, when his wife got home, she pushed him through the window, moaning hideously all the while, "You gambled away the rent money." I still hear those words when I'm holding a big losing position and Susan asks whether I'm out yet. "Why not sell half?" she always asks. I am ashamed to say I never do because I'm afraid there will be a big rise right after I sell.

A Fallen Gambler

The closing chapter in my youthful education on gambling was the downfall of my tennis instructor, Jim Noriley, whom I idolized. He had the best ground strokes I have ever seen. Artie would chauffeur me two hours each way to take the lessons. Noriley presided at the Alistair Cooke estate where, in a gesture of noblesse oblige, he was granted free use of a beautiful covered linoleum tennis court in exchange for teaching the Cooke children. Noriley had a classic backhand stroke with a big behind-the-shoulder backswing in the tradition of Don Budge. He had already taught just such a backhand to the two best juniors in the East, Herb Fitzgibbon and Barry Negri. Now it was my turn.

Artie and I sped up the Belt Parkway to get to the lesson on time. When we arrived at the Cooke estate, Noriley greeted us in a state of disquiet. First, he informed us that he had just finished an exhibition game with Don Budge and Jack Kramer and was very tired. Next, he pointed to the chirping birds, visible through the skylight. "Do you hear that? It's going to rain furiously and I have to pick up a good friend at Belmont. We'll have to cancel the lesson."

Artie and I were very familiar with the performance of horses in the mud. We were, perhaps, even more familiar with compulsive gamblers who had degenerated into ghosts of their former selves, sacrificing family and career for the chance to place one last bet on an old friend in the third. My lessons with Noriley were canceled and my dad and I went back to Brooklyn. Ultimately, Noriley lost everything through gambling at the races and other related vices. He ended living a hand-to-mouth existence as a consultant at tennis camps run by his former students.

I'm often reminded of Noriley's downfall when I read in *The National Enquirer* about this or that star's losing streak at Vegas and the fight with his wife that ensued as she tried to pull him away from the table. Throughout history, there are numerous verified stories about princes who lost their fortunes on the throw of a die. My favorite compulsive gambler story is of Count Mazarin who, on his deathbed, lost a toss on who would pay for his funeral, one second before he died.

A Harvard classmate, Andrew Beyer, once was scheduled for a senior final when a sure thing was running at Belmont. Figuring that the odds were much greater that he'd hit a winner at Belmont than he'd pass the exam, he went to Belmont. He has never regretted his decision and is now one of the most respected turf handicappers in the world. You can catch his wisdom in his regular column in the *Washington Post*.

Two Hustler-Speculators at Work

Some 40 years later, on July 2, 1994, through the kind offices of Kevin Brandt at Kidder Peabody, I had the pleasure of playing table tennis against former World Champion Marty Reisman. The locale was the seedy New York Table Tennis Club on West 50th Street at 11th Avenue, where the prostitutes, drug pushers, and other assorted lowlifes outside are thicker than the flies on the walls. Although Marty's cardinal rule is to bet only on himself, he is considered the world's foremost master of hustling in racquet sports. As I have dabbled in that field myself from time to time, I came loaded for bear.

For his warmup, Marty went through his usual *tour de force* of trick shots, including shattering a cigarette standing on its end at the far corner of the table (his killer forehand drive has been clocked at 112 mph), playing a few practice points using the edge of his racquet instead of the face, and playing with his eyeglasses instead of a racquet. When I let fly with my best shot, he turned disdainfully and began to walk away, only to kick up his right heel and return the shot for a winner off the edge of the table.

I started playing lefty to convince him I was even worse than I am. After the game began with the 15-point spot he gave me, I quickly shifted to my right hand and was able to relieve him of a few bucks.

Next, I beat him after receiving a 10-point spot from him, but he had to sit playing in a straight-backed chair. Then, in true Niederhoffer fashion, I put all my winnings on what looked like a sure thing. Marty would spot me 5 points, but he could score only if he hit a book at the end of the table. I realized I was a guaranteed loser after he hit the book on his first 10 serves. I bought out for 99 percent of the bet and ended the day a winner of $1.

Later that evening, Marty recounted a sad story. After earning blood money hustling ping-pong from the age of 13, winning 17 National Championships and a World Championship exhibition match in Japan, and touring with the Harlem Globetrotters for three years, he made a big score by becoming a partner in a Chinese restaurant just a stone's throw away from the West 96th Street Table Tennis Club he ran. He then embarked on a career as a stock promoter and investor. He sought out penny stocks on the high-flying Vancouver and Denver stock exchanges and arranged for his friends to participate in the buying. He started with $4,000 and ran this into a profit of $1.5 million. On his best day, he made a profit of $500,000, and this came on stocks he had bought for 10 cents or less per share. "Where has this been all my life?" he thought.

He was a player, benefiting from the prospects of big contracts with China, sponsorship by the Morgan interests, fund buying by Steinhardt and Soros, possible listing on the AMEX, and patent applications soon to be filed. I had a feeling of *déjà vu*. The story could have come from one of the classics of the previous century, such as *Get Rich Quick Wallingford*.

"But what about commissions on those stocks?" I asked.

"Well, I paid the full commission of 2 or 3 cents a share, and when I bought a stock quoted at 2 cents to 3 cents, I never paid more than the offer. When I got out, I sold at the market." Based on the iron law of house take, I calculated that the vig (the vigorish, or mandatory payment to the dealer) was 100 percent and that, by the end of his foray, the brokers and dealers had all his money, regardless of how astute the greatest hustler in history was at stock picking.

"So how did it end?" I asked.

"Well, let's just say I held on too long. I got reamed in the crash. But all my stock picks initially went up 50 percent. Now I'm a much smaller speculator. But my friends made money; they got out first and of that I'm proud."

"And how did your broker end up?"

"Well, he did just fine. In fact, I figured I paid him more than $1 million in commissions on my initial $4,000 investment." For Marty's peace of mind, I didn't add the bid/asked spread, which I calculated as coming to twice the commissions.

The pervasive gravitational impact of the house take is well illustrated in N. M. Moore Jr.'s autobiographical memoirs of a professional gambler. The story starts when Bo, his illiterate best friend—a man with a philosophy of "Get the money, and get it honest; but if you can't, get the money"—proposes they team up to cheat Cleo, another "friend."

Having no particular fondness toward Cleo, Junior goes along with Bo. The two set up a "peep" at Junior's house, Bo tips Junior to Cleo's hand, Junior wins, and Bo takes 10 percent off the top. Soon, however, Cleo wishes to get back at Junior, and Bo, unknown to Junior, helps Cleo. This goes on five or six times, and Cleo and Junior discover that each time they beat each other it is for less money than they started with originally, and Bo keeps gaining. Bo had been playing the two of them against each other and quite literally taking their money right out from under their noses. Because Bo took his 10 percent every time, he helped Cleo or Junior cheat the other. After five or six times, Cleo and Junior could get only 50 percent of their original money back, and Bo walked away with their original 100 percent.

I sent Marty a copy of the *Crossroader*. He came in smiling the next day with a folder full of all his transactions. "I forgot one thing my father, the bookie, taught me. The house will grind through a sack of gold."

Those of us who have had the misfortune to play in casinos understand an unusual phenomenon. Often, no one at the table walks away a winner. The house take of 2 percent to 5 percent a pot inexorably adds up when 40 hands are played in an hour. The take is so small and the dealers are so adept at diverting chips to the box that most players hardly even see the deposits. Brokers in low-priced stocks and futures are equally adept at taking five times as much from each pot without attracting undue attention. The high variability of the action, especially when dealing with required margins of 5 percent to 10 percent in futures, provides a nice *divertissement* in this regard, as do plenty of free lunches, frequent breathy phone calls from sexy brokers, and the constant barrage of elaborately produced research reports and invitations to professional seminars and roadshows, always replete with the attendant amenities.

Rake versus Ruin—The Vig

The derivatives markets have no compunction about quoting spreads with an implicit house take of 25 percent. A quote of 0.3 percent to 0.4 percent for an at-the-money straddle, with three days until expiration, is standard. One of the biggest dealers routinely quotes a 100 percent markup on such markets. I try to educate the dealers with some comeback like "Please don't put that in writing. If my customers found out I considered such a quote, they would have you and me locked up." If they don't shape up, I close the account and send them a copy of selected pages from the saga of N. M. Moore Jr.

Except for the opening in stocks, there is not a single price at which the public trades in any market. There is a bid price and an asked price. In stocks, the bid/asked spread of $\frac{1}{4}$ on a \$10 stock quoted on NASDAQ comes to 2.5 percent. Not bad, until you realize that with a turnover occurring four times a year, the entire 10 percent a year secular trend that favors stock market investments is erased. A typical bid/asked spread in futures such as silver or soybeans is $\frac{1}{2}$ cent on a \$5 item, which comes to 0.1 percent. For bonds, the most liquid market in the world, the bid/asked is $\frac{1}{32}$ on a \$100 item, or 0.03 percent. These small spreads, plus a comparable amount for commissions, don't look like large hurdles to overcome in isolation; they come to less than $\frac{1}{10}$ of the percentage level for stocks. What an illusion. The bid/asked spread plus commission plus bad execution quickly adds up to a staggering load.

For perspective on why frequent payment of rakes on speculative trades leads to ruin, consider playing the following game with a brokerage house. Each day, you flip a coin. If it comes up heads, you win \$1; if it comes up tails, you lose \$1. But on every toss the broker takes out 20 cents. What are the chances of ending a winner after 200 tosses? The answer: About 1 in 100,000. And the 20 cents a toss is probably an underestimate of the house vig in all but recent years. Commissions ran from \$100 to \$50 not all that long ago. The bid/asked spread on most of the actively traded commodities, such as gold, grains, and stock market futures, comes to \$50 per contract, although it descends to \$32 for the most widely traded bond contract. So the vig per complete round-turn trade in the 1970s and 1980s came to between \$82 and \$100—let's call it \$80—to take account of recent discounted commissions.

Even though futures firms have recently begun to discount their services and commissions to \$15 a round-turn for a member of the public trading five or ten contracts a day, the outcome hasn't significantly changed.

The high vig relative to average variation will gradually grind down the public. But sometimes Mr. Leverage beats Mr. Vig to the punch. Leverage of 50:1, typical of the futures markets, gives the public plenty of chances to face gambler's ruin.

Table 8–1 shows the mean average percentage of moves per day for actively traded contracts in the mid-1990s. Moves of 0.80 percent a day are typical. The average close-to-close move in futures ranges from 0.36 percent in the British pound to 1.42 percent in copper, with a mean of 0.8 percent.

Let's assume that Joe Public, who has a bank roll of $2,000 to lose, puts up $1,000 to control a future with a face value of $50,000 fluctuating $400 per day. The fluctuation as a percentage of bank roll is 400/2,000, or 20 percent. A very small move against Joe—say, three average daily closes in a row, or one daily move of three times the average—is enough to cause a 100 percent loss of margin and 50 percent of the bank roll.

See why gamblers' ruin works to make it almost impossible for the average public speculator to stay in the game, even if he can overcome a 20 percent house take? Bottom line: The public loses to our friends Mr. Vig and Mr. Leverage. In my experience, Mr. Leverage gets the job done 20 percent of the time and Mr. Vig, the other 80 percent.

When I was a young student at Harvard, the entire statistics library consisted of only fifty books on one shelf. Today, Wiley alone publishes 160 books in its probability and applied probability series. In the 1960s,

Table 8–1. Average Daily Price Changes (Close to Close) 1994–1996

	Dollars	Percent of Change (Average Absolute)
Bonds	$ 500	0.47
S&P	1250	0.36
Deutschemark	400	0.21
Swiss franc	550	0.36
Yen	675	0.49
Pound	350	0.36
Gold	140	0.35
Silver	300	1.20
Copper	310	1.42
Crude	220	0.96
Heating oil	269	0.97
Unleaded gas	290	1.12
Soybeans	250	0.60
Corn	125	0.80
Sugar	157	1.24

there was just one book on probability, Wiley's *Introduction to Probability* by William Feller—required reading for anyone with an interest in variations. The section on gambler's ruin left a vivid impression on me.

There was much talk of real-life gamblers brought to ruin by infinitely rich adversaries, and of how increasing stakes led to pronounced changes in the outcome of the game. A key section contrasted protection versus expectation. If people avoided unfair bets, "it would mean the end of all insurance business. For the careful driver who insures against liability obviously plays a game that is technically unfair."

The eerie correspondence to the fundamental problems of speculation—when to go for it based on edge and variability, with how big an initial stake; what stakes; when to stop—was all too clear.

Feller's book is filled with earthy, real-life vignettes. For example, after discussing how speculators with high initial capital can often have a reasonable chance of achieving a small return, but also a small counterbalancing chance of fatal ruin, Feller tells this story:

> A certain man used to visit Monte Carlo year after year and was always successful in recovering the cost of his vacations. He firmly believed in a magic power over chance. Actually his experience is not surprising. Assuming that he started with ten times the ultimate gain, the chances of success in any year are nearly 0.9. The probability of an unbroken sequence of ten successes is about 0.37. Thus continued success is by no means improbable. Moreover, *one* failure would, of course be blamed on an oversight or momentary indisposition.

The classic gambler's ruin problem, which applies to all speculative situations, can be framed this way. A speculator with initial capital of C plays a game with a casino: he wins \$1.00 each play with probability P, or loses \$1.00 with probability Q, which is $1 - P$. The speculator plans to stay in the game until his capital appreciates to A or depreciates to ruin at 0. It can be shown that, in such a game, the speculator's probability of ruin is:

$$\frac{(Q/P)^A - (Q/P)^C}{(Q/P)^A - 1}$$

Plugging numbers into the formula, a speculator who has a 60 percent chance of winning each play, and who starts with \$1.00 and tries to run it to \$10.00, will face a 66.1 percent chance of ruin for the session. Because he has a 33.9 percent chance (100 percent − 66.1 percent) of finishing the session with \$10.00, his expected final bankroll is \$3.39. He started with \$1.00, so he expects to gain \$2.39.

Table 8–2 summarizes the expected gains for a gambling session, given initial capital C and probability P of winning each day. With a 60 percent chance of winning, the size of the bankroll becomes critical. By starting

Table 8-2. A Gambler's Expected Gain

	Capital								
Probability	$1.00	$2.00	$3.00	$4.00	$5.00	$6.00	$7.00	$8.00	$9.00
100%	$9.00	$8.00	$7.00	$6.00	$5.00	$4.00	$3.00	$2.00	$1.00
90%	7.89	7.88	6.99	6.00	5.00	4.00	3.00	2.00	1.00
80%	6.50	7.38	6.84	5.96	4.99	4.00	3.00	2.00	1.00
70%	4.72	6.16	6.21	5.66	4.86	3.94	2.98	1.99	1.00
60%	2.39	3.65	4.16	4.17	3.84	3.28	2.58	1.78	0.91

with $4.00 rather than $1.00, the speculator increases his expected gain from $2.39 to $4.17—an increase akin to the winning edge held by strong, well-funded players in a poker game. Above a $4.00 bankroll, the decreased risk of ruin is more than offset by the diminished benefit of achieving the $10.00 goal. For example, with capital of $9.00, ruin is very rare, but the upside is only $1.00 ($10.00 − $9.00).

This idealized formulation of the gambler's ruin problem demonstrates the tradeoff that arises in practical trading. The speculator wants to bet lightly enough, relative to his capital, to fend off gambler's ruin, but heavily enough to make his desired rate of return. Unfortunately, the real-life speculator doesn't know his true odds of winning on each trade, so he can't look up the optimum betting levels in a table.

When the odds of success are less than 50 percent, the situation changes. Whereas the player with an edge should bet small, trying to grind out a profit, the player with the worst of it is better advised to go for the home run, betting the maximum, because this is the only way he can end up a winner. This explains, in part, why casinos have limits on the stakes that players can use against them, and why the exchanges have established position limits on what the public can hold.

Periodically, when I meet people who have traded actively in the markets, I explain how gambler's ruin, house take, and leverage combine to make the chances of winning negligible. I usually add an empirical nightmare to the mix. Price tends to move inexorably to a ruin point within the trading day, only to bounce right back once the traders get tapped out. I am met with initial skepticism, which gives way to disillusionment and then to anger when the truth of my basic point is realized. "You mean all the time I traded I was just making my broker and his floor trader rich?" my listeners ultimately ask. It's so stunning, they usually don't comment when I say that there is a beautiful harmony in the way they fulfilled their role in the market ecosystem.

Eventually, they go home and gaze balefully at their old brokerage statements. They then come back to me with "Vic, you're right. I feel much better. On my actual trading, I didn't do too badly. The reason I tapped out was the commissions."

One such friend, who lost everything in silver, couldn't take the shocking realization at first. "Yes, I lost, but I kept thinking that if I had sold instead of bought I would have made as much as I lost."

"But Joe, it doesn't matter whether you bought or sold. You were sure to be a loser regardless." When the realization finally seeped in, he went back to farming Christmas trees.

The judicious balancing of (a) initial capital and the size of the speculative position with (b) the extent of the trader's edge and the variability of price, is the central and problematic equation of speculation. How much to bet on each card, without facing too great a risk of ruin, when the house is using four or eight decks, is a key variable that is considered in all the good blackjack books. In poker, adjusting the size of your bets to your stakes, skill, and opponents is so key that it might be considered the fundamental requirement of success.

The tendency of a small edge against on each trade to lead to certain loss in the long term (say, 50 trades or more) is a fundamental law of speculators. Anyone who doesn't pay attention to it is guaranteed to go broke. Conversely, by keeping the number of transactions low and reducing the house take to a minimum, chances of success are increased.

"We've got to have an edge" is how the casinos put it when confronted by counters and other wiseguys. It all makes so much sense in the context of dazzling floor shows, the cheap meals, the fine hotels, and the ubiquitous floor managers ready to comp any gambler with more than $1,000 to play a hand. "Bet you had fun," the signs say as you leave Vegas. But don't expect to win if you play for a large number of rolls. The chance of winning in American roulette—for example, in 10,000 bets where the house take is only 5 percent—is close to zero. Compare that to the chance of winning in a typical options trade, where the house edge normally ranges between 12 percent and 50 percent. Are there any words in the English language that express 10,000 times less than zero?

Expanding the context to life itself, we all face opportunities for gain or loss each day—perhaps attending a school function with the kids, or asking that attractive person out on a date, or choosing a job, or deciding when to retire. To get to that school meeting, you're going to have to drive, and you might get a ticket or, worse, have an accident. That special person might slap you down, sapping your self-confidence. Life can be seen as a series of speculations. To conduct it successfully, you must balance at least six variables: initial capital, commitment size, house edge, variability of play, quitting point, and duration.

THE ROAD TO RICHES IS PAVED WITH BODIES

In a haunting novel about gambling, Dostoyevski's hero reaches his hand out to gain caresses from older seductresses prior to making a series of losing bets at the gambling table. Freud's take on Dostoyevski's antihero is that the "vice" of masturbation is replaced later in life by addiction to gambling. The mixed feelings of passion for playing the game and guilt for being impassioned with the game are the equivalent to a childhood compulsion to masturbate.[1] Edmund Bergler, an American student of Freud, extends this theory to say that gambling replaces the feeling of guilt from a boy's Oedipal longing for his mother. For an adult gambler, losing becomes "self-punishment" for early transgressions. In a desire to rectify these transgressions, the gambler then *wants to lose.*[2]

Something about the aura of concentrated attention focused on the outcome of a spin of a casino wheel brings out the gambler in all but the greatest stoics. The same goes for the flashing prices on the market screen. On occasions when a visiting friend is leaving town early, I sometimes break a personal rule and allow him to stop by during trading hours. Invariably, he will blurt out that he'd like to participate with me in 1 percent of my action for the day.

I frequently run across speculators who seem to be on an inexorable journey to ruin. One of them was a very good friend's brother. After the 1987 crash, he convinced himself that the economy was in a 1929-type scenario. There would be a rally but then a deluge. Whenever stocks began to decline rapidly, he rushed in to sell S&P futures. After he lost heavily on 12 such consecutive trades, decimating his equity by 80 percent, I suggested he limit his risk by buying index puts instead of shorting futures. In the worst case, if the puts should expire worthless, the most he could lose would be the premium he paid, as opposed to the theoretically infinite risk of being short the futures. He tried the puts on six more occasions and experienced another six consecutive losses. Finally, I suggested he take a break from trading. "The market will always be there when you get back, and you'll be able to think much more clearly about the market while you are not involved."

He replied, "I can't get away from the market. Something big might happen while I'm waiting for the big crash. I don't want to be away when it happens."

Having seen many gamblers and speculators in a similar state, I asked him to take his business elsewhere. He hasn't spoken to me since.

After all the horror stories I heard in my youth and saw firsthand as I climbed the ladder of life, I've become risk-averse. Whenever a perilous situation emerges and I start losing, I think back to the gamblers I've seen lose everything. I have a vivid memory of a famous sugar broker on the Coffee, Sugar & Cocoa Exchange who speculated, lost, and committed suicide. His theory was to buy sugar when it fell below 5 cents and to sell it above 8 cents. It worked many times until, in one move, sugar went up to 40 cents a pound, a loss of thirtyfold on margin.

GAMBLING AND SPECULATION

Gambling and speculation are equally effective in sending people to the poorhouse. It's just as easy to atone for guilty feelings about childhood in one as the other.

The dangers of speculation were vividly outlined in an 1870 classic by William Worthington Fowler. It is a good antidote to excessive risk taking and vig paying, which are the two guaranteed ways of going to the poorhouse. Here are some of Fowler's key admonitions:

> These are the men whose sole business is stock speculation. When they have once entered the street, they never leave it except in a pine box or a rosewood case, according to circumstances.
>
> Hear them talk, and you would suppose they lived on hope, rather than on those delicious ragouts and choice wines which Delmonico, or Schedler, or some of the other famed restaurateurs furnish them. Those saddest words of tongue or pen, "it might have been," enter largely into the thoughts and conversation of the thoroughbred speculator. *If* and *but* are the most frequent conjunctions in his vocabulary. His whole life is a series of regrets, and strange to say, these regrets are more often for what he might have made, but did not, than for what he has actually lost.
>
> Gambling in stocks, after following a legitimate business, is like quaffing brandy after sipping claret. When once a man has fairly committed himself to speculation, his imagination soon grows to lend a hideous fascination to the objects of his pursuit. An evil genius seems to hold possession of him. He takes no note of time, save as an interval between his gains and losses; the thrill of the one and the pain of the other, grow duller as the years wear away, until at length he becomes the optimum eater of finance, living in a world peopled by phantoms which haunt his waking hours, and flit through his dreams. The unsubstantial pageant vanishes as the alarm bell of his ruin peals out, and he awakes to the desolation of reality.
>
> The story of the whole shifting tribe of operators is little else than a dreary catalogue of losses—losses, not of money alone, but of health, character, heart and life.
>
> Men come into Wall Street with fortune, credit, reputation, hope, strength unbruised, confidence in their fellow-men unworn; they leave it without money, credit, or reputation; with shattered nerves, a blunted sensibility, a conscience seared, a faith in mankind destroyed, and hopes crushed by a Giant Despair. They lose everywhere, buying stocks, selling stocks; by failures of their brokers, by frauds of their contractors, by panics, by corners, by tricks and stratagems of the market.
>
> The field of speculation was never more dangerous than now. The market is full of stocks *watered* to five times the amount represented eight years since. Men in Wall Street are treading upon the hardly cooled lava crust which covers a financial volcano; an eruption may whelm them any day in one common ruin.[3]

I have these and other passages taped on all my trading walls. The watering of stock in certain initial public offerings today would make even Fowler blush. The values are multiples of sales or Ph.D.s. There are no earnings or debt to water. *Barron's*, *The New York Observer*, and numerous investment newsletters often carry hilarious stories about the public's gullibility in buying such issues. The stories generally end with a short in the stock indicating their ultimate target is zero. Yet comprehensive enumerations on the performance of new issues show that the returns from buying them at the offering are comparable to the 10 percent a year from buying listed stocks. I consider shorting stocks a gamble with an initial house take of 3 percent or more, and 10 percent a year going against me, with a variability of, say, 50 percent a year. No way can I end up a winner in such a gamble. Nor can anyone else, as far as I can see. The number of hedge funds specializing in shorting is constantly diminishing. Periodically, the rating services will summarize their returns as something like -20 percent a year. But this drastically underestimates the loss, because all those that went belly up during the period are taken out of the pot.

Whenever a short position starts going against me, I get a pain in the stomach and I think about my father's admonitions and the suicides. It's just a matter of time until I'm ready to throw in the towel on all my outstanding positions. I regularly buy hundreds of S&P futures contracts and am willing to accept losses of many points. But when I'm short just 20 contracts and it goes even 1 point against me, I feel as though I have severe ulcers and rush for a bottle of Maalox. I believe that my body's response has great survival value. Soros has a similar litmus test. When his back starts to ache, he knows it's time to extricate.

My fear of total loss on shorts has so far prevented me from ruin, but it also has taken me out of some fantastic opportunities for greatness. I had a similar problem in my squash game. My best opponents would say, "Niederhoffer is very consistent. But he never goes for greatness. I still think on my best day I could beat him."

I was able to play an entire match with no errors. I played with a short backswing—as those of us fortunate enough to have been coached by Jack Barnaby learned to do—and with my long legs and arms and uncanny anticipation, I was able to hit back just about anything they could hit to me. This edge, combined with my patented slice and my ability to bury the ball on the side walls while leaving a wide margin over the tin gave me the strategy that was good for a world championship in the game.

But I could never consistently gain the upper hand over Sharif Khan, who frequently made four or five errors in a game—more errors than I would make in an entire match. Sharif won the North American Open five years in a row before I upset him in 1975. His edge over me was in his willingness to take chances, make mistakes, and hit a lot of shots on the rise. My record against Sharif was three won and ten lost. I believe that had I not been so conservative a player I could have beaten him more frequently. But it was the same problem: I was too risk-averse in my playing. I could never go for the home runs.

Likewise, I'll never be a Soros. To go for broke takes the instinct of the professional gambler. As Stanley Druckenmiller, currently the number one trader at Soros's Quantum Fund, puts it, "It takes courage to be a pig."[4]

PROFESSIONAL GAMBLERS

All the great professional gamblers—sooner, later, or often—experience total bankruptcy because of their willingness to throw every last chip on the table, even for the sake of a "spec" or proposition bet. To me, this is like offering to bet someone $100 that the next person to sit down at the bar will order a bourbon and water. But beware, most proposition bettors maneuver the input in advance. Amarillo Slim's bet that his hound dog could retrieve a stone thrown in a pond is typical. To mark the stone, the bettors placed an "x" on it. The previous evening, Slim had placed an "x" on every stone in the pond. Anthony Holden, in *Big Deal: Confessions of a Professional Poker Player*, described the legendary poker game between Johnny Moss and Nick the Greek. The game is said to have lasted five months, and ended with the Greek's legendary line, "Mr. Moss, I have to let you go." The Greek is thought to have lost over $2 million in the game.

Johnny Moss was no exception to the rule that professional gamblers are ever ready to face total ruin. Holden spoke to Moss's wife, Virginia, who told him that their wedding night was spent at the poker table. After a couple of hours, he had lost all his money. But, undaunted, he reached behind him and fumbled around until he found his new bride's left hand. He pulled the engagement ring off her finger and tossed it into the middle of the table. Holden asked Virginia if she had been upset about having her engagement ring staked at the poker table. Sure, she said, but if she hadn't given the ring to him, "Johnny would've ripped mah whole finguh off." Moss won that pot, by the way; 60 years later, Virginia was still wearing the ring.

TITANS TO BE

My poker playing at Harvard was a mixed bag. In my first years, it gave me the stake to pursue my studies in speculation and squash. But in my senior year, I dropped everything in a poker game against better players. Artie had to drive up to Harvard to bail me out. I was embarrassed beyond belief when he insisted on paying my $2,000 loss directly to the kids who won it from me. Now, I want to cry, remembering how I subjected Artie to forking up the family's entire life savings for my stupidity. But I have been good at realizing unintended consequences from my activities. One consequence came later in Chicago, from a game of two-man poker I played with Russ Shields, the brightest student in my Ph.D. class. It turned out to be one of my greatest coups. Russ was from Kansas and had trained as an entrepreneur at an early age by serving as a "go-fer" in his family's gas-drilling business. By 15, he was responsible for the drilling, extraction, maintenance, and transportation for 150 separate wells. To simplify the process, he learned how to sort and store data on IBM laboratory equipment.

Growing up next to the Wichita Country Club, Russ learned that he could play golf with a putter. He was able to hustle his way into spending money by challenging his opponent to a nine-hole game in which he would use only the putter. Russ added to his links winnings with gin rummy. He relied on a combination of card counting and observation of where his opponents placed their cards to give himself an unbeatable edge.

At Cornell, he found it easy to pay his way through school and acquire a nice car by playing poker with his classmates. Unfortunately, the loser in one of Russ's popular dorm-room games (in fact, the loser whose car Russ had accepted as payment, in lieu of a much larger cash debt) was the son of one of the University trustees. When the news of the boy's unfortunate wager filtered back to the Dean, Russ was persuaded to take a leave of absence. He finished up his undergraduate work at the University of Wichita, where nepotism did not interfere with a hustler's *modus operandi*.

When he came to Chicago, Russ deployed his talents at the tabulating machine by keeping up with the collections and reimbursements for a local office of the Blue Cross. Never one to shy away from a challenge, Russ suggested to his employer that he could perform the accounting function for all of the Chicago area's 500,000 subscribers. Along the way, he also worked as assistant director of the National Opinion Research Center at the University of Chicago, where he fine-tuned his computer skills.

Russ was not only an experienced poker and sports hustler, but also an excellent programmer, fluent in the machine language used on all IBM computers. This skill came in handy when Russ fully computerized the subscription and billing procedures of *TIME* Magazine for Time, Inc.

I admired Russ, seeing in him a little of what I might have become had I been raised in Kansas, and we became friends. But with our mutual backgrounds in the school of hard knocks, it was inevitable that we would land in a no-limit game of draw poker.

RUNNING A PLAY

"Russ, I got the nuts. I bet $1,000. How many will you take?"

"I'll take . . . one," Russ answered.

"You will? Good. In that case, I'll stand pat . . . and Russ, I tap you. Put in all your money."

"Vic, I think you got nothing. As the Duke of Wellington, one of my father's heroes, put it when he threw his last division into the fray at the battle of Waterloo, 'In for a penny, in for a pound.' Here's 10 G's. I call you for the whole pot."

"Russ, the Iron Duke never lost a battle. You're no Duke. Iron bars on your window won't save you from what I might have."

"OK, Vic, stop the banter. This is serious business now. What've you got?"

"Three kings."

"Son of a . . . I have aces up. I'll have to give you a note."

"Russ, since this is going to be the last hand of poker you and I ever play, I'll spill the beans. I set you up. You need to read your Yardley.[5] When we played the other day, and Myron was sitting next to me, I deliberately let him see my discards and my busted hand when I stood pat and bluffed you out of a $50 ante while I was holding nothing. I knew Myron hated my guts and would be sure to tell you that I had nothing. So I set you up for the three-of-a-kind call by making Myron the unwitting accessory in my gambit. And I purposely was very unobtrusive and quiet in making my bet, knowing you would expect me to act that way if I was bluffing, because bluffers usually are very blatant for fear you might not notice their bid. Yardley spells the whole thing out, and I followed it to the letter."

After my game with Russ, I decided that poker theory had much more practical value for the speculator than the study of statistical distributions with infinite variances, then in vogue at the university. The random outcomes, with uncertainty about the holdings of competitors; the judicious blending of acceptable risk and return, given the chips; the importance of calculating odds while making judgments about the opposition's psychology; and the Iron Law of House Take—the similarities were glaring. But at least, in poker, millions of real-world scholars had practical experience with the game.

PRIDE GOETH

I conducted such a study at Chicago and, for a beautiful halcyon year or two, thought I was a master. But shortly thereafter, I got into a game well over my head with Oswald Jacoby, a charter member of the pantheon of bridge and poker greats hailing appropriately from Brooklyn. Every pot I played, he tapped me. When I folded, he showed me his worthless hand. On the rare occasions when I called, he wasn't bluffing. He held the lock hand.

I lost 125 percent of my net worth—about $5,000—in one such game and ignominiously had to borrow the money from my wife to pay up. But that loss has been a beacon to me. I stopped gambling then and there. I have never played a game of poker since, nor have I bet on anything else. Whenever I start to lose big in speculation, I think back to Jacoby, to my father bailing me out at Harvard, and to all the broken glass in Brighton. I feel despair and abysmal gloom, the weight of my sins crushing me to the ground. But professional gamblers and speculators seem to be made of some other stuff. The only emotion they feel after a terrible loss seems to be embarrassment. Hence, I will never be a billionaire. I have lost too often to have the necessary guts. I suppose with six private-school tuitions to pay for, along with my unconventional work habits, I might have a hard time starting over again if I shot my whole bolt. I have read hundreds of gambling books, whether from a vicarious desire for self-flagellation or an attempt to improve my speculations, I don't know. Unfortunately, becoming an expert in any field takes much more study and practice than I've devoted to poker. Offering advice without expertise is aggressive ignorance. To update my knowledge of how poker can help the speculator in the modern world, I enlisted the aid of John Conolley, former editor of the New York paper *Street News*, and an accomplished modern poker player. Together, we read dozens of classics from among the 150 books on poker in the Gamblers Book Club reading list. The major precepts of poker, along with the rules for good speculation, are distilled in Table 8–3.

Table 8–3. Some Rules of Poker and Speculation

Poker	Speculation
Never play with scared money.	Trade with a reserve equal to at least five times your required margin.
Never play when you're upset.	Don't trade around funerals or after a fight with your spouse.
Know the risks. It's easily possible for an expert poker player to have a bad run of a year, two years, or even longer. It's also possible for a poor player to have a winning streak.	Take account of gamblers' ruin. Any one trade or series of trades can go badly astray. Make sure your stake and backers are big enough to support it. Before increasing the volatility of your returns, be sure you have the capital to handle the swings.
Don't let a few hours without a hand bother you. Nobody owes you a hand, and you don't *have* to be in the pot. Keep your risk small when you don't have an edge. Increase your risk as your edge increases. Not only will this increase your expectation, it will make your play more opaque.	The market will always be open. Wait for a good opportunity and then barrel in, subject to gamblers' ruin.
Don't play for the lucky draw. Luck is your enemy. Use your skill to overcome the effects of luck.	Don't trade just for the sake of trading.

Table 8–3.   *(Continued)*

Poker	Speculation
Moving from medium-size games to large games increases your risk out of proportion to the stakes, because large games usually have disproportionately high antes, which changes the set of skills you need to win.	Be careful when you trade the Japanese markets. Price-fixing deals there raise the commissions to a considerably higher proportion of the stake, unless you trade an inordinate size, in which case they will get you with the spread.
Consider quitting if you're on a losing streak. If you're running bad, your opponents will lose their fear of you and will use more deception.	Trouble comes in bundles, especially if your counterparts smell blood.
The difference between a good, steady player is high-risk techniques. The steady player won't make the spectacular killings, but he won't go broke as often, either.	Go for the jugular when you have a winning position.
You must give action to get action. Learn and get good at all forms of poker. Be a generalist; get the reputation of someone who gives action even when he doesn't have the best of it. Not only will this get you more action when you do have the best of it, it will also enable you to trim people who aren't familiar with the game or the game structure (ante, limit, blind) they're in.	Let your broker make a decent profit on small trades. Accept some quotes for small amounts even when you know you don't have the edge. This will improve your liquidity and opaqueness for when you will need them.
The reputation of being a sucker is invaluable, unless you're a sucker.	Always downplay your winnings and emphasize your losses.
If you sit down in a game and don't see a sucker—then *you* are the sucker.	Who's going to pay for the yachts and eight-figure bonuses of the successful players?
The average player knows enough to try to deceive, so he always acts strong when he's weak, and vice versa. Thus, a player who slams down his chips strongly is trying to intimidate. A player who pushes his money in like it's breaking his arm is about to show you the Holy City.	Consider reversing big up openings and buying small up openings.

(Continued)

Table 8–3. *(Continued)*

Poker	Speculation
A player who is fiddling with his chips and jiggling his foot up and down is anxious to play. Handle with care—don't bluff.	When the market goes up in the few minutes before an announcement, be careful about selling.
When a player does something unusual, he probably has a strong hand. If he's bluffing, he'll be careful not to vary his patterns.	When a market has its largest open of the last six months (for example, if the yen opens up 150), it is probably not a bluff and therefore should not be reversed.
Never give away information. Don't show hands you don't have to show. Especially don't take the ego trip of showing a strong hand when you're throwing it away. This informs your opponent that you can be pushed off a strong hand, and will invite him to play more aggressively against you. When throwing away a strong hand, do it quickly. Hesitating will make your opponents think you're tight.	Don't share your trading strategies with your friends. Your broker doesn't have to know how smart you are. When you close your position out at a loss, do so with alacrity.
Memorize your hole cards or hold'em hand the first time you look at them, then don't look again. Looking repeatedly shows that the cards aren't memorable. In draw poker, don't sort your cards. This ain't gin.	Don't call your broker for quotes. It gives away your hand.
Play aggressively. You can generally count on betting, rather than checking, as the way to get the most value from a good hand. And remember, it takes a stronger hand to call a raise than to make a raise.	Trade aggressively when you have an edge, even if it's small.
If you think you're a close second in a multiparty pot, raise. Even though the best hand will probably raise back, you will drive out weaker hands and some hands so that you only have one hand to beat.	If you are in a position that you would like to be out of, or that is moving against you, it is often to your advantage to double up. This trade might encourage others to come in with you and allow you to get out at a better price.
On the last round of betting, don't bet just because you think you have the best	Don't stay with a position unless you are willing to stay with it a little

Table 8-3. *(Continued)*

Poker	Speculation
hand. Bet only if you will have the best hand if *called*.	longer than expected, should an adverse move occur in the near term.
Deception is best used against one player in a small or medium pot. In large pots, no one can be bluffed. In multiparty pots, not everyone can be bluffed. And it only takes one to catch you.	Don't try to muscle the market before an *economic announcement*. People are already playing it close to the vest.
Don't use deception against weak players. They won't be able to follow your normal thinking, let alone your devious thinking. Play straightforward, show down the best hand.	When your position is going your way, don't get out while thinking you can get back in at a better level. Your "cleverness" will often prevent you from taking the available profit.
Win big pots right away. *Never* give an opponent a free card in a large pot, and only rarely in a medium pot. When you have a big hand, give free cards in a small pot to get more action.	On those beautiful occasions when an unexpected bonanza comes your way, take your profits at the close.
Concentrate. Don't chatter. Be quiet, look, and listen, whether you're in the hand or on the bank. Learn your opponent's habits.	Don't waste energy emoting or spending time on other pursuits during the trading day.
In loose games, pairs and small two-pairs go down in value. Come hands—four-flushes, outside straights—go up in value because of increased pot odds. Bluffing, even semibluffing (bluffing when you have a possibility of making a good hand) becomes questionable.	During periods of extreme volatility, or prior to a string of economic announcements, trade only if you have very strong reasons and can hold through an initial adverse move.
Some hands play better in a multiparty pot; some play better head-up. Know the difference.	Some trades work better in liquid markets. Others work better when only one market is open. For example, when bonds are open and stocks are closed, you don't have to worry about a crash scenario when bonds drop.
In tight games, bluffing and semibluffing go up in value, but legitimate hands go down in value. Some hands go way down in value.	During periods of calm, trade aggressively if you have a solid edge.

(Continued)

Table 8–3.   *(Continued)*

Poker	Speculation
When drawn out by a player who shouldn't have been in the pot, don't get angry, get happy. Congratulate his nerve. Egg him on. You'll break him.	Congratulate your unworthy competitors after a good month. Urge them to raise more capital. Send them a special gift commemorating their coup. (The escort services are open on weekends.)
Bet vigorously with a *strong hand that looks weak;* your opponent will put you on a bluff. Note that if an opponent bets all the way with a dangerous-looking board (visible cards in stud games), he could be bluffing. If he bets and keeps on betting with an innocuous board, he's probably betting on strength.	When the explicit news announcements are negative for your positions, yet the position goes in your favor anyway, trade aggressively.
The beginner's poker face is the most transparent expression in the world. You must control your emotions before you can control your face. Convince yourself that the cards don't matter; the outcome of any given hand doesn't matter. Right action is all that matters. You'll get your poker face.	If you have an edge in the markets, convince yourself that the outcome of a single trade doesn't matter. What does matter is trading according to your edge.
Minimum depth of thinking in poker:	Minimum depth in markets:
What do I think my opponent has, plus, what does he think I have, plus, what does he think I think he has? This is minimum.	What is the effect of an announcement? What is the expected number? What is the anticipated reaction to "above" or "below" expectations? Has it been discounted or leaked?
In a high-low split, never enter a pot unless you have at least some possibility of winning both high and low. Playing for one way only is like playing with a 50 percent rake-off.	Give yourself more than one way to profit from a trade. For example, get out if its up either the next two days or the next week.
Violate any of these tactical rules if it will accomplish a specific purpose. The usual reason for violating a rule is to convey false information, either about your hand or about your style of play.	Let your counterparts think you're a fish, always losing, but with incredibly deep sources of capital. In that way, they'll be encouraged to reach to take your trades directly rather than marking them up as the broker them to another player.

RUSS RAISES THE STAKES

I was wrong in thinking that my last game with Russ would be the end of poker between us. Shortly after I cleaned him out, Russ dropped out of school to take over the data processing for the Chicago Blue Cross and the credit checking operation of Credit Bureau Systems, the predecessor of Trans Union. He expanded these operations into the Chicago-based SEI Company, a consulting firm with over 300 employees and about $25 million in sales. Along the way, he developed specialized billing software for cellular telephone companies which has become the industry standard, and he won such plum consulting clients as the Social Security System and the CIA.

Russ walked into my office about 20 years after our infamous game. He told me that because I had been the only player who had ever been able to get the better of him at cards, in appreciation of my acumen and sagacity he had come to ask if I would be willing to join him in a business venture that was then at a critical "go-or-no-go" stage. My decision to invest would mean his ability to go forward with a start-up company he had formed for developing a computer-based map of every highway, street, and road in America. The data would be stored and organized using software code Russ had initially developed in the course of his doctoral studies and had fine-tuned on his subsequent consulting assignments.

Russ went on to apply this sorting technology with great success in his consulting company, eventually hitting on an especially exciting field— one that may benefit almost every consumer in America. Much of the average motorist's time is wasted traveling on roundabout routes or simply being lost. Wouldn't it be nice to have a computerized map of streets and highways directing motorists painlessly to their destinations? That would be accessible by keystroke and oral command, enabling a motorist to navigate roads anywhere on the globe using satellite-based transmission of the cartographic data, not unlike the automatic-pilot technology available to airplane pilots?

"So, Vic, are you in for a million?"

"Well, Russ, since you always had my vote as the brightest guy in the school, and now we've seen our classmates go on to wealth and Nobel prizes, I figure if anyone could make a go of this thing it would have to be you. I'll call."

Ten years later, after hundreds of millions of dollars spent on R&D and millions of lines of computer code, the system is working and is widely available throughout the United States and Europe. Almost certainly by 2000, virtually every American car will feature navigational systems exactly along the lines predicted by Russ a decade ago. *Reader's Digest*, in the August 1996 issue, predicts that these computer maps will become as popular as car radios.

Russ and I still have one point of disagreement on this project, however. I claim that Russ was hustling me when he first approached me to invest, as he assured me I would see an immediate return on my money, within a year at most. But he knew I was "in for a penny, in for a pound."

Occasionally, I have the pleasure of using my knowledge of gambling/speculation for direct profit. My friends often come to me with some speculative proposition where the rake and turnover guarantees total loss. I start by explaining, "You're throwing out your money on that one; stay away. I don't recommend our own program, and our rake is just one-quarter of that."

Usually, my friend mumbles something like, "I'm afraid you're party to the 'not-invented-here syndrome.'"

That always gets my dander up. So I shoot back with, "Yes, I am a bad person to ask, because I'm in the industry. I have extensive computer support and other resources available to replicate any quantitative method I thought was any good. If I'm not using this or that rival's method, it's because I have it and found it to be of no value. If, on the other hand, they achieve superior results using a qualitative method, how long can you expect them to keep coming up with superior insights? How long can one person be ahead of the pack, be a man for all seasons?" I then send them a copy of Bacon's "Principle of the Ever-Changing Cycles."

Finally, if the client is still not convinced, I inquire if he would give me the privilege of shorting just one unit of the fund he is considering investing in. In the rare instances when the client takes me up on the offer, I have in each instance made about 50 percent on my humorous wager. When I receive my check, I then call the client and demand that, in addition to the 50 percent, he must send me another check for his interest gained on the $100 or so he didn't have to invest in the fund before I shorted it. This usually enrages the client until I send him back both checks and tell him to forget it.

CHAPTER 9

———·•◦•·———

Horse Racing and Market Cycles

There is no danger of the public ever finding any key to the secret of winning. The crazy gambling urge and speculative hysteria make that a certainty. But if the public play ever did get wise to the facts of life, the principle of ever-changing cycles would move the form away from the public immediately.

Robert Bacon
Secrets of Professional Turf Betting

Whenever I am dry in the mouth and lumpy in the throat; whenever it is hot, glaring August in my spleen; whenever I begin calling on the Lord to smite the next dealer who quotes me a wide market; whenever I find myself educating two or more floor managers in one day about the definition of a limit order and why mine should be filled; whenever I wish to knock the hat off the clerk who tells me "Locals only" to explain why I'm not filled; and especially when I can't lift the phone to make a trade for fear the market will tick 5 percent against me—then I account it high time to close up shop and go to the track. Nothing is so good for the inside of a gambling man as the outside rail of a racetrack. I don't bet the ponies myself, but I love to learn and I love the excitement. I've found that everything about speculation becomes clear at the track, perhaps because of the deep-seated affinity that people have for horses. It was a capital crime in the 19th century to steal a man's horse. A similar penalty might be recommended for speculators who don't steal an occasional day at the races. But leave your credit card at home—certain rogue bond traders currently under indictment often ran up six-figure credit card debts during their excursions to the track.

The thrill of the race. The beauty of the horses and the track. The hurdle of beating those insurmountable odds. The emotions of the bettors as they cheer their horses on. Truly the sport of kings. The favorites that go off at short odds are just like the high-flying nifty-fifty stocks favored by growth mutual funds. Expected earnings performance is above average, profit margins are high, and the government isn't planning to regulate them out of business. The long-shot, high-odds nags are the same as the value stocks, the companies valued at price earnings of 10 or less, the plays available at less than book value that are favored by contrarian investors such as David Dreman and intrinsic value theorists such as the revered Benjamin Graham. The odds-on favorite growth stocks do show winning earnings more often than the long-shot value group. But when those earnings go up, the price payoff is frequently lackluster in the former group and shockingly good in the latter group. On the other side, the occasional disappointing earnings of the growth stocks can cause a disastrous loss when expectations are revised downward. Disappointment among the value stocks frequently leads to a small loss because things were expected to be bad.

The trainers at the race track are like corporate executives. The trainers receive prizes for winning and fees for getting the horses in shape. But that's not enough to pay for college for the kids and summer homes. To facilitate, they maneuver their horses into situations where a winning bet will pay the bills. (In fairness, the most successful trainers who have horses that run for big purses don't bet on races because of the conflict of interest.) Similarly, executives of large companies receive substantial salaries and perks for performing their job. But the real money, the pin money, comes from stock options, stock bonuses, and stock buying and selling at propitious times. The owners of large blocks of stock of publicly traded companies—for example, Dell Computer, Microsoft, Turner Broadcasting, and Wrigley—are like the owners of the horses.

No one doubts that the public must lose at the races in order to pay for the prize money, stable care, employees, and upkeep of the land, building, and equipment. The racetracks' 20 percent take pays expenses. The rest is second nature. The racegoers are investing in the sport of kings, and to participate, to taste that excitement, they pay a contribution on each race through the pari-mutuel pool. If they bet like other members of the public, they know they'll lose.

The public—the bettors in the stands and the patrons of OTB parlors—are the same people who buy NASDAQ stocks at 5 percent bid–asked spreads, trade low-priced stocks at the market on inactive exchanges, and buy leveraged forward contracts or off-priced diamonds over the phone.

The track record of the handicappers in the *Racing Form* is like the track record of the best stock pickers in *Barron's* or the *Wall Street Journal*. And if George Soros is the Sultan of Speculation, Sweep is the King of the Card.

It's only a small stretch to see that the same models apply to markets and racing. An Exchange and its associated brokers have the same relative upkeep as the track. The CBOT and the NYSE are Hollywood Park and Belmont Park. Who pays for it? Not the brokers and dealers who take out $20 billion a year. Not the floor traders, the jockeys of the exchange, or the insiders and large hedge funds. Just you and me.

WATCHING THE WHEELS TURN

The chief reason speculators should go to the track is that the central dynamic that keeps the wheels of commerce turning is more clearly visible at the races than anywhere else. The ebb and flow of the horses are like the moves among the markets. Each market has its own running style: early speed, late closers, "sitting chilly" off the pace. The trading day is the race; different issues maneuver for position, players watch the action feverishly, each 15-minute call gives a clue as to how the race will finish. The difference in opinion—among bettors on a race and between bulls and bears on an Exchange—creates the fray.

Every day, the conditions change and the fate of each horse is directly affected by the others. Just as a horse can get caught in a speed duel, boxed in, or fanned wide, the price of one issue can be suppressed by the performance of another. Bonds will influence stocks, and both can move currencies, which in turn may move crude oil prices. Each part moves another—at racetracks, in the markets, in the environment, in life.

I learned about speculation at the races from a colossus of wisdom. Let me tell you about the man who opened the gate to the wonder world of turf handicapping for me.

BOOKIE AND THE EDUCATION OF A YOUNG GAMBLER

Bookie was born and raised in the shadow of Sheepshead Bay Racetrack in Brooklyn. He earned his first paycheck shoveling manure and performing other menial backstretch duties for a local trainer. Before long, his diligent work was rewarded and he was given the responsibility of placing the trainer's bets. This seems like a mindless task today, but 75 years ago the state of affairs at the track was entirely different. Bookmakers were still permitted to offer a secondary wagering market in direct competition with the racetrack's own pari-mutuel pool. This allowed for odds discrepancies that could work in favor of a customer who had the initiative to seek the best return available. It also enabled the horse player to place bets at odds known in advance, as opposed to the current system where the player doesn't know the odds until the final bets are totaled.

Bookie still lives on in most futures markets. For anyone who can figure out discrepancies in the floor traders' or locals' quotes, greener pastures may be waiting.

Bookie was sharp. He could multiply and divide numbers in a flash. He spent the morning clocking the workouts of imminent starters, and he hired sentries to report the body language of the entries in each race as they appeared in the paddock. One rule he always followed was never to bet on a horse that had an erection in the paddock area. This made the horse lag. But most important, Bookie knew which market makers liked to open with favorable odds for underdogs and favorites. He hit them before the odds had a chance to adjust to the flow of money. The techniques he used are almost identical to those that sports bettors use today to hunt for better odds on pro football games and those that speculators in markets use in determining how close to the open to place their buy and sell orders during strong up and down days.

A master of the art of discretion, Bookie often spread his bets among eight or ten different bookmakers. Because he kept his deposits with each one relatively small, the bookmakers were never the wiser. He often left the track with thousands of dollars, and the bookmakers never noticed.

His favorite wager was to participate with the trainers when their horses were sent out to win after a poor performance the previous time out. He liked especially to bet on a horse that was claimed a few races ago, showed early speed in the most recent race, and then fell way back out of the money and off the finish by the end of the race. The trainers generally supplemented their living by betting on their horses. How better to do it than to bet on one from their own stable, going off at long odds because the public won't touch it due to its recent performance? Best of all was going with the trainer after he had reclaimed a horse at a higher price than the price at which it was recently claimed away from him. Trainers and others aren't likely to lose money paying up for merchandise they previously owned.

One doesn't have to be very astute to see how comparable forces could work with trades by insiders in companies or dealers in fixed-income securities after some recently disappointing earnings performance.

After years of saving (coupled with a few well-timed wagers), Bookie pooled his resources with another stablehand and bought a cheap claiming horse. Unfortunately, his eye for horses was not equal to his gambling prowess. After the horse was claimed, it proceeded to finish off the board four starts in a row before breaking a leg at the furlong pole in the fifth. Heaping insult upon injury, the track officials summoned Bookie to remove his dead horse from the track at his expense.

Sheepshead Bay folded in 1933, but by then Bookie was already convinced that a career change was in order. He noticed that among all the jockeys, owners, trainers, gamblers, and other assorted people at the track, only one group consistently made money. Instead of trying to pick winners against old man "take," Bookie decided to join the money-makers: as a bookie.

One of the best things about Bookie's career change was that it made him a master of psychology. "The customers play the same tunes in their everyday life that they do when betting with me. If they're careful, they bet the favorite to show. If they're swingers, they go for the long shot to win."

Bookie often told me that he had the best job in the world. He was guaranteed a profit on every transaction. He carried no inventory, and his office was in the open air of Brighton. Accounts receivable were hardly ever a problem because his collector, a 225-pound handball doubles player, arranged payments. True, Bookie's margins weren't as high as those of the major brokerage houses for derivatives transactions, where spreads of 0.2 percent bid to 0.6 percent asked are routinely quoted—a profit margin on cost of 200 percent. But Bookie's clients were not as naïve as the customers who blithely accept such ruinous trades, and, with the 5 percent to 15 percent margins, Bookie had the luxury of looking forward to repeat business. Nor did he have to rely, as many brokerages do, on risk disclosure documents or lengthy disclaimers at the bottom of his offerings to get the leg up on the plaintiff when the chickens came home to roost. Any such disputes could be settled amicably and promptly by the collector, to "mutual benefit."

If only public speculators would pay as much attention to—what Mark Cramer, of my favorite horse racing author, calls—the "the gravitational pull of the house take," as horse bettors do, the public would have lots more chips. At least Bookie was up front about it. He'd tell the customers who bet with him that they couldn't win because the 15 percent vig was too great. In fact, he offered his customers a 10 percent rebate on all their race wagering at the weekly settlement. But the brokerage houses, the bank dealers, et al., routinely quote such spreads and concurrently write market letters recommending this or that "risk reversal" or "volatility" strategy. It makes my blood boil even to write about it, but possibly the forces of competition, communication, and morbidity will have a salubrious impact.

Bookie viewed himself a philanthropist who glued families together. "My bettors are looking to rise above the humdrum of life. They wish to live the impossible dream. Without me, they'd be running after women, drinking themselves into oblivion at a bar, or falling in with undesirables. I help keep the dads at home, let them take the family out to dinner in the evening, improve the sex life, and prevent the kids from getting into trouble without anyone to watch over them."

However, he was the first to admit that even though it was impossible to beat the races, you could reduce the rate of loss by placing bets at the track. When you bet with a bookie, you don't know whether your horse is going to be an overlay or underlay, because the final odds are determined at the start of the race, to say nothing of that great edge track patrons get from reading the ticker flashes on the tote board.

When I first met him in the mid-1950s, Bookie was an anachronism at the checker tables. He wore a silk suit, a matching handkerchief and a black duster, regardless of the heat. In addition to his mathematical prowess, Bookie had a photographic memory. He could remember the results of what seemed like every sporting contest for the past five years. He took a liking to me, and one day I asked him what the secret of his success was.

"Well, I'll tell you what, your Uncle Howie likes to join me on my marathon five-mile swim to Rockaway. Why don't you join us next time and I'll tell you my methods. Your uncle can look after you."

"Well, I can go two buoys and then come back. Perhaps you could give me a brief introduction."

"You're on," Bookie said.

The next day as we backstroked past the first buoy, Bookie told me, "Most important of all is integrity. The customers have to believe in my fairness or else they won't come back.

"Second most important is guts. You have to have the courage of your convictions to take a big bet every now and then even if you can't lay it off before the race.

"Finally, you need initiative. You have to give the customer something exciting all of the time or else he'll get bored. The parlay where the customer bets on two or three races, and each must win for him to collect, is particularly attractive to both me and the customer. I get to take my cut out of each race and the customer gets the possibility of winning a big stake from a small initial investment."

At this point, I was getting winded. But I managed to gather enough breath to ask, "Bookie, what's the secret of winning consistently without risk, the way you're famous for?"

"Live a good, balanced life. When I make this swim to Rockaway, I always take a partner, even if he's a stiff like your uncle. Something might happen, and he'll be there to help. I don't drive my car at 90 miles an hour either. If I start taking bad risks in my personal life, I might take too big a risk in making the book, and get blown out. I have to develop the habit of behaving in everyday things the same way I do in business. That way it becomes habitual to do the right thing. Swimming to Rockaway with a partner is about the kind of risk I should take in business. Being bitten by a shark is still about 1/100th as likely as being hit by lightning."

By now we were at the second buoy. I was tired and had to swim back. Visions of sharks swimming swiftly beneath me always engulf me when I swim out from shore in deep water. I'm a poor swimmer to boot. As I turned back for shore, Bookie suggested I join him someday at the track and he'd show me what it's like firsthand.

"My dad would beat my brains out if he found out."

"Well, it's up to you. You're starting to speculate in stocks, aren't you? You'll learn much more about stock market action from turf speculation than from all your financial manuals put together."

On the day after my swim with Bookie, I was to make my first trip to the track. As I lay in bed the night before, I imagined my father's reaction to a request for a visit to the track.

"No. How many times must I tell you that I don't want you to be a gambler when you grow up? It will ruin you."

The next day, fortuitously, my dad was working the 8:00 A.M. to 4:00 P.M. shift, so he would be none the wiser. So began my apprenticeship to Bookie. I followed him like a disciple as he performed his daily routine. After playing some checkers at the West Fourth Street Park, he would cross Coney Island Avenue and stop by the West Fifth Street handball courts to see if there was any action there. I met Bookie at King's Highway and East 11th Street, where limousines carrying handicappers left for the flats at Aqueduct.

As it turned out, both my father and Bookie were right. I learned more about speculation from my study of racing than from all my training as a student in the economic programs at Harvard and the University of Chicago, and as a teacher at the University of California. Like most players, I got hooked on the races and wasted many productive hours and hard-earned dollars there.

But it's an ill wind that blows no good. Bookie encouraged me to apply the same statistical calculations to horse racing that my father applied to handball betting. Before long, I owned the results charts on all thoroughbred tracks, and spent countless hours combing through past-performance data in pursuit of that ever-elusive edge.

Bookie showed me how he could lay off bets, wagering on one side to win at odds, and then betting on the other side at better odds so he would be sure to make a profit regardless of which side won.

"That's called a *dutch* book," he said. "When bookies were allowed at the track, before the track decided to monopolize the action, that's how I made all my money. Why take a risk when you don't have to? But now everyone's smarter, and I'm older."

ELEMENTS OF HANDICAPPING

Bookie's sentries paid particular attention to bandages on a horse's legs. If there for the first time, they tended to indicate stiffness. Most important of all is information on the horse's disposition. The horse can't tell you it doesn't feel like racing today. But it can fight the groom and jockey when they try to mount. It can refuse to walk in the post parade, or show bad manners, or indicate its disinterestedness in the race at hand. I never bet on a horse when I get such signals.

When I see a horse listlessly walking to the starting gate, I am reminded of a market that has recently had a big move. Volume suddenly dries up and trading is light. Buyers and sellers are telling me they are not happy with the recent price. In the same way, the horse is saying, "I don't want to race."

Another technique Bookie employed was betting on a recently beaten favorite. A variation he particularly liked was to bet on a horse that had been ridden by a top-notch jockey and had performed miserably in the previous high-visibility race. His thinking was that professional pride would lead to a particularly effectual race the next time out. Along the same lines, he liked to bet on horses that went off as odds-on favorites in the previous race and got beat. He figured the bettors, with bad memories of such a horse, would avoid it, thereby improving the odds he would receive on the next race. Unfortunately, since that time, betting the beaten favorite has become such a cliché with the public that it's now one of the worst bets at the track. Betting random numbers would give a better return. Newspapers, such as *Sports-Eye*, provide on-line tabulations of the performance of such horses at each stage in the meet. At Aqueduct, for example, in the winter meet of 1996, the chances of such a horse winning were 0.20 versus 0.12 for the average horse in the race.

I have since seen endless variants of betting on the beaten favorite in speculative markets. One twist my friend Steve Kagann uses is to buy stocks that have shown a price decline of at least 50 percent and are the subject of highly unfavorable newspaper publicity. After adding some bells and whistles to the selection techniques, he has been gaining a return of 15 percent more than the market. Another variation is to buy stocks that have suffered a huge decline and that insiders have started to buy. A study I made of such companies in the 1970s showed highly superior performance, but I have not updated the results.

Michael O'Higgins, in his masterly book, *Beating the Dow*, provides numerous workups showing the performance of such systems as buying Dow companies that show the highest dividend yield, worst predicted earnings change, or lowest current price/earnings ratio. All such retrospective systems show above-average results.

I apply these methods to speculating on bonds and stocks. After a big rise, the public likes to jump in. A fall inevitably occurs and causes disillusionment. After such a beaten favorite sends me its signal of being well intentioned, I like to step up to the window.

Since my racing days, many books have appeared categorizing the chances and returns of past performance. A fine compilation appears in *The Mathematics of Horse Racing*. *Sports-Eye* contains a potpourri of categories associated with winning at each major track listed in the "stable" (sic) of contents. I show in Table 9–1 winning factors at Aqueduct along with the corresponding speculative maneuvers. Unfortunately, the statistics don't cover the expected payoffs associated with the various factors. Even if past performance were a useful guide, the tabulated results could not be used to make money.

One day I shared with Bookie some rudimentary calculations I'd made showing stock market factors along with profit expectations. He was not impressed. "That may work for an easy game like stock picking, but in racing all the angles are much more sophisticated. Furthermore, you can't have just one system for all occasions since the form is always changing. Read *The Secrets of Professional Turf Betting*, by Robert L. Bacon. You'll find it's the real thing."

Bookie's words were prophetic. I consider Bacon's *Secrets* one of the best books I've ever read. I go back to it for a fresh supply of ideas when I get in a rut. And it's mandatory reading for all new employees in my firm.

Table 9–1.   Racing and Market Win Factors

Racing Factor	Chance of Winning	Market Analogy
Highest win percentage	.19	Most frequent rises
Highest money earner	.20	Best performer
Fastest average speed in recent races	.21	Best recent relative performance
Best jockey in race	.17	Executive buying
Best trainer in race	.17	Owner buying
Highest win percentage on wet track	.15	Best performance in bear market
Closed strongly last race	.16	Buying at close
Beaten within one length of winner in last race	.16	Second best performance in industry
Favorite in last race	.20	Bullish consensus was highest
Won recent race in same class after drop-down	.16	Second earnings report after deficit
In trouble last race	.10	Declined after announcement
Dropping in company	.10	Delisted
Impressive qualifier	.11	Excited interest at road show

I can do potential speculators no greater favor than to urge them to read this book. Nearly all the material in this chapter delves into the principles I have learned from it, and their corresponding applications to market speculating.

THE TAKE

Every cent of the track's operating expenses is paid for by the public through the take: Jockey fees, purse money, track upkeep and amortization, track profits, taxes, and executive salary—all these come from the take, which runs from 15 percent to 25 percent of the money bet on each race. Hence, the racetrack handicapper must compete against a staggering disadvantage. A 20 percent profit is considered an above-average return for an investment in a mutual fund, but this is roughly what the racegoer must overcome just to break even! This figure does not include the cost of admission, racing programs and newspapers, transportation, or any of the other expenses the handicapper will incur.

With the odds stacked so heavily against them, it is no coincidence that average racegoers are big losers. They may make money in the short term, but eventually they are overwhelmed by the take and breakage (the rounding down of the payoff to the next lower $0.10 or $0.20, depending on state law) and the percentages wear them down. Because of breakage, the take is greater on bets to place and show. Bettors are even more unlikely to come out ahead if they don't bet to win.

Surprisingly, a handful of handicappers at every track are able to grind out a profit in the long run, according to Bacon. Who are these professionals, and what characteristics separate them from the average Joe? According to Bacon, their first and foremost rule is: "Copper (bet against) the public's ideas . . . at all times." It stands to reason that if the great majority of racegoers are losers, then the winners must be doing something differently. The importance of being a contrarian in markets is well covered in books and columns by Dave Dreman.

A more up-to-date insider's guide, *The Book on Bookmaking*, has some sobering words of advice for those who bet the horses. "If you insist on betting horses regularly, eventually you must lose. The only advice I can give you is obvious: You will lose less if you bet less."[1]

THE CONSENSUS

About 95 percent of today's racegoers arrive at their selections using exactly the same information. With the *Daily Racing Form* in one hand and the track program in the other, the average patron goes to battle with his competitors at the track. But after analyzing the same figures, trip commentaries, and articles as everyone else, it stands to reason that most of these players will arrive at the same superficial conclusions.

One afternoon, in my Suffolk Downs days, I wagered on a horse that was shipping in from Maryland and dropping in class. According to a story in the *Daily Racing Form* several days prior, seven of eight such horses had won at the meet, and three of them had paid over $20. In addition, this particular horse had finished second in his last start, appeared to be in excellent form, and was drawing the leading rider for the meet.

As the horses lined up for the start, I beamed with confidence. The public had vigorously supported my selection, driving the down price from 5–2 to 8–5 in the last flashes. At the height of my exuberance, I turned to an elderly gentleman next to me and remarked, "This four horse can't lose." He looked at me and said, "Kid, you must have read the program."

I looked on disbelievingly as my sure thing proceeded to run a badly beaten fourth, and this same gentleman collected on the $12 winner. It wasn't until several years and many dollars later that I truly appreciated the wisdom of his comment.

Many bettors at the racetrack arrive at their selections after only a passing glimpse at the *Daily Racing Form* or a consensus of public handicappers. As if they had no regard for their hard-earned money, they don't hesitate to bet half a day's wages on 10 minutes of half-hearted research. Later, they cite poor "luck" as the cause of their losses.

Many view the business of turf speculation as the embodiment of the easy life. According to the naïve, perpetual losers, those who are fortunate enough to consistently draw an income by betting on the races have been issued a license by the racing gods to make money without ever being forced to do any real work.

What the public doesn't realize is that a professional horse racing analyst generally spends 16 hours a day going to the racetrack, compiling statistics, and watching videos for trip information, not to mention poring through all of the available information on the day's entrants and establishing a theoretical value for each of the starters. Most would consider such behavior obsessive, but it's a game where only a few can survive, financial disaster looms boldly, and the margin for error is slim. There is always an up-and-coming gunslinger, faster and better than his predecessor, armed with the newest technology, and educated by all of those who have come before him lurking in the wings.

DISCIPLINE

Former world chess champion Emmanuel Lasker once offered the following advice to aspiring competitors: "When you see a good move, wait—look for a better one." One can always be more informed, more prepared, better equipped to make a decision.

Among the losers at the track are racing enthusiasts who possess a wealth of knowledge about handicapping and the horses themselves. They have the records, the contacts, and the experience, but they lack an essential quality: discipline. Track novelist William Murray calls it "an iron ass"—the ability to sit there and not bet. You may select a high percentage of winners and have some strong insight, but if you don't have the discipline to wager on only the two or three races a day that you feel offer the greatest profit potential, then you'll never reap consistent profits. Successful athletes, business executives, and gamblers alike spend the majority of their time and energy trying to discover and cultivate an advantage. In many cases, the fine line between success and failure is distinguished by an almost immeasurably small edge. Unfortunately, in addition to outsmarting his peers, the racegoer must also overcome the 20 percent take. To make money, an extremely large advantage is necessary.

The one advantage the price taker holds over the market maker is the opportunity to be selective. Bookmakers of all forms (casinos, banks, and streetcorner types) are paid a premium for quoting two-sided markets. To make them earn their money, the speculator must watch many prices before selecting the optimal trade.

Imagine being a golfer who could eliminate all of the holes that were played poorly, or a slugger who faced only those pitchers whom he hit exceptionally well. The golfer's handicap would improve and the hitter's batting average would rise.

An old adage that originated at the racetrack contains wisdom that is universally applicable in many different competitive forums: "You can beat a race but you can't beat the races." When an advantage arises, press it! Otherwise, regroup and wait patiently for the next opportunity to buy value.

EMOTION AND SELF-DOUBT

Walk through the grandstand section of any racetrack and study the people. Observe their mannerisms, their gestures, voices, and facial expressions. Sense the emotion: the pervasive fear, anger, sadness, and shock—and that all too rare love of the jockey and joy of winning.

A race is an emotional roller coaster. The buzz of the crowd amplifies as the horses round the turn and head down the home stretch. At the wire, the masses erupt when two horses appear to cross the wire together. Minutes later, the photo reveals that the favorite has been beaten by a nose. Some fans throw their programs in disgust, others criticize the ride by the jockey—who, they clearly feel, cost them their hard-earned money. Some argue that the race was fixed, others sit in disbelief, as if they have lost their inheritance or grocery money. Many probably have. To the side, three men revel in self-adulation: "We knew this six horse couldn't lose, Mikey, this one was ice cream." Tomorrow, these people will probably be among the majority again, agitated and hurt that the gods of racing luck have suddenly forsaken them.

One thing is sure. Among the emotionally charged, you will not find one single long-term winner. Where are they? According to Bacon: "These quiet professionals are quite inconspicuous unless you look for them, because there are so many careless gamblers, crazy amateurs, jumping from one crackpot idea to another betting on hope and fear." I show this passage to any trader in my office who is showing color or palpitation. It's a quicker fix than a course in meditation.

Simple, one would think: the turf speculator must remove all emotion from the decision-making process in order to maintain objectivity. Ah, but this is easier said than done. Just like the stockbroker who sells indexes at the low tick in the midst of a severe decline, after mentally adding on car payments, mortgages, and orthodontist bills, the turf handicapper usually loses his nerve at exactly the worst moment. In the face of danger, one will generally do what is instinctual as opposed to what is logical.

The professional has no fear of losing because he has no emotional attachment to his money. His bankroll is merely a means of keeping score. Because he is confident that he will succeed in the long run, he is not susceptible to the pressure of failure. The professional will make objective selections regardless of the situation. But adrenaline often interferes.

The emotions a speculator feels as he screams to his broker for a fill, angrily watches the price scrolling across the screen, sadly leaves the office after tapping out, or expectantly opens the newspaper to check the moves of his stocks and mutual funds are those of the racegoer. Videos of speculators in my business show them chain smoking, screaming at their brokers, or yelling at their subordinates. These expressions of emotion have within them the seeds of destruction.

To counter this in my operation, I enforce a ban against all jocularity and temper tantrums. For the same reason, I try to avoid all phone calls except urgent ones involving my kids. I don't even like to take my wife's calls because I tend to become too high strung. Unfortunately, she knows more about the markets than I do, so her opinion of my trades amplifies my state of mind.

My mentor, Irving Redel, passed on some good advice to help control emotions. Whenever someone, including family, asks him how he's doing, he answers, "Fair." As far as his family knew, he was faring the same during the 1979 gold run-up, when it was a disappointing day if his profit didn't exceed seven figures, as during the dull markets in the decade ending in 1996, when gold frequently stuck in a $5 range for months on end. On those rare occasions when the gods of fortune have been kind to me and a friend asks me, "How is the trading going?" I sometimes augment Irving's "Fair" with "Not as badly as usual." But my friends are on to me. Now they respond, "that must be very good indeed."

I get vicarious pleasure from someone who wears his heart on his sleeve, even though I know the enthusiasm must be suppressed to make a winner. When a young man walked into my office in a highly charged state and demanded a job, I listened. He had written a paper at Harvard, "The Econometric Analysis of Speed Ratings of Horse Races." Like me, 30 years earlier, he had subsidized his schooling and his business by betting at the races. He became so good at it that tracks often retained him to give seminars for aspiring handicappers. He played five sports in high school and lettered in golf and football at Harvard. This was our kind of guy and I hired him forthwith. I sent him for prespeculation training to the 1995 session at Saratoga. I nicknamed him "Clock." Here's his report:

"Why is this two horse 13 to 1?" I say to myself while diligently searching for my oversight. Alright, his last two races look very bad, but he got caught in a wicked speed duel two back, and lost all chance in his last race when fanned five wide at the clubhouse turn. Now he's dropping in class, draws the rail (a distinct advantage in the shorter routes over the inner turf course) with almost no speed in the race, and gets a switch to Samyn: one of the best grass jockeys in the world. Certainly, this one is a steal at this price.

3 to 2, 7 to 5, 6 to 5: the tote board hums with activity as the public loads up on the nine horse, and every tick boosts the confidence of the chalk players (those who generally bet on favorites). "This nine can't lose," the man beside me boasts. "I bet him last time, and he was checked early, and seven wide in the stretch. Still, he only got beat by a nose." Others around us contribute their input. "He's much the class here, he ran second to an allowance horse three back," says one. "Krone and Mott are red hot!

[Jockey/Trainer combination]" adds another. "They've had 40 percent winners this meet." Even money! the tote board reflects their sentiment.

I know that I eliminated this nine horse last night (the comment in the margin of my racing form reads, "Sucker bet" in big, red letters) but they're right, he does look good on paper. He has the best speed figures, is the class of the race, and would have won his last if not for a bad trip. Since I haven't cashed a ticket all day, maybe I should play exactas with the favorite and try to win some of my money back.

Four to five! the money is pouring in on the nine horse, but now I turn my attention back to the two. It took me three hours last night to come up with him and now I'm going to jump on the favorite? For shame! How many times do I have to get drawn into this trap before I learn my lesson. Not only does this horse always find a way to get in trouble, but he has also got a bad case of seconditis. In twenty-nine lifetime starts he's got only two wins but nine second-place finishes.

Now with renewed confidence I go to the window and buy a few win tickets on the two horse. 15 to 1? Am I missing something? Well, too late now. They're off. "That's it. Samyn right to the front," I say to myself as the two puts a head in front and saves ground around the first turn. As they race down the backstretch, the rider keeps a firm hold on the two horse, conserving his kick for the stretch run. No one seems overly eager to challenge the two on the front end.

The horses enter the far turn with the two still clinging to a short lead. Forty-eight and four-fifths seconds at the half-mile call. Perfect, they're running pedestrian fractions. The two must still be full of run!

Into the stretch and the favorite is flying, picking off horses one by one as he closes ground from twelfth position to fourth, two behind the leader. "C'mon with his nine horse, Julie!" the man next to me screams as he strikes himself in the hip with his program while trying to imitate the motion of whipping a horse. All eyes are glued to the stretch as they pass the eighth pole, but the two horse is still game on the lead. Samyn shows him the whip, asking for more run, and he responds by drawing away from the other front-runners. The nine makes one last desperate attempt to catch the two, but it's no use. As they approach the wire, I'm already walking toward the window, and watching the disappointment on the faces of the chalkplayers as they realize that the nine will run second once again. Another sucker horse goes down in smoke, and burns the public's money. The two pays $32.80 to win (on a two-dollar bet) and turns a disastrous day into a profitable one. "Easy game," I say to my companion, ironically.

BEWARE OF SWITCHES

Racetracks and financial markets have an uncanny knack for shaking out the faint of heart before they can ever realize a profit. The following is from Bacon's Chapter 4: "Keep Out of Those Switches!"

The average turf speculator has developed many habits that allow him to make a contribution to the market considerably greater than the take of 20 percent. He has no right to lose so much. It's almost as if he did it on purpose.

It's the switch, not the move that beats the public. The professionals bet straight to win. That's where there is the least unfavorable take-and-breakage percentage against the straight position. He never bets place or show; that keeps him out of the amateur's position switches.

The amateur bets to win, only to have the horse run third. He bets for third—but the horse runs second. He bets for second, only to have it run third. Finally, he bets on a long shot to show and it wins the race. And the favorites come in second and third. The payoff for first is $44.80, but only $2.40 to show.

Next, he turns to switching the size of his bet. The amateur lets greed or fear change the size of his plays; he plunges on a favorite that loses, then bets lightly on a fair-priced horse that wins. He is always one race behind the form of a horse and several races behind the rhythm of the results sequences.

He demands consistency in his horses while at the same time being utterly inconsistent himself.[2]

These brilliant insights should be studied by all speculators. Chroniclers of cyclical tendencies in markets might wish to pay homage to Bacon in subsequent work.

Unfortunately, Bacon's nightmare scenario has an uncanny way of expressing itself in real life. Here's an actual experience with a sequence of my trades.

The deutschemark is up a little, but the yen is way up, so I sell the yen. Trend-buying levels are reached in the yen, and it rises 100 points.

The next day, they show similar opens, and the yen again much the stronger. I sell the deutschemark to avoid the trend followers. The Fed intervenes this time against the yen, and it goes down 150 points on the day. The deutschemark is unchanged.

These losses cause me to increase my unit size of trading from 100 contracts to 200 contracts, to catch up.

I buy the Swiss franc the next day, because I know it's usually the most volatile of all major currencies. But it goes up a few ticks at the close. I figure that, with my large contract size, I had better take profits.

That night, the Swiss National Bank cuts the discount rate (an event that occurs frequently following a strong New York close) and I fail to take a profit that would have covered my previous losses.

After this series of losses, I reduce my unit size to 25 contracts so I'll be able to stick with my positions. I buy the pound. It soars and I score a big win that would have totally offset the previous losses if I had stuck to a constant unit size.

I take a stab at my faithful friend, the U.S. T-bond. I'm ahead 3 ticks by shorting it, and I grab my profit at the close. The next day, the T-bond opens down 16 ticks as Europe unloads in sympathy with a weak dollar opening.

The next day, I'm on a roll. I sell the bonds as they decline three ticks to the close. This time I maintain my unrealized profit overnight. After the New York close, a Federal Reserve Board governor argues, in a speech in Japan, that the United States has inflation under control. The T-bond opens up in Tokyo 16 ticks against me.

I decide that the best thing to do is to take a break and just paper trade. Get back to basics. Just listen to the computer. Hypothetically, I make money on twelve straight trades. I am on a paper roll. I'm ready.

I switch back to my maximum position. I buy. The markets move in my favor and I make back almost all my losses. This time I'm going to stay with my system, not anticipating anything. I double the exposure. Just when I'm about caught up, the Secretary of State announces at 2:00 P.M. on a Wednesday that, "Regrettably," Iraq has shown no sign of complying with the demands of the Allies.

The market turns down on a dime and I am almost wiped out.

I don't know whether to cry or laugh as I recall a lifetime of switch-itis. My only hope is to remember:

1. Switch-itis is lethal.

2. Stick to a constant number of contracts.

Stay with a systematic approach. As Wiswell liked to say, "a bad system is better than no system at all."

The lesson: Keep away from switches. As Bacon says: "It's the switches and not the races that beat the public play." A whole volume of books could not record all the possible switches that the amateurs can get themselves into.

In contrast, writes Bacon: "The professionals use one sure way of keeping out of the switches. . . . They just don't play too many races. . . . They don't play the bad races at both ends of the daily programs. They don't play bad races—period!"[3]

The Dow collapsed in October 1929, falling from 360 to 200 in a month. It rallied back to 300 by April 1930, only to fall to 50 in February 1933. It meandered back to 100 at the end of the decade. So the nonchanging cycle theorists trotted out the same scenario for the October 19, 1987, crash, when the Dow fell from 2500 to 1700 in four days.

But instead of falling to one-fourth of its crash low, the Dow proceeded to triple in the next eight years following the 1987 crash.

Speculation is a noble and essential activity that uses every reserve, physical and mental, that you can bring to the fray. But in order to maintain the nobility of the profession, you first have to survive. Always remember that it's not the losses that do speculators in, it's the switches.

THE PRINCIPLE OF EVER-CHANGING CYCLES

This single most important principle about speculation is clearly spelled out in Bacon's book, with numerous examples. I've since seen it applied without attribution to every conceivable field under the sun—fishing, baseball, fencing, election politics. I guarantee you'll kick yourself in a tender spot when you rue all the times you barreled in to invest in that best-performing mutual fund, investment letter, or hot brokerage after you understand this vital, this *cardinal* principle.

Let Bacon describe it in the realm of turf handicapping, and then pursue with me some of its infinite applications in the field of market speculation.

> The collective "mind" of the public imagines that if it could only once find the "combination" for beating the races, it would be all set for life. The public wants to hit on some simple key, shown by numbers in the past performances, and use this key to get richer and richer as racing goes on. The public believes that if it could only once find that past performance key, its troubles would be over. . . .
>
> Few players take into consideration the principle of ever-changing cycles of results, although the minor ups and downs of this principle can be seen at every long race meeting. The would-be professional player must always understand that the form moves away from the public's knowledge.[4]

Consider a simple system that's making money:

> And now [says Bacon of a similar system], we'll see how the principle of ever-changing cycles works automatically. Nobody tells the results to move away from the public's selection methods. Nobody makes rules to cause a "revolution" in results sequences. Here is what happens: First, as the public got wise to the winning ways of the system, the public's bets began to cut the prices on the selections.[5]

Here's a racing example that captures the changing cycles.

Most handicappers would agree that the two most important indicators of winning potential are: (1) past class (at what level has this horse raced competitively?) and (2) current form (how well has this horse been running lately?). It is easy to ascertain past class, although the methods for measuring it may differ slightly. Some players will focus on earnings per start and others may look for the highest level at which a horse has won, but there are no hidden secrets.

On the other hand, form is subjective and difficult to measure. Form is measured based on recent final times, early speed, late speed, workouts, trainer patterns, and the horse's own results cycle. Of these, probably none is more reliable for picking winners than simply how fast the horse ran in his last race.

As a raw number, advanced handicappers have always been hesitant to use the final running time of a race as a significant indicator. Because of the variability of track conditions, little can be gained by comparing races over different surfaces. In the 1970s and 1980s, therefore, professionals began calculating a "track variant" in an attempt to even the fast–slow biases of racetracks. Theoretically, if one were to add the variant to a number that quantified the final running time of the horse in question, one could determine who ran the "fastest" race regardless of racing surface. The result was that those with accurate "speed figures" had a better idea of current form than those without. Many generous mutuels were cashed based on "speed."

In the mid-1980s, many handicapping services touted the quality of their speed figures. Then came the real blow to speed specialists: the *Racing Times*, which was absorbed by the *Daily Racing Form* soon thereafter, began to publish the figures of Andrew Beyer, the man who introduced the concept to many aspiring handicappers in the 1970s. Finally, the general public had access to reliable speed figures.

Suppose the system originally had two winners [at 3-to-1 odds] out of each seven horses played, on average. That meant two winnings of $3 and five losings of $1 each, on dollar plays—all on average, of course. That gave a flat bet winning of $1 on each seven dollars invested. But when the prices were driven down to 5-to-2, the flat bet winning was wiped out. The system just broke even. And finally, at the later odds of 3-to-2 average price, the system lost $2 on each seven bets of $1, even though the percentage of winners (two out of seven) remained the same.[6]

But the percentage didn't remain the same. Handicapped races are very evenly matched, and trying to win takes a lot out of a horse. If it goes all out to win a race, its chance of winning the next race is small. An owner who would send a horse out to win at 3-to-1 will lose enthusiasm at 5-to-2 and will tell the boy, "Don't push him too hard. Win if you can win easy." At 3-to-2, he'll say, "Ride him for the exercise. We're not going for the money." Where the bet used to win two times out of seven, now it wins one time in ten. The public again falls victim to the ever-changing cycle.

Speed figures still play a prominent role in determining odds. Even the most inexperienced handicapper will select a horse because it had the highest Beyer number in its last race. In a study conducted by one of our traders over a two-week period in September 1995 at New York and California tracks, a two-dollar win bet on each horse with the highest speed figure in its last race would have resulted in a 38 percent net loss. What once was a valuable profit-making tool is now a money loser. It has been overbet by the public until it no longer has meaning.

The ever-changing cycle will continue to turn, however, and bettors will become disgusted with their inability to realize a profit. They will discard the Beyer number in favor of the next popular indicator, and horses with good figures will go off at reasonable odds once again.

Keep in mind that the ever-changing cycles work in the short term as well as the long. Bacon points out that "in a long meeting of 40 days there will be at least one radical change. A meeting of 60 days will have at least two. Sometimes even a 30-day meeting may have two changes."[7]

Bacon cites certain tracks where it was common for a favorite to win in the first 10 to 15 days of the session. Horses arrived from all over the country, and the public hadn't a clue how to handicap. It stabbed all over the map for long shots rather than betting the favorites down to unfavorable prices. "Under such conditions," says Bacon, "the horsemen simply step out and grab purses with ready horses. . . . And as long as the public hangs back from betting the logical choices, these ready horses will win and repeat for second easy winnings at overlay prices."[8]

When the public finally settles down to make sensible picks, it's already behind the cycle, for the early winners are tired, and they've picked up weight penalties that obviate any chance of winning. Other horses that were in the money, and have as yet no penalties, are suddenly bet down to underlay prices, so they just go through the motions. The cash goes to horses that were previously running out of the money. The public begins looking for "trick plays and hunches and long shots" and gets plowed under the cycles again.

The early form horses are now rested up, and they've lost some of their penalty weight, so they're prancing home at medium odds, as are a few of the long shots from the second form cycle. If the favorites are bet down by smart money, second, third, fourth, and fifth choices win.

"These," says Bacon, "are just a few of the thousands of examples of the workings of the racing law of ever-changing cycles. Be sure to keep it in mind at all times—*especially* when in a winning streak."[9]

The power of Bacon's idea is staggering.

I didn't know that I was taking advantage of the ever-changing cycles, even as I was applying the principles. I learned from Jack Barnaby to change cycles in the course of my squash game. First, I played deep so my opponent would lay back. When he was laying back, I would come in with some short shots. Not only did I have my opponent laying back so he had to cover more ground, but my percentage of wins was greater because I had my touch after a few points into the game. Next, my opponent starts moving up to the front. At this time, I change and move back to depth again. At the end of a game, the adversary is likely to run all out and get my short shots, so deep ones are more appropriate anyway. As

Jack Barnaby put it: "You're not playing golf out there. You're playing squash."

In sports, this principle is everywhere. The crafty veteran pitcher catches a hitter sitting on an off-speed pitch, and blows a high fastball by him for strike three. The next time out, the batter remembers the last at bat and gears up for the heater, but, with a two-strike count the second time, the pitcher throws a straight change and catches the batter way out in front. The batter shakes his head in disbelief. He would have hit the ball hard if he had waited again on the off-speed pitch.

The commodity speculator notices that the trend followers just had a great run. They're all sitting on lots of cash, just waiting for the next trend. But when too much easy money is made, speculators look to make a fast buck by imitating the big boys, and dealers who study the points know that a change of trend will occur if certain key points are triggered. They start moving prices up to these points in anticipation. The probability of a successful trend-following trade is reduced. The price the trend follower pays for these fills will be much less favorable.

The public can never catch up to the changes in cycles. Just when they're ready to follow a system, it's the wrong time.

These oh-so-fleeting hot hands of market gurus become clarified. An advisor comes up with a successful prediction. For example, Bob Prechter, Elaine Garzarelli, and Mario Gabelli picked the big crash in October 1987. They became prophets. Their followers were flush, and they told their friends about their newfound gurus. But then their fills from following the recommendations of the gurus became a lot worse because they were taking their following along with them. This tends to limit their selections to liquid issues, which are much more likely to be fairly valued.

When I buy a mutual fund or select an advisor to handle my money, I always look for the worst performing advisor or fund in the previous period, not the best. For my 1996 crown jewel, I chose an Indian fund that was down 60% in 1995 when the average fund was up 25%. This put me in a delicate situation when the fund manager called me to schmooze about why I chose him. I shot my whole wad of Indian knowledge. "With the Fiza before the elections, the impact of the July monsoons on crops and romance in Bombay, the spring wedding season, and the suspected Reliance counterfeiting, your insights should be particularly timely." I could almost see the raised eyebrows on the other end of the line.

More people lost more money after the 1987 crash, waiting for a repeat of the 1929 crash, than is pleasant to contemplate.

I apply these principles often in my own speculating. When the world's most successful investor sold stock in his investment company at three times net asset value while thousands of other fine funds were selling without a load *at* net asset value, I rushed in to short. Conversely, on those rare occasions when I'm fortunate enough to select an investment that's a top performer in any period, I break into a cold sweat the longer I refrain from liquidating.

To my credit and Bacon's, I've cleaned up quite a bit since I started looking for changing cycles. Whenever it looked like a repeat of the October 1987 scenario, I've stepped up to the plate to buy, hardly losing at all in the process. But now the shippers are tired. The cycles look ready to change again. The one thing I can say for certain about the coming millennium is that "the public will be one step behind the form cycles."

OLD HAUNTS

I frequently patronized the track in my days at Harvard. In recent years, I have reformed, invariably choosing to spend an evening with the family rather than visit old haunts.

I decided that an update in the 1996 cyberspace era would be appropriate.

I felt like Rip Van Winkle waking to a new age as I entered the track. My well-oiled routines were now as rusty as Rip's old fowling piece. I saw many sights but none I knew. If my beard had hung to my knees, I could hardly have felt more out of place. As I entered the 'skirts of the village—I mean, as I gawked into the vestibule—a ticket taker greeted me as if I were bringing the beer to a centenary reunion. I walked into a stadium capable of seating 50,000. TV monitors displaying race information and information on races at other tracks met the eye in all directions. It was as if Rip's old shanty had been pulled down and replaced with a palace.

I thought at first that I had chosen a night when the track was closed. As I looked around the magnificent stadium, I seemed to be the only patron. Then the monitor in front of me came alive with pictures of horses being walked to the gate. An amplified voice shouted, "It's post time!" Scanning the other monitors, I saw that the handle was $200,000, a respectable figure. The first thought to pop into my head was, "Where did all that money come from?"

I knew, of course, that approximately 90 percent of the handle of a track like this comes from OTB and electronic transfers from simulcast betting at local tracks across the country.

Handicapping has also entered the space age. It's getting difficult to distinguish between handicapping the horses and playing the market. Where once the handicapper could be seen leafing through colored 3 × 5 tout sheets, he now has computer software and 900 numbers. He can access the *Daily Racing Form*—or the *Wall Street Journal*—on a computer. *Sports Eye* features the Computerized Sports Eye Accu-Track Photo Charts, not photos at all but numbered circles showing each horse's position at the quarter-pole, half-pole, and so on. Bettors can call 900 numbers for "24 Hour Race Results," "Best Bet Selections Daily," "Dial-a-Horse," and even "Talk to My Horse—Only one winner picked daily," all of which are not principally different from the "High Quality Quotes at the Lowest Cost," or "Your Broker Is Now Obsolete" services advertised in *Investor's Business Daily*.

Even the complaints of handicappers have been affected by the Information Age. Ian C. Blair, editor-in-chief of *American Turf Monthly*, complained in the February 1996 edition that he hadn't hit an exacta in a year, and that good record keeping revealed embarrassing things about his methods, but also that "every live race [at Turf Paradise] was punctuated by a simulcast event from Santa Anita," which kept him from settling into a groove. An obvious embarrassment of riches.

Some things remain the same, however. The old track denizens still hung over the outside rail, gossiping like Rip's friends in front of the hotel. The horses still made the same old circuit with minor variations, much like Rip's story of the long night. And, of course, the professional still made a sharp contrast with the "public."

While the average Joe is armed with little ammunition, the professional is more than likely equipped with an array of data that includes highly detailed trip notes, analysis of the latest jockey and trainer trends, tailormade speed figures, past track biases, and the form cycles of each individual horse. He can tell you which trainers and riders offer the best value and which are overbet; he can also break each entry down by strengths and weaknesses for age, sex, track conditions, distances, and running styles.

The professional records and follows anything that affects the outcome of a horse race. I've even known one handicapper to keep a detailed record of the tidal patterns for racetracks built near the ocean. A certain bookie in Las Vegas is up on weather conditions across the country, and clients often prefer him to the local weatherman.

In tribute to Bookie and Bacon, it has always been a part of the Niederhoffer training program to take a trek to the local track. Because we all work during the day, the trip is usually to the trotters and pacers at the Meadowlands.

To get the full flavor of hope, anxiety, and money management, we always take the bus. Half the riders on the bus are a good bet to have already taken in the action at Aqueduct in the afternoon.

"I had the daily double at Aqueduct, but the damn bus broke down."

"I was going to bet my whole wad on Red River but I decided at the last minute to bet on him to show—and he paid 38 bucks to win and only $2.30 to show."

Over the years, the names and faces have changed, but one can hear daily that familiar tune of the frustrated gambler. A song of hope, fear, loneliness, and despair. Those who have spent time around a racetrack, casino, exchange, or any other bookmaking establishment can certainly sing along; they know the words by heart. Another generation, new musicians, but the same concert halls and sheet music. The band plays on.

CHAPTER 10

Deception and Charts

A favorite device with him was to institute inquiries in the presence of the crowd around him as to roads and watercourses in a direction which he did not intend to take; even to order maps to be prepared, and roads laid down, as though for instant use. Having thus set every gossip talking and predicting his intentions, he would calmly march directly in the opposite direction.

"Mystery, mystery, is the secret of success!"

By a Virginia admirer from
The Life of Stonewall Jackson

The child is father to the man. If only Artie had been a bookie like Marty Reisman's father rather than a cop, I might be a much wealthier speculator. Artie's advice was, "Be open and truthful. Trust in the other guy and work hard." Marty's dad gave him more cynical advice: "Son, I can't take your action this time. I'd feel bad. That college game—like all too many others—is fixed."

Deception is ubiquitous. From the lowliest viruses to the most sapient human every life form is a master at it. To ignore deception is a sure ticket to disaster. I'm ashamed to admit that when I first studied markets, I accepted as gospel such advice as: "I find the use of long-term charts to be paramount in gaining the proper perspective. Let's face it, speculation is a highly visual experience . . . look for repetitive cycles. Make a note of when key highs and key lows have been made and measure the time between highs and lows." Or, "Markets go through active and inactive periods, trending and nontrending. Pull out a ruler, draw the trendline and get aboard. Although markets have changed, technical indicators have not." Or, "Momentum, like all prices and changes, shows trends. Take a consensus approach with different indicators to determine the trend."

I didn't make up these pithy statements. They are star quotations (with an adjustment or two to protect the guilty) from six of the best-selling books on technical analysis in my local bookstore.

217

I fell hook, line, and sinker for such "reasonable" guidance 35 years ago, and I fear the same bait is being eaten today by others who weren't brought up by bookies or taken aside by older fish. I once followed such advice only to have the predators gather around me like sharks.

It took five major lessons before I learned that things are seldom what they seem.

LESSON 1: THE NATURAL ORDER

The first encounter with deception came, fittingly, at Brighton Beach.

Real estate values in Brooklyn in the 1940s were still low enough for the Brighton Beach Baths to maintain three acres of wetlands, nicknamed "The Desert." Artie would often take me there for nature walks. I was not always an eager pupil.

"Dad, what good is all this nature study in The Desert anyway? Let's play a game of handball."

"Let's just take quick walk through and cool off before going for a swim. I'll show you that not only is nature beautiful, but you can learn a lot from it."

"Who cares? I live in the city. I like buildings and people, not insects."

"Look at it this way. Every great sports technique is learned from nature. Concealing, decoys, distraction, playing dead, Trojan horses. They're key to winning or surviving in all sports."

"What do you mean, Dad?"

"Do you see this dark green leaf where the butterfly has just landed? On it is something that looks like just another green leaf. You can hardly tell it's alive, it blends in so well. But look what happens when you touch it. It's a chameleon. And if it happened to be near a yellowish leaf, it could change to that color also.

"Now, take a look at the leaves on this grass stem. Right in the middle there's a green insect called a praying mantis. It looks like a leaf but if one of those butterflies happens to rest on the stem where the mantis is, it's a goner. The mantis will grab it with its legs and stuff it! But the mantis has enemies also. Look what happens when we scare it."

"Watch out! It just grew by 100 percent and developed two more eyes."

"No, those are false eyes to scare you and the birds away," Artie continued. "Did you ever wonder why Red Kravitz, who has the worst temper, wins so many games, even though he doesn't seem to be as talented as the others? He doesn't even have a natural right."

"That's right, Dad. Even you could beat him in singles."

"But his temper is what helps him. He gets everyone upset by looking dangerous. You see that beetle that looks like it has 100 different colors? You can't make heads or tails of it. Nor can its enemies. That's called disruptive coloration. When you really want to hide, it's good to be no color at all, like the jungle fighters you see in the newsreels, and that's why Red

Kravitz is always arguing, stopping and starting the game. He wants to give the opponents nothing to bite into. In nature, the prey blend in with their surroundings in color and shape, and they're pretty much invisible until they move.

"Take a look at the moth on that branch. It looks just like a twig. Why do you think it blends in?"

"Well, to fool the birds and the spiders."

"It looks dead, doesn't it?"

"Yes. Ever notice how Vic Hershkowitz likes to lay back during a point, pretending he's content to just play a lob back? And then his opponent lobs it back, but Vic moves up to the front again quickly and buries it for a dead killer? It's the same principle. He disguises his position to look like he's playing dead, but then he comes up quickly for the kill.

"Do you remember when we went to the Giants game and Charlie Conerly faked a hand-off, first to the fullback and then to the halfback, and every defender tackled and piled up on both of them near the center of the line of scrimmage?"

"Yes, and then Conerly threw a touchdown pass to Joe Morrison."

"That's right. Conerly camouflaged his play. He pretended the play was dead and then came back to life with a touchdown when the enemy, the St. Louis Cardinals, were off their guard. They call that 'playing 'possum' because opossums do it the same as Conerly.

"This goes on throughout the natural world. You can't be a good handball or football player either without using the same kind of deception and camouflage that nature is up to."

Artie found it much easier to relate to deception in the lower life forms, in sports, and in games than to adopt the defense mechanisms that most of us learn to employ in human survival techniques.

LESSON 2: EVEN CHESS PLAYERS CHEAT

My second encounter with deceit came at the checker and chess boards painted on the stone tables at Brighton.

Prior to the 1940s, direct attacks in the center were the mode. But by my time, every patzer knew an equalizing defense against center attacks. To maintain the initiative, players began to play the hypermodern chess game. The key to success here was an indirect attack on (or defense of) the center through bishop moves on the wing. It was called the "Indian attack" (or defense) by 19th-century European travelers who noticed that the top players in India often used this technique. Traditional methods of advancing the center pawns and occupying one of the center squares with the bishop were passé. Center pawn moves were delayed until the opponent declared an intent.

Deception was highly developed among the players. One common error was the seemingly innocuous practice of writing a move on the scorecard before moving the piece. The Russians pioneered this practice to prevent blunders. It spread within minutes to Brighton. But wily opponents quickly took to reading the written moves as they were jotted down, to gain some extra thinking time. Really crafty players purposely wrote a blunder on their pad and then changed it at the last second to dash the hopes of the eager opponent.

At the beach, one of the legendary chess and checkers players was Jules Leopold, President of the Puzzle Club of America. When not playing games at local clubs, he traveled from city to city solving local newspaper games with a team of experts recruited from the boards of New York clubs. In one classic, he sent the creator of a contest based on rebus puzzles an anonymous letter purporting to be from a 90-year-old man in Augusta, Georgia. He enclosed a copy of a rare, out-of-print book of rebuses published in the late 19th century, and wondered if the creator might find it of interest for $10. The game author then began drawing on the book for subsequent puzzles. After that, Leopold always knew the answers in advance because he had retained the only other extant copy of the book. His moves were so deceptive they called him Loophole.

Good board players are trained to maintain a poker face so their opponent will not suspect which way the wind is blowing. The goal is to surprise the opponent with a trap. The moves themselves are often designed by the master to lull the opponent into false security. World Champion Mikhail Tal describes the deceptive calm before a chess storm: "[My play is] silent till the time comes, unassumingly developing pieces and apparently without serious threatening intentions. The board is dozing, the opponent is calm, and as always in similar situations, an imperceptibly prepared explosion proves extremely effective."[1]

In discussing strategy among top players, Grand Master Znosko-Borovsky states:

> Frequently we have to disguise our intentions, to lull our opponent to sleep, or even entice him into error. It is often necessary that he should not suspect our plans. . . . The real art consists in creating the belief, logically, that out intentions are otherwise than they seem.[2]

LESSON 3: BY HOOK OR BY CROOK

My third acquaintance with deception came on the handball court. I played a match one day against Artie Wolf, the player with the greatest hook serve in the history of handball. He served it at half the pace of champions Vic Hershkowitz and Oscar Obert, but it was just as effective. I couldn't return a single serve. The ball would bounce toward me one second and the next be eight feet away. I always knew it was going to hook, but in which direction? When I tried to randomize by mentally flipping a coin and laying to one side, as recommended by game theorists, Wolf wouldn't serve it with a hook at all and my success rate would drop to zero. In later days, I have heard the expression "faked out of his jock" used a hundred times for some tricky maneuver. But I saw it happen thousands of times to Artie Wolf's opponents.

The trick of the hook serve is to disguise the swing so that the motion is the same, regardless of how you hook it. To do this, you hit the ball from in front of yourself so the other player cannot tell which direction your hands are moving. Then, you strike the ball on the high outside if you wish ultimately to spin to the right. At the end of the swing, you move your hand in the direction opposite to the spin you're putting on it, so that anyone trying to read the hook will be deceived. When playing doubles, you can rely on an experienced partner to call "in" or "out," depending on whether it's going to hook into you or outside of you. In singles, you're on your own.

Aside from Artie Wolf, my father had the biggest hook of any of the top handball players. In his teens, he was one of the best. He played at Oriental Beach against the greats: Ralphie Adelman, Mortie Alexander, and Joe Garber. When he started playing football, his arm got so busted up from repeated tackles that he lost his ability to serve with a natural swing. Yet, the hook serve lingered as a reminder of his once great early game. Because of his training, he was the perfect doubles partner for youngsters with ability, like my Uncle Howie. As a past master of the hook, he was always there to yell "Out" or "In."

Artie became accustomed to deception in sports when he was seven years old. Still flush due to his dad's heavy stock market buying on margin during the Roaring '20s, the family could afford tickets to the 1925 Davis Cup tournament, held at Forest Hills. During the preliminary rounds, he was watching a ferocious doubles match between Australia and France. The singles had already been split 1–1. The winner of this match would doubtless move on to the Cup round. Representing Australia was Gerald Patterson, a former Wimbledon champion who was termed one of the hardest hitters in the game, teamed with John Hawkes, a great volleyer. Against them was the ever-popular duo of the wily Basque, Jean Borotra, teamed with René Lacoste. Patterson poached at 6-all in the fifth set and knocked a volley right into Borotra's temple. Borotra fell to the ground motionless. Hawkes and Lacoste rushed over to minister to the unconscious Borotra. But Patterson, knowing of Borotra's tendency to fake unconsciousness, prodded him with his racquet to test the water.

He was right to do this. Borotra often feigned complete exhaustion on the court to lull his opponent into a sense of carelessness. He was known for playing 'possum and for using his racquet as a crutch or a wheelchair to fake out his opponents. Then, at the crucial moment, to the amazement of his opponent, he would rush the net with alacrity on eight consecutive shots and win handily. Never before had Borotra feigned death, however.

Officials and doctors poured out of the Forest Hills gallery. Not to worry. It was just another of Borotra's offensive camouflage tricks. He recovered after several minutes and his team went on to win 10–8 against his shaken Australian opponents, who took the pace off all their shots during the remaining six games of the match so as not to cause further damage.

Twenty years later, Borotra was banned from playing at Wimbledon after the Second World War. The Germans had appointed him Minister of Sports in the Vichy government, during the occupation of France in the early 1940s. He magically vanished during the later stages of the war. The English suspected him of being a quisling.

In 1975, Borotra called me out of the blue. He now served in a cushy UNESCO job designed to encourage sportsmanship. I had been designated to receive the organization's annual award for refusing to accept the World Championship the previous year on the basis of an injury to Sharif Khan, my opponent. I had told Khan I'd wait for him to recover from an eye injury rather than accept a default. There were no funds available for my ticket, but "it would be important for the cause of world harmony if you could come to accept it." I used up my available savings to attend, then learned at the session that I was a pawn. Washington had terminated funding for UNESCO after the organization dissed the United States one time too many and its president had been caught, with a highly attractive assistant, living high on the hog at the agency's expense.

LESSON 4: PRIMATES AND DECEPTION
(IT RUNS IN THE "FAMILY")

Before the World Trade Center was built in Manhattan in 1970, the area west of Wall Street and Trinity Church contained many picturesque import-export establishments. One of these, run by Henry Trefflich, specialized in supplying wild animals to zoos. Henry collected the animals in Africa and shipped them back to the United States for sale. He was famous for purposely allowing the wild animals on board his boats to escape in cities where the newspaper headlines would be helpful in publicizing his merchandise. I became intrigued by the gibbons, lions, and pythons in the window. Next thing I knew, I owned a Japanese stump-tailed macaque.

When I was attending graduate school in Chicago, one of the favorite treats I liked to purchase for my monkey Lorie (named in honor of my thesis advisor) was a banana split from Baskin & Robbins at the newly opened shopping center on 53rd Street and University Avenue. Lorie liked to eat the banana split with a spoon. But not content with his own treat, he often seized my float when I was distracted by the crowd that invariably formed to play with him. To add a festive atmosphere on these occasions, I set Lorie up for activities I had found in the Yerkes Intelligence Test for apes. One problem involved attaching a string to a banana and then placing a heavy weight on the string to see whether the monkey could free the banana. Another required attaching a banana to a tree branch about two feet above the monkey's reach, and then placing a stool about eight feet away to see whether the monkey would move the stool below the tree branch and retrieve the fruit. Lorie invariably solved all these problems.

When my five-year-old brother Roy visited me at the University of Chicago one time, I was particularly vigilant about protecting his property rights. I brought Roy a float and looked around for Lorie. Apparently, he was hiding under the bed. As soon as I left the room, he snuck out, pushed Roy away from his float, and gulped it down. He knew that if I saw him I would put him in his cage, so he hid until I was gone, and then stole the float.

Twenty years later, I learned that research scholars found repeated examples of deceptive behavior among primates and concluded that the main evolutionary reason for the development of the large primate brain was engagement in deceptive activities that enhanced the primates' ability to find and hold onto a mate.

The classic work in this field has been executed by Richard Byrne and Andrew Whiten, two Scottish primatologists. (Their work, originally appearing in *Primate Report*, is reported by James Shreeve, "Machiavellian Monkeys," *Discover*, June 1991.) Byrne and Whiten were studying the foraging behavior of chacma baboons in the Drakensburg Mountains of Northern Africa. Whiten was watching an adult female named Mel dig after an edible bulb. "Paul [a young baboon] approached and looked around. There were no other baboons within sight. Suddenly he let out a yell, and within seconds his mother came running, chasing the startled Mel over a small cliff. Paul then took the bulb for himself."

Struck by behavior familiar from his own childhood, Whiten mentioned it to Byrne and to other primatologists, and discovered that everyone had a collection of similar tales. Realizing that they might be on the trail of something big, they sent questionnaires to primatologists all over the world. They soon had a database of deception indicating that almost all primates are devious. The only exception, without a single case of trickery, was the Lemur family, our smallest-brained cousins.

The deceptions ranged from simple concealment, such as a chimp that learned to suppress "food barks" when Jane Goodall gave him bananas, thereby not alerting other chimps to come and take them from him, to impressive deceits that seem to indicate the ability of one animal to appreciate another animal's situation. For instance, Dutch primatologist Frans Plooji electronically opened a metal box containing food for a chimp that was alone in a feeding area. As the box opened, another chimp showed up. The first chimp immediately closed the box and waited for the second chimp to clear off. The second chimp walked away and hid behind a tree. The first chimp soon reopened the box, whereupon the second came bounding out of hiding and snatched the food. Byrne and Whiten call this ability to defeat one ruse with another "Machiavellian intelligence," and hypothesize that it is the adaptive behavior that favored the development of the huge human brain.

If a large brain permitted some early hominid to outsmart another hominid in finding food or seducing a mate, the owner of the brain survived to reproduce. And the power to outsmart *that* hominid, or to outsmart the one that outsmarted, is clearly the road to an outsized brain. The authors conclude that this ability played a vital role in the early development of chimp and human mentality.

LESSON 5: DECEPTIVE TECHNICAL PATTERNS

The pivotal event that mended my naïve ways came on a visit to Springfield, Illinois, in March 1964, to meet with John Magee, the dean of technical analysis and author of *Technical Analysis of Stock Trends*—"the definitive work on pattern analysis." His office was inside a decaying, older building. Men with green eye shades stood over drafting tables entering prices taken from the *Francis Emory Fitch Stock Transaction Reports*. Issues of *The New York Times* and *The Wall Street Journal* cluttered the place, but they were at least two weeks old so as not to becloud the timeless nature of conclusions with the ephemera of the present. I got a stiff neck from the chill air. The office was air-conditioned and all windows were boarded up to eliminate the influence of light and weather on the technicians' objectivity.

Mr. Magee had developed a rudimentary beta estimate for each individual stock. He had kindly consented to allow me to test them for consistency.

"Mr. Magee, it's kind of you to let me test the random walk theory on your thousands of charts, especially since you sell an advisory service based on predictive patterns within."

"Victor, come with me to the files we maintain. Look at this chart. A gap up, an increase in volume. Next time, a decrease in volume accompanies the down repetition. A third time. A fourth. All symmetric. Price moving in these well-defined trends all the while. Now, if you believe this is a random walk, I'm not losing my hair and I have a bridge I want to sell."

"But, Mr. Magee, there must be other charts where the price and volume look like this but prices move out of the trend lines."

"Victor, that's what technical analysis, the science of recording on charts the transactions from the ticker tape, is all about. Stock prices move in trends. Volume moves with the trend. Human behavior doesn't change. That's why psychiatrists are the least effective professionals. The market goes right on repeating the same old movements in much the same old routine. Knowing the principles of supply and demand, I can interpret any of the thousands of charts in these bins without knowing its name."

"But can you predict?"

"The market reflects hopes and fears, guesses and moods, needs and resources, all reflected in the price. That's all that counts," he answered.

"Do the same techniques work in commodities?"

"It's reprehensible what they do in commodity markets. Government manipulation and regulation has distorted the regular trends, and that's terrible. These are the basic foodstuffs that the farmer has to sell to survive and you and I have to buy to live. To trade commodities you need to supplement the trend lines with a moving average. When prices move above the moving average, you buy. When prices move below, you sell."

"Does the science of technical analysis change with the times?"

"It's the same. Support and resistance recur again and again in any active stock or broad average."

"What enables you to figure out the two points to draw the trendline through so it can be extrapolated predictively?"

"Why, that's what we have all those experienced draftsmen doing at their desks. They're using pencils to draw experimental lines. As subsequent prices develop, one fits best. It's amazing, mysterious, and phenomenal. Not just the small moves but the major swings of several years' duration appear as though their paths had been connected with a ruler."

"I notice the charts in that architecture cabinet are labeled way back to the beginning of the century. Don't these ever get out of date?"

"On the contrary. The charts hold up over the years. The same old patterns, like this one in the 1935 Atchison Topeka chart, keep repeating. A move back and forth within a channel, but once the trendline is broken, a sustained decline."

This was it. I realized that I was talking to a revered figure in the field—"the Dean," "the Fountainhead," "the Seminal Pioneer," "the Preeminent Practitioner," "author of the best-seller read by a million investors," "a man who helped more investors develop sound principles of excellence than anyone."

And yet, even a novice like me, who ardently believed in patterns, could see that if moths, monkeys, and men practiced deception as a regular survival technique, speculators should pay more attention to it than to Magee's naïve extrapolations and explanations. I decided to make a thorough study of deception before losing yet another dollar speculating.

I figured I'd study deception by proceeding from the smallest to the largest organism. I began with viruses, moved to ants, then realized that deceit is ubiquitous and terminated the study. Viruses use it to invade bodies. Ants use it to enslave other ants. Moths use it to evade hungry birds. Generals use it to defeat brilliant generals. Soldiers use it to live another day. Girls and boys use it to attract each other. Con men use it to profit from others' labor. Magicians deceive audiences who know that the illusion is a trick. Great financiers use it to break suckers they don't even remember the next day. Poker players use it to bluff. Economists use it as the key variable in explaining the organization of the firm. Speculators use it to shake weak hands out of a position at just the wrong time.

Deception is not limited to games, war, survival, predator–prey relations, mating, hoaxes, frauds, or economic transactions. Art itself may be defined as making a thing of one kind appear to be something of another kind. A painter uses deception in the form of perspective to make a two-dimensional object appear three-dimensional. Actors use deception to draw audiences into another world. Mystery writers use it to keep readers guessing until the end of the book. Novelists deceive whenever they twist a plot. The more unlike the things are, the higher the art. Adam Smith, in his essay "On the Imitative Arts," finds opera to be one of the highest arts because it represents people doing what they would rarely do in life: communicate by singing.

ECOLOGICAL THEORIES OF DECEPTION

Zoologists have devoted considerable effort to developing a theory that explains the why, when, where, and how of deception.

Predators don't select prey in proportion to their occurrence. Rather, rare prey is ignored more frequently than its rarity will account for. One plausible explanation is that predators form a search image of the more common prey to enhance the likelihood of capture. Some prey will take advantage of the disproportion by evolving concealing coloration, thus achieving a deceptive rarity. Thereupon, the predator's "optimal search rate" for that prey will decrease, his "stare duration" will increase, and, in plain English, he won't waste his energy searching for deceptive prey.

There are, of course, many possible ways of foiling predators besides concealing coloration. Yet concealing coloration seems to be the most energy-efficient. John Endler breaks predation down into these stages:[3]

1. Encounter, or getting close enough to see the prey;
2. Detection, or perceiving the prey against its background;
3. Identification, discerning that the prey is edible and deciding to attack;
4. Approach (Attack);
5. Subjugation;
6. Consumption.

Predation can be foiled at any stage. A zebra, for instance, avoids the lion at the time of attack through socialization, speed, and disruptive coloration (that wall of stripes rushing by). A stinkbug fights back at the time of subjugation by secreting a noxious chemical. A blowfish waits until the consumption stage to spring his vicious trap.

The particular defense chosen depends on its relative costs and benefits and the evolutionary history of the group. The earlier the interruption, such as concealing coloration, the less the risk of capture and the amount of energy expended.

The zebra, for example, would reduce its risk if the lion didn't see him at all. Running takes up a tremendous amount of energy; if there's another lion down the trail, the zebra will be too tired to run.

There is a cost, however. The energy used for the deceptive behavior crowds out the other life-enhancing features. Balance must be struck.

CIRCUMSPECTION AND DISTRUST: AN ECONOMIC THEORY OF DECEPTION

Oliver E. Williamson, a student of economic sociology, has developed a theory of economic behavior that suggests businesses behave in much the same way as plants and animals, for much the same reasons. His theory, called *transaction cost economics*, holds that "economizing on transaction costs is mainly responsible for the choice of one form of capitalist organization over another."[4]

He proposes a three-level scheme to explain how business organizations, or *institutions*, achieve efficacy: the *institutional environment*, through rules, gives rise to *governance* of contractual relationships within parameters dictated by the beliefs and behavior of *individuals*.

James Madison, in the *Federalist Papers*, was the first American to explore this subject. "As there is a degree of depravity in mankind which requires a certain degree of circumspection and distrust, so there are other qualities in human nature which justify a certain portion of esteem and confidence."

Williamson names this depravity *opportunism*: "the use of guile in pursuit of one's own interest." It is the purpose of organizations to develop sanctions and procedures for governance that maximize profits while taking account of the Machiavellian—or, euphemistically, the "opportunistic"—nature of human transaction. "The mitigation of opportunism plays a central role in transaction cost economics."[5]

Transaction cost economics characterizes the buy-or-sell decision among individuals as having three parts: (1) *price*, (2) *hazards* (including guile), and (3) *safeguards* to protect against hazards. In a society where norms, customs, property rights, contract laws, and courts can be counted on to forestall opportunism, safeguards will largely be dispensed with at significant reduction of price. In societies where opportunism is rampant, safeguards will be extensive, up to and including organizing a hierarchical institution where as many transactions as possible can be kept in-house. Employees will still be opportunistic, of course, but the hierarchical organization is *preemptive*. In other words, internal matters are settled internally, without recourse to the courts. Furthermore, the institution can *shift parameters*, or make new rules to control employees by fiat, and it can also try to create *endogenous preferences:* putting out propaganda to influence the thinking of the employees so they will be cajoled or coerced into respecting the *governance structure.*

PRINCIPLES OF DECEPTION

The ecological and economic theory of deception can be applied in any field. I decided to concentrate my energy on three fields that are pervasive in life—war, sports, and nature—as a preliminary to studying deception in markets.

A theme soon developed from the separate studies I made in these fields. At the outset, two groups competed for survival. Much energy was lost in direct battles. The predators and prey became so adept at their respective offensive and defensive tactics that an indirect approach saved energy for both parties.

Deceptive techniques galore emerged in each field to enable life to go on without all the waste from a direct confrontation. But then, some "genius" among the contestants, whether by thought or happenstance, developed a better method of offense or defense. The technique was transmitted through genes, signs, or sentences. Differential survival of the favorable deceptive technique evolved.

But eventually the other side developed a counter to this new strategy. Defense and offense constantly evolved with each other to maintain a balance. The back-and-forth is called an arms race in the battlefield, and co-evolution in biology.

ONE SPECIES, ALL DECEITS—IT'S WAR

Many animals have evolved one or two forms of deception. Humans, on the other hand, are general-purpose creatures. They cook up a deception when they need one, and they are prone to mix and match the fundamental deceits *ad lib.* When deception isn't called for, they can save their energy.

The easiest place to find spectacular examples of this peculiar human talent is in the field of warfare.

Many experts on warfare consider B. H. Liddell Hart, who served as war correspondent for the London *Times* for 40 years, the supreme authority. Here we have his conclusion concerning the efficacy and extensive applicability of what he refers to as indirection, which is at least a brother to deception:

> When, in the course of studying a long series of military campaigns, I first came to perceive the superiority of the indirect over the direct approach, I was looking merely for light upon strategy . . . I began to realize that the indirect approach had a much wider application—that it was a law of life in all spheres: a truth of philosophy. Its fulfillment was seen to be the key to

practical achievement in dealing with any problem where the human factor predominates, and a conflict of wills tends to spring from an underlying concern for interests. In all such cases, the direct assault of new ideas provokes a stubborn resistance, thus intensifying the difficulty of producing a change of outlook. Conversion is achieved more easily and rapidly by unsuspected infiltration of a different idea or by an argument that turns the flank of instinctive opposition. The indirect approach is as fundamental to the realm of politics as to the realm of sex. In commerce the suggestion that there is a bargain to be secured is far more potent than any direct appeal to buy. And . . . it is proverbial that the surest way of gaining a superior's acceptance of a new idea is to persuade him that it is his idea! As in war, the aim is to weaken resistance before attempting to overcome it; and the effect is best attained by drawing the other party out of his defenses.[6]

Hart reviews dozens of campaigns, ancient and modern, citing chapter and verse of how deception led to the key victory. My own study of the history of warfare uncovered three examples that appear to be typical of many successful campaigns: the decoy, the false gift, and the holdup.

The Decoy

The Old Testament (Judges 4:12) provides an early recorded instance of military deception and subterfuge. A powerful army of Canaanites with "nine hundred chariots of iron" led by Sisera was mounting an attack on Israel. Word of their plans reached the Israelites, whereupon the warrior-priestess Deborah advised Barak of Kedesh to raise a force of 10,000 Israelites and to lead them into hiding on the craggy slopes of Mount Tabor, looming above the valley of the river Kishon. With a small decoy force, Deborah lured Sisera's army along the river bank into a narrow marshy plain below Mount Tabor where the heavy chariots were certain to bog down. This done, Barak's 10,000 swooped down from the mountain and decimated the Canaanites.

The False Gift

The story of the Trojan Horse is well known. After ten years of continued fighting with thousands of men, help from the most effective gods and goddesses, all the latest equipment of war, and the heroic feats of Achilles, Ulysses, Agamemnon, et al., the Greeks were still unable to take Troy. The Trojans had an impenetrable wall. Ulysses finally resorted to deception. He designed a wooden horse and concealed twenty of his ablest soldiers within. The remaining warriors pulled up stakes and sailed to Tenedos. The horse was wheeled into Troy and, in the evening, the Greeks emerged, killed the sentries, opened the gates, and finally destroyed the city.

What amazed me on reading the major source material on the Trojan Horse—*The Odyssey*, the *Aeneid*, and Ovid's *Metamorphoses*—was the cornucopia of deceptive techniques the Greeks used to end the war. I count at least five, all of which could provide a template for all deception that has since emerged:

1. The horse was designed with beautiful carvings to look like a trophy so that the Trojans' greed would entice them to accept the gift ("Beware of Greeks bearing gifts," Laocoon foretold). The doors to the horse were concealed with cunningly contrived bolts.

2. Sinon, a double agent, was left behind by the Greeks. He received substantial payment to tell a million lies about why the Greeks had left the horse behind, and predict dire consequences to Troy if they refused the gift. If the Trojans were to destroy the horse, said Sinon, it would mean certain destruction of Troy, but if they brought it inside, they would invade Greece itself and conquer the grandsons of those who had fought against them for so long.

3. With beautiful reverse psychology, the Horse was designed so that it would be impossible for the Trojans to bring it inside the city without destroying part of the wall which had been the mainstay of their defense during the ten years of siege by the Greeks. Surely the Greeks wouldn't send an attacking force within a gift so unlikely to be accepted.

4. The Greek ships concealed themselves miles away in Tenedos where they were hidden from the Trojan sentries. The warriors inside the Horse remained silent except for the clashing of their armor which was drowned out by the Trojans' revelry.

5. The Trojan prophet, Laocoon, who hurled the spear at the horse to show it was hollow and probably contained warriors, had to be discredited. The Greek gods sent a serpent to eat his sons to make it seem they were angry with him for his lies, and then they ate him.

The Holdup

My favorite war tactic is a variation of the playing-dead technique.

It is early May 1940, and the British merchant vessel *Scientist* is cautiously plying the west coast of Africa, bound for Liverpool from Durban with a heavy cargo including 1,150 tons of chromium and 2,500 tons of maize. The *Scientist's* captain, alert for enemy U-boats and battleships, scans the horizon frequently and anxiously. He sees nothing, however, except for an old rust-stained freighter lumbering slowly toward them, flying the colors of Japan, a country nominally neutral at the time. Through his binoculars, the British skipper read the name *Kasii Maru* on the hull. He sees a number of Japanese sailors, scarves around their heads and shirttails out, lounging aimlessly at the rails. A woman absentmindedly pushes a baby carriage along the freighter's shabby deck.

Suddenly, the *Scientist's* radio crackles with a harsh signal: heave to immediately and refrain from use of the wireless on pain of attack. Simultaneously, the *Kasii Maru* lowers the Rising Sun, hoists the Swastika, and fires a shell across the *Scientist's* bow. The *Scientist* duly heaves to and begins to lower boats. Moments later, the abandoned vessel is torpedoed, sending its precious cargo to Neptune's locker. The heavily armed Germans pick up the survivors of the sunken ship before moving on.

SECOND TO ANTS?

Having addressed various examples of human deception, I still hesitate to claim the crown of crookery for our species. The ease and completeness of ant deception still impresses.

Ants are giants in developing sophisticated deceptive techniques. The parasitic ant, *Teleutomyrmex schniederi*, for instance, can't survive without its host ant, the *Tetramorium caespitium*. By falsifying colony odors of the host ant, the *Teleutomyrmex* is admitted to the nest—ants identify nestmates by scent alone—where it is completely dependent on the host for care. *Teleutomyrmex* has no worker caste, and the queens are adapted for riding on the backs of other ants. Their bellies are concave, they have enlarged pads and claws on their feet, and they instinctively grasp other ants, preferably the queen. "As many as eight have been observed riding on a single host queen, their crowded bodies and clutching legs cloaking her body and preventing her from moving."[7]

They are fed and groomed by the host, even eating the liquid that should go to the host queen. Mature *Teleutomyrmex* queens will lay as many as two eggs a minute, all queens and drones. Nevertheless, *Teleutomyrmex* is very rare, as are all similarly adapted ants.

One beguiling thing about ant deception is that it attacks at the strong point: a riding ant uses the victim's best defense against it. The subtle, energy-deficient use of smell for identification becomes the subtle, energy-efficient means of indenturing the victim's hard-wired behavior.

No matter how fine-tuned an animal's senses of smell, hearing, sight, or touch are, the animal is subject to predators. Because of the chances of discovery, animals have evolved a variety of deceptive strategies.

MIMICRY

Mimicry is the resemblance of one species to another for defensive or aggressive purposes. In defensive mimicry, a palatable species looks like an unpalatable one. For example, flies often bear yellow markings that make them look like wasps, many nonpoisonous snakes look like coral snakes or rattlesnakes, and many insects look like ants, which are the least favorite prey of many species.

In offensive mimicry, the predator looks like the prey. The classic example is a genus of fireflies whose females issue light signals to attract males of a different genus, luring them to a deadly embrace. Sometimes, the aggressive mimic resembles a friend. The saber-tooth blenny looks like a wrass, which is accepted as a cleanser fish by its coral reef clients. But once the blenny gets within biting distance, it's all over.

Mimicry tends to develop in diverse, energy-rich webs. It's particularly prominent in tropical rain forests and coral reefs. Would we be surprised to find outcropping in the rich communities of the market?

To have a true case of mimicry rather than mere camouflage, disguise, or ambush, there have to be three actors: the model, the mimic, and the dupe. You can guess who the dupe is in most market situations: you and I—the public.

The 1987 stock market crash provided a wonderful model. Following 1987, longs would be nervous on Fridays, and should their fears be justified by a down close on Friday, the ensuing Monday should be the stage for a rout.

In actuality, the exact opposite has occurred. In the nine years following 1987, of the 44 occasions when the S&P mimicked the crash by dropping more than four full points on a Friday, it *rose* on the subsequent Monday on 28 occasions. The average rise on these Mondays, into September 1996, was 3.5 S&P points.

What explains the transformation? Many fewer weak longs were around in the post-1987 environment, leaving stronger, better capitalized longs as the remaining holders. The dupes were forced to cover, squeezing each other in their rush to escape their short positions.

On December 18, 1995, Treasury bonds for delivery in March dropped a full point from open to close, after a nearly straight run-up of 13 points. This drop went through the "support line" and seemed to indicate the end of the bull run. The drop closely resembled the drop on July 17, after a similar run-up. The July 17 downturn had been followed by a two-day drop of over two and a half points, and didn't hit bottom (seven points lower than the previous high) for nearly a month.

The resemblance was too close for comfort. Weak bulls who saw the resemblance as a causal phenomenon refused to be eaten alive. Once these bulls were forced out at 117.6 on December 19, the market went on to regain nearly the entire previous day's loss at closing, and touched 122 on January 6 before beginning another downturn.

Playing Dead

The opossum is a master of deception. When threatened, it plays dead so effectively that biologists used to believe that it went into a trance. Modern research shows that the opossum is actually wide awake and alert, and experience shows that he is not to be trifled with while in the playing-dead mode. Anyone who has ever tried to carry a "dead" possum by the tail can attest to the effectiveness of the animal's second line of defense: a mouthful of needlelike teeth.

Playing dead works because many predators will eat only live prey. They know from the wisdom of nature that such prey are not likely to be swarming with maggots and worms. This technique—and its aggressive counterpart, lying invisible and then striking from ambush—is so effective that it is used at all levels of nature. For instance, the hog snake, when frightened, turns on its back and sticks its tongue out. If you turn it over, it will turn itself back. Striking from ambush is favored by organisms ranging from the moray eel to the Venus flytrap.

Ambushes are so common in the market that it's hard to find an occasion when one *isn't* going on. During the week, there are critical announcements that are known to increase market volatility substantially in each market. Mind you, the numbers themselves, which are subject to revision, error, and faulty seasonals, are completely meaningless. But at least they are something for the nervous to hang their hats on. In the bond and currency markets, where normal volatility is at least doubled, the big announcements are the employment numbers (on the first Friday of each month), and the Producer Price Index (PPI; usually on the second Friday of each month). In stocks, the last day of the quarter and the stock options' expiration day (the third Friday of each month) bring radically higher volatility and volume. In the currency markets, the big announcement is the monthly trade deficit. In the agricultural markets, the USDA crop reports are traditionally the key. All players are ready for volatility on announcement days, but they forget to watch out the day before, and sometimes the day after, and that's when the markets can catch them off base. Thursday, September 9, 1993, is a good example of an ambush move. The Producer Price Index was scheduled for release the next morning, at 8:30 A.M. The market waited tensely because the Fed had recently threatened to tighten if inflation symptoms began to show. Instead of drifting aimlessly until the appointed hour, the market made its move before the announcements, when no one was ready.

The inflation indexes are one of the few government releases (in my experience) that are consistently kept secure before release. Always alert to every opportunity, traders have already encapsulated this tendency. The inflation release dates are known as *going-against days*.

Bonds dropped 1½ percent on Thursday, September 9, 1993—their greatest decline in six months. They opened down another ½ percent the following morning, ten minutes before the release. But at 8:30 A.M. they promptly rallied 1½ percent on the announcement of the largest-ever recorded decline in the PPI. A decrease in cigarette wholesale prices had been announced several months earlier and had precipitated a 33 percent collapse in the stock of Philip Morris, which in turn led to 10–15 percent declines in the stock prices of all types of branded consumer companies. That downward slide had finally hit the slow-moving, backward-looking, spuriously seasonally adjusted index published by the Department of Labor, massively skewing the PPI number down.

To test the phenomenon, I looked at the average change in absolute price on the days before and after the employment announcement (the ambush days) versus the average change on all other days. The average absolute change on the ambush day was 10 percent higher than on normal days.

Cases of ambush in the market frequently follow from the action of politicians. On Thursday, January 25, 1996, an official at the Bundesbank voiced his opinion that the deutschemark (DM) was overpriced. He felt that rather than approximately 1.49 DM to the dollar, the rate should be closer to 1.60. The DM moved from 1.4765 at 11:00 A.M. to 1.4870 at noon. I was holding yen at the time, and the effect spilled over. I suffered losses, but many Japanese companies speculating in currencies lost crippling amounts.

Ambushes are a form of offensive death playing. I learned to be aware of it from the writings of Louis L'Amour, whom I often turn to for guidance when I crave wisdom, learning, or adventure. Paraphrasing L'Amour, "When you see excessive volatility, be careful; when you don't see excessive volatility, be doubly careful."

L'Amour's wisdom is useful for survival in the markets as well as in the West. On May 2, 1995, I noted that the bond had opened and closed within the same 105 handle on eight consecutive days. Within the next month, bonds rallied six points for one of the most dramatic gains ever.

My broker called to tell me, "The market is dead, there's no flow whatsoever. The bears have given up playing the short side." I knew that danger lay ahead.

The next day, a relatively unimportant number was due to be announced at 10 A.M. "It's probably going to do nothing on the number," a clerk on the floor called to report. I knew danger was near, but I didn't know whether it was danger for the bulls or the bears. Stationary prices seem to be a favorite trait of the bulls rather than the bears, so I closed out my shorts.

I figured the traders would be out playing golf. That often happens during the summer doldrums, and I always get ready for an ambush during such times. Usually, I'm right. But I and most other traders haven't been able to figure out whether the enemy's more likely to strike with horns or a hug.

Leaving no contingency for profit unexploited, a market for profiting from listlessness and volatility has developed. Dealers in the cash markets routinely quote bids and ask for volatility. Volatility invariably goes down after periods of playing dead, and up after a period of energetic movements.

Longer-term basing actions leading to abandonment of all hope, only to be superseded by a fantastic move, are as common as flies in markets. Silver is a market particularly prone to such role playing. Before the 1979 move, from $5 to $50, silver had languished for years. A more current feigning of death came during the last months of 1995 (see Figure 10–1). Near the end of 1995, silver traded around $5.20 an ounce. The option to buy March silver at $5.20 sold for just 6 cents—a reasonable value, considering that silver had been trading in a 5-cent range for the previous two months. But then, in one wonderful month for bulls, silver climbed to $5.60. The March $5.20 options climbed to 50 cents, a tenfold increase.

Bears disregard quiet markets at their peril. The bulls had merely been playing dead. Sellers had been lulled into a false sense of security. Within a few weeks, bears in price and volatility were killed.

A similar phenomenon emerged in the Hong Kong stock market. During the last quarter of 1995, the Hang Seng index hovered within a percent or two of the 10,000 figure, as if in a dead man's trance. In the first week of 1996, the average stock promptly rose 5 percent.

Soft commodities are notorious for playing dead. The long growing cycle often magnifies the influence of any current vicissitudes of price. Coffee looked to be playing dead through 1993 and 1994. Movement vacillated between 75 and 80 cents. Speculative buyers would have been well justified in losing interest. Sellers of options to buy coffee in the future would have been raking in profits throughout this period. Then, suddenly, within two months, coffee quadrupled in price, wiping out all those who

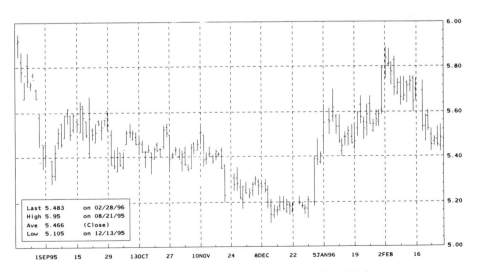

Source: Bloomberg Financial Markets Commodities News, New York.

Figure 10–1.   Silver—Weekly Chart

had become complacent. Recall that after the opossum plays dead, it will, if threatened, administer a lethal bite to those who treat it cavalierly.

I have always been reluctant to trot out a few anecdotes to prove a theory. I believe that playing dead is a central theme of market deception, but, if I'm right, there should be a way of quantifying my belief. I took some preliminary steps with a study of all one-day moves in bonds from the day of the Crash in October 1987 to June 30, 1996, almost nine years in all.

If markets have a tendency to play dead, then the absolute change after small daily moves should be greater than the change after large daily moves. The results support the playing-dead theory. After the 1,296 days when bonds showed a small one-day change, the average change five days later was 1.29 percent. But after the 197 occasions when bonds showed a large change of a full point or more, the average change five days later was just 1.05 percent (see Table 10-1). In other words, volatility was 22 percent greater after the small changes. (The differences are on the borderline of statistical significance, at about 5 in 100 by chance.)

CONCEALING COLORATION

Examples of creatures that practice this deception are legion: the polar bear, the snowshoe hare, the leopard, the Eurasian bittern—which nests in reeds and, when disturbed, extends its long, striped neck and sways with the reeds—and the famous peppered moth, which changed its dominant color phase when the Industrial Revolution changed the color of the trees it inhabited.

As mentioned earlier, a more interesting example occurs among ants. The only method ants have for distinguishing friend from foe is scent. Many predator and parasite species have evolved the ability to fabricate colony scent signals and use them for parasitizing, enslaving, or preying on ants. Hundreds of ant species and thousands of other insect species gain admittance to colonies and are accepted as members. Say Bert Hölldobler and Edward O. Wilson (paraphrasing William Morton Wheeler), "It is as though a human family were to invite gigantic lobsters, midget tortoises, and similar monsters to dinner, and never notice the difference."[8]

Concealing coloration is the most efficient and common form of deception in nature. An animal or plant blends in with its environment. The

Table 10-1. Average Bond Price Change (%)
Following Daily Moves of Different Magnitude

Subsequent Move	Daily Variation		
	Small Change	Medium Change	Large Change
1 day later	0.52	0.49	0.43
5 days later	1.29	1.16	1.05

The size of the bathing apparel is inversely proportionate to wealth and age (Artist: Steve Zazenski).

I am an old trader and I trade the yen (Artist: Marie Keegan).

A romantic Brighton vista (Artist: Rubens Teles).

Early indications: climbing out of the deep end (Artist: Rubens Teles).

Acts of kindness—Niederhoffer castoffs for Joplin's "poor" family
(Artist: Helen Fabi Smagorinsky).

Deception exemplified. Willie Sutton is asked, "Officer, do you mind if I
park here and change the baby's diaper?" (Artist: Marie Keegan).

The emotions on the trading floor (Artist: Harry Pincus).

I know it's time to jump in when I hear a "spine-chilling chorus . . . across the water—a mixture of cries, screams, and shouts . . . the most nightmarish sound imaginable" ("Titanic" oil painting by William G. Muller, 1981).

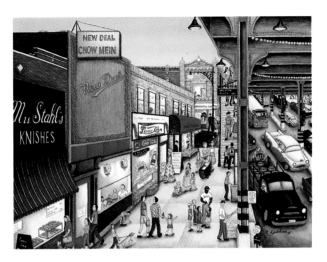

A good meal of Moo goo gai pan from paddleball winnings (Artist: Kathy Jakobsen).

A checkers mecca: youngsters at play (Artist: Linda Mears).

Risky entertainment (Artist: Marie Keegan).

Nothing is so good for the inside of a gambling man as the outside rail of a racetrack (Artist: Victor Gatto).

The universal nature of handicapping (Artist: Linda Mears).

Practice every day—no exceptions (Artist: Linda Mears).

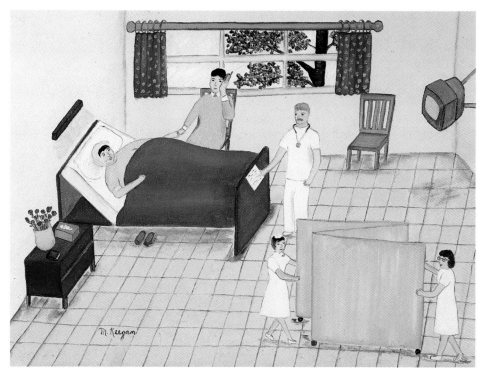

"Get your trading out of here! Go trade pork bellies somewhere else." (Artist: Marie Keegan).

Defending academic freedom (Artist: Steve Zazenski).

The best bargainer: "This would be an ideal retreat" (Artist: Steve Zazenski).

Punishment for excessive use of candlesticks (Artist: Marie Keegan).

Drop a perpendicular (Artist: Marie Keegan).

The camouflaged path of the speculative life (Artist: Milton Bond).

The ecology of the floor (Artist: Marie Keegan).

Marauding markets: bountiful pickings using LoBagola analysis
(Artist: Milton Bond).

Bizarre connections (Artist: Linda Mears).

Brighton in the '50s (Artist: Steve Klein).

moth looks like a twig, the worm looks like dirt, the grasshopper looks like a weed.

To quantify concealing coloration, I like to employ similarities. Each day, I look at a market and choose the moves in the past that most match those that occurred today. My hypothesis is that moves will be inversely correlated with those that occurred following the one most similar day the previous year. For example, consider the Swiss franc. On April 17, 1995, the Swiss franc was up from 87.60 to 89.08, a gain of 2.48. Looking back over the past year, the most similar rise came on March 31, 1995, when it rose 2.97 points, from 85.91 to 88.88. The next day, the Swiss franc went up further, from 88.88 to 89.61, a .73-point gain. Thus, the prediction would be for a decline.

In fact, on April 18, 1995, the Swiss franc went up .95 points to 90.03, so the prediction was wrong. But not to worry; in a test of the eight years ending June 30, 1995, the hypothesis is confirmed. The correlation between the most similar move and the actual move the next day is −0.10. Standard statistical testing shows that results this bad would occur in less than 2 in 100 occasions by chance, thereby confirming that concealing coloration is at work in the Swiss franc.

The Swiss franc is a particularly deceptive market. Of 100 different similarity relations I tested, analyzing the most similar x days out of the last y days, only one showed a positive correlation with subsequent moves.

Considering the prevalence of trading techniques that use similarities as their base (nearest neighbor, neural networks, clustering, and so on), it is no wonder that dealers consistently make billions a year in trading profits by coppering their customers.

DISRUPTIVE BEHAVIOR

Disruptive behavior is the most spectacular form of deception. Naïve hunters have been known to follow a quail for miles while it executes its "sick bird" technique. A squid sprays a cloud of black ink to distract a predator while it makes a getaway. And nobody *ever* crosses a skunk twice, at least not willingly.

But, for a most apt example, let us again look to the ant. *Formica subintegra* uses a form of chemical warfare. When it raids for slaves, it sprays the nest of the victims with unusually large quantities of a chemical closely resembling the "propaganda substances" the slave species uses to warn of danger. This throws the nest into a rout, allowing *subintegra* to carry off victims at leisure.

To appreciate the expression of disruptive behavior in commodities, consider the stock market move around the October 19, 1987, crash. On October 19, the Dow dropped 508 points to 1738. On October 20, the Dow opened at 1856 and then dropped to 1723. At this time, trading was halted on the futures exchanges. The disruptive move scared the daylights

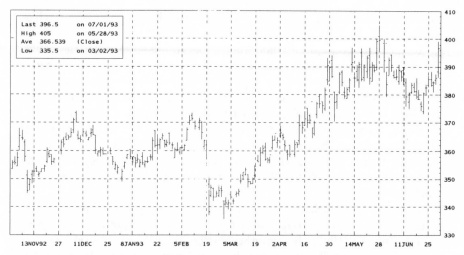

Source: Bloomberg Financial Markets Commodities News, New York.

Figure 10–2.   Platinum

out of all bulls. Those who were left were able to participate in a continuous 250 percent rise in the next nine years.

The April 1993 platinum chart (Figure 10–2) tells a similar story of disruptive behavior to scare off bulls. On February 20, 1993, the price dropped 7 percent, from 357.5 to 337.5. All bulls who wished to prey on the shorts were scared out of their positions. With the weak predators scared out, the coast was clear for platinum to show a sustained rise, which it did.

The markets that most frequently engage in disruptive behavior are the grain markets. After weather events, they frequently trade limit up or limit down for days at a time. It becomes impossible to even record meaningful prices for the computer at times like this, because there is no trading in a spot month to normalize prices. Inevitably, the strong take profit as the weak extricate themselves or go belly up in the process.

TRAPPING

Trapping, the offering of a false gift to get the prey in a vulnerable position, is possibly the most common deceit used by humans. It isn't quite as common among lesser animals, but many other species use it with success.

The angler fish is famous for setting such a trap in its favored coral habitat. It has a cartilage attached to its spine which, when moved in front of a small fish, looks like a worm. When prey comes to snatch the worm, the angler withdraws the cartilage and slips the small fish down its maw. Many species have independently developed similar traps. The trap door spider invites insects to enter a seemingly beautiful vista of luscious nectar. But when the insect tries to taste it, the trap door opens, out comes the spider, and the insect is soon dead.

The trap is so common in markets that I could fill a book with examples. I generally get calls twice a day from dealers who just happen to have an extra X million of some issue available at an attractive price. Invariably, within a second of my grabbing the bait, the trap is sprung and a torrent of selling occurs in some related market.

Big down openings in the currencies are often traps set to spring on those who like to buy on the cheap. During 1995, the Japanese yen opened down more than 50 points on 20 occasions. A period of bliss would emerge as the yen rose 5 points in the first hour of trading. By the end of the day, however, the average decline was 30 points.

In another instance, the British pound finally broke its five-year high and went above $2.00 in September 1992 (Figure 10–3). This was the buy signal many trend followers had been waiting for. The trap was set. Shorts rushed to cover. New buyers surged in, following the trend.

The decline that followed, perhaps the most rapid in any currency in recent years, left the pound at $1.40 just four months later. The 60-cent decline cost $40,000 a contract, which was worse than being eaten alive for many speculators, myself included.

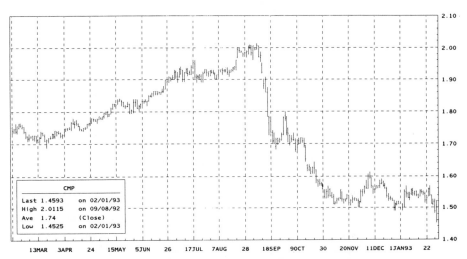

Source: Bloomberg Financial Markets Commodities News, New York.

Figure 10–3.   British Pound

Similar market behavior is so prevalent that it is hard to refrain from smiling at the frequency of the traps. May 1, 1996, two days before release of the dreaded April employment report, the market was as nervous as an expectant father. A leading bank captured the spirit in its market letter: "U.S. Treasury prices were little changed after paring modest gains in Asian trading. Trading was almost nonexistent ahead of the April jobs data amid concerns that the data will promote a plunge similar to those seen in tandem with the March and February job reports." As the next two days wore on, public selling drove Treasury prices down over 2 percent before the number was announced. But the shorts were caught in a vicious trap. Rather than plunging when the number was released, Treasuries rallied sharply throughout the next week.

CHANGES IN TEMPO

The market is not limited to borrowing from nature in the varieties of deception it employs. I have been fortunate to be surrounded by masters of deception in sports. My former assistant, Jon Normile, held the U.S. épée fencing championship for two years. Jon believes that the best way to profit from deception is to employ the fakes, barriers, counterthrusts, second and third intentions, and changes to tempo that he employed in fencing. He warned me away in a memo as follows:

> Take that infamous September 1992 British pound episode, where you almost lost the firm in the severity of its decline while you were long. I interpret it as an example of a "tempo fake." Commence downwards. Unexpectedly, the market closed with the pound up to 1.965.
>
> A fencing analogy can provide an alternative description for this episode. In fencing, one way to construct an effective attack is to change the tempo. For example, a fencer can change his speed from slow to fast. By doing this, he puts himself out of sync with his opponent, who, for a split second, does not know what to expect. It is this window of vulnerability that provides the opportunity for a hit.
>
> In the case of the December pound, the market changed its tempo by delaying its actual move. This delay may have caused some speculators to either misread the market or to simply withdraw. In either case, the speculators lost.
>
> Another example of this kind of "tempo fake" appears on the chart for the December Canadian dollar. Here, we see a sudden bear market starting September 7, 1992, at .8310 and continuing until September 29, 1992, at .7910. In hindsight, there is little doubt as to the direction of the trend: straight down. However, during the course of its run, the market threw a slow pitch. It broke its tempo and stalled out at approximately .8175 for the week of September 13. During this period of stagnation, the market gave mixed signals until it got back on track again and proceeded "south."

In fencing, it is effective to attack and immediately follow with a redoublement, or renewed attack. If the first attack hits, that is fine. You have just scored a point. If it is short and your opponent has begun his attack in response, your redoubled attack will most likely catch him by surprise. In the case of the Canadian dollar, the pause in the middle of its run probably caused a number of speculators to anticipate a reversal. When it renewed its original course it would have caused some pain.

Markets versus Moths

There is a major problem with this descriptive approach to deception. The examples I give are chosen retrospectively to show an analogy between market phenomena and other natural phenomena. The market is rich enough to provide examples to prove and disprove all simple phenomena. The examples have no predictive value. This problem is compounded by the circularity of many of the arguments put forward by writers on the subject of evolution, that "such and such characteristic or strategy has survival value, as evidenced by the fact of its existence, i.e., its having survived." In discussing the evidence for evolution, even many adherents admit that "it has relatively weak powers of prediction. About the only place where there is very strong predictive evidence is in laboratory experiments."

The theory of natural selection has been stigmatized by its critics as an unfalsifiable, trivial tautology. The stigma also fits my market examples.

It is quite likely that what appears to us to be an example of deception could be construed by others as an example of an entirely separate phenomenon, for example, convergent evolution or mere chance.

Because deception is prevalent in many fields and is variegated in its expression, the question naturally arises as to how to predict where and when deception will appear. To get perspective on the answer to this question, consider the lowly puss moth:

> [It] uses camouflage and disruptive coloration for primary defense and various forms of intimidation as well as sheer strength for secondary defense. It never gives up but sits out an attack by responding with a barrage of defenses until the predator goes away, or of course, until it is eaten. A small bird that finds and eventually overcomes one is worthy of respect.[9]

Now if a common moth can muster such an array of confusing defenses, imagine the mind of Mr. Market as he disguises and conceals himself, intimidates and plays dead, in the multifarious manifestations of the price chart. Should we be surprised at how much subtler his stratagems could be than those of the puss moth?

Market life is hazardous.

CHAPTER 11

Sex

They hit their phones like rattlesnakes. In two minutes they had sold out. The position was cut, the profit taken: $6,800,000. They wrote the tickets and sat back exhausted, euphoric, grinning at each other. Sarah let their mood consume her. The sensation was almost sexual. They switched off their screen and went to celebrate.

Linda Davies
Nest of Vipers

NEVER THE TWAIN

"Sex," said Somerset Maugham, "is topic A." When we're not doing it, we're talking about it; when we're not talking about it, we're thinking about it; when we're not thinking about it, it is, with luck, because we're doing it. Hardly any human activity lacks a sexual dimension. And yet, sex and speculation seem to squeeze each other out. Nearly every speculator writes in his memoirs that a good trade "is better than sex." When a woman at a party asks me what I do, I invariably say, "I'm just a speculator." The encounter's over. The only worse conversation stopper is "I'm just a statistician."

Is speculation, then, the only area of life that's not suffused by sex? It hardly seems reasonable. Greed and lust are often more than kissing cousins. Put more delicately, perhaps the two drives—to get and to beget—are siblings. Sex celebrates life, speculation supports it. Both activities succeed best in private. Both are all-absorbing. And both have an air of the shameful about them: primal urges, evidently, drive people to do things they would not speak of.

Does this explain the silence on the subject? After an exhaustive search of the scholarly literature on sex and speculation, I can report that there is no literature. The only effort so far made to connect sex and speculation is the well-known "hemline index"—the idea that market performance is directly related to the shortness of skirts.

The evidence for the theory usually consists of some skimpy skirts from the '20s and the '60s, when stocks were soaring. Next come the inevitable allusions to maxis or the split dresses customarily worn in the '30s and the

'70s, when stocks were in the doldrums. Some ponderous verbiage follows, such as: "It is not unreasonable to hypothesize that the rise in both hemline and stock prices reflects a general increase in friskiness and daring because skirt lengths have limits (the upper thigh); the reaching of a limit would imply that an extreme in mood has been reached." Rounding it off is the hope that a prurient picture of an attractive woman in a sexy mini will auger a bull market. All the research I've seen predates the women's liberation movement, so I must also report that most authors also include a "dirty old man" kind of hope that the Dow doesn't go so high that the minis recede to the unillustrable length.

Ira Cobleigh presents an interesting chart titled "Bull Market and Bare Knees," showing the Dow graph line superimposed on pictures of seven hemlines from 1917 to 1967. He concludes, "We can now state with considerable assurance that there does exist a demonstrable relationship between hemlines and stocks, and in general hemlines are the lead barometer. We may have established a new Wall Street slogan: 'Don't sell till you see the heights of their thighs.'"[1]

In the name of science, therefore, I will sacrifice my privacy, air some family history, and share my personal predilections in order to introduce some sunlight into this dark corner of human nature. Moreover, I will propose two new market indicators (supported by a workout from 1878 to date): the sex-to-speculation ratio, and its cousin, the sex-to-Shakespeare ratio. Perhaps this chapter will open new discussions. Perhaps it will encourage others to speak honestly and thereby contribute to the general improvement of mankind. Maybe it will even spark a new revolution. The Spexual Revolution. The Sexulation Revolution.

My Grandfather's Bent

Sex was a most popular topic with my grandfather. Martin always kept a copy of Bronislaw Malinowski's *Sexual Life of Savages* close to his desk. He also owned a copy of Krafft-Ebing's *Psychopathia Sexualis* and was well-versed in the works of the Marquis de Sade. Martin liked to quote Malinowski and Krafft-Ebing whenever an attractive member of the opposite sex gave him the chance. His daughter Jane recounts that Martin was wont to discourse on primitive sexual customs while helping attractive bathing beauties with their strokes in the waters off Coney Island, 20 yards away from his apartment. If Birdie, who was eight inches taller than he, caught him in the act, she would fairly carry him off the beach in her fury. History repeated itself once when I was 23 and my better half caught me in a similar act. She poured cranapple juice over my head, achieving the desired deflationary effect.

Martin liked to combine music with a little sex and speculation. He took piano lessons from Scott Joplin and doubtless gave Scott many specifics on the emotions of pain, panic, and jubilation that were incorporated into "The Wall Street Rag." Scott taught Martin two rags, "The Pineapple Rag" and the "Pretty Pansy Rag." Martin would close all the windows and hide when Scott Joplin came over, to make the neighbors think Martin was playing. My grandfather wanted only to perform in Joplin's ragtime style. Martin could read music, but not fluently, and he preferred to have Joplin provide a model for him to imitate. He would say, "Show me the chords, and I'll follow it."

Scott Joplin was immensely talented—one of the greatest masters of melodies and rhythm in the annals of music. Yet he was as poor as a church mouse. Martin regularly saved old clothes cast off by his five brothers and his own three kids and carried them personally to Joplin's home in Harlem. The Niederhoffer family derived a warm sense of satisfaction from knowing that Martin had taken a personal interest in the distribution of this apparel. The generous feeling only intensified when Martin told his family that Scott's wife and her many colleagues were so much in need of this apparel that when he arrived at the Joplin home the girls were frequently dressed in little more than towels, sometimes less.

Seventy-five years later, the truth emerged when a researcher into Joplin's life confirmed that the clothes were for the benefit of the denizens of a house of ill repute, which Scott's wife ran and in which Scott resided. By that time, Martin was six feet under. Never in his lifetime, at least, did he have to face the wrath of Birdie, which surely would have descended had she discovered the likely reason for Martin's personal visits to the Joplin residence.

Artie's Allusions

"Eeeeeee-haw! Haow!" The romp of high-heeled boots shook the floor and sent thumps through my chair. "Honor your partner!" sang Artie. "And honor your corner!" He perched on a stool at the head of two squares, playing frantic music on the fiddle. "Now all grab hands and circle to the right. Turn to the center and do the grand square!" Eight men in string ties and pegged jeans clapped and stomped, and eight pretty ladies in crinolines swirled their skirts until they looked like a summer flower garden.

The attractive women are paying a little too much attention to Artie for everyone's good. Artie always had a magnetic impact. He had studied ballet and tap dance as a boy. And he had a natural grace and sense of rhythm that couldn't be taught.

At this party, his conversation was with Adeline, the prettiest dancer, who was dressed in sumptuous silk with a plunging neckline. She was enrolled in a judo class. Even in the 1940s, women were taking self-defense into their own hands.

"Artie, I can walk alone anywhere without fear. I can flip a man."

"That won't protect you. Listen, if a mugger attacks you, don't resist. Give him your money. Don't get him angry."

"But Artie, I've learned how to throw a man."

"Do yourself a favor. You can't fight with a man. They're stronger."

"No Artie, let me show you."

"All right, but I warned you." Artie grabbed Adeline in a full-nelson. His technique was superb, reminiscent of his days as a stalwart of the heavyweight division of the Brooklyn College wrestling team. Adeline was completely dominated. She struggled and writhed. The spectators laughed and urged her to break the hold. But plastered against Artie's 220 pounds of muscle, back-to-pelvis, she stopped wriggling, moaned, and finally, out of breath, called, "Uncle."

My mom, however, wasn't laughing. Afterward, there was hell to pay for a week—for me. My piano practice was doubled. There was no going to the night center for games until my homework was finished. I learned at an early age the ramifications of opening the door to sex on the job.

At work, Artie had ample opportunity to transgress. His job often held the alluring but dangerous prospect of checking the home, even the bedroom, of a lonely and scantily clad young lady when prowlers were in the neighborhood. "Officer, I'd feel so much more comfortable if you stayed a few moments longer to make sure he doesn't come back again while I'm alone in the bedroom." When I play this one out with my wife after a bad day of trading, an all-too-frequent occurrence, I always respond, "Well, perhaps it would help. . . ." But Artie always resisted.

Combining sex with a job is very inappropriate, for a hundred reasons. "Sex belongs in the bedroom, not the office," Artie always told me, and I have followed that advice to the letter except for the time I made a pass at an irresistible assistant of mine when she was just 19 years old. I'm still ashamed except that now we have four kids and have been living together in perfect harmony for the past 20 years.

Artie frequently came into contact with attractive beauties drawn to the phallic nature of his nightstick. The policeman is a walking sex symbol, he wrote in a characteristic passage of his best-seller, *Behind the Shield:*

> The policeman does well for himself in the battle of the sexes. His rugged physique, natty military uniform, sexually symbolic occupational tools, and aura of power combine to make him a figure of virility and undoubtedly have raised his status as a potential husband. Twenty years ago the policeman was a proper boyfriend for the housemaid; today he can successfully aspire to a teacher or a nurse.
>
> In the performance of duty, patrolmen are subjected to greater sexual temptations than members of other occupations. Voyeurism is built into the police job; it is a legitimate function, an aspect of the license and guilty knowledge which may be the basic criterion of a professional occupation.

Even policemen who are only average specimens are quick to defend their honor against any imputation of the lack, or loss, of virility.[2]

Judging from stories prevalent on the Street, the trader also does well for himself in the battle of (for) the sex(es). The first thing a visitor to the floor notices is that the 5,000 female clerks are dressed to kill—attired in outfits reminiscent of the attractive model in the Guess jeans commercial. Apparently, the two main paths to advancement are marriage to a trader or promotion to trader. The broker I use for most of my financial futures assures me that the most successful trader in his pit was previously the sexiest clerk. He insists that all the traders give her the edge on the bid and ask because they like the process of checking out the trades with her.

MY SEX EDUCATION

With the traits I learned and inherited from my grandfather and father, is it any wonder that I now enforce, for myself and my colleagues, a complete separation of sex and speculation. Some representative incidents are worth narrating.

My first exposure to the danger of combining romance and competition came during a 13-and-under handball tournament I was playing in on Brighton Beach's Garber Stadium court. I was never skilled in handball, but I managed, at the age of eleven, to get to the finals. I eked ahead, 21–14, 16–11, and looked like a sure winner. As I wound up to serve, I heard sounds of a crowd approaching. Piercing whistles and *"Bebe,"* *"S'il vous plait,"* *"Oh-la-la,"* and a high-pitched *"Non, non"* filled the air.

The crowd was skipping along in a circle. On the inner rim were men slapping their thighs, clapping their hands, and sashaying along, uttering Indian war whoops. In the middle of the circle walked an attractive girl of about 16, wearing perhaps the first bikini seen on the East Coast. I recognized her as a girl known to have visited the French Riviera, where it was commonplace even in those days for women to go topless on the beach. This assertive lass wanted to make a statement near the Atlantic Ocean. The men crowding around her, with an average age of about 70, could not contain themselves. I kept looking and wondering during the remainder of the match. I ended the loser.

AN ATTRACTIVE REPORTER

I had a hairbreadth escape from loss the next time I mixed sex and competition. At Princeton, in 1974, I was playing in the first round of the National Squash Championship. I was heavily favored because I had won the tournament without losing a game the year before in Detroit.

An attractive female reporter from the *Daily News* arranged to interview me after my first round. While I played, I was thinking about the birds and the bees rather than the business at hand. The next thing I knew, I was losing, 5–0, in the fifth game.

When I played, the crowd always rooted for my opponent. I think the main reason was that I hardly ever lost. A little fresh air is always desirable. When I fell behind in the fifth game, electricity filled the air. Every squash official in the state, in addition to my potential opponents still left in the tournament, rushed to the gallery to cheer on my opponent.

Most of them disliked me, but I could never tell whether it was because I was always winning; because I really was the horse's ass they claimed I was; because I was one of the few Jews in the game; or just because I refused to kow-tow to the effete anglophile snobs who controlled the game in those days. But whatever the reason, I decided right then I was in no way going to give those stuck-up s.o.b.s the satisfaction of seeing me lose.

Meanwhile, my opponent was delaying—arguing with every call, strolling to return the ball, toweling himself off for a minute after every point, calling for a towel to dry the sweat off the floor, and doing anything else he could think of to distract and rattle me.

I normally would have expended my energies giving the referee and my opponent a piece of my mind, but dissipating energy in such situations is a sure ticket to ruin. I know now that it's much better to attend to the business at hand. That's what I did in that match. I just turned on the pressure, forgot about the allure of the reporter, kept my big mouth shut, and went on to catch my opponent, 18–13 in the fifth.

Keep Your Distance

Even more dangerous than crowding out your own pursuits is interfering with others when they have sex on their mind. My first day in junior high school, I wanted to try out for the band. I opened the conductor's office door unannounced. Stepping into the office, I found the conductor preoccupied. (See now why academics make such a fuss about prior appointments.) His shirt was off, and he was locked in a passionate embrace with the captain of the cheerleading squad.

"Niederhoffer, what the hell do you want?" he said.

"Well, I just wanted to try out to play clarinet in the band. I know most of the standard compositions: Mozart, Weber, Brahms, Rossini. . . ."

"Get out of here. Can't you see that Melody is not well? I'm taking care of her."

"But, when can I . . . ?"

"Never. You're hired in the third clarinet section—last man. Now get out of here."

I played in the band for three years. But not surprisingly, after that introduction, I never advanced from third clarinet.

Sex, speculation, and music are flow activities that block out all awareness of the outside world. That's one of the reasons they're so enjoyable. I've often had occasion in my multifarious career to come into contact with guys and dolls engaged in private flow activities. Call it sad, call it funny, but I'm always ready to give better than even money that there's romance in the air. Frank Loesser spoke true in the lyric for *Guys and Dolls*, which is set in the world of gambling and speculation: "When you see a guy reach for stars in the sky, you can bet that he's doing it for some dame."

I have been able to apply those better-than-even-money odds from time to time, to stave off disaster. A typical example: my teenage daughters were taking lessons from a tennis instructor, Gary W. As part of the service, he chauffeured them to and from the courts. I attended one such lesson, detected stars in his eyes, and canceled the lessons. Shortly thereafter, he attempted to kidnap one of his former students, using a cattle prod to discourage resistance. He had equipped a secluded cabin in the Catskills with bondage and other sexual paraphernalia. When the kidnapping failed, he blew his brains out. Romancers who must reenter the real world fall hard.

THE MISTRESS OF THE MARKET

The market is a lonely place. The infinity of political, economic, biological, sociological, and psychological factors that influence it overloads the senses. It's essential to have an oasis, a place where a fresh breeze clears the senses. I found my oasis in the twice-daily, electronically transmitted Telerate columns of Caroline Baum. To me, her work is among the finest literature I have ever read. Her style and creativity are a combination of Franz Schubert, H. L. Mencken, and Emily Dickinson. Indeed, one of my favorites is a poem Ms. Baum wrote about the 30-year Treasury refunding. She also is capable of a Jacqueline Suzanne touch.

In a feature story about her in 1996, *Worth* dubbed her "The Merry Mistress of Bonds"[3] and described her as the most widely read and respected financial writer on Wall Street. Underneath the headline, it ran a full-page photo of her bestriding the littered exchange floor like a goddess. I would recommend that Hanes or Calvin Klein consider the photo for one of their advertising campaigns.

I have read her columns, about six million words in all, at the end of each day for ten years. Aside from the *National Enquirer*, she is my only exposure to Wall Street thinking. She tends in her views to follow the flow of money. When the Fed is tightening, she's usually bearish, and when the Fed is easing, she's usually bullish. When the Fed reverses course, it's a great time to go with. Interest rates tend to move in long

Table 11–1. Shifts in Fed Policy: Discount Rate Changes

Starting Date of Shift in Policy	Starting Rate		Total Number of Easings	Total Number of Tightenings
Nov. 1, 1978	9.50%			5
May 29, 1980		13.0%	3	
Sep. 25, 1980	10.0%			4
Nov. 1, 1981		14.0%	9	
April 9, 1984	8.5%			1
Nov. 20, 1984		9.0%	7	
Aug. 8, 1988	6.0%			3
Dec. 17, 1990		7.0%	7	
May 16, 1994	3.0%			4
Jan. 30, 1996		5.25%	1*	

*As of 9/15/96.

rising trends or falling trends until anticipation of a change in Fed policy. What most people, myself included, tend to forget is that ten-year interest rates gradually moved up from 3 percent in 1950 to 14 percent in 1981 with hardly a blip. Subsequently, they have fallen almost continuously to 6 percent in 1995, with the exception of 1984, 1994, and possibly 1996.

The Fed is leaning against the wind most of the time. The norm is for the Fed to gradually tighten when the economy is expanding, and to ease when the economy is contracting.

The daily flow of Fedspeak emanating from the Rotary Clubs, academic conferences, and leaks to Beltway newspapers, makes one forget the incredible inertia in policy. Much better to look at something objective. I did this by examining every change in policy the Fed has made since its founding in 1913. To be objective, I considered only the qualitative tools: discount rate, reserve requirements, and margin requirements. Incredibly, they rarely change direction. The average run of contracting (raising rates) or expanding lasts about three years and involves seven consecutive easings or tightenings. The changes in the discount rate are listed in Table 11–1. From 1978 to 1996, there have only been 10 changes of direction.

Unfortunately, I'm always going against. When the freight train of Fed policy is rolling over the stragglers, I'm frequently crushed. Time after time, I've found myself long during a bout of tightening. Licking my wounds at the end of a day, I turn to one of Ms. Baum's columns and find something like this:

After NAFTA, the bond market got down to basics. And while it was getting down, it went down.

Market participants chose to ignore the improving economic fundamentals for the better part of the week. The denial took many forms:

Look, they said, at all the cash from the Treasury's $25 billion interest payment that will have to find a home.

Look, they said, at the big muni defeasance calendar that will take Treasurys out of the market.

Look, they said, at the chances for a coupon pass from the Fed to address its seasonal add need.

Realize, we said, that the Treasury is not giving out alms. It is returning to investors what it took away from investors in the form of taxes at some earlier date.

Realize, we said, that the need for Treasurys from municipal issuers will not override the interest rate cycle. . . .

Realize, we said, that it's nice to have a rate-insensitive buyer like the Fed who, unlike the Treasury, creates reserves in exchange for securities. (November 19, 1993)

I'm not too big on bondage, but after a big loss, I often feel like flagellating myself. Ms. Baum's columns have allowed me to do this relatively innocuously—"the sensation was almost sexual."

In February 1994, the Fed started to tighten the federal fund rate after six consecutive years of constant easing. The markets in their wisdom took an immediate dive. The Fed can always be counted on to put a favorable spin on any such rout. Like night follows the day, the Fed trotted out Governor Lawrence Lindsay, formerly a Harvard professor, to downplay the significance of the tightening.

"Once is enough," he said. What fools the Fed must think speculators are. The next day, the markets really got clobbered because now "They" were afraid the Fed didn't mean business. The whole thing became an Abbott and Costello act, and the Fed immediately had to wheel in another Governor to say, "Once is not enough." In reporting the incident, Ms. Baum, in her inimitable way, put the whole thing in proper spexual perspective. "Amen," she concluded.

I am not the only reader to be smitten by Ms. Baum's allusions. Even the well-known ascetic, Alan Greenspan, the very antithesis of spexuality (like most central bankers), had a similar reaction. When he met Ms. Baum for the first time at a cocktail party, he introduced her to his significant other: "This is the one person in the world who can make the flattening of the yield curve sound pornographic."

I introduced myself by writing her a letter. The gist was that I was a mobile home dealer somewhere in Elkhardt who followed her comments on interest rates each day so I could keep up with my notes receivable, and inventory. The boys at the Rotary Club discussed her work each day, and had elected me to interview her for them on the occasion of the annual Home Show at the coliseum. I told her it would be a dream if she would consent to such a meeting. She responded "Dreams can come true."

At our meeting, we hit if off well. Like Peter Lynch of Fidelity, she often measures the strength of economic activity by taking a trip to the mall. I emphasized that unlike Peter Lynch, who often relies on his wife's reports on what's hot at the supermarket to get his 400% returns (Legg's was one of her most spectacular touts), I try to quantify everything before taking a speculation. She liked the juxtaposition of the quantitative and the hayseed. The boys at the office and I were awed with direct contact with our idol.

We started a collaboration on an article about Hillary Rodham Clinton's cattle trading. As you might recall, starting with $1000 initial capital, Hillary Rodham Clinton made $99,537 trading commodities over a 10-month period. Our conclusion captures the flavor. "After examining every one of her trades and checking them against the actual high, low, and close of the day, we have just one question. Rodham's total withdraws from the account totaled $99,537, what happened to the other $463?"

The fixed-income markets of England are not immune from outcroppings of sexulation, even at the highest levels. Ms. Baum reported on the subject in her signature style on Wednesday, March 22, 1995:

> Our interest in the trade numbers is usually confined to the export side . . .
> [but] sometimes, the international give and take is too important to ignore.
> The Deputy Governor of the Bank of England, Mr. Pennant Ray, was
> caught with his pants down, so to speak, when his former paramour spilled
> the beans about their affair to the press.
>
> At a time when everyone else is coming out of the closet, he's going into
> the closet.
>
> Mr. Pennant Ray reportedly cavorted with his nubile young lady in the
> dressing room of BOE Governor Eddie George after banking hours.
>
> The Brits may have a bad track record when it comes to running non-
> inflationary monetary policy, but when it comes to entertainment services,
> nobody does it better. Can you imagine such goings on at the Federal Re-
> serve Board or behind the formidable powers at number 14 Wilhem Epstein
> Strasser, better known as the Bundesbank, "If this were the Bank of France,
> he'd get promoted." A BOE watcher reported, "In France, it's a mark of
> honor."

Mr. Pennant Ray resigned from his position shortly after the news was reported. The chief offense in the British mind appears to have been the locale of the transgression, the Board Room itself. The British are very open about sex, so long as it's behind the closed doors of a cheap hotel. I would suggest that more attention should have been focused on the timing of the supposed indiscretions. If it occurred after trading hours, then it could hardly have interfered with the austere traditions of the "Old Lady of Threadneedle Street."

Some confirmation of my hypothesis is the outcome of the outing of the chairman of a stock exchange in 1994. It was reported in the tabloids that, during evenings, he patronized a spanking establishment where former schoolboys go to play out their childhood experiences with their governesses. Rather than resign, the chairman openly appeared on the floor of the exchange the next day. He received a standing ovation.

I always like to do some experiment and observation with subjects I write about, but I saw no opportunity for quantitative study here. Knowing of my scientific interest, my wife arranged for a stripper to go through her routine at my fiftieth birthday party. In deference to my six daughters, the performance was held in the confines of my office in New York. Just to be on the safe side, I set the performance time for 4:15, after trading hours, on a Tuesday. This is the time at which I have received weekly checkers and chess lessons from Jules Leopold, Tom Wiswell, and Art Bisguier for 15 years. I figured the average age of these gentlemen (80 years) would exonerate all concerned from any charges of unbecoming conduct.

Just as the stripper got into her act, the bonds started moving against me in the cash market. The voice synthesizer bemoaned, "Bonds going down—new low in bonds—bonds below round number—how low can bonds go—Soros selling bonds . . . ." That was it. I left the performance and didn't come back. I did receive a report, however, that Tom Wiswell, my 85-year-old checkers teacher, found the performance particularly exhilarating.

The Chicago Board of Trade bond pit was recently rocked by a sex scandal. A stripper was secreted onto the floor in 1995. After select traders previewed her merchandise, she was allegedly spirited away to an office several floors above, where a paid performance ensued. An independent investigator has been hired to report to the Board on the incident. My guess is that a charge of "conduct unbecoming to a member" will be forthcoming.

Under the circumstances, I figured the only way for me to investigate spexuality would be to interview Pat Arbor, the Chairman of the Chicago Board of Trade. I conducted the interview at the Four Seasons Restaurant on Tuesday, December 5, 1995.

The interview started with Pat revealing that he was not bereft of experience in sexulation. Twenty years earlier, when he was just a member of the Exchange, a paternity suit charged him with having fathered a daughter with a famous Black *Playboy* centerfold. He lost the suit. His daughter, Kelley Arbor (a student at Harvard), shortly thereafter appeared as a *Playboy* centerfold. (Sales of the February 1996 issues of *Playboy* at newsstands around the Exchange doubled from their regular rate.) Understandably, he felt it best to disqualify himself from opining on extracurricular sex among speculators. He did indicate, however, that many well-known Exchange speculators from the 1980s were known to have a predilection for sexual relations outside their marriages. In almost all cases, full disclosure ultimately ensued. The outcome was all too predictable. Between the cost of the divorce, and the members' inability or disinclination to speculate profitably during the proceedings, almost all such members lost heavily and were forced to sell their seats.

History of Sex and Speculation

Sex and speculation have been tied together since primitive times. In the late 18th century, according to former *Forbes* reporter Gregory J. Millman, a little too much spexuality may have caused the collapse of international financial order.[4]

John Law, the promoter of the Mississippi Bubble in 1716, is often credited with pioneering modern central banking. The first link of his career and the horrible consequences that followed came when Edward Wilson's sexy and muscular bare chest excited Elizabeth Villers, the mistress of King William III. She arranged a series of trysts with him. When the fear of exposure became great, she had John Law kill her lover. Law was sentenced to death, but escaped to France. When he wasn't gambling or womanizing, he developed a scheme to convert the French government debt into shares in a stock company that would be granted a monopoly on trade with the French colonies on the Mississippi. He arranged an introduction to King Louis XIV, who accepted the scheme, hook, line, and sinker.

The Mississippi Company was formed amid a speculative bubble that rivaled the tulipomania in the 1650s or the run up of Motley Fool's favorite, Iomega, in 1996. During its height, ladies frequented John Law's drawing rooms, willing to sexulate in return for a chance to buy stock. To heighten the fever, the government hired 6,000 bums, dressed them up as miners, and informed the public that the miners would soon be departing to dig for gold in New Orleans. It didn't work. The whole edifice collapsed and Law died penniless.

According to a financial fax from the world's largest bank, it is still considered appropriate in Europe for governments to create euphoria when selling debt and shares to the public. The theory is that the country benefits when the speculators pay up. In the United States, however, inducing speculative purchases through euphoria is frowned on. In a typical condemnation, Harvard Professor John Galbraith reports that, during many past bubbles, insanity born of optimism and spexuality was at work. In the 1980s, in a slight variation, some vulnerable clients of Michael Milken and Drexel Burnham Lambert who attended the annual Predators' Balls, as they were dubbed, were said to have had the attention of appropriately ascetic prostitutes. This was meant to encourage them in the purchase of junk bonds, many of which were comparable to the Mississippi swindles.

The English had a sympathetic bubble of their own in 1711. But, as Galbraith notes, "It was by comparison a rather ordinary, if exceptionally intense boom and collapse in security prices caused by a comprehensive exercise in official bribery, corruption, and chicanery."[5]

Why do the words *pot, kettle,* and *black* keep flitting across my mind's-eye as I read this condemnation?

In modern times, the techniques have been sharpened. Gene Marcial tells the story of Walda (Mistress of the Universe), a sexy brunette who has amassed a wealth of $20 million-plus by closing sales of secondary equity issues of large, seasoned NYSE companies to sophisticated European investors. Timing these sales to the client's maximum level of sexual ardor is key, she reports. "Timing is everything. I make it a point to ask the critical question about a deal I may have cooking at the most precise time. He pulls me to him and puts his mouth on mine. I whisper feverishly, 'Are you really going to buy a million shares?' My system works, simple as it is."[6]

Sex is essential for propagation, so it's no accident that it evolves quickly to capture the dynamics of fresh trends in markets. During 1995 and 1996, the market for initial public offerings (IPOs) was the hottest ever. IPOs in their first day of trading frequently rose 100 percent by the close. Naturally, brokers who had such issues available became attractive mates. I have been told by many an acquaintance that not a few of their attractive friends have switched jobs and now spend most of their time trading IPOs. They trade sex for a larger allocation.

In September 1996, I wished to buy into a hot new issue with the idea of flipping it at the close on the first day of trading. Rises of 20 percent on that first day have been typical over the past 30 years. The underwriter told me they had to be sure I wasn't a flipper before they decided how much of my order should be filled. My partners immediately indicated that in hot markets like these you have to agree to sleep with the underwriters to get full allocation. I accepted a partial fill.

The 100-year-old books in my stash record similar incidents. The greatest speculator of all time, Commodore Vanderbilt, succumbed to the temptation of a notorious pair of lady brokers who were the talk of Wall Street for a season near the end of his career. Lady Claflin Cook, formerly Tennie C. (a/k/a/ "Tennessee") Claflin, and her sister, Victoria C. Woodhull, set up the firm of Woodhull, Claflin & Co., brokers in stocks and gold. This pair had originally exercised considerable influence over the Commodore on account of their reputations as spiritualistic mediums. The Commodore also enjoyed a certain amount of laying on of hands with Miss Tennessee, who was particularly adept at leading her older customer on.

One chronicler of these events, Matthew Hale Smith, noted that when these ladies first arrived on the scene it was reported that:

> Vanderbilt was to back them for any amount. Vanderbilt denies this, but reputable gentlemen, who have called on him in regard to business transactions, in which these ladies were concerned, have received his assurance

that it is all right. The sisters have been traced to Vanderbilt's house in Washington Place, repeatedly in the evenings, and gentlemen doing business with the Commodore have met him there.[7]

What follies and disasters ensued in this situation can only be imagined. The archives disclose plenty of anecdotal evidence that speculators fail when passion becomes part of the mix. Kenneth L. Fisher has analyzed the careers of seven great speculators who ended as losers. Of these, James Fisk Jr., F. Augustus Heinze, and Jesse L. Livermore lost, according to Fisher, because they were oversexed. Winners generally do not suffer from this predilection.

J. P. Morgan, the great investment banker, was well known for his womanizing. How did he pull it off in those Victorian times, I asked? The author of the definitive biography about Morgan said: "He arranged that he and his wife would never be on the same continent at the same time."

Benjamin Graham, the founder of security analysis and the most revered fundamental analyst of all time, was quite lecherous. Books about him often record that the wives of his closest friends and neighbors had to be constantly on guard. In a typical description, Kenneth L. Fisher reports:

> But beneath the distinguished success and achievement was a man whose life was anything but steadfast and conservative. Ironically, he was a notorious ladies' man, who took on mistresses while gallivanting among his various homes in the south of France, California and Wall Street until his death in 1976.[8]

Ascertaining whether the evolution of followers of the father of security analysis has predisposed them to similar predilections would prove to be an interesting scientific study.

James Fisk, Jay Gould's partner during the notorious Erie Wars and the infamous run on gold that resulted in Black Friday in 1869, liked high living. He chivied Gould into letting him buy Pike's Grand Opera Palace with Erie money, and then moved his offices there. He used the actresses of the opera house company as his private harem. He swelled around in diamonds and fine fabrics, living the life of a sybarite while the abstemious Gould set him up and stabbed him in the back during the gold panic. Fisk, broke and living more or less on Gould's charity, ended up dead at the hand of his girlfriend's other boyfriend. He was 36. Gould, who thought of nothing but business, went on to build a fortune that would have made him a billionaire by today's standards.

Heinze, one of the contributors to the Panic of 1907 through his attempt to corner United Copper, loved women, liquor, and cards. Says Fisher, "His extravagant nights seemingly never interfered with his success—that is, until his extravagance trickled into his daytime activities."

He used his office as a rumpus room, throwing parties that beggared the powers of such words as "lavish" or "extravagant." When the crash came, he lost his banks, his prestige, and $10 million. He died of cirrhosis of the liver in 1914, up to his neck in marital difficulties and malfeasance lawsuits.

Livermore, one of the all-time greats, went from bankrupt to millionaire four times before the Great Depression slammed the door on him and the SEC locked it by outlawing his methods of market manipulation. He married three times, "while keeping an endless supply of mistresses, drinking like a fish, and yachting aboard his 202-foot *Anita.*"

I have been fortunate in my speculative argosy to know many great speculators in the half-billion-and-up league. From time to time, I have asked the survivors the openly vicarious question: "Is it true that women find billions an aphrodisiac and does this create temptation?" I will give a composite answer to protect the privacy of those I may or may not have mentioned in these pages. "Yes, they do. But I don't because it would cost too much money and create too much distraction from my business."

I have posed a similar question to the numerous national champions I have known in various racquet sports: "Do women ever tempt you by asking to join you in your hotel room on the eve of your tournaments?" The composite answer was that if the athletes were not playing in the finals, their response to the temptresses was: "Hurry up to my room."

TRANSGRESSIONS CLOSE TO HOME

I follow in the footsteps of Professor Galbraith, one of my teachers at Harvard, who confessed, 40 years after the fact, to having a dalliance with one of his students. He added two extenuating circumstances: "It was not politically incorrect for such proclivities to be expressed in those days. Also, we have been happily married for the subsequent forty years."

My wife and I met in a similar way in 1977. She and I became acquainted while programming market relationships in tandem. We shared thinking, creating, organizing, and flow charting. Programming with someone is one of the most intimate experiences possible, certainly exceeding on the intimacy scale showering together (which books on sex recommend as a prerequisite for further action). We liked the flow, and one day we programmed no more.

She is aware of my grandfather Martin's and my father's history in these areas, so she can kid me with impunity. When we hold a dinner with other couples and are arranging the seating, Susan is likely to say to my guests, "Oh no, Victor won't wish to be seated next to me. He always likes to sit next to a beautiful woman like yourself."

Yes, I find women who are competent at their trade personally attractive. And I believe that sex, along with music, enables humans to achieve the highest degree of happiness. I have on occasion proposed mutually beneficial romantic activities to unmarried females of my acquaintance (during my 11 years of bachelorhood). The invariable answer was, "Nobody's ever asked me that way before. But no. I know what you propose makes intellectual sense but I can't do it emotionally!" I learned in 1993 that, at Antioch, this kind of dialogue is necessary to preclude a charge of date rape. I was politically correct before my time. In fact, I was so legal that I never got to do anything illegal. Fortune favors the bold in romance as well as in speculation. Faint heart never won fair lady—or a 100 percent annual return.

I make it a rule, however, that, when sex is in the air, it is not the time to speculate. (Nor, for that matter, is it a good time to play other strenuous games.) If the sex has been too good, too much complacency is present. If the advances have been unrequited, there is a tendency to leap at every situation and trade oneself into oblivion.

Corollary: If your wife is too busy with the kids to get involved, as I know is typical of families with many children, your frustration can lead to total ruin as you overtrade and hold out for the most unlikely and unreasonable fills and executions. "If you want something, get a ticket or make an appointment," is the unspoken ambiance that surrounds family life.

Why do sex and speculation crowd each other out? Freud himself championed a variant of this theory. Sexual repression was necessary, he thought, to allow the creative forces of civilization to manifest themselves.

Perhaps biological factors are paramount. We like to think of ourselves as creatures of the mind, but the physical is primary. The least change in body chemistry impairs one's ability to concentrate. A passing girl in a bikini can cause me to lose a sure game of paddleball. Stopping for a meal break is an infallible ticket to losing at poker. Worse, the mind doesn't even know it's impaired until it sees the resultant disaster.

It's not easy to enforce these personal rules. The currency markets where my firm transacts considerable business seem to attract a wealth of attractive professionals, and 50 percent of the brokers and dealers who staff the graveyard shift are women.

It's part of the standard patter in this field to exchange badinage. "Hi, Big Guy. What's up? What are you throwing around today?" I've been asked a few hundred times by brokers of the opposite sex, all of whom I knew to be beauties.

"Oh, I'm afraid I'm AC DC today," I always answer.

THE SCIENCE OF SEX

The hemline theory has been the only attempt to quantify market performance versus sexual predilections or activity.

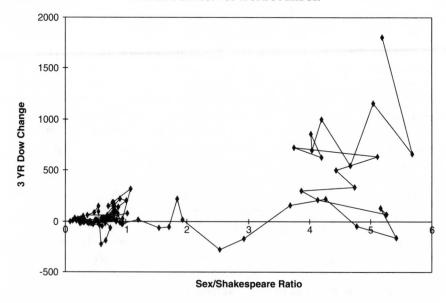

Figure 11-1. Sex/Shakespeare versus Three-Year Dow Change

But there are obvious difficulties in sampling here. Some years have high hemlines and low hemlines in tandem. Furthermore, the shifts in trends in hemlines are rare enough to be consistent with *any* stock market move.

I decided that a fresh effort to trace the relation was in order. To illuminate it, I calculated a yearly measure of the attention our culture focuses on sex and on speculation. By comparing the two, I am able to calculate the leads and lags.

Modern computer databases provide a number of ways to measure the attention that is focused on a particular subject. The number of books published on a subject in a year is one good indicator of the attention it receives in our culture. The World Library Retrieval System offers a database of bibliographic information on 30 million titles contained in libraries around the world. I have counted the number of books published on sex and on speculation each year from 1886 to 1995. The ratio versus the Dow is displayed in Figure 11-1.

To expand on this phenomenon, I thought it might be interesting to consider the number of books about Shakespeare. My theory is that attention to Shakespeare might measure the extent of interest in the best that is thought and said about life. As William Stanley Jevons put it so eloquently in his study in the March 12, 1864, *Atheneum:*

> As these words are universally acknowledged to be the best ornament of the
> English language, it seemed likely that the comparative degree of attention

bestowed upon them at different periods would afford some measure of the degree of good taste then prevailing.[9]

Scrutiny of the data indicates that there has been a relatively modest increase in the number of books about Shakespeare, from 126 in 1886 to 345 in 1995. Similarly, books about speculation have increased moderately, from 10 in 1886 to 51 in 1995. But sex books have increased from 42 in 1886 to 1,842 in 1995. The popular perception is upheld: sex is on everyone's tongue and bookshelf. With numbers like this, the sex-to-Shakespeare ratio has increased from 0.3 in 1886 to 5.3 in 1995. The sex-to-speculation ratio has increased from 10.5 to 36. (See Figure 11–2.)

The market has tended to go up more in the last part of the 20th century, concurrent with the rising ratios, so there is a bias for a positive correlation. But the results show an astonishing positive correlation nevertheless. In 1996, the correlation of the sex-to-Shakespeare ratio with the market change is 0.5, and the correlation of the sex-to-speculation ratio with the market change is 0.3. The odds against numbers as large as these arising through random variations alone are 1,000 to 1 against.

But there is a problem. Steve Stigler calls results like these "bogus" correlations. The Dow change in a year predicts the sex-to-speculation and sex-to-Shakespeare ratios one year later about as accurately as the ratios predict the Dow. Which way does causation run? Because of these subtle artifacts, caution is necessary in using the ratios for prediction. Still, the ratio of sex to Shakespeare stands at between 5.0 and 6.0 as the last decade of the 20th century ends. Such a value calls for a rise of 200 Dow points a year. Watch the book reviews for early indications of a change.

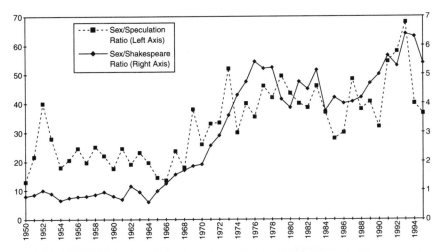

Figure 11–2.   Sex/Speculation and Sex/Shakespeare Ratios

SEX IN THE SPECULATOR'S FAMILY

In their book, *The Police Family*, Artie and my mom, Elaine, describe the sexual tension that police work involves:

> The rhythm of existence switches abruptly every week, reminding the policeman's wife that she is a Cinderella with midnight the pivot around which the family schedule rotates. One "shift" out of three a wife may wait up past midnight in order to "greet" her husband. But the timing is bad: he's all keyed up and she's half asleep. If she is a sensual person, her sexual craving remains unsatisfied during those long nights.[10]

When police officers return home after a late tour, some are eager for sex. The wife may not be in an amorous mood or a seductive pose and may be morosely contemplating the unpleasant chore of cleaning the home or getting dressed for work. The occupational mystique that police officers are supersexed and great lovers may lead to trouble for both the bachelor and the married Don Juan.

> One policeman chose to stop off on the way home for a few beers with the boys so he will be drowsy enough to fall asleep.[11]

They say that children often travel in the same footpaths as their parents. Strangely enough, the policeman and the speculator have similar tours of duty. My father, like most policemen, worked alternate weeks from midnight to 8:00 A.M., from 8:00 A.M. to 4:00 P.M., and from 4:00 P.M. to 12:00 midnight. Each tour is repeated on a three-week cycle. As a speculator in fixed income and currency markets, I work these three shifts every day. In addition to the problems of being keyed up versus half asleep, or amorous versus getting kids ready for school, I have to face a further occupational incompatibility.

On my tours of duty, I don't carry a gun. The crooks I am trying to arrest often beat me up, leaving me black-and-blue and broke. I'm keyed up, but don't feel sensual at all. But my wife is ever resourceful in developing ways to tempt me away from drowning my sorrows with a few beers.

I'm not likely to go out because my bedroom is adjacent to my trading room, and I don't drink. Like most traders, I maintain a separate bedroom from my wife so I don't wake her when the phone rings with news of a fill. When I have just taken a big hit and am ready to throw in the towel, I can count on my wife coming into my room in a seductive mood. "Dear, is there anything I can do to cheer you up?"

"No. There's nothing you or I can do or that anyone else can do for me."

"Look, no matter what happens, we can always start over. We'll get a small apartment somewhere. Like we used to have. The kids won't mind.

We'll visit you in debtors' jail every day, if worst comes to worst. You can play games there, the way Willie Sutton played handball and chess or like the old racquet players did in prison."

"I don't want you to see me behind bars. Find a policeman who can be a good model to the kids and take care of you. Pretend he's here right now . . ."

"You're a very attractive young lady, Susan."

"But you hardly know me, Officer."

"On the contrary, we had your husband under surveillance for a long time and we got to know a lot about you. I'd like to get to know you . . . I mean—on a personal basis."

"Do you always talk so much when . . ."

CHAPTER 12

Returns and Randomness: Academic Style

Twenty to twenty-five! These are the years! Don't be content with things as they are. "The earth is yours and the fullness thereof." Enter upon your inheritance, accept your responsibilities. Raise the glorious flags again, advance them upon the new enemies, who constantly gather upon the front of the human army, and have only to be assaulted to be overthrown. Don't take no for an answer. Never submit to failure. Do not be fobbed off with mere personal success or acceptance. You will make all kinds of mistakes; but as long as you are generous and true, and also fierce, you cannot hurt the world or even seriously distress her.

Winston Churchill
My Early Years

FIVE GLORIOUS YEARS

In the five years from age 20 to 25, I explored the fullness of the academic life as a student at the University of Chicago and as an assistant professor at the University of California, Berkeley. The enemies I fought against were zealous random walkers stationed at the professorial lines, and bigots who wouldn't let Jews in their clubs. By assaulting their fixed beliefs, I split the flanks of an impregnable defense to grab a Ph.D., and I refused to be shut out of their clubs. Fierceness I had in spades, but I cringe now when I recall how far away from the generous and true ideal I was, and how much distress my youthful mistakes caused.

Inheritance, responsibility, and discipline are the charcoal, sulfur, and saltpeter of success, but it takes a spark of luck to ignite the mixture. In a provocative book on the subject, Mary Batten concludes that, with few exceptions, people who made great chance discoveries prepared themselves by mastering the great tool of inquiry introduced by science—the experimental method.[1] Batten's conclusion rings true for me. The only skill I really developed at Harvard, aside from squash, was the ability to use that wonderful method to uncover and integrate regularities. In retrospect, this ability is not trivial. Many deep thinkers consider the ordering and connecting of discrete data to be the fundamental organizing activity of human nature. The successful human, speculator or otherwise, must use this ability to adapt to an ever-changing environment.

The lucky star that gave me the chance to use science to integrate connections and patterns was a tout sheet posted on the kiosk of Clocker Lawton at Suffolk Downs. The sheet had the usual claims: "#1 performing handicapper three years in a row," "pick winners like a pro," "$1 thousand bet that paid off," "45 years of experience free," "+1170% 1 year gain." Clones of these claims can be found in ads in the financial newspapers every day, along with the obligatory invitation to attend an investment "make that turf" seminar.

But Clocker's sheet was distinguished by fascinating commentary relating turf wisdom to the investment world. The wisdom began with derision: "Jim Lorie of the University of Chicago says that by investing in common stocks randomly, you can get a mere 10 percent *annual* return on your money. But by following my system for just $2 a day, you can assure yourself of better than a 10 percent return *in just one day, in just 30 minutes* merely by boxing my choices in the Daily Double!" Clocker's ad ended with the boast, "Professor, stick *that* statistic up your ivory tower! Returns like your measly 10 percent are wholly inadequate for my good customers."

I took up where Clocker left off. I wrote to Jim Lorie indicating that my studies showed it was possible to pick stocks that would appreciate considerably higher than 10 percent a year. I told him there were patterns in price and volume determined by the distance and velocity of the moves—regularities based on humans' inability to weigh recent versus old events, and differences in returns due to volatilities, emotions, liquidating value, and momentum in Fed policies.

Jim wrote back that, along with most of his colleagues, he had found evidence that stock prices were random and efficient, but that it might be nice to have me around to shake the dice. He urged me to apply the same kind of single-minded determination I had shown in my squash game to uncover anomalies in the apparently random character of stock prices. Full of the illusion of hope, I applied to the University of Chicago Graduate School of Business.

I subsequently sweet-talked the dean's assistant at Chicago into allowing me to see my application (one of the rare occasions where I have succeeded in a nefarious pursuit) and found a note from a member of the admissions committee who subsequently went on to win a Nobel prize: "Seems like our kind of nut. Reach to get him." (How he would live to regret these words.) Newly ensconced in my dorm at Chicago, I plunged into research on market prices. The school had an air of ferment in those days. The traditional folklore derived from the horse-and-buggy business case studies clashed with the mathematical techniques then becoming *de rigeuer* in economics to illuminate decision making under uncertainty.

THE LORIE YEARS

Before James Lorie came to the Graduate School of Business in 1951, it was a sleepy place. The university's undergraduate student body tended to look with disdain on kids who cared about business. And around it all, the bad neighborhoods were inexorably approaching the campus boundaries.

James Lorie, a recent Chicago Ph.D., was recruited to revitalize the school. His first task was to appoint a dean. W. Allen Wallis, Chairman of the University's Statistics Department, accepted the Deanship in 1956. Forty years later, he told me that Jim Lorie was almost single-handedly responsible for his accepting the position.

The results of the Wallis–Lorie partnership are now a matter of history. They redefined the School's entire mission: it would deal not with the ephemera of business case studies but with basic disciplines that would be valid under all cases. Their philosophy, which became known as the "Chicago Approach to Business Education," is now so widely recognized as to be taken for granted, but it was highly innovative in the mid-1950s. Lorie worked tirelessly—even to the point of undermining his health—in developing a 10-year plan in fund-raising and, above all, in recruiting. Wallis recalled that Jim "was as effective in persuading people like George Stigler, George Shultz, Sidney Davidson, Barney Berelson, and many others to join us as he was in persuading me to become Dean."

The result was a tremendous change in the school's fortune—in faculty and student head count, and in the increasing eminence of the school. The University of Chicago consistently rates in the top five business schools in the United States and among the top ten internationally. In the past 25 years, the University of Chicago has won or shared eight Nobel prizes in economics—five of them by scholars affiliated with the Business School— versus one for all other business schools combined.

A QUANTUM VARIATION

Jim's recruiting techniques were legendary. He would visit every major university and speak with the most eminent professors in the field. He would invariably ask: "Who are the best people in your field in the generation following yourself?" Acting on this knowledge, Jim invited the emerging talent to visit his school.

The location was a problem, however. The surrounding neighborhood was well known as a dangerous place to live, let alone bring up a family. Jim had a daring and effective solution. First, after fetching a prospective new hire from the airport, Jim would follow a carefully chosen route that avoided the tenements, which then resembled Beirut on a good day. After following the strategically planned route, capped off with a quick tour of the University's Botanical Gardens, Jim would suggest they stop for lunch at a diner several blocks from the University. As they climbed out of the car, the prospect would unfailingly notice, "Jim, you left the keys in the car. I've heard there's a lot of crime in this area."

"That's a lot of hooey. This neighborhood is safer than the White House itself. Not only do I leave the keys to my car in the ignition, I usually leave the door to my apartment unlocked."

And so went the recruiting effort that led to the emergence of Chicago as one of the top business schools in the world. But Dean Jack Gould once added a wry footnote to the daring strategy. Occasionally, Jim's expense account showed a mixed and highly variable distribution. There was the frequent itemization of $3 for a tuna fish sandwich, or $5 for a University of Chicago sweatshirt. But every now and then came a quantum variation, such as $8,000 for a stolen DeSoto. Not to worry. Jim always paid for such items out of his winnings in the stock market.

Jim cut an elegant and well-turned figure around the campus. Contrary to popular stereotype, economics and finance professors are just as interested in turning a profit in the market as the next person, and it is a rare after-hours gathering among such profs when the subject of how to exploit the latest academic theory on market-beating doesn't crop up. Jim's consistently winning record in the market, coupled with his many academic distinctions, made him one of the most sought-after academics for consultation on such matters.

An Historic Chance Phone Call

In June 1961, Jim received a historic telephone call, out of the blue. At the other end was Louis Engel, a University of Chicago alumnus, who was working as marketing and public relations director for Merrill Lynch Pierce Fenner & Smith. Engel had already written *How to Buy Stocks*, which went on to sell over 4 million copies. Now he wanted to develop an advertising program based on the theme that stocks are a good investment. Could Jim provide research data to support the claim? Jim responded carefully, "Well, Lou, this will require a fair amount of research. I'll get back to you with some ideas on how to get the job done properly."

When Jim called Engel back, he said he would like to undertake the research necessary to answer Engel's question. But to do it properly would require time, money, and brain power. Jim proposed a project involving the collection of monthly stock market data—price, volume, capitalization, and dividends for every stock listed on the NYSE from 1926 to the present. To store and manipulate the data would require computers. The Board of Trustees was reluctant to appropriate money for the necessary computer purchases, but was not averse to accepting a Univac as a gift from Merrill Lynch. Jim eventually persuaded Merrill Lynch to contribute $200,000 to finance the program.

Next, the laborious process of transcribing the price data onto computer-readable formats was undertaken. Finally, an associate director who combined a genius for accuracy with a mind that could grasp properly all the new computer technology had to be found. Jim hired the perfect man for this job, Larry Fisher, a real-life embodiment of the classic Dickensian professor: brilliant, affable, absent-minded. The enterprise was off and running.

Engel's call to Lorie led to the formation of the Center for Research in Security Prices, nicknamed "Crisp." Crisp's activities soon led to the development of a database of common-stock prices, volumes, and dividends that became the essential building block for all research in the field of modern finance.

The first studies that emerged, covering rates of return, were revolutionary. Stocks *are* a great investment. Almost any diversified portfolio of ten or more stocks held for five or more years is likely to have a return of 10 percent or more every year. As Engel and his co-author Henry Hecht summarized the study, in *How to Buy Stocks:*

> In all the 2,211 year-to-year combinations possible between year-end 1925 and December 1991, there are only 72 with negative rates of return. And most of these loss periods were for relatively short time spans. For investments held at least seven years, there were only five occasions that resulted in losses; you would have realized at least some profit in every investment period lasting ten years or longer. . . .
>
> When the investment horizon extends at least ten years (as in most planning for retirement, education, and similar objectives), the historic pattern is particularly encouraging. Of the 1,653 10-year-plus periods covered in the table, more than 95% show an annual compounded return above 9.1%, 90% above 10.6%, and in half the periods the return was 13.6% or better. Indeed, in nearly three out of ten instances, the return topped 15%.[2]

Lorie and Fisher's test results have been extended backward and forward, to other stock markets, stock sectors, fixed-income securities, junk bonds, commodities, real estate, alternative investments, what have you. Jeremy Siegel, a professor at the Wharton School who has summarized this work admirably, concludes that U.S. stock returns have been admirably consistent at 6 percent a year above inflation for the past 200 years. Returns on other stock markets have exceeded the U.S. quota. Real fixed-income yields were 5 percent from 1802 to 1870, but have been only 0.8 percent since 1926.[3]

Lorie applied his findings to building his own portfolio of stocks. He would select a stock with a good story, buy it at the open the next day, and hold it for five or ten years, or until it was bought out. He found his stocks by keeping his eyes and ears open to good products. Once discovered, he would ask suppliers, customers, former employees, trade editors, and current competitors what they thought about the stock's potential. It's amazing how much more often competitors are willing to say bad things about their rivals rather than good things about their own firms.

Since I met Jim, I've met all manner of stock-selecting techniques that experts could devise. Almost all the successful ones—from the Beardstown ladies to the proverbial sandy-haired superstar fund-manager profiled as the best of the current lot—use the same parameters as Jim.

An Unfortunate Short

Jim has acquired a reputation as being an exceedingly kind and decent man. Of his giving and productive life, dozens have commented to me unsolicited, "Jim was like a second father to me." He was my benefactor, bailing me out of debt time and again, providing food and a home away from home, arranging for my scholarship to be renewed after it was canceled, hiring me for my first full-time job, and introducing me to Bob Gwinn—my first customer.

By violating what I had learned from masters such as Jim, however, I was almost carried out. Bob Gwinn started as a young salesman at Sunbeam when it was generating $25 million a year in sales. He eventually became chairman, taking the company to over $1 billion in sales before it sold out to Illinois Tool Works.

I told Bob that I had a system for shorting overvalued stocks. The ideal short was RH Hoe, a Chicago-based manufacturer of printing equipment that had seen its best days in the 19th century. Hoe had not earned money in five years. Its stock was trading at $18 a share, and I noticed that it had a preferred stock that was $15 per share in arrears on its dividends. That day, Bob was showing me the factory floor at Sunbeam, and we stood watching the metal-stamping machines and the workers winding copper-wire coils for home appliances. "Tell you what," he said, "I'll give you $25,000 to manage for me using that strategy." I signed my first client and proceeded to short my first stock. It almost proved to be my last.

Over the next few weeks, I watched the stock trade up to 20, then 30, then 40, finally breaking through 50. As the stock rose, I increased my short position, and Bob began shorting it too, through his own account. But when the stock climbed past 50, I started to cover, unable to stand the pain. It was too late, however; a major bear squeeze was on. I covered the last of my position between 90 and 95. I lost the entire initial $25,000 stake plus $50,000 more; Bob and I together lost almost $100,000.

A month after we closed out our position, RH Hoe declared bankruptcy.

One day, shortly after the Hoe debacle, I was moping along Broadway when I ran into Wilton ("Wink") Jaffee, an old Wall Street hand and a veteran of many campaigns. As we talked, I blurted out something about "The biggest boom and bust cycle I've ever seen in a stock was in Hoe." Wink replied with a chuckle, "Oh, yeah, we had some fun squeezing the shorts on that one. Really took some of those midwestern hayseeds to the cleaners."

AN EAR FULL OF CIDER

I had to relearn a lesson taught me earlier by my Dad and Bookie: If anyone offers you a bet on a sure thing, grab your wallet and run in the opposite direction. No matter what the fundamentals of a situation are, be absolutely sure you know whom you are betting against before you put your money down on a "sure thing." There's probably a good reason you're being offered the bet.

A string of bad earnings for a stock serves the same purpose as a disastrous race by a horse. Frequently, it discourages the public from betting on the horse the next race out, when the odds are high enough to warrant a game effort. The same principle applies for a final write-down of billions, the discontinuance of a line, the firing of a chief executive, or a pessimistic earnings forecast. Often, a great success lies just around the corner.

Fortunately, I learned the danger of a short squeeze early in my career and, ever since, I have been leery of going short unhedged. My queasiness paid off in 1980 when I was long gold and short silver. My gold position saved me from total ruin when my short in silver was caught in the infamous Hunt-orchestrated silver-cornering operation. Day after day, I watched silver close limit up. Finally, unable to take it any longer, I covered. I would have been wiped out had I not been hedged in gold.

The best reason for staying away from shorting stocks is the overriding 10 percent annual return for the past 200 years. One way of seeing this is to dig up a long-term chart of the stock market averages. *Barron's*, the *Wall Street Journal*, and *Value Line* often run such displays. The overall impression is a continuous rise of some 100-fold over the past 100 years, with pauses in the 1930s and 1970s, and small downward blips in 1907, 1929, and 1987. The averages exclude dividends, so add in another 100-fold return from dividends.

Since that time, I've seen more money lost by shorting stocks than by any other technique. Even in vast declines, the shorts generally don't prosper because their firepower is withered away by catastrophic rises that unloose them at the top. When such stocks do decline, the shorts are usually so shell-shocked and reduced in circumstances that they don't have the courage to come back in. Further, once stocks start declining, the rules requiring a sale on an uptick manage to conspire to prevent reinstatement of the position even if the old confidence comes back. The typical lament of the short sellers is always, "You're not going to make money shorting stocks until the SEC outlaws 25-year-old investors. They're just too young to understand that the bottle isn't half full." Or, "I told my friends to stay short but I didn't have the guts."

Shorts love to talk about irrational values, the inability to collect full interest on their credit balances, stocks with $3 million in sales selling at market values of $2 billion, artful accounting, declining mutual fund flows, and the like. That's not the problem. These are what musicians would call incidental passages. The problems with shorts is simply going against the returns that entrepreneurs pay investors for lending long-term capital.

The Random Walk Theory

Like so many places before and since, I was a fish out of water in Chicago. I was accustomed to Niederhoffering my classes—attending one or two lectures a semester, then showing up at the final with an original paper on which I expatiated rather than answering the assigned question. This worked fine in the advanced Ph.D. courses. But to get the Ph.D., it was necessary to complete the M.B.A. classes. These courses had homework each evening: case studies, solutions of sources and uses of funds, development of financial statements from journal entries, calculations of discounted cash flow, look-up of binomial probabilities—typical M.B.A. stuff, all very valuable but very hard to Niederhoffer.

The central premise of the finance courses I majored in was that stock prices, interest rates, earnings—information of all sorts—moved in a random walk. Overlaid on this was the concept that neither capital structure nor dividend policy changes the value of a firm. The theory is based on the reasonable idea that all relevant information is incorporated into current prices without systematic bias, and that individual investors could replicate corporate leverage through their own borrowing and lending. Empirical studies looked at from a distance supported this view. Price movements generated by random numbers look identical to those generated by charts; the performance of analysts and mutual funds is inferior to blind dart throwing; correlations between consecutive changes in individual stocks are close to zero; and the track records of market timers is consistently inferior to a buy-and-hold strategy.

The students and professors at school were energized by the theory. I thought of them as a society of ants or bees. Each worker group performs its assigned task, yet all tasks are knit together to create a thriving, self-sustaining community of purposeful toil. One group of students swarmed around the key-punch machine, entering stock prices datum by datum. Others collaborated on lengthy computer programs designed to analyze the price data. Another group of statistically oriented scholars applied mathematical analyses to distribution curves without finite variances.

Professor Eugene Fama, a graduate of Tufts College in his mid-20s, was a leader of the effort. He summarized his findings in 1965, in the most widely referenced paper in the field of efficient markets:

> For many years the following question has been a source of continuing controversy in both academic and business circles: To what extent can the past history of a common stock's price be used to make meaningful predictions concerning the future price of the stock? . . . It seems safe to say that this paper has presented strong and voluminous evidence in favor of the random walk hypothesis.[4]

This theory and the attitude of its adherents found classic expression in one incident I personally observed that deserves memorialization. A team of four of the most respected graduate students in finance had joined forces with two professors, now considered venerable enough to have won or to have been considered for a Nobel prize, but at that time feisty as Hades and insecure as a kid on his first date. This elite group was studying the possible impact of volume on stock price movements, a subject I had researched. As I was coming down the steps from the library on the third floor of Haskell Hall, the main business building, I could see this Group of Six gathered together on a stairway landing, examining some computer output. Their voices wafted up to me, echoing off the stone walls of the building. One of the students was pointing to some output while querying the professors, "Well, what if we really do find something? We'll be up the creek. It won't be consistent with the random walk model." The younger professor replied, "Don't worry, we'll cross that bridge in the unlikely event we come to it."

I could hardly believe my ears—here were six scientists openly hoping to find no departures from ignorance. I couldn't hold my tongue, and blurted out, "I sure am glad you are all keeping an open mind about your research." I could hardly refrain from grinning as I walked past them. I heard muttered imprecations in response.

In an interesting follow-up to that incident, there has been a strange transformation of the four students at the meeting. Each of them has subsequently served as a partner at a major investment firm, applying specialized knowledge to uncovering inefficiencies. One of them is the founder of several mutual funds whose *raison d'être* is to find anomalies. Another stated in a recent paper, which appeared in a prestigious academic journal, "Indeed, stock prices do appear to be somewhat predictable." As usual, the academicians are way behind the form. All the anomalies that have appeared in the published literature that, in turn, has formed the basis of the professors' reformulations are mere ephemera designed to lure the unwary followers of professorial authority into ruination.

COMPETING HYPOTHESES

I used the extensive database at Chicago to extend my findings of the non-random properties of stock prices. The hypothesis, techniques, and conclusions I reached were diametrically opposed to the *idée fixe* of the school. Eventually, a forum for a confrontation was arranged. The venue was the notorious Ph.D. Finance Seminar where, by tradition, no holds were barred.

The tone of the seminar was set before I arrived. Like most graduate students in business, I needed my investment fix (where were my stocks trading that day?) before I could proceed. In those days, schools were not equipped with trading stations for every student, so a call to my broker was in order.

Arriving at five minutes past the hour (classes were scheduled for ten minutes past), one of the illustrious attendees, whose name is now a household word in finance, exclaimed "Horse's ass, Niederhoffer is making a delayed grand entrance." (I had stationed spies to report on the pregame atmosphere.)

I opened by saying that I would show that markets were replete with regularities from the most microscopic tick-by-tick data right up to yearly moves within the decade. I criticized all those who had concluded that markets were random, including most of the professors in the room, as being too heavy-handed in their testing methods to uncover the structure of price variations. Further, I cautioned them that their failure to disprove a hypothesis that no structure existed was methodologically inadequate to support a conclusion that prices were random. When I put it in the vernacular, "You can't prove a negative," pandemonium broke loose.

Heresy! Booing and hissing broke out. Some of the more revered professors stood up to demand that I retract. I expected an old vaudeville-style hook to yank me out by the neck. As I tried to proceed, the group refused to allow me to present the first part of my paper, a review of the literature, on the grounds that they didn't want to waste their time hearing me analyze things they had already read. My statistical techniques and conclusions were challenged on the grounds that stock prices have infinite variances. Any differences in means I found would therefore be of no significance. My samples were challenged as being small and unrepresentative. Finally, it was asserted that, even assuming that my statistical results were accurate, the conclusions I reached were not meaningful because they could not overcome transaction costs, and so could be of no value to anyone but floor traders or specialists.

Looking back, the regularities I presented have stood the test of time. Soros once arranged for me to play tennis against super money manager Oscar Schaefer, a member of the *Barron's* Roundtable, and one of my clients when I started in business in the 1960s. After the game, he asked me, "Are you still doing that up-and-down Friday–Monday stuff you used to, or have you progressed?" Before I could answer, Soros chimed in, "I'm afraid he's doing exactly the same, hasn't progressed at all." That would be shameful in most cases, because markets are always changing. Rigidity creates vulnerability. Yesterday's stars are always today's dogs or, as I like to put it, "Nothing recedes like success."

Yes, the focus of my attention has been remarkably consistent from my days at Chicago. But while the questions are the same, the answers change. The main finding I presented at the seminar, updated 30 years to 1996 is presented below.

I started with a refutation of the strong form of the random walk theory that no information has a systematic impact on the markets. Some absurd papers along those lines were littering academic journals in those days. Findings, for example, that prediction of yearly earnings after the first-quarter interim report was released were no more accurate than those made with just the previous calendar year's results. Along similar lines, other academic studies failed to find the previous path of yearly earnings indicative of the future earnings path. They called this phenomenon higgledy-piggledy growth. These studies, in retrospect, could form the basis for a course in biases in the social sciences. Every defect that sociologists like to warn their undergraduate students away from was represented in abundance. The null hypotheses that the academic studies failed to refute have about the same merit as the theory that eyes do not help reading. But leave it to faulty myopic academic research to not even get into the ball-park on the day of the game.

To disprove the irrelevancy of earnings, I examined the best and worst performing stocks on the New York Stock Exchange in 1970. I looked at the 50 stocks with the best performance during the year, the 50 worst performing stocks, and a selection of 50 random issues, and I focused on their performance relative to both actual earnings and forecasted earnings announced previously.

The study showed that there is a clear linkage between a company's earnings and its subsequent price performance. As shown in Figure 12–1, the median actual earnings improvement for the 50 best price performers was 21 percent. Conversely, the 50 worst price performers had a median actual earnings decline of −83 percent, and my random sampling showed a median change of −10.5 percent.

I also analyzed the price impact of "earnings surprises"—instances where the well-paid oracles of Wall Street fell well short of the mark in their earnings forecasts. Which of the two is more embarrassing, a forecasted average of +7 percent and actual of +21 percent for the top 50, or a forecast of +15.3 percent and actual of −83 percent for the bottom 50?

This striking result has been widely reprinted. I have since updated it and find that earnings are still the key to individual stock performance.

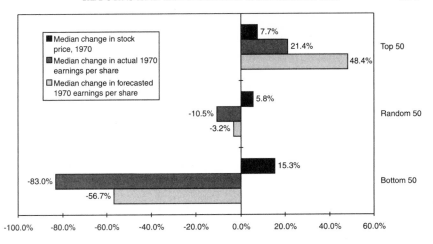

Figure 12–1. Median Changes in Forecasted Earnings, Actual Earnings, and Stock Price, One-Year Horizon

However, earnings predictions are so inaccurate that the price performance of companies with terrible forecasted earnings is superior to that of companies with excellent forecasted earnings.

TRANSACTIONS AND REGULARITIES

I then turned my attention to information that did have predictive content, starting at the most elementary level of the market-making process itself.

Limited orders to buy tend to cluster below the market, and limited orders to sell cluster above. Market orders to buy must be sufficient to overcome the limited sell orders before consecutive rises can occur. Market orders to sell must overcome the buy limited orders before consecutive declines can occur. That's why some can watch a market, as dull as paint drying, as prices reverse up and down hundreds of times in a row before continuations take over. The result is four nonrandom properties:

1. There is a general tendency for price reversal between trades.

2. Reversals are relatively more concentrated as integers where stable, slow-moving participants place their limit orders.

3. Fast-moving floor traders, knowing the locations of these limit orders, take positions at nearby prices, "pocketing the spread."

4. After two price changes in the same direction, the probability of a third change in the same direction as the second is greater than after two changes in opposite directions.

These tendencies are now so well documented that they make their way into many of the investment and finance textbooks. Odds ratios in favor of reversals versus continuations in transaction data normally run at five-to-one.

BLUE MONDAY

Next, I considered whether days of the week showed any differences. I started with the conventional view that certain days of the week are good for markets and others are bad. My original insight came from elemental activities like the relation of a man to his second best friend, the horse. The working stiff gets paid at the end of the week and bets the favorite on the weekends. Horse and handicapper lose because the payoff isn't big enough to warrant extra effort. On Monday, only the poor regulars are left, and they are desperate to earn back what they lost. They bet on long shots just to see the formful horses come in. The same phenomenon is true in markets. Admittedly, the cycles of destruction are a bit more variable (nothing as regular, for example, as the drop in noon temperature in humans, regardless of whether they've lunched), depending on excesses of optimism and pessimism as well as the temperature and day of the week.

A good place to start analysis of daily patterns is by focusing on the moves during the beginning and end of the week. Monday, for example, is supposed to find people gloomy from going back to work and from digesting excessively over the weekend. Friday is traditionally a day of thankfulness because the weekend respite and festivities are at hand.

I reported many such effects, and they still exist today, although often in reverse.

In one such study, highly relevant in my Chicago days (when stocks cleared in four trading days, making Monday purchases less desirable), I found that, in each of the previous 60 years, the chances of a rise in the Dow on Monday was lower than a rise on Friday. The 20-percentage-point negative bias in chances of a rise were millions to one against. Unfortunately, the cycles have changed numerous times since.

The next extension was to combine momentum with seasonality. For example, the action on Monday might be particularly bearish after a Friday that acted less favorably than the norm. The conjunction sounds so simple, but I calculate that the basic idea has made my immediate and extended family of customers a substantial nine figures.

The phenomenon has now become part of market folklore. Articles in the newspapers often refer to it. Yale Hirsch, publisher of *Stock Trader's Almanac*, is particularly adroit at displaying nonrandom effects like this. Here's how he presented a related phenomenon, as recently as 1993: "As discovered by . . . Niederhoffer, Cross and Zeckhauser . . . when the market is down on Friday, chances are three to one that Monday will also decline. In the 1953–1985 period, I found that only 28.2% of Mondays were able to rise after declining Fridays."[5] The chances of a rise in the last four days of the week has consistently run 13 points higher than on Monday. I have supplemented these data with stock market futures data from 1992 to 1995 (Table 12–1).

But these results in and of themselves were not sufficient to make money; they involved discrepancies of 0.3 percent between the best average change and the worst. Commissions at the time amounted to at least 0.5 percent and the bid/asked spread was 1 percent. So, there was never a reason to sell: the comprehensive studies of Lorie and Fisher had shown that the market, on average, was a rising animal. Since that time, others have found the same difficulty.

To make matters worse, I knew even then that results that appeared significant in one period had a tendency to evaporate in subsequent periods. The reasons are legion. If a phenomenon truly exists, shrewd operators discover it and start anticipating it in following periods, thereby evening out the moves. As the moves become evened out, the market (which likes to do its work, like all of us, along the lines of least resistance) finds it's better to take its large declines on days other than Mondays. It's much more likely, however, that a peculiar constellation of factors is in effect at the time and is causing the phenomenon to occur. As ecologists like to say, when talking about food webs in a related context: "There's always a web. But the problem is, the web is always changing."

There's something incredibly naïve about many of the academics who work in fields where financial results might lead to profitable activities. It never occurs to them that shrewd operators who discover a regularity might keep the secret close to the vest. Conversely, most phenomena that are reported in the literature are so weak as to be worthless. Further, the members of the trade generally are not as dumb as they appear. They read academic journals and hire the best graduate students to keep them posted on new findings. When a recurring effect of practical significance is reported, the trade takes advantage of it with great abandon, huge capital resources, and low costs. When the phenomenon is a delusion but many slow-moving outsiders believe in it, the trade is astute enough to front-run the buying and the selling.

The results that academics publish are consistent with these human tendencies. When I published my work on seasonality, I was not unmindful of where my bread was buttered. I withheld the good stuff. Still, the findings on daily seasonality that I chose to publish caused quite a stir in the academic world. Here's how one expert described them:

> The next study of daily return patterns did not appear in the academic literature for four decades. Frank Cross (1973) studied the returns on the Standard and Poor's index of 500 stocks (the S&P 500) over the period 1953 to 1970. He found that the index rose on 62.0 percent of the Fridays, but on only 39.5 of the Mondays. The mean return on Fridays was 0.12 percent,

Table 12–1. Percentage of Higher Next-Day Closes
(Based on S&P Composite Index, 1952–1996)

Year	Friday Close to Following Monday Close	Monday's Close to Next Friday's Close
1952	50.0%	60.4%
1953	32.7	55.1
1954	51.9	63.5
1955	48.1	63.7
1956	34.0	49.1
1957	25.0	53.9
1958	59.6	63.5
1959	40.4	57.4
1960	36.5	53.6
1961	53.8	58.6
1962	28.3	52.8
1963	46.2	60.2
1964	40.4	62.3
1965	46.2	57.0
1966	36.5	50.3
1967	40.4	59.6
1968	39.1	56.9
1969	32.1	54.3
1970	38.5	51.6
1971	44.2	56.0
1972	38.5	58.6
1973	30.8	47.8
1974	34.6	45.4
1975	53.8	53.6
1976	55.8	52.4
1977	40.4	48.9
1978	51.9	53.1
1979	54.7	55.0
1980	57.6	54.7
1981	46.2	48.3
1982	44.2	44.5
1983	50.0	53.6
1984	39.6	45.6
1985	44.2	55.5
1986	50.0	56.1
1987	50.0	55.7
1988	51.9	54.8
1989	51.9	61.1
1990	66.7	48.5
1991	44.2	49.9
1992	53.8	44.2
1993	63.5	42.3
1994	50.0	42.3
1995	51.2	71.1
Average	45.4%	54.2%

Source: 1993 *Stock Traders Almanac,* p. 119. 1994–1995 updated.

while the mean return on Mondays was −0.18 percent. As Cross says, "The probability that such a large difference would occur by chance is less than one in a million."[6]

Frank Cross and I were partners at Niederhoffer, Cross and Zeckhauser for almost 20 years. The referenced study arose from previously published joint work.

REVERSAL OF FORTUNE

Richard Thaler's book, *The Winner's Curse*, is a brilliant exposition of what academics have learned about the nonrational, unusual, and erratic in economic life, and he reviewed our work in a generally adulatory fashion. But whenever a professor touts an anomaly, I have learned that an antianomaly is probably lurking in the wings.

To see how cycles have changed or stayed the same, I calculated the performance of S&P futures, classified by each day of the week, from a month after the 1987 crash to March 30, 1996. There were 2,115 days in all. The average changes in the S&P (in points), classified by the day of the week, are:

Day	Average Change
Monday	.56 points
Tuesday	.21
Wednesday	.29
Thursday	−.10
Friday	−.12

The average: .56-point move on Monday, about one-tenth of one percent, corresponds to five points in the Dow Jones Industrials. The results are not overly spectacular—they barely cover slippage—even if it is a recurring phenomenon. What is interesting is that the changes are almost *exactly the opposite* of the regularities that formed the basis of our discoveries in the late 1960s. Monday is by far the strongest day, Friday the weakest. Because the Monday effect corresponds to only a 1-in-100 shot by chance alone and was selected retrospectively as the largest positive change with no previous hypothesis to explain it, I have no confidence whatsoever that these results could not be attributable to random variations alone.

Just in time to transmit completely incorrect news, as if proving the best possible confirmation of its worthlessness, there comes down the pike a group of academic studies showing Monday to be the most bearish day of the week. As reported in *The Economist* (September 24, 1994):

[An academic] study found disproportionately heavy selling of small parcels of shares (typically by individual investors) on Mondays. . . . Four of every five share price falls on Mondays happened after a fall on the previous Friday. Moreover, when the market rose on Friday, share prices on average gained on the following Monday. The study also found that it is really a Monday morning effect: after 1 P.M. share prices tended to edge up.[7]

As long as the academics and their fellow travelers in the media have their antennas set to transmit the most erroneous news at the best time to wreak the maximum damage, there is hope for those with a contrarian turn of mind. Perhaps there are some who can draw from their own down-to-earth experiences to trade against such "findings" and pocket some winnings.

As Gilbert and Sullivan put it, in celebration of constantly changing Nature, and tastes:

> And it's not in the range of belief
>   That you could hold him as a glutton,
> Who, when he is tired of beef,
>   Determines to tackle the mutton.[8]

The cycles change. I note with some shame that to have traded using the Blue Monday effect I discovered 30 years ago, which has been taken up by almanacs, academics, and journalists, would have cost the investor over 2000 Dow points in the post-crash period.

But it looked good on paper.

AN OUNCE OF TESTING

Since the 1960s, considerable attention has been focused on what has been called the "turn-of-the-month effect." In the classic study on this subject, Robert Ariel divided the months into two halves. He then computed the returns in the two halves, adding the twist of using both equal-weighted and value-weighted indexes. Such clever distinctions are the warp and woof of academic papers. They lend an aura of arcane profundity to what might otherwise have been a straightforward investigative effort. Ariel concludes that the returns for the first half of the month are significantly greater than the returns for the second half.

To find out whether this effect still existed, I looked at the first and last ten days of S&P futures prices in the 106 months from the 1987 crash to August 1996. The average performance during the first ten days of the month was up 2.02 S&P points, and the performance for the last ten days was up only 0.68 S&P points. A noticeable bias during these eight years causes the market to rise on average almost three times as much in the first ten days of the month as during the last ten days. In line with Ariel's study, I have found that seasonals within the month still exist.

THE JANUARY EFFECT

It is interesting to see whether the tendency for the first period to predict the subsequent period is a general phenomenon of stocks, applying, for example, to months of the year as well as days of the week. Apparently, a real effect is going on. The January Barometer has been a famed indicator since close to the beginning of technical analysis. I remember hearing Harry Comer, a technical analyst at one of the big wire houses, giving a presentation on it at a bacchanalian revel held at the Myopia Hunt Club when I taught there in 1962. The correlation between January's percentage change and the next eleven months' percentage change was 0.15. To test the phenomenon, I used data on the Dow Jones Industrial Average from 1935 to 1995. The results confirmed the phenomenon. In 21 years, when January showed a decline, the average percentage change for the next eleven months was up 2.3 percent. A decline in the following eleven months occurred 50 percent of the time. In the 40 years when the Dow showed a rise, however, the average percentage change was plus 8.7 percent, and a rise occurred 80 percent of the time over the next eleven months. (See Figure 12–2.) Applying rank statistics to test these means for

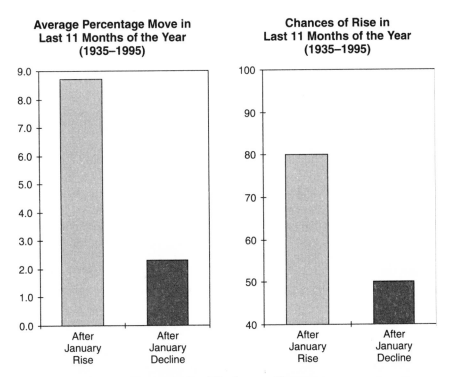

Figure 12–2.   The January Barometer

nonrandomness, one can be 99 percent confident that a nonrandom effect is at work here.

It is interesting to speculate why a result like this would exist, and whether it will hold in the future.

After considering differences in days and momentum, the question arose as to whether the months of the year exhibited differential performance. To test this, I looked at the monthly moves of the Dow Jones Industrial Average and its precursors from 1870 to 1995, and found the average move for each calendar month during this span.

The results show January and August to be the best months, and May, September, and October to be the worst. There was no prior reason to suspect that these months would be the most bullish and the most bearish. To test whether these results were valid, I took all 1,200 changes and put them into a hat. I divided the 1,200 changes into 10 groups of 120 by selecting randomly with replacement, and then chose the most bullish and the most bearish groups. I repeated this process 10,000 times. In only 20 of the 10,000 times did the difference between the most bullish and the most bearish months exceed the 2.5 percent difference from our sample. So we can say that, at least over the past 100 years, January and August have been the most bullish months, and September and October have been the most bearish.

	Mean		Mean
January	1.2%	July	0.8%
February	0.0	August	1.5
March	0.6	September	−1.0
April	0.9	October	0.0
May	−0.2	November	0.5
June	0.3	December	1.1

YEARLY SEASONALS

After considering daily and monthly seasonals, it's natural to move to yearly effects. The difficulty is that yearly data exist for just 200 years. The average human mind can spin 1,000 hypotheses about patterns in those years.

The simplest direct hypothesis would seem to be that, over the years, there are decennial patterns in the moves. Legend has it, for example, that the end-digit-7 ("7") years are particularly bearish. The worst crash in history, making the 1987 crash seem gentle by comparison, occurred in 1907. Similarly, the 30 percent upward move in 1995 was widely heralded in advance as a decennial bullish property of end-digit-5 ("5") years.

To see whether the average change found in the "5" years was nonrandom, I implemented the following procedure to arrive at confidence intervals for the observed results. I took 120 of the 124 yearly market performance results and computer-sorted them on a random basis into ten groups of twelve. For each group, the mean was computed, and the maximum and minimum means out of the ten means were retained. I ran 1,000 such trials.

The results for the "5" years were supportive of the theory: in only 4 out of 1,000 trials was the maximum of ten means above 27 percent, a highly significant statistical result. In only 101 of the 1,000 trials was the minimum of the ten means below −7 percent. We can thus say with 99.6 percent confidence that the "5" years are inordinately good years to buy stocks, and we can be 89.9 percent confident that the "7" years are relatively bad.

The results of the 1870–1993 test appear in Figure 12–3. Returns on the stock market averages are calibrated in percentages along the y axis. Returns are shown for each year, arranged in columns headed 0 through 9, representing the terminal digit of each year. Within each column, the mean return for each year carrying that terminal digit is shown by a small triangle, and a line connects all nine means.

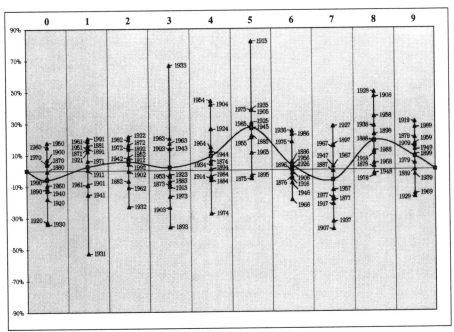

Market returns for the years 1870–1884 are based on the end-of-year prices compiled by the Cleveland Trust Bank, Axe-Houghton and The Cowles Commission for Research in Economics. Market data for the years 1885 onward are based on the Dow Jones Industrial Average.

Figure 12–3. Stock Price Change (with Mean) by Ending-Digits 0–9, 1870–1993

It turns out that "5" years are indeed great years. Their average return of 27 percent is phenomenally high. The "7" years would have been good to avoid, especially from October to year-end 1987, when the average dropped 25 percent. In 1987, the Dow Jones Industrial Average was up by about 2 percent. But for all twelve "7" years that we considered, the mean return was negative, −6.5 percent.

THE FORTUNATE ILLNESS

My presentation on regularities did not go over well. A vigilante committee was formed to ride me out of town on a rail. Wherever I presented papers, there they were with their random-walk guns blazing. And wherever they were with nonsensical papers showing that this or that bit of information added nothing of value, there I was to poke fun at their biases and inadequate testing procedures. The climax came with publication of a paper designed to show that information on first-quarter earnings did not help forecasts of full-year earnings. I had some great fun poking holes in this pronouncement because, statistically and empirically, it was an impossibility. The first quarter, after all, is 25 percent of the full year's results. If the first-quarter earnings were not positively correlated with the full year's results, then the next three quarters had to be inversely correlated with the first quarter. In rebutting the results, I quoted the authors' particularly infelicitous choice of words: "It is curious that the first quarter which represents one-quarter of the total should be uncorrelated with the full year, of which it is part." Warming to the controversy, I remarked, "The authors thus express in their own words and style the skepticism with which they felt others should regard their results." That one word, "style," almost did me in.

At my Ph.D. seminar, a posse of students closely associated with my adversaries showed up to interrogate me. To put my work in perspective, one suggested I expand my study of quantifying the impact of U.S. news on economic time series. Another suggested that my work should be recast to take account of the infinite variance of stock price changes. The members of my dissertation committee started nodding in agreement. Seeing that my goose was cooked, I decided not to give them the sanction of the victim, "I regret that I have challenged your cherished beliefs with my study. But these questions were obviously designed not to illumine the issues, but to do me in." I was ushered out to a chorus of boos. "You shouldn't have said that," Lorie told me afterward. "You just shot yourself in the foot."

It looked like I'd become "all-but-dissertation," the modal degree of the Federal Reserve staff. But luck was a lady. With Jim's urging, the chief randomness professor on my dissertation committee decided it would be better for his health if he reduced his stress by resigning from my committee. Simultaneously, Lorie suggested I put my Ph.D. on hold and accept a position as an acting assistant professor at the University of California, Berkeley. "They're not quite as set in their ways out there, and time can cure most wounds," he said.

Jew or Squash Player?

I was fighting on another front on the squash courts. The year I entered Chicago, I won my first U.S. National Tournament in New York. The next year, it was scheduled for Chicago. At 21, I was in one of those sweet spots in time where I could literally fly around the court. I was virtually unbeatable. But something rankled.

There were five private clubs where squash was played in Chicago. Out of a total membership of some 7,000, one person was Jewish. All of these clubs were happy to have me play as a guest, but none of them saw fit to allow me to play as a member. As a result, I was unable to play at prime hours, bring my own guests in, or purchase food and equipment.

The whole situation was demeaning in the extreme. Twelve months before the Chicago Nationals, I announced that I would not defend my title unless one of the city clubs admitted me. The twelve months passed, and the tournament was played in Chicago without me. I announced my retirement from the game. With a great facade of hand wringing and soul searching, the officials of the squash association and my competitors accepted my resignation with alacrity.

Thus began my five-year hiatus from the game—while I was at my peak. What I would give to have these years back today, with all my knowledge and repertoire of tricks. The only compensation was that my stance made me a hero of the Anti-Defamation League, and I received much favorable publicity for being a young man of principles. The episode also sensitized me to the abuse that minorities experience. Battling on both the random walk field and the squash court was a little too much. However, I believe it strengthened me in following a contrarian philosophy—the only way, I believe, that speculators can prosper.

The Western Frontier

California, the traditional frontier, beckoned. There were many reasons to go West in the good old days: to find new land, to gain elbow room, to trap fur, to dig for gold—or, to get a change in luck, or escape from creditors, enemies, or the law. Put more kindly, people sought a new horizon in the West. Following in their footsteps, I extended my horizons to the University of California, the Free Speech Movement, the antiwar protests, the Pacific, the good weather, real estate, and beyond.

But the frontier always offers new opportunities. California can find something for its bold young men to do besides clear land, surf the Pacific, gain consciousness, talk mellow, bathe in a hot tub, and enjoy free love.

The West in the 1960s was at the vanguard of the investment frontier. Sparked by the Lorie–Fisher rate-of-return studies, the first index funds, pioneered by the Wells Fargo Bank, emerged. In 1996, the former bank subsidiary manages $145 billion of such funds, and the industry itself accounts for one-third of the $3 trillion total of mutual fund equities under management, with the Vanguard Group itself managing over $50 billion of such assets. In 1996, the Vanguard Index 500 fund held assets of $20 billion and showed a 15 percent annualized return over the previous eight years—3 percent above the norm. This superior record is certainly due to low expenses and low turnover. I speculate, however, that part of this superiority stems from competitors' tendency to concentrate in the wrong stocks and industries.

My introduction to Western culture came when John McQuown, head of the burgeoning quantitative research group at the Wells Fargo Bank, invited me there to calculate low-cost ways of managing portfolios of stocks that would duplicate market returns. The Chicago studies had shown that randomly selected purchases of listed stocks yielded returns averaging 10 percent a year over long holding periods. In practice, however, mutual funds were not delivering this kind of return. To add insult to injury, many of the funds charged investors hefty fees for the privilege of returns worse than random performance.

THE GOODMAN TECHNIQUE

I reject the cynical view that the faculties of research universities are replete with underworked, overpaid, petty-command society lovers who are completely indifferent to teaching their students. I also reject the popular stereotype that an academic's teaching methods atrophy once tenure has been received.

My own experience on each side of the lectern disproves both concepts. At the University of Chicago, I took courses from Professor Leo Goodman, who received tenure at the youthful age of 25 and adopted a socratic teaching method that made the learned Greek philosopher seem an autocrat by comparison. Leo's teaching method contained no frills. At his lectures, he would distribute a copy of one of his papers and tell the students to read it for the next class. Dismissed. At the next lecture, he asked for questions. If yes, he answered; if no, a new paper was assigned.

I adopted Leo's methods for my own classes. I didn't have to wait for student evaluation to know that I couldn't fill Leo's shoes. At the first graduate investment class I taught, 250 students showed up. In retrospect, the dean must have spread the word that I was a rising star with secret techniques of making money. Attendance steadily diminished at my classes. Only two students registered for the class in the fifth and final year that I taught it.

I have looked up the first paper I wrote at the University of California, Berkeley, "The Alphabetical Properties of Stock Prices," and am happy to report that there has been one reference to it. But, it is too limiting to measure the value of a paper merely by what the student and subsequent citer get out of it.

Nor do I agree with the implications of Martin Anderson's provocative work, *Imposters in the Temple*, that all university professors care about is seeing their papers published, to the exclusion of its utility to anyone else. Anderson points out that 93 percent of all papers published in the humanities department are never referenced by other papers. The author benefits just as much as the reader.

Such was indeed the case with my alphabetical properties paper. I frequently buy companies on the basis of the first letters of their name, without regard to what each company does. During bubbles in biotech stocks, for example, any company with "bio" in its name is likely to rise precipitously. When the value of such companies is measured in terms of price/Ph.D.s, or price/patents, I know its near time to pull the plug.

Similarly, when the technology companies are out of favor, I avoid all companies with "tech," "-onics," or "computers" in the name. During the doldrums, such companies are bound to fall to half of book value, regardless of their long-term value. At times like these, the best contrarian fund managers put their fingers in the dike.

I have subsequently generalized my approach to take account of the geographic properties of markets. Whenever I make big money in a country, I take out a map and look for the countries, that are the nearest. If one country's interest rates are yielding a 40 percent real return, chances are that the one just across the river or over the mountain is close to the mark. I have a big Rand McNally map posted in my trading room, and I frequently consult it in this regard. As I write near the end of 1996, my fund's biggest killing has come from buying Turkish Treasury bills. The nominal compounded returns of 120 percent a year and more in the context of an 80 percent inflation rate seemed just too good to resist. But the map was somewhat deflating in this case. Investment in Iraq is against the law for U.S. citizens.

THE CHIEF RABBI

Not surprisingly, during most of my lectures, the students were bored stiff. To lighten things up, I often asked the students to relate how their own personal experiences applied to the subject. The usual reaction was total silence. To break the ice on such occasions, I employed a technique I learned from Sir Francis.

In *Memories of My Life*, Galton recounts how he overcame a similar reticence at a meeting of the British Association on the study of mental imagery. He merely related the story of the revered and venerable Chief Rabbi of Danzig. One day, the rabbi's house caught fire, and among the many valuables lost in the blaze was his prize wine cellar. The Jews of the city took counsel as to how to restore the rabbi's loss. After many initial proposals to build him a magnificent edifice were downsized and finally rejected, the congregation hit on the following scheme. Every member of the faithful throng should visit the rabbi's house on an appointed day, and bring with him a bottle of wine, which should be poured into a giant vat set up for the purpose. And so it was done.

After the departure of the last visitor, the rabbi eagerly hastened to the vat to taste of his neighbors' kindness. When he turned the tap to fill his glass, however, he found to his dismay and wrath that pure water issued forth. Each of his benefactors had said to himself, "What matters whether I put in a spirit which costs money, or water which costs nothing? My own contribution will make no sensible difference to the total result."[9]

TIME SERIES CHARTS

The gambit worked for Galton, and it often works for me. One day, after I had recited this tale, a distinguished, white-haired gentleman stood up and introduced himself as Harold Weaver, a professor of astronomy. He was in charge of investments for the Board of the California Astronomers Association and was auditing my class to stay up on current trends in the academic world. He had applied some of the techniques of astronomy to analyzing stock market interactions. "You see, in astronomy, a typical problem is to predict where a planet is going to be in its orbit around the sun. We know where planets are at various times and our job is to predict where they are going to be in the future. Kepler solved that problem through diagrams like this [here he unrolled a scroll-like chart], and Newton formulated the laws that explained why all objects move in this fashion. Now with stock market data, the problem is more difficult because there is a large random element to these moves. Take the interaction between the stock and bond markets, for example." Professor Weaver then brought out a chart of 1969 moves in stocks and bonds.

Presented here is a more timely 27th anniversary chart covering the monthly moves from 1989 to August 1996 (Figure 12–4). These moves are graphed as a time series, putting three dimensions onto two. (If you need a fourth dimension, you can vary the color or thickness of the lines.)

Oddly enough, the picture that emerges shares a common appearance with a map of the universe. For a long time, astronomers have known that the dispersion of galaxies in the cosmos shows regions of accumulation surrounded by regions of desolation. This is the same configuration that

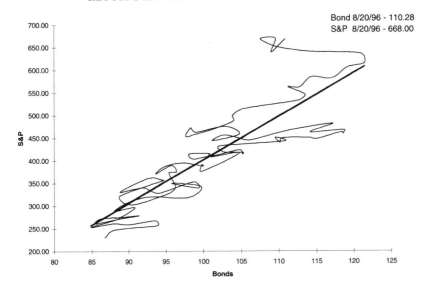

Figure 12–4.   Weaver Chart of Bond/S&P Movement,
(November 1987–July 1996)

emerges when we plot two commodities on a graph. There seem to be areas on the graph that show a lot of activity and have a high frequency of price occurrence. At the same time, there are areas with little or no trading activity. Prices quickly move through the low-frequency areas to the high-frequency areas. This is a satisfying observation for those of us who believe that everything worth anything is reflected in the financial markets.

"Notice that most of the lines move in a northeast or southwest direction," Professor Weaver commented. "In fact, 75 percent of the lines are NE or SW, and 25 percent are NW or SE. This illustrates what you call the tendency to comovement between bonds and stocks. There are three times as many moves in the same direction as there are moves in opposite directions. This corresponds to a correlation between stocks and bonds of 60 percent. The key is what happens after such events."

Figure 12–4 has many interesting features. I urge the reader to take a careful look at it and extract the kernels contained within. Near the top right are the 1996 data points. And they clearly don't fit. The bond level of 110 is much too low to be consistent with an S&P of 670. How will the divergence be resolved? A bond rise? A stock decline? Or a new paradigm? Be my guest.

"Now, just as Kepler was able to predict the motion of the planets from diagramming planetary motion, the fellows at the Astronomers Association are using such diagrams to predict stock market movements."

"Professor, what's the secret? How do you go from descriptive element to predictive?"

"Why, Dr. Niederhoffer, that's why I'm here." Thus, a beautiful friendship was born. The attempt to answer these queries has taken up a good part of my creative thinking over the past 30 years. My most recent effort involved taking the tangent of the angles between the intersection of two consecutive lines and ascertaining whether these tend to be followed by any recurring moves to the horizontal direction (a stock market prediction) or the vertical (a bond market prediction).

I often use such diagrams for stock market trades, and I made some good money on each of them until 1987, when stocks again were way too high for bonds. The discrepancy corrected itself in one day, October 19, 1987. The relation held pretty well through year-end 1993, until bonds went down 10 percent and stocks stayed the same in 1994. 1995 was a good year, with bonds and stocks going up 10 percent and 20 percent, respectively. Then the whole thing began to head down in 1996, which has an eerie similarity to 1987. Stocks registered a rise of 10 percent in the first six months and bonds went down 10 percent.

THE SUBJECTIVE NATURE OF ACADEMIC RESEARCH

I taught at Berkeley for a few years following the free speech movement, and I was there during the height of the protests against the war in Vietnam. The protests were quite extensive, frequently closing down the streets of Berkeley; on several occasions, protesters occupied key buildings and thoroughfares on campus. The protesters often picketed in front of Barrows, the Social Science building where I lectured. When I attempted to break through the protest lines, I invariably got choked by the tie. Since that time, I have been reluctant to wear such badges to work. I unfortunately work in a trade where I cannot hide my bad performance behind a veneer of respectability. While pursuing success, I might as well be comfortable and prepared for escape.

While at Berkeley, I learned once and for all that academics are as biased and subjective about their trade as anyone else. The occasion was the brouhaha that arose in response to an article that Arthur Jensen wrote about the causes and varieties of educational achievement. Jensen and I shared a common interest in the work of Galton, so I looked him up when I arrived at Berkeley.

I will not discuss Jensen's research; Charles Murray and Richard Herrenstein have performed that task admirably in their magnum opus *The Bell Curve*. But my experiences with the lynch mob of professors and students that followed Jensen around should be a caution to all budding speculators who might be tempted to take the latest academic findings as gospel.

Jensen reported the results of his research in the *Harvard Educational Review* in 1969. His paper on this point, a model of scholarly precision and caution, with 169 index references and numerous tables, summarized hundreds of separate psychometric studies.

The paper caused an uproar, and numerous professors and graduate students wrote to the University of California paper, the *Daily Californian*, demanding that Jensen be banned from further research and removed from the faculty. Students rioted on the grounds of the Sociology Department, threatening to shut down the University if these demands were not met. Posters with Jensen's face appeared around campus, captioned "WANTED FOR CRIMES AGAINST THE HUMAN RACE."

After a little checking, I learned that the University had on the premises only two copies of the issue of the *Harvard Educational Review* containing Jensen's article. Thanks to some help from a friend who worked in the library, I found that both copies had been checked out to professors in the Genetics Department. It became apparent that no sociology or psychology professor could have read Jensen's article in the University library. I then called the *Harvard Educational Review* to check on the subscription status of the professors who had written bitter diatribes against Jensen, supposedly after reading this article. Not one of them had a subscription. To anyone who would listen, I pointed out the near impossibility of the professors' ever having read the article. Their ideological predisposition was so great that they were willing to condemn a scholarly article they had not read.

A conference was duly arranged and held in the Biology Department building, the agenda of which was to lynch Jensen and to allay the sensibilities of those who brook no questioning of whether there is universal equality of aptitude among individuals. There were the expected diatribes: "We should perhaps thank Burt and Jensen for reminding us that arrogance, ignorance, and prejudice have been fellow travelers of the mental testers ever since Galton"; "The belief in value-free procedures is not only incorrect but potentially dangerous"; "Jensen's approach is not really a remedy, but a prescription for ignoring the problem," and so forth.

It is no wonder, after comments such as these, and some so much worse that I deem them unprintable, that Jensen once referred to the aversion to the genetic hypothesis as "the most powerful taboo in the field of science."

Always ready to defend a disciple of Galton from the slings and arrows of collectivists, I arranged to act as Jensen's bodyguard when he gave class on campus. I brought my squash racquet to his classes and helped maintain order after the University Police had been outflanked. I found these lectures extremely enjoyable and challenging. And I learned that Jensen has the hide of a rhinoceros. No matter how much is thrown at him, he coolly faces his critics and rebuts all their arguments with facts, data, and logic.

I use his tough approach to my advantage whenever I feel the weight of conventional thinking going completely against me. My views on markets always seem to be completely against the weight of the best academic research and the most astute political commentators. Invariably, I find these learned commentators know infinitely more about the subject at hand than I do. I find their views compelling but, invariably, a ticket to the poorhouse. That's why I tuned out of all media except the *National Enquirer* shortly after I left Berkeley. Like many successful life forms, I tried to remain invisible and incommunicado to ward off the wisdom of those who knew more than I did. This worked for over 20 years or so, until I started offering units of my fund to well-heeled investors. My partners and I were lucky enough (once we overcame some bad initial results in the birthing process) to be rated near the top of the pack. This doubtlessly temporary and nonpredictive result has thrust us into the limelight again. Hardly a week goes by when I am not requested to disseminate my views to the masses.

Often, I am asked to appear at forums where investment bankers are hyping their products with a quasi-academic justification for support. Invariably, a clash occurs when I find myself saying things like: "Are you really serious about that mumbo jumbo, or is this just designed to generate commissions? There is absolutely no scientific justification for you." At an August 1996 Bloomberg Forum, I finally crossed the line. My counterpart this time was espousing the view that long-term holdings of commodities had historically yielded the same kind of return as stocks. By adding such to the portfolio, the investor could improve his position on the return–risk isoplanes. Before I could excuse myself, I blurted out, "The last time I heard such pablum, Metallgesellschaft had gobbled it up and lost $2 billion or so in the process." That was it. I realize that I have become as superfluous in the world of forums as I have become in many other fields. I vowed then and there that I would have to abstain from such efforts in the future. I am as unfit to be a member of the promotion-of-the-public club as I was to get into the Gentile club of Chicago 30 years before.

Although I respect the literary critic Harold Bloom, I don't agree with his view that "the academy . . . [is] always dominated by fools, knaves, charlatans and bureaucrats . . . ."[10] My experience with the biases and arrogance at Harvard, the stereotyped random walk views at Chicago, and the witch hunts at Berkeley have convinced me that professors are made of the same stuff as you and I. I revere the character and intelligence of some professors, but I find that making their living in an occupation where the customer doesn't determine remuneration and where their tenure is independent of performance leaves them susceptible to behavior and postures that most of us wouldn't find acceptable in our butchers, bakers, and electricians.

This knowledge gives me an edge when a professor deigns to descend from the lofty slopes of academia to the world of speculation, usually with a minicomputer in hand. Invariably forthcoming is a demonstration of how the latest developments in neural networks, fuzzy logic, stochastic programming, nonlinear differential equations, or chaos theory can open market secrets. Shortly thereafter, I can be sure to read how, in a hexagonal-shaped room with furniture the Museum of Modern Art would be proud to display, a professor and a handful of the brightest Ph.D.s from Cal Tech, Stanford, and MIT are now accounting for 5 percent of total NYSE volume each day. When I add up all the 5 percents I've read or heard about, it comes to well above 100 percent.

FINAL DAYS IN THE WEST

It took one final incident to carry me out of the academic community. One day, a former student grabbed me by the tie in an airport and started pushing me around. "Professor Niederhoffer, you may not remember me. I was one of your students in Business Administration 133. I just wanted you to know that you were undoubtedly the worst teacher I have ever had in my entire life. I've lodged a complaint."

The student's complaint was correct, but I had some defense in his case. He had turned in as his term paper an article copied verbatim from a prewar issue of the *Journal of Finance*. References to "par value," "railway bonds," and "holding companies" abounded and gave him away. Fraternities of that era stored old papers written by the earlier brothers that might be turned in subsequently as term papers, when uninspiring professors or a bout of drinking precluded a more personal approach. (The most recent citation in this one was dated 1938.)

Soon thereafter, I received a note from Dean Richard Holton, "Professor Niederhoffer, could you stop by my office? I've received a letter from a student with a bee in his bonnet about your teaching style, and I'd like to give him the courtesy of a response." When I arrived at his commodious office, he reported the student's complaint as follows:

"You always seem to speak extemporaneously. You often engage your students in badinage. You rarely wear a tie. You put your sneakers up on the desk. You invariably lecture about your own work, either denigrating or usually ignoring erudite contributions of the founders of finance. You spend more time talking about hobos than about the great Benjamin Graham.

"Now Professor, we consider you one of our stars here. When it was announced at the faculty meeting that you had accepted an assistant professorship here, there was prolonged applause. This student seems to have an ax to grind against you. What do you have to say for yourself?"

After reflecting, I concluded that it was high time for me to cut my teaching career while I could still leave with a modicum of dignity. As a squash and tennis teacher, involved one-to-one with students, I seemed to be a natural. But when I tried to extend this method to the teaching of finance in a classroom, I was a failure.

About two weeks later, I met again with Dean Holton. "Well, Victor, have you thought about our conversation? You know, I've been watching you, and I like you. But there's the question of your teaching style, for one thing. And there's something else, too . . . you have to realize that there has never been a professor here to receive tenure who combined an active business career with full-time academic responsibilities. You'll have to give up one or the other."

"But Dean, I make only $9,000 a year, and all my students graduate and take jobs with a $14,000 starting salary. How can I survive and raise a family?"

"Well, that's the sacrifice you have to make to teach at a prestigious university like Berkeley. I made it. And if you choose to stay I don't think you'll regret it. But you have to decide soon."

My decision was not long in the making. It was back to New York to play in the real world of markets and to take another run at the squash tournaments.

CHAPTER 13

——————•◦•——————

Connections to Monitor

[A] rumor that the Secretary of the Treasury is going to sell, or loosen up gold; a bill is to be introduced into Congress; it is to be essentially modified, to be defeated or passed; the Spanish minister walked rapidly out of the White House one morning; the Secretary of State sent an important dispatch to a high official at Washington; the fares on an important railroad are to be reduced, or certain roads are to be consolidated.

Matthew Hale Smith

MARKET CHAINS

The classic discussion of interdependence comes appropriately from *The Origin of Species*, where Darwin states that every being is connected, albeit obliquely at times, to every other being. With tongue in cheek, he related the health of the British nation to the number of cats in an area. The cats eat mice. With more cats there are fewer mice. But mice devour the nesting sites of bumble bees. The bumble bee pollinates clover eaten by cattle. The English nation must have its roast beef made of cattle. He concludes the chain:

> Hence it is quite credible that the presence of a feline animal in large numbers in a district might determine, through the intervention first of mice and then of bees, the frequency of certain flowers in that district[1]

A chain with as many links made and lost some of the biggest fortunes during the early 1970s. "El Niño" (The Infant) is a weather pattern that occurs every few years because of a weakening of the westerly winds in the Pacific Ocean. The flow of cold bottom water is reduced, and surface water in South America, including the Humboldt Current in Peru, warms. This reduces Peru's anchovy harvest, which needs colder temperatures to thrive. Anchovies are a key ingredient in poultry and cattle feed, so farmers are forced to substitute soybean meal for the reduced fish meal. Increased demand for soybeans raised the spot price of soybeans from $3.40 to $11.00 a bushel during 1973.

El Niño chains spread because fish meal is a key ingredient of feeds. All livestock and household pets consume a feed consisting of three classes of ingredients: (1) grains, such as corn or wheat; (2) grain by-products like corn gluten; and (3) protein supplements such as fish meal or soybean meal. When protein supplements increase in price, producers substitute soybean meal, immediately causing soybean prices to rise. Ultimately, the producers jump between classes. The impact of price rises then spreads to grains and grain by-products.

The impact of chains like these on markets is called "the domino effect." Bones and bodies crash into neighbors and markets. In mid-1996, the copper futures market decline of 25 percent, caused by the Sumitomo losses caused by Sumitomo rogue trader, Yasuo Hamanaka, ultimately caused the silver market to fall below $5. Aluminum, lead, and nickel then fell by 5 percent; and the dominos fell on near neighbors, including the Australian dollar, world grains, the U.S. dollar, U.S. bonds, and the U.S. stock market. Only when the dominos were hoisted by the confirmation of Federal Reserve Chairman Alan Greenspan did the markets rebuild themselves again. Finally, by the end of June, copper advanced 10 percent from its low, and the S&P Index promptly rose 6 points in relief in one of its largest increases in the previous year.

Moves in stocks are so frequently attributed to chains, ripples, rotations, rolling readjustments, and synchronized global improvements that such explanations have become banal. The story, "Jitters among high-flying stocks spread like a ripple over the surface water to technology giants" or "Rotation of interest in value stocks from the high multiplied US market to the more undervalued emerging markets" is guaranteed to appear at least ten times a week in the financial news. In a *fin de siècle* touch, such a commentary must be followed by: "The decline spread to the high-tech stocks recommended on the Motley Fool Bulletin Board."

Modern traders are highly sensitive to connections. When *BusinessWeek* and the Smick Johnson Report simultaneously reported, in June 1996, that unnamed sources said the Fed would not tighten at its next Open Market committee meeting, they immediately characterized it as an attempt to bail out technology stocks, then cratering on the NASDAQ.

All markets are buffeted by chains. Rumors of the Fed buying, Soros selling, a change in the size of an auction, a rogue trader, or a natural disaster regularly cascade through market prices. In an ironic twist, they affect the cavities of dogs and the dental practices of veterinarians (which I monitor through the number of advertising pages in *Veterinary Medicine* magazine). Unfortunately, like many speculative causes, the chains do not communicate their ultimate impact on the market until after the evil has befallen. If only I could induce the chains to communicate their impacts in advance, it would be far better for my profits and the health of my German pointer, Rolph, and my Black Lab, Mia.

I persist in employing chains quite as extensive as Darwin's to predict market moves, but I am more likely to start with a stock market. One of the striking interrelations that characterized the 1960s, when I first started speculating, was the high correlation between moves in the Hong Kong stock market and the American Stock Exchange. The ups and downs looked so similar that, if given two unlabeled charts, it was impossible to tell which market you were looking at. By 1995, the relation disappeared. The hot sector of the U.S. market was now high-technology companies. Mutual funds specializing in such issues were up approximately 40 percent. But small, volatile stocks in Hong Kong lay dormant. The key to a surge in Hong Kong, according to various experts, would be a bubble burst in the United States, which would cause a mountain of money to be shifted to Hong Kong from Japan, Europe, and the United States. Sure enough, high-technology stocks cratered near the end of 1995 as Fidelity/Magellan Fund shed its holdings shortly after touting their eternal value. The Hong Kong market promptly rallied 15 percent in the first two months of 1996.

In an interesting twist, almost all emerging markets now dance to the tune of Hong Kong stock movements. Hong Kong residents control so much wealth that the Filipino and Mexican markets are in desperate trouble when Hong Kong so much as hiccups. On March 11, 1996, Hong Kong had its third largest decline ever, falling 7.5 percent in a day. The Asian markets showed a sympathetic drop. Ironically, the cause wasn't missiles dropping in the Straits of Taiwan, but fear that a balding central banker, sometimes called "the Green Machine," in Washington, DC, might tighten the money supply as a result of some random employment report numbers.

Feedback loops in emerging markets often boggle the speculator's mind. Many emerging market portfolio managers base their country exposure on U.S. monetary policy. When the Fed eases, they rush like lemmings to the Hong Kong, Singapore, and Mexican markets, because these countries export a high proportion of GNP to the United States. When the Fed tightens, they jump to India, Korea, and South Africa—countries with distant connections to the United States.

The relations between markets seem to have always been a part of the speculator's lot. When the venerable Barings and Company first went into bankruptcy in 1890 from losses in Argentina, U.S. equities promptly responded with a panic of unprecedented dimension. When my grandfather Martin traded with the Boy Wonder, the first question a trader asked another on disembarking from the train or ferry was, "How's London?" The Boy Wonder preferred to speculate out of London so he could be nearer to the source. During particularly violent crashes, such as the panic of 1907, he hopped the first trans-Atlantic steamer to inspect the carnage directly. Nothing has changed. Every speculator worth his salt must track the moves of U.S. stocks traded in Tokyo and London, how the Asian markets traded from open to close, and what the European stock markets did after yesterday's New York close. This is all part of getting a handle on what is in store in the United States today. Conversely, futures on foreign stock markets traded in Chicago move tick for tick with the moves in the Dow and the U.S. dollar during the New York trading day. The headline "[Emerging Market] Quiet Awaiting U.S. Data" is ubiquitous in the financial news.

REASONS FOR INTERRELATIONS

The reasons markets are interrelated are so varied it's difficult to know where to begin. Language, energy, carbon, genetics, social relations, and economics all play a part. Language is a good starting point.

We are linked with words. Most people share a common heritage through reading books that have been read by millions of others throughout the ages. Every book we read relates us to all who have turned the same pages. Even if we don't read or talk, we still communicate and share a sense of culture through television, the Internet, movies, and the like. Social icon Marshall McLuhan expressed our new digitized approach to communication with lofty pronouncements, such as "The New Electronic Interdependence recreates the world in the image of a global village."

Yet, in 1607, John Donne wrote in *Devotions*:

> No Man is an Island, Entire of Itself,
> Every Man is a Piece of the continent,
> A Part of the Main. . . .
> Therefore never send to know for whom
> the bell tolls;
> It tolls for Thee.

Since the development of the steam engine and the telegraph, we've shared information almost instantaneously. The current shibboleth is that cyberspace will inevitably lead to the decline of the nation-state. The ties that bind grow tighter.

The physical reasons for our interdependence stem from the laws of conservation, especially the conservation of energy. Regardless of its form—solar, heat, light, gravity, wind, mechanical, chemical, nuclear, or electrical—when energy metamorphoses from one state to another, the total quantity does not change. In one of the first efforts to explain the duality, mutuality, and reciprocity of the properties of matter, W. R. Grove, in *The Correlation of Physical Forces*, wrote:

> There are, for example, many facts, one of which cannot take place without involving the other, one arm of a lever cannot be depressed without the other being elevated—the finger cannot press the table without the table

pressing the finger. A body cannot be heated without another being cooled, or some other force being exhausted in an equivalent ratio to the production of heat; a body cannot be positively electrified without some other body being negatively electrified, . . .

The probability is, that, if not all, the greater number of physical phenomena are correlative, and that without a duality of conception, the mind cannot form an idea of them; thus motion cannot be perceived or probably imagined without parallax or relative change of position.[2]

The links we share with all life forms through a common genetic heritage is, to a large degree, the underlying theme of modern biology. It is believed that multicelled plants and animals sprang from a common ancestor two billion years ago. If all that lives is descended from a single cell, it is not surprising that the chemical processes that make us all tick are similar. There is a "high probability that we derived, originally, from some single cell," writes Lewis Thomas in *The Lives of a Cell*, "fertilized in a bolt of lightning as the earth cooled. It is from the progeny of this parent cell that we take our looks; we still share genes around, and the resemblance of the enzymes of grasses to those of whales is a family resemblance."[3]

On a more philosophical level, the animal, vegetable and mineral worlds are constantly being transformed one into the other. Guy Murchie expressed this nicely:

All the kingdoms interact upon one another continuously. When a farmer plows his field, in effect the human kingdom (a man) is persuading the animal kingdom (a horse) to induce the mineral kingdom (a plow) to influence the vegetable kingdom (corn) to grow food. The kingdoms don't always harmonize, however, and bitter wars are fought between them . . . with the so-called lower kingdoms winning at least as often as the higher or more intelligent kingdoms.[4]

So many vital elements and physical and chemical processes are necessary for the formation and continuation of life that one is tempted to rejoice that we made it at all. One essential link is carbon, the friendliest element of all. Carbon links the living and nonliving world; it is as important to life as the share of stock is to the market. Because of its friendly structure, carbon has a unique ability to connect with other atoms, be they carbon, oxygen, hydrogen, or nitrogen.

"You will die but the carbon will not," Jacob Bronoski wrote in the *New York Times* (October 13, 1968), "its life does not end with you. . . . It will return to the soil, and there a plant may take it up again in time, sending it once more on a cycle of plant and animal life." Thus, individual carbon atoms are indestructible. As a community of living organisms must perpetuate itself by replacing the life-sustaining carbon, the actions of decomposers such as bacteria, fungi, worms, and so on, which serve to liberate the carbon in dead bodies and recycle it in the soil for plantlife, are paramount. Similarly, the stock market can only sustain itself by recirculating the shares of stock between varying groups of buyers and sellers. The actions of brokers and specialists in transforming orders from institutions and the public into bite-sized chunks maintains the balance of markets.

Societal ties are determined, to a degree, by our rather mundane desires for status, prestige, approval, affection, security, and power. These sociological variables are impacted by a host of factors, including family-rearing practices, religion, and other social mores, which, in turn, are affected by culture, time, and nationality. For instance, trust determines our willingness to do business with outside agents. But trust itself is determined by a web of personal relations and social structures that reassure us that punishments for bad faith and rewards for good performance will be forthcoming. Case in point, in the markets, millions of dollars are transacted on the trading floor with nothing more than eye contact or a wave to seal the bargain. Hardly one in a million of these transactions is disowned, even though there are often hundreds of thousands of dollars to be gained by a bad-faith refusal to recognize the bargain. Presumably, social sanctions, reputation, and efficient communications among traders prevent malfeasance. (The use of audio tapes and video cameras can also be a deterrent.)

The affinities and regularities involved in choosing customers and suppliers is called clientelization. Rather than search for the best price randomly or through systematic screening, buyers and sellers tend to move along well-trodden paths to trade again and again with the same counterparties. Whenever I send a broker to the floor to trade, I face this problem. It takes two or three years before the other brokers will recognize my guy, unless he happens to be unusually good at lining the other floor traders' pockets with bad fills for me. To get around the problem, I sent attractive females to the floor when it was still a great rarity for women to trade. They got recognition all right. But, in heated battle, the men pushed through them like a knife through butter to trade with their larger and more aggressive male counterparts. When I visited the floor and invariably found my traders the most popular of all, I never knew whether to attribute it to their ability, personality, sex appeal, or inexperience.

Goods also must conform to social norms before entering the higgledy-piggledy of the market. It is not socially acceptable to trade in body parts, cures for diseases, or sacred icons. I don't like to admit to friends that I tend to put on my maximum exposure during volcanoes, earthquakes, and panics. On the other hand, the value of some stocks is so clearly embedded in lifestyle decisions that speculators ignore that fact at their own risk.

The auction of items from the Jacqueline Kennedy Onassis estate at Sotheby's, in May 1996, is an excellent example of the link of the economic, political, and social in setting prices. Numerous items sold almost grotesquely over their estimated value. In aggregate, the sale netted $37 million versus a preauction estimate of $3 million. Why? And will the prices hold? Anyone who can answer accurately can look forward to a great career in speculation.

Usually, I don't follow the herd. Ken Rendell, a leader in appraising collectibles, was particularly vehement in calling the bubble unsustainable, but I couldn't resist a little speculation. The wires reported a book signed by Jackie was hammered down at $71,000. At the same time, I had an opportunity to buy, for $7,000, a letter from Jackie to a nurse, describing how to treat Jack Kennedy. The 10:1 ratio seemed favorable, so I bought. If there were only some way to short the sale of her books, I'd feel much more comfortable.

The economic reason for markets' interrelation flows from the wide substitutability and complementing of goods to consumers and producers. The substitute for hamburger is not only poultry, pork, or fish; it is a trip to the movies, a ride to a Dairy Queen, a game of Nintendo. As the price of hamburger rises, there is a corresponding increase in the price of chicken and pork, which, in turn, makes hamburger less unattractive. Demand for it increases;—there is a negative feedback effect on the price of hamburger. There is also an increased incentive to devote resources to produce hamburger. When markets are interdependent (and all of them are), the prices of all products must be simultaneously determined.

What we buy and what we sell is equal. You and I receive income in the form of wages, interest, and rent from the capital, machinery, and land we lend out to firms. When these firms make a profit, they pay it out to us in the form of dividends or an increase in book value. Looking at it from the viewpoint of the firms, their costs are our wages and rents. And their profits are what they have after deducting their costs from our spending. A firm's cost plus profits is equal to its revenues, which is our spending.

Many economics books illustrate this interrelation (see Figure 13–1). The consequence is a never-ending feedback loop between spending and revenue. It is because everyone's spending will become income for someone else, and this affects our spending, that a little change in one area of the flow will have wide-ranging impact on the others. In cyberspace jargon, the feedback loops in our economic systems transmit viruses.

How much easier it would be to encapsulate price relations in speculations if they were fixed in stone. But price is determined by desire as well as scarcity. The components are ever-changing. I believe von Mises's view on price relations is worthy of posting at the scene of all speculative battles:

> It does not indicate a relationship to something unchanging, but merely the instantaneous position in a kaleidoscopically changing assemblage. In this collection of things considered valuable by the value judgments of acting men each particle's place is interrelated with those of all other particles. What is called a price is always a relationship within an integrated system which is the composite effect of human relations.[5]

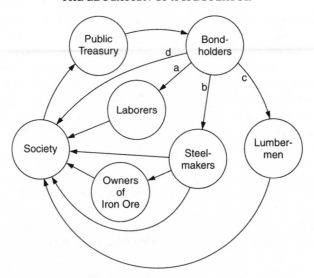

Figure 13–1. The Circular Flow

Dr. Bo informs me that a good veterinarian must be a master at ferreting out barnyard interconnections. For example, unhealthy pigs are often part of a web involving the bad sex life of the farmer and his wife. The unhealthy pigs lead to a worried farmer. The worry leads to bad sex. The bad sex leads to reduced appetite for food. So the desserts are eaten by the pigs rather than the humans. And that has the same bad effect on pigs that it has on humans. "To break the cycle you have to start somewhere," he once told a farmer in a barnyard chat. "Here are pills that I usually use as an aphrodisiac for dogs. Take some yourself and I think your problem will be solved."

Bogus Intermarket Relations

No account of intercorrelations would be complete without paying due respect to bogus interactions. Steve Stigler points out that the great economist Jevons found a correlation between sunspots and business cycles in the 1800s. Subsequent analysis has shown the correlations to be an artifact of trends in both series (business cycles predict sunspots just as well as sunspots predict business cycles). Jevons developed an elaborate explanation of the interrelations of sunspots to rain, monsoons in India, trade with Europe, and business conditions in England. Statistically speaking, Stigler says, many of the links are real in the aggregate, "but individually they get swamped by noise."

Connections need not be confined to the short term. It's dangerous to generalize about forces affecting long-term moves in markets. What appear to be grand interrelations can often be replicated with random numbers. If one market is a random multiple of another plus a random error term, then overlapping graphs look highly predictive. This is one of the reasons that 99 percent of the visual correlations of two time series are spurious.

Most of the charts and graphs used by intermarket analysts suffer from an elementary version of this statistical fallacy. The charts feature prices of various markets superimposed one on the other. Usually, they exhibit common trends, especially because they are not adjusted for the cost of carry. All production numbers, for example, increase with population or GNP. And almost all price series move up with inflation. A five-year chart has just ten semiannual datapoints. It is unlikely that there will be more than three turning points in each series. Naturally, it will look like one series moves either up or down or before, after, or in conjunction with the other, with rises in one preceded or followed by a decline in another.

Stigler sent me an interesting chart from the journal *Nature* "explaining" that the decline in the German birthrate was caused by a decline in the stork population. Stigler commented, "This chart would be right at home in most books on technical analysis."

No sooner did I receive it than one of the major business magazines ran the same chart with different labels to show that central bank purchases of U.S. Treasury securities explained the decline in U.S. interest rates (Figure 13–2, p. 302).

LEININGEN AND THE MARKETS

My introduction to connections came when I was a kid. The family stayed awake each evening, listening for Artie to come home safely from his 4:00 P.M.-to-midnight shift. When he arrived, he'd sit by my bed and tell a story to help me fall asleep. One of these stories, based on "Leiningen and The Ants," and the ensuing discussion we had about it, formed the cornerstone on which I have built my speculative fortunes. Come back with me now to 1950 in Brighton Beach, right next to the elevated trains, as Artie tells you a story:

> One day, a day very much like any other day in the foothills of the Andes, a mountain lion chased a rat for sport and for lunch. The rat vanished down a hole, and the frustrated cat tore at the hillside, widening the hole, in a vain attempt to reach the rodent.
> The rain, washing down the hillside, continued the work of a cat. As the years passed, the hole widened to a cleft, until eventually the hillside collapsed. And there revealed lay the glittering gold veins of a mother-lode, that would attract a generation of precious metal prospectors.

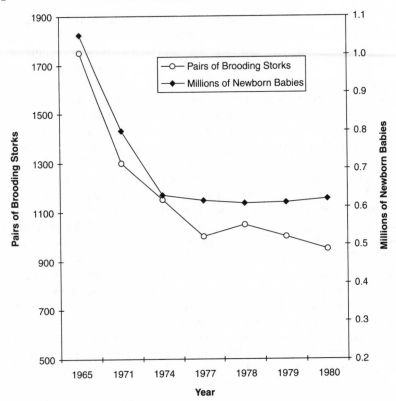

Figure 13-2. Declining Number of Storks Bring Fewer Newborns

Horsetail plants grew up all around the site—a plant, like humans, with an affinity for gold, and known to absorb some four ounces of gold per ton of plant material.

Attracted by the sight of the horsetails and the confirming residue in the pan with which he tested the mountain stream, a prospector built a hut and staked his claim. But little did he know of the massive army of ants that would soon descend on him like a square-mile sized blanket of gnawing death. The shadow spread across the hills from east to west, then down-wards, downwards, uncannily swift, and all the green herbage of that wide vista was mown as by a giant sickle, leaving only the vast moving shadow, extending, deepening, and moving rapidly nearer, as thousands of millions of voracious jaws bore relentlessly, mercilessly down upon him.

Had he asked the Indians, they could have told him not to build there. And so soon enough the man's bones, and those of his horse and dog, joined the silent gold-bearing rocks in silence.

"You know, Vickie," Artie said, "this kind of thing still goes on today. In Brazil, they're cutting down the rain forest for lumber, roads, and pastureland for cattle, not leaving enough greenery for the ants to eat. So now the ants are forced to wander for shelter and food. They're on the march again, bearing down upon the Indians, who are fleeing before them in terror. And when there is terror in Brazil, there is terror in Texas. Everything is connected. Change one thing in nature and everything else is affected. It's the mark of wisdom to understand the connections."

HUMILITY IN INTERRELATIONS

All who study interrelations seriously will eventually conclude that they are ephemeral and unstable at best. For this reason, ecologists say (usually after an anecdote or two showing such things as how increased DDT led to an increased insect population or to lethal doses stored in eagles): "Such complex interrelations must be understood before they are tinkered with."

I agree. In one of the more obnoxious manifestations of childlike behavior, officials in presidential administrations (past, present, and, undoubtedly, future) are proud to boast of their high college board scores. Yet, they readily admit that they have never taken an economics course. How odd that they should believe that high college board scores alone entitle them to rule the economy. Secretary of State James Baker was the leader in the "them that can't do teach" school. His approach, in the opinion of Bundesbank President Otto Pöhl, was the approximate cause of the October 1987 crash.[6]

The fragmented, shifty, and random nature of market interrelations, I discover, is a source of great pain to me. Such failed efforts to influence markets without taking account of interrelations makes me leery of ever treating markets in isolation.

A prerequisite for success in dealing with the immense landscape of market interrelations (or any other system) is humility. I realize that even though I have devoted my business life to ferreting out connections among markets, I don't have adequate tools or knowledge to study them properly. I feel like Br'er Bear in the Uncle Remus story when he risked his life to see the moon in the swamp, only to see it vanish before his eyes each time. In the meantime, Br'er Rabbit waltzed away with all his chips. But maybe if I work harder and smarter I'll catch a lasting connection.

THE OCTOBER 1987 CRASH

Perhaps the most vivid market interactions in most observers' eyes are the moves in the bond, stock, and currency markets that precipitated the October 19, 1987, crash. In the ten months prior to the crash, the Dow Industrials had risen some 37 percent, from 1900 to 2600 in the face of a 20 percent decline in U.S. bond futures prices, from 98 to 78.

A differential return of 57 percent begins to hurt when you're playing it for a "regression" to the mean. Some representative yields provide a snapshot of the relative returns available:

	Yield at Year-End 1986	Yield before Crash	Yield at June 30, 1996
30-year bond	8.2%	10.2%	7.0%
3-month T-bill	5.7	8.7	5.1
Dow stocks	3.6	2.6	2.5

In the old days, differentials between dividend yields and fixed-income yields tended to be reversed. (To prove this would take a book in itself.) Suffice it to say that the differential between bond and stock yield before the 1987 crash rose to 7.6 percent, near the highest in history. In mid-1996, the differential is just 4.5 percent.

Foreign investors did not countenance the 1987 differential. The dollar dropped 10 percent during the prelude to the 1987 crash. Bond yields of 10 percent were not adequate to induce the stolid Swiss and the patient Asians to hold U.S. debt in the face of a declining dollar. The feedback process worked the other way also. On days when the dollar dropped, U.S. bond prices went into freefall.

The die was cast on Sunday, October 18, when Secretary of State James Baker intervened. He announced on the TV program "Face the Nation" that unless the Germans took steps to buy more American goods, the United States would allow the dollar to decline further. That was enough. The self-correcting mechanism to hold the stock market in balance was broken. Worldwide markets suffered the greatest loss in wealth in human history.

"Baker did it," German Bundesbank President Pöhl told his governors the next day, before revisionist historians and servile spinmeisters could work on him.[7] How right he was.

On the day of the crash, the dollar lost 1 percent against the European currencies and a bit more than a half percent against the yen, as would be expected. Copper and soybeans, the bellwethers in metals and agriculturals, were down almost 6 percent. Oil was down 1.5 percent, and gold and silver, harbingers of disaster, moved up 2 percent and 4 percent, respectively. Even before the U.S. market opened, the Hong Kong market had declined 11.1 percent. It then closed for four days, only to open 25 percent lower (Table 13–1).

By the day following the crash, October 20, the feedback process was at work to contain the calamity and signal what was to come. Bonds rose almost 7 percent in one day, their largest one-day rise ever, making dollars

Table 13–1.   Key Daily Price Changes Surrounding the October 1987 Crash

	Friday to Monday 10/19/87	Monday to Tuesday 10/20/87
Bonds	−0.20%	6.80%
Swiss	0.90	−1.90
Pound	1.14	−2.05
Yen	0.61	−2.10
Silver	4.02	−12.00
Copper	−3.81	−11.77
Gold	2.20	−3.96
Heating oil	−1.73	−0.30
Crude oil	−1.63	−0.35
Soybeans	−1.53	2.24
Corn	−3.72	3.22
Sugar	−3.64	−3.98
S&P 500 futures	−28.61	7.30
S&P Index	−20.40	5.23
DJI	−22.62	5.90
Tokyo	−14.90	9.29
London	−10.84	−12.22*
Germany	−9.39	−1.40*
Hong Kong	−11.15	(Closed)

*On Wednesday, October 21, in Europe, London closed up 7.9 and Germany closed up 5.7 percent.

of earnings in the United States more valuable. The yield differential between stocks and bonds moved almost the entire distance back to the year-end 1986 levels in one tumultuous day. And the dollar recovered 2 percent against the foreign currencies, signaling that Baker would not do it again. The next day, copper and silver each declined 12 percent, indicating that U.S. industrial activity would not be going at full tilt for the foreseeable future. And stocks recovered about 114 Dow points, about ⅕ of their decline the previous day, on their way to a relatively continuous 100% gain over the next eight years.

I took a page out of my Uncle Howie's book by snatching defeat out of the jaws of victory. My U.S. stock holdings were decimated by the 25 percent decline in the U.S. market. My Hong Kong holdings took a nose dive (nay, went to zero) in the face of a 40 percent decline in the market. I started the crash with a huge position long U.S. bonds, but I sold it in the heat of the battle, to cover margin calls on my equity holdings. (I blame it all on my wife and my first customer, Tim Horne, both of whom warned me to stay away from stocks on the Monday morning of the crash. Their calls goaded me to buy more.)

The memory of the crash lives on in the collective consciousness. As soon as stocks closed on October 19, the crash day, the Fed intervened to buy Treasuries. Fixed-income prices registered their largest gain in history, rising more than 10 percentage points in one day in the long end. Since that time, stocks have pretended to recede into another crash on at least 50 occasions. Speculators rush in to sell stocks and buy bonds. This is a vivid real-life example of what psychologists call the recency effect. You remember the last place you parked your car, but you tend to forget the previous places. This survival trait is helpful in orienting us in time and space when finding a book, a thought, or a ring, but it's a killer in the markets. More money has been lost by shorts in such maneuvers than in the October 19 crash itself.

Prices during those crises show a peculiar relationship: as stocks go down, bonds go up, which causes stocks to go down, which then leads to bonds' going down.

CORRELATIONS BETWEEN MARKETS

Most advances in a field come after a good descriptive base is developed. Science historians, for example, often remark that only after Mendelev developed the periodic table of elements could the atomic theory of the elements be formulated and refined. Similarly, Copernicus's accurate calculations of the planets' distances from the sun made it possible for Newton to formulate his theory of the elliptical orbits of planets.

A good way to start to understand the ever-changing but inextricably linked markets is to look at their actual connections over a reasonable base period. Some correlations among daily changes of most of the major U.S. markets appear in Table 13–2.

Several clusters of markets appear to behave like identical siblings. The Swiss franc, British pound, and Deutschemark triplets are correlated from 70 percent to 90 percent with each other. The lowest correlation of the yen with any of the European triplets is 0.40, corresponding to moving in the same direction 70 percent of the time. Similarly, stocks, bonds, and Eurodollars are correlated from 40 percent to 60 percent, like fraternal triplets.

Except when clustering with siblings, stocks are negatively correlated with every other market, ranging from −0.07 with sugar to −0.15 with the currencies to −0.23 with gold. Similarly, bonds are negatively correlated with all other markets, ranging up to −0.27 with gold. Sugar and soybeans appear to be the least connected to all other commodities, with no correlations ranging above 15 percent in absolute value, except for the surprising 25 percent correlation between beans and gold.

Aside from the clusters, the highest correlation of all is the negative correlation between bonds and gold −0.27, thereby upholding the popular

Table 13–2. U.S. Commodity Correlation Matrix: Average Daily Close-to-Close Changes, January 4, 1993 to April 25, 1995

	Swiss	Yen	Pound	DMark	Bonds	Gold	S&P 500	Crude	Beans	Euro $	Sugar
Swiss	1.00	0.56	0.69	0.91	(0.09)	0.14	(0.18)	0.06	0.04	(0.07)	0.04
Yen	0.56	1.00	0.41	0.55	(0.13)	0.14	(0.15)	0.02	0.01	(0.09)	0.02
Pound	0.69	0.41	1.00	0.71	(0.03)	0.06	(0.11)	0.01	0.03	(0.02)	0.06
DMark	0.91	0.55	0.71	1.00	(0.09)	0.12	(0.17)	0.05	0.04	(0.04)	0.06
Bonds	(0.09)	(0.13)	(0.03)	(0.09)	1.00	(0.27)	0.60	(0.11)	(0.14)	0.61	(0.15)
Gold	0.14	0.14	0.06	0.12	(0.27)	1.00	(0.23)	0.14	0.25	(0.14)	0.08
S&P 500	(0.18)	(0.15)	(0.11)	(0.17)	0.60	(0.23)	1.00	(0.14)	(0.07)	0.40	(0.15)
Crude	0.06	0.02	0.01	0.05	(0.11)	0.14	(0.14)	1.00	0.05	(0.02)	(0.01)
Beans	0.04	0.01	0.03	0.04	(0.14)	0.25	(0.07)	0.05	1.00	(0.09)	0.12
Euro $	(0.07)	(0.09)	(0.02)	(0.04)	0.61	(0.14)	0.40	(0.02)	(0.09)	1.00	(0.08)
Sugar	0.04	0.02	0.06	0.06	(0.15)	0.08	(0.15)	(0.01)	0.12	(0.08)	1.00

stereotype that gold is a harbinger of inflation but dispelling the equally hoary thought that gold goes down during periods of declining bond prices (rising yields) because it costs too much to finance. Surprisingly, gold is negatively correlated -0.23 with stocks, but positively correlated 0.25 with beans.

The stock market and bonds appear to be prime movers, correlating highly with most of the other commodities. Stocks are correlated (negatively) about 15 percent with the four currencies, confirming the popular feeling that when the dollar gets weaker, the stock market tends to go down. But, contrary to popular belief, a rise in long-term interest rates and weak bond prices tend to be associated with a weak dollar. The correlation between bond prices and foreign currency (per unit of foreign currency) is negative, about -0.15. The popular view is that when bond prices go down, the foreign currencies should go down because U.S. interest rates are more attractive, which makes U.S. dollar-denominated investments more attractive.

INTERNATIONAL CONNECTIONS

Biologist Robert E. Ulanowicz is on the right track when he points out that the methods of physics, with their "materialist/reductionist approach," are inadequate to describe the positive feedback loops of living systems. The mathematical approach focuses on individual reactions—or transactions—and looks for a straight chain of cause and effect from one incident to the next. Ulanowicz holds that, as one widens one's scale of observation, new properties of systems emerge. Looking closely, one might see the sequence C-D, such as "cow eats corn." However, when one expands the observation, one sees the loop A-B-C-D-E-A: "man plants corn, market carries corn to cow, cow eats corn, market carries cow to man, man eats cow." The man-corn-market-cow-man relationship has become stable and highly efficient. What started out as a chance configuration of separate parts takes on proper ties of the whole itself.

Ulanowicz believes that these loops, once they are established, have, besides the characteristic of "autonomy" (the loop is not part of any outside cause–effect chain), "emergence" (they emerge as one widens one's observation) and "formality" (the loop is the plan that guides the action). They also have "growth enhancement selection" and "inducement of competition." Growth enhancement is a characteristic of all positive feedback systems. The loop will select members that make it work more efficiently such as in the replacement of grass by corn. Loops induce competition as a result of selection. Herefords first competed with and finally drove out longhorns, for instance, and the beef loop grew more "ascendant," or, in economic terms, "really began cranking out the cash." As you can see, not only does the cause-and-effect phenomenon spin in this loop, it radiates from the loop in all directions. You can also begin to see, considering the breadth and depth of the global economy, what scale of observation is required to understand the feedback loops. Just think of how many loops are not yet detected.[8]

All these complexities arise when one tries to tie down international economic connections. Besides the usual problems of multiple causality, figuration, emergence, formality, instability, and uncertainty, the differences of culture, language, politics, legal systems, reporting systems, enforcement mechanisms, and taxation must be taken into account. All this is compounded by the enigma of exchange rates. The values used to measure in one country must be converted into the exchange rates of another country.

The theoretical underpinning of the global linkages of economies and exchange rates is one of the most complex in all of economics. In the most thoughtful study to date on this subject, McKibbin and Sachs start with a simplified model that predicts:

> . . . a fiscal expansion under the conditions of floating exchange rates and high capital mobility—the relevant conditions of the 1980's—leads to an expansion of output, a currency appreciation, and a trade deficit. A monetary expansion in contrast, leads to an expansion of domestic output, a currency depreciation, and an ambiguous and likely small effect on the trade balance.
>
> . . . The overall effect on the world economy is, of course, the result of the simultaneous application of policies throughout the global economy.[9]

But this model intentionally doesn't take account of such factors as the effects of trade deficits, the impact on prices and wages, or the role of expectations in changing behavior based on the anticipated final outcome of the process. To come up with answers taking account of these effects, the authors develop new methods of solution involving game theory, simulation, and good guessing.

One manifestation of the difficulties involved is that economists can't even agree on the major determinants of foreign exchange rates. There are three competing theories. The balance-of-payments approach focuses on the flow of short-term and long-term money going in and out of the countries. The portfolio-asset-management approach focuses on expectations about the returns and risks of holding currency assets within an efficient portfolio of other assets. The technical-analysis approach, favored by 90 percent of practitioners, focuses on price movements as predictors—moving averages, filters, Elliott wave theory, Fibonacci numbers—the kind of mumbo jumbo that this book has hopefully provided a caution against.

Amid such fogginess, it is no wonder that politicians have jumped into the fray. Whenever one of my friends tells me to read an old article about another country (the *National Enquirer* is unfortunately limited to stories of hairbreadth escapes, unusual romantic age differences and practices, royalty, and medical breakthroughs in the international field), I know what I am going to find. There will be talk about the necessity for global cooperation, economic integration, international linkage, coordination of macroeconomic policies, worldwide interdependence, and global indexing. The solution is to share information, improve communication, develop new and more realistic models, create fair rules of the game, and establish an entity to plan and enforce supranational interests.

Futurologists Alvin and Heidi Toffler are the champions at coining terms to express our unprecedented interdependence. It's a "borderless world," an "electronic cottage" out there where "planetary consciousness" is interrelating data and "linking concepts in startling ways" into "larger and larger models and architectures of knowledge." The interrelated changes they see coming in our civilization (encompassing technology, family life, religion, culture, politics, business leadership, values, and sexual morality) are due to the clashes between the newcomer, the knowledge revolution, and the old-timers, the industrial revolution and agricultural revolution.

JAPANESE CASE STUDY

Perhaps my own experience trading the yen during 1994 and 1995 will illustrate how one small speculator tries to carve out some profitable space in the borderless electronic cottage. 1994 was the year when the U.S. bonds, small stock, and dollar:mark and dollar:yen markets plummeted by more than 10 percent each, wiping out a trillion dollars of U.S. wealth in the process. The popular explanation for the decline was that foreigners decreased holdings of U.S. assets because of fears of further declines in the dollar.

Apparently, "They" were experiencing a kind of positive feedback: the more the U.S. market declined, the more likely it seemed that the decline would continue, thereby leading to further selling of dollar-based U.S. assets like stocks and bonds.

This fear had a historical verisimilitude. In April 1986, for example, it would have cost a Japanese investor ¥185,000 to buy $100,000 of the current 8 percent U.S. bond in the futures market. By the end of April 1995, the falling dollar had reduced the value of the 8 percent bond to ¥84,000. A decline of 55 percent on principal can begin to hurt even the stoical Japanese, who are accustomed to waiting 30 to 50 years to see a payoff, and who can offset such losses over a life expectancy four years longer than their more short-term-oriented U.S. counterparts. (By the end of 1995, however, the value of that bond had advanced 50 percent to ¥125,000.) The J. P. Morgan derivatives research group uses calculations like these to develop benchmarks for predicting the value of the dollar versus the yen. As far as I know, however, there have been no quantitative studies of the validity of this method or the accuracy of the predictions. I forgive the Morgan firm in this case. Of the numerous counterparties I have the pleasure of dealing with in this burgeoning field, they are the laureates.

As the yen rose in value and U.S. fixed-income markets cratered during 1994, I was able to make some good money by taking account of feedback relations. Whenever U.S. stocks took a big dive, I figured that "They" would be on the alert to arrest any declines in the dollar in subsequent periods. Whenever the dollar started declining against the yen around the Tokyo lunchtime (10 P.M. EST in the United States), I figured that "They" would take steps to prop up the dollar for the New York opening. I bought the dollar on those occasions, and, nine times out of ten, shortly after I bought, news of central bank intervention would make the rounds. I haven't figured out yet whether the central banks were following me, whether brokers were confusing me with them, or whether chance was at work, but interventionists and I were making our moves at the same time. At any rate, the strategy was sufficient to make me the most successful fund manager in the world in 1994.

Indeed, the correlation between changes in the dollar and U.S. stocks during 1994 was highly positive. The daily correlation was about 30 percent. On 18 days, for example, the dollar declined by more than ½ percent against both the deutschemark and the yen. The average decline in stocks on those days was 6 Dow points; the average decline in bonds was ½ point. For the 17 days when the dollar rose in price by more than ½ percent against the yen and the deutschemark, the average rise in stocks and bonds was, respectively, 12 Dow points and ⅓ percent in bonds. Because the bonds declined about 13 percentage points during this period, the rise in bonds was particularly nonrandom. Exemplifying a cruel penumbra that prevents those with short-term horizons from achieving great wealth, the subsequent moves completely reversed this effect.

But easy ways of making good money disappear in time. During 1995, a different web emerged. The U.S. stock and bond markets rose continuously even as the dollar continued to drop. On one horrible occasion, from March 5 to March 7, 1995, the dollar dropped from ¥93.50 to ¥88 in 36 terrible hours, and this after having declined four big figures in the previous five days. I thought the carnage had gone far enough. Newspaper headlines foretold imminent disaster should the decline not be arrested. The dollar's status as the world's reserve currency and the viability of Japan itself were questioned. An old-faithful type of rumor began to make the rounds again: that MITI and MOF—the Japanese industrial and financial planning authorities—were urging Japanese institutions to sell their $50 billion of U.S. bond holdings in exchange for deutschemarks.

Surely, I thought, "They" will step in now. But when I bought the dollar/ yen this time, I found myself standing alone in front of an avalanche. Within the hour, the yen moved down a further 2.5 percent against me. I had forgotten that it is possible to drown in a river whose average depth is 2.5 feet. Because I was leveraged about 10 times, I managed to lose 25 percent of my assets within an hour. It turned out that I was premature by about four hours. Starting at 4 P.M. on March 7, the Japanese, through their counterparts in central banks in New Zealand, Australia, and Hong Kong, started buying the dollar while the dollar bears were counting their winnings. It reversed almost the entire move before the dollar bears knew what had hit them.

Bloodied but unbowed, I rushed in to buy Japanese stocks. A rise, I figured, would bail out the Japanese economy. The Japanese are the U.S. politicians' favorite whipping boys because their success precludes a charge of racism when the flames of xenophobia are fanned, I figured that U.S. interests would benefit from a healthy Japanese stock market.

The Japanese are also large buyers of U.S. Treasury debt. That debt must be bought if the U.S. government is to pursue its compassionate agenda without reducing itself to the bone. Ultimately, a harmonious resolution of the conflict between the East and the West emerged. Pictures of a U.S. trade representative threatening his Japanese counterpart with a samurai sword appeared in the media. No way would the *gajin* be this indelicate in public unless a peace accord had been reached. I bought Japanese stocks heavily. The next day, a face-saving trade deal was announced. But instead of rising, the Japanese stock market promptly declined 5 percent from open to close, as often happens when rumors of good news are confirmed. To make matters worse, the dollar rose 2 percent against the yen on temporary euphoria, leading to a 7 percent drop in the value of my unhedged Japanese stocks. I couldn't stand another 25 percent loss like the March yen fiasco. I threw up my hands in disgust, and dumped my holdings. As usual, selling out when fear is greatest is the worst time to sell. In the ten months after I sold out, the Japanese stock market marched up inexorably by 40 percent from my bailout point.

A JAPANESE FIELD TRIP

Because so much of my wealth is chained to Japanese activities, I thought that a visit to the source of much of the fluctuations in my fortune would be in order. To gain perspective, arms, ears, and eyes, I traveled throughout Japan in the fall of 1994 with six daughters, mother, mother-in-law, and Susan. The first thing I wanted to see was how much a Big Mac cost— the global standard of the determinant of exchange rates. McDonald's uses local supplies, so the cost of a burger is a good proxy for the local cost of living. Even with some holes, this theory probably has more horse sense behind it, and better predictive power, than alternative explanations of exchange rates. I found that the cost of a Big Mac and french fries in Japan was three times the cost in Hong Kong, but only twice the cost in the

United States. A fish sandwich, however, was only 50 percent more than the comparable U.S. cost.

The fruit in Japan was beautiful, but I decided that paying $75 for a cantaloupe or $50 for a peach would be prohibitive for my entourage of ten.

I then stationed myself outside a large office complex to count how the Japanese were doing on the conformity index. Of the first 300 male office workers I tallied, 299 of them were wearing white buttoned-down shirts. I concluded that the proverb "The nail that sticks out gets hammered" still applies, and that treating Japanese market participants as followers rather than leaders would be in order.

The Japanese have a love/hate relationship with the *gaijin*. I tested this by showing up unannounced at several traditional Japanese establishments. The invariable response was, "No food. Please go."

I have always found loyalty to be a key quality among speculators. The Japanese are renowned for their loyalty to family, friends, and pets. To tap into it, I visited the famous memorial to Hachiko, the dog that accompanied its master to the railroad station each morning for eight years and waited patiently for him to return in the evening. When his master died, Hachiko waited patiently for ten more years until he died heart broken. My family visited the statue and I found numerous tourists worshipping at the shrine.

Within eyeshot, I could see a string of the high-tech "love hotels" Japanese executives use to reduce the tedium of a 70-hour workweek and 20 hours of commuting. This blend of the traditional and the modern somehow reassured me that the Japanese would endure for yet another few years after successfully solving their problems for the previous 3000.

"You gotta have *wa*," or harmony, is the stereotypical western view of Japan. When Kinugasa, the famous baseball player, was asked to comment when he left the hospital with a dislocated shoulder to play in his 1,532nd straight game, he remembered, "If I played, it would hurt for a day. But if I didn't play, it would hurt for a lifetime." When I visited the stock exchanges, the floor traders clapped their hands and sang company songs as stocks rose.

The Japanese business landscape is dominated by stable, cooperative partnerships linking industrial, trading, and banking concerns in a thick relation of interlocking ownerships and directorships, preferential purchasing arrangements, and social networks. These links are a manifestation of the Japanese desire for *wa*. The ratio of wholesale to retail sales in Japan (about three, which is double that in the United States) must be a manifestation of *wa*.

I do not place too much reliance on the Federal Reserve's assurances that it runs an airtight operation vis à vis the dissemination of information to the Japanese. The *wa* between government and industry at the numerous sake-fueled Kobe beef revels and other venues surely permits the dissemination of economic numbers like the U.S. trade balance many hours (or days) before traders in the United States can profit from it. "We're not a sieve like the Japanese," a former Fed governor angrily shot back at me after I queried him on the security of Fed data before an announcement. I attempted to butter him up ("Governor, your insights are intriguing"), but he hung up on me when he realized that I did not regard him with the abject reverence that those in the command sector come to expect. I still find that the moves in Japanese markets on the day before important numbers are announced in the United States are invariably on the mark. I especially like to note the move in the dollar/yen when it trades in Tokyo from zero GMT to 6 GMT, because this sings like a canary.

When I left Japan, the exchange rate was hovering about 100. I vowed that I would never underestimate the resilience and vitality of this long-lived society. Whenever news of a potential crisis emerges, I buy right into it. Emperor Akihito's dynasty has ruled relatively continuously for some 2,660 years. I have confidence that this able, polite, loyal, and conformist civilization will manage to solve its problems for the foreseeable future.

A Japanese–American Web

The web of relations is always changing in its leads, lags, direction, and magnitude, but there is a certain continuity in the pathways. Let's trace two such links that are usually operating at all times.

A typical move in U.S. stocks might start like this. The U.S. bond market goes up, perhaps because Tom Baldwin, the largest bond floor trader, has detected some weak shorts with stops one or two ticks above the market. The dollar follows. The U.S. stock market immediately rises because of the increased value of U.S. earnings with the lower interest rates. Then high-grade copper, a primary industrial metal, moves up in anticipation of greater investment spending. The Japanese stock market drops because U.S. assets are now becoming more attractive to foreigners. But this makes gold decline because inflation is likely to be lower with a strong dollar. With inflation down, something has to be less attractive. It is time for meats, grains, and soft commodities to recede because there will be less purchasing power left for them. But if European and Japanese assets are going to decline, soon they will pull down the U.S. stock market. And the cycle will be ready to reverse. All this in a minute or two, 10 or 12 times a day.

A more complex set of interrelations is always near the surface. For example, increased Japanese industrial activity is good for Japanese stocks because they will have more revenues and earnings. But the increased demand for credit to finance this expansion will be bad for Japanese bond prices. During 1994 and 1995, the correlation between changes in Japanese bond and stock prices was about −0.18. The oft-reported rumor that MITI

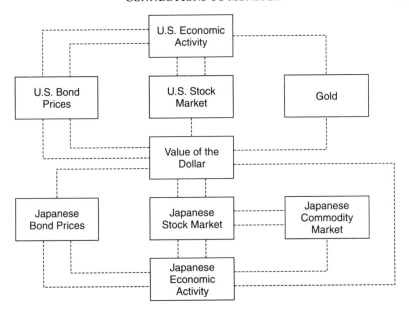

Figure 13–3.   The U.S.–Japanese Web

is insisting that Japanese insurers sell their stock holdings and switch to bonds to meet their obligations has a statistical verisimilitude to it.

During the 18 months ended June 30, 1995, the Japanese 10-year bond yield declined relatively continuously from 3.5 percent to the lowest yield ever, 1.9 percent, a price gain of 10 points. At the same time, the Nikkei moved down from 20,000 to 14,000.

As Japanese economic activity increases, there will be a demand for more dollars to finance imports of American goods. This will raise the value of the dollar, lowering the value of the yen correspondingly. As the dollar goes up, Japanese exporters become more competitive, thereby increasing the prospects for Japanese stocks.

Take account of the ever-changing leads and lags in these relations, and you have a good framework to understand markets. A simplified diagram of some of these relations appears in Figure 13–3.

INTERNATIONAL CORRELATIONS

To provide some concrete information on linkages, let's consider concurrent comovements and countermovements in these variables as they exist in the mid-1990s. Again, the best place to start is the correlation matrix. Consider the interrelations (for the first time in history, I believe) between daily changes in most major foreign and domestic equity, interest rate, and currency markets.

Because there are 78 separate correlations, it is hard to summarize the linkages in one or two sentences. But several regularities emerge. For example, the U.S. and European fixed-income markets are highly correlated. Also, the European equity and fixed-income markets move very closely together, but opposite from their currencies. The highest correlations are those between European fixed-income markets, with the German and French bonds showing the highest correlation of all, 0.78 (excluding the Swiss franc and the Deutschemark at 0.95). The U.S. stock market is correlated about 0.5 with the English and French markets but only 0.13 with the Nikkei. (See Table 13–3.)

All currencies (expressed in futures terms as value in dollars per unit of foreign currency) are correlated negatively with their respective stock and bond markets. The pound, for example, is correlated −0.26 with English stocks (FTSE in Table 13–3); the yen correlates −0.13 with the Nikkei. All fixed-income markets are correlated about 0.5 with their stock markets, except for Japanese stocks and bonds (JGB in Table 13–3) at −0.18. The stock markets of the European countries are correlated about 0.5 with the European fixed-income markets, and the English and French stock markets are correlated 0.73 with each other. There is a high positive correlation of Japanese bond prices with the European bond prices, indicating that they are substitutes for those trying to get a return on assets, thereby connecting interest rate moves all over the world.

The Canadian dollar and Japanese bond seem to be the least interlinked, having no absolute correlation greater than 0.26 with any other market. The yen is correlated positively (0.26) with the Japanese bond, negatively (−0.13) with its own stock market, and negatively (about −0.20) with all foreign stock markets.

It is nice to know from a descriptive viewpoint what the correlation between changes has been in the same period, but the more profitable question is whether there are predictable leads and lags. For example, does the change in the Nikkei today have an effect on the Bund tomorrow? We have tested all such forward intercorrelations. None of the coefficients exceeds 0.10 in absolute value, corresponding to just a 55 percent change of a comove.

PROFITABILITY OF INTERMARKET TRADING

The direct and indirect effects on markets work themselves out over varying time periods, with separate and ever-shifting relations. Furthermore, many of the relations appear to manifest themselves only after key trigger levels are exceeded in the leading market. And this is as it should be. Easy money should not be available. Speculators, looking to make money when

Table 13-3. International Commodity Correlation Matrix: Average Daily Close-to-Close Changes, October 6, 1993 to April 25, 1995

	U.S. Bond	Bunds	JGB	French Bond	Swiss	DMark	Pound	Yen	$Can	S&P500	Nikkei	FTSE	CAC40
US Bond	1.00	0.48	0.08	0.44	(0.16)	(0.15)	(0.10)	(0.18)	0.11	0.51	0.00	0.42	0.41
Bunds	0.48	1.00	0.10	0.78	(0.16)	(0.14)	(0.14)	(0.10)	0.13	0.39	0.03	0.49	0.60
JGB	0.08	0.10	1.00	0.06	0.14	0.15	0.08	0.26	(0.05)	(0.01)	(0.18)	0.00	0.00
Fr Bond	0.44	0.78	0.06	1.00	(0.17)	(0.17)	(0.12)	(0.12)	0.15	0.31	(0.01)	0.45	0.57
Swiss	(0.16)	(0.16)	0.14	(0.17)	1.00	0.95	0.75	0.59	(0.25)	(0.16)	(0.16)	(0.30)	(0.34)
DMark	(0.15)	(0.14)	0.15	(0.17)	0.95	1.00	0.77	0.59	(0.25)	(0.14)	(0.17)	(0.28)	(0.33)
Pound	(0.10)	(0.14)	0.08	(0.12)	0.75	0.77	1.00	0.44	(0.12)	(0.12)	(0.08)	(0.26)	(0.27)
Yen	(0.18)	(0.10)	0.26	(0.12)	0.59	0.59	0.44	1.00	(0.19)	(0.16)	(0.13)	(0.19)	(0.24)
$Can	0.11	0.13	(0.05)	0.15	(0.25)	(0.25)	(0.12)	(0.19)	1.00	0.15	0.05	0.16	0.20
S&P500	0.51	0.39	(0.01)	0.31	(0.16)	(0.14)	(0.12)	(0.16)	0.15	1.00	0.13	0.57	0.51
Nikkei	0.00	0.03	(0.18)	(0.01)	(0.16)	(0.17)	(0.08)	(0.13)	0.05	0.13	1.00	0.13	0.14
FTSE	0.42	0.49	0.00	0.45	(0.30)	(0.28)	(0.26)	(0.19)	0.16	0.57	0.13	1.00	0.73
CAC40	0.41	0.60	0.00	0.57	(0.34)	(0.33)	(0.27)	(0.24)	0.20	0.51	0.14	0.73	1.00

an interest rate, stock market, foreign exchange, or goods market gets out of line with others, watch like hawks, waiting to swoop down for a low-risk profit whenever a market is not properly aligned and defended. If a regularity became too glaring, it would immediately be washed away by all the hawks.

There is always a market somewhere where divergences can be rectified. But the problem is to recognize a divergence. I have a similar problem when I play checkers or chess. When my teacher is there, he can raise an eyebrow or sit back to indicate a good move is possible—that I should *think*. I play great under these conditions, visualizing moves ahead like a champion. But when no one is there to tell me to reflect, I'm 50 percent worse.

Because most markets trade somewhere 24 hours a day, as soon as perturbations in one market occur, the ultimate impact is registered and projected instantaneously by arbitrageurs and speculators. A speculator must constantly take account of the impact of moves in the local market, the other markets it is linked to, and the consequences the ultimate move will have on the local market, in a never-ending spiral. But that isn't enough. What matters is the expectations that the participants in one market have as to the impact from other markets. No wonder it's so hard to make a profit.

I have based my entire career in speculation on quantifying interrelations between markets. The complexity of these relations, always dizzyingly random in their import and almost uncountable in their extent, appears overwhelming. But gluing it all together is a simple economic fact. When asset prices and interest rates change in one venue, the relative attractiveness of assets all over the world is affected because of changes in the desire to buy and sell currencies.

Although I believe I was the first to analyze these connections systematically, my joy of discovery is tarnished a bit by five factors:

1. The interrelations are always changing. Just when you think that sugar is the key to soybeans or oil is the key to the dollar, the relation turns around and belts you in the eye.

2. I have, over the course of 16 years, taught my ideas to many employees who have subsequently left my firm and started businesses of their own based on these ideas. My former employees, such as Monroe Trout, my brother Roy, Tim Lee, Peter Hansen, Toby Crabel—the list is endless—now manage at least $1 billion in hedge funds, managed accounts, or commodities funds among them, so all the obvious interrelations are dissipated the very second they show their beautiful faces.

3. Books such as *Intermarket Analysis*, and articles on intermarket analysis in the trade press are considered standard required reading for aspiring market players. When something becomes that commonplace,

it's over the hill for sure. (Fortunately, at least for me, most published literature seems to consist of little more than discussions of various market charts that are superimposed on each other and sometimes move in similar or opposite directions. Like most books on market analysis, these have not advanced beyond the dark ages of the 16th century when a patient's diseases were cured by application of astrology and alchemy.)

4. Computerized black boxes tracking all major interrelations instantaneously are widely available to all market participants. When a group marketing one of these black boxes for detecting interactions came to sell me their product, a program very similar to one I first developed in 1979, they proudly told me that one bank had purchased more than 400 for its traders.

5. The top traders in the world have formed a breakfast club to discuss the current day's interrelations so that they can jump in ahead of the crowd at the open. Oh, well, I generally trade through 6 A.M. each day, in Japan and Frankfurt, so I'm not much good as a contributing member for a breakfast club. I like to read heroic stories to my kids in the morning anyway. And I don't figure there's too much room at the top for those who purchase gurus' secrets. I think I'll pass.

Indeed, the field of intermarket analysis has become so sexy that a 456-page book has appeared on the subject. Yet only 41 pages of the book carry any reference to intermarket analysis. These pages display 19 charts of various markets superimposed on each other. Interspersed with them is some weighty prose about how inverse trend relationships, positive correlations, and market trends are interrelated and feed on each other. The TED spread, monetary indexes, the 14-week stochastic, and the difference between the 180- and 50-day moving averages are noted and integrated with the interrelations. I couldn't find a single mean, correlation coefficient, or other number to summarize the graphical relations. The author concludes in a fashion characteristic of the field:

> While the economic, fundamental and technical factors are crucial to forecasting the trend of bonds and stock [sic], there are some important intermarket relationships that could not be ignored. Crude oil prices, for example, is [sic] an important determinant of the direction of inflation, interest rates, and the fixed income market. . . . Interest rate sensitive groups tend to follow developments in the bond market. Gold is a barometer of inflation. . . . Awareness of these intermarket relationships could enhance both market pricing and stock selection. Without due consideration to those relationships, market analysis would not be complete.[10]

Perhaps there is still hope.

CONNECTIONS TO MONITOR

In a lively turn-of-the-century study of connections speculators should monitor, Professor Henry Crosby Emery of Columbia focuses on the key interrelationships—droughts, rains, new inventions, discoveries, freight rates, legislation, political complications, bankruptcies, strikes, riots. Perhaps a politician feels that the nutrition of the poor should be improved, or a northwesterner in Texas decimates livestock, or "two grasshoppers had been seen in the neighborhood of Fargo or that [the Sultan of Speculation] had been observed that morning speaking to his brokers with a scowl on his face. . . . It's all epitomized in the familiar saying that 'Wall Street discounts everything.'" As you have probably guessed, the speculator isn't Soros and the politician isn't Clinton. In fact, the speculator is Hawker and the politician is Bismarck. The date of publication is 1896.

Emery concludes that successful speculation may be defined as "the struggle of well equipped intelligence against the rough power of chance."[11]

In our own day, the connections are so extensive, so manifold, that this list appears to our minds as an excerpt from a child's primer. Here's my own late-20th-century list of intelligent connections that I, the speculator, monitor to reduce the tough powers.

An order of pizza at the White House (war alert);

Tankers low in the harbor (heavily laden—oil abundant);

Cars at the mall *à la* the Beardstown ladies, or in the company parking lot, *à la* the Motley Fool (good sales or employment);

Bright sun, ample rain (bumper grain crop);

Full moon (a change in trend);

Long cigarette butts (good times coming);

Big Gulp cups half-full in the dumpsters (discretionary income up);

Traffic at airport (business vigorous);

Thin newspapers (no jobs and advertising);

Cold summer (bad harvest, possible ice-age);

Excess snow (increasing energy prices);

Heavy wind (moderation in temperatures);

Trial verdicts (possible riots' impact on insurance companies);

A delayed announcement (bad news coming);

Monsoons or weddings in India (romance, romance—more consumer spending);

A world championship cricket or baseball game (no volatility or liquidity);

A hawk in winter (early spring);

The travel plans of Soros (activity in a new market);

Active beaver lodges (more absorption of water—less rain, higher grain prices);

High migrating bird counts (bad weather makes them fly low);

The new century (boom in tourism in Italy, good times for software developers);

Sickness of a president (the market abhors uncertainty);

Age distribution of the population (old people are good for bird watching and bonds business).

Not much has changed.

CHAPTER 14

Music and Counting

If I write a symphony an hour long, it will be found short enough.

Ludwig van Beethoven

MUSIC IN THE MARKET

Everywhere Artie went, there was music. He heard music as he stepped through life; he hummed it on the street, danced to it on the beach, played it on the violin in the house. Behind the shield, they called him "The Music Cop."

A neighbor once apologetically asked me, "Your father seems like such a nice and learned man. But has he lost his marbles? He's always singing out loud to himself."

I just said, "No, he's just happy." But the proper response should have been, "Wherever there is harmony, order, rhythmic proportion, there is music" or "All life is music if you play the right note in proper time and harmony." Artie was one of those fortunate men who had music in the soul.

The tune Artie liked best was the theme from the third movement of Schubert's Quintet in A Major (The Trout) for piano and strings. The melody opens on A, with a simple D major chord and then moves back to A, from which it leaps to E and then falls back to A again in diatonic intervals in its dominant A major harmony. The pure happiness, the images—of a clear brook bubbling, of trout easily escaping the fisherman, of birds singing—this simple melody evokes are beyond description.

Many musicians, my father included, want this selection played as an epitaph at their funeral. My father, unfortunately, had his wish fulfilled at the prime of his life, at the age of 63. The family violin teacher, Gregory Zaritsky, performed it.

When the markets are moving in my favor in a nice, gentle way—never below my initial price—I often think of the Trout Quintet. We have a piano in the office. If the felicitous moves repeat often enough, one of the musicians who seem to gravitate to my employ is sure to dash out a few variations of the Trout. If we happen to be making money for or doing business for Soros, the variation preferred is the fast fourth movement, a beautiful rondo in the Hungarian style.

When I'm long, the charts of a market in a gentle uptrend often remind me of the musical notation of the Trout Quintet. An example of such a market is the DJIA from February to May, 1996 (Figure 14–1). First, the market experiences a gradual rally from the opening price of 5400 up to 5700. Then, a downward move back to 5400, meandering up to 5600, then falling off.

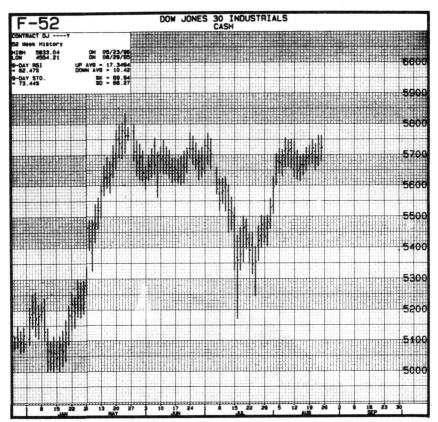

Figure 14–1.   Dow Jones Industrial Average

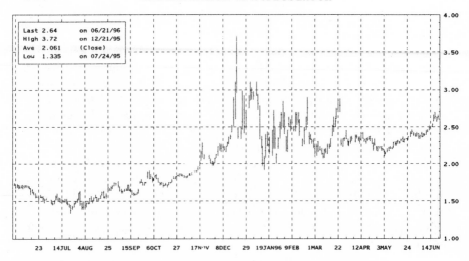

Last	2.64	on 06/21/96
High	3.72	on 12/21/95
Ave	2.061	(Close)
Low	1.335	on 07/24/95

23 14JUL 4AUG 25 15SEP 6OCT 27 17N·'V 8DEC 29 19JAN96 9FEB 1MAR 22 12APR 3MAY 24 14JUN

Source: Bloomberg Financial Markets Commodities News, New York.

Figure 14–2.   Natural Gas Price Graph

Another frequent work I hear in the market is Haydn's Symphony No. 94 ("The Surprise"). The surprise is a simple fortissimo chord in the second movement, designed "to make the women jump." In a contemporaneous review of the work, a lyrical critic wrote:

> The surprise might be likened to the situation of a beautiful Shepherdess who, lulled to sleep by the murmur of a distant Waterfall, starts alarmed by the unexpected firing of a fowling-piece.[1]

Right after lunch or before a holiday, the markets have a tendency to meander up and down in a five-point range above and below the opening. The pattern is similar to the twinkling C-major fifths of Haydn's symphony. Often, a startling move is imminent (the December 1995 jump) as is evident in Figure 14–2. It warns us not to be lulled to sleep by the murmuring of the water, or, worse yet, by thoughts of a beautiful, slumbering shepherdess.

FUNERAL MUSIC

Near the end of Artie's life, when he was struggling with cancer, he was more likely to hum Handel's "Passacaglia." The grave theme introduced in the bass in G minor, subsequently repeated in countless variations, evokes a finality to a life of endless striving to be good. "Let's listen to

Sonata quasi una Fantasia.

To Countess JULIA GUICCIARDI.   Op. 27, N♡ 2.

Abbreviations: M. T. signifies Main Theme; S. T., Sub-Theme; Cl. T., Closing Theme; D. G., Development-group; R., Return; Tr., Transition; Md. T., Mid-Theme; Ep., Episode.

I. Adagio sostenuto. (♩ = 52.)   L. van BEETHOVEN.

a) It is evident that the highest part, as the melody, requires a firmer touch than the accompanying triplet-figure; and the first note in the latter must never produce the effect of a doubling of the melody in the lower octave.

b) A more frequent use of the pedal than is marked by the editor, and limited here to the most essential passages, is allowable; it is not advisable, however, to take the original directions *sempre senza sordini* (i. e., without dampers) too literally.

Figure 14–3. Beethoven's "Moonlight" Sonata

this together," Artie would say to me. I didn't understand why a tear crept down his face until it was too late.

My brother Roy inherited musical genius from my parents. I knew he was walking with the gods when, at the age of five, he'd listen to a piece played by my sister Diane on her flute, or by Artie on his violin, and would play it back perfectly on the piano. Like many musicians, however, Roy's genius was helped along by family influence. Artie took Roy to Suzuki violin lessons twice a week and played along with him, always the only father among the ten mothers at the session.

I took Roy away from a life of professional music at the age of ten, when I bought him a TRS 80 computer. He started with computer-composed music. But I corrupted him with the material world of speculation. I started him programming futures systems rather than symphonies. After ten years working in my ensemble, he left to start his own group.

He carries on the musical tradition when the notes of the market don't come back to their proper tonic. "All too frequently, the piece we play is Mozart's *Requiem*," he says. The very act of composing it filled Mozart with thoughts of death. The evening of his death, Mozart called his friends to his bedside to sing it through with him.

Music in a minor key evokes tragic emotion in Western listeners. When the market's in the process of destroying us, someone in our office is likely to play Beethoven's "Moonlight" Sonata (Figure 14–3, p. 325) on the CD player. Just as the music starts, a colleague is sure to intone dolefully, "Oh, the bond," or "Oh, the yen." The steady, rhythmic three-note oscillation between G sharp and E, followed by the slowly varying thirds all starting and ending within a one-note range, cast a musical pallor on the accompanying market movements. The gold fluctuations for most years after 1980 show a similar pallor to all but the most steadfast bulls (Figure 14–4). The passive, range-bound, slow moves of the market, moving listlessly from peak to valley, closely parallel the dark, sustained, repetitious pianissimo melody of the sonata as it searches for a resolution. When I flashed the chart of the gold and the "Moonlight" Sonata next to each other at a meeting of Swiss bankers, there was a spontaneous round of hearty laughter. I'm afraid there was a sprinkling of tears also.

I seem to have acquired the dubious distinction of being the inventor of LoBagola analysis, named after an African Jew who reported a foolproof way of capturing elephants in the wild. Herds of up to 100 elephants went on a roll once a year, trampling everything in the area near LoBagola's village. After opening a path of crushed vegetation and damaged property, the elephants would invariably return on the same path.

The Beethoven Sonata op. 109 (Figure 14–5) is full of LoBagola patterns. One bar starts at a high D and cascades to low G and back. The same trick is used in the next measure, starting at high C and tumbling to low C and back. A quick turn into the D# key, and then the notes move

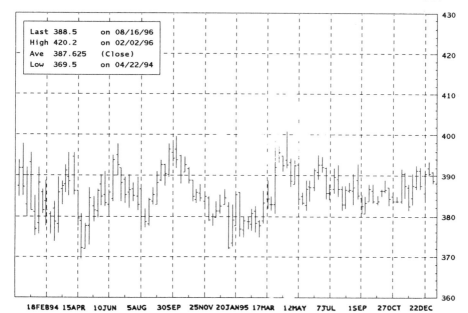

Source: Bloomberg Financial Markets Commodities News, New York.

Figure 14–4. NY Gold Price Graph, 1994–1995

Figure 14–5. Beethoven's Sonata op. 109

back over themselves in a path reminiscent of the elephants' back-and-forth trample.

LoBagola patterns in the markets are common. A good example is the Treasury Bill futures markets from 1976 to 1992 (Figure 14–6). The yield started in 1977 at a rate of 5 percent and moved in three years to 16 percent, then back, in just a year, to 6 percent. Again, the yield rolls to 17 percent, back again to 7 percent, then to 11 percent, and finally back and forth a few times. The silver futures market chart (Figure 14–7) also shows a similar LoBagolan movement from $5 to $50 and back to $5 in a six-month period.

There are no markets in African stocks that exemplify LoBagola patterns. However, the weekly chart of Yapi Kredit Bank in Turkey (Figure 14–8) shows the apparently universal nature of LoBagola patterns. It rose from 0.01 to 0.04 in the five months before the December 1994 banking crisis, and then fell right back to 0.01 in the subsequent five months.

Not all movements start with quiet and move to activity. Some music is so violent that it is scary to read and to play. The Skryabin Prelude in D#

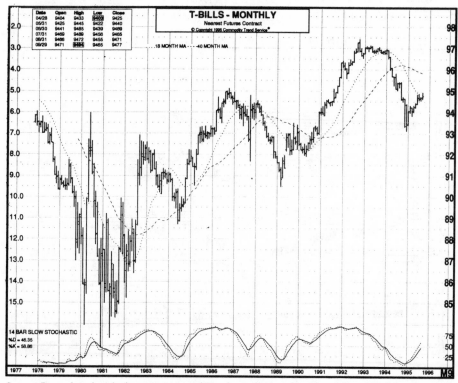

Source: Reproduced with the permission of Dearborn Commodity Trend, Inc. All rights reserved.

Figure 14–6.   Treasury Bills, 1977–1996

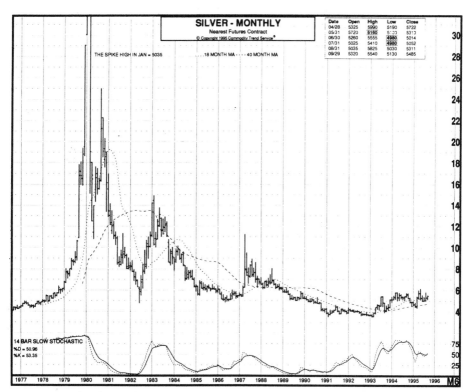

Figure 14–7. Silver Futures, 1977–1996

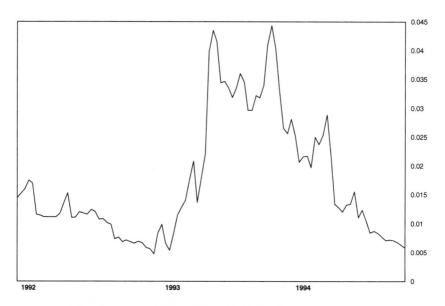

Figure 14–8. NST Yapi Kredit Bank, May 1991–May 1996

329

12.

Figure 14–9. Skryabin Prelude

Minor (Figure 14–9) is an example. The wildness of the moves brings back memories of violent soybean futures movements up and down between $5 and $10 every couple of years (Figure 14–10).

Although it doesn't have any predictive value, there's one kind of market music that no one likes to hear—the coda of the first movement of Beethoven's Ninth Symphony:

> Its slippery chromatic bass, and the awesome moans above it, remains a paralyzing experience. That is the way the world ends.[2]

The moves of the stock market on October 19, 1987, the bonds on March 8, 1996, when they dropped the limit of three points, and the 5 percent decline in the dollar:yen ratio on March 8, 1995, came close to ending my wrongly positioned world. (Note the one-year anniversary.) But I regained my bearings the next trading day in each case, and the suffering was lifted with an Ode to Joy of a rally.

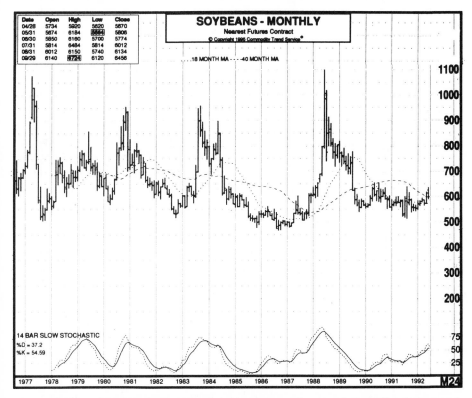

Source: Reproduced with the permission of Dearborn Commodity Trend, Inc. All rights reserved.

Figure 14–10. Soybeans, 1977–1992

Unfortunately, Beethoven's ability to trade currencies was not as great as his composing. He agreed to stay in Austria for payment of 4000 florins a year from three noble benefactors. But Beethoven lost purchasing power when Austria devalued in March 1811. As much ahead of his time in litigation as in art, the Shakespeare of music had no compunction about suing his benefactors to make him whole, even though two of them were near bankruptcy themselves.

PURE MUSIC

After a period of violent moves in the market, I like to return to basics— something that doesn't require risking the end of my world.

One way I play during these times is to sell calls and puts at a strike price equal to the current price. The process is as close to a pure play of mathematics as speculation ever becomes. I estimate the future variability based on similar episodes of panic. Then I compare the quotes emanating from the dealers' black boxes. If I think they're off key, I hit them.

The whole kit and caboodle reminds me of Bach. He wrote music of extraordinary perfection and purity. Bach strives "for the detection of the perfection of harmony . . . but such perfection is attained only when all parts work together . . . without any confusion."[3] Bach's facility with mathematics (he constructed a fugue with six voices for Frederick the Great on the spot) is on a par with that of the greatest options and spread traders I have had the privilege of knowing. All of them are former math team champions or professional card counters. The Swiss-based drug companies have the most high-powered mathematicians on the firing line, trading options. According to dealer scuttlebutt, the Swiss regard their options strategy research as being at least as important as finding new drugs.

Bach's work was full of surprises. He often used startling ensembles of instruments, or changes in key or harmony, to build moods of terror, grief, or weariness (the influence of his 20 children, perhaps?).

I often find that, after a startling move in an underlying market, a new mood of gloom or perhaps of exultation pervades the trading environment and is reflected in the price of options. Usually, volatility is high and delivers an extra return because many unhedged buyers and sellers of the underlying desperately desire to buy protection from a big move against. However, just as Bach returns the harmonic structure back to the original, the mood of the market dissipates and the option prices return to normal levels.

Despite Bach's mathematical genius, his music is to most scholars the most personal and least contrived. Haydn, Mozart, Beethoven, and almost all other musicians since have held Bach in awe. I have been fortunate to employ Dr. Michael Cook, a Ph.D. in mathematics whom I met after I attended a musical he composed. His grandfather, Deems Taylor, wrote some timeless words about Bach's music 60 years ago:

Hearing it, one is conscious of being in the presence of something warm, generous and friendly, a personality of infinite sympathy and understanding. And yet it is hard to think of anyone's sitting down to make music like this. I never think of Bach as scratching inkily, scowling and erasing, trying out this and that upon a handy and well-tempered clavichord. I see him, rather, out under the morning sun, pruning, raking, watering; tending things—fresh, green, growing things, quivering with life, that put forth tendrils and leaves, that bud and blossom and bear fruit before one's very eyes.[4]

Yes, I feel that way too, especially when I smell the grass after a nice rain when I'm short the grains.

PREDICTIVE MUSIC AND MARKETS

The literature of music and charts is so vast that I would have to be ignorant indeed if I couldn't pull together a few visual correspondences or historical resonances.

To remove my speculations from the fuzzy lane, here's a simple algorithm for translating chart notation into musical notation. Take the total range of the previous day (or 50 points around yesterday's close) and divide it into eight intervals or notes starting with middle C as the previous close. Then take each half-hourly price, round it, and assign a note to it. You'll often hear nursery tunes in the manner of "Three Blind Mice" when you sound it out. To get some rhythm in there, take account of the variability within the times. No wonder jazz musicians call their music "charts," and orchestra conductors often find their performers studying stock futures charts during rehearsal breaks.

I have taken to drawing a five-line treble clef around the price movements of markets during a day or week. When Artie heard music on the radio, he often consulted a dictionary and found the piece from the melody transformed into the key of C. I use this volume sometimes to identify the music I'm looking at in the charts. I have yet to quantify whether the final resting place can be figured out from the opening theme.

The lines I draw, and the angles between them, look like the work of the mystics who litter the speculative field. They call the fitting of such lines Elliott wave theory. According to Elliott wave theory, prices move in cycles of five-part impulse waves with the trend, and two-part corrective waves against the trend. Because of the many variations possible, Elliott "theoreticians" agree that the wave analysis orders probabilities but it does not provide a road map. The waves are of indeterminate magnitude and duration, and there is no objective algorithm for assigning the wave count. The combination makes for a fuzzy, mellow, nonfalsifiable environment.

The world champion Elliott theoretician is acknowledged to be Robert Prechter. In laudatory reviews of his current work, *At the Crest of the Tidal Wave*, revered industry leaders refer to its:

Icy logic and stunning originality, scholarly precision, brilliant and important long range research.

Prechter's 1978 book predicted the super bull of the 1980's. After an analysis of wave II, wave four of I, and wave four of III Prechter writes in 1995, "The grand supercycle bear should carry to its expected target within the range of the previous supercycle fourth wave, between 41, and 381 on the Dow. . . . This long standing forecast is no longer something for a future time. Rather it is the expected range for the low of the bear market we now face."[5]

Other Elliott theoreticians interpret the current action as merely a corrective wave, and they predict a Dow of 10,000. It is comforting to know the range in advance. (For my sacrilege, please anticipate a scurrilous attack on my work from a true believer in Elliott theory or some related technical nostra.)

Not surprisingly, it is a common occurrence for two prominent Elliott theorists to differ vociferously on which section of the wave we are in.

Programs have been developed to reduce the ambiguity. A satisfied user reports, "It's like having a room full of Ellioticians doing counts for you full time except that it never gets tired, never makes a mistake and never takes a coffee break." The programs cannot overcome ambiguity, "which happens in Elliott analysis frequently." So, as a price series unravels, "the program's previous preferred count will be replaced by a new one."[6]

A symptom of the sterility of Elliott wave theory is its lack of dialogue with other scientific analysis. For instance, if "laws of growth" are evident in crowd behavior, one would expect that this phenomenon had been observed in other areas such as epidemiology, population biology, or population models.

A way of building a base of Elliott analysis and the related mumbo jumbo of Fibonacci and Gann might start with consideration of the logarithmic spiral (which embodies the Fibonacci series). It is found in spiral nebulae and in shell formations. What is the reason for its appearance? In the case of shells, it has to do with growth phenomenon. What about nebulae? Presumably, the reasons are different—gravitational law?

And in markets? Why should Fibonacci ratios control retracements? Perhaps they are building on the detritus of the market. To grow, the market needs to build on itself; it sucks in material (new investors) from the environment; turns it into waste (takes their money); then builds on it (the change in price attracts new money).

I conducted a search in the scientific literature for all of 1995; nowhere in the literature on population biology or epidemiology was there any reference to Fibonacci series. If the technique had some predictive value, some modeling value, one would expect it to have been picked up in these fields.

EMOTIONAL MOVES

Music has the power to bring out different emotions arising from the deepest experiences of the listener. Some music fills me with power, infinite pleasure, or, if the markets are moving against me, with a sense of tragedy. I have unfortunately not reached the sublime heights envisioned by Beethoven for, "Ye who ever truly understands my music is freed thereby from the miseries that others carry about in them."[7] I have, however, been known to imitate the maestro's conducting style during the trading day. When conducting, Beethoven liked to use body language to communicate the emotions of the music. Louis Spohr, in his biography, gives an eyewitness account:

> Whenever a *sforzando* occurred, he flung his arms wide, previously crossed upon his breast. At a *piano*, he bent down, and all the lower in proportion to the softness of tone he wished to achieve. Then when a crescendo came, he would raise himself again by degrees, and upon the commencement of the *forte*, would spring bolt upright. To increase the *forte* yet more, he would sometimes shout at the orchestra, without being aware of it. When it began the *pianissimo*, Beethoven, to signify this in his own way, had crept completely under the desk. Upon the ensuing crescendo, he again made his appearance, raising himself continually and then springing up high at the moment when, according to his calculations, the *forte* should have begun.[8]

I try not to emote during the trading day. But if the markets are going wildly in my favor, I am prone to spring on top of my trading desk and spontaneously shout a "Yes!" or two. More likely, however, I am found under the desk, quiet as a mouse, hiding from some misery.

Beethoven deservedly achieved renown during his lifetime. The whole world was at his feet. "People no longer come to an arrangement with me. I state my price, and they pay,"[9] Beethoven said. When I state my price in the markets, I find, to the contrary, that the people who hear about it invariably rush to sell just below and buy just above, thereby preventing me from trading at all.

The maestro's conducting gave rise to one of the most touching incidents in the history of music. After the finish of the scherzo, during the first performance of the Ninth Symphony in 1824, Beethoven fell far behind his orchestra. The soloist, Fraulein Unger, gently tugged at his sleeve and led him to a seat. The audience came to realize that Beethoven had composed and conducted while deaf. Such a cheer went up from the audience as has never been heard since.

I am often way out of sync with the market. On such occasions, Soros has been known to tug at my sleeve, albeit not as gently as the Fraulein. "Victor, did they carry you out, yet? Whatever you do, don't trade for me until you've had your feet in the grave for a few weeks." My partners have a more direct trick. When I'm on tilt, they tape the phones up so I can't conduct any orders to the pits.

I don't mean to imply that I consider my trading worthy of comparison with the maestro. Rather, sometimes I'm tone-deaf. Nor can my trading be compared to Mozart, "who just made up nursery rhymes—the nursery rhymes of heaven." I share at least two defects with Mozart. First, it is now believed that the reason for Mozart's poverty during the last years of his life was an addiction to gambling. I'm not addicted, but, like Mozart, I tend to pay the casinos too much vigorish—a sure path to destitution. My second defect illumines the greatest puzzle about Mozart: Why was the beauty of his music not more appreciated by his contemporaries? The answer, advised Emperor Franz Josef of Austria, was that Mozart wrote too many notes.[10] I make too many trades.

My problem, Soros told me, is that I'm "always in and out with trade after trade. The market is a mathematical hypothesis. The best solutions to it are the elegant and simple." Mozart was aware of his defect and changed during his late 20s to a simplified style. It is harder to change when one is a semicentenarian.

CONTRAST AND REPETITION

Music arises from the most basic impulses. The vocal cords make sounds, the body and feet make rhythmic movements, and the mind transforms these sounds and movements into music. Joseph Machlis, in *The Enjoyment of Music*, says it perfectly: "[Music] has retained its connection with the springs of human feeling, with the accents of joy and sorrow, tension and release. Its procedures have been shaped by thousands of years of human experience; its expressive content mirrors man's existence, his place in nature and in society."[11]

While all agree that music is the universal language, the language of the emotions, there has never been a satisfactory definition of the expressive quality of music. Aaron Copland put the problem this way: "Is there a meaning of music? My answer to that would be 'Yes,' and 'Can you state in so many words what the meaning is?' My answer to that would be 'No'."[12]

The basic texture of early Western music stems from point-counterpoint (or note against note), which is a highly developed art that has many compositional rules and resulted in the great Baroque masterworks. One key step in its development was the invention of musical notation.

Paul Griffith and Roland DeCande make this point nicely in *The Heritage of Music*:

> The particular glory of Western classical music is its heritage . . . which is possible because it has a means of record: it has notation . . . . In western classical music, however, the model is that of the novel, with emphasis on what is new and what has never been expressed before . . . . Nevertheless, it

remains broadly true that the essence of non-Western music is continuity whereas that of western music is change (Until notation was invented in 1000 in the West, Western and Eastern music were similar.)

Then suddenly a great change took place. Since music could be notated, it could become polyphonic, and since it was polyphonic it necessarily began to extricate itself from the generalized concept of mode.[13]

If I say, as most musical scholars do, that Western music emphasizes individual rights, the pursuit of happiness, Magna Carta, the Declaration of Independence, and all that, I'm going to step into endless controversy. I can say, however, that the Eastern markets show much more continuity than the Western ones. I frequently make money in the Hong Kong or Indian stock market by playing their trends after a big move (with certain subtle adjustments). The serial correlation of one-day changes in the Bombay Sensitive Index, the Indian Stock Market Index, from 1994 to 1996, was 0.11, a figure significantly higher than the 0.01 for the S&P during this same period.

The most common form for almost all Western music is called the A-B-A form—statement, departure, return. The two A's impress the melodies on memory. The B provides contrast. Much of Western fiction is written in this or a closely related form.

The A-B-A form dominates the market. The beginning of a day is marked by up moves in one segment of the market and down moves in another. After a period of transition, the moves in the segments are reversed.

Finally, the opening theme is repeated, usually with vigor, in a coda at the close. To keep the audience in suspense, however, many deceptive cadences are thrown in along the way. Then, just before the close, the contrasting themes are recapitulated. Ontogeny recapitulates phylogeny in the original key. The final irony in market music is that the contrasting theme wins out often enough to prevent anyone from making too much money by betting consistently on the A-B-A form. One of the musicians who works for me says the market is like a jazz piece when you know all the players and know the rhythm, but you can't predict where the opening theme will be resolved.

DISSONANCE AND RESOLUTION

The trademark of Beethoven's, Mozart's, and countless other immortals' music is the sonorous capture of the composer's passionate and sometimes painful struggle for clarity and resolution. Indeed, the traditional central theme of classical music composition was that dissonant intervals or harmonies must be resolved into consonance. In the old days, perfect harmony was the rule—primes, fourths, fifths, and octaves were standard, with the very rare major or minor second creating a moment of dissonance that the rest of the piece would resolve. Many listeners were jarred by even the suggestion of repeated dissonance. The Italian theorist Artusi attacked Monteverdi for attempting to "corrupt, spoil, and ruin the good old rules" by using tonal combinations like major and minor sevenths that "are harsh to the ear, offending rather than delighting it."[14] Another example of such a musical purist was Rossini. The story goes that he could not be roused from bed until an attendant played a loud major seventh at his bedside—at which point Rossini's ears would be so offended he leapt out of bed to silence the noise.

Once, a floor trader on the NYSE came to me with the idea that stock market moves are similar to a symphony. He played the Dvorak Cello Concerto for me while his sexy girlfriend admired my squash trophies. He then showed me a one-to-one correspondence between the score notes and the stock market moves for the year. I gave him a six-figure initial capital to test his theories. Within three days, he lost 100 percent of the stake plus. He left town as poor as Berlioz, who spent the last six years of his life dejected, destitute, and unacclaimed.

RULES FOR SUCCESS

I was very fortunate to study music from the age of three. I learned with a portable, color-coded paper keyboard that covered the piano. It worked for me. By the time I was five, I had perfect pitch and could sight-read any piece as well as I can play it today. At seven, I could play the notes of the Bach three-part inventions and the Beethoven Sonatas. At nine, I could play the Mozart clarinet concerto, at the "B" level, without any lapses in fingering. However, my tone was and is dismal.

I preferred hustling pennies and nickels in money games at the beach to practicing my instruments. Fortunately, my parents allowed no such choice. Each day, my father sat me down at the piano and urged me to play. If I claimed that my clarinet was broken, he'd take out a screwdriver and adjust the keys. If, while he tried to repair it, I'd try to sneak away to the beach, he'd catch me and drag me back to the piano bench. If I refused to practice my piano scales—my Czerny, Hanon, and Beringer—he'd sit and wait to grab me if I tried to escape.

When I was six years old, our family decided to take a vacation in Florida. But for me it wasn't all recreation: there was no break from my daily piano lessons. We found a music shop that rented instruments, and my mom and dad paid the storeowner 50 cents for the privilege of allowing me to practice daily on the only available piano, strategically located in the store window.

The cliché holds that parents often repeat the virtues and mistakes of their own upbringing. Thirty years after my dad "channeled" me, my first daughter, Galt, refused to take her piano lesson. While her piano teacher, Robert Schrade, a gentleman I revere as the modern embodiment of Bach, waited at the piano, I tried, unobtrusively, to pull Galt toward the piano. I grabbed one arm. "You have to take your lesson." My wife grabbed the other. "You can't force her. You'll make her hate it."

Galt let me know that unless I let her go she'd report me to the family abuse authority and have me locked up. Between us, we almost pulled her arms out of their sockets, all the while trying to hide the donnybrook from Schrade. He started to play a transcription of a Strauss waltz. It broke the stalemate. I won the tug of war. Amid her muffled sobs, I escorted her to the piano as if I had no care in the world. I told him later, "It was the most embarrassing moment of my life." He said that he just thought of the unbroken circles of parents and children provoked to similar scenes.

I still don't know if I did the right thing. I've since related the story to friends, and many have expressed regret that their parents did not force them when they were reluctant music makers. On the other hand, Galt now plays the drums, not the piano, even though one of her early teachers referred to her as "highly gifted at all keyboard instruments."

RULES FOR MASTERING AN ELEMENTAL ACTIVITY

The training methods for musicians have advanced the competence and brilliance of musical performance and composition far beyond the achievements in any other field. By borrowing from the training techniques of the musician, the prospective master of any other elemental life-sustaining activity, such as speculation, can walk with the gods and stand with giants. Here's a compilation derived from stitching together the training techniques of Artie, Robert Schrade, and Ferruccio Busoni, a virtuoso pianist and composer of the 19th century.

For Music Mastery	For Speculation Mastery
1. Allow no day to pass without practicing with your instrument.	Study the market every day.
2. Get to know how your equipment is made and how it performs under all weather conditions.	Visit the exchanges. Be wary of rain and wind, and learn how to program in an assembly language.
3. Start each day of practice by playing a single tone with varying degrees of touch and dynamic quality.	Start with the stock market first.
4. Play one hand at a time where required by technical difficulty.	One position is enough.
5. Never fool around, even when no one is listening. Perfect practice makes perfect performance.	Don't boast or tell friends how great your system is or throw a few contracts in "just for fun."

(Continued)

For Music Mastery	For Speculation Mastery
6. Whenever you make a mistake, go back and repeat the passage correctly when no one is around.	Keep a record of all your losing trades. Were you in over your head?
7. Master all the technical aspects of your play and get in condition months before your performance. Then, when you perform or compete, you'll be able to concentrate on the intellectual and refined aspects. Shading and dynamics create great performances.	Paper trade before you start. Save up adequate capital. When you trade, vary the size of the position based on your assessment of the distribution of return and risk.
8. Play from memory. You can't soar when you're looking at a transcript. But take notes and keep a diary of all the pluses and minuses after you play.	Calculators or computers should not be consulted during the trading day.
9. Get into the performance hall an hour in advance, and acclimate yourself to the environment. Don't talk to anyone or shake any hands before or during your performance.	Get to work by 7:10 A.M., not 8:10 A.M., just ten minutes before the markets open.
10. Study the most elemental pieces and decisions from the standpoint of an expert. You will be astonished at how difficult it is to play a Czerny, or even a Clementi Sonatina perfectly.	How would Soros have traded that one lot?
11. Don't become stale trying to overcome the difficulties of a piece. Come back after a breather, and approach it from the beginning as if you didn't know it.	Take a break when you're losing.
12. Cultivate and nurture all emotions during practice. Open the floodgates during performance. But restrain ostentatious, visible emotions when performing.	No high fives, crying, alibiing, or bemoaning missed trades during the trading day.
13. Surround yourself with great masters of your art. Attend their performances. Study their books. And pay up for their lessons.	At least four books by Soros, and three about him are available.

For Music Mastery	For Speculation Mastery
14. Don't have sex just before, or during, your play. It will crowd out the climax your performance should create.	Stay away from badinage with those former models who cover you.
15. Don't replay the notes or fingering you missed during a performance. Once you look back, you'll be off on all the coming music.	Forget about the great prices you could have traded at. Should you enter, add, or exit *right now?*

If you're a Bach, don't worry about rules. In responding to compliments on his organ playing, Bach said, "There is nothing remarkable about it. All you have to do is hit the right notes at the right time, and the instrument plays itself."[15]

MUSIC AND COUNTING

Music and counting are inseparable. Gottfried Liebnitz, coinventor of calculus, said, "Music is the pleasure the human soul experiences from counting without being aware it is counting." The thought is a variant of the Pythagorean number mysticism. The Pythagoreans discovered that when the lengths of two vibrating strings are ratios of whole numbers, the tone will be harmonious. For example, a ratio of two to three produces a perfect fifth, and a ratio of three to four produces a fourth. Without realizing the mathematical relationship of the tones, a listener can easily describe the pleasant feelings the harmony evokes.

But, as anyone exposed to the grotesque sound of a synthesizer can attest, the frequency of vibrations of a musical note is as small a part of music as the palette of colors and a paintbrush are to a work of fine art. A late friend, Jack Koopman, the leading eye of the antique silver industry in the 1980s and 1990s, gave me a variation of this rule when I asked him whether a recent fall in the price of silver would depress the price of the fine museum-quality presentation pieces he was selling. "Victor, the price of silver has as small an influence on these pieces as the price of lumber has on the fine Chippendale chest you see there."

One attempt to combine music and counting is contained in the Schillinger System of Musical Notation. Joseph Schillinger, a teacher at Columbia University, was a mathematician and composer who counted among his private students George Gershwin, Oscar Levant, Benny Goodman, and other major musicians. In his work, he claims to have developed a general theory of music and melody.

Among his bag of tricks is a method for functionally transforming melodies from one style into another. For example, mapping a melody of Bach into the style of Liszt, according to Schillinger, is a process that can be achieved through counting.

Study of Schillinger's work leads me to see some analogies to the work of Ralph Elliott. A few pictures of spirals, a mathematical treatise on symmetry, a chambered nautilus, a dropped perpendicular, a formula for Fibonacci series, some quotes from Le Bon on crowd behavior, an allusion to the seminal work of Pacioli on divine proportions, some illustrations of the sculptures of Michelangelo or da Vinci, and the inevitable reference to the arrangement of leaves on a stem—these forms of mysticism describe everything and predict nothing.

The German poet, Heinrich Heine, expressed what seems to me to be the definitive thought on music counting:

> Nothing is more futile than theorizing about music. No doubt there are laws, mathematically strict laws, but these laws are not music; they are only its conditions—just as the art of drawing and the theory of colours, or even the brush and palette, are not painting, but only its necessary means. The essence of music is revelation; it does not admit of exact reckoning, and the true criticism of music remains an empirical art.[16]

Arthur Schnabel, the great mid-20th-century pianist, thought the essence had to do with silence rather than sound. He said, "The notes I handle better than many pianists. But the pauses between the notes—ah, that is where the art resides."[17] There is nothing in the 100,000 volumes in the Brown Mathematics Library that ties down the music-mathematics interface. However, anyone who has looked at the mathematical proof of a theorem, using letters and algebraic symbols as raw materials, and compared that process to composing a musical piece, using as raw materials symbols for notes and instruments, knows that the activities are identical twins. Thus, IBM, in its heyday, recruited musicians as programmers, and almost all the speculators at my firm have been, are, or could be professional musicians.

DIFFICULTY OF COUNTING

That's not to say that decision making based on systematic recording and logic is easy or accurate. Most modern psychology texts feature an array of illusions, biases, selective attentions and errors in perception, reasoning, and judgment. These problems occur because perception and the like are heavily skewed by an individual's background and past experiences.

A well known optical illusion presents two lines of equal length, one with open arrows, the other with closed arrows at both ends. The difference in the direction of the arrows creates the illusion that the two lines are of different lengths. When viewing such deceptions I tend to lose confidence in the accuracy of my vision. Yet vision is not the only sense subject to confusion. Comparable illusions fool our sense of touch, taste, smell, and hearing.

Errors in judgment are particularly frequent in choices involving uncertainty and risk, the meat and potatoes of all speculation. The usual error here consists of using a rule of thumb such as availability, anchoring or representativeness, instead of a formal logical analysis. Even our formal reasoning often breaks down due to errors of the undistributed middle, particularity of premises, or content. (A good exposition of these lapses is contained in Zimbardo and Gerrig's *Psychology and Life*.)

Counting, like music and speculation, may thus be thought of as mirroring the human experience. In my view, you can't have one without the other; everyone is essentially a mathematician. Buy or sell something, hang wallpaper, paint, or dance, and you are exercising the mathematical faculty.

How to Count

I learned the importance of counting at an early age from two polymaths separated by an ocean, a century, and an even wider gulf in social status. The first counter was Francis Galton, the inventor of weather maps. I came across his work when I studied the influence of weather on sporting outcomes, a necessity for every would-be speculator.

Galton's favorite motto was, "Wherever you can, count." He always traveled with a pin and an index card so that he could discreetly make tabulations of anything that struck him as noteworthy. Some statisticians—Steve Stigler and other numbers lovers (me)—consider him the greatest counter of all time, and it is well to study his methodology carefully:

I frequently make statistical records of form and feature, in the streets or in company, without exciting attention, by means of a fine pricker and a piece of paper. . . . If I then press it upon a piece of paper, held against the ball of my thumb, the paper is indelibly perforated with a fine hole, and the thumb is not wounded. The perforations will not be found to run into one another unless they are very numerous, and if they happen to do so now and then, it is of little consequence in a statistical inquiry. The holes are easily counted at leisure, by holding the paper against the light, and any scrap of paper will serve the purpose. It will be found that the majority of inquiries take the forms of "more," "equal to," or "less," so I arrange the paper in a way to present three distinct compartments to the pricker, and to permit of its being held in the correct position and used by the sense of touch alone. I do so by tearing the paper into the form of a cross that is, maimed in one of its arms and hold it by the maimed part between the thumb and finger, the head of the cross pointing upward. The head of the cross receives the pricks referring to "more"; the solitary arm that is not maimed, those meaning "the same"; the long foot of the cross, those meaning "less."

It is well to write the subject of the measurement on the paper before beginning to use it, then more than one set of records can be kept in the pocket at the same time, and be severally added to as occasion serves, without fear of mistaking one for the other.[18]

COUNTING EDUCATION

The second counter I learned from was Artie. One beautiful summer day when I was seven, I was stunned by the sight of my dad making marks on a big yellow pad while he was watching the best handball players in the world compete at Garber Stadium. After each point, I saw the notations: OTWK—off the wall killer; KW—killer, winner; DW—drive winner; DE—drive error; A-ace; AW—angle winner. My dad was calculating the chances of winning the next point after runs of winning and losing points of different magnitudes. He also recorded the duration of each point and the percentage of winners and errors for each game, contingent on various leads. "Why are you doing that, Dad?" I asked. "Who cares when you get the points as long as you know who's best?"

"Did you ever notice how Moey Orenstein, the greatest doubles player ever, usually gets behind, 15–11, and then goes on to win, 21–19?"

"Everyone knows that. He gets behind early so he can take in more bets at better odds. Then, he comes in with his patented overhand, off the wall, dead killers, hit with a backspin."

"That's right," my dad said. "But notice how when he's playing a tournament match or a nonbetting trophy match, like the match he played against Vic Hershkowitz for the unofficial world title, he doesn't get behind ever.

"Take Artie Wolf. Lots of times, he gets way ahead at the beginning of the game, with his three-foot hooks and off-the-wall dead killers. But then, he starts playing safe. He doesn't want to take chances any more. All of a sudden he's taking balls behind the long line and lobbing them back instead of going for the shot. Most players are much more afraid about losing a game they're ahead in than losing one they start even from. Their game suffers when they play safe."

A game is like a piece of music. The tempo varies as the players change the speed of their hit and the celerity of their offensive and defensive moves. The rhythm of who's winning and how hard the players try for each point starts changing, based on the score. Finally, the harmony of the game changes. The players vary their shot combinations according to the score, what's been working for them, and how much energy each has left.

I began to count musical time. The only way for someone not naturally gifted to match the right and left hands on a piano keyboard, or to keep time with an instrument or the voice, is to work out the fractions of the rhythm. I always practiced with a metronome. I still hear that metronome ticking when a market is moving. Once a market gets in a groove, the speed of the ascent or descent beats out a cadence each hour or day. When it breaks tempo, it is often the signal for a new melody or some discord to appear.

I then started to count in card games. My kids are still amazed when I tell them I know all their hold cards in Casino. Counters know their opponents' likely holdings and the remaining cards at all times. This is quite an advantage. Counters also have an edge in many activities that are not obvious to noncounters. In playing Monopoly™, for instance, the champs always count the chance and community chest cards that have gone out (there are only 18 of each). In Scrabble™, the counter gains the edge by keeping track of the balance of the 100 tiles that have not been played. This affects the probability of drawing good and bad tiles in subsequent draws. In lotteries, counters track popular numbers to avoid sharing a tied prize. (The high numbers are generally the least popular.) In speculation, the counters track the remaining contracts or options that have to be offset to avoid delivery, knowing that the weak longs will bail out before expiration. To give counting its due there are so many areas that the speculator needs it that a prerequisite for the job might well be Galton's pricker and paper.

COMPUTER-ASSISTED MOVES

Counting, speculating, music, and family came together in 1979 when I attempted to quantify the predictive properties of markets. I've eventually come to believe that markets are so sensitive, so interrelated, that a shooting star changes soybean prices in Holland. When Mexico sneezes, Hong Kong catches a cold. I likened it to a market symphony played by millions of strong and weak insiders and outsiders, conducted by the gods of chance, performed at the exchanges, ultimately to be reviewed by critics in advisory services, brokerage houses, and the media. And always the common struggle between dissonance and consonance, equilibrium and disequilibrium, stickiness and animal spirits.

To become proficient at the movements of the markets, I'd have to appreciate its music.

Serendipitously, my insights coincided with the introduction of the TRS-80, the microcomputer manufactured by Radio Shack that initiated the information age. I bought a few computers, started counting, then looked for a few harmonious musicians. The first one played the piano, cello, and violin, was gifted at mathematics, and, best of all, had been trained by Artie. With credentials like that, I figured I had to go for him, even though he was only 10 years old. I hired my brother Roy.

I am familiar with all the theoretical Darwinian stuff about emotions having a functional role in eliciting appropriate responses to emergency situations. The modern view is that emotions set off a chain that moves the individual to homeostasis. But in real life, those sinking feelings in the stomach, palpitations of the heart, and dryness of the mouth as prices spin about prevents me from the ascetic decision making necessary to even out the battle. When I allow emotions to get the upperhand; I find myself eternally unhappy, angry, disgusted and surprised. To reduce their influence, I directed Roy to model my emotions with a computer. He modified one of the now readily available computer voice synthesizer programs so that it ran concurrently with the stream of prices coming off the Quotron. When a price would move to an extreme, the computer delivered market commentary in a robotic male voice: "New low in crude." "Oh, copper!" "Breakout in silver!" "Beans limit up!" "Yen at the round number." "How low can gold go?" "One minute to the open. . . . Traders, ready your tickets." "Stocks at a new high." "Soros selling." "Intervention in the currencies." "Leak in bonds." "Number in three minutes."

An unfilled buy order elicited the response "Locals only, you're not filled." "2000 ahead of you." "Henry bidding for 3000 above you." If a sell order went unfilled, "Very quiet, light on the bid, heavy offers," "Locals out playing golf today." The emotional atmosphere that formerly pervaded our trading room was thus diffused.

The computer was programmed to calculate each trader's profit and loss on a real-time basis. When the losses hit a predetermined target, the computer generated a demoralizing utterance. How deflating to rush into the trading room to communicate all-too-human emotions and then hear the computer beat you by two or three seconds, with exactly the proper intonation, ". . . tapped out. Call it a day. . . ." Paul DeRosa, who heads one of the 38 government bond dealerships and has been involved in all aspects of the business for 25 years, told us that the computer was so realistic it eliminated the need for the proverbial trading manager and squawk box that the old-fashioned houses still use. The only problem was that it was infuriating to have a kibitzer over our shoulders 24 hours a day, especially when we were losing. We disconnected the program and gave the computer another musical job.

I need to know what's happening in the markets. But it's dysfunctional to be tied to the screen. I hooked up a music synthesizer to the computer, linked it to the interface between the computer and quote screen, and generated a program that would give a musical summary of the markets. I used piano tones for stocks, strings for interest rates, the cello for short-term rates, and the violin for the 30-year bond. The Japanese yen was registered with the high flute, corresponding to the favorite instrument of Japan, the *shakuhachi*. The English horn, the French horn, and the Alpenhorn stood in for the other currencies.

Unfortunately, the output was so cacophonous I had to turn it off after a second or two, just like the voice program. Ultimately, we had to teach the computer to compose music in harmony so it wouldn't sound so bad.

MUSICIAN AND COUNTER EMPLOYEES

The second employee I hired was playing on the office piano one day while I was trading. I was desperately hanging on to a losing trade when I heard a technically flawless, soulful rendition of Gershwin's *Rhapsody in Blue*. I looked around to upbraid my brother Roy, the only person I knew who could play that difficult piece. Instead, I found Paul Buethe, then a 23-year-old University of Nebraska graduate and Columbia M.B.A., our newest hire in the Mergers and Acquisitions Department. I told Paul what he could do with his music during trading hours, when I was nursing a big loss. He apologized and said that he should have known better. The main activity of the students and professors in his M.B.A. program was to sit around, watch quote screens, and conduct mock trading programs.

I suggested to Paul that a man who could play piano like that belonged in our trading division, where life and death hang in the balance every minute rather than over the course of a nine-month merger deal. He became my trading partner shortly thereafter. Paul specializes in developing trading systems based on analogies to the worlds of music, sports, and physics. The systems are so complicated that they can be tested only by hand. The musical connection between us has proved harmonious. We often share our sorrows after a huge loss by playing a duet, perhaps the Funeral March from the second movement of Chopin's Sonata No. 2 in B Flat Minor.

We were joined by Steve Wisdom, whose bent was counting rather than music. Before I hired him I asked him to teach a course in multivariate statistics to our summer trainees. The trainees had taken similar courses at Harvard, Stanford, and Yale. Without exception, they independently evaluated Steve's teaching as superior to their college classes.

The music-counting connection has been a good one for us. Paul, Steve, and I have now been partners for 10 years. We know each other's music so well that when one of us goes on vacation, no conductor is necessary. The others know exactly what parts to play.

DANGER OF END

Is it accident or predestination that life so often imitates art? In the 1840s, Hector Berlioz asked his mentor, Jean Lesueur, to attend a performance of Beethoven's Fifth Symphony. The Fifth starts with the most famous four notes in music, the Morse code for "V," ta-ta-ta-tum: three quick notes and a long, unmeasured lower one. I've seen the markets open like this a million times, especially after a big rout on the previous day. Hope springs eternal, so the next day is likely to begin with a few short, small, spastic trades slightly above yesterday's close. Then the big boys end the respite with some truly violent selling that leads to liquidation at drastically lower prices. Beethoven tears back and forth between the main themes in the first movement "without a break and in wild abandon." Finally, before the development, Beethoven puts a big silence "articulative as well as dramatic."[19]

On October 20, 1987, after the stock market crash had sent the Dow down 500 points the previous day, the market opened with a few short up ticks from follow-up buying based on the overnight rise in bond prices. Then the liquidation began again in wild abandon. The tension became so unbearable that trading had to be stopped on all markets except the Chicago Board of Trade Major Market Index.

"The silence was dynamic." The Fifth is a victory symphony. Its path is from strife to triumph, ending with C major chords played by thunderous trombones, contra bassoons, and shrill piccolos, a hurricane of bullishness. "But the goblins were there," E. M. Forster says in *Howard's End;* and he adds, "They could return." There was a dynamic silence instantly—until out of the clear blue sky some sustained buying in the major markets began. By the end of trading on October 20, the Dow had risen 200 points, almost half the previous day's carnage, and the seeds were planted for the greatest bull market in history, encompassing a tripling in the next nine years. But a few goblins returned occasionally—on Thursday morning, October 20, when the averages opened below the old lows, a case in point.

Music was never the same after the Fifth Symphony. Nor would markets ever be the same after the October 1987 crash, the February 1980 COMEX silver crash, or the June 1996 copper crash. Berlioz in the 1840s urged his mentor, Lesueur, to attend a performance so he could understand the change. But Lesueur, a man fixed in the old ways, hesitated. Berlioz continues:

> I kept on at him, solemnly pointing out that when something as important as this occurred in our art—a completely new style on an unprecedented scale—it was his duty to find out about it and to judge for himself. . . . He yielded and let himself be dragged to the conservatorie to hear the Fifth performed.[20]

After the 1980 silver crash, I asked Artie to spend a day with me at the COMEX to see the carnage. At first, he hesitated, "I have to grade papers."

I told Artie that there was music, beautiful and horrible, in the market just the same as in the singing of birds or the baying of hounds chasing game. "The visit to the pits will expose you to a crowd that can't be missed in a lifetime." He agreed and I escorted him to the World Trade Center.

When the Fifth was over, Berlioz found Lesueur in a corridor, striding along with a flushed face:

> Ouf! Let me get out. I must have some air. It's amazing! Wonderful! I was so moved and so disturbed that when I emerged from the box and attempted to put on my hat, I couldn't find my head. Now please leave me be. We'll meet tomorrow.[21]

At the COMEX, while Artie watched the market gyrate up and down, hundreds of floor traders fought like vipers in a bottle, reliving the 1979–1980 rise from $5 to $50 and back to $5 again in each 15-minute interval. While we were there, I received a call. My major client needed my help in launching a bear raid on the all-world stock markets. My head started spinning. "Well, Dad, did it blow you away?" "Vickie, it reminded me of the mobs I had to control in Union Square during Labor Day agitations or after the Dodgers won the pennant. I'll see you later. I have to get to work." The next day, Berlioz hurried to Lesueur's school.

> But it was easy to see that my companion was no longer the man who had spoken to me the day before, and that he found the subject painful. I persisted, however, and dragged from him a further acknowledgment of how deeply Beethoven's symphony had moved him; at which he suddenly shook his head and smiled in a curious way and said, "All the same, music like that ought not to be written."[22]
> "Don't worry, master," I replied, "there is not much danger."

I called Artie the next day for some Monday morning quarterbacking.

"Wasn't that amazing? Did I exaggerate when I said it was the most exciting music you'll ever hear?"

He was reticent. Finally, he replied, "These powerful forces, they're like an avalanche. How can you withstand them? Remember the bodies of the big-shot speculators I had to deliver to the morgue? You're in over your head."

"Don't worry, Dad," I replied, "There's no danger. I have it all quantified."

CHAPTER 15

The Ecology of Markets

It is interesting to contemplate a tangled bank, clothed with many plants of many kinds, with birds singing on the bushes, with various insects flitting about, and with worms crawling through the damp earth, and to reflect that these elaborately constructed forms, so different from each other, and dependent upon each other in so complex a manner, have all been produced by laws acting around us. When we reflect on this struggle, we may console ourselves with the full belief, that the war of nature is not incessant, that no fear is felt, that death is generally prompt, and that the vigorous, the healthy, and the happy survive and multiply.

Charles Darwin
The Origin of Species

THE FIELD AT THE BOARD

The modern way of studying any species is to examine what it is doing, what it eats, whom it is eaten by, and what sort of environment it inhabits during its life cycle. Charles Elton, a pioneer in ecology, put it in homely, unforgettable terms 70 years ago: "When an ecologist says, 'There goes a badger,' [the student] should include in his thoughts some definite idea of the animal's place in the community to which it belongs just as if he had said, 'there goes the vicar.'"[1]

So, here comes the speculator trying to study the markets. In view of the complex webs and multifarious habitats of the players, the ideal vantage point for such a study would be a satellite. The proper equipment would include X-ray vision, a time machine, and ESP. I have to settle for the next best thing, a visit to the exchange, but I can do so only once or twice a year. The visit fills me with so much emotion that I am wrecked for days afterward. The exchange has been the scene of many of my greatest triumphs and tragedies. But for a few lucky breaks, I would have been shipwrecked and cannibalized there.

As I enter the exchange, I see inscribed in the stone of my mind's eye the words, "Abandon hope, all ye who enter here." As I walk through the

350

turnstiles, admitted by the latest digital identification systems, my emotions race.

First comes exhilaration, the glory of the hunt. I hear the baying of the hounds, the energizing music of Beethoven's Fifth Symphony, the stormy pastoral music of the Sixth. This is what I was born to do. Here I was long billions of bonds, right before the biggest rise ever, in the fury of the October 19, 1987, crash. Here I achieved a hundredfold return in a year when I was courting my better half. Here I often affect the wealth of the world by $10 billion in a second when I lob a few thousand of my friend's contracts on the hyenas, vipers, and sharks in the pit, all frantically waiting to strike. Here I am treated like a "whale" visiting a casino. "Yes, I'll take that message in the private pool, then scan the media room before indulging . . . in baccarat."

On one occasion, the charged state I achieve on the floor almost electrocuted my wealth. Lightning struck at the opening of stock market futures trading in Kansas City in 1982. I bought a membership and high-tailed it to a better life on the Kansas City floor. Before I knew it, I owned 50 percent of the open interest of the total outstanding stock market futures. "But futures should be trading at 8 percent above cash!" I kept exclaiming as the futures tumbled down one full point per hour to a discount of 3.00 points to cash. Ultimately, for our mutual protection, my partners and I instituted a rule that I was never to trade from the floor of an exchange again.

Exhilaration is invariably followed by deepest melancholy. What tragedy lurks in these pits. I sold my bonds in the cash market right after the close on October 19, 1987, and couldn't buy them back for three days. I am always just a day or two early in every position I enter or exit. How does the market always know to make the real move after I'm forced out? How often I've sat staring at the screen at the end of a day, waiting for prices to change in my favor even after the market has closed, my head in my hands, thinking, "I'm lost."

I've lost so often here that the count is almost laughable. In the old days, the stock exchange floor was famous for tomfoolery. Typical pranks included squirting a member with perfume (all members were males), holding an umbrella over an official's head, inducing a visitor to take his hat off, tossing darts, fomenting a fracas between two irate brokers—who commenced their milling at the board and then adjourned to an upstairs meeting room where the fight was carried to the bitter end. If a member took a customer to visit the floor, a wag was sure to scream, "There goes another of his victims!" A favorite amusement was to wake an elder statesman with the roaring from a dozen leathery lungs of, "Josh," "Josh," "Josh."[2] On the futures exchanges, the noise level causes the elder statesmen to retire upstairs too early in their career for that joke. In the canyons of Wall Street nowadays, the members of the stock exchange are much too dignified for such frivolities. The weight of maintaining a monopoly in a stock while holding restricted orders from customers, trading for one's own account, and making a market for the public tends to crowd out the typical fun of schoolboys, squirrels, seals, and monkeys.

On the Chicago futures exchanges, the attendees are still full of tricks. The brokers will take bets on who can hit a softball out of Wrigley Field, or wager who can throw a hard ball across the Chicago River. During quiet moments on the floor of the Chicago Mercantile Exchange, members often purchase a beach ball from the local Rand McNally store and toss it around the floor. The stripper they secreted onto the floor of the CBOT in 1995 was meant in jest, before the politically correct turned it into a tragedy. While I was on the floor, I saw the brokers collecting money for a game of "bag of bucks." The winning dollar picked out of the bag was worth a $10,000 prize.

Whenever a big order comes into the currency pit, a roar goes up: "The Sheik!" When Soros comes in, the brokers yell, "The Palindrome!" Rumors about the source of each large order come straight out of the bond trading of the Roaring '20s, the era of the great Gatsby:

"He doesn't want any trouble with anybody."
"It's rumored that he was a German spy during the war."
". . . , he was in the American army during the war."
"You look at him sometime when he thinks nobody's looking at him, I'll bet he killed a man."[3]

On the floor of the Chicago Mercantile Exchange, rookie traders are greeted with a unique rite of initiation. A trader will stick a card in the shape of a shark's fin into the rookie's collar, and as he walks into the pit, trading stops as the members yell, "Shark!" This custom parallels that of a century before at the New York Stock Exchange. Upon the entrance of rookies, traders would roar, "New Tennessee."

Most animal behavior textbooks are filled with studies on territoriality. Who among us hasn't been warned away or attacked by a bird or a dog when we have come too close to its space? From hummingbirds to kittiwake gulls to lions defending a pride, animals will fight to maintain their territory. In the same way, members of the exchange are notoriously territorial about their positions on the floor. A spot on the floor is "owned" by a member and is one of the most valuable perks of membership. In 1996, a member who was forced to leave the exchange for personal reasons sold his place on the floor for $1 million. The brokers, like the birds, will, if necessary, fight to the death for their territory in court and in the ring. Among the more cerebral option traders on the IMM, verbal blows may be exchanged.

The antics on the trading floor make me angry. Traders have time to joke, gamble, and fight for million-dollar positions because they take out a vig from every trade that goes on the floor. The "only vig." My vig. My two brokers in Chicago are nicknamed "Butcher" and "Pockets." They're eating me alive right in front of my eyes. And if I ever fall, like Buck in *The Call of the Wild*, they'll devour me in a second. That is what a certain blue-blooded Morgan firm tried to do to me after the crash. I'll get my revenge. Those merciless sons of guns.

My frustration ultimately turns to higher thoughts. After all, these creatures on the floor are merely trying to make a living. Their education and heredity have prepared them to survive in certain niches. Those who survive are more successful in the struggle of market existence, so they transmit their modus operandi and chips to family and friends. Admittedly, they survive by digesting and recycling the liquidity of the public. I'm just part of that public, fulfilling my role.

Rather than rail at the exchange, I should appreciate the natural beauty of it. Who would rail at the savanna for providing a forum for lions to eat wildebeest and zebras to eat grass? The exchange is but a market ecosystem. I don't fulminate at the racetrack or the casino when the customers are charged for entertainment and hope. Why should I hold the exchange to a higher standard?

After a few hours on the floor, the tumult carries me out of the nitty-gritty of limits, stops, and making money. I see the pits as trees, the members as vultures and insects, my counterparts among the banks and dealers as giraffes and kangaroos. Soros is not my friend, customer, or mentor anymore; he is a lion, fulfilling his role of maintaining the animals below him by culling the weak so don't kill each other off. The exchange is no longer in the Chicago financial district or the Wall Street environs, but in the African Serengeti.

After exposure to the symphony of emotions on the floor, I feel drained—the same way I do after playing a five-set match in an important tournament. But I still am left with a host of questions. What principles explain and order all the disparate behavior?

What explains the fluctuation in volumes of contract traded over time? Why did the gold contract vanish on the IMM but continue albeit at one-third its old level in New York after the Hunt fiasco? Why do brokers drive fancy sports cars? What is the source, the driving engine that powers all of this activity?

Philosophical musings like these lead me to seek a market model to explain the seemingly disparate and chaotic phenomenon. The activity moves, deception, games, niches, connections, structures, hype, rules and regulations—there seemed to be a systematic set of principles that hold the whole kit and caboodle together. I turned to the science of ecology for guidance.

ECOLOGICAL PRINCIPLES

There are almost as many definitions of ecology as there are ecologists, but the one given by Krebs in the standard textbook in the field captures the flavor of the linkages best: "Ecology is the scientific study of the interactions that determine the distribution and abundance of organisms."[4]

I call the study of the webs that link the players the ecology of markets. The way I study it is the same way ecologists study spiders, birds, and snails. I look at what the players do when they're at home, the kind of home they live in, how they capture and defend, who eats their waste, and how they are recycled when they die. Instead of studying them in their webs, nests, and shells, I study the market players on the trading floor, in the brokerage house, and in cyberspace. All the individual ecosystems are linked, creating a supramarket organism through myriad interrelations.

Ecology has developed certain principles that are invaluable in explaining these interactions in every environment. I cannot begin to provide an adequate summary of ecological concepts; a typical ecology book has a glossary with 1,000 new words, about as many as are taught in a first-year language course. But two principles are so pervasive and important that any attempt to apply ecology to another field must take them into account.

1. *The ultimate source of energy.* Living things require energy to keep distinct from their physical environment. An ability to use energy and to interact with physical forces is the primary characteristic that distinguishes living things from the nonliving. The ultimate source of energy is light from the sun.

2. *Organization of communities.* Communities are organized by feeding relationships—who eats whom. Elton expressed the regularity 70 years ago, in a landmark study:

   > Food is the burning question in animal society, and the whole structure and activities of the community are dependent upon questions of food-supply . . . animals have to depend ultimately upon plants for their supplies of energy, since plants alone are able to turn raw sunlight and chemicals into a form edible to animals. Consequently, herbivores are the basic class in animal society. . . . The herbivores are usually preyed upon by carnivores, which get the energy of the sunlight at third-hand, and these again may be preyed upon by other carnivores, and so on, until we reach an animal which has no enemies, and which forms, as it were, a terminus on this food-cycle. There are, in fact, chains of animals linked together by food, and all dependent in the long run upon plants. We refer to these as "food-chains," and to all the food-chains in a community as the "food-cycle."[5]

The energy principle and that of the feeding web were combined by ecologist Raymond Lindeman in 1942. He referred to the species in the food chain as producer, herbivore, and carnivore. He visualized these trophic levels as pyramids of energy transformations. At each level, less energy is available because of metabolism and the inefficiency of biological transformations.

The concept has been enlarged over the years by the inclusion of decomposers, whose purpose (as discussed in macabre detail) is to remove wastes and digest the indigestible. Ambrose Bierce, in *The Devil's Dictionary*, aptly sums up this process with his definition of edible: "Good to eat, and wholesome to digest, as a worm to a toad, a toad to a snake, a snake to a pig, a pig to a man, and a man to a worm."[6]

MARKET ECOSYSTEM

I propose that each futures and foreign exchange market is held together by a web of public, dealer, large speculator, and broker players interacting with each other and their market environment. Food and energy, in the form of losses, is created by "the public" and other slow-moving participants. The primary consumers of these losses are the foreign exchange and fixed-income dealers—banks and investment brokers such as Bankers Trust, Chemical Bank, Goldman Sachs, Citibank, Morgan Stanley, Salomon Brothers, and Union Bank of Switzerland. The secondary consumers, who feed on the banks, are large successful hedge funds, including Quantum, Tiger, and Omega. At each step, the orders and volatility are broken down into manageable slices and recycled among the participants in the web by decomposer species such as floor traders and telephone brokers. Table 15–1 shows the relations of typical ecosystems in the earth's biota. The market ecosystem is in the last column. A system diagram of the major market relations appears in Figure 15–1.

PUBLIC PRODUCERS

"Who's winning here?" a certain well-known real estate mogul—who is as famous for his lechery as for his deal making—likes to say to the poker players at the casino he owns. "You are," the players respond with a laugh. The public market player should treat his certain losses with the same commendable disinterest as the poker player answering the mogul or the ecologist contemplating the niche of the badger.

There are many "publics" in the sea of markets, but most of them are shy about wearing their badges. They can be found among futures traders, stock flippers, market timers, system clubs, and tape watchers. But because of the high morbidity and mortality within these groups, membership is always in flux. Perhaps the best way to identify the species is by behavior—inflexibility, ignorance, arrogance, myopia, hesitancy, undercapitalization, overconfidence, spendthrift ways, and hopefulness.

I am not ashamed to admit that I am occasionally part of the public. I often trade with dealers in foreign exchange paying a 5-point bid/asked spread when my exit point is a 25-point profit or loss. Further, I have been known to accept a derivatives or options trade where, if I exited

Table 15-1.   Trophic Levels in the Earth's Ecosystems

	Producer	Herbivore	Primary Carnivore	Secondary Carnivore	Decomposer
Tundra	Lichen, reindeer moss	Caribou, reindeer	Wolves, Arctic fox	Polar bears	Low microbes, effect of freezing temperature
Pond	Algae, phytoplankton	Zooplankton, crustaceans	Dragon flies, mollusks	Bass, trout	Bacteria, fungi
Meadow	Herbaceous angiosperms	Flies, bees, spiders	Beetles, wasps	Sparrows, crows, deer, ferrets	Bacteria, fungi
Ocean	Blue-green algae	Amoebas, radiolarians	Crabs, lobsters	Tuna, swordfish, shark, turtle	Barnacles, coral
Savanna	Grasses, sedges, acacia trees	Zebras, wildebeests, impalas	Cheetahs, hawks	Lions, leopards, jackals	Vultures, hyenas, bacteria
Market	Public, government	Dealer	Large speculators	Large hedge funds	Locals, vulture investors

instantaneously after entering, my loss would be 50 percent of my cost. And, like other suckers, I occasionally bite when my stock broker calls with a mining stock selling at fifty cents on a Canadian exchange.

My life expectancy in such activities would be lower than that of a mouse playing with lions. Yet I persist. The life-enhancing factor is that I usually try to take the opposite side of public trades.

The role of the public in this field is to be eaten. Anecdotal evidence supporting this role can be found in the work of Stanley Kroll, a well-respected futures broker who rose to prominence in the 1980s. Despite his success, he became discouraged because none of his customers made money. None of the other brokers at his brokerage had a customer who made money either. And the same was true at all of the other major brokerage houses where he worked. To be fair, an updated report in the mid-1990s is not as negative. The president of a discount brokerage with 10,000 customers reports that 10 percent to 20 percent of its customers make money. Most treat the exercise as an entertainment.

In light of this performance, it is no wonder that public futures traders are rare. As one veteran futures trader who, like me, has seen it all, said, "The public is mostly gone, replaced by managed systems traders. They are much harder to figure out, and much harder to trade against." And yet the public persists.

The CFTC publishes a biweekly report of all trades by commercial users, large speculators, and the public. A large speculator is defined as a

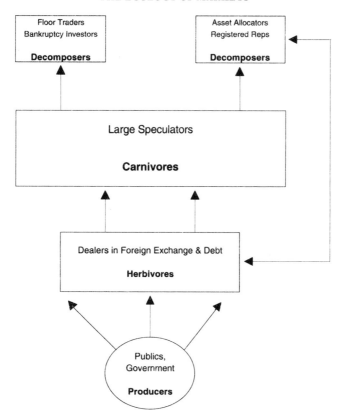

Figure 15–1. The Market Ecosystem

"noncommercial" trader whose position at the end of the trading day exceeds a predetermined volume of contracts. For example, a large speculator in IMM Eurodollar futures is either long or short over 400 contracts at the close. The remainder of the volume of contracts traded in quantities lower than the required reporting levels is classified as public trading.

A compilation of the percentage of the open interest held by small speculators in various markets during June 1986, June 1991, and June 1996 appears in Figure 15–2. Public participation is clearly dropping. In 13 of the 16 markets listed, including the two largest markets—bonds and stocks—the percentage of public participation was lowest in 1996. Average public participation in 1996 was 27 percent, down from 35 percent in 1991 and 34 percent in 1986. Overall, these percentages empirically show small traders' participation declining by approximately one-quarter.

Public participation is down, but it's still substantial in absolute terms. The public accounts for 30 percent of the total open interest in many futures markets. In June 1996, for example, the total open interest for all futures contracts was 10,380,585. Assuming the public controls 27 percent of these contracts at a face value of $50,000 per contract and a margin of $2,500 per contract, the public participation in futures markets totals $140 billion with a margin outstanding of $7 billion.

MANAGED FUTURES PUBLIC

Who are they? One public for the futures market is visible and easy to define. They're the group that responds to advanced, mechanical, space age, effortless approaches, guided by supertraders, winners of speculating championships, who "won't let you make critical mistakes." They attend intense, real-time seminars limited to eight attendees, where visionary pioneers of high integrity and discipline teach them how to find the exact lows and highs with 99 percent accuracy. They can claim an immediate 120 percent tuition refund if the return is less than 200 percent or the drawdown exceeds 5 percent. And sometimes they hire agents to manage their money.

The performance of the public in the managed systems business is difficult to pin down. Accounts under management have grown from $2 billion in 1981 to $25 billion today. It's a lucrative profit center for brokers, floor traders, and brokerage houses (or futures commissions merchants, as they're called in the industry). According to the rating services, the returns delivered by managed futures are a few percentage points a year greater than stocks. Although I am a participant in this industry and have been known to hit the number-one ranking, I have grave doubts about the validity and reliability of the reported results.

The most important limitation in the reported figures is that they are retrospective. The funds that are eager to report at the end of the period are the successful ones. Just as misleading are all the funds that start out reporting but withdraw at the end. A related phenomenon is that, in its first year of reporting, a fund tends to show extraordinary returns. My friend, Joel Rentzler, once discovered that the average first-year return of funds filing to be registered as commodity trading advisers with the CFTC was well above 50 percent.

Another grave limitation is that the results are reported by the futures trading advisers themselves. Except for audited results, there would appear to be many a slip between the cup and the lip by the time these stellar results get translated into the public's bottom line.

Put all these limitations together and add the usual stuff—improper weighting by initial value, selective reporting of stellar performers, fattening up a contender—and the end return has more uncertainty about it than the proverbial kicks of Prussian horses. One way of reducing uncertainty

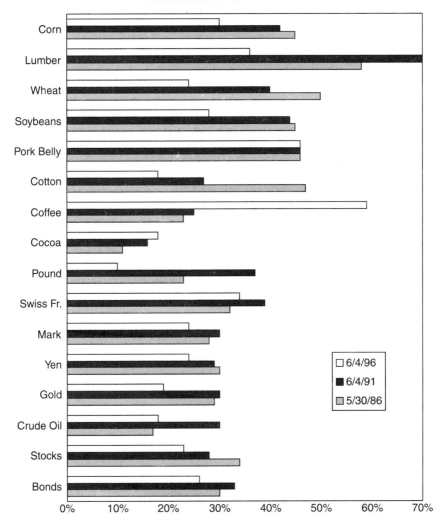

Figure 15–2. Public Participation as a Percentage of
Total Open Interest in Major Markets

would be to compute the prospective performance of a preselected group
of public funds to the belly-up point or the end of the year, depending on
which comes first. Such calculations invariably show sharply lower returns
than the reported figures.

As to some real-world experiences of those who participate in managed
futures, a recent court case, against a brokerage firm I use for a large part
of my currency business, provides insight. The claimants were toilers in

the entertainment industry who lost big in managed futures and were awarded punitive damages totaling five times as much as their losses. In assessing the industry, expert witness Richard Teweles, author of *The Commodity Futures Game*—in my opinion, the best book on futures ever written—stated:

> After the outrageously high fees and commissions, it would be a miracle for someone to make money on these futures programs. It's good as amusement for rich people, like playing poker or going to the racetrack; it's exciting while you're playing, even if you lose in the end. The only people who make money are the brokers.[7]

John Allen, the plaintiff's attorney, after analyzing the various vigs and costs, cut to the bottom line:

> Who, in his right mind, would invest in managed futures, if he knew he had to make 34% in one year just to equal the yield of a T-bill?[8]

The time has come for some kitchen talk. I am a major participant in the managed futures business. The funds I manage plus those of my former employees account for a significant percentage of the industry's activity. The sixtyfold return (after all fees) I've made for my first customer, Tim Horne, over the past 13 years, while certainly unsustainable, adds a certain degree of legitimacy to my activities. I'd like to believe that my niche is to collect an agency fee from my customers for allowing them to participate as large speculators.

On the other hand, I'm part of an industry that has no compunction against offering programs to the public with breakevens in the 30 percent and up area that Mr. Allen describes. The higher purpose that such programs serve is commendable. The fees help pay for the overhead and the entertainment of good people. I have to believe, however, that those who pay the piper often fail to see it in this lofty light. An awareness of the shadows, currents, and whirlwinds of my business made me delay hanging up my shingle as a full-fledged member for the first 25 years or so, when I was looking in the window.

OTHER PUBLICS

There are other publics besides those who dream of hundredfold returns with the 20 times leverage available in futures. Those who trade in and out of stocks with high bid/asked spreads should expect to be devoured. Anyone who makes a practice of flipping investments where the vig is high, relative to the variation, is a good candidate for a similar fate. The $3 trillion U.S. mutual fund industry is fueled by public buying. As of mid-1996, the net inflows were running at $35 billion a month. In the spirit of the mutually beneficial transactions that characterize capitalism, it is well that the public has profited enormously from its bullish tendencies. Fund families have allowed the public to participate in the high returns available previously only to the rich. Further, some funds, such as Fidelity and Vanguard, have actually beaten the benchmarks. Yet, most studies show the public's performance from holding mutual funds to be inferior to a simple buy-and-hold strategy by a percentage point or two. The $30 billion or $60 billion annual public underperformance in the aggregate is a small price to pay for the benefits of diversification, liquidity, and high return potential that the industry offers.

One objective way of identifying a public is by the returns that are targeted. Horace Lorimer, one of the most sagacious 100-year-old men in my library, gave some benchmarks in 1897 that have stood the test of time:

> You must learn not to overwork a dollar any more than you would a horse. Three percent is a small load for it to draw; six, a safe one; when it pulls in ten for you it's likely working out West and you've got to watch to see that it doesn't buck; when it makes twenty you own a blame good critter or a mighty foolish one, and you want to make dead sure which; but if it draws a hundred it's playing the races or something just as hard on horses and dollars, and the first thing you know you won't have even a carcass to haul to the glue factory.
>
> I dwell a little on this matter of speculation because you've got to live next door to the Board of Trade all your life, and it's a safe thing to know something about a neighbor's dogs before you try to pat them. Sure Things, Straight Tips and Dead Cinches will come running out to meet you, wagging their tails and looking as innocent as if they hadn't just killed a lamb, but they'll bite. The only safe road to follow in speculation leads straight away from the Board of Trade on the dead run.[9]

As Lorimer makes clear, the Boards of Trade of Life are not confined to Chicago. And, in all fairness, I should add that the Chicago Board of Trade is my favorite board, one where the rider can get the best work from his horse of any I have found.

GOVERNMENTAL CONTRIBUTORS

With the regularity of the moon, the government enters the debt market four times a year to raise money to add to and pay off or refund its existing debt. The refundings generally take place in the second week of February, May, August, and November; a short note, a long note, and a bond are auctioned off on successive days.

The feeding habits of the crocodile provide a caution and a lesson, especially for speculators in the market equivalent of the Everglades, the Amazon, or Australia. The crocodile captures prey and doesn't eat again for two weeks. But when the crocodile is hungry, no life smaller than a rhinoceros is safe in its vicinity. Two terrible features add to the crocodile's efficacy. First, it disguises itself as a log, close to the beach, and then sprints at speeds upward of 25 miles an hour to capture its prey. Second, the crocodile has an exquisite memory. It hovers exactly where it last saw potential prey; for this reason, experienced fishermen know never to fish in the same place twice. The crocodile never forgets where it was the last time, and is likely to lie in wait.

The gloom surrounding the government refundings is enough to make a speculator give up the whole ball of wax. First, there is the monkey business about getting Congress to increase the debt limit. Next comes the fear that the Japanese will refuse to buy our debt unless interest rates increase dramatically. Finally, the end-of-the-world stuff: if no provision is made to pay off past debt, the government debt burden will grow unrestricted. Hyperinflation is around the corner, another stock crash is imminent, energy or agriculture prices are going through the roof, and the government dealers themselves have little or no interest in bidding at any price. A government dealer is sure to prepare a sober report noting that, just to pay off existing benefits at present interest rate levels, the government will have to tax more than 80 percent of personal income in the year 2020 and beyond.

As I add the final details to this work, in August 1996, the 30-year refunding has been held and, as if to prove my point, the headline on the Dow Jones newswire has exclaimed, "Central bankers' appetite for U.S. Treasuries may be waning" amid much moaning about the terrible prospects for this auction. A government dealer has been quoted as saying, "The downside is if you don't get their [central bankers'] buying, the Treasury would lose a key area of support and demand would dry up."

Something has to give. And before the gloom can be dispelled, the government must make a substantial contribution of energy to the marketplace.

According to its own balance sheet, our government's borrowing comes to about $4 trillion, or about $15,000 for every living person in the United States. In this unfortunate state of economic malaise, the Japanese are equal to Americans. The selling of the debt provides the market ecosystem with an important input of energy. Fortuitously, by tradition, government dealers agree to bid on the debt without demanding a commission. But by maintaining an inventory in such debt the dealers incur considerable carrying costs. Unless the value of that debt goes up after dealers shell out their capital, the markets will grind to a halt.

And yet, somehow, the government is always able to borrow. Knowing what we do about the loss of energy at each level of the pyramid, it would be surprising indeed if there was not a tendency for that debt to go up in price after the dealers buy it.

The most volatile day of the auction is traditionally the Thursday on which the 30-year debt is marketed. Its importance to the debt market might be compared to the seventh game of the World Series. Table 15–2 contains the moves of bonds relative to the 30-year Treasury auction date for the 27 auctions since the 1987 crash. On average, bonds go down one-third of a point in the three days preceding the auction and back up (one-third of a point) 3 days after (Table 15–2 and Figure 15–3). Such a large differential is significant from a statistical, economic, and ecological viewpoint. The $2/3$-point pick-up on the debt of $60 billion a year provides some $400 million of energy to keep the markets going. This seems like a small price for the government to pay to satisfy its needs.

Ever mindful of the latest trends, the Treasury is constantly reshaping its borrowing mix. It stopped selling 4-year notes in 1990 and 7-year notes in 1993. Since February 9, 1994, the 30-year bond has been offered only twice a year. In 1996, the Treasury has changed the timing of its ten-year auction by adding two special monthly auctions outside the quarterly cycle, presumably making it harder for market participants to lie in wait.

The Primary Consumers

The primary consumers of the "publics" are dealers, banks, and brokerage houses. Year after year, publicly held banks and brokerages report annual profits in the $10 billion range from their foreign exchange and fixed-income trading. Presumably, this is augmented by comparable profits at privately held and nonreporting divisions of larger publicly held entities. Athletes know that the real test of a champ is how well he or she performs on an off day. Bankers Trust showed championship form in 1995, eking out a $900 million profit from its trading operations. This was especially impressive because the bank was recovering from devastating adverse publicity in connection with its 1994 activities.

Some interesting data on foreign exchange revenues of publicly held banks appeared in a Salomon Brothers survey from 1995. Table 15–3 lists the foreign exchange revenues of 22 banks for the years 1991–1994. Just one bank on the survey showed a net loss at any time, namely Bankers Trust, with a $54 million loss in 1994. Typical annual revenues ranged

Table 15-2. Bond Movements Preceding and Following Auctions

Auction Date	Price	Days Preceding Auction					Days Following Auction				
		−10	−5	−3	−2	−1	+1	+2	+3	+5	+10
May 12, 1988	6847	−138	−144	−35	−29	−13	47	25	−78	−131	−143
Aug. 11, 1988	6647	−97	−300	−219	−144	−19	−6	−25	16	3	−19
Nov. 10, 1988	7115	−113	−194	0	−6	19	−59	−22	−28	−147	−191
Feb. 9, 1989	7147	−140	−146	−131	−171	−153	−75	−97	−125	−88	−197
May 11, 1989	7059	−119	−72	−82	12	40	213	213	216	272	372
Aug. 10, 1989	7969	−65	−181	−6	−6	16	−82	−185	−135	−119	−113
Nov. 14, 1989	8131	16	−22	9	−6	−9	31	25	−50	−12	−50
Feb. 8, 1990	7550	−59	−81	10	44	38	115	37	75	0	−63
May 10, 1990	7250	204	151	22	−15	66	156	218	178	150	203
Aug. 9, 1990	7336	−216	−288	53	81	87	−43	−59	−37	−159	−340
Nov. 8, 1990	7389	3	−38	−106	−97	−28	103	194	213	203	288
Feb. 7, 1991	8043	103	141	−12	−41	−50	81	53	66	28	−59
May 9, 1991	7939	18	−85	−4	6	6	−134	−62	−146	−115	−84
Aug. 8, 1991	8027	169	163	10	−53	−53	−13	19	56	125	190
Nov. 7, 1991	8477	150	7	54	119	100	40	56	112	87	−44
Feb. 13, 1992	8561	−91	−150	−119	−122	−110	3	−59	−6	−25	160
May 7, 1992	8580	85	78	47	22	−25	112	118	165	150	162
Aug. 13, 1992	9357	71	46	−69	−113	−116	41	−9	44	66	−62
Nov. 12, 1992	9264	34	116	1848	100	75	0	−6	19	28	−31
Feb. 11, 1993	9814	84	0	−22	−10	72	16	3	50	175	307
May 13, 1993	10202	−44	−175	−178	−159	−103	12	−13	−78	−16	72
Aug. 12, 1993	10883	38	63	0	−12	−28	28	47	19	59	372
Feb. 10, 1994	10995	−225	−144	−28	25	−16	56	0	16	−100	−291
Aug. 11, 1994	9938	−94	−247	−122	−82	−82	72	53	194	66	32
Feb. 9, 1995	10053	178	84	−57	−47	−41	−28	−25	44	88	116
Aug. 10, 1995	10972	−132	−35	−85	−94	−60	−96	−74	−24	−6	76
Feb. 8, 1996	11969	10	−72	10	−6	3	0	90	103	−53	−416
Observations		27	27	27	27	27	27	27	27	27	27
Average Chg.		−13.7	−56.48	−32.30	−29.78	−14.22	21.85	19.07	32.56	19.59	9.15
T Statistic		−0.6	−2.2	−2.03	−2.06	−1.13	1.44	1.08	1.64	0.89	0.23

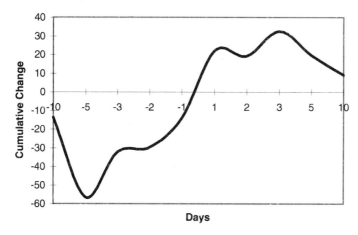

Figure 15-3. Cumulative Bond Movements
Relative to Auction Day

from US$807 million for Credit Suisse Holding to a measly US$75 million for Commerzbank of Germany.

The Financial Times reported that the foreign exchange profits of dealing banks in 1995 was up about one-third from the 1994 levels. The dealing banks are very good at going about their trade and must be compared favorably to such other herbivores as the kangaroo and the bee.

Author and professor Robert Aliber of the University of Chicago, one of the shining lights in foreign exchange, has analyzed the abnormal profits of banks in the foreign exchange markets in recent years. During one of his periodic field trips to dealing banks, he scheduled a visit to my office directly after a bank meeting. But he arrived 15 minutes late, with a poignant reason for his lateness. The chairman of the money center bank he had been visiting had kept him waiting while he, the chairman, negotiated the year-end bonuses of three foreign exchange traders who had made the bank $250 million over the year. Professor Aliber concluded that the foreign exchange profit of money center banks is inordinately large relative to the capital they employ in these activities. He believes these profits compensate dealers for the persistent needs of importers to buy foreign exchange and the eternal desires of hedgers to reduce risk.

Paul DeRosa takes another track. He notes that bonuses to foreign exchange dealers are typically one-fourth the level paid to counterparts in the fixed-income field. He attributes the low ratio to the knowledge of bank managers that it's the system that creates their profits. The two key contributing factors are the wide bid/asked spread and the use of limit and stop orders by slow-moving participants.

Table 15–3. FX Trading Revenues 1991–1994

	$U.S. Million			
	1991	1992	1993	1994
UK				
Barclays	384	510	267	136
HSBC Holdings	528	678	566	525
Lloyds	127	241	174	161
Nat West	239	457	359	286
Germany				
Commerzbank	30	74	75	85
Deutsche Bank	237	242	286	177
Switzerland				
OS Holding	502	626	807	777
Swiss Bk. Corp.	586	669	641	595
Union Bk. Swtz.	545	641	615	522
Netherlands				
ABN Amro	278	357	346	316
United States				
Bank America	246	300	298	237
Bankers Trust	272	331	191	−54
Chase	215	327	356	280
Chemical	289	476	468	222
Citicorp	709	1,005	995	573
First Chicago	95	110	105	42
J.P. Morgan	85	262	179	131
Canada				
Bank of Montreal	118	135	132	110
Bank of Nova Scotia	86	106	112	133
Canadian Imperial	230	266	197	204
Royal Bank	233	246	221	205
Toronto-Dominion	132	134	119	113

Source: Salomon Brothers Inc.

I believe the dealers play the role of the house, in imitation of the casinos in Las Vegas and Atlantic City. In 1995, cash foreign exchange trading amounted to about $1.2 trillion a day in volume—of which approximately one-third involves the public with banks and two-thirds is directly between the banks in the interbank market.

In a typical foreign exchange transaction, a bank will quote a market of $/¥ 100.05/100.15 on 1 billion yen. The banks spread amounts to 0.10 percent, or 10 cents per $100 of each trade. Assuming the orders are balanced, the bank's profit would be one-half the spread on each transaction. Multiplying the figures out, the average amount gained by the bank per year would be:

$$\tfrac{1}{2} \times 0.10\% \times \tfrac{1}{3} \times \$1.2 \text{ trillion} \times 250 \text{ trading days} = \$50 \text{ billion per year}$$

The amazing thing, then, is that reporting banks make *only* $8 billion to $10 billion a year from their foreign exchange business. Assuming that those amounts come to 80 percent of total revenues, the profits come back to a figure close to the amount estimated from the bid/asked spreads. No wonder many holders of foreign exchange do not bother to hedge unless they expect at least a 3 percent move against their holdings.

One factor that tends to enhance the banks' profits is the lack of a central clearing mechanism for foreign exchange. A customer must, for all intents and purposes, exit a position at the same house where the trade was entered. Consequently, the bank always knows which way a customer will go. Because money must be deposited in advance, most customers desire to leave the bank just enough funds to cover the size of their positions. This enables the bank to know which way the customer will go once it has used up its available margin funds. For example, assume a customer with $10 million on deposit, as a 5 percent margin against the value of foreign exchange, holds long positions of $200 million. If the customer asks for a quote, the bank will know he has to sell dollars and will be inclined to quote a bid/asked spread that is biased to a low dollar bid. Customers placed in this position remind me of the ads for the Roach Motel: easy to check in, very tough to check out.

No matter how hard I try to reduce this edge, the banks are always one step ahead of me in closing down the pass. Just before I extricate from a trade I like to call the banks and ask how much I can add to my position. "Victor, why are you going to all this trouble to jerk us around? We know you never add to a winning trade," they say. Somehow, they always know.

However, as in all systems where one species preys on another, there is a constant evolution of the techniques that both groups use to maintain their margin of benefit. One technique the banks utilize with good effect requires that all customers deposit money in advance of a trade, purportedly so the banks will not have any credit risk on the transaction. The banks justify this deposit by alluding to the differences in settlement times and banking hours in various countries when the transactions are settled. In 1974, Bank Herstatt, a small Austrian bank, went bankrupt in the midst of clearing some $700 million in foreign exchange transactions. This risk, called Herstatt risk, has been used ever since as an example of the great risks banks face. Payment up front results in major benefits for the bank. In addition to the Roach Motel bit, the customer's funds can be invested at a profit by the bank, to the extent they earn more in the Fed funds market than they pay as interest.

Customers have their own tricks to balance the equation. One strategy is to unload positions on several banks simultaneously, so that the banks are forced to get out at a loss when the trades start coursing through the system. To prevent this from happening, banks frequently delay making a quote until the other counterparts the customer might be trading with have indicated a direction. "You're in line," I often hear when I have a trade of some real size to do.

On the rare occasions when I am able to get out of a trade with a bank without an immediate loss, I invariably get a call from the sales manager at the bank the next day. "Vic, my dealer complained. We thought we were seeing your whole business. But whenever you call to ask for a quote, we hear your activity with others over the squawk box. We're making you five-point spreads. And we're beginning to wonder why."

"Well, Aziz, the reason is that you make $1 billion a year on transactions like that. You don't hear me complaining about the 90 percent of trades I have a loss on, do you?"

Another technique customers use to maintain the balance is to place trades through brokers to maintain transparency. But the banks have comparable lines with the same brokers. They seem to know after a while exactly who is trading, and what his position is, by the size and style of the trades they receive. To supplement the intuition, most banks also maintain computer programs that indicate the likely direction of each trade and whether the customer tends to be a trend follower, a pyramider, or a stop-loss kind of operator. In the absence of technology, I understand that, in certain markets like the yen, it is customary for all the dealing banks to talk with each other on a daily basis to keep track of who is long and short.

FIXED-INCOME HERBIVORES

Turning to the fixed-income sector, dealers make a comparable bid/asked spread profit. Trading again is on the order of $1 trillion a day. The spread on a typical transaction would be $100^1/_{32}$ to $100^3/_{32}$ or a $^2/_{32}$ spread, which is .0625 percent per $100 item. This is of the same order of magnitude as the 0.10 percent spread on the foreign exchange trade.

Unlike their foreign exchange counterparts, the government dealers do not insist on a "security deposit." Nor is the customer locked into a particular position with a bank; government securities can be delivered against each other at various clearing banks or brokers.

Perhaps because of this lack of edge, government dealers typically refuse to quote a two-way market. The standard patter goes like this:

"Linda, Niederhoffer here; kindly offer $10 million on the long bond."
"We're at $100^{3/32}$."
"I buy."
"Bob [Dealer], you can sell $10 million of the long bond to Niederhoffer."
"That's agreed."

The broker protects himself from being exposed the wrong way on a trade by knowing the customer's direction in advance. Finally, the time between the salesperson's relay of the offer of a trade and the dealer's confirmation that a trade has been made enables the dealer to guard against a move against him during the 10 seconds or so that the trade is open.

To maintain balance, customers often get several dealers on the phone simultaneously. Then they choose the bid or offer that is the best of the competing quotes offered. When I traded for certain big operators, I had a trading room with a dozen direct lines and 20 phones. When we traded, a team of traders would come out with their portables, cellulars, and jerry-built phones, so we could all get quotes simultaneously and hit the brokers before they could react. But the dealers quickly adapted. Before I could utter the words "Kindly bid $100 million bonds, Niederhoffer," I often received a call from my Merrill Lynch broker. Merrill Lynch had heard from its Pittsburgh office that we were in the market selling in volume, and had adjusted the quotes correspondingly.

CARNIVORES—HEDGE FUNDS

We turn to the highest link in the web, the carnivores—the lions, eagles, elephants, and whales. In the market, these top predators are the hedge funds. Mainly raised from wealthy individuals, these funds were said to total $70 billion as of mid-1996. At the top of the heap is the Quantum Fund, which has achieved returns of 35 percent a year for 35 years or so. The sheer size of Quantum is staggering. A $1,000 investment in Quantum in 1962 would have grown to over $1.5 million by 1995, assuming reinvestment of all distributions and no taxes. For each successful hedge fund, of course, there is another that has bombed out. Every year, major hedge funds bite the dust. The survivors then become stronger, and the retrospective returns are seemingly more profitable. The successful funds are much bigger than the unsuccessful ones. According to industry reporting services, hedge funds have averaged 20 percent a year in recent years and are, in aggregate, wildly profitable. Assuming that the combined size of these superpredators is around $70 billion and that they take out 10 percent a year above and beyond a simple buy-and-hold strategy, there is an additional $7 billion a year of energy that must be supplied by the public.

What's the hedge funds' secret, when they can't make it on the bid/asked spread the way the dealers do? Certain naïve commentators attribute the return to a constant interchange between government officials and traders, which seems to mark all the successful funds. It is in the interest of governments to know what the traders are going to do, and vice versa. This helps the successful operators position themselves in the direction of the flow. The big operators look for situations where business, governments, and dealers would benefit from some market event. They then join hands and circle to the left.

Some operators facilitate the interchange with luxurious game-preserve holdings. For those without a game preserve, benefit can be found in the revolving doors of Washington. Legions of former high government officials either work at these firms or provide advisory services. For those too low on the totem pole to compete in this direction, a spouse who works at a central bank or a good friend at the United Nations is always handy. A regularly scheduled tennis game with a central banker or a country president is also helpful. Unfortunately, I own no game farms and my wife is usually busy with four kids. Besides, "Dr." Greenspan's slicing base-line game does not complement a serve-and-volley game like mine.

Yet there is still the difficulty of accounting for how all that information enables the predators to overcome the bid/asked spreads. Certainly the returns have been abetted in recent years by the tendency of hedge funds to borrow short and invest long in equities and debt. During a rising market such leverage works great; but something deeper is going on. Dealers have uncertainty as to the likely variations in the value of the inventory they hold to conduct their business. The uncertainties surround the optimum quantities to hold and the prices to pay and charge. To maintain access to credit, it is helpful for dealers to lay off risk by trading with speculators who are willing to facilitate their hedging. Like insurance companies, some large hedge funds are willing to accept these risks in exchange for a profit. Because dealers generally maintain an inventory of goods to conduct their business, on balance speculators buy goods from dealers. For this, the dealers charge a price.

The ability to conduct their business while remaining insulated from fluctuations in the value of their inventories enables dealers to specialize in the relatively secure activity of capturing spreads rather than speculating on value. Banks and suppliers are willing to provide more credit to dealers who are able to insulate themselves from price fluctuation. Frequently, the dealers can engage in a higher volume and a more profitable business than they could handle if they were not able to lay off their inventory risk. The dealer's total reward as well as the reward per unit of risk is enhanced by the activities of the large hedge funds.

Decomposers

The death and waste products of living things provide resources for decomposers. The most common decomposers are bacteria, fungi, worms, mites, snails, crows, and hyenas. In most ecosystems, the number of species specializing in decomposing is considerably greater than the number involved at the producer and consumer levels. Ecologists applaud the action of decomposers. For example, Darwin figured with ebullience that the earthworms near his house formed a new layer of soil seven inches deep every thirty years.

Brokers play the decomposer role in the market ecosystem. They break orders into digestible sizes. The three main categories of broker-decomposers correspond to the stage an order is in. Commission house brokers solicit the order, floor traders digest it, and then bankruptcy specialists come in and recycle the carcass or contract, before or after bankruptcy.

The commission house specializes in introducing public customers and hedgers to the market and in communicating orders to other reducing agents in the pits. Total brokerage commissions on individual stocks was estimated at $5 billion in 1995. For their services, most brokers provide a flow of information about the market and 24-hour access to the floor. I pay particular attention to the earnings all-stars and the supply/demand estimates of brokerage house analysts. These help me explain my losses when I go astray.

The major decomposer group, the members of the major commodity exchanges, digest the order once it is sent to the pits. They number over 5,000 in the United States alone. The legends of BMWs, gold Rolexes, yachts, and the tens of millions of dollars taken out annually by large floor traders are recounted frequently enough to have a ring of plausibility. The value of the seats (memberships), as shown below, proves that there is good money to be made in these roles:

Exchange	No. of Seats	Seat Value, Mid-1996,* in Millions
CME	625	$0.6
CBOT	3,661	0.6
NYMEX	816	0.4
NYSE	1,366	1.2

*Midpoint of bid/asked spread.

Most broker remuneration comes from the bid/asked spread. Both Chicago exchanges report volume in 1996 of about 1 million contracts a day. Assume that the total volume of transactions on all U.S. exchanges is 3 million contracts daily. Let's say one-third of these are between the public and a member, and the rest are member-to-member. The average spread on a commodities trade is approximately one-tenth of a point on the S&P, or $50 a contract. Half of this is the vig. With 250 trading days in a year, I calculate the vigorish as:

$$3 \text{ million} \times \tfrac{1}{3} \times 250 \times \$25 = \$6.25 \text{ billion a year}$$

This figure is about half the take by foreign exchange dealers, government dealers, and hedge funds.

As of mid-1996, the price of seats on the Chicago Mercantile Exchange had fallen about 40 percent from the highs just one year earlier. The vig must be going down at a vigorous rate.

Floor trader profits represent the reverse side of the losses on slippage by the public. The flow of funds between the two groups is enhanced by certain diabolical tendencies that prices seem to have: they go to the worst possible levels of the day when public activity is at its highest point. It is uncanny how often prices move to their lowest levels when the public is most vehement about selling, and vice versa. Furthermore, prices have a way of moving to levels that are designed to scare traders out of a good position just before moving to a level that would have generated a substantial profit. These tendencies, in aggregate, account for the amounts that reducers take out over and above the bid/asked spread. The public thinks of these losses as slippage.

Like the other groups, reducers also attempt to become more efficient at pursuing profits at the expense of others. Books have been written on bagging trades, front-running, running stops, excessive spreads, and so on, since at least 1660.

Some decomposers are not content to recycle nonliving things. Certain fungi, including porcelain fungus and ferns such as mycorrhizae, grow on living things. There is beauty in the specialized and efficient way in which each living thing fulfills its role in the grand design, but I object when I find my counterparts decomposing my chips and body while I am still alive.

I became a meal for my formerly grateful and deferential counterparts at the height of my losses during the March 1995 dollar:yen debacle. Into my parlor and over my phone came a variety of organisms that rushed to prey on my body. First, my friends called to report rumors that I was in trouble. Next, my brokers called to increase my margin and to urgently demand immediate payment of the paper loss on my holdings at the lowest point they had reached during the fraction of a second they were against me the worst. Then, broker after broker called to review my current financial condition and to reduce my credit. Finally, my bankers called to register their concern and demand repayment of all outstanding loan balances. Shortly thereafter, they reduced my line of credit by 50 percent. The vultures were circling and the maggots were all over my body even while I was still alive.

As the market dropped, my weak customers called to ask: "What is your plan? Where is your stop loss?" "They put so much pressure on me," I told my brother Roy, "I could hardly think straight. Did you have any problems like that?"

"With me, they were in my office, monitoring my positions," he said.

During the midst of the carnage, I received a call from the leading weekly covering my industry. Before running the story, they wanted to confirm a rumor that I had gone under. I was able to persuade them that I was viable, despite the 50 percent loss in assets under management that my firm had suffered. I stated that I had just had 16 consecutive, highly profitable months and was entitled to one losing month. "Even the Harlem Globetrotters lose once every 25 years or so," I said, trying to adopt a populist note. But they ran the story anyway. For ten weeks, it was nip and tuck, especially when my clearing bank got wind of the article and pulled my firm's credit.

When death-row inmates are marched from one activity to another, all the other convicts chant, "Dead men coming." I thought I heard this chant over Reuters, Telerate, and the Internet as I monitored the carnage.

After eight years without a loss, Capablanca, the chess wizard, lost a game to Richard Reti in the New York International Tournament in 1924. There was stunned silence, then wild applause. "Soon the news traveled to every chess player on the continent. Reti was king of the hour. Such moments are to chess players what the flush of victory is to generals in the field," the tournament book proclaims. Yet, Capa came back and was undefeated in the rest of the tournament. Similarly, I came back after my March debacle, finishing down only 3 percent on the month and gaining over 60 percent in the next 12 months.

Paul DeRosa, the one speculator I would put in a class equal to Soros, was also going through a period of drastic decline. His funds managed a drawdown of 60 percent from a high in January 1995 to a low in June 1995. "I managed to make several hundred million for my friends and partners over the previous five years, and no one contacted me. But as soon as I dropped about a fifth of this, every newspaper and wire service in the country wanted to parade my losses on their pages. Where were they before?" he wrote me.

I am a loyal friend. When he was down in the dumps, I came in, accounting for 20 percent of his fund assets in one hard moment. He recouped in July. He told me he was inspired by following a friend playing in the U.S. Open. After several bogeys in a row, the player hit an errant tee shot so far right that he hit a provisional ball in case the first was hopelessly lost. When he finally found his original tee shot (with the help of half the gallery and a USGA official), he was blocked out by a towering wall of trees and buried deep in the punishing Shinnecock Hills rough. Despite his unenviable predicament, the amateur fought back! He muscled an improbable sand wedge over the trees and then bounced a three wood onto the front fringe before holing the chip for a miraculous par four. Somehow, with a combination of grit, patience, and a little luck, he scrambled around, gained back several shots, and wound up with a very respectable 71, just a few shots behind the leaders in the world's most difficult golf tournament.

Fortunately, three of five games take the laurels in squash. When I lost the first, I often heard ecstatic cheering for my opponent, the same way I hear it when other top traders have a losing quarter. But by the end of the match, the cheering had a tendency to turn into grave frowns, furrowed brows, shaking of the head, and muttering of, "that lousy Niederhoffer."

There is a majesty and horrible efficiency in the speed with which vultures, crows, and worms recycle nutrients and minerals trapped in the vegetable and animal world. Knowing of the recycling chain, I try to prepare in advance to move away before I get eaten. Better not to march on death row in the first place.

However, in my illustrious career, I was unfortunately thought to be "condemned" once before. During the aftermath of the 1987 stock market crash, I sold some bonds short against futures I owned. But futures closed limit up several days in a row, preventing me from offsetting my cash position with the matching futures. Although I had been a preferred client for seven years, trading tens of billions of dollars to our mutual profit over that time, the prestigious publicly held investment bank that facilitated the trade threatened me with bankruptcy proceedings and attachment of my assets unless I covered immediately. I was able to pay them off in one or two days. But, to be spiteful, I sent them a check instead of wiring them the funds. I learned from the saleswoman handling the account that the president of the bank had personally decreed that I subsequently be blackballed. Since then, that bank has had many presidents. And, in the intervening eight years, I have received numerous calls from its sales force suggesting that I open an account with them. "You'd better check your blackball list. I'm forbidden to enter your august club," I advise them.

RULES AND REGULATIONS

Seemingly disparate phenomena become all too clear within the market ecosystem model. Margin requirements play an important role in keeping the wheels of futures commerce turning. The legendary swiftness with which large amounts of money can be made or lost in futures trading is primarily a function of the relatively low margin requirements in these markets. The minimum margin requirement in the stock markets is now 50 percent; in the various commodity markets, margin requirements generally lie in the range of 2 percent to 10 percent. These margins are set by the various independent commodity exchanges and their clearing firms, with oversight from the Commodity Futures Trading Commissions (CFTC) and National Futures Association (NFA).

Determining the margin requirements in a given market requires the wisdom of Solomon. The calculation must be consistent with the survival of the exchanges. The margins must be low enough to encourage the public to turn over its trades with sufficient velocity to provide the vig that the web needs to operate on. They must also be low enough so that, when the public cries uncle—"Get me out of the position right now!"—the exchange members can feed on the slippage—another profit center.

The exchanges walk a tightrope. Margins cannot be too high, or new players will be discouraged from entering the system. But if margins are too low, players will be tempted to overtrade, thereby bankrupting themselves too frequently, with the result that they will not return to the game. When margins are set at, say, 1 percent, a 1 percent move in prices will either double your money or wipe you out. That's too much risk for a one-day bet. The average customer is not too enthusiastic about the prospect of coming up with another $100,000 or so after seeing his life savings go down the drain in a one-day move exacerbated by margin liquidations.

Margin also plays an important role in protecting members against their customers' bad debts. It has been the industry's unfortunate experience that a customer who suffers a complete loss has a tendency to walk away from the debt knowing that, except in the most egregious cases, it will not be worth the member firm's while to chase after the money owed. Price limits and marking to market help ensure that customers stay in the game and help the members collect on losses before the situation gets out of hand.

One of the virtues of the minimum 50 percent margin requirement for the public in the stock market is to make most stock market investors long-term holders. The turnover of stocks on the NYSE is less than 100 percent a year, and institutions seem to have a higher turnover than the average member of the public. As a result, margin liquidations, gamblers' ruin, excessive trading, bandwagon psychology, brokers' maneuvers, and the host of other factors that cause the public to get eaten in the futures and foreign exchange markets, operate to a much lesser extent in the stock market.

Maintaining Rent

Other exchange rules are designed to maintain an orderly fulfillment of the public's role. For example, most exchanges have rules prohibiting participants from crossing a trade directly. An exchange member must be a counterparty to each trade. Thus, it's guaranteed that the public participant must pay a bid/asked spread. The one major exception to this rule is the opening and close on a Nikkei stock market contract traded on the

Osaka Stock Exchange. But the mandatory minimum commissions there are so high that they more than compensate for the vanishing bid/asked spread. Stock markets have traditionally allowed the public to trade at the opening with others at an opening price. When my volume is small relative to others, I invariably trade individual stocks at the opening.

Some of the more famous guidelines that traders are taught from day one are now seen in proper perspective. "Limit your losses with the use of stops" is the gist of rule number 1. It hurts, but it's much less painful than ruin—or so goes the explanation. Variants of this rule include: "Bulls make money; bears make money; but pigs get slaughtered," "Cut your losses short," "Don't fight the trend," and the related "Always trade at the market." The rule may or may not have intrinsic value, but it surely encourages maximal turnover and minimal credit losses for brokers.

The use of stops makes a certain amount of common sense. It also enables the reducers on the floor to make some money by moving prices to levels where stop orders will be triggered, a technique known as "running the stops." When you are "stopped out," you will take your losses at an "acceptable level" that has been predetermined so your brokers will be protected against your being a credit risk.

I have never used stops, even to bail myself out. Somehow, having a fixed rule to exit provides my adversaries too great an advantage. It would be the equivalent of automatically defaulting in a game if an opponent hits a series of good shots. A proper alternative to the use of stops is to trade with a low enough percentage of money at risk so that disaster won't knock at the door.

PUBLIC'S BULLISHNESS

The public has a psychological predisposition to take the bullish side of trades. This is especially true for new entrants in the market, almost all of whom prefer the long side. Why this is so is a matter of academic debate. Some believe it is a function of a perennially hopeful, optimistic bias, and that hope is emotionally correlated with an expectation of a rising price. It is also possible, however, to see the long-position bias as a function of a predisposition to "ownership." Going short in the stock market is a high-friction transaction: borrowing costs, dividend payouts, and the concomitant difficulty of borrowing thinly traded stocks are involved. Even more important, it is difficult for the amateur investor to get comfortable with the idea of selling short. Selling something you do not own has something of the arcane, not to say the sinister, about it. The existence, in the over-the-counter stock market, of a "Short-Busters Club," which sells itself as a sort of righteous, crusaders-against-evil type of organization, testifies to the emotional bias against selling short.

THE GOLD ROLLER COASTER

In late 1979 and 1980, a terrible thing happened to the dynamics of the system. Gold and silver went up and up; gold advanced steadily from $300 to $800 an ounce, and silver advanced from $5.00 to $50.00 an ounce. This was good for inflation bugs, hard-money types, and survivalists, all of whom were in their heyday (and still live on in vestigial form in certain publications). But it was terrible news for the locals. Prices went up so fast they never had a chance to get out of their short positions at a profit.

Hedgers who owned gold and silver found themselves in a similar predicament. They usually sell futures against the physical metal holdings they might be in the process of refining or selling. If futures prices move against them, they must pony up more margin, but there is not a comparable increase in the credit they receive for holding their physical goods. To make matters worse, many hedgers were holding their inventory in a form that could not be delivered against their short positions in futures.

In July 1995, I had dinner with Dr. Henry Jarecki, one of the two or three largest hedgers in the world at the time of the 1980 run-up in gold and silver prices. Dr. Jarecki informed me that he often had to ante up $10 million a day in additional margin just to carry his hedges during the run-up. (Fortunately, a chance meeting with a banker hungry for business at the height of the crisis resolved the problem.) His mother-in-law turned out to be an old Brighton Beach resident who knew my father well. We made a cellular call to her from the restaurant. "Oh, yes, Artie the cop. He was a great guy. Very smart. Blond hair. Played tennis beautifully. Became a professor. Had three kids. But one of them became a commodities gambler."

Hedgers generally had access to credit and were able to survive the run-up, but such was not the case for many of the exchange members. On the Chicago Mercantile Exchange and the New York COMEX, some exchange members faced total ruin as their short positions in silver, taken on in the normal course of market making, reached hundreds of millions of dollars in deficit. The CME and the COMEX, attributing the rise to manipulation by the Hunt family, finally broke the back of the bull market by decreeing one day that it would no longer be permissible to buy gold and silver futures except as a short-covering transaction. In other words, it became illegal to become a "new" buyer of silver futures. This is a difficult road for a bull to travel. Usually, it takes both buying and selling to keep things in balance.

Immediately following the decree, the price of silver collapsed, opening "limit down" day after day and taking gold along with it. Exchange members were bailed out. The Hunts were hoist with their own petard. Not only did they suffer ruinous losses on their silver positions, but they were subsequently sued for market manipulation and violation of position limits. They eventually settled for $400 million. Another consequence, however, was that the public was so traumatized by its losses on its long metals positions that now, more than 15 years later, investors are still licking their wounds. The Chicago metals market, which used to trade 50,000 contracts a day, is now virtually nonexistent. Silver has fallen to as low as 7 percent of its former high. And gold trades listlessly at around $390 an ounce, give or take $20, for years at a time.

In an interesting ironic twist, the COMEX and its board members were sued by all parties. The longs sued because the Exchange had banned buying. The shorts sued because the Exchange hadn't acted fast enough. I was short silver throughout the entire run-up and lost a few million in the process. I would have been entitled to a refund of about one-third of my losses as my share of the settlement, but I had been so disgusted with the whole situation that I had thrown out my records about seven years after the fact and couldn't find anything to offer as substitute proof. To compound the problem, my accountants had filed for bankruptcy and lost their records as well. If you have a big loss as a speculator, I advise you to keep those records for a long, long time. You never know where the dust will settle.

History has a way of repeating itself. In the autumn of 1993, the copper market rose on the London Metal Exchange (LME). According to one rumor, a squeeze had been orchestrated by one of the largest Japanese trading firms. The Exchange, in its wisdom, saw absolution. It placed a limit on the amount by which a near-month contract in copper could exceed the next distant month's contract. David King, the chief executive of the LME, when questioned on the tactic, was quoted as replying irritably: "It's got nothing to do with protecting anybody. . . . Obviously, the fact that LME contracts are used as the global reference price does place an additional obligation on us to ensure as much as possible that . . . prices are in line with what one expects them to be."[10]

This explanation seemed adequate until May 1996, when copper stood at $1.30 a pound. But several large carnivores didn't believe that the supply-and-demand situation warranted such a price. Their short selling brought about the disclosure of the Sumitomo Corporation's $2.6 billion loss from rogue trader Hamanaka, and a decline in the price of copper by 40 percent in the next month. Several months before, Sumitomo's chairman had referred to Mr. Hamanaka (Mr. Copper) as "the most honest person I have ever met." There is just concern in the industry that the reforms emerging from this disaster—such as requiring more margin—may cripple trading.

COMPETITIVE EXCLUSION

The determinants of the fluctuations in the number of predators and prey form the heart of most textbooks on ecology. Graphic methods are typically used to solve simultaneous differential equations covering the effects of numbers, the growth rates, and the carrying capacity of the environment. One conclusion is called the Principle of Competitive Exclusion. No two species with similar styles can occupy the same niche, nor can two species that are completely competitive coexist. Examples of fruit flies or paramecia grown together in a culture provide a laboratory verification of this principle. The inability of two completely competitive markets to coexist, such as Chicago and New York gold, or CBOT stock futures and IMM stock futures, provides empirical confirmation in the market.

A little manipulation of the parameters in the equation invariably leads to a related conclusion. Coexistence is possible by segregation into separate niches. The usual example used here is the coexistence of giraffes, which eat the leaves of trees, and grass-eating wildebeests in the African Serengeti. In markets, the niches are so specialized that it would take a whole book to describe them adequately. The biggest contracts in the world—Treasury bonds on the CBOT, and Eurodollar futures on the IMM—are traded just seven blocks from each other. One is determined by a three-month rate, and the other by a 30-year rate. Yet, they move tick for tick with each other 24 hours a day, thereby providing a nice real-life example of finding the proper niche.

Studies of such principles and of corresponding examples lead to the formulation of certain basic questions. For instance: How do plant and animal relations determine distribution and abundance? What keeps such a structure going, maintaining it in balance and preventing it from self-destructing in markets? Without attempting to develop an elaborate model, it would seem apparent that a constant stream of new matter or money must be provided by the producer organisms at the base of the pyramid so that each higher level of the pyramid can pay for its activities and growth.

At any given level of the pyramid, the players cannot maintain themselves unless net money coming in at least equals net money going out. Huge costs are involved in maintaining the physical environment within which the players ply their trade.

The public is the basic producer that must provide this new energy. There must be a constant stream of new members coming back to take up the slack caused by those who have fallen. Their net contributions each year must provide not only the costs of running the system, but the profits that the higher levels take out. The consumers (banks, hedge funds, brokerages) must not be greedy, however. They cannot take out a greater proportion of the public's resources than can be refreshed from new entrants. Otherwise, the system will diminish its own food supply and hinder itself through excessive competition, which, in extreme cases, can lead to extinction. We thus see that, in market webs as in all such webs, there is a close commonality of interest between predators and prey.

Homeostatic Functions

How is the harmony of such interests maintained? One of the common features that all life possesses is a mechanism for maintaining orderly conditions. This tendency is called homeostasis. In system theory, it is called negative feedback. Standard college textbooks on biology, such as Beck and Liem's *Life*, devote a few hundred pages to homeostatic and negative feedback mechanisms, treating the subject with the same attention they give to the biochemical and cellular bases of life, and the biology of organisms and populations. They show that every function of the living organism can be understood as performing this dampening function on the influences of the environment. Furthermore, even when not subjected to environmental changes, these systems must be working to maintain constancy.

> Metabolism converts nutrients into available energy or building blocks. Excretory organs separate the unwanted by-products of metabolism which they eliminate from useful materials, which they retain. The status quo, especially of chemical composition, is thereby preserved. In death, homeostatic mechanisms have been overwhelmed.
>
> The concept of homeostasis is a great central idea of biology. It permeates every aspect of biological organization.[11]

The immune system is the defense mechanism that neutralizes invasion by foreign micro-organisms. The purpose of the excretory system is to remove waste that would upset the chemical balance of the body. In the field of markets, Exchange officials and commodity regulatory agencies such as the CFTC and NFA provide a function similar to that of the white blood cells, which find foreign bodies and identify them for the leukocytes to kill. (We will not compare this latter group to market participants here.)

A common homeostatic behavior in humans is temperature regulation. If the temperature rises above the 98.6°F optimum for normal human activity, sensors on the skin detect it and signal the brain that a rise has occurred. The brain relays the information to the effectors that increase blood flow to the skin. This induces perspiration. The loss in heat, caused by evaporation, lowers the body temperature. When the body cools below a certain point, a comparable mechanism is set off, this time reducing blood flow and causing shivering. This activity generates heat through physical activity, thus raising the body temperature.

In markets, the role of temperature is played by price moves in other markets. These provide negative feedback to bring the offending price back into its equilibrium level. The situation is complicated by price followers. Should price move a certain amount from equilibrium, followers are likely to take speculative positions in the direction of the move from equilibrium. This provides a positive feedback that increases the movement away from the old levels. When these moves bring price to a level unwarranted by relative scarcities, it is the function of the moves in other markets to bring the offending market into equilibrium. The problem is that nobody knows what the equilibrium level is until at least the morning after the fact.

Federal Reserve Chairman Alan Greenspan and ex-Governor Wayne Angell have made much of the signaling function of gold. If gold goes up too much, the Fed knows it has to slam on the brakes to keep the inflationary temperature down. At the annual COMEX dinner I attended in 1992, I heard then-Governor Angell (who has since departed the Fed for greener pastures at Bear Stearns) describe how his first desire would be to fix the price of gold at a permanently low level by central bank sales whenever it rose above $350. But he gave up the idea (wild applause) because gold's homeostatic function would be ruined. The abject deference the Governor enjoyed at the dinner, while he floated a trial balloon that would have ruined the livelihood of the 1,000 or so attendees, was a testament to the monstrous control that governments exert over business through their affiliates such as the Fed and certain other three-letter agencies.

Soros loses no opportunity these days to disseminate his view that markets can, on occasion, be destabilized by the activities of speculators. He calls for the creation of a new "World Organization" to regulate such activities. This thesis was first stated in *The Alchemy of Finance*, where he lists examples of positive feedback in his experience, when prices continued to diverge from some norm as information concerning these divergences triggered other reactions that, in turn, added fuel to the fire.

Positive feedback can certainly occur. Richard Dawkins, for example, has a chapter in *The Blind Watchmaker* on such explosion in brawls, world conflicts, and nature, showing how the tail of the peacock probably evolved through a variant of positive feedback. Larger tails are preferred by females, so males with larger tails reproduce with greater success. The trait of having large tails became more prevalent as the gene pools of both sexes began to reflect this sexual preference. The average tail length is a "compromise between utilitarian selection tending to make tails shorter (for longer flight) and sexual selection tending to make them longer."[12]

Even within the body, with all its homeostatic mechanisms, the balancing process breaks down if the temperature strays too far from the 98.6° norm. If body temperature rises above 105°, for example, the metabolism speeds up. This generates intense heat, and the process can progress faster than the body's ability to cool itself, thereby leading to heat stroke and death. This is why I make my kids get out of the Jacuzzi after a few minutes. Similarly, low temperature can slow the metabolism, leading to decreases in temperature until death from hypothermia occurs.

The activities of trend-following funds, using stops to protect themselves, and of dealers hedging their options exposure, can lead to moves that temporarily accent the original move away from equilibrium. But just as the body is organized by a myriad of homeostatic negative feedback activities, so the markets are balanced by the harmonizing influences of other markets. Speculators observing these relations directly or indirectly use these moves to bring markets back to proper levels. If such speculators tend to lose by these activities, they will not prosper or reproduce.

There is a reason that homeostasis or negative feedback predominates in all natural and human ecosystems. Most living things function at or near their optimum levels. Controlled regulation within this range is highly useful. The interacting markets and the activities of contrarians or value investors are the main forces for homeostasis in markets. Let those who would seek to substitute a supranational hand into the equation ponder Darwin's noble thought:

> It is good thus to try in imagination to give any one species an advantage over another. Probably in no instance should we know what to do. This ought to convince us of our ignorance on the mutual relations of all organic beings, a conviction as necessary as it is difficult to acquire.[13]

"The Secretary of the Treasury did it."

Finale

―――――――・◆・――――――

Take account of ecology. Where does the other side live? What does he eat? Does he respond best to slow or fast lures? Always consider the rhythms. Try to synchronize your activities with how fast or slow the currents are moving.

Everything is hooked together. To get good results, pay attention to language, science, economics, literature, religion, and art. Remember Hamlet, "A man may fish with the worm that hath eat of a king and eat of the fish that hath fed of that worm."

If you must know how good you are, enter a contest or tournament, but remember that completely different techniques are appropriate here from those that win in the normal day-to-day fray. The winner of a contest has nothing to lose and therefore takes much more risk than would be appropriate for you or I even to consider in the usual course of events.

Above all, be a contrarian. Once you hit a winner you're very unlikely to find a winner in that same place. The best fish swim deep and all fish are not caught with the same flies.

Everything is affected by the weather. When the moon is full the easiest pickings are often nearest at hand. The wind is your friend but often the direction of the wind changes the play and the response of the prey.

The weakest prey are the easiest to catch. When you see red on the battlefield, prepare to reel in the biggest winners.

Stay calm. Keep your emotions in check. A loud voice can upset your concentration and give away your position. The time for exhilaration is after you've bagged the winner and you've gone home to reflect on what you did right or wrong. Adapt a scientific approach. Keep records of what's working and what's not. Once you analyze the record you will be able to see what changes have the best likelihood of success. Especially if you're doing badly, change something. Try another tack—change your bait. But be humble enough to know that there are many others better than you at the game and try to learn from these legends. Many of the greats offer seminars for "reasonable" fees and are happy to share their wisdom with you.

The cycles are always changing. Winning techniques for the morning are completely different from those at noon or the close.

When I read the likes of this guidance, my first reaction was despair. My god, someone beat me to the punch. All my best insights have been discovered by others and disseminated widely to the public in books already available at my local bookstore.

But then I realized that these insights were not about speculative market angles but angling recommendations on how best to catch fish. It would appear that fishing techniques, and fish themselves, in fact, offer lessons for the speculator.

Steve Stigler, the statistical consultant to my speculation business, shared what he called a "Galtonian flavored" Texas government study, "Heritability of Angling Vulnerability in Large Mouth Bass," which he felt would help me become a better speculator. You've probably noticed that you get different results after the trend followers have made money a few months in a row. Well, this fish experiment will give you some insight.

The study Steve sent had segregated bass caught three or more times with artificial lures (and therefore considered to be from vulnerable stock—represented by the grey bars in the chart) from those not caught at all (those with a more wary disposition, represented by the dark bars).

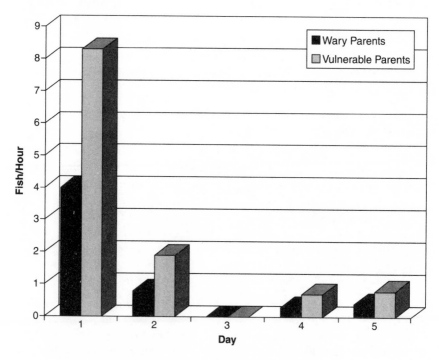

Angling Vulnerability of Largemouth Bass

Fishing on Wall Street—the intrepid fisherman.

When the two groups were allowed to spawn, the offspring of the vulnerable parents were caught twice as often as those from the wary parents. The study concludes:

> Where it is desirable to maximize catch rates, such as catch-and-release fisheries or urban fishing programs for the disabled, stocking large mouth bass with high angling vulnerability would obviously be beneficial.[1]

Without in any way meaning to denigrate the compassion of such an intervention, I am going to write my Congressional Representative a letter demanding passage of a law to compensate victims of vulnerable parents such as mine.

SOME BRIGHTON BARGAINS

Grandpa Martin was the world's worst bargainer. He once came uncomfortably close to buying the Brooklyn Bridge, so to speak. When he was running the family fruit business, two businessmen from the "Grand Central Development Authority" approached him with a top-secret proposition. The management of Grand Central Terminal had decided to close the information booth. Why take up all that valuable floor space when the ticket agents could answer questions? So as not to create a public protest, the change was to take place quietly over a weekend. If Martin would deposit $25,000 in cash with them, the franchise space was the Niederhoffers'. Think of the throngs of hungry commuters who would converge on their store each day. Fortunately, the family was able to pay only the finder's fee and thereby avoided the con.

In a testament to "There's a sucker born every minute," the crooks found a gullible customer willing to pay an even higher price—$100,000! It was not a pretty scene when a pair of brothers in the fruit and vegetable business showed up at Grand Central Station the day after handing over their life savings. Lumber and tools in hand, they had come to build shelves for the nectarines, lettuce, garlic, tomatoes, and so on. The inevitable followed: the cops had to show the brothers the way out. It's not easy to admit you've been conned. The brothers showed up every day for years afterward, shaking their fists and screaming at the clerks inside the information booth. They became a regular attraction for out-of-towners and a passing amusement for commuters.

Artie closely vied with Martin for the bad bargainer title. We would frequent Katz's Delicatessen, the largest in the world, at Houston and Ludlow. Police officers have generally received "most favored customer" status at restaurants, coffee shops, and the like, because their presence helps to maintain security. Ruby, a retired policeman who manned the cash register, adjusted tickets accordingly.

My father's partner, Miltie, finishes a big meal and walks right past Ruby without paying. In hand he has an additional two dozen franks and a pound of pastrami to go. As he reaches the door, Ruby offers yet more, "Hey, Miltie, take this salami for your son in Korea too."

My dad and I follow on the heels of Miltie and present our check to Ruby. "What did you have?" he asks. "Well," my dad answers, "we had a couple of corned beef sandwiches with french fries, a coke, and a coffee. It was great. The fries were nice and hot."

"That'll be $2.80."

"$2.80?" Dad asks incredulously, pointing to the salami tucked under Miltie's arm.

"Oh, I'm sorry, you're right," Ruby replies. "I forgot the coffee. That'll be $2.90."

My father was a born loser in business. And he knew it.

Artie was uncomfortable with the higgledy-piggledy of the market. He never bargained for an item. Whatever the stated asking price, he paid it, no questions asked. And if the product was defective, the meal less than satisfactory—well, "Buyer beware." "So what of it; I bought it. We'll know to keep the Hades away from that store next time," he would say.

Unfortunately, I inherited Dad's reluctance. Perhaps my insecurity in asking for a price reduction was more out of a fear of being told "no"—that same kind of "no" I feared when I asked a girl for a date when I was young—than from a taboo or higher value that prevented my dad from bargaining. I carried this defect with me for years, well into adulthood. In one painfully memorable incident, I found that my reticence probably cost me $15 million. When I started my business in 1965, my partners asked what split I proposed. I was ashamed to ask for the 90 percent I believed I was entitled to and could have copped as the only full-time employee. I said, "How about equal?"

A bad bargain in fruit stands.

I now make it a practice to bargain for everything. I am not able to maintain one persona in business negotiations and another in my personal spending habits. Thus, it helps to practice in the personal arena what I must perfect in the business field. If the speculator is not able to bargain for the best deal, I would advise that he ask a trusted friend to carry the ball.

Bargaining is a way of life for many merchants. The very idea of their asking price not being subject to change is ludicrous to them. Business is based on a series of mutually beneficial transactions between consumer and purveyor. It's perfectly proper to state your wishes and estimate the degree of benefit (the price) that fits your resources at the moment. As soon as I ask a merchant for a price, I now add the word "asking" just a nanosecond after he states the price.

Then I follow with "That's a little over my budget. Is there any adjustment possible for cash or a quantity purchase?" If I'm in a hurry, I simply say, "What's the best dealer price on this?" If the owner appears pious, I look dolorously at him and say, "Look, we're both in the same boat. What do you need on this?" Sometimes I cannot refrain from smiling as the words slip out. As a result, I've averaged about 50 percent off retail, with not a single purchase at less than 10 percent off, on virtually all the items I've purchased from owner-operated establishments. These negotiations provide me with practice for my own business, where I must ask for and receive a tighter spread in order to survive. Hopefully, I've also paved the road for subsequent customers who won't be considered quite as naïve a class. Best of all, I haven't ruined the game for the merchant or me.

In asking for a market quote, I make it a general practice, well before I trade, to contact several dealers to see which way they are leaning. Information is unfortunately subject to the law of diminishing returns. If you're looking for the best price on a car, there's a point at which prices converge. In the markets, after you've heard from the third dealer, there is little to gain in the narrowing of the bid/asked spread. When I've called my third dealer, I'm ready for a little judo. Dealers like to trade against me once they know which way I'm leaning. I let them do it. If I'm planning to sell now, I'll leave a limit order to buy on their books, and vice versa. For example, if the current bond price is 101.08 and I intend to sell at 101.31, I will leave an order to buy at 101.01. "Now, don't read me," I add. This puts them in a frame of mind that is beneficial to me; they are good at putting two and two together. Next, I simultaneously call several dealers to get a market. I ask each to tighten the quotes, never accepting too wide a spread even if the bid price proposed by one of them is better than any competing price. Finally, I choose the best of the lot. This process takes about two seconds. It's the little things you do that add up to victory. I figure that the extra $\frac{1}{100}$ of 1 percent I save in face value on each transaction by this process is good for at least 50 percent of my total profits over the course of an average year.

A Modern Panic

As I put the final touches on this book amid a stinging rebuke from my beleaguered editor, another panic has occurred on Wall Street. This was certainly one of the most widely advertised in history. One magazine after another weighed in before the fall with early July articles anticipating a panic in the stock market. That's always the signal for me to take out my buying crutches.

It didn't hit 10 percent on a close-to-close basis, but on Tuesday, July 16, 1996—a record-breaking day for stocks, with 688 million shares exchanging hands on the NYSE alone—shouts of "It's down 10!!" resounded all around the big bearish trading floors. The S&P dropped to a low of 601.25, 11 percent lower than its close of 675.88 on July 1, just ten trading days earlier. During that same day, the NASDAQ index fell 57.08 points from its high of 1065.33 to 1008.25, a gnat's eyelash above the round number of 1000, and fully 19 percent below its May 31 close. In one horrible 45-minute period, the S&P futures dove from 625 to 610.25, 10.4 percent below the July 1 close, as technology mutual funds, finding that there were no buyers of individual common stocks at any price, sold index futures to achieve liquidity. Supposedly sophisticated mutual funds have now replaced the famously maladroit odd-lot short sellers as the bellwether of excessive selling.

Global Bourses were hammered in sympathy. Australia and Thailand hit new eight-month lows, and almost all others declined at least 2 percent on Tuesday. The tornado in New York had not yet even begun. If that wasn't a panic, then Jesse Livermore never went belly up.

The funnels of particularly violent tornadoes have been known to pluck the feathers off chickens. The July 16, 1996, stock market tornado and its aftermath did equivalent damage to technology stockholders. Many of the tech superstars, such as America Online, Ascend, and Iomega, dropped 10 to 20 percent from the open to 1:30 P.M., only to close up on the day when the funnel spun off. Motley Fool favorite Iomega was representative, falling 20 percent during the day to 19⅞. It was continuing a 63 percent decline from its high seven weeks earlier, despite the heroic efforts of chat line users with portable computers and cellular modems advising calm in the midst of the storm. Advice to hold on from someone holding a large block of stock is always suspect, particularly during a tornado.

Mutual funds also rode the violent roller coaster. The major fund families activated their emergency 24-hour phone crews to calm panicked investors. Equity fund redemptions reached a record level.

During the height of the vortex, I managed to lose 15 percent of my assets in one hour, without the benefit of any "Steady as you go" from my colleagues. Horrible rumors reached the Street that I was in deep trouble. "You should be in trouble like I am," I told my brokers when they requested extra margin. With a cravenness all too typical of those who make a practice of jumping in over their head, I desperately closed my positions out at break-even after the Dow rallied 200 points in an hour. Then, the Dow rallied another 50 points after I sold.

After the damage was done, reports in the major newspapers referred to Tuesday's action as a massacre, a murder, a bloodbath, a butchering, a rout, a black hole, a deep plunge, an unmitigated disaster. Comparisons were made to unmentionable predecessors. However, papers like the *New York Times*—which, I'm happy to say, now regularly contains one of the most sophisticated and useful stock market commentaries available—made efforts to contrast the hiccup of Tuesday the 16th with the crash-and-burn aftermath of October 28, 1929, and October 19, 1987.

As usual, the powers that be patted themselves on the back for the great job they did in averting catastrophe. "The circuit breakers broke the stampede," read the propaganda in the newspapers. On the contrary, as stocks approached 30 Dow points from where the S&P futures would lock limit down for 30 minutes, weak holders of stocks rushed to sell before the door was closed—thereby exacerbating the decline. On the other hand, markets did break the decline. While the stocks were riding the descending funnel, short-term yields dropped 0.2 percent. The net result was to undo the previously anticipated increase in the Fed funds rate, the cause of the decline in the first place. As the interest rate on the long bond dropped below 7 percent, speculators like myself rushed in to buy. Within a few minutes, the Dow was up on the day.

CANDLESTICK ANALYSIS PUNISHMENT

Every evening, in an elegant bar in Tokyo, an attractive 40-year-old woman descends a carpeted marble staircase. As she smiles and waves to the throng of patrons below, raucous laughter greets her amid shouts of *"Da meh! Ikenai! Ya meh teh teh!"* ("No, that's awful! Get away! Stop!"). As she descends the last step, the men grab their privates with one hand and laughingly wave her away with the other.

The occasion is the nightly entrance of Toshiko-San, a glamorous Japanese lady once married to a prominent older member of the Diet (Japanese parliament). When she found that her husband had been carrying on with an attractive geisha, she severed her husband's genitals and, in a typically ritualistic Japanese approach, pickled them. After five years in jail, she emerged to great celebrity and became the proprietess of a successful Tokyo nightclub.

Stylized ritual has manifested itself in the world of Japanese technical analysis. The Japanese have developed a form of charting called candlestick analysis. The candlestick consists of a vertical line (the "shadow") showing the high and low for the day. A rectangular bar (the "body") is superimposed to show open and close for the day. The body is black if the day's close is lower than the day's open. If the opposite holds, the body is white. Some of the evocative names for candlestick patterns include White Blossom, Evening Star, Hanging Man, Pregnant Woman, and Doji—a key pattern connoting a session in which opening and closing are at the same or nearly the same price.

Among a number of weaknesses in candlestick analysis techniques, the most obvious fault is visual. What often looks like a trend is more than likely mere camouflage designed to part the weak players from their hard-earned yen. Second, no quantitative studies have ever been made of the technique's results, so virtually any conclusion can be drawn from the charts. Everything is explained, nothing is proven.

And candlestick charts have two further defects. Many of the patterns are based on the conjunction of three or more events. When each event has a probability of 1 in 4, the chances that one will find this pattern on a given day are 1 in 64. That's just not enough frequency for any scientific analysis in the year or two of observations that could, in some reasonable sense, be imputed to be relevant to the present. The other peculiar problem is that many of the patterns appear to be subject to varied interpretation. What looks like an Evening Star pattern to one person might be classified as a Doji by another.

So when Mr. Normile, our star fencer, entered the office on October 22, 1993, after the bonds had fallen a point, and announced to us that the fall was quite predictable because bond prices had been in a Black Doji Star pattern, I felt impelled to instruct him in the error of his ways. The next time he entered the offices, the traders were ready for him. "Oh, no! *Dah meh! Yah meh teh!* Don't *doji* us!" Mr. Normile is certain to think long and hard before he gives us another pat explanation for a big move in the market.

LoBagola

One of the most common themes in speculation is a roaring market going to unprecedented highs or lows. The examples are so common that they're almost too mundane to enumerate—the move of silver from $5 to $50 in 1980; the move of dollar:yen from 105¥/$ to 80¥/$ in 1995; the move of coffee from 80 cents to $2.65 in 1994, or of soybeans from $4 to $12 a bushel in 1973—all these, in the space of two to four months, spring to mind. These are the moves that get the speculative juices flowing, that make hundreds of millions of dollars for the big players, and that spark the interest of the masses for years after. If only the public could reap just a small fraction of the percentage gains the big players so deftly take out. But these stampedes, bubbles, self-fulfilling prophesies, et al., fill me with dolor, morbidity, and lassitude. Chances are good that I'll be on the wrong side, providing liquidity and money for the big gainers on the other side, and expediting my own demise. To make matters worse, after losing a bundle and being forced out of my position, the inevitable is sure to happen: just as soon as I get forced out, the price promptly moves down exactly the same path with about the same velocity as the big bull move.

I felt that I had to examine my errors and approach these moves systematically from a new perspective. After searching through all the advanced mathematical treatises, from catastrophe theory, genetic algorithms, and chaos theory to Fourier analysis, nonlinear differential equations, and neural networks, I was about ready to call it quits. I found that these techniques were great retrospectively but invariably had nothing to say on a predictive basis. Finally, I found the panacea in the wisdom of a 19th-century philosopher from Africa.

Following the destruction of Herod's temple in A.D. 70, the Jews were driven from Palestine, and a number of them wandered the coasts of North Africa. In the ensuing centuries, members of this tribe traveled south, becoming the principal inhabitants of some of the oases of the Saharan desert. Some of these Jewish people ultimately settled in the country of Dahomey, now known as Benin, which lies between Ghana and Nigeria.

One village populated by this tribe lay in a tropical rain forest. The land surrounding the village, known as the terrible Ondo Bush, was filled with dense, five-foot-high underbrush. The temperature exceeded 115°F in summer, and it rained continuously three months out of the year. The village was subject to the relentless depredations of elephants, leopards, lions, reptiles, and marauding packs of great apes who would destroy huts and tear apart anyone or anything in their path. The residents lived in coconut fiber huts mounted on 15-foot-high pilings made of bamboo stalks, to avoid the reptiles, vermin, and resultant floods.

How this information came to be revealed to the West is a tale in itself. One of the more resourceful members of this community found himself, at the age of about ten, an inadvertent stowaway on a Scottish steamer anchored offshore. He and his pals had paddled a canoe out to investigate the strange apparition, and the sailors indulgently let the boys explore the ship. The boy was below in the stoke-hold, watching the firemen stoke the boiler, when the captain gave the order to cast off. The boy's companions jumped overboard to swim to their canoe, only to be instantly devoured by sharks. Emerging from the hold, the boy beheld the plight of his companions. Bewildered, terrified, and alone, he gave himself to his unfathomable fate. Brought to Edinburgh, the boy subsequently received an English education. He eventually returned to his native Dahomey to great acclaim, whereupon he wrote an extraordinary memoir of his experiences, *LoBagola: An African Savage's Own Story*, published in 1930, of which the above is merely the preamble.

In his opening pages, LoBagola describes in great detail how the villagers defended themselves from marauding monkeys and elephants. In the case of the monkeys, the villagers were forewarned by a great chattering noise, loud enough to herald the arrival of the pack when still hours and miles away. Upon hearing the noise, a dozen men and boys, armed with poisoned spears,

LoBagola waits for a move.

would position themselves in the trees in an attempt to kill the chief monkey—clearly identifiable as he walked behind the "mother monk," the leader of the pack. If the chief could be killed, the rest would turn and flee. But if the chief was not killed, then terrible destruction would befall the villagers and few would escape serious injury or death.

From the elephants, there was little to fear most of the time, as long as everyone stayed out of their way; they traveled in groups of 50 to 100 and were easy to avoid. The villagers would capture them by digging pits camouflaged with bamboo and shrubbery, and would then kill them singly for their ivory. But occasionally the elephants would go on a "romp," and nothing could stop them. When on a roll, the elephants would trample, uproot, and destroy anything and everything in their path, regardless of how many might fall into a pit, or otherwise be waylaid. And LoBagola says that if elephants pass by one way on a roll, they will surely return by the same path, whether a day, a week, or a month later. Thus, the villagers knew how to place their pits in their quest for ivory.

In my world, the greatest source of disaster is the annual move of one commodity or another to unprecedented highs or lows, a move of deadly suddenness that crushes everyone in its path, scattering the remains of the unfortunate for the vultures to pick at. In studying this problem, I call the brand of my dogma that attempts to deal with unprecedented price moves *LoBagola analysis*. Participating in just one of these moves with a reasonably sized position would have achieved riches beyond anyone's wildest dreams.

On the phone, before making a trade, I listen to the background noise from the floor. If I hear the monkeys chattering, I refrain from the trade for a while. If the floor sounds like the seventh-inning stretch at a baseball game, then danger is not imminent and a trade is warranted. When I hear those elephants trampling, on a roll, I try to sit on my hands. I try to wait for the funnel, the eye of the storm, to pass. No force can withstand the immense weight of the elephants. The key is to find the balance between the roll and the aftermath. After the elephants have passed, after the earth-shaking has abated and the stench of animals no longer clouds the air, I carefully climb down from my perch and look around for opportunities. After the elephants destroy an area, other species often descend to pick up the debris. There may be bountiful pickings in what's left. I use this knowledge to play the fixed-income and commodity markets of a currency than just LoBagolaed.

My fund was the top-ranked fund in 1994. The media rushed my doors. During one beautiful month, my picture was featured in *Business Week*, the *National Enquirer*, *Financial Trader*, and the *Wall Street Journal*. When reporters asked me for the secret of my success, I revealed it: LoBagola analysis. I was pleased to learn from Jim Lorie that when he saw the article about me in the *Wall Street Journal*, with LoBagola's picture in place of mine (compliments of my partners), he burst into the most hysterical laughter of his life.

But there is a problem. For each of these LoBagola moves that retraces itself on the same pathway, there are numerous countermoves that start to retreat against the original roll, but then turn around in the direction of the original roll. In other words, it appeared that the elephants were returning along the same path, but they were only pretending. And several other moves start so abruptly, with limit up or down days, that it's impossible to follow them before the roll is over.

Our response to LoBagola at present must be: Although there are "rolls" in commodities, there appears to be no way of systematically profiting from them. And yet, as LoBagola observes, the one thing known about elephants on a roll is that they will return by the same path *at some time*. The African native is patient. He sets his trap where he knows they will retrace their steps.

VALUING THE GOODS

A certain kind of businessperson will take on any job under any circumstances, provided there's a profit to be made. This kind of type-A personality is halfway between a hoodoo and a real estate promoter on the personality tableau. We've all run into this specimen at great cost and far too often. Artie liked to buy roofing material from this type of seller, only to find the roof and the roofer washed away with the next rain. Many roofing material salespeople seem to gravitate to the selling of leveraged commodity contracts or NASDAQ stocks. They tend to operate from Fort Lauderdale, San Diego, or other resort communities, usually reserving their calls for a time when you're sitting down to dinner with the family or trying to steal a romantic moment with your significant other.

I am all too prone to buy stocks from such sleaze, as long as the discount from some previous standard—yesterday's price, last year's book value, the average performance of mutual funds—is high enough to trigger some computer screen.

I thought I had the worst case of this disease on record, until I read Meyer Liben's hilarious but haunting story, "Pinkerton: The Enchanted Isles." Pinkerton was a broker in the distressed stationery line, but, in reality, would deal in virtually any commodity—smudged file cards, misprinted rubber stamps, offcolor composition books, envelopes with the glue missing, postal scales off by a cent, and the like. He ran his business for the moment, without any sense of the future; he kept no inventory and never bought until he had made a sale. Like myself, he believed there is a market for everything. He had only two business rules: (a) the price had to be right, and (b) there had to be a buyer out there—a greater fool, so to speak—who would take the product off his hands.

Eventually, Pinkerton changed his ways. He formed a profitable partnership with a more conservative businessman in another field. The partner, who dealt in quality and value, ran an operation where credit, customer satisfaction, and repeat business were paramount.

Like Pinkerton, I do my buying and selling with complete disregard to fundamentals. If the price of rice is down in Tokyo, I sell wheat in

Minneapolis. Who cares if locusts and boll weevils are descending on the crops. When the price of Hong Kong stocks goes down three days in a row, I buy copper in London. No matter if there's about to be a general strike at all automotive plants, or if the warehouses are overladen with copper. My statistical interrelations will subsume, or so I believe.

I realize there's something wrong with my approach, but I'm following my lights. But, like Pinkerton, I long for another way—a fundamental, value-based approach, rather than the ephemeral technical jargon that spits out of my computer. The kind of formula that Dave Dreman writes about or that Warren Buffett champions—buying stocks in the lowest quartile of price to book value, or price to sales, and selling those same stocks in the highest quartiles. I realize that most of the excess returns from such strategies were realized in the 1970s and 1980s. And, for every study showing that value is superior, there's another one showing that the growth companies, those with highest price/earnings ratios, invariably showed superior performance.

There's at least one thing I can do: I can stick to fundamentals. Not for me the buying based on rotation, cycles, insider trading, odd-lot shorting, and the million other technical tricks that supposedly affect price. Au pairs for my kids, yes; but not pairs for stocks. When it comes to stocks, I'm strictly a fundamentalist. The balance sheet and the income statement are my two-page bible. Forget about psychology.

Still, I need to hold on to a rudder, at least in my stock trading. So I strive for value regardless. Something goes against my grain when a company is sold at 30 times annual sales and valued at $2 billion, when I know that the same company could not qualify for a $1 million bank loan and most likely would go into bankruptcy were it not for assorted jesters on the Internet holding it up. But I need a little test just to add some scientific ballast to support my holdings in case things don't work out as planned.

For the past 15 years, *Value Line* has been publishing a weekly list of companies selling at the greatest discount from book value. The list provides a real-time source of value stocks available for the asking and testing. Unlike the rankings of group 1 through group 5 stocks, there is no hornet's nest of problems with transaction costs and the dating of the issues received versus the pricing of the hypothetical portfolios. (I have always feared that these problems explained the lackluster performance of the *Value Line* mutual funds versus the record-beating world-class performance of the ranking system itself.)

To test, I took a sample of 30 stocks with the lowest price/book value ratios in the last issue of *Value Line* published in each of the past 10 years. Then I calculated the returns of such stocks for the next year and compared them to the S&P returns. The results, as shown below, are a mixed bag. In six of the 10 years, the value stocks underperformed. An investment of $100 in the value stocks would have appreciated to $250 by the end of the period, compared to $280 for the S&P.

Price Performance of Companies with Widest Discounts from Book Value

Year	Average Price Change	S&P Index Change
1986	−3%	15%
1987	0	2
1988	39	13
1989	11	27
1990	−39	−7
1991	20	27
1992	47	4
1993	20	7
1994	6	−2
1995	18	34

Thank god, like Pinkerton, I only buy in for 5 percent of the deals when it comes to buying and selling value stocks. My belt-and-buckle business of trading futures based on the numbers has at least paid the bills and sent my kids to good schools. I'm afraid that buying value stocks might lead to bankruptcy. Value stocks look good on paper but, in the event that this distressed merchandise doesn't sell, it's good to have a reliable money-making program to fall back on.

CHINESE FIREDRILL

One game I've never been beaten in is Chinese handball. The game is played like ordinary handball except that the ball must hit the ground before hitting the wall. The game is called "Chinese" because, to most schoolchildren, China is somewhere "down there," below the concrete. The game survives in New York because the velocity of the ball off the wall is much slower than a regular handball shot. This economizes on the seven and one-half feet of space between the sidewalk and the wall in the Brighton environs.

I find that Chinese handball has much to teach me about market practices. A limit order is a good tactic for Chinese trading, but a market order works best for handball trading. The direct market order against a quickly moving target frequently leads to a fast rebound against. The game is then over before it starts. To slow the process and blunt the other side's power, I use limit orders. I don't win as fast, but the losses are a lot slower in coming. Just as the ball lasts a lot longer in Chinese vs. regular handball, I find my capital enjoying a similarly enhanced longevity.

In my teenage years, I traded Chinese handball for Chinese firedrills. It was a rare day in Brighton that any of us was able to lay legitimate claim to the use of a car. Most of the time, the car emerged secretly in the middle of the night from the parents' garage amid much stealth and trepidation. The punishment for being caught was dire—grounding for a month or more. When some lucky delinquent was able to produce a car, a bevy of boys piled in for a ride. The game of choice was the Chinese firedrill. At a traffic light, we all summarily piled out of the car, ran around to China on the other side of the world, and piled back in before the light turned or an imperial policeman stopped the fun. Trading on the electronic markets after an important announcement, with the Internet chat room geeks madly scrambling to change their limit orders and pick each other off, is strangely reminiscent. Little did I know that, in the juvenile tradition of the Chinese firedrill, there would be an even more ridiculous and destructive adult counterpart in speculative markets.

The game is described in a 1996 SEC report about the wide spreads in the NASDAQ markets. These spreads were reported to be approximately four times as large as those for securities listed on the NYSE and AMEX: on average, approximately .40 on a $20 security. Because of these large spreads, I do not trade NASDAQ stocks. The reader can probably ascertain by now that the very thought of giving up 2 percent to get in and out of a trade before commissions is antithetical and loathsome to me. My usual technique of putting in a Chinese limit order to capture the spread in my favor doesn't work in NASDAQ stocks because limit orders for the public are not given priority, even if at more favorable prices than dealers' bids and asks.

The way these wide spreads have been maintained now emerges amid much publicity. If a dealer dared to post a ⅛- or ¼-point spread instead of the standard ½-point spreads typical for all but the most active stocks, he was subjected to a variety of tortures. The narrower market was referred to as a Chinese market with all the opprobrium the word connotes to children in their juvenile pursuits. The trader who set the Chinese market was subjected to humiliation in the form of anonymous phone calls, not unlike the prank calls children make. In one case, reportedly taped by the SEC, the anonymous caller "in a phony Chinese accent ordered chop suey, moo goo gai pan, or other Chinese food, in an apparent allusion to the understanding among market makers not to make 'Chinese markets.'"[2]

Moo goo gai pan is one of those dishes ordered mainly by westerners who are entirely unfamiliar with Chinese cuisine. As far as I know, the major locus of moo goo gai pan is at Brighton Beach. My family ordered it on those rare occasions when we could afford to eat out.

I conclude, therefore, that the anonymous caller must have been one of the boys from my youth who, like Tom Sawyer, never grew up. How tragic that a market as big as NASDAQ, often reported to be bigger than the

NYSE, has allowed such a tradition to flourish. But how nicely it all fits in with the public's proper role in the game.

ARTIE'S LAST GAME

Checkers with my father was a routine pastime. We would take the time to renew the age-old battle of father and son, but on the friendliest of battle-grounds—the checkerboard. Conversation flowed freely during the open-ing moves, which are standard. In the 35 years we played checkers, I never beat Artie. Near the end of our last game, on December 28, 1980, Dad said, "You have a good move." After some time, I saw the solution. I could sacrifice a checker, and he would be forced to jump. And after my next move, he would be unable to move, blocked by his own piece. In checkers, the player who moves last wins.

"Great, you finally beat me. I'm blocked on the board the same way the cells are blocked in my body. You're the master now."

I won my first game from Dad, but he lost his life a few weeks later, smothered by his own wayward cells. (He had been battling a lethal lym-phoma for seven years.) I realized later that he had seen this final position coming many moves before and purposely played toward it. His skill, not mine, gave me my first and final victory over him. And it was the most tac-tical checkers game of his life.

Just a few weeks later, I was sitting with Dad in Memorial Hospital. At 4 A.M., he woke, looked at me, and said, "If you are here at this hour, I must really be on the way out. I know how you hate hospitals."

"Dad, I still love you, even if I do feel that you pick up lots of conta-gious diseases from hospitals. Do you feel like you're going?"

"I have more to live for than any man. And I have been the happiest man alive with my teaching and my wonderful family. I have no regrets. I've never done anything but good.

"But it's time for some final advice. Are you sure that all those techni-cal figures of yours can take account of fundamentals like wars, elections, volcanoes? I've had to deliver lots of bodies of destitute bums to the morgue from the Bowery, and many of them had more statistics on them from the *Morning Telegraph* than you compiled from your Investor Statisti-cal Laboratory and CompuStat files."

With the same combination of outward bravado and inner trepidation with which I would one day assure George Soros that I knew the tricks of the tides, I responded, "Dad, don't worry. I've got it all under control."

"Whatever you say you can do, I know you will. Take care of Mother and the kids. And be careful." A minute later, Artie made, as far as I know, the first request in his life, "Vickie, do me a favor. Go out and get me some ices."

That was it. Eight hours later, he died.

Artie's death shook the foundation upon which my life was built. Shortly after, I gave up my wife, home, wealth, daily nurturing of my children, business partners, meat and poultry, trophies and racquets. I cried for Artie every day for the next five years.

Finally, I felt I had mourned and sacrificed long enough and gradually started rebuilding. My good friends, natural drive, and love of music stood me well in the end. Tom Wiswell and I began playing board games; I courted the future Mrs. Niederhoffer; I played piano with Robert Schrade, a gentleman who embodied Artie's character traits. I developed a surrogate familial relationship with George Soros in which tennis, chess, and speculation held us together. I've since regrouped on all fronts. Unlike some who disintegrate upon the death of a loved one, Artie's legacy led me to new highs.

I think of Artie whenever I give my kids a tip on form, especially when I tell them to do it the right way and forget about winning, or whenever I hear of a noble, unselfish act, regardless of how small and seemingly insignificant. Artie represents to me everything that is best in human nature and, especially, fatherhood. He is a model to which I hope to aspire if I am lucky. He often said to me in a schmaltzy way, "Vickie, I was always there for you when you wanted, wasn't I?" I hope that my loved ones can say the same of me too.

Since Artie died many people have told me that he was like a second father to them. He was the kindest and most loved man I have known. In a kind world, he would not have died so young, but his legacy is a constant reminder to me of how to live wisely, creatively, lovingly, with respect for others. His life work is spread about the world in an infinite number of ways, both large and small. In the end, I take comfort in knowing that Artie lives forever through the life enhancing impact of his example and spirit.

GOING DUTCH

The favorite play for full-time bookies, as well as most other gamblers, comes when they can "dutch" a bet—lay off the bet at better odds than the original proposition, so that the bookie wins regardless of the outcome. Bookie often was able to dutch the book when I played paddles against a much older and stronger player. He'd wait until I fell behind at the beginning of a game. Just when the crowd thought there was no way I should even be on the court with someone that much stronger and more experienced—"He's only 11"—Bookie would bet $100 on me at 10-to-1. He'd be overwhelmed. Then I'd make my comeback. I'd get up to serve and hit angle serves, running off 10 points in a row. With the crowds begging for mercy and hoping that the kid would win, Bookie would quietly step in again. He'd bet $550 on my opponent at even odds. The net result: Bookie wins $450 either way.

During my market forays, I am often on a similar trajectory. A market takes a big move. I reverse. I'm always too early, and, like lightning, I'm down 50 percent on my margin. When I double up, usually prices go to my direction and I'm gold. My customers generally say, "If only you'd wait just one more day, you'd have all the money in the world."

Forty-five years after Bookie, I have another backer who runs a Dutch book off me: my director of marketing. On one occasion, I was talking to the head of another trading firm and mentioned with praise that I was all set for marketing because all my activities were covered by Callah. He looked at me with amazement for a second and then burst out, "That's funny. He's our director of marketing also." We've since nicknamed him "Hats" in honor of his ability to wear 50 different hats, depending on the situation.

Shown here is a sketch of a floor trader deciding which of several hats to wear at the beginning of a day: the worker, the businessman, the soldier, and so on. We use it as a logo on all our communications with Hats. A typical incident will put these circumstances in perspective. One of my partners is tied up on the phone. I ask what's wrong. "My wife is upset. Hats won't get out of her office." She works for an asset allocator, and Hats has commandeered her office as a makeshift conference room and is pitching another trader's services. At the time, we were enjoying a great run in the

A marketeer of many hats.

markets and thought our marketing campaign was firing on all cylinders. Then we learned from an industry journal that Hats was busy raising a substantial sum for a competitor, in case we stumbled. I thought of Bookie wringing his hands in delight when he succeeded in dutching one of my games, assuring himself a profit whether I lost or won.

The funny thing is, I admire Hats for his tricks. If truth be told, there's a little bit of Hats in all of us.

PLEASE HOLD ALL SEMINAR TICKETS

When I traveled around the country selling companies, I frequently stayed at hotels that served as headquarters for salespeople of "multilevel" direct marketing companies such as Amway and Niagara Cyclo-Massage. A revivalist atmosphere prevailed. The salespeople would sing company songs to psych themselves up for the selling ahead. Storytelling and playacting recent sales coups were *de rigueur*. Finally, a 15-foot sales chart would appear, showing how close each salesperson was to winning various contests for meeting sales goals.

I am reminded of these meetings by the atmosphere that pervades commodity trading seminars. First, the leader describes his or her great successes. Then an approach to riches is mapped out, but the ultimate decision as to how to apply the approach remains in the hands of the attendees. Next come testimonials from satisfied clients who have attended the seminar before.

Does it never occur to these seminar participants that anyone who truly had a system to beat the markets would never waste time and money in marketing such a wonder? Or that, even if one could find some genius who was willing to share the secrets for a fee, the ideas would be dated and of no practical value by the time they were disseminated, because of the principle of ever-changing cycles? Or that the prior attendees, testifying to their successes, are suffering from hindsight bias. Or that there is a selective bias among attendees to talk only about their successes and to gloss over their failures.

THE BEST BARGAINER

I have been very fortunate to have, as a mentor in my business, Irving Redel, a gentleman who, among his other outstanding attributes, is the best bargainer I've ever met.

His crowning glory in negotiations, however, has to be the time he bargained for some tax relief. The town fathers of a wealthy township in New York rejected a request from him for a tax abatement on some vacant land near the center of town, rejecting his request on the basis that unimproved land had to be taxed at a high rate to preclude speculation.

The next thing the town fathers knew, an old minibus was parked next to the fanciest property in the neighborhood. As its passengers disembarked onto a well-manicured street, a certain incongruity became evident. All but one of the passengers, male adults, were dressed alike: black suit jackets over black pants; at their temples, long, spiraling curls cascading to their shoulders. Their chest-length beards flowed over white shirts, and perched on their heads were small black caps or black, broad-brimmed fedoras. In the forefront stood one carrying a sextant, tripod, tape measure, and log books. This man spoke to a tall, prosperous-looking gentleman with a receding hairline, attired in sports clothes.

"Yes, this will make a wonderful retreat for 50 or 60 of us, when the summer days get so hot in Crown Heights," the one carrying the sextant said.

"Oh, yes, a grand retreat indeed," answered the other, in a booming *voce fortissimo*. Next, they all marched toward the town square. One of the black-capped men entered a gourmet grocery store and inquired whether the cookies and cottage cheese on display were kosher.

All along the street, curtains were carefully drawn aside, venetian blinds were ever so slightly parted, oak-paneled front doors were discreetly inched open as the citizenry strained to assess the situation. Merchants leaned out of doorways. Husbands at desks miles away received phone calls from anxious spouses. Before long, the entire community knew the story.

Irv had decided to donate the land to an Orthodox Jewish sect in the Crown Heights section of Brooklyn as a summer retreat for worship and study.

Strangely enough, within a week, Redel was contacted by a delegation of the town fathers. "We have reconsidered your request for a tax abatement and find that your case, after all, may perhaps have some merit." Irv replied, "Well, I'm glad of that; I would never have wished to upset this quiet Jewish community with a retreat facility for Jews."

A solution was reached: Irv made a substantial contribution to the Congregation. The town fathers lowered his taxes. Perhaps speculators aren't so bad after all.

TRADING SUSAN

I like to keep in touch with prices 24 hours a day. If I have a position and take a break, even for a few seconds, prices are bound to go to my exit level the instant I am gone. More to the point, prices move in a rhythm. If I get out of sync with the rhythm, my trading goes awry. The speculation game is like poker. Everything that has happened up to the present determines future strategy.

Once, I went too far. I brought a portable screen into the delivery room while my wife was giving birth to our fourth child. In the midst of her excruciatingly painful contractions in a 40-hour labor, I stole glances at the screen and tried to trade out of my positions on my cellular phone. I could hardly refrain from breaking the illusion when the obstetrician complimented me on my diligence in keeping the family posted. Finally, Susan yelled at me (the only time she's done so in 18 years), "Get out of here with your screen. Go trade pork bellies."

Doc Bo

After all is said and done, the admonition "Physician, heal thyself" comes to mind. While I have had good fun denigrating and decrying the gurus others use, I must admit to consulting an oracle of sorts from time to time.

Successful speculation is nothing more than a scientific, systematic, and economical way of hastening the inevitable. There is not one secret to it. I would be remiss, therefore, if I tried to give you my own special techniques, for they would certainly be outdated by the time you could put them to use. High on the list of mistakes a speculator can make is to base trading strategies on blind faith in a guru.

However, I rely heavily on our in-house guru. He doesn't reside on the summit of Parnassus; he lives in a closet in the basement of my house. I met Steve ("Dr. Bo") Keeley, world traveler, veterinarian, national paddleball and racquetball champion several times over, and hobo, at a racquetball tournament in San Diego, where he was the reigning National Champion. Then and there, I formed a financial and personal partnership with the Bo that has lasted 30 years. I share vicariously in all his adventures.

During the six months a year that Bo is not riding the rails or tramping the world, he generally lives at my house. He keeps in contact with his fellow 'boes, so I'm always getting reports on current economic conditions on Skid Row and the rails. Opportunistically, I take advantage of one of the Bo's lingering survival traits. He is always alert in the evenings in case a "bull" should emerge to search the freight. I've tried to calm him by telling him that there is a universal code of brotherhood among policemen and their progeny, so there's nothing to be afraid of in my house. Yet, he likes to keep moving. If I yell to him that the Central Bank is in and that we have to run for our lives, he rushes to help me call a few extra dealers in Japan to ward off the sneak attack.

Here, for the first time, I will reveal the key indicators we have developed.

Railroad car loadings in the early 20th century were once a key harbinger. Market players focused on the statistic with the same simple-minded attention they devote today to such ephemeral numbers as the money supply and unemployment claims. But railroad figures fell into disuse as other forms of transportation—trucks, cars, and planes—rose in popularity. Doc Bo and I, however, have improved on the early statistics.

First, the difference between a hobo who hops freight to travel from job to job and a tramp who doesn't work, is that the hobo reads the *Wall Street Journal* before using it as insulation and the tramp simply uses it for insulation. The hobo:tramp ratio is a good indicator of the employment situation because it rises directly with the number of available jobs. Hobos are inveterate readers because they have so much time to fill waiting for freight cars to arrive, so a good first indicator of the employment situation is the number of issues of the *Wall Street Journal* found underneath the bridges where hobos congregate. The number of freight cars passing by fixed points is a direct indicator of economic activity. As recently as February 15, 1996, speculator Vic received a bulletin from Dr. Bo that freight cars were going through key locations in Jacksonville, Denver, and Salt Lake City at twice their normal rate. The number of freight cars was also increasing. The employment situation was obviously good, so I stayed short the bond. Sure enough, the February employment statistics showed an 800,000 increase, one of the largest ever, and bonds dropped three points.

After hopping off a freight, Dr. Bo likes to take in a movie at one of the 24-hour cinemas on Skid Row. The price of admission is good for a movie flop—a night's sleep. The amount of popcorn being sold in the movies, indicated by litter on the floor, as well as other unmentionable activities in the aisle, is a good representation of the economic tides for the lowlifes who attend. When he leaves the movies, Bo likes to count the smiles:growls ratio. Those with thin wallets are generally happy when the income distribution becomes more equalized. If they're not doing a lot of smiling, relative to the fat cats, it usually means bad times for employment.

The next stops for Dr. Bo are veterinarian clinics. Dr. Bo is a veterinarian by training but gave up the practice to play racquetball. Still, he likes to stay in touch with his fellow vets. We turn the contingency into profits. Unlike human medical care, vet bills must be paid for out-of-pocket. Dental work on dogs is a highly sensitive leading indicator of consumer expectations and well being. When owners anticipate good times, they feed their dogs richer food, which causes cavities and gum problems. If the disposable income is available, a visit to the vet is scheduled. In the Spring of 1996, Bo reported that business at vets was quite brisk. I shorted bonds on this intelligence.

After visiting the vets, Dr. Bo likes to follow the bums into "the Sally." The Sally here is not the venerable government bond dealer. It's the Salvation Army. By calculating the beef:potato ratio in the meals they serve the bums, or the number of suits and shirts on the apparel racks, Dr. Bo gets a good indication of available disposable goods in the working sector of the economy. The missions are a hotbed of information in this regard. They collect food from fast-food establishments. If there are six donuts per hobo for dessert, look out—business at the ubiquitous donut diners is down. Another good indicator, incidentally, is the length of the lines at soup kitchens. Long lines indicate bad times.

After a good night of worship, food, and sleep at a mission, Dr. Bo takes in the fast-food establishments. The amount of food left in the dumpsters is a two-pronged indicator. On one hand, it varies with economic activity. But on the other hand, the harder the times, the less that's eaten. I will not reveal the adjustment the Bo and I have developed, except to point to the amount of sodas left in the Coke and Big Gulp cups in the dumpsters.

Bo and I pay particular attention to the kinds of boxcars traversing the rails. A disproportionate mix of coal cars, with its augury of cold weather, has a pervasive impact on all speculations. A shift to oil cars tells that energy is on a roll.

Automobile carrier trains—"portable parking lots" in 'bo language—are a key indicator. Not only do they tell where auto stocks are going much before the weekly sales figures are reported by *Ward's*, but by examining the sticker prices one get a leg up on the inflation numbers. Along with employment numbers, the PI sisters are the two keys that move markets the most, month to month.

Not all indicators are as easily interpreted. "As I return to the red-light areas conveniently located near the freight yards," says Dr. Bo, "I find the same sidewalk princesses plying their wares year after year. It doesn't take a lot of smarts for a 'bo with a small wallet to establish a correlation between economic conditions and the cost of the cookie. The fluctuations are wild and evident. I have never been able, however, to figure the lead time of the indicator."

The Bo and I like to get a grasp on the government sector by monitoring the movements of circle tramps. These tramps ride the rails to collect food stamps in three to five locations in a circle of cities around the country. Each has a few social security numbers and a verifiable address (generally under a bridge), and stays one hop and two steps ahead of pursuing social workers.

The standard exchange rate for food stamps is 50 cents off the face value. When the circle tramps find government handouts less plentiful, it's a good indicator of the "lean hog" type of operation our politicians like to run with taxpayers' money.

The fundamental hobo indicator may now be revealed. The size of cigarette butts on the ground is directly proportional to the health of the economy. The hobo is always on the lookout for a discarded butt. And when he has to smoke one very short "snipe" after another, then hard times are here. The original smokers are so strapped they are smoking right to the ends so as not to waste a penny. To be fair, Rose Wilder Lane, in the *Discovery of Freedom*, was the first to note international differences between the size of discarded butts. But I believe that Bo and I are the first to track changes systematically within a country over time.

I recently made millions by applying this theory in Brazil. My agents there noted an increasing prevalence of long butts on the ground, and I rushed in to buy Brazilian stocks.

A NIXON CONNECTION

Everywhere, there are myriad interconnections. During the 1960 presidential election campaign, William McChesney Martin, chairman of the Fed, did John F. Kennedy a favor by maintaining a restrictive monetary policy before the election. This strategy always favors a challenger. As far as Richard Nixon was concerned, Chairman Martin's tight policies led to recession and Nixon's defeat. Who would have thought that this sequence would be a major factor in explaining the market trends of the 1970s?

Nixon wasn't going to risk having a similar economic slowdown wreck his reelection chances in 1972. He appointed Fed Chairman Arthur Burns to make sure interest rates didn't rise to politically inexpedient levels again. He believed, however, that an excessively stimulated economy would lead to rises in inflation and interest rates. With the dollar already under pressure, he suspended gold redemption by foreign central banks and imposed domestic wage and price controls in late 1971. The resultant liquidity helped stoke the flames of a strong stock market.

At the same time, the dollar was under pressure by foreign banks. They fought the trend by buying dollars. The newly created dollars caused a worldwide liquidity explosion. Demand for energy and food increased. Coincidentally, it was a time when grain and petroleum reserves were low. The inflationary pressures naturally found their way into grain prices. With the final oil supply disruptions of the 1973 Israeli war, OPEC was in a great position to raise prices.

By 1973, the Federal Reserve was trying to reverse the damage by tightening liquidity. The U.S. stock market suffered a horrendous drop. Unlike the 1930s, this was a time of rising, not falling, consumer prices. Using month-end prices, from their peak in December 1972 to their trough in September 1974, a real performance index on the S&P 500 fell by about 52 percent. This was not as bad as the 1929-to-1932 fall of 79 percent in real terms, but it was more than enough to caution investors on stocks for quite some time.

In the 1970s, the stable conditions of the 1950s and 1960s were under attack. The economy was suffering from an escalating inflation rate. Our political leaders, whose attention to their own needs was combined with ignorance or ineptitude, seemed unable to tame the inflation monster unleashed by inadequately restrained monetary growth. High inflation rates drove up tax rates. Increased social welfare programs and government regulation drove up the cost of government and created great uncertainty in long-term corporate planning. Corporations were slow to pass along cost increases, which hurt corporate profitability. The gigantic rise in oil prices created further havoc in energy-dependent industries. The Nixon Watergate scandal wounded public confidence in governmental ability. For

President Jimmy Carter, the end came with the humiliation of the Iranian hostage crisis.

This environment created the changes in political attitudes that enabled Ronald Reagan to become President. Under Paul Volcker, the Fed tightened monetary policy considerably, and inflation was brought to heel at the price of a very severe recession. With the reduced demand, real energy prices began a significant decline. Tax reform and lower inflation greatly reduced the tax burden on capital income. Increased defense spending and new foreign policy succeeded in restraining Soviet attempts at continued expansion, and, along with a failing Soviet economic system, combined to bring the communist system to an end. With stocks depressed, it was to be expected that valuation levels and stock prices were due for a major reversal, even though the profit rebound would take some time to catch up. Interest rates would fall as inflation fears subsided.

But major reversals bring casualties. In the late 1970s, it was assumed that price increases would bail out borrowers, particularly those producing petroleum, such as Mexico. The recession, the rising dollar, and the falling real oil prices, along with an overvalued peso, soon brought Mexico to default. The savings and loans, in particular, had already been driven close to ruin by rising interest costs set against low-yielding long-term mortgage portfolios. The efforts to prop them up, combined with partial regulatory reform, created an ideal environment for financial speculation. The combination of tight monetary policy and easy fiscal policy, in an environment where capital investment in the United States looked increasingly attractive, also led to a much overvalued dollar by the mid-1980s, which hurt trade-sensitive industries. With increased profitability and low stock valuations, an era of great merger speculation began. The banks that had just been burned on Third World loans were getting ready to fry on real estate and leveraged buyout loans—given that traditional lending to corporate borrowers was no longer that strong and was subject to more competition from the commercial paper market. In Japan, rapid monetary growth was financing a major speculative bubble in real estate and stock prices as the overvalued dollar gave the Japanese great trade advantages and increased confidence.

Partly in response to the competitive pressures brought on by the high dollar value, the economy slowed in 1986, cooling inflation. Stock prices rose as interest rates declined. The liquidity provided by an easing of monetary policy in 1986 helped fuel a stock market into clearly excessive valuations. Soon this liquidity was being felt in inflation, which in turn brought about Fed tightening. The stock market seemed immune until reality caught up in the startling drop in October 1987. The Fed eased in response, and the decline was soon forgotten.

The lesson learned by a new generation of investors was: Take advantage of market reversals to buy into the secular bull market. Inflation continued to rise, though at far more reasonable rates than in the 1970s, necessitating renewed Fed efforts at restraint. The real estate bubble came to an end under the pressure of revised tax laws. The resulting crisis in the banking and S&L industries ensured that credit expansion would be restrained as banks tried to rebuild their capital. The Fed moved to eliminate inflation following the 1990–1991 recession, and at least brought inflation back under control. Corporations battered by foreign competition and corporate raiders became more efficient and increased their profitability substantially.

The factors influencing major changes in valuation were now mixed. The political situation regarding tax and regulation became more negative again under Presidents Bush and Clinton. But the prospect of a prolonged and profitable expansion was a powerful counterforce, as was the final collapse of the Soviet Union. The election of a Republican majority in Congress in 1994 raised the prospect of great strides in dealing with the problems of budget deficits, excessive government, and high taxation. At the same time, corporate downsizing and continued efforts to improve profitability helped raise the long-term profit outlook. Major changes in computer and communications technology helped renew hopes for improving economic growth potential. A massive move toward mutual fund investing—driven by low short-term interest rates, the record of stock returns in the prior 15 years, and a growing realization by the low-saving Baby Boomers that they had better accumulate some net worth for retirement—continued to drive up stock prices through 1996.

Basic secular and demographic trends drive events to a certain degree. Yet, moves made by key players or groups in society can influence outcomes. The pressures for an end to the old monetary regime were there. But if Nixon had not acted when, how, and why he did, the results might have been different. Had restraints not been placed on U.S. financial instruments, the Eurodollar market might never have grown and the worldwide stimulus might not have been as pronounced. Had supply conditions not been as tight, it might not have been inelastic oil prices that zoomed, and overall inflation might have been less. Had changes been made respecting depositor risk at the time of financial deregulation, events of the following decade would certainly have been different in many areas. Everywhere, there are the myriad interconnections.

CONSONANT DISSONANCE

They laughed at me when I went to England to tell an audience that music and speculation were similar languages for expressing rhythm and emotion. "Over the past year new breeds of financial astrologers are looking heavenwards for guidance," the *London Times* commented in a roast of me and my theory. The headline: "Should You Watch Your Dog's Wagging Tail to Pick Shares?" set the tone for the story. In a nice touch, they employed a timeless technique of deception to help me dig my own grave. A sexy reporter called me prior to the piece's running to ask me to dig up publicity photos. I was up for a favorable story. In actuality, the picture was used to accent my buffoonery.

"I cannot imagine Mercury Asset Management (the Fidelity of England) using such relations," the Cavendish column in *Sunday Business* reported. In an objective recounting of the reaction to my views, the *Wall Street Journal* reported that many of the Englishmen present were laughing at me for a less benevolent reason. I speak in a Brooklyn accent, and my theories lack humility. It's just not British to boast of your success. They were alluding to an out-of-context remark in which I said I owe all of my success (omitting the caveat "however meager it may be") to quantifying such relations. The European financial networks carried interviews with several pillars of the British financial community who expressed their skepticism about this new fangled and curious but evanescent method.

Anyway, the guiding principle of music and markets starts with a central tone and a gravitation back after departing in various tension-provoking dissonant intervals. Lowly speculators and great composers are compensated if they are skillful in resolving the tensions.

Into the tug of war between the buyers and sellers enter those with merely incidental interests in the outcome. The public rushes in to buy, propelled by thoughts of tremendous profits arising from inflation, innovation, or shortage. Weighty academic research is sponsored or hauled out to inflame the public stampede. Trend followers blow the bubble higher; for support, they trot out numerical calculations based on data from the 1970s or a collective memory of the alluring profits that this or that legend may or may not have once achieved before bankrupting his public investors, who barreled in based on the legend's results.

Whenever I am severely criticized, whenever I am in turmoil, whenever my ethics and modus operandi are questioned, I have a patented method of resolution. I take out my pencil and quantify. And then, based on the outcome, I go out and trade.

If my theory is correct, then the opening notes of a market would tend to be repeated at the close. This would seem like a simple, testable hypothesis that could be approached in a scientific fashion. Unfortunately, I cannot provide definitive evidence of whether money is to be made by betting on the opening theme to recur. The January Effect in stock is suggestive (after a rise in January, the remaining 11 months are about 1.6 times more likely to go up after a rise than after a decline).

To provide some beef in this nebulous area, I examined the largest market in the world, the U.S. bond market, to see whether the opening theme tends to set the final resting place. I studied six years, 1990 through 1995. I defined the main theme as the direction in which the bonds moved from the close the previous day to noon of the current day. After the 805 rises to noon, the bond rose a further $4/100$ of a point to the close. After the 754 declines to noon, the bonds declined a further few hundredths of a point. Such a difference supports the theory, although it is not a practical difference. The difference wouldn't cover commissions and slippage, which come to at least $6/100$ of a point.

I also noted that the bonds tend to return to the home key an inordinate number of times. They close unchanged about twice as frequently as they close up or down one tick, a highly nonrandom event.

CODE OF BRIGHTON

Ten thousand times in my life I have stood on a court, racquet in hand, referee on his chair, crowd watching, ready to battle an opponent. From those 10,000 experiences, I learned two important points about equality.

First of all, I learned that we are all different. Some players are fast, some hit hard, some take risks, some are smart, some are coordinated, some work hard, some have an overpowering drive to win. When Thomas Jefferson wrote in the Declaration of Independence that "all men are created equal," he meant equal in *rights*, or before the law, not equal in *abilities*. In life, as on the courts, inequality pervades our experience.

Every time my opponent and I stand on a court, each of us has the same goal: victory. Bound by the rules, we take an infinite number of paths and game plans to achieve victory, or what Jefferson called the rights to "life, liberty and the pursuit of happiness."

However, it is understood that games, like life, need referees to settle disputes, to judge close calls, to provide such interpretation of the rules as may occasionally be necessary. The best referee is one you hardly notice, whose name you do not recall, who seems invisible to the fans. Referees who take too active a role are intrusive to the players and audience. Instead of "enforcing" fairness, they almost seem to impede it.

No referee has even taken more than one-quarter of the points I won and redistributed them to my opponent. If otherwise, I would certainly have stopped playing and my opponent would have given up trying to improve his game. The whole level of the game would decline into mediocrity. When I play well in the income game, I often find the referee taking way more than half my points, each year, with a further half of the balance due when I kick the bucket. Does he really expect me and others to try very hard in such a situation? Those who doubt supply side economics should try playing a few matches with a referee in the opponent's pocket.

There are two ways of getting things in this world: through voluntary trade between individuals or through dispensations and commands from an interfering referee. When the state protects life and property and eschews redistribution, prosperity prevails and people can afford to speak, criticize, meet, play games, and worship freely. But when the "ref" routinely redistributes your hard-won points to the other side or changes the rules on you, you are unlikely to be motivated to play your best game.

I picture politicians as professional gangsters. Their goal: to pluck the maximum number of feathers from chickens with the least amount of squawking. Not relevant to a book on speculation, you say? On the contrary, I apply this theory time and again to predict how politicians will act when confronted by violent moves in the markets. For instance, after the Mexican bailout in 1995 both Democrats and Republicans were unanimous in praising themselves for their altruism in saving Americans from the Mexicans. Ross Perot was just as vehement in decrying the act as a waste of taxpayer money.

My take is that the last thing in the world the elected politicians wanted to hear about in 1996 was a further devaluation in Mexico. Without a devaluation, Mexican treasury bills yielded 50 percent to 100 percent returns. I rushed to buy with abandon. As one political operative after another patted themselves on the back for their actions in the bailout, I rubbed my wallet in glee. The profits I made from applying the lessons I learned about equality led to considerably better than average returns for my clients.

My friend, Doug Casey, sees boundless opportunities in South America. They have been to the abyss and are beating a hasty retreat. I am told that good squash players find the transition to jai alai quite felicitous.

A LONG TWO MINUTES

New York, 8:30 A.M. It has been a wild ride overnight; thunderclouds have been forming during the hours the U.S. markets are closed. The Bundesbank has scheduled a press conference at its headquarters for between 8:30 A.M. and 9:30 A.M. Suddenly, the fate of Europe as a collection of nation-states versus a unified common market; free-floating versus fixed and administered exchange rates; recession or expansion throughout the world—all these hinge on the conference. Most of the Big Boys already know the outcome in advance. The rumor is that the Bundesbank will increase its discount rate. Overnight, the dollar has been cratering. World bond markets are plummeting, and the Hong Kong stock market, down 4 percent, has led the other Asian equity markets into the sewer. If they follow through and increase the rate, there could be panic on the scale of 1907, 1929, or 1987. Or so the plummeting graphs on the screen indicate.

As always, we're going against, heavily long, hemorrhaging.

Finally, the tension snaps. The headline flashes across the screen: BUNDESBANK LEAVES INTEREST RATE UNCHANGED. Immediately, the dollar rises 2 percent against the European currencies. Bonds go up 3 percent. The Dow rises 50 points on one or two trades in London. "Stops are being run." The phone rings. A broker tells us that a large trend-following fund is buying heavily. "Let's jump in to buy before the other funds get triggered. There's a pivot ahead," I say. "Wait, what's that?" CORRECTION flashes across the newswire. The Bundesbank actually increased the discount rate and the repo rate 50 basis points.

The dollar retraces its 2 percent rise back to even, then falls another 2 percent. We're hosed. The funds are reversing; the big hedge funds are adding to their short dollar position. World stock markets are careening, whiplashing investors like the tail of some enraged dinosaur.

It's near an anniversary of the October 1987 crash, and the Gann and Elliott wave theoreticians have been predicting Armageddon in the stock markets. My first client calls, "I hope you're not long stocks for me."

Our chronic bear from the Mediterranean is on the phone: "Buy me 100 puts on the S&P."

"It will have to go down 15 percent in a month before you break even; there's a 30 percent vig on the spreads alone," I shout.

"I don't care what the price is. Buy at the market. We're gonna free-fall," he responds.

But now there's light at the end of the tunnel. The PPI is released. It's down 0.1 percent. That's great. We might be saved; the PPI was expected to be up. Bonds immediately run up the ladder 1½ percent. "Put in a limit order to buy. What? Baldwin's bidding for 1000 ahead of us? Buy cash instead," I shout. In a frenzy, everyone grabs a line. Too few hands on deck today, so the receptionist is recruited to call Salomon and the cleaning lady is given Citibank's number. "Hurry up. Get the hobo out of the closet so he can get an offer from UBS." But the speakerphone gets jostled, setting off a deafening feedback. We can't tell whether the brokers have heard our responses to their offers or not.

"Maybe we should wait for the unemployment claims due out in a few seconds. Run some computer simulations to see what happens on days like this. Oh no, claims are down. That's bearish." What a roller coaster. From rags to riches to rags in three generations. That's when there are opportunities. Here's when I take out the cane. "Check the computer. What's the impact of dollar, bonds, and stocks—all down in conjunction with a Thursday PPI announcement? Crude's down; that means bonds should be up, gold down. That's bullish for the Nikkei."

"Witter's on the line. We're in trouble. They just raised our margin from 5 percent to 20 percent. You have 30 minutes to come up with $20 million or else they close you out and cancel your line," my partner pants.

"How many dollars is Lopez long? Close out his positions. I'll book the trade. We have to meet margin," I say.

"You'll have to talk to Victor about that. He's our risk-control officer. Yes, and trader also," my cohort barks into the speakerphone. One of our asset allocator customers is on the line. He noticed that we just lost 25 percent for him. "Victor, where will you stop yourself out?" he asks, trying to feign a nonchalant curiosity.

"I don't have any," I say.

"Then would you kindly consider reducing our positions by half?" he replies. "We're hedged with another trader who's against you but you've tripped our risk exposure parameters."

"I'll be happy to close out all your positions. But in that case, I assure you I'll never trade for you again," I respond.

"#!?*ing Niederhoffer says he won't trade for us again if we interfere," I hear him shout through a poorly muffled phone. "We're having a board meeting with our major Japanese client on it this instant," he purrs back. "We'll be back to you in a jiffy with their decision."

"You really shouldn't be calling me during trading hours," I admonish.

What else could go wrong? The computers are down. "Calculate our losses by hand. What's our current yen exposure? How much do we have to cover to meet margin? Are we still solvent?" Troubles always come in bundles. Our backer and supporter from day one, Refco, just issued a margin call. Dittmer personally approved it. "With crude below $18 a barrel, your margin secured by your oil holdings is no longer adequate." We're going to have to liquidate something, but what? Our treasurer is on the line. Harris Bank just called. There's a fail in a bond delivery that is going to cost us $20,000 a day.

The Quantum direct line rings. "Sell 1000 bonds at 23, that's a limit of 5 ticks below the market." Just what we need, Quantum sending a bearish signal to the markets against us when we're on the ropes. "Do you have a fill for us on that yet? Good, sell another 1000 at 18." they command.

And another order comes in: "I have a fill: You sold 200 bonds at even. Nice trade. You already have a half-point profit. Oh, excuse me, is this Roy?" "No." "Oh, I'm sorry. That fill was for R. G. Niederhoffer's firm, not yours. We pressed the wrong button."

"Victor, your attorney is on line five. One of your neighbors filed a lawsuit against you. He says to ask you what the prospects of selling your house are," my assistant chirps.

The computer drones, "Victor, you're tapped out." My partner plays the Funeral March on the CD player. I double up. I've heard this music before. Things couldn't be worse. "Put on the 'Wall Street Rag.' Good times are coming. Send a Niederhoffer signal. Buy 100 millions D-Marks of DM," I say. But there's a problem. We're in line. Our order can't be executed. Tudor Jones is buying ahead of us and all phone lines at our brokers are busy with their other big customers. "In that case, place a sell stop 100 points below the market. That's sure to change the tide when they try to run our stops."

Susan comes in. "Can you make sure the kids finish their piano practice while I show the exterminator where the termites are? Wow, you look like you've been through a deluge. Everything OK?"

"Oh, no, business as usual."

New York, 8:32 A.M.

Notes

<hr>

CHAPTER 1

1. Julius and Francis Butwin, *Favorite Tales of Sholom Aleichem* (New York: Avenel, 1983), p. 1.
2. Herman Melville, *Moby Dick* (New York: Random House, 1930), p. 6.
3. Norman Rosten, "Under The Boardwalk," *The Brooklyn Reader: 30 Writers Celebrate America's Favorite Borough*, ed. Andrea Sexton and Alice Powers (New York: Harmony, 1994), p. 189.
4. Elliot Willensky, *When Brooklyn Was The World, 1920–1957* (New York: Harmony, 1986), p. 178.
5. Don Lynch, *The Titanic: An Illustrated History* (New York: Hyperion, 1992), p. 142.
6. Gerald Loeb, *The Battle for Stock Market Profits* (New York: Simon & Shuster, 1971), pp. 275–77.
7. Edwin Lefèvre, *Reminiscences of a Stock Operator* (New York: John Wiley & Sons, 1994).
8. Ibid., pp. 186–87.
9. The correlation coefficient measures the closeness of relationship between two variables such as these. It is a measure of the simultaneous variation of two quantities and reflects the common influences they have. When they vary directly and linearly together, the correlation is 1.0, when they vary inversely and linear, it is −1.0. A correlation of zero means that neither quantity can be predicted from the other by a linear relationship. We will also use the regression coefficient, discovered by Galton, which is the correlation coefficient normalized for prediction by the ratio of the magnitude of the two variables.
10. Paul Dickson, *Baseball's Greatest Quotations* (New York: Harper, 1992), p. 482.
11. René Lacoste, *Lacoste On Tennis* (New York: Morrow, 1928), p. 166.
12. John Thorn, ed., *The Armchair Book of Baseball* (New York: Macmillan, 1985), p. 241.
13. Quentin Reynolds, *I, Willie Sutton* (New York: Da Capo, 1993), p. 233.
14. Willie Sutton with Edward Linn, *Where The Money Was* (New York: Viking, 1976), pp. 96, 144.
15. Quoted in David Spanier, *Inside the Gambler's Mind* (Reno: University of Nevada Press, 1987), p. 160.

CHAPTER 2

1. Scott Joplin, *Collected Works* (New York: New York Public Library, 1971), p. 181.
2. Lefèvre, pp. 113–14.

3. Forest Davis, *What Price Wall Street?* (New York: Godwin, 1932), pp. 212–38.
4. Henry Clews, *Fifty Years in Wall Street* (New York: Irving, 1908), p. 727 ff.
5. A New York Broker (John Ferguson Hume), *The Art of Investing* (New York: D. Appleton, 1888), p. 138.
6. Quoted in Matthew Hale Smith, *Twenty Years Among the Bulls and Bears* (Hartford, CT: Burr and Hyde, 1871), p. 553.
7. Henry Clews, *Twenty-Eight Years in Wall Street* (New York: Irving, 1887), p. 19.
8. Edward G. Riggs, "Wall Street, The Stock Exchange" *The Quarterly Illustrator*, I (April–June, 1893), p. 355.
9. William Worthington Fowler, *Ten Years in Wall Street* (Hartford, CT: Dustin & Co. 1870), pp. 319–20.
10. Riggs, p. 387.
11. Garet Garrett, *Where the Money Grows* (New York: Harper, 1911), p. 13.

CHAPTER 3

1. Joseph Fontenrose, *The Delphic Oracle* (Berkeley: University of California Press, 1978), pp. 1, 5.
2. George Rawlinson, trans., *The History of Herodotus*, Great Books, Encyclopedia Britannica (Chicago: Benton, 1988), vol. 6, pp. 21–22.
3. Frederick Poulsen, *Delphi*, trans. G. C. Richards (London: Gyldendal, 1921), p. 27.
4. Joseph Faltenras,
5. William Greider, *Secret of the Temple* (Louisville, KY: Touchstone, 1987), p. 240.
6. Harry Browne, *Why the Best Laid Investment Plans Usually Go Wrong & How You Can Find Safety & Profit in an Uncertain World* (New York: Morrow, 1987), pp. 43–44.
7. Will and Ariel Durant, *The Story of Civilization, 7, The Age of Reason Begins* (New York: Simon & Shuster, 1961), p. 601.
8. Ibid., pp. 586–87.
9. Quoted in William S. Beck, "The Rise of Science," in *The Realm of Science*, ed. Stanley Brown (Louisville, KY: Touchstone, 1972), I, p. 94.
10. "Fundamentals of Mathematics," *The Realm of Science*, ed. Stanley Brown (Louisville, KY: Touchstone, 1972), III.
11. Beck, p. 102.
12. Carl Sagan, "Can We Know the Universe? Reflections on a Grain of Salt," *Great Essays in Science*, ed. Martin Gardner (Buffalo, NY: Prometheus, 1994), p. 105.
13. Martin Gardner, *Science: Good, Bad and Bogus* (Buffalo, NY: Prometheus, 1989), p. 319.
14. Ibid., p. 99.
15. Richard Gregory, ed., *The Oxford Companion to the Mind* (New York: Oxford University Press, 1987), p. 579.

16. Christopher Scott, "Paranormal Phenomena: The Problem of Pro," *The Oxford Companion to the Mind,* ed. Richard Gregory (New York: Oxford University Press, 1987), p. 579.
17. Ibid., p. 580.
18. J. A. Wheeler, quoted in Martin Gardner, *Science: Good, Bad and Bogus* (Buffalo, NY: Prometheus, 1989), p. 191.
19. Ibid., p. 192.

CHAPTER 4

1. Howie Eisenberg, "Second Place Is Some Place," *Ace,* October, ???? pp. 22–23.
2. Lacoste, pp. 176–77.
3. Quoted in Alexander Cockburn, *Idle Passion: Chess and the Dance with Death* (New York: Plume, 1974), p. 59.
4. Elliot Aronson, *The Social Animal* (New York: Freeman, 1992), p. 148.
5. Frank Taussig, "Is Market Price Determinate?" *Quarterly Journal of Economics,* 25 (May, 1921), pp. 394–411.
6. Paul H. Cootner and Sidney S. Alexander, "Price Movements in Speculative Markets: Trends or Random Walks," *Industrial Management Review,* 2 (1961), pp. 7–26.
7. Paul H. Cootner and Sidney S. Alexander, "Stock Prices; Random versus Systematic Changes," *Industrial Management Review,* 3 (1962), pp. 24–25.
8. Thomas Tooke, *Thoughts and Details on the High and Low Prices of the Last Thirty Years* (London: John Murray, 1823), part II, p. 131.
9. *American Meteorological Journal,* 1, no. 12 (1884), p. 160.
10. Ibid., 1, no. 4 (1885), p. 543.
11. Ibid., 1, no. 3 (1884), pp. 77–79.
12. Alfred Cowles and Herbert E. Jones, "Some A Posteriori Probabilities in Stock Market Action," *Econometrica,* 5 (1937), p. 294.
13. Victor Niederhoffer, *"Non-Randomness in Stock Prices: A New Model of Price Movement,"* Harvard College, March 1964.
14. Victor Niederhoffer and M.F.M. Osborne, "Market Making and Reversal on the Stock Exchange," *Journal of the American Statistical Association,* 61, no. 316 (Dec. 1966), pp. 905, 908.

CHAPTER 5

1. Harry Cowles, *The Art of Squash Racquets* (New York: Macmillan, 1935), p. 13.
2. Jack Barnaby, *Winning Squash Racquets* (Boston: Allyn & Bacon, 1979), p. 249.
3. Dickson, *Baseball's . . . ,* selected quotes.
4. H. S. Wolf, *Studies in Stock Speculation* (Wells, VT: Fraser, 1924; reprinted 1966), p. 77.
5. Robert W. Colby and Thomas A. Meyers, *The Encyclopedia of Technical Market Indicators* (Burr Ridge, Illinois: Irwin Professional Publishing, 1988), pp. 508–554.
6. Francois Voltaire, *Candide or Optimism* (New York: Limited Editions Club, 1973), p. 123.

7. Barnaby, *Winning*, p. 152.
8. Robert Lenzner and Stephen S. Johnson, "Harvard is Knee Deep in Securities," *Forbes*, Nov. 29, 1995, p. 106.

CHAPTER 6

1. Sholto and Reuben Percy (Thomas Byerley and Joseph Robertson), *The Percy Anecdotes* (London: for T. Boys, 1821–1823), XII, p. 111.
2. Mahlon Hoagland and Bert Dodson, *The Way Life Works* (New York: Times Books, 1995), p. 158.
3. Dante Alighieri, *The Divine Comedy*, Inferno, Canto 3, trans. Lawrence Grant White (New York: Pantheon, 1948), p. 5.
4. Hoagland and Dodson, p. 21.
5. Richard Thaler, *The Winner's Curse: Paradoxes and Anomalies of Economic Life*, (Princeton: Princeton University Press, 1992), p. 63.
6. Johan Huizinga, *Homo Ludens: A Study of the Play Elements in Culture* (Boston: Beacon, 1950), p. 1.
7. Mark Twain (Samuel L. Clemens), *The Adventures of Huckleberry Finn* (New York: Heritage, 1884).
8. John Updike, "The Pro," reprinted in *The Norton Book of Sports*, ed. George Plimpton (New York: Norton, 1992), p. 161.
9. Peter Bjarkman, ed., *Baseball and the Game of Life* (New York: Vintage, 1971), xvii.
10. Dickson, p. 278.
11. Ibid., pp. 155–56.
12. Huizinga, p. 37.
13. Ibid., p. 5.

CHAPTER 7

1. Quoted in John Bartlett and Justin Kaplan, eds., *Bartlett's Familiar Quotations*, 16th ed., (Boston: Little, Brown & Co., 1992), p. 505.
2. Sholto and Reuben Percy (Thomas Byerley and Joseph Robertson), XIX, pp. 8–9.

CHAPTER 8

1. Quoted in Anthony Holden, *Big Deal, Confessions of a Professional Poker Player* (New York: Penguin, 1990), p. 137.
2. Ibid.
3. Fowler, p. 33 ff.
4. Quoted in Jack D. Schwager, *The New Market Wizards* (New York: Harper, 1992), p. 208.
5. Herbert O. Yardley, *The Education of a Poker Player* (Channel Islands: Guernsly Press, 1957).

CHAPTER 9

1. Ferde Rombola, *The Book on Bookmaking* (Romford Press, 1984), p. 111.
2. Robert Bacon, *The Secrets of Professional Turf Betting* (New York: Ameripub Co., 1975), pp. 23–27.
3. Ibid., p. 27.
4. Ibid., p. 29.
5. Ibid., p. 30.
6. Ibid., p. 33.
7. Ibid., p. 33.
8. Ibid., p. 34.
9. Ibid., p. 28.

CHAPTER 10

1. Quoted in Amatzia Avni, *Danger in Chess* (London: Cadogan, 1994), p. 100.
2. Ibid., p. 104.
3. J. R. Krebs and N. B. Davies, *Behavioral Ecology*, 3rd ed. (Boston: Blackwell, 1991), see chap. 6.
4. Oliver E. Williamson, "Transaction Costs Economics and Organization Theory," in Neil J. Smelser and Richard Swedberg, eds., *The Handbook of Economic Sociology* (Princeton: Princeton University Press, 1994), p. 86.
5. Ibid., p. 81.
6. B. H. Liddell Hart, *Strategy* (New York: Meridian, 1991), p. xx.
7. Bert Hölldobler and Edward O. Wilson, *Journey to the Ants* (Cambridge: Harvard University Press, 1994), p. 123.
8. Hölldobler and Wilson, p. 125.
9. Denis Owen, *Camouflage and Mimicry* (University of Chicago Press, 1980), pp. 139–40.

CHAPTER 11

1. Ira Cobleigh, *Happiness Is a Stock That Doubles in a Year* (Bernard Geis Associates, 1968), p. 114.
2. Arthur Niederhoffer, *Behind the Shield: The Police in Urban Society* (Garden City, NY: Doubleday, 1967), p. 120.
3. Jim Melloan, "The Merry Mistress of Bonds," *Worth*, April 1996.
4. Gregory Millman, *Around the World on a Trillion Dollars a Day* (New York: Bantam, 1995), p. 42.
5. John Kenneth Galbraith, *A Short History of Financial Euphoria* (New York: Viking, 1993), p. 43.
6. Gene Marcial, *Secrets of the Street* (New York: McGraw-Hill, 1995), pp. 216–17.
7. Matthew Hale Smith, p. 275.
8. Kenneth L. Fisher, *100 Minds That Made the Market* (Woodside, CA: Business Classics, 1995), p. 69.

9. William Stanley Jevons, *The Atheneum.*
10. Arthur Niederhoffer and Elaine Niederhoffer, *The Police Family* (Lexington, MA: Lexington Books, 1978), p. 87.
11. Ibid., p. 88.

Chapter 12

1. Mary Batten, *Discovery by Chance* (New York: Funk & Wagnalls, 1968), p. vii.
2. Louis Engel and Henry R. Hecht, *How to Buy Stocks* (Boston: Little, Brown & Co., 1994), pp. 289–96.
3. Jeremy Siegel, *Stocks for the Long Run* (New York: Irwin, 1994).
4. Eugene Fama, "The Behavior of Stock Market Prices," *Journal of Business*, 38 (January 1965), pp. 34, 105. Quoted in Thaler, *The Winner's Curse*, p. 53.
5. Yale Hirsch, *Stock Trader's Almanac* (Old Tappan, NJ: The Hirsch Organization, Inc., 1993), p. 118.
6. Thaler, p. 144.
7. "What a Difference a Day Makes," *The Economist* (September 1994), p. 84.
8. Isaac Asimov, *Asimov's Annotated Gilbert and Sullivan* (New York: Doubleday, 1988), p. 79.
9. Galton, *Memories of My Life* (London: Methuen, 1908), pp. 272–73.
10. Robert Andrews, *The Columbia Dictionary of Quotations* (Columbia University Press: New York), p. 5 (Harold Bloom interview in *Criticism in Society* (ed. by Imre Salusinkski, 1987)).

Chapter 13

1. Charles Darwin, *The Origin of Species and the Descent of Man* (New York: Modern Library, n.d.), p. 59.
2. W. R. Grove, *The Correlation of Physical Forces* (London: S. Highley, 1850), p. 126.
3. Lewis Thomas, *The Lives of a Cell* (New York: Bantam, 1974), p. 3.
4. Guy Murchie, *The Seven Mysteries of Life* (Boston: Houghton Mifflin, 1981), p. 362.
5. Ludwig von Mises, *Human Action: A Treatise on Economics* (Chicago: Henry Regnery, 1963), p. 392.
6. Steven Solomon, *The Confidence Game: How Unelected Central Bankers Are Governing the Changed Global Economy* (Simon & Schuster: New York, 1995), p. 372.
7. Ibid.
8. Ulanowicz, Robert, *Growth and Development, Ecosystem Phenomenology* (New York: Springer-Verlag, 1986), p. 000.
9. Warwick J. McKibbin and Jeffrey D. Sachs, *Global Linkages* (Washington, DC: Brookings Institution, 1991), pp. 6–7.
10. Michael E. S. Gayed, *Intermarket Analysis and Investing* (New York: New York Institute of Finance, 1990), p. 378.
11. Henry Crosby Emery, *Speculation on the Stock and Produce Exchanges of the United States* (New York: Columbia University, 1896).

CHAPTER 14

1. Quoted in Michael Steinberg, *The Symphony* (New York: Oxford University Press, 1995), p. 216.
2. Quoted in Harold C. Schonberg, *The Lives of the Great Composers* (New York: Norton, 1981), p. 122.
3. Quoted in Christopher Wolff, *Bach, Essays on His Life and Music* (Cambridge: Harvard University Press, 1991), p. 396.
4. Deems Taylor, *Of Men and Music* (New York: Simon & Shuster, 1937), pp. 33–34.
5. Robert Prechter, *At the Crest of the Tidal Wave* (Gainsville, GA: New Classics Library, 1995), p. 67.
6. Desmond MacRae, "Catching the Wave, Elliott Style," *Financial Trader*, 3 (May 1996).
7. Quoted in Joseph Machlis, *The Environment of Music* (New York: Norton, 1977), p. 272.
8. Quoted in John Amis and Michael Rose, *Words About Music* (New York: Marlowe, 1995), p. 115.
9. Schonberg, p. 114.
10. Ibid., p. 103.
11. Machlis, p. 9.
12. Amis and Rose, p. 17.
13. Paul Griffith and Roland DeCande, *The Heritage of Music, Classical and its Origins* (Oxford: Oxford University Press, 1990), pp. 9–10.
14. Machlis, p. 9.
15. Amis and Rose, p. 186.
16. Ibid., p. 2.
17. Robert Andrews, *The Columbia Dictionary of Quotations* (New York: Columbia University Press, 1993), p. 613.
18. Galton, *Memories*, p. 315.
19. Steinberg, p. 29.
20. Ibid., p. 32.
21. Ibid.
22. Ibid., p. 33.

CHAPTER 15

1. Charles Elton, *Animal Ecology* (London: Methuen, 1971), p. 64.
2. James Medbery, *Men and Mysteries of Wall Street* (Wells, VT: Fraser, 1870), pp. 145–47.
3. F. Scott Fitzgerald, *The Great Gatsby* (New York: Simon & Shuster, 1992), p. 48.
4. Krebs, p. 3.
5. Quoted in Robert E. Rickles, *Ecology* (New York: Freeman, 1990), p. 175.
6. Ambrose Bierce, *The Devil's Dictionary* (New York: Dover Publications, 1958), p. 83.
7. Quoted in Richard Karp, "Bad Actor?" *Barron's*, July 1, 1996, p. 20.

8. Ibid.

9. George Horace Lorimer, *Letters from a Self-Made Merchant to His Son* (Toronto: Briggs, 1902), pp. 195-96.

10. David King, CEO of London Metals Exchange,

11. William S. Beck et al., *Life* (New York: Harper, 1991), p. 14.

12. Richard Dawkins, *The Blind Watchmaker* (New York: Norton, 1987), p. 195 ff.

13. Darwin, p. 62.

FINALE

1. Gary Garrett, *Heritability of Angling Vulnerability of Large-Mouth Bass* (Texas Parks & Wildlife Department, December 31, 1993), pp. 1–4.

2. Floyd Norris, "At Nasdaq, Time to Repent and Grow Up," *The New York Times*, August 11, 1996, section 3, p. 1.

Select Bibliography

Alighieri, Dante. *The Divine Comedy*, trans. Lawrence Grant White. New York: Pantheon, 1948.

Amis, John, and Michael Rose. *Words About Music*. New York: Marlowe, 1995.

Andrews, Robert. *The Columbia Dictionary of Quotations*. New York: Columbia University Press, 1993.

Aronson, Elliot. *The Social Animal*. New York: Freeman, 1992.

Asimov, Isaac. *Asimov's Annotated Gilbert and Sullivan*. New York: Doubleday, 1988.

Atkinson, Rita, et al. *Introduction to Psychology*. New York: Harcourt, 1993.

Avni, Amatzia. *Danger in Chess*. London: Cadogan, 1994.

Bacon, Robert. *Secrets of Professional Turf Betting*. New York: Ameripub Co., 1975.

Barnaby, Jack. *Winning Squash Racquets*. Boston: Allyn & Bacon, 1979.

Bartlett, John, and Justin Kaplan, eds. *Bartlett's Familiar Quotations*, 16th ed., Boston: Little, Brown & Co., 1992.

Batten, Mary. *Discovery by Chance*. New York: Funk & Wagnalls, 1968.

Beck, William S. "The Rise of Science," *The Realm of Science*. Louisville: Touchstone, 1972.

Beck, William S., et al. *Life*. New York: Harper, 1991.

Bierce, Ambrose. *The Devil's Dictionary*. New York: Dover Publications, 1958.

Bjarkman, Peter, ed. *Baseball and the Game of Life*. New York: Vintage, 1971.

Browne, Harry. *Why the Best Laid Investment Plans Usually Go Wrong & How You Can Find Safety & Profit in an Uncertain World*. New York: Morrow, 1987.

Butwin, Julius and Francis. *Favorite Tales of Sholom Aleichem*. New York: Avenel, 1983.

Carret, Phillp L. *The Art of Speculation*. New York: Hugh Bancroft, 1930.

Churchill, Major Seton. *Betting and Gambling*. London: James Nisbet & Co., 1894.

Clews, Henry. *Fifty Years in Wall Street*. New York: Irving, 1908.

Clews, Henry. *Twenty-Eight Years in Wall Street*. New York: Irving, 1887.

Cobleigh, Ira. *Happiness is a Stock That Doubles in a Year*. Bernard Geis Assoc., 1968.

Cockburn, Alexander. *Idle Passion: Chess and the Dance with Death*. New York: Plume, 1974.

Cootner, Paul H., and Sidney S. Alexander. "Price Movements in Speculative Markets: Trends or Random Walks," *Industrial Management Review*. Vol 2. 1961.

Cootner, Paul H., and Sidney S. Alexander. "Stock Prices; Random versus Systematic Changes," *Industrial Management Review*. Vol 3. 1962.

Cowles, Harry. *The Art of Squash Racquets*. New York: Macmillan, 1935.

Darwin, Charles. *The Origin of Species and the Descent of Man*. New York: Modern Library, nd.

Davis, Forest. *What Price Wall Street?* New York: Godwin, 1932.

Dawkins, Richard. *The Blind Watchmaker*. New York: Norton, 1987.

Dickson, Paul. *Baseball's Greatest Quotations*. New York: Harper, 1992.

424   SELECT BIBLIOGRAPHY

Durant, Will and Ariel. *The Story of Civilization, 7, The Age of Reason Begins.* New York: Simon & Shuster, 1961.

Eisenberg, Howie. "Second Place is Some Place," *Ace.* October, 1979.

Elton, Charles. *Animal Ecology.* London: Methuen, 1971.

Emery, Henry Crosby. *Speculation On the Stock and Produce Exchanges of the United States.* New York: Columbia University, 1896.

Engel, Louis, and Henry R. Hecht. *How to Buy Stock.* New York: Little, Brown & Co., 1994.

Fisher, Kenneth L. *100 Minds That Made the Market.* Woodside, CA: Business Classics, 1995.

Fitzgerald, F. Scott. *The Great Gatsby.* New York: Simon & Schuster, 1992.

Fontenrose, Joseph. *The Delphic Oracle.* Berkeley: University of California Press, 1978.

Fowler, William Worthington. *Ten Years in Wall Street.* Hartford: Dustin & Co., 1870.

Galbraith, John Kenneth. *A Short History of Financial Euphoria.* New York: Viking, 1993.

Galton, Francis. *The Art of Travel.* London: John Murray, 1883.

Galton, Francis. *Memories of My Life.* London: Methuen, 1908.

Gardner, Martin. *Science: Good, Bad and Bogus.* Buffalo, NY: Prometheus, 1989.

Garrett, Garet. *Where the Money Grows.* New York: Harper, 1911.

Gayed, Michael E. S. *Intermarket Analysis and Investing.* New York: New York Institute of Finance, 1990.

Gregory, Richard, ed. *The Oxford Companion to the Mind.* New York: Oxford University Press, 1987.

Greider, William. *Secret of the Temple.* Louisville: Touchstones, 1987.

Griffith, Paul, and Roland DeCande. *The Heritage of Music, Classical and its Origins.* Oxford: Oxford University Press, 1990.

Grove, W. R. *The Correlation of Physical Forces.* London: S. Highley, 1850.

Hart, B. H. Liddell. *Strategy.* New York: Meridian, 1991.

Hirsch, Yale. *Stock Trader's Almanac (1993).* Old Tappan, NJ: The Hirsch Organization Inc., 1992.

Hoagland, Mahlon, and Bert Dodson. *The Way Life Works.* New York: Times Books, 1995.

Holden, Anthony. *Big Deal, Confessions of a Professional Poker Player.* New York: Penguin, 1990.

Hölldobler, Bert, and Edward O. Wilson. *Journey to the Ants.* Cambridge: Harvard University Press, 1994.

Huizinga, Johan. *Homo Ludens: A Study of the Play Elements in Culture.* Boston: Beacon, 1950.

Jarvie, Grant, and Jospeh Maguire. *Sport and Leisure in Social Thought.* New York: Rutledge, 1994.

Joplin, Scott. *Collected Works.* New York: New York Public Library, 1971.

Karp, Richard. "Bad Actor?," *Barron's.* July 1, 1996.

Krebs, Charles J. *Ecology, The Experimental Analysis of Distribution and Abundance.* New York: Harper, 1994.

Krebs, J. R., and N. B. Davies. *Behavioral Ecology,* 3rd ed. Boston: Blackwell, 1991.

Lacoste, René. *Lacoste On Tennis.* New York: Morrow, 1928.

Lefevre, Edwin. *Reminiscences of a Stock Operator.* NY: John Wiley & Sons, 1994.

Lefevre, Edwin. *Wall Street Stories.* New York: McClure, Phillips & Co., 1901.

Lenzner, Robert, and Stephen S. Johnson. "Harvard is Knee Deep in Securities," *Forbes,* November 29, 1995.

LoBagola, Bata Kindai Amgoza Ibn. *LoBagola: An African Savage's Own Story.* New York: Alfred A. Knopf, 1930.

Loeb, Gerald. *The Battle for Stock Market Profits.* New York: Simon & Shuster 1971.

Lorimer, George Horace. *Letters from a Self-Made Merchant to His Son.* Toronto: Briggs, 1902.

Lynch, Don. *The Titanic: An Illustrated History.* New York: Hyperion, 1992.

Lynch, Peter. *Beating the Street.* New York: Fireside, 1993.

Lynch, Peter. *One Up on Wall Street.* New York: Penguin Books, 1989.

Machlis, Joseph. *The Enjoyment of Music.* New York: Norton, 1977.

MacRae, Desmond. "Catching the Wave, Elliott Style," *Financial Trader.* May 1996.

Marcial, Gene. *Secrets of the Street.* New York: McGraw-Hill, 1995.

McKibbin, Warwick J., and Jeffrey D. Sachs. *Global Linkages.* Washington, DC: Brookings Institution, 1991.

Medbery, James. *Men and Mysteries of Wall Street.* Wells, VT: Fraser, 1870, rpt. 1968.

Melloan, Jim. "The Merry Mistress of Bonds," *Worth,* April 1996.

Melville, Herman. *Moby Dick.* New York: Random House, 1930.

Millman, Gregory. *Around the World on a Trillion Dollars a Day.* New York: Bantam, 1995.

Mosteller, Frederick, and David L. Wallace. *Inference and Disputed Authorship: The Federalist.* Reading, MA: Addison-Wesley, 1964.

Murchie, Guy. *The Seven Mysteries of Life.* Boston: Houghton Mifflin, 1981.

Nadi, Aldo. *On Fencing.* Sunrise, Florida: Laureate Press, 1943.

Newcomb, Simon. *Principles of Political Economy.* New York: Harper & Brothers, 1886.

Niederhoffer, Arthur. *Behind the Shield: The Police in Urban Society.* Garden City, NY: Doubleday, 1967.

Niederhoffer, Arthur and Elaine. *The Police Family.* Lexington, MA: Lexington Books, 1978.

Niederhoffer, Victor. *Non-Randomness in Stock Prices: A New Model of Price Movement.* Harvard College, March 1964.

Niederhoffer, Victor and M.F.M. Osborne. "Market Making and Reversal on the Stock Exchange," *Journal of the American Statistical Association.* December, 1966.

Osborne, M.F.M. "Brownian Motion in the Stock Market," *Operations Research,* vol. 7, no. 2 (March–April 1959).

Owen, Denis. *Camouflage and Mimicry.* Chicago: University of Chicago Press, 1980.

Percy, Sholto and Reuben. *The Percy Anecdotes.* London: T. Boys, 1821–23.

Plimpton, George, ed. *The Norton Book of Sports.* New York: Norton, 1992.

Potter, Mary C. "Remembering," *An Invitation to Cognitive Science: Thinking, Vol. 3.* eds. Daniel N. Osheron and Edward E. Smith. Cambridge: NIT Press, 1990.

Poulsen, Frederick. *Delphi.* trans. G. C. Richards. London: Gyldendal, 1921.

Prechter, Robert. *At the Crest of the Tidal Wave.* Gainsville, GA: New Classics Library, 1995.

Rawlinson, George, trans., *The History of Herodotus.* Great Books, Encyclopedia Britannica, Chicago: Benton, 1988.

Reynolds, Quentin. *I, Willie Sutton.* New York: Da Capo, 1993.

Ricklefs, Robert E. *Ecology.* New York: Freeman, 1990.

Riggs, Edward G. "Wall Street, The Stock Exchange" *The Quarterly Illustrator*, I, April–June, 1893.

Rombola, Ferde. *The Book on Bookmaking.* Romford Press, 1984.

Rosenzweig, Mark R., Arnold L. Leiman, and S. Marc Breedlove. *Biological Psychology.* Sunderland, MA: Sinauer Associates, 1996.

Rosten, Norman. "Under The Boardwalk," *The Brooklyn Reader: 30 Writers Celebrate America's Favorite Borough.* eds. Andrea Sexton and Alice Powers. New York: Harmony, 1994.

Sagan, Carl. "Can We Know the Universe? Reflections on a Grain of Salt," *Great Essays in Science*, ed. Martin Gardner. Buffalo, NY: Prometheus, 1994.

Samuelson, Paul. *Foundations of Economic Analysis.* Cambridge: Harvard University Press, 1947.

Satterthwaite, Frank. *The Three-Wall Nick and Other Angles.* New York: Hold, Rinehart and Winston, 1979.

Schonberg, Harold C. *The Lives of the Great Composers.* New York: Norton, 1981.

Schwager, Jack D. *The New Market Wizards.* New York: Harper, 1992.

Scott, Christopher. "Paranormal Phenomena: The Problem of Pro," *The Oxford Companion to the Mind*, ed. Richard Gregory. New York: Oxford University Press, 1987.

Siegel, Jeremy. *Stocks for the Long Run.* New York: Irwin, 1994.

Smelser, Neil J., and Richard Swedberg, eds. *The Handbook of Economic Sociology.* Princeton: Princeton University Press, 1994.

Smith, Matthew Hale. *Twenty Years Among the Bulls and Bears.* Hartford, CT: Burr and Hyde, 1871.

Solomon, Steven. *The Confidence Game.* New York: Simon and Schuster, 1995.

Spanier, David. *Inside the Gambler's Mind.* Reno: University of Nevada Press, 1987.

Steinberg, Michael. *The Symphony.* New York: Oxford University Press, 1995.

Steinmetz, Andrew. *The Gambling Table.* London: Tinsley Brothers, 1870.

Sutton, Willie, with Edward Linn. *Where The Money Was.* New York: Viking, 1976.

Szalza, Ginger. "Roy Niederhoffer: Filtering Out the Noise for Profits," *Futures*, December 1994.

Taussig, Frank. "Is Market Price Determinate?" *Quarterly Journal of Economics*, May 1921.

Taylor, Deems. *Of Men and Music.* New York: Simon & Shuster, 1937.

Teweles, Richard J., and Frank J. Jones. *The Futures Game.* New York: McGraw-Hill, 1987.

Thaler, Richard. *The Winner's Curse, Paradoxes and Anomalies of Economic Life.* Princeton: Princeton University Press, 1992.

Thomas, Lewis. *The Lives of a Cell.* New York: Bantam, 1974.

Thorn, John, ed. *The Armchair Book of Baseball.* New York: Macmillan, 1985.

Tooke, Thomas. *Thoughts and Details on the High and Low Prices of the Last Thirty Years.* London: John Murray, 1823.

Twain, Mark. *The Adventures of Huckleberry Finn.* New York: Heritage, 1884.

Ulanowicz, Robert. *Growth and Development: Ecosystems Phenomenology.* New York: Springer-Verlag, 1986.

Voltaire, François. *Candide or Optimism.* New York: Limited Editions Club, 1973.

Von Mises, Ludwig. *Human Action, A Treatise on Economics.* Chicago: Henry Regnery, 1963.

Webb, Robert I. *Macroeconomic Information and Financial Trading.* Cambridge: Blackwell, 1994.

Willensky, Elliot. *When Brooklyn Was The World, 1920–1957.* New York: Harmony, 1986.

Wolf, H. S. *Studies in Stock Speculation.* Wells, VT: Fraser, 1924, rpt. 1966.

Wolff, Christopher. *Bach, Essays on His Life and Music.* Cambridge: Harvard University Press, 1991.

Wyckoff, Richard D. *Wall Street Ventures and Adventures Through Forty Years.* New York: Harper & Brothers Publishers, 1930.

Zimbardo, Philip G. and Richard J. Gerrig. *Psychology and Life.* New York: Harper Collins, 1996.

Index

429

Sex *(Continued)*
scandal in England (BOE), 251
science of, 257–259
sex-to-Shakespeare ratio, 243,
258–259
sexulation Revolution, 243
in the speculator's family, 260–261
Shakespeare, 158, 168, 259, 332
sex-to-Shakespeare ratio, 243,
258–259
Sharpe ratio, 134
Shatkin, Hank, 25
Sheepshead Bay racetrack, 15, 197, 198
Sherry-Netherland Hotel, 19
Shields, Russ, 186–187, 193–194
Short, selling, 45–46, 268–269, 376
Shreeve, James, 223
Shultz, George, 264
Siegel, Jeremy, 266
Sigmund, Karl, 144
Silver, 138, 181, 377
crash, 1980, 348. *See also* Hunt,
Bunker
futures (Figure 14–7), and music, 329
weekly chart (Figure 10–1), 235
Silver, Sam, 10, 87
Simmel, George, 144
Simon, Julian, 151
Singapore, 295
Skryabin Prelude in D#, 328, 330
Slobodkin, 144
Smick Johnson Report, 294
Smith, Adam, 226
Smith, Matthew Hale, 254, 293
Snead, Sam, 30
Society for the Prevention of
Disparaging Remarks Against
Brooklyn, 9–10
Sociology:
figurative, 144
interpretive, 144
of sports, 144
Soros, George, 2, 3, 14, 26–27, 31, 39,
45, 69, 74, 84, 95, 101, 108, 114,
125, 131, 133, 150–154, 176, 185,
196, 252, 271, 272, 320, 321, 323,
335, 336, 340, 346, 352, 353, 373,
381, 399, 400
South Africa, 295. *See also* Africa
Soviet economic system, 408, 409
Soybeans graph, and music (Figure
14–10), 331
Specialists, 106

Speculation:
books published on, number of, 258
as a game, 145–149
and horse racing, 197
rules for:
from music, 339–341
from poker (Table 8–3), 188–192
and sex (history of), 253–256, 257
successful (a definition), 320
Spencer, Herbert, 73
Spiritualist, 75–76
Spohr, Louis, 335
Sports, 129, 220–221. *See also* Baseball;
Football; Game(s)
analogies, 347
indicators, 78–81
and life, 144–145
principles, 214
racquet, *see* Racquet sports; Squash;
Tennis
sociology of, 144
Sports-Eye, 202, 215
Squash, ix, 2, 24, 26, 27, 30–31, 44, 56,
82, 95, 100, 105, 110, 128, 213–214,
246, 262, 283, 289, 291, 292, 374
discrimination in squash clubs, 283
English Let rule, 26
Standard & Poors Index, 104
Stanford, 75, 291, 347
Statistics/probability, 178
fallacies, 300–301
Steinhardt, Michael, 176
Stigler, George, 2, 264
Stigler, Steve, 2, 259, 300, 301, 343,
384
Stock Trader's Almanac, 411
Stoop ball, 134–135
Stops, use of, 94, 376
Strachen, 112
Suicides, 18, 19, 145, 182, 184
Sumitomo Corporation, 142, 294, 378
Sunbeam, 267
Sunspots, 300
Superbowl, 78, 81, 82, 145
Supernatural phenomena, 76–77
Sutton, Willie, 31–33, 261
Swiss Bank Corp., 366
Swiss National Bank, 209
Swiss/Switzerland, 304, 306, 316, 332,
366
Switches, 208–211
Synchronicity, 84
Synthesizer, 29, 341, 346